Just the Right Note

Just the Right Note

Mary Beakey Guziejka

*To my very dear friend,
Helen - with love
and fond
memories!*

Mary M. Guziejka

Bard Brook Press ◆ Belchertown, Massachusetts

Published by:
Bard Brook Press
27 Wilson Road
Belchertown, Massachusetts 01007
www.bardbrookpress.com

First Edition
December 2012

ISBN: 978-0-9834931-1-2

Printed in the United States of America.

DEDICATION

For my wonderful Mom and Dad, Mr. and Mrs. Andrew Beakey
Anna Scannell, my uniquely inspirational music teacher
and her niece, Louise Dunn, my drama coach

ACKNOWLEDGEMENTS

I want to acknowledge the loving support of my family through
my years of teaching, travel and adventure, including:
My loving husband, Edward M. Guziejka;
My brother, Richard A. Beakey and his wife Lillian;
Susan M. Guziejka, our oldest daughter, who, sadly has passed on,
and her loyal husband, John Thompson;
Eric Guziejka, my son and his wife Kelly,
and their lovely children Kim and Mike;
Amy Guziejka Sawyer, our youngest daughter and her husband Dave,
and their wonderful children, Michael, Emma and Eva.
My hope and prayer is that one day they will read and treasure this book,
Just the Right Note,
with a song in their hearts.

Also, I want to thank my editor, Susan Mitchell, and book designer,
Eileen Klockars, who guided me through the book publishing process.

Many, many thanks to all the above loving,
kind, and beautiful people.

CONTENTS

PREFACE

The following is the text of a speech given by Mary Guziejka in November 2009, at Sanborn School in Andover in honor of the 30th anniversary of the Harvest Festival that she had implemented in November of 1979. Her audience was the entire school, parents, and members of the Senior Center, but she directed her comments primarily to the students of Sanborn School.

What is the first thing you would do if someone gave you a gift? If the gift was something you had dreamed about for years? If in your heart you were almost sure you would never receive it, and then you did? What would you do first? You would say thank you. Probably you would say, "*Thank you very, very much*". Then, after that, what might you feel like doing? I will tell you what I would do and I am sure many of you have already thought of the answer.

Give something back …give something back that would be equally as nice, equally as big and equally as long lasting; something that would let the giver *know* how much you cared about the gift that had been given to you. Sometimes though, that is hard to do.

Many years ago, the Town of Andover gave me the 'gift of a lifetime' and I would like to tell you about it. I had worked here in your school for twelve years. During that time I always had a dream, a great big dream, one that I was afraid would never come true. That dream was to travel and study overseas. I always, in particular, wanted to live in England. So I decided one day that if I didn't *try* to live in England I would *never…ever* know if I could.

The first thing I had to do was apply for a sabbatical. A sabbatical is time off away from work to study at a University and learn. Then I could bring new knowledge and experiences back to my teaching in the town of Andover. I was a little nervous about the application, but…I did it! I wrote a letter to the Superintendent of Schools asking please, would he and the School Board grant me a paid year's leave of absence to study at the University of London, England in the Music Education Division. I told them I wanted to give the children in Andover new experiences, help them learn about England and travel and study.

Dr. Seifert and the School Board granted me a year away from teaching in Andover, while still receiving half my salary. He took care of all the necessities and after that, in June, when school ended, my family and I left for England so I could attend the University of London! My husband, Edward, came with me as well as our youngest daughter Amy, nine years old, and our son Eric who was 17 years old.

We found a house to rent and everywhere we went people were wonderful to us. Not much time had gone by when we had people coming forward from everywhere to make us feel at home, comfortable and wanted. The English could not have been friendlier.

As I was learning, studying, traveling, and making wonderful friends in England, I kept thinking, *how can I ever repay* Andover for having done something so wonderful for me? How can I ever give back all the joy and pleasure and experiences that I was gaining every single day? I had said thank you to everyone who helped me move, but that was not enough.

During my year of study I visited many, many schools: rich schools, medium-rich schools, poor schools in very poor areas of London, medium poor schools and the richest school of all, Eton College, just outside London, next to Windsor Castle. It is a private high school. Prince William and Prince Andrew attended school there as well as many other famous people.

While visiting Eton College, I heard about a program that I would have loved to carry out here at Sanborn School. But the students at Eton were older and their project could not easily be done by young children *your* age.

At Eton, each student adopted an elderly person to care for in the village. The student was responsible for helping that person whenever necessary, as in raking leaves, shopping at the village store if the elderly person was not feeling well, and similar chores all year long. The students were not paid to do this. It was a service. However, the high school students and the older people became such good friends they grew to be like family. That is a wonderful way to feel. You see...when people grow old they are alone much of the time. Why? Well, many or most of their friends and family members may have died, or their own families may have had to move away because of jobs or various other reasons. So, having a student come by every day or two was a marvelous thing for the older person and equally as good for the student. The students learned to give of themselves to others. The boys from Eton College and the elderly people grew to love each other and became wonderful friends.

I was still searching for something wonderful I could bring back home to Sanborn and the Town of Andover besides my music studies. Then the very thing I was looking for happened right beneath my nose and with my own little girl. Amy was nine-years old at that time and attended an English school called Park Hill. (The children in the Park Hill School loved her because she 'spoke funny'. Why do you think they said that to her? Well, it was because she spoke English with an American accent.)

This is what happened in Amy's school. Every year here in the United States we celebrate Thanksgiving in November. In England they have a similar celebration, but it is held in October and they call it a Harvest Festival, (which is what we are celebrating right now).

Since I was a visiting teacher I was invited to go out with the children to visit the elderly people in the area near the school and I chose Amy's group. First, all the students went into the auditorium where there was a huge display of food and baskets and packages that they and their parents had donated, and another huge display of flowers in pots, and other displays of just about anything you want to name.

All the school children had written letters, drawn pictures and also had pictures of themselves to give as gifts. I was in awe. The huge stage was full all the way to the back and gifts also lined the steps down from the stage. After looking at all the gifts, we were asked to sit in the auditorium because there would be a speaker. The Minister from the church spoke to the children and parents. Then Mr. Kitley, the principal, spoke about how important it is for children to learn to give to others, to adults or other children, *but most especially to the older adults in the area*; to learn to take care of the older adults, to visit with them, and bring them small and thoughtful presents. After Mr. Kitley spoke, the Minister gave a blessing and we all said a few prayers and then, much to my surprise, the best was yet to come!

We were divided into groups and each adult was given six or seven children per group. We were handed names and addresses of all the people we were to visit during the day while we distributed the gifts. I was amazed. I had never, ever done anything like this in any of my schools before. We left the school in our groups and walked all over our school vicinity, covering the whole territory on foot. No busses. English people are great walkers.

I was in charge of one group, but never having seen this done before I did not know what to expect. We went to our first home, where an old man sat on a chair on the stoop in front of his house. The sun was shining on him. He was waiting for us. He was visited each year so he knew we were coming. The children knew him by name and all gathered around him and sat and talked and talked. He told them about fighting in World War I…he had fought in the trenches. They were enthralled by his stories, as was I. We stayed a long time listening to him. No one was in a hurry to leave. One of my little boys had given him a present of a can of baked beans. He held the can close to his chest as he spoke.

But the can of beans was not the most important thing for the older man. What was the important thing? Who can tell me? Yes, you are correct. For that time we were there, he was not alone, as he usually was. For that time, he had friends who would listen to him and his stories, and in turn, he listened to them. He sat in the sun listening to the children' stories with tears coursing down his cheeks. It was a touching scene.

I was absolutely moved by the whole experience and wished I could have captured it on a camera. He sat on the top stoop, some children stood around his back; others leaned on his legs and some sat on the steps in the front of his feet. I was sorry to leave him, he looked so happy, even with his tears, but we had to move on.

We went on to other houses of older people, gave them pictures and stories and gifts of food and flowers. But most importantly, what did the children do? They listened intently, and talked to and with all the elderly people, taking home with them the stories to tell their moms and dads.

I went home with Amy that night and I knew exactly what I wanted to do when I returned to Sanborn School in Andover the following autumn. I wanted to have a Harvest Festival and accumulate gifts and flowers and stories for elderly people and then deliver them, just the way it had been done at Amy's Park Hill School in England. I wanted the children in Andover to see and feel the warmth and sunshine in the eyes of the elderly people when they received children into their homes. I wanted the students to talk to the elderly and to listen to their stories. I wanted the children to enjoy the art of giving and listening.

I then felt I found the way I could repay the good people of Andover for the gift they had given me. The following year, when I began teaching at Sanborn School again, I organized a Harvest Festival with the help of many other people. I want to thank Mrs. Maureen Wood, mother of Susan and Helen, Mrs. Atkinson, mother of Richard, and Mrs. Kachen, mother of Susan and another daughter, plus Scott's Mother, Sheilagh Livermore. I want to thank all these mothers from the bottom of my heart, especially if any of them happen to be here today.

Without them the Harvest Festival would not have been the success it obviously has turned out to be. They were lovely and dedicated hard workers. I was able to continue the Harvest Festival with these ladies for four more years until I decided to move abroad once more. When I left Sanborn again, I did not go on sabbatical. I went permanently to live and teach music, drama, dance and high school band to children of all ages in schools in Okinawa, Japan; Izmir, Turkey; La Maddalena, which is an island off of Italy; and London, England.

Now I am retired and home for good and very honored to have been invited to attend and speak at this Harvest Festival on its 30th anniversary. THIS IS THE GIFT THAT KEEPS GIVING!!!

PRELUDE

West Ruislip Elementary School
West Ruislip, England, September 1995

"To be or not be or not to be,
that is the question,
Whether t'is nobler in the mind
To suffer the slings and arrows of outrageous fortune
Or to take arms against a sea of troubles
And by opposing end them..."

Hamlet
—Shakespeare

In 1995, the fifth and sixth graders of West Ruislip Elementary School in West Ruislip, England, embellished their bodies and fortified their minds with Shakespearean characters, ones they loved and had chosen on their own with my guidance. The Shakespearean passage had a message for the student, and it did not matter if it was short or long, the students found a meaning in it for them.

I was a new teacher at the West Ruislip school, which was situated about twenty miles due west of London, England. I wanted to begin the year with something exciting and different for my students in order to gain their love and, unknowingly to them, cause them to want to learn more and more in a spontaneous fashion. I would despise myself if the students were bored whenever they had me as a teacher and be upset with myself if I could not encourage them to enjoy the Fine Arts!

At that time, I had been working for the Department of Defense Dependent Schools for more than ten years. I usually taught music, drama and dance, and at West Ruislip, I also taught the talented and gifted classes as well. (In Izmir, Turkey, I also taught high school band). After some careful thought, I decided to incorporate Shakespeare into my curriculum of music and drama. Why Shakespeare, you might ask, since it is allegedly too difficult for students at that age? Well, let me share my story, and then see what you think.

Shakespeare was a wonderful and unsurpassed writer; no one has come along to top him or move ahead of him in my estimation, and in the estimation of people far more brilliant than I! A few people had told me the fifth and sixth grade students were far too young to study Shakespeare, but they proved they were not. I chose many short paragraphs for them to learn. We discussed the words and meanings in class, deciding about this 'saying' or that, and in particular, from which of Shakespeare's plays did this or that 'saying' emanate.

Then, the exciting part came when I told them they could dress in Shakespearean type costumes. At first, the plan was to have a parade of Shakespeare characters walk through the school, into the other classrooms, and then outside and around the school. As time went on, and the students became more enthusiastic about Shakespeare, they decided to orally deliver some of their favorite Shakespearean passages. Most of the students were delighted that they would be delivering speeches, and it did not matter how short or long the speeches were. No child was eliminated and no speech was ignored.

The students all understood what the words meant and why they were saying their particular speeches.

They designed their costumes on their own, with help from me, the music teacher, drama coach, square and folk dance teacher, talented and gifted program teacher, and whatever else the school's administration asked me to do. But singing was always an important component of whatever I did. In the end, all their learning and my teaching became incorporated into a massive production of song, music, drama and dance.

I scheduled the performing times in advance to give each of the other teachers time to work it into their schedules. The students in each class listened to the speeches, admired the costumes, and asked questions. Then my Shakespearean 'actors' would parade to the next classroom. With each stop, the performances grew better and better, more dramatic and more enunciative in a distinct Shakespearean way. I was delighted with the students whose words were clear, expressive, and dramatic. They obviously understood all the words they were delivering to the classes. Some of the students were a bit shy of course, but none were left out. Even the quieter students still delivered something, if only a sentence or two, that had been written by Shakespeare himself.

Living in England, (most of the military families were there for at least two years at a time or more), it had not been difficult for the more outgoing children, who could be 'hams,' to copy the accent and speech of the English people. When some younger students raised their hands with questions, my most eloquent speakers were able to explain their speeches in their American accent, and then zip right back into the character they were performing. Consequently, the parade was a huge success! The audiences were pleased, as were the performers. I was 'over the moon with delight.' (An expression I said often and the students seemed to love.)

Of course, the following school year had to be better than the previous year, so I developed a curriculum that offered a more complete study of Shakespeare. In the fall, I arranged for the fifth and sixth graders to take a trip to the Globe Theatre in London where Shakespearean plays are still performed to this day. Sadly, the original Globe Theatre burned down a long time ago, but the new one is every inch the same as the old one. To prepare for this trip, I compiled a group of Shakespearean speeches, and then offered the students the opportunity to choose the one or ones they liked the most to memorize and deliver. The students chose the ones that meant the most to them, but before they were able to do that, they had to fully understand the speeches, and I helped them with that.

We traveled to London by coach, (bus) and by the time we entered the Globe Theatre my students were primed and ready. But, what happened next, even I was not prepared for. I never dreamed that the students would be invited by the gentleman in charge to give their speeches up on Shakespeare's stage in the Globe Theatre. This was as big a surprise to me as it was to the students! The children were absolutely up in the air with joy! We were not in costume unfortunately (too difficult to coordinate that when traveling into London by bus). But the students were invited to speak in front of whatever audience was at the Globe Theatre at that time.

There were many teachers and their students from various English schools, along with a few tourists. They all enjoyed hearing our American children with their American accents pretending to have English accents. Many came forward to congratulate the children when all was finished! What a treat that was for all of us…chaperones too! It was the crowning glory for the students and for their teacher! I believe the students just about flew home that day without wings, they were so thrilled with the experience.

Following that delightful trip, I chose a Shakespearean play for my fifth and sixth graders to study during the winter months. Their favorites were *Midsummer Night's Dream* and *Comedy of Errors*.

None of the Bard's plays are adviseable for fifth and sixth graders unless they are altered to some degree, so I found suitable abridged versions for them to study. I felt the version I had was quite appropriate due to the fact that all Shakespeare's words were still there, just the overall length of the play was shortened. The author had done a remarkable job in restructuring those two plays. I am afraid I do not have his name in order to do him justice since the book I borrowed has long been returned to its original owner, a lovely and generous English lady, Mary Andrews. She had been hired to be the base's 'Host Nation Teacher' long before I arrived at West Ruislip School.

That winter, one period a week for the fifth and sixth graders was dedicated to the study of those two plays, while the other period of the week was for music, dancing, singing and playing instruments. Many times as we studied the plays, music and dance, they all merged together, which was wonderful for both the students and me.

Then in the spring, the students, several parent chaperones and I, traveled to Stratford- Upon-Avon, which was the thrill of a lifetime for most of the students! We toured the Shakespeare Museum, picnicked on the bank of the famous Avon River, and went for a ride in a boat on that same river.

The day ended with the students attending a production of the famous *Merchant of Venice*. It was an 'unabridged' production and I was a bit nervous about whether fifth and sixth grade students would be able to sit attentively through the play. I had prepared them in advance, relating facts about the plot, characters and some of the language. But I was still anxious.

The play opened and as it went on I awaited the 'blow of boredom' to fall on my students. It never did. In fact, during

Mary Guziejka in Anne Hathaway's cottage garden

the first intermission, the girls quietly rushed over to tell me they loved the play and most especially they loved the beautiful lady who played the role of the young woman who disguised herself as a male lawyer in the courtroom.

The boys came to me next, having politely waited their turn, to say they also enjoyed the *Merchant of Venice*, but in a different way. The boys were more deeply concerned about the Jewish merchant. It was obvious as they talked to me that they felt sorry for the merchant who was in deep trouble. All went well, and the children and I considered the day a huge success. I had watched closely for any fidgeting or talking or other signs of boredom, but none happened. The students were glued to the play and the speeches and I was thrilled.

So now, would you be willing to argue that fifth and sixth grade students are too young to study Shakespeare? I believe the secret to having them enjoy Shakespeare is to have them 'act out' some of his plays. At least, it worked for me!

> *"Imagination*
> *Is more important*
> *Than knowledge…"*
>
> **—Albert Einstein**

My time in West Ruislip, England teaching music and Shakespeare was a thrilling experience for me, but only one of many I've had over the years.

Now I'd like to relate how this mystical, magical, musical journey of mine began, this lifelong yearning and love for performing, playing, and teaching music, drama, and dance.

Chapter 1
Childhood and Education

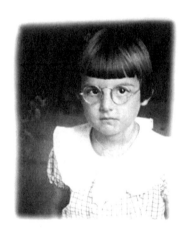

Mary Beakey, age 4

When I started this story of my life and music and memories, I wanted to start with: "I was born!" I wanted to open my story with that powerful phrase until I remembered Charles Dickens, the famous English author whose writings I love, used it first; not wanting to plagiarize or be plagiaristic, I decided to use the phrase only after I gave him the credit. Therefore… I WAS BORN!

A few weeks after I was born my father walked over to Miss Scannell's Furniture Store with me resting in his arms, presumably to see Miss Scannell. That is where my folks bought their small pieces of furniture after they married. At that time they had one little boy, my brother Richard. Evidently, my father also knew Miss Scannell taught children to play the piano, so he went excitedly into her store with this new baby… ME…swaddled in a blanket. I was born in May, and it was relatively warm out when he walked into her store and said, "Anna… this little girl of mine is going to learn to play the piano, and I want you to be her teacher."

Miss Scannell approached my father, stared at me, chucked me under the chin, and gooed and gahhed. Then, being a pompous sort of lady, Miss Scannell puffed up her short body, put her hands on her hips, and said in an authoritative, raspy voice, "If I have anything to say about it she will take lessons from me and she will play well!" I can still hear her bossy, raspy, but loving voice as I write this. She talked that way all the time I knew her.

So, from the child's mouth, now grown up and almost gone…I begin my autobiography, consisting mostly of:

MARY…MUSIC…and…MEMORIES

As a small child I always wanted to play piano and be on stage. I remember that so well, that at this moment…it almost feels like…yesterday! Well, not quite…but…I also always wanted to act. I cannot understand that too well now since I was a shy little girl. However, I was fortunate to have a mother and father who wanted the best for me and worked toward that aim. But then, I was born during the depression (which lasted from 1929 until World War II started in 1941), and the best for me was not easy to come by, for either my brother, born in 1928, or me in 1931. Money was scarce, it was just not to be had.

However my parents worked hard and I was able to take piano lessons. My piano teacher, Miss Scannell, was, compared to us, very rich. She was also rich in personality and rich in knowledge of the piano and children. She owned two beautiful baby grand pianos, one was black ebony and the other, which came later, was a lovely brown mahogany wood. These were safely ensconced in her music room in a large home in the "Highlands," which at that time was the posh section of the city of Lowell.

But then, anything would seem large compared to the four tiny rooms of the apartment in which my family lived. There were four tiny apartments in the building arranged in twos. Two on one side, up and down, and two on the other side, up and down. The apartments were joined together in the front by a porch with banisters and railings.

The apartment had one bedroom for my parents and another for my brother and me. One could barely walk around the double bed in my parents bedroom to get to the one small closet. There was a bureau with four drawers, two large and two small, and a large mirror. The small and narrow space between the bureau and their bed was the path to the closet. I remember always wanting to go into their bedroom so I could look into the huge mirror. Mirrors were scarce then and I was fascinated by it as a little girl. I loved seeing myself!

I slept in a black iron crib until my feet hung out over the floor, and that is no exaggeration; my brother's single cot was just about two feet away from mine. In our room there was absolutely no space for a bureau (and my parents probably had no money to buy one either). All our clothes, the few that we had, were either in our shallow, narrow closet, or in our parents' bureau drawers. There was a window to the left of the tiny closet in our bedroom.

Eventually, as I grew taller and older, my mother allowed me to sleep on the divan, which was in the small living room. In the morning she scooped up the bedding, tucked it away somewhere, and the living room looked as though no one had slept in it at all.

The kitchen was also small. There was a cold water faucet protruding over a long, rather narrow, black iron sink. We had no central heating, just a black 'do everything' fat-bellied stove with an oven. It had oil burners in it and it heated the house as well as the food. We were 'lucky' my mother said many times when we complained about the stove. Most other black iron stoves burned wood. But ours had two kerosene burners inside of the wood burning area. That made it much easier for my mother to do the cooking. She cooked on top of the black stove, and also placed her black flat iron on it to heat for ironing. I have that famous iron here in my kitchen to this day. It is so very heavy that I do not know how she ironed anything without burning our clothes. I surely would have singed everything I owned had I tried to iron with it.

The last room was the toilet. It had no windows leading to the outside, but there was a transom opening into the tiny passageway that led from the kitchen to the living room. For the toilet to have had a regular sized window, it would have had to open onto the hallway/ stairway area that led up to a second apartment. Everyone going upstairs could have peeked in and one could not have that…so no window.

But our home was a small and cozy domicile, especially to someone of my young age. It was the only home I knew until I was nine years old. I remember vividly to this day my mother's rocking chair in the kitchen in which she rocked me each night. I also remember clearly when my mother decided she would not rock me anymore! I do not remember the exact day of course, but I do remember the time frame. I went to bed and cried softly into my pillow so she would not hear me; I was angry and very sad. I loved the kitchen, the rocking chair and I loved my mother, and I NEVER wanted to be put to bed. I never wanted those precious moments I enjoyed with her to end.

The small living room had a fireplace mantle, but the fireplace was blocked, boarded up tidily, for some reason. The living room had three windows, with some space in a corner between two of the windows for an old upright piano that someone was giving away. It had some broken keys, keys that did not play at all, and I cannot remember how it got into the house. But I eventually learned to play piano on it despite the condition it was in! My parents had no money to buy a piano, but lucky me, this one was free and it was mine! I loved it and so began my music career.

I remember well the mantle over the closed up fireplace. The couch/bed for me was beneath the mantle. I used to hang my tan, lisle, long stocking on the mantle at Christmas waiting for Santa Claus to come. My brother and I always found an apple and an orange in the toes of our stockings. Probably one of my earliest memories was when the Christmas tree was placed in the right hand corner of the small living room, to the right of the radio, and my father lifted me up to the very tippety-top, which seemed so very high at that time; he wanted me to 'help' him put a star on the top of the tree! Obviously I loved it since that scene is still in my mind's eye now.

Of course, there was no television then. We did have a radio that was between the two windows in the front of the living room. It was a tall wooden cabinet radio and every day after school I would sit on the floor with my ear to the radio, listening to one of many daily series such as, "Stella Dallas," "Superman," "Jack Benny," or "Fibber McGee and Molly." I especially loved the opening of the program called "The Shadow." The voice on the radio always eerily said, "He He He He, Heee" in a sneering sound…and then continued with a spooky version of the words, "The Shadow Knows…" My brother and I argued on occasion about what programs to listen to and who got to have his/her ear closest to the cloth covering the speakers. Because he was three years older, he usually won, but he would let me sit next to him.

We had a narrow side yard, which seemed awfully big when I was small, and a little plot of land in the back, with enough room to play a little baseball game with my brother and a friend or two. We had hardly any yard in the front, just a tiny plot of green grass…weeds, most likely. My mother also had a clothesline in the backyard, which she must have shared with the lady upstairs.

One thing that comes to mind now was the day my brother dug a hole in the back yard that was so very deep he told me we were almost in China, and guess what? I believed him! I still remember seeing the layers of different colors in the earth and I kept looking for the children from China, but none came… sadly for me. I was so very innocent at that time.

The backyard also was host to several 'baseball' games which were really more like kickball, depending on the ball that was used. We called it baseball since we had three bases to run and touch and then 'home'. Another thing about the yard was this: it had a sad, dead, tree trunk taller than my brother. It just stood there doing absolutely nothing except when we played baseball and then it became home base. It was also a neutral spot when we played tag.

Because of that dead tree trunk and my yearning for trees where there were none, I made certain that the acre of land in Dracut where Ed and I built our home six years after we got married, and where we have now have lived for more than fifty years, had many trees. Never a season or day goes by that I do not look at my trees and love them, even in the winter when they are bare and drab and dreary looking. They still speak to me.

And, speaking of trees, I remember looking out of the window on Queen Street at the time of a huge hurricane which destroyed virtually everything around us, including our one huge, and lovely tree at the front of the house. It was so large its roots had partly erupted out onto the sidewalk. I loved that tree. It was so beautiful. I was devastated when the storm tore it down, but I never told anyone because my brother would have laughed at me.

We also had a door leading out from the kitchen to a small shed which held our boots and shovels, sleds and gardening tools, and a rake. On the long, narrow side of the house stood my mother's garden, which I also loved. I enjoyed watering the flowers when I was tiny. I had a very happy childhood.

I went to Miss Scannell for piano lessons and loved it. I loved the sound of the piano in my living room, and I loved Miss Scannell's black, baby grand piano. At that time, my brother also took piano lessons from Miss Scannell but I assume he disliked it, because after a while he stopped going. But before he quit, one day, when the two of us went for lessons, my brother took a different route home without my knowledge. Because he was three years older than I was I thought he was just about an adult, and I felt he was very important. That day he said to me, "Mary, we're lost." Those were the very words he used.

With a break and a tremble in my voice I said, "Can't you find the way home?"

"I'll try," he said, with a smile on his face...and we walked and walked and walked seemingly twice as far as usual; in my fright, it felt like we walked for hours. Meanwhile, he was enjoying his joke tremendously, with a big smile on his face. After a little while I started sobbing, then sniffling and finally bawling!

Suddenly, he said, "Oh, look, cry baby, there's our house." Richard was smiling and laughing because I was crying and only then did I realize he had been playing a joke on me. To this day I can still see Stevens Street and the drugstore on the corner where we were when I realized we were not really lost.

Mickey

We had a dog named Mickey. I loved him more than anything in the world. I would stoop down and hug and hug him, never wanting to let him go. I would say loving words to him and he would jump all around me and even knock me over. He was my greatest friend in the world then!

One day, without my knowledge Mickey followed me to school. I don't know how he got out of the yard but most likely, in my haste, I had not closed the gate tightly. He was smart, he kept a good distance behind me. I arrived at school, opened the big front door, and hung up my coat in the hallway on a black iron hook before going into my classroom. I sat quietly in my seat and waited for the salute to the flag and the song "America" to begin. Then...in ran Mickey and he jumped into my lap! I was so surprised, shocked...I didn't know what to do. I knew he should not have been there, yet there he was...on my lap and licking my face with his tongue.

The teacher, whose name I cannot remember, seemed very cross and asked, "Why did you bring your dog to school, Mary?" I timidly said in a tiny voice near to tears, "I didn't bring him, he must have followed me..." The tears were beginning to well up in my eyes.

"Then, HOW did he get here...?" she asked, coming closer to my chair and speaking in an angry tone of voice. I was still fighting off my tears when the teacher seemingly made a decision. She sent another child upstairs to fetch my brother from his class and he was told in no uncertain terms when he came into my classroom to "TAKE THAT DOG HOME!" My brother was not at all happy with me at that time, thinking I had deliberately brought Mickey to school.

Memories, memories...the children in my class taunted me after the dog episode by always pointing at me and singing jeeringly, "Mary had a little dog, (instead of "little lamb") little dog, little dog, Mary had a little dog whose fleece was white as snow, (Mickey was a white dog, by the way!) He followed her to school one day...etc." Then they finished with, "It made the children laugh and play, laugh and play, laugh and play, it made the children laugh and play which was against the rule." I was taunted with that song for months whenever we went out to the playground at recess. I must say my mother made sure Mickey never followed me to school again.

Another time though, poor Mickey got out of the yard in front of my eyes,, and just ran off! I don't know exactly how he got out, but he ran out and was hit by a car on Branch Street, which was only a few yards away from our home. Someone, I believe it was the man who hit him with his car, kindly brought Mickey back to our apartment carrying him in his arms. He knocked on the door, presumably after asking people in the neighborhood who owned the dog, and said to my mother, "Lady, your dog ran out right in front of my car. I couldn't stop any quicker than what I did. I am so sorry." He was a nice man and seemed genuinely sorry for the dog and for us since, of course, I had already started to cry.

My mother called the Veterinary Hospital for someone to come and get Mickey, although we had no phone of our own at that time, never had one until we moved a few years later, so I do not remember how that happened. Mickey's paw was torn off with only a small piece of skin left attached to the paw. I can still see it hanging, even today in my mind. The vet said he would send someone right away to pick up our dog. The man who came to get Mickey looked at the paw while poor Mickey was crying and whining, and said, "It is a very bad break."

My mother replied, "I am sorry but we have no money for his surgery, none at all."

"Well then," uttered the man, "I will have to tell the Vet to put him to sleep."

I kept grabbing on to my mother's arm whining and crying since I obviously did not understand what was going to happen to our dearest Mickey.

"Is he going to die?" I cried, hoping for a good answer. No answer came from the man who gently picked Mickey up in his arms, and left.

After he left, I threw myself on the couch/bed and cried my eyes out. I am not sure what my brother did because he also loved Mickey. We were all upset, but my mother, in her staunch way, said, "There is nothing more we can do about this, so go to your room and stop crying."

Well, I moped around the house for several days trying at my young age to understand what making our pet Mickey 'go to sleep' meant. But after the 'death' of Mickey, the most horrible thing was the little boy upstairs. His name was Donnie. He came down by my window and hollered in a sing-song voice, "Ha ha Mickey's going to die-y... Ha ha, Mickey's going to die-y." He sang the song for several days and never gave up. He was the meanest child I ever knew! Whenever he sang at my window out in the back of our bedroom I cried all the more. Donnie loved it when he could torment me. He absolutely thrived on it, and since I was sensitive and prone to crying he was then prone to carrying on endlessly in his meanest ways, no matter what was wrong.

Days and weeks went by and I had to continue with the business of growing up, playing piano, smelling the flowers in my mother's garden and trying to do well in school. Then one day the doorbell rang. Mickey, at that point, was the furthest thing from my mind since I had resigned myself to the fact that he was not coming back; this may have been six to eight weeks after mother sent him off to the Vet.

My mother opened the door. Mickey was at the front door in the arms of the doctor. There was a huge long cast on Mickey's leg up to his front shoulder. The Vet tenderly placed our dog down on the floor and Mickey wagged his tail furiously and barked little barks and tried to jump up on each of us. His cast went thump, thump, thump, and banged the floor as much as his tail wagged. Mickey and my brother and I were so excited that we were over the moon with delight in surprise and amazement.

Then my mother amidst all the noise and confusion said very somberly,

"Doctor, we have absolutely no money to pay for this. I cannot possibly pay for the dog's surgery. You will have to take the dog back to the pound!"

"Not to worry, Mrs. Beakey," the vet replied, "we experimented, we took a chance and it paid off. Now if another dog has the same type of problem Mickey had, we will know how to fix it. He is yours to keep and *no cost to you!*"

My mother sat down, looking a little dazed and a bit weak. Tah Rah! We were all in HEAVEN it seemed! My mother began smiling, but my father had not yet returned from work. I was so young and involved with myself, typical of that age, that I do not remember anything else after that. But, what a wonderful ending…dear Mickey lived to be approximately 15 years old!

Once Mickey recovered I continued playing with him as much as possible. I loved being out of doors with him. I had a playmate. One day, although I was told NEVER to tie a rope to Mickey, I did. That particular day I wanted to tie him to the fence so he would stand still and let me play house with him. I was only about seven years old. I did not notice that the rope was long. I tied him to the fence area outside the kitchen door. The long rope allowed him to race up and down the side garden. He ran this way and that.

Finally I wanted him to stop and play with me up close, so I grabbed him and tried to hug him, which meant I had to stoop down to his level. I squatted down, my feet on the ground with my bottom also near the ground. For some reason, Mickey grew terribly excited; he started running around and around me, which I delighted in. I did not realize though that I was being wound up in the rope. Then, he must have spotted a dog on the street and he took off quickly as a bolt of lightening, arriving at the front fence in a second, leaving me entangled in the rope which was wound around my neck.

The fence where the rope was tied was on one side of me, and Mickey was at the other end pulling, and I was *caught* in the middle with several turns of rope around my neck and upper body. I was about to choke to death. Luckily my mother happened to look out the window. In what must have been a state of horror, she scrambled to fetch a knife out of the kitchen drawer and ran out into the yard. I still remember seeing her cutting the rope off of Mickey. Obviously, I did not die, but it was certainly a close call. That memory will never leave me.

After the rope was cut, I don't remember what happened. My mother may have taken me to the hospital, but then, maybe not. There is no one left for me to ask. I do know, that a terrible thing almost happened to me, and in retrospect, having had three children of my own, I understand better what horror my mother must have experienced that day.

❈❈❈

There is another rather embarrassing story about me. I thought about not relating it, but then it did happen, I still remember it, so here it is. I must have been six or seven years old. We were still living on Queen Street and I attended the Franklin School.

We had horrible bathrooms in school in those days, absolutely HORRI-BLE and frightening…at least to a six-year-old girl. They were in the dark cellar of the school. They were dirty looking, and seemingly the lights were never on when we had to use them. I hated going downstairs to use the bathroom. I was scared! I was in the same classroom with the not very loving or understanding teacher who was angry when my dog, Mickey, came to school. I felt the need to urinate but told myself, "I can wait, and do it at home."

Well, I wiggled and fidgeted for a little while. But then, in my feeble attempt to hold back what might come out when I did not want it to come out…I failed. In those days we called it a 'Number Two'… and… a 'Number One'.…they both came out. I was horrified! I could not move, I did not know *what* to do, as I sat in my seat, frozen to the spot. Several minutes passed and then suddenly I saw the teacher go to the door to call someone up the hallway. Then my brother appeared at the door…just like before when he came to fetch Mickey.

"I know what the teacher did," I said to myself. "She called for my brother to take me home! Oh, what shall I do, what shall I do?" and I started to weep. Of course, at that age, it never occurred to me that the smell might tell the teacher something had happened. I was upset when my brother came in and took me by the hand and angrily dragged me to our house. In my mind's eye, I can still see me being virtually pulled up the street by the hand, and crying at the same time. I was absolutely mortified, embarrassed, and…of course, scared…I cried all the way home!

❈❈❈

My brother and I attended the Franklin Public School. I was there from kindergarten through fourth grade. Then, for some reason the Franklin Public School was closed, rented or given away, I know not which, to the French Catholic Parish where we attended Mass every Sunday. The school was actually directly across the street from the French Catholic Church, which was named "Notre Dame de Lourdes" meaning Our Lady of Lourdes. My school was now to be run by the French Nuns who had the title of, "Les Soeurs de la Croix," which, when translated, means, "Sisters of the Cross."

French was never spoken in our home; my father was not in love with the language although he was born and brought up in Sherbrooke, Quebec, Canada, as was my mother. But, she was French and he was of English/Irish descent. (As an adult, and not in front of my parents, I always said that they fought the French/English war all the time!)

He wanted no French spoken in his house and that was that. My mother's family originated from Normandy, France and their name was 'Leclerc.' My father's family came from Ireland and England. His father's last name was 'Beakey' and his mother's last name was 'Worth.' In our travels abroad as adults, my husband Ed and I, researched all the countries and names and places from where our parents originated. It was most exciting. Ed's parents were both born in Poland and landed in Massachusetts either just before or just after their marriage, whereas my mother's family originated in France and moved to Sherbrooke, Quebec, Canada, and my father's father was from Ireland while his mother was from England.

I always wanted to learn French so I could communicate with my cousins each summer when the three of us, my mother, my brother Richard, and I, would go to Sherbrooke, Quebec, for a few weeks. So, I asked, nay, begged my mother to let me attend the French School instead of a different public school, and my mother said, "Yes!" I was thrilled!

Timid and nervous as I was, I nevertheless entered the French School. By then I was going into the fifth grade and stayed in the same school until I graduated four years later from the 8th grade. (To this day I wonder how my mother convinced my father to let me learn French and in a French School!)

I learned to speak French fluently and rapidly thanks to the good nuns. I had no choice since that was all that was spoken in that school! No English words were spoken in their daily lessons at that time!

I remember vividly my first day in the fifth grade at the French School. I walked into the classroom with my mother and the Sister greeted me with, "Bonjour, Marie. Comment ca vas?" I looked at her shyly and did not know what to say. Then she added, "Je m'appelle Soeur St. Vincent de Paul." She was still smiling kindly at me. Obviously she was trying to make me feel at home. But then, seeing I knew little if any French she started speaking in English. She had a classroom of fifty-two students…and *horrors*, most of them happened to be boys.

She said to me, smiling as she spoke, "I know just where I will place you in the group; I will put you right in the middle of all those boys. You see," she said… smiling all the while, "they all talk too much and with you sitting there in the middle they will not be able to talk to each other as easily." She nodded with satisfaction, placing both her hands inside the opposite sleeves of her black and gray robe.

I inwardly croaked at the thought of sitting in that section but I was left with no choice. My mother departed with a smile and a wave of her hand, leaving me to sit helplessly amidst the boys! The remainder of that year is a blank at this point except for one other incident. (Looking back today on all those occurrences, I imagine it all must have been so difficult for me that I blanked most of them right out of my mind).

In order to help me learn French more quickly (and I must reiterate, no English at all was spoken in the school) the nuns, all of them, not just my fifth grade teacher, but whenever another sister needed an errand and saw me somewhere, as in the hall or at recess etc., would send me on errands. For example, they would send me to tell another classroom teacher something in French. They would tell me what to say in French and make sure I understood what I was saying and also make me repeat it to them several times. I felt terrorized at first; I was extemely bashful to begin with and terribly afraid of making mistakes all the time.

But then, with the help of these nuns, who were very kind and patient with me, I learned how to speak French. Each time I went on an errand it was easier than the last time and I eventually grew in confidence and language ability. I suffered no more from the intensity of the shyness I first had. The nuns thought I was very special and they all treated me beautifully, and with great patience. I felt singled out and important somehow and that in itself made me feel right at home!

Most of all in my four years at the French School, I loved my sixth grade teacher whose name was Soeur Jean Bernard. I loved her so much that one day I asked a friend,

"Would you like to come with me to see Sister Jean Bernard at the convent?" It was a long distance away, but we had fun on the walk thinking out loud to each other of the surprise the sister would have when she saw us at her door.

We found the convent, rang the big doorbell by giving it a crank, and another Sister answered the door. She showed us into a parlor and then rang a bell hanging on a large wide strap in the hallway, which was evidently to call Sister Jean Bernard to come down. Sister was so surprised to see us that she was virtually nonplussed; nevertheless, she recovered from her surprise and asked us into a sitting room, talked with us and gave us treats. The visit worked out beautifully, Sister seemed pleased and so were we. I don't recall ever doing it again, or why we did not. However, my friend and I loved the visit, we loved Sister, and she seemed to enjoy us.

At the French School we wore uniforms. They were black from stem to stern and on top of the black collar we had a separate white collar that circled the neck and joined in the front. Then we had a little black bow tied in the front at the neck. I cannot remember what the boys wore; I believe they wore dark pants and a white shirt, when it was clean...plus a tie at the neck also. I enjoyed wearing a uniform because we all looked alike and in a time when most of us had very few, if any, nice clothes to wear, the uniform gave us 'equal footing'.

As my French speaking and understanding capabilities grew, I decided I wanted to sing in the church choir where everything was sung in Latin or in French. Learning any language is much easier when one is young and singing is a wonderful way to learn and understand many words; I trace my love of singing to that time.

In the sixth grade, I set a record of going to school a little early each day for the whole school year in order to sing in the choir for daily Masses. I never missed one day of school or of church! I guess I had developed a strong constitution that year and also loved what I was doing. I was given a present of a religious statue for having perfect attendance that year.

Unfortunately, in the seventh grade, I grew ill and had to miss school and missed attending Mass as well. I also had a miserable teacher. Our classroom was across the street in a small building next to the beautiful church, along with the eighth grade class. This seventh grade teacher would throw her 'clacker' at any child who may have been talking to someone at the wrong time. If she missed her aim, the clacker hit someone else, but that never seemed to bother her.

I was hit on the head once and I was not talking. The teacher threw her clacker at my dearest friend, Peggy, but it hit ME on the side of the head. I must say the clacker really hurt when it landed. It was made of wood, had a hinge and two sides to it to 'clap' together which signified, "*Be quiet or else!*" The teacher also had a fat, strong arm! Peggy always seemed to talk when she shouldn't. She is still my dear friend and I love her, but I have never forgotten that awful bruise on my head that day! Unfortunately I was left with a dreadful fear of Sister St.Charles Ovide from that day on.

When I was in the seventh and eighth grades, the older children sang at ALL the funeral masses. I loved music at that time. I loved playing piano and I loved singing, not that I was a good singer, but no matter, I loved it! The choir and organ were up high in a loft looking out at the altar and the entire congregation. I would stand right down at the front of the loft with the organ way in the back and 'sing my head off' as they said back then. The songs I loved most of all were the French Christmas Carols, as in "Il Est Nee Le Divine Enfant…" (I can sing that tune in my head even now, many, many years later)…I did not love the hymns that were sung at the funeral mass, but they were a close second to the Christmas songs and had to be done.

Time went by, as it always does and I graduated from the eighth grade. I don't remember receiving any honors or special mention, but that did not matter to me. I was thrilled to have graduated and hoped I might be able to attend Keith Hall, a private Catholic High School.

Sadly, Keith Hall does not now stand on the hill where it was perched. The marvelous house was a beautiful piece of architecture, but was torn down about thirty years or more after I graduated so an overpass could be built. Today, people wish it had not been demolished but it is far too late for that now. Also sad, our Notre Dame de Lourdes Church is gone; it was torn down along with the building where the seventh and eighth graders were taught. It was such a beautiful old church! (Keith Academy, which was a few yards up the street from Keith Hall is still standing. It was not ripped down but was converted into apartments or condominiums).

Keith Hall

I had begged my mother to send me to Keith Hall, absolutely begged, almost got down on my knees as I recall. She had taken me to see Lowell High School, which to my young eyes was absolutely huge. Of course now it is bigger and has more than quadrupled the enrollment it had then. But, I was too afraid to go downtown by myself to attend that monstrous looking high school. There were so many students, seemed like a few thousand, but I know now it was not that large, probably a few hundred students. I was frightened out of my wits for many reasons. I was scared I would get lost; not have any friends or just generally not know what to do.

Mother investigated Keith Hall, found out the cost, which was terribly expensive for us at that time, and then decided to find a job. She went to work so I could attend Keith Hall. (My brother, three years older than I, was attending Keith Academy). We were staunch Catholics and Keith Hall was a Catholic School run by the Sisters of St. Joseph, (not to be confused with the French High School, which was called St. Joseph's High School).

When mother and I went to inspect Keith Hall, we loved it right away. It was small, warm and cozy, with lovely architecture. I was so anxious to be selected as a student I had my fingers crossed and was very nervous. Mom rang the doorbell, and a Sister answered.

"Good afternoon," the Sister said. And then my mother, a little hesitant, asked, "Would you have room in your school for my little girl in September?" Politely and with a lovely smile, sister said, "Do come in and I will call Sister Superior. We will talk about the enrollment then. Come...sit in this office. I will call her right away. Do make yourselves comfortable," she said with a gracious smile, pointing out chairs on which we were to sit.

We sat down and I fidgeted, of course. I always fidgeted when I was nervous or worried about something. My mother whispered, "Sit still, Mary." So I quickly pulled my feet together and waited patiently, or impatiently, I am not sure which at this point, knowing how much I did NOT want to go to Lowell High School. I was a 'nervous wreck.'

Sister Superior entered, went to her desk, and sat down. We had politely stood up when she entered the room, which is something I learned in the French School, although I am sure my mother knew to do that as well. Sister Superior smiled, a lovely, beneficent smile, and then spoke to my mother asking, "Mrs. Beakey..."

"She already knows our name," I said to myself in much surprise. But, of course, she already knew our names. I was so nervous that I did not remember mother had already given her name to the other Nun who met us at the door.

"You wish your daughter to come to our school?" continued the Sister Superior.

My mother answered, "Yes... I do. We are Catholic, and Mary has already attended a French Catholic School on Branch St. and she would very much like to continue on with her schooling here in your Catholic environment with your Sisters of St. Joseph."

"What are some of your daughter's redeeming features, such as her grades in school, her attendance record and her hobbies?" asked Sister Superior.

Mother replied, "My daughter did not miss one day of school when she was in the sixth grade. She loves music and sang at all the funeral masses while in the seventh and eighth grades. She earned excellent grades, is fairly fluent in French and she plays the piano very well."

After that, I sat up much straighter and then the Sister Superior said, "Mary, tell me about yourself!" I muttered and stammered and showed my shyness, but Sister smiled very benignly at me which prompted me to say, "I really want to attend this school Sister...may I?" And that ended my speech. She said she would let us know very shortly after all the lists had come in.

"Meanwhile," Sister Superior said, "let me show you around our lovely building."

We saw a gracious building, although small. I loved it immediately. On the right of the entrance there was a very long room, the sophomore home room. On the left of the entrance was the tiny library and Sister Superior's office. Far back on the same floor was a tall set of stairs. Toward the back of the lower part of the stairs was another room, a beautiful small chapel. I loved the chapel immediately.

We went upstairs and perused three other rooms; the freshman room, the junior room and another room where Latin was taught. The senior class had the privilege of being on the first floor, in back of the superior's office.

On the way out, having opened the beautifully carved door, I whispered, "Mom do you think they will accept me to be their student?" Mother, always proud of how I managed my schooling whispered, "I think they will." And, they did.

I couldn't wait to start. The tuition by today's standards would be considered peanuts, about enough to pay for a meal for two in a modest restaurant. I think it was as much as sixty dollars for one year. But in 1944, with our country still fighting in World War II, sixty dollars was a huge amount of money. That was going to be very hard to come by for my mother, but she did pay for the tuition...somehow!

I attended Keith Hall all four years and I played piano frequently since none of the nuns were musicians. Often Sister Columbiere, in whose room music classes were held, asked me to play either classical music, or popular tunes for singing and once in a while for dancing. The girls were not too thrilled having to listen to me that often, and I don't blame them, however how could I say no when Sister Columbiere insisted?

I loved every part of high school, even pacing up and down on the grass saying the rosary on certain holy days or Easter, or even daily during Lent. I loved the smallness of the school building. And I loved the nuns, some more than others, of course, but they were all nice to me and none of them threw any 'clackers'!

I'm eternally grateful to my mother, (a saint in my eyes), because she stood on her feet eight hours a day packing cookies to help support our family and earn the money to send me to Keith Hall High School. But talking about my mother's work leads me to my next chapter.

Chapter 2
Family Life

Praising what is lost, makes the remembrance dear..."
All's Well That Ends Well
—Shakespeare

Leclerc family, circa 1912;
Mary's mother, standing in the middle, in back of youngest sister

Jeanne and Aurore Leclerc (Mary's mother) circa 1912

My mother and father had little education. My father had no formal education as a child, but after moving to the United States in his early twenties, he attended night school with the Marist Brothers. He found this wonderful opportunity by knocking on various doors and asking: "Do you have anyone here who could teach me to read?"

I always admired the fact that my father sought out someone to teach him to read even though he was already an adult and married. After all there could have been a modicum of shame attached to the fact that he could not read. Nevertheless, he persevered and eventually someone answered one of the doors on which he knocked with a, "Yes, do come in, I would be happy to help you." I am so proud of him even now, that I want to share that story with everyone. It must have been difficult and perhaps embarassing for my dad to learn to read so late in life. But he did and he was thrilled. He always told us he could only read on a sixth grade level but my brother and I felt he read at a higher level. He used to read some children's stories to us, but mother was the one who read to us the most.

My mother was a bit luckier than my father. She grew up on a farm in Sherbrooke, Quebec, Canada, as did my father, but she was allowed to attend school near her home until the sixth grade. When she finished sixth grade, she was told she could not attend school any more since her many sisters needed her help; either to deliver their babies or take care of them after the babies were born. My mother's family had eleven children and she was the tenth one. My father's family had twelve children, of which he was the youngest.

In those days, the early 1900's in rural Canada, there was very little, if any, money to be had. Jobs, outside of farming, and education were scarce. Most families had farms to grow their own food, and some to sell. They needed many children to grow up and work on the farms. In my mother's family, the youngest of the eleven children, Jeanne, was the luckiest since she was able to attend all the levels of school and graduate from high school. She went on to a job as a secretary, married, had two children and her husband worked at a non-farming job. They were not rich, but they were comfortable.

When my mother and father married, the wedding was performed in Sherbrooke and the same morning they were married they boarded a train at 7 a.m. and traveled to Lowell, MA. Evidently they had heard jobs were available in Billerica for machinists; my father was a machinist. He was hired by the Boston and Maine Railroad. My mother stayed home and had two children, Richard,

Jeanne and Aurore, 1946

and then me, Mary, three years later.

How does one talk about the most wonderful mom in the world? Where does one start? She was ballast for me, always knew what to say or do even though she had no formal education beyond sixth grade. She was a reader, a thinker and a do-er par excellence! She was strict, firm and loving, yet at the same time fun to be with in a quiet way.

However, when she was in Canada with her sisters, a different side of her personality came flooding out in waves. She was funnier, livelier and happy as a lark all the times we were there. I thoroughly loved the summer days when we would go to Sherbrooke to visit her sisters. They were all comical and fun to be with. Two of them were especially humorous, and the others were patient and nice while listening to the humor going around in the group. The sisters enjoyed having us visit each summer. They loved me and I loved them and their families. We were always hugging and holding and laughing with each other. My oldest and closest cousin is now 95 and in the last stages of Alzheimers. I love her and miss our lifetime relationship terribly…even today! Her sister, Terese, who is approximately eighty-five years old is also a good friend and has just now lost her husband who was in his nineties! I miss them all but Marguerite, affectionately called, "Margo," with a French rolling of the 'r', was the number one in my thoughts as a child!

❧ ❧ ❧

My mom was a reader and would read whenever she could. She conscientiously read to Richard and me every night for many years. Those were such happy moments, kneeling by her chair under the lamplight, or sitting on her lap listening to mom read!

Because mother loved to learn, when she decided my brother and I were old enough, she made sure we visited Boston to learn its history. She used her Boston and Maine Railroad Pass, which was a 'perk' given to the families of the employees of the Boston and Maine Railroad where my father worked. We could travel to Boston free once a month with the pass. (Also, we could travel free to Canada once a year).

On the way to Boston, mother would always point out the Bunker Hill Monument in Charlestown, which we could see from the left side of the train just before the train arrived in Boston. When I was five-years-old, that was an incredibly exciting experience for me! My brother Richard came with us during many of these trips, but since I was so young, I only remember a few of them. I remember mostly the ones where my mother was able to take pictures of us using her maroon colored box camera. (She could take eight photos on one roll of film). I was always so excited whenever my picture was taken. I could hardly wait to see what I looked like!

Mary and her mother on the Boston Common 1935

Mother would pack a lunch for us and off we would go to see something worthwhile and free... 'free' was the important word then because if it wasn't free we could not afford to go. In Boston she made certain we went to whatever was useful for our education. We went to see the State House on the hill with its beautiful gold dome! We also went to the Boston Gardens and the Boston

Commons many times. We fed the ducks, saw the swans, and sometimes rode on the Swan Boats. The ones that 'pulled' the boat looked like real swans to me as a little child. I was very, very happy on all those trips to Boston and I will never forget them.

We saw Paul Revere's House more than once, and the cemetery where famous people were buried. And let us not forget the Old North Church! That cemetery across from the Old North Church always fascinated me as a child! We also went inside the famous ship, Old Ironsides, many times. Then, being in the same general area, we explored Bunker Hill and almost always had a picnic on the hill! The museums were never left out, but at that time of my life, the famous historical sites were more exciting. It is one thing to read about Paul Revere in a history book, but how much more exciting to go as a young child into his house!

Today, Boston has what is called a Freedom Trail, which takes travelers to all the places I mentioned above. I have traveled that trail several times as an adult with friends from other states or countries and they too enjoyed it all tremendously.

But we did more than travel to Boston for recreation. My mother took us by bus to Lakeview to swim. My brother and I played in the water. I tried to swim, but never learned how until I went to college...all I seemed to do was splash and sink into the water. However, we played on the beach and returned home by bus. We did not have many of these trips by bus because they cost money, but my mother saved her pennies, and we went as often as she could afford to take us.

I also remember being taken by the Swanson family to Crystal Lake and another time to Maine, which was a rather far drive for all of us in the car. I will never, ever figure out how all of us got packed and stuffed into one car. The Swansons had four children, so there were four adults and six children all packed into a car probably built in 1935. I seem to remember I was always hidden away under my mother's legs or on her lap during the few trips we did take with the Swansons.

Mom had her box camera with her at all times and took pictures of different events. I used to look at a special picture all the time when I was little girl, wondering how that photograph came to happen. It was a photo of me sitting on the grass at the Boston Common, with my mother bending over to tie my shoe. I had my beret on my head and eyeglasses on my nose and I seemed smilingly happy. (Yes, I had to wear glasses as a small child. Other children in school always teased me by calling me 'four eyes', which made me unhappy and unsure of myself. I wore glasses until I was about twelve years old. Evidently in those days, if a child had a 'crossed' eye, no operation was to be had, but glasses with a certain type of lens straightened out the problem eye after a few years of being called 'four eyes'. Yuk!)

Today though, as I struggle to remember and write these events, I would have to say my favorite sites when I was a small child were the historical sights in Boston and the beaches.

Problems in Our Family

As I mentioned earlier, my father worked in Billerica, MA for the Boston and Maine railroad. He would take the train to and from his job. The train, filled with Boston and Maine employees would arrive daily in Lowell at 4:20 p.m. One day, while we were still living in the apartment on 28 Queen Street and I was about seven or eight years old, my mother said firmly and definitively one afternoon, "Mary and Richard, go meet your father at the train and be careful of the cars when you cross the street. Richard," she continued, "Go now so you won't miss the train and hold Mary's hand all the way to the station. Don't let her run into the street." Mother's voice was strong and firm, no cajoling, no explanations, just a direct order that we had to obey.

Well, for a little girl, the train station seemed a long walk away from our home. I wondered why mother was sending us to meet our father so far away since we rarely were allowed to go off by ourselves. We scrambled down the street, and waited for the train. My father eventually appeared, coming down the train steps with a group of other men who worked for the Boston and Maine Railroad Co. The B & M repair stations were in Billerica and since hardly anyone had cars at that time, the B & M railroad sent a train to Lowell so their employees, free of charge, would arrive at their workplace.

The first time we were allowed to go meet the train, Richard held my hand all the way and especially when the train chugged into sight. Dad, coming down the steps and seeing us, was so surprised that he came home with us most pleasantly. The next time though, and many times after, were not quite as pleasant. He would stop at a barroom with the other men, which was on the way to our home on Queen Street, and send us home alone, saying, "You two go along home, and tell your mother I will be there in a few minutes."

I was surprised, and Richard said, "Come on home with us now, Dad. Mom has supper all ready to go onto the table." But, my father replied, "No. I am going to have a few beers first with the men and then I will be home. Tell your mom what I said."

So off we went, home to mother. She said very little but we could tell she was disappointed. My father's 'few minutes' began to last more than an hour or two each day. I grew very worried about him. When I was young and he finally arrived home, he would seem 'funny,' different, like something was wrong. Sometimes he was angry...very angry!

Each day all seemed to grow worse and no matter what ruse my mother would tell us to use with our father, it never worked. He would NOT come home with us. Oh, he always came home eventually, but he was a little tipsy (not a word I actually knew then however). After a while things began to be unpleasant in our home and I did not really understand why. I just could not figure out what was happening since before that time we had so much fun together on our trips to Boston, on picnics, or just to downtown Lowell.

I prayed and prayed every night...kneeling by my bed, and I told God I would be so good, I would be such a very good girl all the time, if only He would make my father better. "Please, God, make my Father be good, make him come home with me at night after work...I will be a good girl, I promise...I will always be a good girl..." At that time, I was so young and knew so little that I felt that if I were good, or even better than good, all would be much nicer in our home. You see, when father came home tipsy, he was sometimes jolly and fun, although too much so, and sometimes he was just plain angry!

So much of that time in my life was sad and difficult. I continued to think that if I behaved all the time, and was a really good girl, God would change things, make everything better. Nothing worked, however, no matter what I tried. I went to church daily while in the French Catholic School. I went to communion daily as well, after I made my First Communion when I was seven years old. I prayed, implored God to make things better, but nothing seemed to change.

When my father's problems with alcohol developed to an extreme, I was probably in the seventh or eighth grade. My mother was forced to look for a job because dad was not always able to work. Mother acquired a job at 'Educator Biscuit,' (a cookie factory) more commonly known as 'The Crax' at that time. It was located on Jackson St. not too far at all from our home on Appleton St.

(We had moved from the apartment a year or two earlier).

Her working hours were horrible from my perspective as a child. For example, she worked one week from six a.m. to two p.m. That was not too bad since I liked having her home when I returned from school. But not having her home in the morning was hard. Then the next week she would work from two p.m. to ten p.m. which made my morning great, but not the evening. Nights were lonely. My brother and I got the meals mom had either cooked for us ahead of time, or my brother helped assemble some for both of us.

We did not have too much fun in those days, my brother and I. In addition, our house was full of strange people, which leads me to tell you about the house on Appleton Street. One day, my mother announced that we were moving out of our apartment on Queen Street. I had to stop and think that over a bit. I loved our little four room 'nest' even though I had had to sleep in the same room with my brother and then, after a while, my bedding was moved into the living room. But at that very moment I could not figure out why we had to move.

Mom went on to explain, "Mary and Richard, sit down and let me tell you what is happening next." Richard stayed standing and I sat down to listen. "Our new house on Appleton Street is a big old house; it has ten rooms, is made of brick and you will love it."

Well, hearing that, I was elated. My imagination went to work and it grew so busy that I never heard the remainder of my mother's story then. My 'busy as a bee' mind took over and all I could picture in my mind was this gloriously huge house and made of *brick* and I would have my very own large bedroom with a lovely bed! I would be able to run all over this big brick house and around it and up and down stairs.

Wrong! I was most definitely…wrong! Moving day arrived and I remember now sitting flat on the floor in the kitchen of the new house crying and blubbering. I said to mother, in a small sounding voice with tears flowing from my eyes, "Mom, where is my bedroom? I thought I would have a room for myself." I had looked all over and could not seem to find what might be my bedroom.

Mom gathered me in her arms, placed me on her lap, although I was about nine years old, and said, "You will have a room, Mary, in time, but not right now." I did not understand any of her words. Puzzled and with a complete lack of understanding, I said,

"I will have my room, but I cannot have it now?"

"That's right," Mom said. "All the rooms upstairs are rented so we can earn some money, and for now we will live in these two large downstairs rooms all together."

I looked at her, aghast and horrified and, in my nine year old whining tone of voice asked,

"You mean we will sleep in here and eat in here and live in here too…all of us? All of us will live in these two rooms?"

"Yes," Mom said, "but soon, you will have a room for yourself." Mother was not one who coddled anyone. She was a bit hard-hearted by necessity. I did not understand why until I was much older, but in looking back now, I realize she had hardly any choice. I slid off of her lap, looked at the upturned bucket on the floor and cried out petulantly, with a bit of anguish hovering around in my vocal chords, "But where will we sleep?"

She explained fully and firmly, meaning no questions were to be asked, "You and I will sleep in the living room at night, and Dad and Richard will sleep in the kitchen. In the daytime we will put away the bed sheets and the clothes, which is why I have these couches; we can sit on them in the daytime and open them up and roll them out at night to make beds."

I was so taken aback, absolutely aghast at what I heard, having imagined all this time I would have my own bedroom, that I plunked down onto the upturned bucket and cried my eyes out. I can still see the picture of that little girl named Mary, sitting on an upturned bucket, sobbing away in the kitchen/bedroom.

I suppose eventually I stopped, but I have no memory of any of that. All I know is that for quite a while mother and I slept together on a pull out living room couch. I guess the plan worked for the two of us, and in time, I loved cuddling with mom at night.

'The Crax'

For my mother, the Educator Biscuit Company was a hard place to work. But she had to find a job to help pay for the mortgage on our 'Rooming House.' Rents brought in very little money in those days. My father sometimes worked and sometimes did not, either because he did not feel well, had been drinking too much, or work was 'slack,' as they said then. Therefore, there was no choice for mom! She had to work! She felt fortunate to have a job at 'The Crax,' as the company was nicknamed, but her job required her to stand virtually in the same spot for eight solid hours a day. She packed boxes with cookies. I will try to explain what I saw once when I was invited in to see her at work.

There were moving belts of empty boxes and cookies and each belt was timed so the cookies or the boxes came down on the belts seconds apart. They were timed to the second, so one had to be fast. Mother was 'a packer,' so she placed the proper amount of cookies from the cookie belt into the boxes that came down the box belt.

She was so quick and so good at what she did that fortunately, (or unfortunately depending on how one looks at it), she was given more belts and more runs of cookies to pack than some of the other young women. She had as many as six belts to take care of, and all the belts were carefully timed to deliver the cookies or boxes to the 'packer' at a certain speed. The belts never stopped moving unless something broke down in the machine.

After twenty, or maybe close to thirty years, at the Educator Biscuit Company, mother grew deaf. The noise from the engines and the belts and the motors was so loud and so invasive that most everyone lost their hearing while working at the 'Crax'. (There were no government organizations overseeing safety standards in those days).

Despite all that, mother was proud that she was good at her work. Her meager pay was sorely needed in our home. She continued on at the 'Crax' until she was sixty-two years old. When mother retired on her sixty-second birthday, and on her first free day at her home, she almost collapsed in her easy chair, not literally, but mentally from sheer fatigue and relief. I remember that well. Her first salary was fifteen dollars per week for a 40-hour week, eight hours per day, five days a week. Anyone reading this today in 2011, would laugh at such a small paycheck, and might say, "Everything was cheap then!"

But everything was not cheap then. My mother's paycheck had to pay the mortgage on our 'rooming house,' for our food, clothing and other expenses. Fifteen dollars a week, $60 a month, did not go far, and I am eternally grateful that she was frugal enough to be able to afford to send me to Keith Hall instead of Lowell High School. My mother was a saint in my eyes. She was always wonderful, kind, generous to a fault, and a hard worker for many, many years. I miss her terribly!

It was not until I was probably ten or twelve years old that I understood that my father had a severe alcohol problem; sadly for him and sadly for us as well, alcohol had gotten the better of him. The remainder of his life, and ours, was difficult and fraught with his hospitalizations. Besides being hospitalized for his alcohol problems, the alcohol opened the door for other physical problems and also he had several accidents.

One time a roof caved in on him and a few other people who were attending an auction in a barn in Billerica! He was severely hurt and landed in the hospital for a long stay. Another time, when he was much older, his legs started to break, not both of them at once however. First one and then, in a couple years, a second one and on and on for about ten years. He broke his femur bones, each bone broke twice, one high up on the femur by the hip and the other, just above the knee, and the pattern repeated itself on the other leg.

"When he was good, he was very, very good, but when he was bad,
he was horrid!

I found that verse as a little girl in a nursery rhyme book. It stayed in my mind for, well…forever it seems, since it is still there… only because it seemed to fit my father's situation. I was ashamed. I did not want anyone I knew to see him drunk when I was an older child, and I did not want to be with him while he was that way. And to top it all off, on nights when he was extremely 'happy' he would come home and wake me up and bounce the bed with me on it and laugh and laugh and laugh.

There were times though in his life when he was wonderful, since he was recovering from one fracture or another and could not go out of the house to buy a drink. But as soon as he could walk once again, he would say, "Clara, I'm going out and I promise I will only have one drink. Just one. No more!" Then the whole cycle would begin once again. My mother helped him through the thick of all of this while working full time at the 'cookie factory' as it was jokingly called, since my father couldn't hold onto any job at that point.

My dad's very last accident, the fifth one, broke one of his hips which left him totally bed-ridden, meaning no walking at all for 82 days. After that, he came home and spent many months trying to pull himself together to learn to walk all over again! He was unable to walk for approximately nine months. This entire 'breaking of bones' occurred over the course of ten or more years during the last ten years of his life. Also, because of his alcoholism and his constant anxiety, he developed psoriasis all over his body. He was miserable, sad, and lost much of the time in the grip of alcohol and depression in his later years. We all stood by him, trying so hard to help him as much as possible until he died at age 73.

When my mother retired at 62-years-old, she began helping me. I was married with two young children. My husband Ed had problems with his back and had many surgeries and was unable to work. She looked after my children, and did the general house-keeping while I was off teaching. She was her happiest, it seemed to me, spending her days with our children before they were old enough to attend school. She read to them, rocked them, played with them and taught them as well. I was happy she was with our children and in our home. But there are still times when I wish I could have been home with my own children. (Although I thank my lucky stars I was a teacher since I had the summer off—two months and two weeks—as well as school holidays and vacations.)

We worked it out quite well in all those years. My mother and I did not have one single argument. The only time she ever became angry with me when I was an adult, was when I made her go to the 'hearing doctor.' That threw her into a tailspin. (Amazing how life repeats itself. I lost my hearing working in a poorly sound-proofed room with the high school bands in Turkey. I clearly remember myself saying, "There is *nothing* wrong with my hearing!")

My mother said the exact same words to me while grumbling and groaning as I took her to the hearing doctor. He found that her ears had been damaged from the noise in the factory. Now that I am deaf I understand better how she felt and the worse my hearing grows each year, the more I understand.

Toward the last ten years of her life mother could hear practically nothing. She read lips and read notes we would write and kept her wonderful personality, but I was heartbroken for her. In her last years, she would smile and listen and ask for me to repeat something. By the third repetition, I was sometimes practically sitting upon her lap. (I called it 'knees to knees'). We did our best but mother must have felt or seen the exasperation on our faces, and then she would laugh at us and say "Is *that* what you were trying to tell me?"

And now, one last incident that involves my mother and father. After Ed and I married, we drove my mother and father into Boston at Christmas to see the famous Christmas tree and lights in the Boston Commons. On one of these visits, when my father was in a wheelchair, I had Ed park the car up near the State House. I told my mother and Ed to walk on down with our daughter Susan, who was nearly five years old, through the Boston Commons. I would roll my father in his wheelchair down the sidewalk, the longer way around, since that would be easier for me to do, and we would all meet at the stores below to gaze at the beautiful Christmas displays.

I started pushing my dad in the wheelchair, as Ed, my mother, and Susan walked straight down through the Common on the grass. It was dark by then. I came to a corner where we had to take a sharp right turn. I had forgotten there would be a steep hill to travel down, so when I turned the corner, the wheelchair with my dad in it started rolling at a great speed on its own. I had to run to catch up with it and then struggle fiercely at the same time to hold it on the steep hill so my poor and crippled dad would not fall out of the chair, or have it turn over with him in it! My father was trying hard to drag his feet to slow down the motion of the chair but to no avail. Then I realized there was no sidewalk. What used to be a three-lane road had become a four-lane road since we last visited Boston to see the Christmas lights. It was now a 'one-way' street, with all four lanes facing us. I was on the road with traffic coming towards us as we rolled down the hill!

What seemed like a lovely evening out with my family after working all day became a nightmare as I tried to hold back the wheelchair with my father. Glaring car head-lights faced us and the fear of being hit by one or more cars was driving me insane! We arrived at the bottom of that steep hill safely somehow, but my whole body was absolutely ringing wet from perspiration due to fright and holding back all that weight in the chair while trying to avoid an accident. I was so exhausted that all I wanted to do was get back in the car and go home. Of course, none of that could be done, nor would it have accomplished anything. We still wanted to show our daughter Susan the windows in Boston all decorated for Christmas!

When my father and I finally met up with my mother, Ed and Susan, I breathlessly tried to explain what had happened. My father had been scared also, but by then he was in better condition than I. However, I forced a smile on my face and kept pushing my father on the gloriously level sidewalk while Ed, Susan and mother looked at all the beautifully decorated store windows. However, I did *not* push dad back up the hill to the car. I sent Ed to fetch the car and he picked us up on a level part of Tremont Street. It was an unforgettable night.

Things won are done,
Joy's soul lies in the doing!
Troilus and Cressida

—Shakespeare

Chapter 3
Musical Education

Time went on and my piano practicing went on. I improved because Miss Scannell, my teacher, always said with her special giggly type of laugh while pointing her index finger at me, "If you don't practice, you know what will happen…and you don't want to be a *dumb cluck*, do you?"

Then she would laugh and with that laugh, I knew she was mostly teasing me; however, for some reason, those words helped me get better and better. I loved Miss Scannell. The words, and the way she said them, made me never want to be a 'dumb cluck' if I could help it, so I practiced on my piano faithfully every day. As I grew older it became quite comical when Miss Scannell would ask me if I wanted to be a 'dumb cluck,' but as a young child I took her quite seriously and worked hard to avoid that fate.

However, I must tell you that there were some days, maybe many days that I did not want to practice. On those days my mother saw to it that I did practice. When my mother became stern she folded her arms or put her hands on her hips. Then we knew the time had come for Richard and me to do what we were told, or else…!

Miss Scannell did wonderful things with her piano pupils. For example, she introduced us to the Symphony. Now this was during the latter years of the Depression, and few in our class could afford to go to Boston and…to a Symphony! However, Miss Scannell saw to it that we did. We went on the train; because my father worked for the railroad, my mother had a free pass for me and for herself, but I imagine that the others had to pay for their fare.

When we left the train in Boston we made our way over to Symphony Hall in a large group with Miss Scannell telling us the following in her funny little raspy voice, "You keep a tight hold of each other's hands…do **not** let go! I don't want any of you to get lost in Boston!"

When we arrived at Symphony Hall, Miss Scannell gathered us around her. She was a tiny lady, probably about four feet ten inches tall and also plump. Because she was older she had difficulty running or rushing around. I can still hear her authoritative voice and see her determined demeanor as she stood at the huge double doors of Symphony Hall.

She stood there, short, with a massive bosom, hands on her hips and yelled at us in her raspy voice, "We have 'rush seats' and we paid 35 cents for them, and *that*…is a *lot* of money; we are to sit in the highest balcony way up in the sky. Now, what I need you children to do is this. When the doors open, you have to **rush** up the stairs as fast as you can and go to the very top balcony. *do not* stop on the way up…and sit in the very front seats of that highest balcony so no one else can take them! You go as fast as you can and wait for us. Spread your bodies out over the seats. We will be there right after you." (By that she meant that she and the other chaperones would be coming up behind us. We could run fast up the stairs, but the older ladies could not!)

Then she added once again and most authoritatively, "We adults cannot move as fast as all of you can, so make certain you run fast!"

We waited with baited breath for those huge doors to open; many long steps led up to those doors, and I can still see us perched precariously on the long top step waiting and waiting. When the doors finally opened, we scurried away like squirrels shot out of a cannon, up one flight of indoor steps and another and another, with all of us racing to grab the seats; we made it to the top set of stairs ahead of anyone else in the crowd. In a short time all our bodies were sitting on or lying across some seats! I saved one for my mother.

Miss Scannell was quite gratified to see that this symphonic experience worked so well with her little group and the parents. She decided we should go to the symphony once each year. She devised a plan; each student would give her a quarter once a month. She would save the quarters to buy the seats for the concert each year. This idea to save a quarter a month gave us all a sense of responsibility which was important in our young lives. Each month I almost got down on my knees to beg my mother for that quarter to take to Miss Scannell at the first lesson of each month. Of course, my mother would never have denied us that experience—the 'hard worked for' quarter was produced each month.

Each year we enjoyed the trip to the symphony tremendously. Miss Scannell prepared us in advance for the music that would be played during the concert, which allowed us to understand what the conductor was doing on the podium and improved our overall enjoyment of the music. We children all loved the experience and gained much knowledge each time we went.

I do not remember if, as the years went by, we always sat in the 'rush' seats. I do have a vague recollection when I was a bit older, of sitting down on the 'floor' section at a round table and on separate chairs. I must have been in my early teens since I seemed to have been most enthralled by the ladies and young girls sitting around us on the floor section because many of them wore long gowns. I could not take my eyes off of them at times. That was thrilling for me. I believe it may have been a Christmas Concert, but my memory for that event is not as clear today as it is for the first few symphony concerts we attended with

Miss Scannell in Boston. And, I wonder how much those seats must have cost then?

But not only did Miss Scannel have us attend concerts at Symphony Hall, she also had us play the piano there as well. Beginning when I was about nine years old and continuing until I was in college, she entered us in an event that was similar to a contest, except there were no prizes awarded. We had to play pieces that had been chosen by a group of judges based on our level of skill. Miss Scannell had us practice those pieces for months. Then at the appointed time, we went to Symphony Hall to special rooms set aside for the contest. We played our rehearsed pieces for the professional judges who critiqued our effort. The judges usually wrote a small paragraph about our playing and then rated us as superior or excellent, very good or good, or fair or poor, and made suggestions as to how we could improve.

Fortunately, I was always rated near the top or a little below. I must admit, I worked hard each year to play better and better. By the last couple of years in high school, I received ratings of 'Superior' and 'Excellent.' Having her students participate in this contest each year was a marvelous and most unselfish thing for Miss Scannell to have done for us. She encouraged and worked with us on our special pieces of music every step of the way. I cannot praise my dear Anna Scannell enough.

While I was practicing to play in Boston for the judges, I also gave various recitals in and around Lowell. For example, Miss Scannell chose me to play for the Association of the Blind once in a while. At that time of my life I was very, very shy. Playing the piano was fine and usually easy for me, but afterwards the blind people wanted to either touch me or feel my face. I found that part extremely difficult. I understood why they did this, but to have someone run their hands over my body and face, even in a gentle and nice way, made me stiffen like a board. I managed somehow and I think I only played for that association a few times. My dislike, fear, or shyness for what was happening must have shown; I may have been in tears about it at home, knowing how sensitive I was at that young age.

I also played once at the Opera House in Lowell when I was in my teens. The lovely old building is gone now, but I remember clearly accompanying some people who were on stage but not singing opera. I was paid, probably no more than five dollars, if that much, but it was so exciting to have earned a bit of money nevertheless. That stage and theatre were used for all kinds of performances and on several occasions I played the piano there, all of which prepared me for what was to come in my life.

Mary's Concert

Then, what I consider to be the most important period in my life, I had my own recital on a real stage with an audience in Kitson Hall in the Lowell YWCA Building! My *own* recital...*all alone* on the stage...was something I worked toward for a long time! That, for me, was the height of happiness!

I wore a white gown...my mother had made it for me on her trusty sewing machine. When I was about four or five years old my mother bought a sewing machine. I have it here today in my house. She paid a quarter a week to the store where she had bought the sewing machine until she owned it. Unfortunately, I do not remember the exact price but I'd estimate it cost about thirty-five dollars. Mother was so thrilled because it was a new one...a brand new, never used Singer Sewing Machine. She made all our clothes, and some for my one doll!

And so here I am today, having taught music for more than fifty years in school; given piano lessons in my own home; and still playing on my lovely Baby Grand Baldwin Piano at least once each day, sometimes for long periods and sometimes just for shorter ones if only to keep my fingers nimble. I do so enjoy Mozart, Beethoven, Chopin, Bach inventions and a few other easier pieces. I never play for an audience now since I grow too nervous and my hands are very arthritic...but I treasure all that I have and enjoy it to the fullest when I am alone!

And to think that it all began when I was just a little baby and my father took me into Miss Scannell's furniture store and proudly stated, "Anna, this baby is going to take piano lessons from you and she is going to be a pianist and go to college." As I grew up, Anna Scannell often pointed her finger at me and told me that story. And I never tired of hearing it!

Chapter 4
Childhood Memories

When I was about twelve or thirteen years old and we were living in the Appleton street house, my mother bought some white eyelet fabric. I loved white fabric (and still do). She brought the fabric home with a pattern and left it on the sewing machine.

The next day when I returned from high school about 2 p.m., my mother was at work. Well, since I was in high school, I decided I could follow a pattern and could surely make my own dress which would help my mother, and show her how well I could do on my own.

"*Hmmmn*"…I thought and decided, "I can do this by myself. I will sew it today while Mom is working and surprise her with it in the morning."

I already knew how to sew on the sewing machine; well, I knew how to sew a little. I set about sorting the pieces of the paper pattern, then I laid the pattern pieces down on the cloth on the table and some on the floor (since the table was too small) and started cutting away. I was having a marvelous time. (Patterns then were not as easy to follow as today's patterns since nothing was printed on them and the cut out work of each piece did not help much.)

However, something strange and odd developed. I did not seem to have enough fabric to finish making the dress. I thought I had done everything correctly, but as I looked at it, in what I thought was the 'all put together dress,' something was awfully askew.

"Ohhhh…What have I done," I asked myself. "What has happened?" I began to get worried, then depressed, first about the dress, then about the money wasted and my own stupidity. I had not saved *any* cloth! I had just haphazardly cut here and there on the previously existing whole piece of cloth. I had cut up large pieces of cloth that could not be used again for the dress. All sizes of wasted cloth were strewn across the floor.

My mother came home and must have looked it all over while I was sleeping. The next morning, pointing to my work, she said, "Mary, you had not bothered to lay down the whole pattern, all the pieces, and fit them together on all the cloth."

"Therefore" she said, "you have no more cloth with which to finish your dress." She pointed out how I had wasted much needed fabric and therefore none of the pieces I cut would ever fit together for a dress. I dissolved into tears and cried…and then cried some more! I felt so bad about wasting fabric and money…my mother's hard earned money. It broke my heart to think about it.

Mom was a dear person however, and told me not to cry anymore; she looked over the whole mess, thought a while about it and then said, "I can save whatever fabric we have and use it. Just you wait; I am pretty sure I can fix it up for you."

She went downtown at some point later that week and bought some brown and white check fabric. She fiddled with it all, cut and sewed this; cut and sewed that; and voilà! I had a new dress. (I must admit, it was not my favorite dress but I had to wear it anyway, no one was allowed to waste money in those days.) I gradually put it in the back of my closet and 'forgot' to put it on now and then.

I never, ever again, want to wear white eyelet with brown and white check. UGH!!! The worst part was mother had to cut the cloth so that one band of white eyelet went around the skirt area, then the next band was brown and white check and the third one was the white once again and fourth the brown and white check. I can still see myself skulking around in the dress when mother asked me to wear it. The dress was awful looking from my point of view, but I would never have said that to my hard working mother who diligently put this disastrous type dress together for me and all due to my mistake!

The Bloomers and the Swing

My mother not only made my dresses, but she made my 'bloomers.' I always thought bloomers were fine until one day some older child laughed at my bloomers. I was probably six years old when I realized bloomers were not the 'thing' (as they say today.) After that I was self conscious about them and tried hard not to have them show.

But that was difficult considering six-year-old girls are constantly upside down or sideways or skipping and running and jumping with skirts flying. No female child in those days ever wore shorts or slacks since there were either none available or it was not considered appropriate attire. This particular day two little boys who lived across the street asked me if I would like to swing with them. I had always thought they were so lucky…they had a rope swing with a wooden seat attached to the roof of their front porch.

Of course I said, "Oh yes, I would love to swing with you!" So, over the narrow road I went from my house to theirs. We were having so much fun, taking turns swinging, and singing rhymes that seemed to fit with the swinging until the grandfather of the boys appeared out of nowhere and started yelling at me in his gravelly voice telling me to go home.

"You are a dirty child," he hollered rudely. "Go home and don't ever come back. Go…be gone, I don't want to see your face back here again…showing your dirty underpants, you should be ashamed!! Don't you ever come back here again!"

He yelled a few more times. I was totally shocked and did not know what to do. He angrily pointed his finger at me indicating I should leave. I sadly and sheepishly got off of the swing, ran across the street, opened the door and flew into my mother's arms in the kitchen, crying and crying. I felt I would never stop! When she was able to stop my tears from flowing a bit, she stared at me with her lovely blue eyes, and asked what was wrong while wiping my tears away.

"What happened, Mary, why are you crying so hard? Did someone hurt you? Tell me what happened."

"The old man across the street…" I was sobbing and hiccupping so hard I had trouble talking. "The old man across the street told me never to come back and play with the little boys again. Momma, he said I was dirty and I know I am not dirty; I washed up with you this morning. You always keep me clean!" I cried some more. I was hysterical, blubbering as I tried to speak while my nose was running,

"Mom, the Grampa across the street yelled at me….saying I was…saying… I was a dirty girl and I was showing off my underpants, and that…it was a dirty thing to do!" All the time I was saying this I was once again sniveling, choking and crying as though my heart would break, "Mom, I'm not dirty. Why did he say that to me, why did he send me home?"

Mom kept trying to console me, but I was still a mess…a sobbing mess. "He told me"… sob…"he told me never to go back to play with the little boys"… sob…"again!" I began to calm down while in my mother's arms and then I could explain everything more coherently. "The boys will have to swing alone…without me! I will never go back there again!" I muttered out loud to myself as I clambered out of my mother's arms.

I don't remember now how any of this was resolved and I do not know if my mother said anything to the old man, but I never again went across the street to that house…*ever*…for any reason!

The Rumble Seat

Another of my childhood memories, is a cuter one. Uncle Ernie, from Sherbrooke, Quebec, had a car with a rumble seat. No one we knew, other than the Swanson family in Billerica, had a car and no one else that we knew ever had a car with a *rumble seat*! No one had money to buy a car then. My family never had a car when I was growing up. In fact, my parents never owned a car!

To our great pleasure, Uncle Ernie and Aunt Jeanne, my mother's sister, and their two children, Normand and Suzanne, our cousins, or in French, "mes cousines," came to visit. We had other relatives in Waterbury, Connecticut and Uncle Ernie, wanted to take all of us to Connecticut in his car. What a treat for me! My mother's brother, Uncle Louis and his wife, Aunt Medora, and their girls lived there. It was a little far for us to travel, but Uncle Ernie said all would be well. I was extremely excited to ride in a car...and...in a rumble seat too! Of course, I must admit, my mother had to explain to me what a rumble seat was!I could hardly wait to leave in the morning.

We got started after breakfast. The two mothers rode in the rumble seat with three of the children, and Uncle Ernie and my father rode in the front two seats with my brother, Richard, since he was the oldest, and biggest. Can you imagine two adults and three children sitting in a rumble seat all together for a five or six hour drive, if not more? And one must remember, back in 1937 there were no highways.

Well, we did it...we got packed and finally left Lowell. Getting into the rumble seat left a large impact on my young mind! I was as happy as could be, going somewhere in a car, since that was a novelty for us. We had *never* gone anywhere in a rumble seat car. (Mr. Swanson's car was a regular four door car). This would be a marvelous adventure for us as far as I was concerned.

Well, after we got going, things changed a bit. The wind became cold...and colder...and coldest! I ended up huddled under my mother's legs with my cousin under her mother's legs; the two boys took turns sitting between the two men or with us ladies in the back!

Each child did have a turn to sit in the front between my dad and uncle, we all took turns doing it; each time the car stopped we changed around trying to figure who would sit in the front the next time.

I can still hear us arguing, "My turn...no, your turn...no it isn't...it's my turn"...and on and on it went! What a cold and dreadful ride that was. It was memorable...in an awful way. To this day, I remember the ride vividly. We must have stopped for bathroom breaks on occasion, but I do not remember them. I only remember the cold and scariness and the dreadful fatigue that eventually enveloped me since it was a long ride to Waterbury. Because of the cold, we did not see any scenery at all, which was what I had expected when dreaming about this 'wonderful' trip to Connecticut in a rumble seat car!

Somehow though, we all survived the ride to Waterbury in spite of the cold, and had a really good time in Aunt Medora's house with her two girls. I was happy to see they had a bathtub…we did not have one…I was absolutely thrilled. All together there were six children while we were there and, I thought to myself, "I just know we could act out a show about Snow White by using the bathtub as a coffin. Of course we can put on the show, we will use the bathtub for a coffin and ask our parents to come to see us act it out."

I told the other children, including my brother, about my plan and said, "I know all the songs and I will teach them to you."

Oh, the wonderful memories; I remember well directing the play of Snow White and the Seven Dwarfs with my cousins. I was a bossy one and told them how to do this and that to make the play really successful. I was about six or seven years old when I saw the movie in Lowell and I fell in love with the story. (I was about the same age when I went to Waterbury in the 'rumble seat.')

"My Aunt Medora and Uncle Louis must be very, very rich," I thought. "They have a bathtub when none of us do." We play acted the whole time we were visiting my cousins, except for when we ate and slept. Each of the girls took turns playing Snow White, and the boys, my brother and Normand, played the Prince and the dwarf parts. I really do not remember who played the part of the Witch! It was all a funny jumble and we made up all the words as we went along.

Plays and musicals and singing and nursery rhymes always made an impression on me and stayed with me all my life…at home…and much later with my three young ones, and in teaching my own school children. Snow White is a warm memory in my heart to this day!

Train to Canada

When I was about six or seven years old, we also took a train ride to Canada. As I mentioned before we had a free pass to go to Canada on the train because my father worked for the Boston and Maine Railroad. We could go out of our country once a year and my mother, brother and I certainly took advantage of it.

One time we were lucky enough to stay the whole summer at Stoke, Quebec, Canada, which was a small town with a small lake. Uncle Ernie and Aunt Jeanne had bought a tiny summer place on that lake. I felt they were very rich also because they too, had a bathtub in their main house! They also were the ones with the rumble seat car, but they had turned that in for a regular car of 1935 vintage, a black Ford as I recall! Uncle Ernie let me sit on his lap one day and drive the car…meaning, as I look back now, pretending to drive the car, although at my young and tender age, and knowing nothing about cars, I thought I was actually driving it as I held on to the steering wheel while sitting on his lap…up the road we went from the lake house toward the town. I was so happy!

We were spending that summer at the lake with my favorite cousins. We were all close in age. If I was seven years old, Normand was six and Suzanne was five, and my brother was ten. The cottage itself was small, but that did not seem to matter one iota as we all squeezed in and enjoyed it to the fullest. I could not swim but tried to learn, and my brother could row the boat. The other two cousins were in the same position as I, since they were young they had not yet learned to swim. But the four of us fumbled and paddled around in the lake, throwing each other down and splashing around. Who cared if we could swim or not?

The cottage had no indoor plumbing, no bathroom at all. The 'outhouse' was out of doors to the side of the cottage. It was a tiny single room with a door and walls and a flat roof and my goodness, did it stink! I looked at it and said, "UGH!" To go to the bathroom at someone else's house was an ordeal for me, shy as I was, and not wanting to show my 'dirty' underpants, (I still remembered the old man using those words), but somehow I managed.

At one point, Suzanne used to throw stones into the outhouse while I was in there. The door did not reach right to the floor, it was at least a couple of feet above the floor. She would scale the stones in at me from the outside while I was sitting on the rough, wooden seat trying to do Number 1 or Number 2! (I think now she must have been jealous of me.)

The first time it happened I thought, "Oh dear, that was her time to 'get even' with me I guess." Finally, after many stones were thrown at me, I told my mother. She told her sister and Suzanne was punished and her mother, my Aunt Jeanne, insisted Suzanne must never do it again; but she still threw the stones anyway, much to my dismay, while I sat on the 'throne'!

Another episode occurred with Suzanne. She knew I could not swim and had never been in a rowboat, so the first time we children got into the boat she stood up and started rocking the boat furiously. She had no fear of anything it seemed. Again, I yelled and hollered and screamed. I was terribly frightened, and I was sure mother and Uncle Ernie saved me from 'drowning.' (Actually they were near me all the time; but I was too young to realize I was not in any real danger. I only saw, in my mind, a little girl drowning!)

Again Suzanne was punished, but things never seemed to change between us. Poor Suzanne never enjoyed my presence when I came to Sherbrooke and I really and truly never knew why since I tried to be her friend. Later on I realized that she was the youngest in her family and always seemed to be given whatever she asked for and/or was allowed to do what she wanted. When I arrived, things changed since I was company and they only saw us once a year if we were lucky. I probably got all or most of the attention, and Suzanne evidently did not like that.

The first year we went to Stoke Lake was a poor year in Lowell. The B. and M. Railroad was in a slow time and we had no money at all, so we stayed all summer at Stoke Lake. Consequently, I fell in love with the lake. It was small but the water and surrounding scenes were all beautiful to my young eyes. (I did manage to go back to Stoke Lake once as a young adult. What to my younger eyes had been a high mountain in front of the house, I discovered was a slight hill. The lake was extremely small, and the cottage was minute. All this made me wonder how we managed so well with four children and three adults. How on earth did we all sleep in there?)

Those were delightful summers for me since we could never have afforded to go on a vacation if we had not had the railroad pass and been able to visit close relatives. I believe we may have gone to Aunt Jeanne's for three or four consecutive summers at the lake. Other summers, we visited them at their regular home. A visit at their home was heavenly and a most rewarding time with laughter and good humor all around. We had picnics outdoors on the front lawn and sang as a group. We had none of that at our home in Lowell becaue of my father's problems. I treasure, still, those loving and exciting times in Sherbrooke. I looked forward to the summer visits all year long. They were meaningful and happy occasions…especially in the eyes of a young child.

I must add here that my mother had two sisters in Sherbrooke, and two other sisters who lived further away. The older sister, Tante (Aunt) Marianne was the funny one, always laughing, guffawing, teasing and hugging; she lived to be ninety-seven years old. She was quite a bit older than my mother and Aunt Jeanne. She also had a rental home on the other side of Sherbrooke and her husband had a car. They all seemed so rich to me then, in comparison to my family.

They would all come to visit at Stoke Lake or the other sister's home when we were there. Aunt Marianne had at least six children, one died in World War II at Monte Casino. His name was Adrian and he was driving a tank when he and the tank were bombed. (As an adult, while working as a teacher in Italy, Ed and I went to find the cemetery where Adrian was buried so we could take pictures of his grave and its lovely and inspiring monument. I wanted photos of the grave for his family who were never able to go to Italy, and for me as well, since as a child I dearly loved Adrian).

Aunt Mary's daughter, Margeurite, affectionately called Margo, has been my dearest friend since I can remember. She is about fourteen years older than I. She is still with us here on earth but not doing very well in a Sherbrooke, Quebec care facility. She is 95 years old now and has Alzheimer's, losing more memory all the time. I was closer to her than any other relative when I was young, other than my own dear mother, brother and father. She was wonderful, always happy and singing like her mother. Unfortunately, she became poor after she married and lived on a farm. The poverty, and all that accompanied it, did not deter her though. She maintained a home for five top notch children, and in spite of little or no money, did very well with the important things in life, such as love, friendship, gaiety, and thoughtfulness.

Uncle Ernie at some point had built some bunk beds at the Stoke Lake house, two sets, side by side, with a divider, which would easily sleep eight people, or more, if you were children. My mother always came without our dad at those times. When I was younger, I assumed he could not join us on these lovely vacations because he was working. Now I know differently.

We used to walk, we four children, for what seemed like miles to pick up the bread in the village each morning. It seemed very, very far, but it must have been only one mile, each way. One day, the scamp, Suzanne, did it again. She encouraged me to save the crust of the two loaves while she pulled out the innards and we all ate them. I, frankly, did not enjoy eating the innards of a loaf of bread with no butter but then, she obviously did. It must have been the attention she would get after this fiasco that she was looking for. When we returned to the cottage there were two loaves of bread but with nothing inside the crust. Aunt Jeanne knew immediately who the culprit was…Suzanne. She was punished again. I don't believe my brother, who was so much older than we three little ones, was with us that day. Had he gone with us to the store, he most likely would have stopped all this from happening.

Nevertheless, with all its little peccadilloes, the summers at Stoke Lake were a smiling, and loving time of my life as a child. I can clearly, to this day, see us walking to buy the bread and eating out the innards, and the boat rocking event and numerous other happenings while at Stoke, more of which I will not list now. My mother's relatives were always fun to be with and…they loved hearing me play the piano!

Seven Years Later…or More

Normand, who was the older of Aunt Jeanne's two children, played the violin for several years so there were times when we visited that he and I would play duets together. We were not the best, but our parents were thrilled with the performances and I must say, I enjoyed it all.

One day when I was about fourteen years old, Uncle Gerry, my cousin's husband invited us all to the bar. The country bars were family friendly in those days. Everyone went. Well, despite that, I was uncomfortable when we first arrived, but grew more comfortable as time went on. Uncle Gerry went around telling all the people in the bar room how well I played the piano, so…you guessed it! I was asked to play the piano: Mozart, Chopin, Beethoven and Bach and I also loved one of the Hungarian Rhapsodies by Liszt; they were all my favorites. I was a bit nervous as usual, but played the best I could, and before you know it, although I was only fourteen years old, a drink was bought for me and placed on top of the piano…alcohol drink, that is. I played another composition, and another two or three drinks ended up on the top of the upright piano. Uncle Gerry was constantly by my side that day saying, "Play more…play another one" or "keep playing…"

On and on it went. When I finally left the bar room with my large group of family members, the entire top of the piano was covered with drinks, all placed one beside the other going from treble to bass, or top to bottom! It was unbelievable! Evidently I pleased my audience and that was their only way of telling me how good I sounded to them. Of course, I did not drink any of them; I was, first of all, too young, and there would be no way anyone could drink all those drinks that were lined up on top of the upright piano…and stay alive… or… play the piano! But it was certainly a memorable afternoon for me!

The quality of mercy is not strained
It droppeth as the gentle rain from heaven
Upon the place beneath.
It is twice blessed.
It blesseth him that gives and him that takes.

The Merchant of Venice
—Shakespeare

Chapter 5
Recitals and Junior Miss Contest

Pleasure in the job
Puts perfection in the work.

—Aristotle

The concert…*my concert* (as I liked calling it in my mind then…although Miss Scannell called it a recital), was held in the YWCA Recital Hall in Lowell. They had, what I thought then, was a lovely recital hall. (Looking at it today, it is still a lovely recital hall but rather small). I was fifteen years old and…*I was the star performer!*

Miss Scannell told me though, that a star performer must have a partner, as in a co-performer. I thought that over, and decided she was correct. (I would not have been allowed to disagree much in the matter anyway. Miss Scannell was always and most definitely, 'the Boss'). However, when I learned who was to perform with me I was a bit upset. The co-performer would do dramatic readings! The girl, Barbara, was a friend of mine, somewhat, but that is not why I was upset. I felt more dignity would be added to the performance had there been another musician playing an instrument, or singing, preferably singing, rather than 'speaking.' Well, Miss Scannell disagreed with me, and of course, since I was young and she was the captain steering the course, I did not win the battle.

I was going to play classical pieces by Beethoven; *Fantasie Impromptu* by Chopin; Bach Two Part Inventions; *The Hungarian Rhapsody* by Liszt; and a composition called *The Sea* by MacDowell. (I especially liked it since it made me feel I was in the ocean water riding the waves.) Barbara's 'readings' or 'skits' were interspersed between a group of piano solos. Miss Scannell was the boss over the program and placement of pieces, and in spite of my woes and fears all went well; the concert was in extremely good taste. I was deliriously happy since at that age, it was the biggest event in my life!

My mother was there to hear me play, but my father said he was too nervous to sit through all of it, so unfortunately…he resorted to a few drinks to calm himself down and he never did come to the recital at all. I was quietly saddened by his absence, but then, I had to cope with it as we in the family had to cope with all that my father did at that time. My brother, Richard, was in the Navy, so naturally, he was not there; the recital occurred during the end of World War II or slightly after. Actually, Richard left home at or around the 15th of January 1945 to enter the Navy the year the war ended. The concert was in the spring of the year following his departure.

Many of my friends attended though, as did many of the good friends and family of Miss Scannell, and her pupils and their parents. My dear and oldest friend, Maguerite Thibeau, and her mother were there; they were so special, they cheered me on wherever or whenever I played or sang in a concert. This was a thrilling event for me, the *crowning glory* of my fifteen year old life and I felt like I was walking on air. I had many compliments and a few bouquets of flowers. I never slept a wink the whole night after the concert since I was so exhilarated and deliriously happy. But, then…I was soon to learn there would be other 'crowning glories' coming along down the 'pike!'

The following year two good friends, sisters Barbara and Ginny Broe, one year ahead of me at Keith Hall, came looking for me one day. Barbara said excitedly, almost jumping up and down, while Ginny smiled broadly, "Mary, we have been looking all over for you. We have a form here we want you to fill out." She was almost out of breath and had a paper in her hand. I looked curiously at them, not knowing what they were talking about.

Quizzically, I asked of both of them, looking at one smiling face and then the other, "What kind of a form? What for? Why do you want me to fill it out?" as I quickly scanned the piece of paper.

Ginny, with an even bigger smile on her face, replied excitedly, "There is a contest coming up in Lowell at the Memorial Auditorium and we want you to enter it." I was so shocked I didn't know what to say.

"Mary," she continued, "we are sure you could win, you play piano so beautifully and that's why we want you to fill out this form." And in an even more excited voice, rising in pitch, she added, "You might win all kinds of wonderful prizes! We went down to the office to pick up a form for you." Barbara added excitedly, "You might also win the big prize and be Miss Junior Miss of Lowell! But…you have to go through tryouts first and if you are selected to play we know you could win big prizes at the final concert!"

I looked hesitant, I am sure, not ever being one who could jump into anything without knowing what was going to happen. When there was a moment's hesitation in Barbara's speech…tremblingly… I said, "What is the contest for?"

Ginny replied slowly and carefully making sure I heard all of her words, "It is a contest…(she paused and then said with great volume and enthusiasm as the end of her sentence bellowed off into the air!)…to crown the new Junior Miss Lowell for the year!"

Of course, I had not even known there was an old 'Junior Miss' before but then, a new movie had come out recently called, *Junior Miss*, and I am sure this contest evolved from that, but at that moment, I knew nothing of anything like that, nor did I know at that time about the film.

"Oh dear, oh, Ginny…I can't do that. I am too nervous to get involved in anything like that and also I am sure I would never win! I am just not good enough!" Tremblingly, I then reiterated more firmly, "I…can't do it. I just can't! That is impossible…I don't play well enough, I can't do it!" My voice seemed to have risen an octave and I was frightened.

Ginny, with great patience and determination then said, "Mary, all you have to do is sign here, then we will help you take care of the remainder of it. You don't have to do anything after that but wait! Just sign here on this dotted line. We are so positive you will do well; wouldn't it be wonderful to be named Miss Junior Miss of Lowell of 1947?"

Ginny and Barbara were becoming more and more excited while waving the form in my face and pointing at where I should sign the paper and I was becoming more and more scared! I was caught in the middle. I liked the girls, they had always been kind and loving to me, and I wanted to do what they said but I was frightened, totally frightened; I had very little mind of my own at fifteen years old, and not too many friends either since I was still painfully shy…unless I was acting or playing piano.

"Mary, here's my pen, just sign here," Barbara gently urged me forward to lean on the table for signing. She insisted, "You can do it, Mary, we know you can do it!" They were cheering me on like football cheerleaders, "You are *too good* at playing the piano *not* to try out for it," Barbara said!

I must say, they won this battle and I waveringly signed the form and that was the end of it. They then left me as they scooted on to their classes…I was trembling all over as I hesitatingly went to mine! My mind was soaring ahead of me, a mile a minute and I kept asking myself, "Was I right to do this? Should I have signed that paper? I have not asked my mom or Miss Scannell…what will they say?"

I found out soon enough. Miss Scannell did *not* approve at all and my mother was the opposite. She felt I should go ahead with the plan and try out for the finals. I felt good about that but I did not feel good about Miss Scannell and her negative thoughts about the contest.

From then on I moved from one jittery day to another wanting to 'try out' and *not* wanting to 'try out!' Then, it happened. One day I was notified by mail that I was selected and if I went ahead with the plan I would have to go to the 'try outs' on three different days, meaning, if I performed well in the first one, then I would move on to the second and then again, maybe move on to the final tryout.

"Oh my," I thought to myself. "What will I do?"

I talked with my mother about it again and then Miss Scannell. My mother still wanted me to continue as planned; and as you may have guessed, Miss Scannell did not. She did not budge from her decision, not one iota. However, this was one time my mother and I went over her head…well… just a little! Miss Scannell assured me she was not angry at our decision, she just thought this contest did not have enough dignity or clout to it.

I wanted to play *The Sea* by McDowell since it was such a showy piece of music and it demonstrated my capabilities in a big way. I made the waves in the ocean roar and tumble. But Miss Scannell, knowing far more about these things than I did, vetoed that idea. She told me I should play the *Fantasie Impromptu* by Chopin. She insisted! (That is a piece where most people in an audience, who did not know much about classical music, thought I was playing "I'm Always Chasing Rainbows…")

Miss Scannell felt that the *Fantasie Impromptu* by Chopin had more dignity than *The Sea* and would carry more weight in the eyes of the judges. Miss Scannell, always the clever one, insisted I play *The Sea* for the tryouts. If I passed all three tryouts then she wanted me to play *Fantasie Impromptu* by Chopin for the big night. At each tryout I came out on top in my category and then, finally, I was selected for the *big* event! I almost fainted and I do not remember how I even got home that day.

Eventually, the big night arrived. The contest was held in the Lowell Memorial Auditorium. I had never played in that giant size auditorium before or in *any* auditorium that large! It was a beautiful place, and still is today.

The acoustics in there were marvelous and the seats were filled with people. My mother had made a white evening gown for me; I felt as though I looked rather 'swell!' The program finally started; Miss Scannell refused to come, but my mother was there. My father's nerves kept him away, again. There were dancers, and dramatic readers, like my friend Barbara, and there were singers and pianists and out of all that talent, everyone who performed did relatively well, considering what their venue was…but…*I won the big prize!* I became "*Miss Junior Miss of Lowell* 1947!"

A newspaper reporter was there from the *Lowell Sun* interviewing me after the program while we were back stage. I was in such a state of shock that to this day I still do not remember what I answered him when he rapidly questioned me. I still have the article that was in the newspaper, actually it is in my mother's album; I was so proud of it. "Imagine!" I kept saying over and over again to my-self, "I'm Miss Junior Miss of Lowell!" Then again, I would think, "I'm being in-terviewed by the *Lowell Sun!*"

My whole body was trembling and I was foolishly, (it felt like) smiling con-tinuously and stupidly not knowing what to say in answer to the reporter's many questions. My shyness had taken over. Thank goodness my mother was standing next to me and helped me get through it. I do not know to this day how she got from the audience to the stage!

A photographer from the *Lowell Sun* took a photo of me holding my bou-quet of flowers and of course, wearing my new white evening gown. Rather funny to look at today since I looked so stiff and awkward and scared, but nev-ertheless, I won...and the photo shows me holding flowers and smiling! I was also interviewed by a reporter from the local radio station, and then...after that...was offered the lead role in the play called, *Junior Miss.*

Besides the offer to be Miss Junior Miss in the play, I had numerous other surprises and presents. Each large store in Lowell presented me with various awards, as in: an evening gown from Lemkins, a store from which we could *never* afford to shop; a radio from another store; a record player with some records from somewhere else (the case that held it was made to look like a suitcase, it had a cover and a handle and could be carried from room to room); a gold watch from Scott's Jewelry; and finally, a whole wardrobe as in a spring coat, a dress, shoes and stockings, and the 'whole nine yards,' from the Cherry and Webb store in Lowell.

Keith Hall Junior Chosen as Lowell's "Miss Junior Miss" *Feb. 25, 1947*

Miss Mary Beakey, 193 Appleton St., Chosen at Junior Miss Dance in Auditorium

LOWELL—A 16-year-old Keith Hall junior, who likes jive, but studies classical music, was last night named "Miss Junior Miss" of Lowell.

Mary Beakey, a brown-eyed blonde, won out over 10 other competitors in a contest that climaxed a "Junior Miss" dance at the Memorial Auditorium. Wearing a flowing white eve-ning gown of satin bodice and marquisette-over-satin skirt, with sweetheart neckline and illusion yoke, Miss Beakey was present-ed a bouquet of red carnations

Mary is Miss Junior Miss of Lowell

Strangely, although as the winner of the contest, I was promised the lead part in the play *Junior Miss*, I was told several days later that the director, for some reason, had a consultation with Barbara and her mother, and that Barbara would have the part and I would play the older sister. Of course I was upset... very upset. I wanted to scream and yell, "that is my part, that was what I worked for...you can't give it away, you just can't take it away from me!" But...they did. Barbara was given the part in the play that was originally designated for me, the winner of the contest!

I was absolutely devastated as only a teenager can be, to have worked so hard for this prime part and to have won the contest and yet see the major and most sought for prize given to someone else; that was just not fair! I wanted to yell and scream all over my little world...but I didn't. I meekly took on the part of the older sister although it was not suitable for me since I was not older...I did not look older...*I was just not older*!

The first day of the rehearsals, when I learned about the change, I cried all the way home. I can still see myself walking home alone from downtown Lowell with tears rolling down my cheeks and then in my mother's arms at home...she was most understanding and helpful but nothing could be changed as she discovered the next day. My mother had looked into it, and all was to stay the same!

Barbara became the Junior Miss in the play. The worst part of the play for me then was that I had a boy friend in the play, being the older sister, and we had to *kiss*. Ugh! I was terrible in that role, at least I felt I was. I felt rigid as a board, all over! I had never kissed a boy at that point in my life and here I was, forced to do it on stage and in front of the whole audience! It was horrible. I must have looked like a stiff, grown up doll up on a stage for all to view. But, I did it, I worked my way through that horror, and that was that! I have never forgotten any part of that contest, nor the 'kiss!'

In spite of my fear and stiffness, the experience of the contest and the play helped me in my future life. The opportunity to be in that type of drama at the age of fifteen, led me to be involved in drama and music through college. Then, those experiences carried me along in my music teaching career. For all of that I am thoroughly grateful to this day. The play, *Junior Miss* was successful, (or as successful as any play can be with young and inexperienced players performing in downtown Lowell); and, with me, stiff old me...having to kiss a boy but... being in the play was all that mattered to me after a while and I learned a strong lesson, which I never forgot!

All my music performances and acting roles made me realize how important drama and music are to children in school. It places them in another sphere, another spot in their lives where they can feel important and successful. I have never had any regrets about my years with Miss Scannell and her niece who was my drama coach, Miss Louise Dunn. They were able to take an extremely shy child (me!) and turn her into one that was able to step forward and help many children in the future while teaching music, acting and dance.

Who is Miss Dunn, you are probably thinking? Miss Dunn was an elocution teacher. The word 'elocution' is not as commonly used today as it was back then, but it is the teaching of the art of speaking correctly. She corrected me constantly. She was a wonderful teacher and gave me many ideas I used in my career later on. She taught us speeches by Shakespeare, among others.

There were other dialogues in which we would act out all the parts in a solo narrative such as 'Patterns' by the poet Amy Lowell. I loved that one. From my child's point of view, the last sentence really jarred me since it had in it, what in those days would have been called a 'swear' word. It ended with a most disillusioned and horribly saddened young lady whose lover was killed and the last words of the very long poem are, "Christ, what are patterns for?"

Miss Scannell was the one who suggested my mother take me to Miss Dunn for lessons since I was in need of stage presence and diction. When I walked on stage to play piano, I was told I walked 'as stiff as a board.' My arms were always stuck to my sides; I had no looseness in my body. I was always dreadfully nervous! Well, Miss Dunn fixed that. She started right from the beginning with me and worked hard to loosen me up and to get me to feel comfortable about myself. I loved every bit of what we did together and I loved her. She was tall, thin and lovely and always had a beautiful and encouraging smile on her face. I was in little skits, dramas, funny and/or serious, and also recited some super monologues. Every bit of it certainly helped me during my teaching of music, drama and dance in the future.

❧ ❧ ❧

A reporter from the Lowell newspaper went to interview Miss Scannell on the occasion of her hundredth birthday. (She lived to be 104 years old.) The write up in the *Lowell Sun* filled up a whole page.

I was teaching in Okinawa, Japan at the time. Someone sent the paper clipping to me and I read it and smiled from ear to ear. Anna had told the reporter who interviewed her about some of her special pupils, of which I was one. (I was not her most accomplished pupil though, since as I improved, she also improved and went on with younger students to even greater and better events in their lives. A few of them even gave concerts in New York City. I always wanted to do that very thing, prayed for it even, but Miss Scannell was not that far along in her teaching when I was her student and probably was not as sure of herself).

When I returned home from Okinawa during the summer of her hundredth year, I rang her doorbell and was shown into her living room. Anna was sitting on the couch with her feet dangling. (She was very short and with age had grown shorter!) I went up to her and kissed and hugged her; she was extremely happy to see me. We chatted a bit as I snuggled next to her on her couch, and then I said, "Anna, I read the account of your hundredth birthday; it was wonderful! However…I have a question for you. Why did you tell the reporter I was teaching in Taiwan?"

She looked at me in her usual rather gruff and funny way and barked at me in her raspy voice, "Well…where were you teaching?" Then I made myself more-comfortable next to her on her couch and I smilingly said, "I was not in Taiwan, I was in Okinawa! Okinawa, Japan!" She snapped right back at me and said, "Close enough!" Of course, I laughed, she laughed and we hugged each other. She was always amazing.

Four years later I was with her the day she went into the hospital. We had another loving and sweet visit. We always talked about the same things; recitals, how shy I was, how great it was when I played piano in Boston all those years. We both loved reminiscing! She talked about different pieces of classical music, my favorites and hers. After a short visit I departed with loving goodbyes and a promise to return.

I went back to my mother's apartment and in a few hours, the phone rang. It was Miss Dunn, my drama coach, and Anna's niece. She said, "Mary, Anna has passed away. She just went to sleep, a short while after you left her."

> *Tomorrow and tomorrow and tomorrow*
> *Creeps in its petty pace from day to day*
> *To the last syllable of recorded time*
> *And all our yesterdays*
> *Have lighted fools*
> *Their way to dusty death!*
> *Out, out brief candle!*
>
> **Macbeth**
> **— Shakespeare**

Chapter 6
High School Adventures

I loved going to the small Keith Hall High School up the street from my house, but, of course, being a much smaller school, I never had as many choices in our school as I would have had in the Lowell Public High School. But never mind, I was thrilled with everything those years; I loved all my schooling and my weekly lessons of drama and piano.

Keith Hall High School was in an old and beautiful building. The Sisters believed it had belonged to a wealthy family at one time. How it got into the hands of the Catholic Church I have no idea, or no memory of it, if I was told. Nevertheless, it was a lovely old building. Unfortunately, many, many years later it was bought from the church and then torn down to make room for an overpass. I was upset when that happened but I guess one has to make way for progress!

In back of the principal's office was a beautiful small chapel. I went to the chapel often by myself, and drew great comfort from it. It was small, peaceful and serene all the time. It was like a silent but beautiful escape from reality for me.

There was a long flight of stairs in the hallway leading to the freshman room upstairs, and one room for the junior class; then the last room on the second floor was for typewriting and stenography classes. The third floor was the attic and above it, a marvelous and old cupola, of which there was a vague story about a thwarted love and a lady going up to the tippety-top all the time to look for her loved one. It may have been all 'made up' by some of the girls. I never did find out. I feel, even to this day, that the story was undoubtedly true.

Another interesting feature of the school was the walls of each room; they were covered with sheets of metal, which left nothing underneath uncovered. It was not smooth metal, it was designed to be 'bumpy' but in a nice way, allegedly to cover wall paintings. We were told that priceless hand paintings existed on the walls underneath but unluckily for us we never did see them.

The sophomore teacher, Sister Columbiere, had a piano in her home room, which was the longest and biggest room in the school. I assumed it must have been the 'drawing room' when it was a home and family members would 'withdraw' to it after the dinner meal! Meetings of combined classes were sometimes held in the room, as well as sermons from the priest who would come over during Lent to preach several times during Holy Week.

Music classes were also held in the 'drawing room' because it had the only piano in the school. I was asked to play many times, probably too many for the liking of the girls in my class, but then, I had no choice whatsoever. When Sister said, whichever Sister it was, "Mary, come play the piano for music class..." I had no choice but to cooperate whether the other students liked it or not! I played hymns and classics and also some popular songs for the girls to sing depending on what I was asked to do by the Sister in charge.

I must now mention Sister Josephus since she taught History and English, and in particular, I remember her most of all from my senior year. I always loved learning English, reading and grammar and the like, and thought possibly I would be an English teacher one day instead of a music teacher, but then, I had excelled so much in my music and in playing piano during the four years I attended high school that the idea of being an English teacher became shelved. However, Sister Josephus made my imagination run wild between Shakespeare and Charles Dickens and the marvelous English poets and their poetry. I did enjoy all her classes so much.

Of course, along with all the above, we had algebra and geometry classes (not my favorites) and all kinds of history classes which I relished. We also studied chemistry but up at the boys' school, Keith Academy and in their lab, since we had no provisions for a laboratory at all.

Nothing spectacular occurred inside little Keith Hall High School, other than our normal classes. But when Lent arrived, and if the weather was fine outside, we would sally out of doors and parade back and forth around the grounds each day saying a rosary. One time when we were about to say the rosary I was asked to be the leader and I was just thrilled! I can still see the group parading up and down and fingering the rosary while I delivered the Hail Mary...and then all the others answered with...Holy Mary Mother of God, etc.

The only thing that disturbed me was the fact that my French capabilities were ignored. I was already very skilled in the French language upon entering the school. My mother told the Sister who taught French that I was quite fluent in French, and asked the Sister if I could go ahead into a more advanced class. My mother was more forward in her thinking than the nuns were in 1944. The answer was, "No, Mrs. Beakey, we cannot do that."

My mother then asked, "What will my daughter do when you have beginners' French?"

The Sister replied with, "Why, Mrs. Beakey, Mary can sit next to some of the girls that need assistance. She can help other students." (A bad plan from our point of view since it did nothing to fill my needs). Sister then said, after noticing my mother's displeasure and disappointment, "I am sorry but there is no other way we can help Mary in French studies. We do not have enough teachers or enough students to study advanced French. You will have to be satisfied with Mary helping others." So, that is what I did for the next two years. I helped the girls who really did not want me to help them. It was a complete waste of one period a day, but there was no recourse.

The boys' school equivalent of Keith Hall, Keith Academy, had a football team. Football teams need a cheerleading squad…so on one day in the spring of my second year, a notice came to Keith Hall that there would be tryouts for football team cheerleaders. That excited me! I went over to the boys' high school to 'tryout.' (It was just a short way up the street from our school). Many other girls were also going for the tryouts. We all 'tried out' many times, we did many cheers, and yells and jumping up and down, and guess what happened? You are absolutely correct. I was chosen to be a cheerleader. (I never thought I performed very well at the tryouts to be honest, but the other girls, as I watched, were noticeably worse, actually some of them were pretty bad.)

I was a cheerleader for the last three years of my high school days and in the last year I was chosen to be the Captain of the squad. All my elocution lessons were put to good use and I cheered away to the point where I enflamed my vocal chords once…but I was thrilled and didn't I love it so?

I wore a large all white, knit sweater with a royal blue flared skirt. On the sweater was the large initial "K" for Keith Academy. I went down to the Lull and Hartford Store with my mother; it was famous for sports equipment and of course, cheerleading sweaters and letters. The store had letters that represented all the schools in the surrounding area. They had the skirts as well, but skirts changed each year since girls grew over the years and the styles changed as well. One sweater lasted for three years though, since they were all quite large to begin with. Many times we had to wear other sweaters underneath since the weather here can grow quite cold near the beginning of November and football games were held until Thanksgiving. I remember all the jumping, yelling, and routines we had to learn and how crazy we all became when Keith Academy won a game. Cheerleading did so much for me in terms of making me more confident.

Besides cheerleading, one other thing happened to make my senior year the best ever. The senior class held tryouts for its annual play titled: *Our Hearts Were Young and Gay* by Cornelia Otis Skinner. I tried out for the lead and won it and Pat Evans won the co-lead. We were to be sisters in the play. The play was staged in the Lowell High School Auditorium. That was a success for me, and a confidence booster. I guess, in retrospect, I did well in high school despite the fact that we were quite poor.

I was sorry to leave Keith Hall, but at the same time, happy to have been accepted into Lowell State Teachers College, its name at that time. (It is now part of University of Massachusetts and growing larger every year!)

I had also fallen in love at the end of my senior year. I fell in love with a man named Ed, who took me to my Senior Formal and dated me a few times. We eventually married after I graduated from college and had worked at teaching for one year. We are still a warm and loving couple, now married 59 years. Although we have certainly been through thick and thin together, we are still 'going strong' as the saying goes.

Chapter 7
Eddie

Mary and Eddie — June 27, 1953

I mentioned in my last chapter that I met a young man named Eddie. I now call him Ed. He was lovely, tall, kind, generous and funny and never, ever, forced himself upon me as some young men did at that time, or tried to do.

I was in my last year of high school when my 'best friend' (turns out she wasn't at all, but pretended she was), introduced me to her brother Eddie. I had never dated much; my mother did not really allow it. I only had two 'boy friends' in my life. One was Ray McNamara who was sweet and also gentlemanly. He was fun to be with and had graduated from college. He was five years older than I, which seemed to me at that time, to be very old. We dated a few times. The dates consisted of a walk in the park, a visit at my home, a visit at his aunt's home where he lived, that…was considered 'dating' at that time.

Ray was gentlemanly and a lovely friend. I was elated. I thought I was the only girl in my school without a 'boyfriend' before Ray came my way. Well, one day I asked my mother if I could go to a dance hall out at Lakeview. I told her I would be going with Helen. "Mom, I promise, I will not come home with anyone but Helen."

Mom said, in her stern manner, "Make sure you don't. Also do not take a ride in anyone's car. You make certain you go by bus and come back by bus!"

I promised and off we went. I am not sure at this time just how Helen and I got to Lakeview but probably by bus. We did not have many dances, well, I didn't, since, as I had said, I had a certain amount of shyness that still hovered and lingered around me and I suppose my body language showed it. I seemed to be stiff, and not relaxed most of the time.

Helen was lacking nothing. She was not the least bit shy which may be what attracted me to her in the first place since shy people tend to enjoy being with 'forward' people. Actually, she was a 'flirt.' But the worst thing happened. At the end of the dance, I could not find Helen. I looked and looked and finally she came looking for me with some young man and said, "Mary, you will have to go home by yourself. I am going with 'Ted,' or whatever his name was.

I stood there agape. My mouth opened and nothing came out. Suddenly, I said, "You can't leave me, how will I get home?" She never answered and suddenly, she was gone. That was it.

I was scared and miserable. Lakeview was far from Lowell (twenty minutes seemed far to me in those days), and I had to take the bus alone. I scarcely knew how to take the bus with someone, let alone take it to Lowell by myself. We also had to change at a stop in Lowell. To this day I do not remember how I arrived home, and safely, but I was left feeling pretty bad about my 'best' friend. Besides which, my Mother was furious…

Well, a few months went by and somehow Helen and I got together again, as, 'best friends.' She obviously had some characteristics that I wished I had at that time, as in her forwardness and her gaiety…Helen was always laughing. By then I had met Ray and she met Gary. They were buddies. They were gentlemanly and fun to be with and once in a while we met them and walked in the park.

Ray gave me a ring he wore on his finger. I guess that meant we were friends. I assumed it meant we would be friends for life and I would in turn love him and never leave him. *Yikes*!!! How little I knew about life!

Then everything came to an end. My Aunt Clara and Phyllis came to visit. I was happy to have them come of course, but then the weirdest thing happened. We planned, my mother, aunt and cousin, to go to Hampton Beach for one overnight. We would all sleep in the same room since none of us had much money. Helen was invited also. Not sure how I managed to talk my mother into that after Helen had left me alone at the dance.

We five, mother, Aunt Clara, Phyllis, Helen, and I went by bus to Hampton Beach. I was thrilled, since this was my first trip to Hampton Beach to stay overnight. The boys, Gary and Ray, said they would meet us at the dance hall. The Hampton Beach Dance Hall was a big thing at that time. If you went to that dance hall, you were 'special' in other girls' eyes. If you never went, you were nobody at all!

We established ourselves in our one room. We two girls would sleep on the floor, which was fine with us, and the three older ladies would sleep in the beds. The next thing I knew it was time to go to the dance. I could hardly contain myself. I was so excited! I was a mess. Not a spotted or dirty mess, just a mess emotionally! Having *never* done anything like this before, you can just imagine how thrilled and pleased I was! Helen and I dressed up and primped or did whatever one does at sixteen years of age to look pretty for a dance, and suddenly, when we started out the door, Aunt Clara said to me in her most officious manner, "Wait for us, we are coming along also."

I exploded inside, then timidly asked "*What?*"

Aunt Clara repeated, "Your mother and Phyllis and I are coming along with you. You certainly did not think we would let you go alone to a dance?"

I looked at my Mother and said, pleadingly, "*Mom?*"

Mom understood and answered me with, "We will sit on the sidelines and you will not even know we are there." She knew I was upset, but she had to be nice to her guests also. Of her own volition, my mom would not have gone, well… maybe…she would not have gone. She most likely would have waited in the motel room, reading until Helen and I returned from the dance.

Out we went. I had a face that was so low it almost touched the sidewalk. Helen was sarcastic and rude about the whole turn of events…the adult ladies chaperoning us at the dance! The ladies did as my mom said, sat on the benches along the wall and watched. Somehow the night went by, but nothing worked quite right. I danced a few dances with Ray. He was not a very good dancer. I did not dance at all with Gary; never saw Helen much and then suddenly, while walking on the sidewalk back to the hotel, (I have no recollection of where the adults were) Helen muttered at me in an authoritative voice, "You have to give me that ring!" as she pointed to my finger.

I just looked at her blankly. The only ring I had was Ray's ring. He had given it to me just a few days earlier. It was Ray's own ring, but meant to be a friendship ring. I was sorely puzzled and what hit me next almost knocked me over. Helen put her hand out and said, in a horrible, nasty tone of voice, "Hand me the ring Ray gave you! It's mine now!"

I meekly, near tears said, "What…what do you mean?"

She snapped at me, "Ray and I are a couple now and you have to give me his ring. He said to get it from you."

Dumb and witless old me gave it to her and then she left me standing speechless by myself on the sidewalk! I am not certain to this day how we both got back to the rented room and slept on the floor together as well. It must have been awful!

After breakfast the next morning it was time for the ride home on the bus. Helen and I were sitting together but not speaking to each other. I sat there and looked at her hand with 'my' ring on her finger!

The next few days were a blur for me. I was teary and moping around and not understanding anything. I remember doing nothing other than sitting and rocking back and forth in my mother's antique rocking chair, (which now sits proudly in my living room) and I could say nothing to anyone.

Obviously I was naïve, innocent and probably what one might call…stupid. I was not sure if I felt worse about losing my boyfriend, (I thought he was my boyfriend) or losing my best friend or feeling I was a loser to begin with. Somehow, I got through it and, as usual, life went on.

Where does Eddie come in? He was Helen's brother. I was still seeing Helen once in a while in school, and her brother Eddie was a lovely and nice person. I invited him to come with me to our senior formal, at Keith Hall. Of course, Helen and Ray came with us, but then, I had put all those feelings about Ray away since I had Eddie and that was *all* that mattered to me at that time. I then went on to Lowell State Teachers College to work toward my degree and Ed went back to the Navy until his time was finished.

❧ ❧ ❧

I must tell you about another high school incident that involved Helen and me. I had a winter tweed coat. Helen happened to have a tweed coat that winter also. They were the same style but each had a slightly different shade. One day, after school, I went to put on my coat; I was at the coat rack at Keith Hall, and couldn't find my coat. I looked everywhere. I spoke to the nun in charge telling her my story, and she said she had not seen it.

However, there was one coat left hanging on a hook and no one else left in the school, which implied someone had taken the wrong coat. I tried on the other coat, since I needed something to wear in order to get to my house. I was in despair, since the 'other' coat, which looked a little like mine, did not fit me very well. The shoulders were too narrow and the sleeves too short…and yes, I might have been able to button it but then, I hung out all over.

Sister said, "Mary, wear it home, you need something on you for the walk to your house, this is winter and the weather is freezing cold!"

I looked at it on me, despairingly, and replied to Sister, "You are right, Sister, I have to go home." It was already growing dark out and it was only about four o'clock. I put it on and started out the door, and went on down the street, feeling weird with a coat that did not fit. I had almost arrived at my house when I noticed a figure walking toward me, but rather far away. The figure looked a little unusual to me. The closer we got to each other I soon realized the figure was Helen dressed in a coat that was much too big for her, sleeves hanging down, shoulders drooping and too long. With utter surprise, I said aloud to myself, "She has my coat on!"

Finally we met up, and I said, "Didn't you know you had my coat on? It's much too large for you. Couldn't you tell the difference?"

Helen mumbled something and we hastily changed coats on Appleton St. Lucky for me, I was near my house but she had a long walk to go home to hers!

❧ ❧ ❧

In Helen's home there were, besides 'unfaithful' Helen, other brothers, six, to be exact, and one other very bossy sister. There were eight children total in her family, but two were already married when Helen and I were in high school. I grew to know the family better when I began dating Helen's brother, Eddie.

Her older brother Henry, was the star of the family. During World War II he had been a paratrooper and jumped at the Normandy invasion and other war zones. He came home unharmed and filled with medals…and then went on to University of Massachusetts.

(l-r) Guziejka brothers—Stanley, Mitchell, Edward, Chester, Sabin, and Henry

I felt quite honored one day when Henry asked me to help him with a composition. As it turned out, I helped him with several papers since he was studying French and had many problems with the French language. He also liked the way I wrote his composition. I felt so good about my paper work, which was written for Henry and he was in a University, which meant 'my' work was being accepted on a college level. I was thrilled!

Time went by, as it always does, and Helen married Ray. Fortunately, I was forgiving and still thought Ray was a good guy right up until and after their divorce twenty-five years and two children later. She had become an alcoholic and to this day, sadly, still resides in a state nursing home and in terrible shape. It was all quite sad for her family. She had a boy and a girl. Unfortunately, her daughter, Gail, has now died but her son is a podiatrist and lawyer and doing very well.

But for me, well…I got the best of the lot; Eddie. We have been married for 59 years, and to be most exact, 59 years today, June 27, 2012 as I sit writing this. We had three children also and all were and are wonderful!

Chapter 8
Lowell State Teachers College

After graduating from Keith Hall in 1948, I went on to Lowell State Teachers College. I went through my whole four years there in the Music Education Department, with piano and singing recitals; acting and student teaching; and regular classes in *one* building! Now, more than 60 years later, the school has become the University of Massachusetts of Lowell and has many, many fine and beautiful buildings.

I walked to school, it was only a mile or two each way. Once in a while a friend who had a car would offer me a ride to my home, but I was most careful…I had to know who it was. That person had to be someone I knew well or I would never get into the car. Of course, as I write this paragraph I remember once when a 'friend' offered to take me home and I accepted. Let me tell you, I never did that again. He pulled the car over a few blocks from my home and decided I must 'neck' with him. I settled that pretty fast. I got out of the car and walked the remainder of the way home. We never spoke to each other again after that episode. In retrospect, he was awfully strong and very insistent, but I fought back and left the car.

I was still going out with Ed. When I say, 'going out' I mean, he was still my beau, but we really did not 'go' anywhere at all. He had a car, he worked and I only went out one night a week according to my mom's dictates and had to be in at a certain time…or else! That was fine since I had lots of homework and piano practicing, both of which took almost all my time.

I stayed up late working on my Chopin pieces or Mozart or Beethoven or Grieg or Liszt and of course, my finger exercises and scales. Finger exercises are extemely important. They help one to be a fine pianist and I wanted to be a 'fine' pianist at that point. Three to four hours a day of practicing on my piano was not unusual, which left little time for sleep.

I was a nervous wreck the first year of college because I wanted to do well, but at the same time I was afraid of everything. I tried not to show this fear, nor did I tell any of the other students…but I was scared.

The upper classes were small, so we, the freshmen music education class, ended up having the largest enrollment of music students. And we, in the music department, were only twenty-four students, twelve boys and twelve girls. Elementary school teaching classes were larger, but not by much. There were approximately eighty other students enrolled in freshmen elementary teaching. Our class enrollment was the largest of all the students studying music and elementary school teaching combined. Consequently, there were few music students throughout the other three levels as compared to the freshman class.

As a result, we all grew to know one another fairly well. When there were concerts for the more important holidays we were all in them. When we had musicals or shows we all participated. All the freshmen students majoring in Band/Orchestra played with the older students for all concerts. All of us also sang in the Big Chorus with the older students as well, since there were never enough students in each level to make a large enough chorus. The combined larger sound was marvelous; it was 'music to my ears.' I loved all of it, and every single thing in which I participated in all the four years of my college days.

In our choruses or recitals we always sang or played classical music. However, there were a few times for some fun and games. Every spring we had 'Amateur Antics.' It was usually a hilarious show. Sometimes some of the acts were serious but you can rest assured, ours was not. We had some young men in our group who had marvelous senses of humor. The first time we performed for Amateur Antics our freshman show was not only entertaining it was hilarious.

I gave a speech, a Shakespearean speech that was altered with humor to fit the occasion. I believe it started with "Friends, Romans, countrymen, lend me your ears..." Someone in the class had gotten hold of a humorous and altered edition of some famous speeches by Shakespeare. They were a riot to deliver and funnier still to hear. I delivered one of the speeches wrapped up in a sheet, trying hard to look Roman, which of course, I wasn't and I had a marvelous time. Our show was so funny and well delivered that we were *positive* we would win the Gold Medal. Guess what? We did not. I am not even sure where we placed now, all these years later, but I do not believe it was even second place. Each year, we discovered later, it was usually the more serious plays which delivered a serious message that won. Therefore, crestfallen, we went back to our groups and decided the prize was not so important, what was important was that we all had a great time and worked together as a group; that was what mattered that night.

Vito Selvaggio was a seriously wonderful friend to me all my four years in college. He was older, had been in the service as had Al Tatarunis, my other good friend who was a junior at that time. They had been through rigorous training, and were certainly far more mature than I, the young girl from Lowell who never went into the military.

We had recitals once each week throughout the school year. Each music-student was required to perform three times during the two semesters at one of the weekly recitals; twice in our major (mine was piano) and once in our minor (mine was voice). I did not have a wonderful singing voice, which upset me terribly in the beginning of my training. My singing teacher, Mrs. Vose, told me that I had a voice like a child. I had 'no overtones' and those were her very words. I was heartbroken that night after my lesson, but...never mind. It proved to be a boon while teaching little children since their voices lack 'overtones' also!

At one point we had to write our own classical composition. Mine was called "Little Peter." I based it on one of the Bach Inventions, two pages long with a repetitive melody alternating from right hand, (treble clef) to left hand, (bass clef.) I succeeded in doing what I set out to do and was definitely pleased with the outcome.

Vito surprised me one time during one of the recitals when he played my composition, 'Little Peter,' on his clarinet! I was stunned, overwhelmed, and absolutely beside myself with sheer joy and happiness. I can still see him in my mind, on the stage...and as he finished he waved for me to stand and accept the compliments from the audience. Vito was short and I was tall, and he possessed a crackerjack sense of humor. He would often say to me, "If you were short and I was tall I would *marry you!*" He was and still is a great guy.

After each recital in which we performed, we had to meet with the head of the music department in his office the next day. He would then critique our performance. I have already mentioned that our music department was small, which made all of us care how the other one performed and/or was graded. During each recital three music teachers gave critiques of the students playing their instrument or singing, (similar to the auditions I attended in the Boston Conservatory with my teacher Anna Scannell).

On the day following a recital, a crowd of students gathered in the hallway sitting on the steps that led up to the gym, waiting to hear what criticisms, if any, our fellow students would receive.

Well, one day it was my turn to see Cyrus Thompson. He was the music department 'Head' and a very large man with an Adolf Hitler style mustache. I went to his door and knocked. He asked me in and said, "Sit down, Mary."

Then there was a long pause as he sat and fiddled with papers that were strewn in front of him on his desk. He then looked up and stared at me for what seemed a long time. I waited to hear if I received an 'A' or a 'B' or whatever, and the reasons why. The first words out of his mouth were, "I don't like your hairdo! I want you to change it. Do something different with it. It spoils your appearance and it does not look good while you are up on the stage performing."

I was absolutely taken aback by his remarks. In my utter disbelief all I could do was stare at his mustache that looked like Hitler's. I felt I was frozen in place as he talked while his mustache moved up and down.

First of all, my hair style had nothing to do with my playing, and secondly, I liked my hairdo. It was plain and simple, no curls, just bangs and long straight hair and perfectly clean at all times. Knowing my temperament, I was angry but I was also very sad and I had all I could do not to cry in front of him. He muttered something else that I could not understand, stood up and asked me to leave and said, "Would you please send in the next student?"

I fumbled my way out of the door and saw Al Tatarunis and Marcia (they later married) and five or six other seniors and/or juniors waiting to hear my score. I was a freshman and they had all thought I played piano beautifully and were anxiously waiting for the results of my meeting with Cyrus Thompson. I looked at all those young men and women who always seemed to be so kind to the younger classmen, and I burst into tears. I tried to tell them what Mr. Thompson had said, but with tears starting to pop out of my eyes all I could do was choke and utter a few words, "He...he...told me...(choke and sniff)...he did not like...my...hairdo!"

And after that I dissolved into more tears. Good old Al and the others were upset and felt no student deserved to be treated that way. I am not sure what they said or did about this, nor do I remember if my grade was changed, but the next day I heard that a body of students went to see Cyrus Thompson. I do not remember what else happened, exactly, but what I do know is I have loved Al and Vito and Marcia and the others ever since. Vito and Al are still nearby, but many of the others have moved on or left us due to age and illness. Our whole group of music students on every level were close, we were so few and had so much in common...which was love for *music* and thence...each other!

As an aside, Al came to my rescue several times, through chance a few times and through his good natured spirit and generosity at others. Al had and still has now, a great sense of humor, and is a fine musician. His love of music came issuing forward when he played or sang in schools or parties or in churches. I learned so much when I worked with him in Danvers, of which you will learn more later. As I write today, he is still singing in churches in Massachusetts, New Hampshire and Florida in the winter!

On another note, all the music classes together studied and sang the famous

Handel's *Messiah* in the spring (and some other compositions that were equally serious and beautiful sounding whose names escape me at the moment). For the formal concert, we wore black robes and white collars and the delivery, I was told by my family, friends and the audience applause, was smashing.

The final concert we each had to give in our senior year, was the most important one of all from my point of view. Two or three of us played in the concert. I played the piano and the singing was done by one or two others. I played large and demonstrative pieces of music such as, *The Hungarian Rhapsody*, a group of Chopin, some Bach and a large Beethoven piece that went on and on. I was good, I played well and I knew it. I liked what I accomplished. Ed was not able to attend unfortunately. He was in the hospital having a couple of surgeries. They surely were scheduled at the wrong time! My ever faithful and proud mother was there, but my father could not attend for the same reasons he always had. Miss Scannell was of course, present. All went well and I was 'proud as punch,' as the saying goes. I will never forget that evening!

❧ ❧ ❧

In addition to enjoying music throughout my life, I also loved swimming. I had finally learned to swim while in college. A Red Cross representative came to the music class asking for someone to volunteer to go to overnight camp to learn to be a swimming instructor, lifesaver, and first aid person. The camp would last for two weeks and it was held immediately after school ended.

I raised my hand. (Something good always seemed to happen when I raised my hand). I loved swimming and wanted to improve my skills. I was accepted, all expenses paid. (If not, I would not have been able to go to the camp).

We were in the water about ten or eleven hours almost continually each day. Of course there were food breaks and bathroom breaks. I was absolutely water logged and whether one wanted to learn or not, you did not have much choice since you were *always* out in the water over your head. You could not put your feet down. We also learned much about small boats and boating in order to save someone if a boating accident occured.

All of my experiences at Red Cross Camp were good ones. For example, each night the staff held a type of concert, playing popular music, not classical. There were several water safety instructors who also loved music and played well. They needed someone to play with them on the piano so I raised my hand and up I went. I was so excited, like a child. This type of experience had never happened before. Of course, all ran smoothly and the instructors and I enjoyed each other.

There was only one *not* so exciting experience for me. It was the first time this had ever happened to me but I found out later in my life it was not to be the last.

One student, a graduate, from our college but not from my class, seemed to want, nay, insisted upon sleeping next to me. I did not care for her simply because she was all over me, in a rather physical way…and very persistent. Also, the room was so crowded with beds that each cot was a hand's space away from the other cot…we practically breathed in each other's faces, they were so close. Then after trying to find a different place to sleep without her breathing into my face and 'touching' me where I did not want to be touched, I was finally pulled aside by another friend who told me to avoid that woman. She said, "Come with me and I will find you a place to sleep in our cabin."

Therefore, like magic, I disappeared from the woman's sight. She did not know where I went, could not find me right away and consequently, she was sleeping in her corner alone. I did not know with whom she slept and I was not really interested. I was deliriously happy that the other friend had come to my aid because I really did not know what to do in terms of sleeping and where to go and with whom to talk…such a dunce I am…I should say, such a dunce I was. I should have spoken up and demanded my space, but that was not who I was at the time. I hope by now I have changed…just a little anyway!

Chapter 9
Practice Teaching

To become a teacher, one has to first go through a difficult period of time called, 'practice teaching.' With my shyness and fearfulness, I found some of the practice teaching to be wonderful, but miserable at the same time. I prepared, and prayed and hoped and mostly it was not too bad. Of course, there is always going to be *one* supervisor who doesn't like someone!

The college required the music students to 'practice-teach' during their last two years of our four years of college. At the same time, we still had studies and classes to attend here and there during the week. In between times we then had to scurry about looking for our next tour of duty and, in the evening besides doing our homework, we practiced our instrument, which was piano for me.

In looking back, there must not have been as many jobs available for music specialists as there were for elementary school teachers. Therefore someone in the Education Department, decided we should major in both areas. I majored in music, (where the work was detailed and tougher than I expected), and minored in elementary school teaching through 8th grade. That meant I was qualified to teach any elementary classes grades 1 through 8, or any music classes grades 1 through 12.

What did we do with all our other classes, ones where we had to listen to lectures and take notes, etc? Well, the professors had to fit them in around the elementary school practice teaching, which was not easy, for them or for us.

Somehow I managed fine in the first year of student teaching, and I found I absolutely loved teaching music, and enjoyed the elementary music teachers in the buildings where I was assigned. They were all helpful, friendly and understanding, since they had all been through the same routine once before in their lives. Then, the last year came along and…it was a tough one.

I was placed in a first grade classroom. (My memory fails here a bit. I'm not sure if I was in the first grade daily for six weeks, or a few days a week for a longer time.) I was assigned to go to the Washington School in the Highlands area of Lowell. I walked since I had no car. The walk was at least two miles and I walked with my arms filled with treasures I would need to help the little first graders along the road to success. I was happy and looking forward to all of this in my own anxious way.

Well…on the first day, and in the *very* first half hour of entering that first grade classroom, before the children arrived, all was horrible! The teacher's name was Alma Ward. I walked into the room and began to introduce myself, sweetly, and with a smile, and was ready to thank Miss Ward for having me in her classroom when she broke into my speech and expostulated with the following remarks, "*I do not want you here…I did not ask for you to come…I asked to have no one come to my room from the music department!*"

Without taking a breath, she continued, "*You will be very unhappy here, because I will see to it that you are. So leave…just leave…and go…right now!!!*"

I thought I would faint. I was sure I was in the correct room; I was so upset I did not know what to do.

Charlie Brinkman was a music student also; he too was assigned to this room, the first grade, with Alma Ward. For some reason, she kept him on. She dismissed me, never looked at me again, and turned around and with a sweet expression on her face talked to him. He stayed; I left.

I did *not* know what to do, where to go, how to handle this. I was upset and have never forgotten, even today, one iota of it at all! I stayed in the school corridor for a little while trying hard to think, but I couldn't. I started whimpering to myself, "What should I do… what should I do, where should I go? Should I go home or go back to school?" I repeated this phrase over and over in my mind. Then I gathered up my things and some courage from somewhere, and walked another mile or two to the college with all my treasures for the children.

I was so upset that when I got to my one building college, I still did not know who to see or where to turn. I went towards the front offices, and sat down on a couch in the hallway with my arms still encircling all the little treasures I had accumulated for my first lessons in Alma Ward's first grade class.

I was totally crushed, in absolute misery, felt unloved, thought I might fail the term and then what? Always in the back of my mind was how hard my mother had to work to keep me in this college. How would she feel if I flunked out of this course because of this woman? I knew I had done nothing wrong…

As I sat there completely broken down, Miss Wilson came along. She was an older woman, maybe in her early sixties, very sweet and kind and taught music education classes at our college. She looked at me, bending over the couch a bit, and said, most kindly, "Mary, what is wrong? What has happened?" She sat down on the couch next to me and added, "I thought you would be in the first grade now having a wonderful time with the little children!"

The minute she spoke so kindly to me I burst into hysterical tears. She sat next to me, and comfortingly, put her arm around me and asked, "What has happened? What has gone wrong? Can you tell me?" Then, with her arm around my shoulder Miss Wilson helped me to rise from the couch and said, "Come with me into my office, I'll find a drink for you and we will have a nice talk about what has made you cry like this."

She almost carried me into her office; thank goodness it was just down the hall a few yards. She closed the door, gave me a box of tissues, and waited until I had calmed down a bit and then…let me talk. I repeated all of Miss Ward's words and mannerisms and Miss Wilson, absolutely floored by what I said, could barely speak coherently!

"But how…how…on earth could anyone treat you this way? What is wrong with her? If she had a problem with having student teachers she should have been more forthcoming; she should have told *us* of her difficulties. We never would have sent you to her!" Miss Wilson then said, in an officious but comforting manner, "I will take care of this, don't you worry. We'll work something out, you can be sure of that!"

To this day, I do not know how or when I finally got to my home, which was another two miles away in the other direction. My arms were still hanging onto the treasures for the first graders that I now felt like throwing away. After I finally dragged myself into the house, I saw my mother was not there; fortunately, she was at work since I needed to be alone to think.

Miss Wilson knew I had to teach in the first grade as part of my student assignment and I wondered how on earth she could fix this miserable mess. I also knew I still had to teach in that particular first grade since all the other assignments had been handed out and the available rooms and teachers were all full, all assigned, and there was no other place for me.

Miss Wilson looked into everything for me and within the next day or two, I was called into the elementary teachers director's room. The director was sweet and understanding and said most kindly, "Mary, I totally understand how you feel. Miss Wilson and I had a long talk. We have worked together and produced an easier schedule for you…and please understand this; you are an excellent student and will be an excellent teacher. Do not, above all things, let this affect you any further." She then went on to say, "The problem is all fixed."

What they had done was this: I was to teach, still, in Miss Ward's room but she was never to be in the room with me at the same time. Whenever I taught a lesson, I would be helped and supervised by a professor from our Lowell State Teachers College who had once been an elementary teacher. The times had been worked out, and each time I went, I never saw Miss Ward's face again. She left the room when I entered it and never looked at me once. Each time I went in to that first grade, I found a professor from the college sitting at the desk waiting for me to teach a lesson. She was a nice lady and most kind; she knew all the details of my discomfort and Miss Ward's anger.

Amazing! I could not believe this was happening. I rallied, was able to pull myself together, feeling comfortable with the other supervisor. I worked hard and I also loved the first grade and I received an 'A' in my student teaching! I was extremely comfortable and at ease with this other lady, the professor from the elementary section of the college, and she was pleased as she could be about my work with the children and my steady progress during the one semester.

All I could think of after this whole affair finally ended was, "How lovely everyone was to me!" Miss Ward wasn't…but then, I never wished Miss Ward any harm. She certainly threw me into a spin though. Had it not been for Miss Wilson finding me crumpled up on the couch like a soggy mess, I don't know what I would have done.

My four years at Lowell State Teachers College came to an end. I gave my last concert, the biggest and most important one in my eyes, held at the end of our senior year in music education. I was thrilled with the reception I received from the audience and my final grade was an 'A'; one could not do better than that.

I remember wearing a lovely long gown and being most at ease and my mother was there with Miss Scannell. Ed was not there since he was in the hospital for an operation on his knee and then his foot. All my college friends thought I played beautifully, and Miss Scannell and my mom were extremely proud and had huge smiles on their faces as they hugged and kissed me!

There was not much to do at the college following the concert. All that we had left now was the graduation. Ed and I had become engaged on April Fool's Day 1952, his humor came into play at that time…and that…I will never forget. We married one year later in June on the 27th, 1953! This was certainly a gigantic year for me. *I was finally a full-fledged music and elementary school teacher and soon to be… a BRIDE!*

To business that we love we rise betime
And go to't with delight

Anthony and Cleopatra
—Shakespeare

Chapter 10
Middleton Junior High Graduation

During the second semester of my senior year at Lowell State Teachers' College, a gentleman came into one of our classes with the professor. He told us he was looking for a student teacher to volunteer to come to Middleton Junior High school to teach the graduating class of 8th graders for one day a week to help them put on a really nice graduation. A new building had just been erected for the junior high classes and in the same building they had a lovely new auditorium. He wanted the graduation to be special for the parents and students with music and caps and gowns and the like!

The school's regular music teacher was unable to take on the project because she was expecting a baby soon and her husband was about to have 'open heart' surgery. Middleton Junior High needed someone to take her place for the next eight weeks before graduation and then be at the graduation itself to conduct the whole program.

I looked around rapidly at the other students in the class. They just sat there. No one seemed interested in his proposal, so I raised my hand and said, in my best speaking voice and with absolute sincerity, "I will be glad to go to Middleton and put on a graduation for you!" He said that was wonderful and looked pleased, so I smiled and probably looked as happy as a circus clown. He said he would talk with me alone after class.

But, the professor dismissed me right then so I could discuss the responsibilities with this gentleman and not keep him waiting in the hallway for the class to end. It seems he was the Superintendent of Schools for Chelmsford *and* for Middleton. Chelmsford was the next town over from our college but Middleton was at least a forty-five minute drive away from my home in the other direction. I had no car, but felt I could work out that problem later since my brother was out of the Navy and had bought an old car. Maybe he would let me drive it one day a week. I had worked hard with Ed to learn to drive and I had my license.

The gentleman's name was Tom Rivard. He introduced himself again and we shook hands. He gave me directions on how to get to Middleton, and to where the school was. I also told him that I had no choice on the days I could go; I could only practice teach on a Thursday due to our school schedule at that time of year. With a broad and happy smile on his face, Mr. Rivard said, "That will be just fine, just fine!" and he shook my hand warmly.

He seemed so pleased at that moment. We talked it over a bit more, and when we parted company, he left with the same large and lovely smile on his face. I was thrilled and delighted to have this opportunity and that none of the other students had been interested in this volunteer position.

When I got home I told my mother and she helped me figure out how I was going to get to Middleton Junior High every Thursday. This was in the spring of 1952 about eight or so weeks before graduation from the college. My brother Dick had bought an old car and my mom asked him to let me use it on Thursdays. Dick grumbled and did not like that at all but Mom said, "You have no choice, Richard. You have to help us out at this time and that is all there is to it!" So, of course, he did!

So, off I went on Thursdays to Middleton for the next eight weeks. I would also be there to direct the graduation in June. I was nervous, and almost sick to my stomach the first day of teaching, but the funniest thing happened which chased all my fears away. The two gentlemen who taught the two eighth grades were so wonderful to me and so firm and consistent with their students that I had not one problem whatsoever with discipline; the cooperation on the part of the graduating students was almost, but…not quite…exemplary.

After a while, the situation became funny, from my point of view. The two male teachers stayed in the classrooms while I taught. Not one child was allowed to do one thing out of line, or one wrong thing, or even look the other way while I taught. There were boys and girls in each class but more boys than girls, which could have been most difficult and especially at their age level. Many of the boys were at least fifteen and sixteen years old, some had stayed back a year or two on the way up to the eighth grade, but they obviously 'made it' and were finally graduating.

We learned the songs that I felt were correct for this somber and serious occasion. They sounded…well…pretty good, but not perfect since the students had not had much training previously. But that was fine. The class behaved well, and did all that they were told to do.

The funniest part occurred while I sat on the piano bench in the new auditorium. I was playing the traditional *Pomp and Circumstance*, and the two male teachers were there and they were making sure that the boys and girls walked to the beat of the music. One teacher even hit the floor with his stick on the beat, yelling, "right, left, right, left"…so the students would step at the right time to the beat of *Pomp and Circumstance*. It became almost hilarious, but I managed to simply smile and not lose my aplomb.

Those two lovely gentlemen teachers never left my side during any of the lessons, therefore the students began to do well. I loved every minute of my teaching and toward the end of the eight weeks, the students began to feel really good about what they were accomplishing in terms of singing and marching in and out to the beat of the music. Once the final practice with the graduation robes was done I knew all would go well on Sunday, the big day. And it did. I was 'proud as punch' and happy I volunteered. That way I could add this teaching job and the directing of a graduation to my curriculum vitae. It would give me a better opportunity to find a job, since music jobs were fairly scarce at that time.

Once the eighth grade graduation was over, Mr. Rivard told the college Music Director he would like to pay me a substitute teacher's wage. I was surprised when he said that, but then, the Music Director replied, "Unfortunately, the college will not allow a student to be paid." Mr. Rivard saw my disappointment but added he would give me a recommendation filled with praise for my work and attitude. He said, "Mary, I doubt you will have *any* trouble finding a job!" He said this sentence with an emphasis on the words: "any trouble finding a job."

❄❄❄

Superintendents from schools in the area were starting to come to the college to interview students for prospective teaching jobs. A man named Warren Bennett came to school and into our classroom one day. He was looking for a music teacher for the Bedford, MA school district who could teach English to the seventh grade classes, manage a home room and study hall duties *and* teach music to all the elementary school classes, of which there were many. I went for the interview. No one else did. Mr. Bennett was so sweet to me…he could not have been better. He was charming and had a broad smile on his face all through the interview. Also, Bedford was not too far away and my fiancee Ed and I were planning to buy a used car, so I would have no problem getting to work.

Before Mr. Bennett left the classroom where the private interviews were being held, *I had a job*!!! He told me what the salary was. I was floored by the amount and filled with rapture and joy. The salary then was $2,500 per year and because I was teaching music, I was given an extra one hundred dollars per year! So all together I was to make $2,600 my first year of teaching. Having never earned more than a dollar an hour teaching children how to play piano in my own home, (I taught fifteen students), I thought $2,600 was a mountain of money!

The next few days flew by and I graduated from Lowell State Teachers College in June 1952.

About two weeks after my college graduation, I received a letter of praise and 'thank you' from Thomas Rivard. With this letter I also received a check for $120, the same amount a substitute teacher would have earned, to cover the cost of my time spent teaching for the Middleton eighth grade graduation. I was so suprised I almost fainted. Mr. Rivard was not breaking any 'rules' at that point since I was no longer in college. How kind of him, and in a short while (about five years) he would be kind to me once again!

> *The quality of mercy is not strained*
> *It droppeth as the gentle rain from heaven*
> *It is twice blessed…*
> *It blesseth him that gives and*
> *Him that takes.*
>
> **The Merchant of Venice**
> **—Shakespeare**

Chapter 11

First Full Time Teaching—
Bedford School

The summer following graduation went by quickly and slowly at the same time. I was extremely eager to start teaching and yet, at the same time I was happy to enjoy the lovely days of summer with Ed, my fiancé!

Ed and I, after much discussion, finally set our marriage date; it was to be a year from June on Saturday the 27th, 1953. I was deliriously happy about everything! It seemed as though everything I had worked for all my young life had come to fruition; I was marrying someone I loved very much; I had a new job when no one else in the music department from the college had one yet; I had a loving family, and I was doing exactly what I wanted to do. What more could one ask for? (Ed and I had even shared the cost of buying a second hand car so I could drive to my new job).

The middle of summer brought mail about what to expect in my first job. There were papers to be signed, etc. I did all that was expected and then drove over to Bedford, through Lowell, and then through the town of Chelmsford, which was not very far away from Lowell. I had to make this drive alone to be sure I knew how to find the schools. I eventually found them and discovered the three schools were all clustered together on the same large plot of land. With that discovery, I felt I was in good shape and able to ride off on my own to start my new job when the day arrived.

I was extremely excited that first day; I felt like I was going to explode… and, to my delight, I also found I had no problem driving to the schools in Bedford.

Of course, we must have had some teachers' meetings before school started but they are absolutely gone or hidden in my memory. The very first thing I do remember is opening day, my very first day of being a *real* teacher!

I was assigned to a homeroom in the building that housed one fifth grade, one sixth grade, two seventh grades, one eighth grade and one ninth grade. My building was not a big building, but old, prestigious and dignified looking. The building still stands today, and I still admire its gracious architecture.

I went to see my old school in 2010 and went inside. The Town Hall offices of Bedford now inhabit the former school building and it is in excellent shape for its age; it has been redone inside and outside. I particularly wanted to see *my* auditorium where I spent much of my time working with the children on drama, singing and dancing. I was delighted to see it had been restored but left unchanged, so to speak. The only rooms that were totally rebuilt were my homeroom and the principal's office! They are now offices for city administrators. As I walked through the building I felt waves of nostalgia and happiness flowing over me!

Opening Day of School, September 1952

I was always brought up to be very polite, particularly, with elders, therefore…what happened to me that first day shocked me…!

I was excited on the first day of school as I drove into the parking lot. I parked my Ford and walked over to the door that I already knew was my own entrance, since my room was situated to the left of that particular side door and I had been in my classroom several times ahead of the opening of school. One needs to be prepared! I was so excited and nervous that I almost hollered out loud…"*I have my own room!*" But…I contained myself!

Rooms designated for music teaching **only** were very scarce. Schools rarely had any rooms specified for arts (I speak now for the 1950's and 1960's and onwards. I am sure that today, things may have changed a bit). But at that time, music and art teachers usually had to work out of other teachers' rooms, which was difficult on both sides of the coin.

I was as nervous as I could possibly be yet, I felt euphoric. I had a silly smile on my face as I walked up the slight incline toward the side doorway after parking my car. A crowd of students was huddled in and around the doorway and down the steps. Above the incline were six fat, and very steep cement steps upon which to walk to finally be able to open the huge doors. As I started up the incline, prepared to say "Hello," smiling still, and of course, "Excuse me?" since I was planning to go through the small mob of students and into my room, a loud bell pealed; it almost rang off its perch it was so very loud; and instead of the students making way for me so I could go through the crowd, *they* rushed, nay, raced…in a body and up the steps. I was seemingly invisible to them as they flung open the huge door, leaving me alone on the ground, and on both my knees, positioned like a dog, and with my books scattered all around me on the pavement! Yes…they had knocked me down and then disappeared inside the building!

I was absolutely stunned, and totally surprised, plus, my two knees were quite sore, and a bit bloody, having hit the pavement first, plus… my nylons were torn! I was not sure what to do…my only recourse, it seemed, was to pull myself up off of the steps from where I had been pushed by the rushing mob, brush myself off, pick up my armful of materials and try to walk up the stairs and on into the corridor. All my dignity had flown away…disappeared. How does one walk sedately into her first classroom with holes at the knees of her nylon stockings and blood flowing from *both* knees, trickling down her legs? I was a mess and close to tears but somehow able to hold them back. Fortunately, nothing was broken in my body but I must admit all my decorum had been devastated and I felt dejected! None of the students knew what happened to me, or even cared to know! I was just amazed! Not one had stopped to help me up or ask if I was hurt! If any ever looked back at me I was not aware of it!

I pulled myself together the best that I could, heaved open the huge door and looked around the hallway; I found my room, right where I knew it would be, the first door on the left. I let out a big sigh as I deposited my goods on the desk, which was in the front of the room near the door. I sat down quickly at my desk on an old chair on wheels and then… it began to whirl almost uncontrollably around on the floor. That angered me so much that I got up and grounded the chair somehow, sat on it and rested my body and my nerves briefly. After a minute or two or three, I then decided to get up again and start over. Although my knees hurt, the blood had stopped trickling which made me feel better. I had to whip off my nylons, they looked worse than the knees, and I spent the day with no stockings on, which in those days, would have proved to be embarrassing. But then…what else was there to do? Nothing… but get up and get better fast. I managed somehow to overcome my small peccadilloes, and decided all would improve in time.

I then gazed around the room in my daze while sitting on my lively wheeling chair and much to my pleasure, saw an old upright piano to the right of my desk. Puzzled, I remembered it had not been there before, when I last came to this building and looked at my room. The door stood between my desk and the piano. That piano would be mine for the year.

"Ugh," I moaned to myself, "it looks terrible, like some of the notes might not even make a sound." It did appear to be a wreck after closer inspection… awful…the piano was dusty, and old, and decrepit looking. The keys were absolutely used and wasted, but I thought, "*Hmmmn*, at least it has *all* its keys, so it will have do for now. I will ask to have the piano tuned, maybe Mr. Bennett will see to that for me." And then…my day started! My heart started to flutter as I heard some noise. I turned quickly to my right and saw sixteen boys and girls troop into the room, or should I say, race into the room, pushing and shoving each other, with the boys vying for the back seats!

One could say I had a comical, crazy and cuckoo start; dignity had absolutely flown out of the room and did not come back for a while…it was a difficult day, no question of that, with several highs and a few lows, and nothing in the middle. However, after a few weeks all went relatively well and the remainder of the year was just great! I must confess…with all its trials and tribulations I enjoyed my Music/English teacher position very, very much! Yes, along with music education I taught two seventh grade English classes a day, and held a daily study hall!

My homeroom students only numbered 16; that was a helpful start. They were a small and very enjoyable number, and, as a result, they and I became very close in time, almost like family, and I would give anything to meet one of those students now. They would be in their mid sixties today which seems astonishing to me.

Everything felt extraordinary…I had graduated… I had found a job…I was in Bedford… teaching, with torn nylons and bloody knees, and loving it all! Ultimately, for five full years…I was deliriously happy.

Back to Reality

A fifth grade and sixth grade were housed in the Junior High building since the other two buildings were overcrowded. It was my responsibility to teach music to them. I was overwhelmed for a while since all I could think of was, "How on earth will I see all these children once a week for one music lesson?" I did not get upset…for a change, I just decided to take it all one day at a time, or one step at a time, and I was sure it would eventually work out somehow!

I was issued a schedule for Junior High classes, which gave me the times of the changing of classes. Then, another schedule saying I was to teach two seventh grade English classes per day and music classes to each of the other students in that building as well. Then I was to monitor one study hall period per day for my own homeroom students. After that schedule began, then I would go around to all the elementary classroom teachers and ask them to schedule my music class into their time frames. Scheduling for the elementary school children became a daunting effort, I must admit. Teachers did not always like to change their existing schedules although they did like the thirty or forty minutes of freedom provided for them while I was in their rooms. All I could say to myself was, "You can do it, Mary…you can do it!" And, somehow, I did!

The hardest class to teach in the Junior High when I taught music, was the eighth grade. They were huge, big fellows and very mature girls; I think most of them in that class were around 15 and 16 years old which I felt was rather old or advanced, chronologically speaking.

If I had to choose from that building which students I enjoyed the most at the beginning of the year, I would chose the seventh and the ninth graders. I guess it can sometimes happen that a few, allegedly, 'bad apples,' can all land in one room. However, having said that, we managed nicely, *after a while*! And…I discovered they were not really 'bad apples.' They were just untaught. The preponderance of them had no manners and came from the surrounding farms and had no desire to attend any school classes whatsoever. Most of the students in the eighth grade did not want to be in school, cared naught about learning anything, but were not old enough to quit, it seemed, or their parents would not allow that to happen. I feel I helped change that during the first year although it took a zealous effort on my part since the students' attitudes did not change overnight.

A 'funny' episode happened to me with the eighth graders. I once found a boy drawing pictures of me that made me look most voluptuous in certain areas, almost nude, and very offensive, so I brought him, with the drawings, to Miss Sheehan, the principal. She was a gem. I do not know what she said or did to Frank, but he was a jewel after that episode. I still remember his full name, even to this day. Amazing! I had to have been very angry over that episode for me to send anyone to the principal's office! It is not something I would normally want to do…I always liked to think I could handle my school teaching problems by myself but I felt this episode of drawing my body parts in a naked way, was totally uncalled for and had to be stopped quickly.

As you already know, my duties in the seventh grade classes were to teach seventh grade English. That worked out fairly well since I grew to love teaching English. The seventh graders and I got along well, and they also tried very hard…so the result was we came out on top. They enjoyed my playful style of teaching and also the fact that we sang a lot and were able to write compositions about our music lessons and outdoors and their farms. All went well in the English composition department, which left the children quite content. I was then able to proceed with the reading portion of their English class and all went along quite smoothly as well.

Naturally, I also had a text book to follow for the grammar end of the English lessons; that part is always a little trickier since children do not usually enjoy grammar lessons very much, but I found many tricks to help them understand grammar, and as a result, I felt we all managed rather well.

Music in the Junior High

I had no songbooks with which to teach music to the upper classes, therefore I taught all the Junior High classes how to sing patriotic songs and Steven Foster songs, and lovely, traditional Christmas songs. These were all songs from my own collection but I only had one of each song, which meant I had to make copies somehow.

Xerox machines were not in service or even thought of in Bedford in 1952 but I soon learned to use the messy mimeograph machine. There was only one in the building! I had to be inventive somehow, which I was. Naturally I had quite a bit of music at home and brought in all that was suitable and appropriate for my Junior High students and I duplicated everything. It is a wonder I was never arrested for breaking the copyright law!

None of the school children in Bedford had ever had music lessons. The Junior High girls loved to sing but the boys were resistant to singing, having never been taught singing before. I pondered how to win over these older students, since the younger ones loved all I did in music classes. Then one night, I had what I thought was a brilliant idea. I decided to have the students illustrate some of the songs we would learn. I won them over by starting with art work and colored chalk on the blackboards.

I felt that if those who would not sing with me were punished for not singing or not attempting to sing, they would *never* want to sing, and I did not want that to happen. Therefore, I taught folk songs, all of which contained stories in the words and music. I decided I would have some of the boys and girls (they all eventually took turns) illustrate the story of the folk song they were learning on the chalkboard, while the remainder of the group sang. Guess what? It worked! They were so busy sketching and drawing and coloring the stories of the songs while the remainder of the class sang that they started to really enjoy themselves; then the melodies became familiar to them while sketching and coloring as the others sang and before you could blink an eye some of the boys who had never sung a note before were singing along with the others while drawing and coloring.

My idea grew like 'topsy' and after a short while all the students wanted a turn, which was only fair. Then we thought the chalkboard was a little dreary so we used colored chalk on long and wide sheets of manila paper, which were spread over the black boards and attached with tape. (All schools then had enormous rolls of manila colored paper so I decided to put them to good use.) Some of the illustrations were so well done we wanted all the other children and teachers to see them so we taped them up in the hallways of the first floor. The students were quite proud of themselves. I still have a photograph of seventh graders displaying their collage of hand colored pictures depicting the stories sung and told in the songs of the old west.

Their illustrations were wonderful. One unit was of cowboys and another of machinery, including trains, tracks, engines, and even smoke pouring out of an old engine, and another was of some children in town and birds in trees. The students also loved the patriotic songs. And then it was Christmas time, which is always a wonderful time in a music teacher's classroom.

I found early in my teaching career that by the time Christmas rolled around, once the carols and secular songs started to be learned, the students began 'to eat out of my hands' so to speak. It proved to be a most successful venture. Before the school year was finished all the boys who had never sung before, sang in lovely voices. My eighth grade boys, with their changing voices, also sang and seemingly with much enjoyment. The music room, cum seventh grade homeroom, consisted of marvelous collages of picture-stories and lovely singing voices along with happy children! I was in 'seventh heaven' in the seventh grade… and extremely happy with my position in life! I told all my older students what some of my plans were for the Christmas season and they could hardly wait for that time to arrive!

Elementary Classes

Along with junior high building I had two more buildings in which to teach, which housed the remainder of Bedford elementary students. I cannot tell you accurately the number of children I taught, but it was many. I usually would have taught each class one time per week, but if and when the classes might have numbered too many I would then be forced to see some of the children only every other week. Fortunately that did not happen too often.

The children in the building facing the junior high building were third and fourth graders and one fifth grade. My building also housed one other fifth grade, which was taught by a dear lady who became a lovely friend, Esther Wein. She would help me with anything if it meant her children would learn happily and meaningfully. She was a marvelous teacher!

The other building across the way was a very old and square wooden building. I can even remember today that its color was a worn out yellow; it was pale and very old looking. That particular building had classes from third grades through fifth grades, but at this time I do not remember how many classes were in it. My 'car pooling' friend, Eddie Byrne, who graduated from Lowell Teachers College with me, taught fifth grade in that building.

The third building was a modern style building, attached to the old yellow building, and in an L shape; it was a one level, brick building, which looked new. It had many, many large windows, which made the inside bright and airy, unlike the old buildings. That new building contained all the little ones, children of first, second and third grades. My schedule was so full that I do not remember teaching first grade, at least during that first year.

I taught in all those rooms. At first it was difficult, learning the grade levels, the buildings and the rooms and the teachers' names; it was confusing and took a while for me to become adjusted...but somehow, in time, everything worked out fine. I had to be patient. But once we, the teacher and students, all knew each other, the days became most pleasant.

Tales of Woe

I like to tell the bad and the good, or the wonderful and funny, or the not so funny because they all exist in the life of a teacher; here are a couple of tales of woe.

In my seventh grade homeroom, I taught English. I had one very small class of seventh graders and another teacher had a larger room filled with seventh graders. They came to me on such a mixed up schedule that I never knew where I was it seemed. Between teaching English two periods a day and having home room for a third period, and one study hall, plus all the other buildings for music, I was never sure whether I was coming or going.

I was not discouraged; I loved my job and I loved being busy. The children in the other buildings, unlike the junior high students, had their own music books which I used for their music lessons. That helped immensely.

The principal, Margaret Sheehan, and Mr. Bennet, the Superintendent, (the gentleman who interviewed me at the college) were absolutely wonderful to me; they were extremely helpful and most concerned for me, hoping I could work all the wrinkles out of my very large program of many classes and many levels. I did finally succeed with the scheduling and with the utmost cooperation from them.

I'd like to share with you a few vignettes that will make you either laugh or cry as you read. The first two I feel are negative, but then I'll move on to the positive. On the whole though, there were absolutely more positives than negatives during my time in Bedford.

My First Upset

Miss Bessie worked in a room across the hallway from my homeroom. She was a lady in her sixties or seventies. I had just turned 21 years old in May, therefore she seemed ancient to me. She had always taught music to her classroom children before I became the music teacher. When she had to turn her class over to me for music, I found she did not like what I did or how I did it. (Or maybe she just wanted to continue with her own class and in her own way with her form of music). Whichever it was, as I was teaching her class one day, in my seventh grade room (since the piano was located there), she must have been listening at the door. Suddenly she stormed in raging mad, grabbed the textbook from my hands, and said, in a most stern and angry voice, and in front of the students, "I am going to teach music to my own class from now on."

She then took over and made *me* leave *my* room. She ordered me to leave! Well, I was not going to argue or fight in front of the students, so I left. I was absolutely embarrassed and totally unsure of my next step and…being the type of person who could never confront anyone…I must admit I was near tears! I was not sure what to do and I am still not sure what I did, except I must have told the principal, Margaret Sheehan.

Miss Sheehan must have taken care of the matter somehow because I taught Bessie's class once again and in my own room. That is all I remember! Miss Bessie never spoke to me again, not even a 'good morning' after that episode…*ever*! (I did not miss that too much, I must add!) Her class and I got along beautifully, I enjoyed them and they enjoyed me. I never did know what happened to cause me to have the children again for music and I was not about to question the principal, but I did have the children each week and we had a great time together learning many songs.

My Second Upset

The first time I entered a second grade room, the teacher told me…in front of her class, and in her ugliest voice, that she did not want me in her room…*and*… not to come back! That was that. It was embarrassing to say the least. The worst part was the poor students did not know what to do or say or how to act with me.

The teacher, Loretta was an unpleasant woman, but I had a job to do and I had no choice. The students could not come to my junior high school room, that was not allowed. But…thank God I had such a wonderful principal in Margaret Sheehan who handled these foul situations. She spoke to the teacher, and after their conversation I returned to that classroom on a regular basis. However, it was not an easy thirty or forty minutes of teaching in Loretta's class each week. During the entire year, she would *not* leave the room when I was teaching her students, therefore I was always uncomfortable in her class.

I did what was necessary though to teach music in that class and felt quite good about everything by the end of the year. The children and I were comfortable with each other, but the freedom in the room was missing, unfortunately. I was under a strain all the time and so were the students. Nothing ever changed with Loretta. She remained as nasty as she could possibly be to me, all the time.

The Old Upright Piano Incident

After I had been in Bedford for a while I felt I was succeeding to a degree, considering the jumbled up mess I received for a schedule. Then something happened in the auditorium that could have led to a fatality!

I had access to another old upright piano in the auditorium of the junior high building. The auditorium was small, and very lovely, with old woodcarvings on the walls all around the large semi oval room, and a stage at one end. It was decorated most beautifully in that respect.

When I started rehearsing for our Christmas program I asked Miss Sheehan if she would have any objection to my classes being doubled up and then, consequently, using the auditorium in which to sing since two classes together would not fit comfortably in my classroom.

The auditorium had three levels of steps that ran across the front to the sides of the stage. With two classes in there together standing on the 'step-risers' I would have plenty of room for the two classes (or even three of four), when it came time to rehearse a large group. She agreed that the idea was a good one and told me do it! She said she would talk with the teachers and there would be no problem 'as far as she could see.' She was so perfect in my mind; I loved her and she was wonderful to me always!

To my thinking, the students would have double the amount of music, or more, and we would accomplish so much more and much faster by practicing in the auditorium. Also the singing would be absolutely beautiful in the auditorium as compared to my small and cluttered room, since the acoustics would cause the students' voices to resonate.

Then…when it was time for the choral singing in the Christmas Pageant I was planning, (no one knew about that yet), I would have a place in which to practice.

We were approaching Thanksgiving, and my junior high students were most affectionate, polite and friendly with each other and with me. They had grown to love what I did and I had grown to love all of them for what they were and what they enjoyed doing with me.

(By the way, the stage in the auditorium is still there today, as I said previously. I went to see it just a short while back. It was smaller than I remembered, but still beautiful. The whole auditorium looks the very same, clean and newly painted and presently being used for Town Meetings).

Now, on another 'note', I am sure you will all agree, an upright piano could be dangerous unless it is resting against a wall. It is large, cumbersome and very, very heavy. But you must understand, I could not teach with the back of the piano leaning on a wall and playing it with my back turned to the students. Impossible. I had to have eye contact with the singers all the time instead of playing with my backside to them. Of course, that meant I had to move the piano from the wall in the auditorium to have it positioned at an angle, (not against a wall) closer to the students which allowed me to play the piano while maintaining eye contact with the students.

One day when we had finished a practice for our Christmas Program and the time had come for the students to go back to their classrooms I needed to ask two strong boys, and of course myself, to move the piano, gently, gently, and slowly, slowly, back against the wall. However, before I could say *one* word…simultaneously, and with much enthusiasm, three or four boys raced to the piano yelling, "We'll move the piano for you Miss B!"

My mouth opened and yelled, "Don't touch it!" *and*…at the *exact* same instant Mr. Bennett and another man opened the door on the opposite side of the auditorium just as the piano *crashed* to the floor onto its backside with the keys resounding while sticking up in the air!

What happened was this: the boys, in their zeal to be helpful, all pushed the piano from the keyboard side *and* at the same time; therefore, the piano being an upright, it fell…*backwards* on to the floor with its keyboard sticking up in the air and its sound vibrating all over the large room.

Thankfully…the falling piano did not hurt anyone, although it did land on the toes of one boy's foot, but luckily only smashed down the tip of the shoe leather, never touching his actual toes! I was so fortunate, so blessed, as were the four boys who pushed. All was well…except for the piano and my embarrassment at having had that happen in front of Mr. Bennett and his guest. You may find what I am about to say next hard to believe, but this is the exact truth! The man with Mr. Bennett was *the safety inspector for the schools in Massachusetts…here from Boston, MA!* yes…he was *the safety inspector!*

To make matters worse, he witnessed that awful spectacle. The door opened at the exact instant or one moment later. I was an emotional mess inside when I discovered who he was, not to mention how upset I was that the boys might have been terribly hurt!

I was extremely mortified, not angry *at* the boys, necessarily, though they were not supposed to have done that. They were trying hard to be helpful, but went at it too fast and without permission and…of course, I felt very bad. I was absolutely beside myself with fear and I expected to be castigated by Mr. Bennet and Miss Sheehan! I thought I would have a black mark on my record.

When Mr. Bennet found time to be alone with me in his office after the Safety Inspector left, he was absolutely kind and gentle and a real jewel. After a few minutes alone with him in his office and when I knew he was not outraged at me, he began to laugh and laugh, probably at the whole situation and to my dismay, the two of us ended up laughing until tears rolled down our cheeks. As he laughed, I cried tears of happiness because no one was hurt. The incongruousness of a piano being pushed over at the same time…the very same minute… the safety inspector appeared in the room was unbelievable to both of us. It might not ever happen again in my lifetime…(it never did.) And since no one was hurt, we could then laugh again in weak relief!

Another Small One

I should title this short story 'a blessing.' For some reason this picture has stayed in my mind all these years. I was at a point in my elementary school teaching in Bedford where things were not coming together as smoothly as I had hoped. The reasons, in my mind were:

First, I had too many classes; secondly, some teachers were not as cooperative as others; thirdly, some were similar to Bessie in the sixth grade and just did not care at all, one way or another, whether their students were happy, learning, doing a 'good job' or whatever else. These teachers just did their thing, matter-of-factly, it seemed to me, and it seemed the students did not come first in their eyes.

One day I went into Marge Merrick's fourth grade room. She was an older lady, probably near retirement age, which then seemed ancient to me. She was always smilingly friendly, and told me she loved having me in her room once a week. I could have kissed her when she said that but I managed to restrain myself!

In order to have the children's voices sound the way they should while singing, I had to have them feel relaxed *about* singing. Straining their voices by singing too loud or trying too hard, or not trying at all, or singing in loud harsh tones would not be what I wanted from the students. Therefore I focused on ways to relax them and at the same time keep them under control.

I loved drama, so I decided to have the students dramatize the songs, most especially the songs that leant themselves to dramatization, of course. (Not all songs lean in that direction). Dramatizing usually always works beautifully and leaves the children very happy.

This particular day I chose a new song for the students and they loved it. It would not be familiar to anyone now, it would be ancient at this point in time, but I remember the melody like it was yesterday but not all the words.

"*In a rocking chair sat Mae, rocking, rocking, all day*
In a rocking chair sat Mae, rocking, rocking all day....
Then, since I have forgotten the middle part, I will jump to the ending...

"*She was queen and he was King*
loud the wedding bells did ring...
rocking, rocking all day."

Unfortunately, that is all I remember, along with the melody, but the story told of a young woman daydreaming while rocking in a rocking chair...her dream was that of a prince wanting her hand in marriage...he gave her a ring and they eventually rode off on horses to get married.

Well, for some reason, the melody maybe, or the words, or both, or maybe even my presentation with the pantomime...made that a favorite of the class. The sweetest part was Marge Merrick herself, the teacher. I can still see in my mind a benign smile on her face all the time, as she rocked away in her own rocking chair, as though she was daydreaming of some wonderful experience in her earlier life as we sang that song. Whenever I came into the room, she always reminded the children and me to sing her favorite song at the end of class, which they loved to do for her. The memory of this and Marge Merrick is still a sweet and poignant one in my heart and mind today.

Presentations to Parents

I will not describe all five of the Christmas pageants we presented in Bedford, but I will tell you about the most successful one. I will also share a few memories of other productions throughout my five years as music supervisor/teacher.

We produced a few musicals, one with sixth graders called, "Who Stole the Tarts?" That one was based on nursery rhyme stories. The children and parent audiences loved it. Kathleen Harrington, the teacher of the class, was an outstanding helpmate and was so proud and thrilled with the whole performance, as was I. She worked with me steadily, encouraging me always; she was a marvelous *helpmate* and a great homeroom teacher! It was performed on a stage but I cannot remember which one. It was not the one in the junior high building, consequently another stage cum auditorium had to have been built somewhere in our sprawling school(s) but I do not remember exactly where at this point.

Kathy knew how important these shows were, in that, and I cannot repeat this often enough, the children felt proud of themselves. Without exception, they all felt good inside their very own being! One could see it and feel it by their demeanor and disposition; their behavior was exemplary. It is important for children to feel that way about themselves. All their other work improves as a result. They were sixth graders then and performed in another show with me when they were seventh graders.

One other musical, which I directed with the junior high students and that was most successful was, "The Mayor of Casterbridge." One of the students, Richard Frohock, developed outstanding singing and acting ability and he fit the part well in terms of size and maturity. He played the lead in the musical; he was the Mayor of Casterbridge. His singing was wonderful as well as his acting, but then, maybe I am biased.

Since the students' earnestness was so all prevailing, how could one not fall in love with these students and their musical productions? They really wanted to be better and succeed in whatever project I introduced to them through the years. I still have lovely eight by twelve photographs of the "Mayor of Casterbridge" when all the students were in their costumes. The photographs were taken the night of their performance! The parents of these students were so very thankful. They told me they had never seen anything like that before in Bedford!

This type of work was a huge and enormous effort, but I must reassure the reader, it was not a single teacher project since it needed the cooperation of other teachers and parents and that cooperation was obviously very present, which thrilled me! Many of the parents wanted to help whenever the time came for the Christmas pageant and the spring musicals and eventually the square and folk dancing.

I also had the complete cooperation of the 'shop' teacher who built the scenery for the performances with the junior high students as part of their class. All was wonderful! What more could I have asked for? I was in my glory during those five wonderful years. Like Topsy, I also grew…in my learning and teaching!

The acting was superb and convincing, the costumes, thanks to parents and the home economics teacher were great and all went 'singingly well.' The "Mayor of Casterbridge" was my first operetta except for the very small *Hansel and Gretel* I had produced at the Lowell Girls' Club a year or two before. That too, I repeated in Bedford during one of the five years I was there.

The cast of "The Mayor of Casterbridge" Bedford, Mass. circa 1953

As they say, 'I caught the bug.' I continued with shows like this through my whole fifty years of teaching and still, today, feel good about what was accomplished with students through music, drama and dance! I did so enjoy directing musicals and plays with children of all ages!

Folk and Square Dancing

I began square dancing classes with the upper grades and they loved them. My reasons for beginning these dances were: parents wanted their children in junior high to dance, but I could not stand to see these boys and girls, while in puberty, cuddling and huddling, in a fox trot or a waltz. They were awkward, very stiff; more mature ones liked to dance, but most did not.

One of the junior high teachers was attempting to teach this type of dancing and when I asked her if she enjoyed it, she replied, "I absolutely dislike teaching this type of dancing. The students are just not old or mature enough for ball room type dancing. Some are, but they are very few, while the others just look uncomfortable and stiff and awkward.".

I mentioned that I enjoyed teaching square dancing and folk dancing, and wondered if she would prefer that I teach that style of dancing rather than the more mature type. She was *most* pleased with my offer and offered to assist me.

We put our 'heads' together, and figured out all the details; I notified parents and of course, Mr. Bennet and Miss Sheehan, both of whom gave immediate approval since they did not enjoy seeing those dance classes that seemed so uncomfortable for the students. All this took a while, nothing happens overnight as we all know. By the time it was all decided I was raring and ready to go.

I not only taught the junior high students how to square dance and folk dance, I also included all the students in the school. The younger students learned traditional folk dances; many were German dances. The students from third grade up learned the square dances. It was a wonderful time for me, and all the children. The square and folk dancing was always a happy time and it helped the students improve in many ways, i.e. in courtesy, rhythm, feeling confident, interacting with the opposite sex in a courteous way and enjoying it at the same time.

I always found the following to be so sweet. When we did not have the proper number of boys and girls in a square at a performance for parents and friends or, in a classroom, an upper grade classmate would always volunteer. The older students were happy to help out with the younger ones when it came to dancing. My heart always beat with great joy when I saw a boy, for example, who used to be a real 'toughie,' volunteer...yes! volunteer...to be a partner with a young child and he felt no humiliation at all. After that particular dance ended one could see his pride in himself...he just felt really *good* inside and all over. *That* is a wonderful thing to find in a 'tough' young boy.

In retrospect, I recall that the students were happiest when they were help-ing with younger children and that pleased me. They had clear, honest and happy expressions on their faces the whole time. Then, it reached a point after a few more dances for audiences where they were almost begging to help all the time. I was thrilled with the loving way they handled the small children in their square dances. That type of behavior happened often since it was always difficult to find the correct and even numbers of boys and girls in most of the dances. This behavior, once it is instilled within children will stay with them, of that I am certain, since I saw the development amongst the older children through the five years I worked in Bedford and I was happily satisfied with their progress and demeanor!

All the children learned to love the special dances and we held square and folk dance festivals for parents each year. Actually that is where my dance festivals began; they all started with my wonderful classes of children in Bedford in 1952.

My Wedding Day

Before my second year of teaching began, June 27,1953, came along. That was the day Ed and I were married at St. Peter's Church near my home. It was a lovely day and a difficult day in several ways.

I loved my wedding gown, it was a 'blush' pink, almost white. I was deliri-ously happy as any bride is on the morning of her wedding. Sadly, my father did not want me to marry, so he put up a terrible fuss that morning; he said he *was not going to walk down the aisle with me!* I was almost in tears at the back of St. Peter's Church...but, eventually, thanks to my brother and his persuasion, all worked out well. (I doubt that the persuasion was pleasant...) My father did walk down the aisle as I hung onto his arm almost tugging him along, and in one of the the photos I can see I was leading him, as opposed to him leading me happily down the aisle. He was not in the least content and nor would he have been, no matter who I married. I guessed it was an 'only daughter leaving home' syndrome.

I recovered from that since my marriage to Ed was the most important thing at that moment. Ed was to approach the altar from the left side door as I waited at the altar rail, and then Ed would come up that short aisle with my brother who was the Best Man! My father and I stood waiting and waiting, probably only a few minutes but it seemed forever to me. For a fleeting moment I felt like the bride who was being left at the church! Finally Ed came down the aisle, but oh…no…it seemed to be the wrong aisle! I was so confused and concerned I was not sure what to do or what had happened.

It seems Ed was supposed to have come in from the side door then walk over to me at the altar rail, accompanied by my brother…as I mentioned above. Then my father would step back and be out of the picture and go to sit in the pew with my mother. However the door from which Ed and my brother were to enter was locked! Ed and Dick, *plus* Mr. Bennett, my Superintendent, who was also invited, were left waiting at the locked side door and could not come in. No one in the church realized they were stuck outside the side door. Later on in my life it was a funny situation…we did enjoy a few laughs about it now and then… but for a few minutes as I stood at the altar, it did not seem a bit funny at all!

To this day I do not know if Ed came in the correct side door or if both men and Mr. Bennett scooted around to the front entrance and Ed came down the middle aisle!

The marriage ceremony eventually came to an end and we all went to the banquet at the famous 'Rex' building, which had a restaurant and ballroom area for my one hundred or so guests. It was a grand day but the bride ended up crying in the ladies room. Why? Because my father performed in a manner that was unexpected and not enjoyed by me due to his alcoholism. Miss Scannell, who also attended the wedding, found me in the ladies room crying. She snapped at me in her usual matter-of-fact style, hands on her hips and bossy as ever, saying, "Why on earth are you in here crying? You should be in the hall dancing with your husband and happy!"

Of course, she knew already without me having to tell her; my father was completely intoxicated and acting like a fool, and I was embarrassed! Miss Scannell, in her inimitable style said, "Pull yourself together, don't be so silly, go out there and have a good time. This is your big day…it does not matter what your father says or does!"

Since all my young life I had listened to her directions, I dried my face, fixed my veil and scurried out of the ladies room to *try* to enjoy the remainder of my special day with Ed!

My First Graduation Ceremony

Naturally, it fell to me to direct the Bedford Junior High ninth grade graduation ceremonies since it was filled with music: *Pomp and Circumstance* and the recessional, plus some singing on the part of the graduates. This was my very first time doing anything like this since my own graduation, except in Middleton when I was still in college, and I must admit I was very nervous. This was in June about two weeks before my wedding. Yes, I had had successes throughout the year, but still, I was quite nervous.

I taught the ninth grade graduates, to walk sedately and in time to *Pomp and Circumstance* as in Middleton, although I never needed two men with long sticks to help the students walk to the beat of the music. I also taught them some classic religious songs, one was Bach's *Jesu Joy of Man's Desiring* and one other, the name of which I cannot remember; they sang beautifully. Ed could not attend for some reason, but my mother and her friend were in the audience as well as many, many parents and their friends. Although the class was a small graduating class, the auditorium was full!

The minister from the local church came forward to give an invocation, and then a few speeches were made by various officials. Songs were sung between each speech, and most importantly, the diplomas were handed out to the graduates. There were a few students who won some awards and a few short speeches were given in honor of the awards. Then the ceremony was over and it was time to leave…the graduates would walk out to the music of *Pomp and Circumstance* one more time.

I must admit to being quite nervous through this whole graduation since I had never done anything quite like this one before. Therefore, I confess, much to my embarrassment something went awry and this is what happened!

All the program was finished, and I, with a sigh of relief started playing the *Pomp and Circumstance* march, not noticing at all that the minister had stepped up to the microphone and was about say one more prayer. *I just never saw him!* Therefore, I started to play *Pomp and Circumstance* while the minister's mouth was opening and the ninth graders, seeing this happen, all had *huge* smiles on their faces, knowing full well I had made a *major* mistake! They began marching down the steps and out of the auditorium to the beat, and right on the beat I must add.

"Hmmn," I thought, "they have such broad smiles on their faces; they are pleased with their graduation ceremony," I decided. "My goodness, I have never seen them all smile so much and be so happy at the same time. How wonderful!"

Wrong! They were beaming at me, each one of them, as they walked down the steps and the aisle because *I had made a mistake!* I had started playing too soon. The minister was standing at the side of the stage waiting to give his final prayer when I marched all the ninth graders out of the auditorium. *And...*I truly did not realize this mistake until the whole procession was fully finished and not a student was left in the auditorium.

Then...I happened to look to the stage and only then did I see the minister. He "ahemed" and said in his officious and low droning voice..."Not to worry, Mrs. Guziejka, not to worry..."

Of course, the moment I realized why he was saying, "not to worry, not to worry," I saw his speech in his hands, looked at my program, and my face flushed with complete and utter embarrassment! I was near tears as I tried to tell him how sorry I was that I had made such a terrible mistake.

He left the stage reassuring me all the time as he walked down the steps, that all was well and not to give it another thought. I walked out, eventually, when everyone had left; I felt so embarrassed, and through my tear blinded eyes saw my car and my mother and her friend sitting in it. Once I was in the car, I bawled like a baby. It took me about ten minutes to recover enough to drive home. Tears dripped down my face all during the ride from Bedford to Lowell!

❦ ❦ ❦

It was September 1953, and the children were coming into the lunchroom and Mr. Bennett and I happened to be sitting together at one of the first graders' tables. It was a short legged table, very low and close to the floor! I do not remember why we were at that particular table except, perhaps, one of us was there first and the other person sat down to chat. Mr. Bennett said to me, "How do you manage with that last name of yours, Mary? I will never, ever learn to say your new married name correctly."

A sweet and obviously precocious first grader happened to be walking by slowly with her tray of food and overheard the Superintendent's words. She was so cute and funny as she put her tray down, most carefully, on our table. She looked squarely at the Superintendent with her hands on her hips, and said in a darling, but bossy, six year old voice:

"Mr. Bennett, didn't you know that 'Guziejka' rhymes with 'salt shaker'? Try it...say Guziejka...salt shaker." He did as he was told, with a huge grin on his face and then the little girl said, "Now…you will never forget it." She picked up her tray and calmly and nicely went to the next table to eat her lunch with friends. We were left alone in happy and quiet hysterics…

The Christmas Pageant

The schools were located in the 'downtown' area of Bedford, Massachusetts. The center of the pretty town of Bedford had a 'green,' a large plot of grass starting at the steps of an old church, which was set far back from the road, and moving broadly, way up to the sidewalk. At the beginning of my second year of teaching, September 1953, I looked everything over and decided I would talk with Mr. Bennett and Miss Sheehan and see what they would have to say about having a Christmas Pageant on the 'green.' Holding the pageant in front of the old church could not help but make the pageant more significant for the Christmas nativity scenes I had in mind, and the festivities which would follow. It would also add great dignity to the performance.

Both the Principal and the Superintendent thought the idea was wonderful but how would I do it? I left them with great assurance that I would find a way to do it and then get back to them about it.

I immediately went to talk with the friendly and helpful 'shop' teacher; Industrial Arts is the more correct title, but 'shop teacher' was what he was called at that time. His name escapes me although I can still see his welcoming and smiling face. He said he would be willing to have his shop classes build a staging area and carry it over and do whatever I felt was needed to make it all just right.

"Mary," he said, with a large reassuring hand on my shoulder, "my students would also benefit from that type of thing; I think your idea is a wonderful one, and I am certain my 'shop' kids will love it!" He ended our conversation most emphatically with a terse command of, "Let's do it." He was usually a very serious man who never showed this type of excitement, but he seemed thrilled now.

My plan was to have the nativity scene situated on a stage in a frozen position, as the students would be representing statues, no dialogue; we would have curtains to cover the scene until the time for it to be shown, then the curtains would close at the end of the religious segment. That scene would appear during the first half of the performance and the chorus would be standing on the risers below the staging and over to the side, singing the appropriate Christmas carols. The second half of the program then would consist of Santa Claus songs and the like, such as *Winter Wonderland, Jingle Bells, Rudolph the Red Nose Reindeer,*

White Christmas, etc. We also would have a volunteer gentleman from town to be Santa!

How did I have the piano moved over there? I cannot remember, but I feel my wonderful 'shop' teacher did the whole move for me with his classes and his skills and his truck. I know I had to have accompaniment for the songs the chorus would sing so therefore I needed the piano.

My students were not quite skilled enough at this point to sing a cappella, meaning, 'without musical accompaniment.' First of all, I was new at the Bedford schools, and a cappella singing had never been taught before. Possibly in another year or two we could accomplish that, but not at that stage of my teaching in Bedford. I also planned to invite the audience to join in on songs towards the end of the performance, which I knew they would love and definitely a piano would be needed. The children would sing the more beautiful and religious type songs first, about the nativity and then the last half of the program we would sing the secular songs.

The upper elementary grades, would also be the in the chorus along with the junior high students. The nativity scene would present Mary, Joseph, and baby Jesus and some angels; baby Jesus would be a swaddled baby doll.

"My goodness, how can I accomplish all this alone?" I wondered. I was always great with ideas but they ran amuck in my head and grew and grew in size. "Hmmn," I thought to myself, as I stared at the gorgeous old church and the green, "I will need help if I am going to accomplish all of this."

Then…I knew exactly what I had to do. I would send out letters to the parents of children in the grade levels involved and ask for help. Then, as a few days passed, I discovered word of mouth was more than ample, better than the notices which were sent home. I ended up with more parents than you can imagine helping out with costumes and scenery and other items that were needed along the way. The production grew like 'Topsy!'

The Great Plan

I sent letters inviting the parents who wanted to help to come for a meeting in my room; when the group of friendly parents came to school to meet with me, I told them about all about my plans and they reassured me that all would go well. They insisted they would be supportive and do whatever I wanted or needed. One mother said with a very authoritarian voice, "Mrs. Guziejka, you just call me and I will round up the teams!"

Since we were to be a choir, and choirs always wear something special, the ladies made dozens of red capes, with white collars and red bows to be placed on the white collars for the children in the chorus. I do not remember the number of children performing that evening but it would have been between one hundred and two hundred participants since it included the junior high through ninth grades and elementary school children starting at the third grade. The capes, collars and bows looked beautiful when finished and they remained with my choruses year after year, as long as I was in Bedford. (Which at that time I thought would be forever since I was so happy in my work. I was young and naïve at twenty-one or twenty-two years old!)

My plan was to have all the children in the chorus promenade, two by two, from the school to the 'green,' a good long walk I must say, around the buildings up the side of the green and then down the center aisle of the 'green' to the step risers and stage! While they were promenading, the audience would stand or sit along the side. The children's glowing faces and smiles showed how happy they were on this the big night of the Christmas performance!

I decided it would be nice if the students each had a 'candle' to glow on their faces. But candles were dangerous, so we decided the students could use flashlights instead to shine on their faces from under their chins, as they processed around the corner from the school to the 'green' and the nativity scene. To make the flashlights *look* like candles we had another group of parents make covers designed to look like candles. No child was omitted, tryouts were not necessary, every child would learn to sing, and sing well! Every student had a cape and a 'candle' illuminating his or her face. It was a stunning procession!

Darkness had settled in early as usual in December, so the procession of the choir in costumes with a 'candle' glowing in their faces, made all the children look beautiful! The little children looked absolutely adorable coming around the corner and up on the green and singing...with me urging them on. They sounded sweet as could be and looked equally as lovely. With their 'candles' glowing, they sang Silent Night and a few other easy carols while processing as I sang along with them.

Once they were stationed on the step risers to the side of the nativity scene, and after the curtains swung aside to show the nativity scene, they sang other simpler Christmas songs *but*...some in two-part harmony. Yes. I was proud of how they sounded and with no accompaniment, which is called, 'a cappella' singing. I can still 'hear' it now...a cappella singing with children's voices singing two part harmony makes the sound beautiful. The entire audience loved it.

The nativity scene ended, the curtains were closed, and then the chorus and I proceeded to sing Rudolph and Jingle Bells and a few others to end the program being accompanied by me on the very old and most used piano, but…in tune! We even produced a Santa Claus in the last half of the program who went around in the audience handing out fruit and candy to the parents and their other children. It was a successful event and I was absolutely thrilled at the reception from the audience.

This Christmas Pageant was performed each year in all the remaining years I was in Bedford. The performances grew a little smoother each year and the ladies did not have to make many capes since they were all made and put away for the next performance

My husband Ed and my mother and father came to see and hear that first Christmas Concert along with Ed's father. He was most impressed that everyone could say the word, *Guziejka*… Mrs. *Guziejka*, that is. He kept repeating in his broken English while clapping his two hands together, " Edjiu, Edjiu, oh… the people…they can say, Goo-J-ka…very good, very good!!!"

My First Child

After I had worked nearly three years in the Bedford schools I became a mother. I had a darling daughter named Susan Mary, born April 2, 1955. She had fair skin, beautiful blue eyes and weighed six pounds and seven ounces at birth. I was elated, as was my whole family. She was a marvelous baby; I stayed home with her for a few months and then had to return to teaching in Bedford. The School Department had given me a 'leave.' I worked until just two months before Susan was born and returned to the Bedford after summer ended in August.

I have always thanked God for my marriage, my baby, and my fortitude at being able to have my baby and work also. I must say times were still poor and ragged in our country however…Ed and I felt we were rich and prosperous in our marriage, our new baby, and in money since Ed also worked and two incomes to us at that time seemed like a huge amount of money. We certainly were naïve in many respects as I look back now, but then, we were extremely young! We had a lovely small apartment upstairs in my family home, my mother was happy about that and the rent was extremely low to help with our budget; when Susan came onto the scene there was also an extra room on the same floor for her crib and bassinet and bureau. All was absolutely fine in my naïve mind and I went back to work in September feeling like a queen.

All my years in Bedford were happy, lovely and profitable educationally speaking for both the students and me. The school children were great, they loved me and I loved them. Small musical shows were still being put on by me; students were also square dancing and folk dancing outside and inside, and singing beautifully in their classes and at the traditional concerts...the Christmas Concert went on each year and the town loved it...all was well and I thought I had the world by the tail.

Why I Left the Bedford School System

I was happy in Bedford, even though I had still not acquired a room of my own, or an office yet. I was no longer teaching out of my seventh grade room. A new teacher had been brought in to teach English and since the school was growing so fast, I would have had no way to continue at the pace I had been going. After Susan was born, I taught only music, dance and drama. I had no more seventh grade English classes or home room duties. I missed that part of my teaching, but nevertheless I still taught music to the junior high students; they and I still had close contact with one another.

I discovered early that music teachers mostly lived out of the trunks of their cars but...I became lucky! I was told I could use a small attic room, very small, I might add, up on the third floor of the junior high building. *I was thrilled to have my own office!* I was 'tickled pink.' School had ended, I was happy about my past years, I did not...ahem...make any more mistakes at the other graduations, and most importantly, I felt I was doing a good job...we were all still dancing! So...all was well.

I felt competent enough about my skills in teaching that when I discovered the Music Department was going to hire a Director of Music for all Town of Bedford schools, I decided I would apply. Also, I felt almost certain I would be hired due to all the innovations I had begun and also because I seemed to be liked by the students and the parents. I felt I was fairly well organized in my music program and had done well with the students in spite of having a baby. Mr. Bennett and Miss Sheehan applauded my work in my evaluations and verbally as well whenever a situation presented itself.

I sent in my application for the position of Director of Music. Then, somewhere in the last few weeks of school, after the application was presented to the School Board, Mr. Bennett called me into his office and asked me to sit down. After a few minutes of hemming and hawing he then said with a sad expression on his face, "I am so sorry, Mary, but the school committee changed their minds. They decided to go on as usual with the Music Department just the way it has been. There will be no Director of Music this year."

I was disappointed of course, but rallied and replied with a smile, "Oh, Mr.Bennet, that *is* too bad, but I am alright with it now that I know. You have given me an office, albeit small, I can make my plans for next year, and I am very happy here with you in Bedford. I am truly very happy here and I do take great pleasure in working for you."

We parted company and off he went smiling and cheerful, as did I. "Hmmn!" I thought to myself, "Mr. Bennett is great to work with. He is always so fair and open and honest and also has a good sense of humor."

Time went by. School ended for the summer, and I used the last two 'work days' cheerily writing down what I needed to purchase for school supplies for September, and most importantly, what I wanted to improve upon for the approaching year, as in what new musicals could be done, how to improve on the Christmas Festival on the green, what new records to buy for my square dancing classes, when I had a knock at my office door.

I thought, "Who on earth would be coming up so many stairs just to see me?" I wondered. It was a long walk up to my tiny attic office, and the stairs were awful too, constantly curving every third step or so. The only other teacher who shared this minute space with me, and in another small alcove, was the P.E. teacher when he changed his clothes. The P.E. clothes were left behind on the floor so I could smell them, and with no exaggeration, they literally *stunk!*

I opened the door and I saw a man. His name was Keith P., another name I will never forget. It was the man who was hired within the last year or so, to teach high school music in the brand new and beautiful high school building. He was a nice enough man. We had talked a bit over the past year or two, but did not really know one another well at all. Suddenly, I started thinking, "Why is he here to see me? This has never happened before."

He looked at me rather officiously, no smile, which was unusual, and in a rather domineering and intrusive way said, "I have come to see your schedule for next year."

No explanation ensued from his mouth, just a pompous, "I have come to see your schedule for next year."

I looked at him with a puzzled stare, I am sure it looked puzzled since I *was* puzzled! I asked, "Why would *you* want to look at *my* schedule?"

He still stood there expectantly, facing me with his hand out, waiting for the schedule, and then said, "I am the new Director of Music and I want to see your schedule for next year's classes."

I stood up quickly and stated firmly, "You can't be the new director. I was told the school board was not hiring one this year."

"Well," he said, "they hired me and that is that!" Emphatically, once again he said, "I *do* want to see your schedule."

I was totally befuddled and aghast…and I *would not* give my schedule to him. Instead, I left my office. I walked out on him and left him standing there… and dashed over to Mr. Bennett's office across the pavement from my building and into the old building facing the auditorium.

I was inwardly seething; I cannot tell you how angry I was! Here was a new man, he had taught here only one or two years, and had done no extras, just taught high school band; a nice enough man, yes, but then, I had gone through five years of all kinds of classes and situations, had been most successful, praised by all, parents and Miss Sheehan and Mr. Bennett, and gone far beyond the call of duty…and now…this! How could they possibly have given him the Director of Music position after telling me there would be no such position available this school year?

I roared inwardly and rushed down the stairs, virtually ran down the hallways, crossed the median strip quickly between the two schools, and bolted up into Mr. Bennett's office. I knocked on his door and he asked me to come in. There was no secretary there that day; we were all alone!

"Oh, Mary," he said with a smile, and stood up when I walked in, "I'm glad to see you. Please, do sit down." I sat and stared at him for what seemed a long minute, and he could see immediately I was upset. He asked, "What's wrong, Mary? I have never seen you so upset."

In a hard tone of voice I replied, "You *must* know what is wrong," emphasizing the word **must**. "Keith P. came to my office door just now asking for my schedule for next year.

He told me…" and my voice was cracking since by then I had lost my bravado and I felt like I would be a weeping fool in a minute. I could feel those ever present tears beginning to form, "…he told me he is the new Music Director!"

I then pointed at Mr. Bennett, not crying yet, but angry and with a firm voice, "You told me after I applied for the job, that there was *not* going to be an opening this year for that position."

Mr. Bennett stirred, obviously uncomfortable, in his chair. I then went on and continued with, "How could you do this to me? You always told me you liked my work all these years." My voice was growing louder and more strained as I spoke. "You could never give me enough praise and also, we have never had a bad or harsh word between us about anything."

I was close to crying at that point and my voice was beginning to crack. He saw I was upset…and then…I started to cry. He searched his pocket and gave me his clean handkerchief to use to mop up my face and have a good and long blow of the nose. Then Mr. Bennett rose from his chair and came closer to me. He put his hand on my shoulder and once more stated, "I love your work, and Miss Sheehan does also, we *all* love your work here."

Then I raised my voice a bit more, my crying had stopped, as I angrily retorted, "Then why was I told there would be no director's job when I applied for the position? You told me there would be *no* Head of Department position for this coming year and now I am told by Keith P. that *he* was appointed Head of the Music Department!"

Mr. Bennett seemed shamefaced, but, answered calmly and said, "Well, the school committee said they would not hire you because you were a woman and you could have babies. He is a man and therefore will not have any babies. That is why you were not hired to be Director of Music."

I was totally shocked! He made it all sound so simple and succinct. I answered angrily through my tears and hiccups with, "I already had one baby, I only missed two months of work, and I have been most successful here in spite of having a baby at home." Now, sobbingly, with his large handkerchief to my face, I said, "How can you let them do this to me?"

"Well, Mary," Mr. Bennett said, "they have. I tried to change their minds, but they would not listen. They absolutely refused to hire a woman for the Music Director's position."

As I mopped my tears with his handkerchief once again, sniffling at the same time, I countered with, "I will just have to look for a new job. I can see none of my hard work has been appreciated here."

I stood up and he came to me and put his hands on my shoulders and said in his nicest voice, "But, Mary, you love it here, you will never leave us. I know you won't."

I looked at him, and although I thought he was a lovely person and had been very good to me for the past five years, he certainly was lacking backbone, and I said to myself, "Just you watch me...I will find another job and I will leave."

Sadly, and with much confusion still hovering in my angry mind, I left his office.

I went home to Ed and my baby, Susan, and as I held her I cried some more. Ed could not console me. Finally, I was able to pull myself together and by then, I knew just what I would do. Since I was so angry and also very sad, at that point I felt I could move mountains! I called Mr. Rivard the next day; he was the Superintendent who paid me for my teaching work after the graduation I directed in the Town of Middleton. I knew he would have some advice for me or even know of a job opening in some other town nearby. I told him how I felt about *not* being hired because I was a woman and could have more babies.

He felt bad for me, and felt what had happened in Bedford was wrong. He did not talk against Mr. Bennett, but he thought a minute about my plight and asked me if I would like to work for him, only in Chelmsford this time. I was startled. My object in calling him was only to ask if he knew of any openings for 'women who might have children some day' never thinking he might have an opening in one of his two schools.

I asked, "Are you serious?" as my voice rose an octave..."You have a place for me...an opening?"

He replied, "I have an opening for a sixth grade teacher and I know you are certified for teaching grade levels one through eight and music; it is in a small building in Chelmsford called the Quessy School. It has only four classrooms and is not too far from where you live. You would be the music teacher for the whole building."

"How could I do that? How could I manage both the sixth grade and music lessons at the same time?" I asked.

He thought awhile and then said "That would be no problem at all, our new sixth grade teacher in the same building will teach math each day in your room while you teach music in all the four classes. Mary, you are qualified for both music and elementary education so that presents no problem. Also," he continued, "you are a fine teacher. While you teach music in Bob Armstrong's room, he will teach math in your room and so on and so forth with the other three classes." I had graduated with Bob Armstrong and liked him very much as a friend.

I was absolutely stunned. I not only liked Mr. Rivard but I also respected his way of managing situations, and he liked my work in Middleton and here I was, being hired almost minutes after I left my last day of school in Bedford. I was so happy...*words cannot describe the joy that was entering my whole mind and body*!

The following day I drove to Mr. Rivard's office in Chelmsford and signed the contract. He then drove me to the ancient, but beautiful looking Quessy School building in West Chelmsford. It was a darling old building and I loved it.

And so, it seemed that with almost no effort at all on my part that I had acquired a new position for September. Part of my young mind was not sure how it had all happened and so fast! I did *not* notify Mr. Bennett in Bedford that I would *not* be returning until the very last day possible according to my contract, which was thirty days before school resumed in September! I just could not bring myself to do it...since I was still sad over the whole incident.

But at the same time I was absolutely flummoxed...baffled... happy, and thrilled that a new job came to me so easily and that I had stood up for my rights by myself and for the first time that I could remember.

> *To thine own self be true*
> *And it shall follow*
> *As the night, the day*
> *Thou cans't not then*
> *Be false to any man!*
>
> **Hamlet**
> **—Shakespeare**

Chapter 12

Chelmsford School Experience
The Quessy School

A new saga...a new beginning...a wonderful opportunity...one seventh grade music class, and three sixth grade music classes once a week and everything else that goes with being a sixth grade teacher except for **math**. I never dreamed I would ever be a sixth grade teacher and now, there I was! *Wheeee*!!! I felt that was most impressive; Mr. Rivard seemed to have great confidence in me, which pleased me excessively. I was quietly excited about everything! One thing in particular that excited me was that I did *not* have to teach **math**, which was and still is, a weakness of mine! And my schedule was full! What an unbelievable opportunity just entered my life due to one single, solitary phone call made at a propitious moment!

I already knew how to find the school so off I went to the inevitable teachers' meetings for two days, which were held in a bigger school with the superintendent, Mr. Rivard and the principals. My principal at the Quessy School was a teaching principal, named John C. who had been an adult student with me in college...meaning he had entered college older than I, no doubt having been in the military service prior to that. Since there were only four classes in the Quessy building, a full time principal was not needed.

The two days of meetings passed quickly and then, over I went to the Quessy School on the children's first day and I felt just great. I got to know the students a little the first day (one cannot do it all in a single day) and I found them to be most pleasing. Also, the drive was pleasant and not too long, only about twenty to thirty minutes from our third floor apartment in my mother's home.

I do not have many specific anecdotes to share about my two years at the Quessy School. However, I enjoyed teaching Reading/English; all my drama skills forged ahead while we read. The children loved reading and playing some of the parts of the people in the reading books. (Their reading books were very old editions and I personally thought they were relatively boring! Newer and more interesting reading books for sixth and seventh graders surfaced not too long after I left the Quessy School). However, in my inimitable dramatic fashion I tried hard to make all my reading groups interested in the stories and as a result, the students' reading skills improved. Those were the school years of 1957-1959 and great things in teaching reading had not as yet begun to happen in our public schools. Hence, I decided I would have to be inventive.

I had students with a wide range of abilities in my class. I mean a *really wide* range. I had children who were barely able to read and on the lowest level possible, with IQ's hovering around 80, which is extremely low. These children were then considered to be 'slow learners'. I also had a few students with high IQ's (one girl scored 150 on an IQ test...which was remarkable!) A few other students were just beneath that and the remainder of the students were in the average range.

"What on earth does one teacher do with a little over thirty students in a classroom and with such a wide range of intelligence?" I asked myself this question almost daily after school started while searching my mind in an effort to be inventive, keep their interest and have them learn!

I had divided the children into groups according to their abilities to teach reading, but all the groups seemed to find the reading instruction dull. I never wanted children to think reading dull.

Inevitably, I began to use my drama skills to help the children with reading and to encourage them to enjoy more of what they were trying to learn. I also found that, as with my seventh-graders in Bedford, having the sixth grade students draw illustrations of words they were learning made reading far more interesting for them. And when they needed help sounding out words, I used silly drama to help them. They giggled and tried to imitate and we all began to laugh and feel happy.

"Whatever it takes," I kept saying to myself. If I could stand on my head to help them read, I would...(I could not stand on my head if someone paid me... what was I thinking?)

If reading was difficult to teach because of the wide levels and ranges of intelligence of my students, Social Studies was even worse. There is, in my opinion, nothing worse than students sitting in rows during Social Studies and each student taking a turn to read a paragraph, one after the other, often in a boring, stumbling tone since many words meant nothing to them. That was the 'style' of teaching when I was a child and some of it was still being done in the 50's. I remember having to do it in my youth at the school with the nuns and in our freshman year in high school! One child after another up and down the rows, reading a paragraph. No one really kept anything in their minds for further use since it was all so boring, and not understandable to many of the students.

"Well," I thought, "something has to be done!" I decided to use drama and focus on Julius Caesar, since we were studying that particular period of life in Rome during our Social Studies classes. I consulted with the art teacher for the Quessy School about this project and asked him if he would like to join us with his lessons.

The art teacher at the Quessy School was peripatetic. He appeared at the classroom door to give a lesson about once every two weeks. However, as he and I began to talk about the many learning problems of students in my class, and as we got to know each other, he did his best to come to my class once a week. He became a boon to my teaching and a wonderful teacher to my students.

The art teacher thought focusing on Julius Caesar was a wonderful idea. He came to help us, and at times was able to give us extra classes during the week. And, will *wonders never cease*…we, the children and I, decided we would write our own *play*! Yes, our own drama of that time period! Naturally, I helped each and every one of them, but the more the students did themselves, the more excited they became and the better they read and wrote; even my slower students were excited and started to try to read more often and they all thoroughly enjoyed the art aspect of the entire project.

The students were thrilled! Instead of the children dragging into school lethargically as they did at first, they now came in quite excitedly once we had started our many small or big projects. The brighter ones took over, in a good way, helping the others write the dialogue based on the facts in the history book. The art teacher began his project with large and colorful scenes of Rome covering every free space of our classroom's walls. The children enjoyed creating the scenes. This went on for about three months and much learning took place.

When the play was written, all the children brought in bed sheets to dress as Romans. (With the help of some parents, we laid the sheets on the floor and a student would lie down on the sheet for measuring and cutting. We used pieces of rope at the waist to hold the sheets on the students).

They loved putting on their costumes when it was time for us to do history! Stop and think how fascinating it is to be a child and do chapter learning in school while dressed in the costumes of that day. I, personally, would have loved every minute of it at that age level had I been able to learn in that type of situation as a child. The costumes give the child another person to deal with; they are then outside of their own bodies and minds, so to speak!

My plans were executed beautifully and I was thrilled at the students' enthusiasm. We wrote the small play together. Because of our work with the Art Teacher, our huge classroom windows resembled places in Rome, Italy. Then, we put on our small play for the three other classes. It was designed as a learning adventure to be performed in the classroom, not on a large stage for an audience full of parents and friends. However, parents of my students were invited and many came and stood around the edge of the room as their children performed.

The artistic work was simply great! The children were so proud of themselves. We even had the dramatic scene with the words where Julius Caesar dies, uttering, "et tu Brute?"

We performed our play separately for each of the three classes in the building with some parents at each; the acting principal attended the last one. On his way out of my room he looked most somber, and with no smile on his face. I walked with him into the corridor. I guess I was expecting a good word from him. Instead he said, and *this* is a direct quote, which I could never in a million years forget,…

"You should have stayed where you were before…in Bedford…teaching music." He then walked off and away, going upstairs with his class.

I was furious. I had happy children who were proud of their progress; lower IQ children learned about Julius Caesar and Roman History in a way they could never have managed before and the brighter ones learned to research facts and write a play. The classes absolutely enjoyed doing the research and the readings and were asking me when we could do another play. Although I was furious, I maintained my smile since I was so very proud of my students; I just could not let them think I was angry or disappointed in them.

Later, the acting principal sent a message to me asking that I take a period out of my music class time and come watch him teach Social Studies, (history and geography) so I could learn the real way to teach Social Studies. I did…and it was horrible! The children sat in rows in the classroom, and one paragraph after another in the textbook was read aloud by each of them in a dull voice going from child to child, and row to row.

When the class ended, I thanked him for inviting me, but left saying to myself, "*Never…never…*will I teach that way…no matter what he says or even if he tries to force me to do it. **Never!**" That was the worst teaching I had ever witnessed.

Thanks to the support of parents and the art teacher, I continued to teach beyond the dull and often boring textbooks. I bought a few copies of *TIME* magazines for the students to share. They enjoyed studying the current events. What did they learn from that? Number one, they improved their reading. Two, they learned about current events, as well as geography, since none of them knew about Cuba, i.e. where it was, how they spoke and who on earth was Fidel Castro anyway? But we surely did learn much about Cuba and Castro before we were finished. Once we ended with those articles we read this or that article in the magazine looking up further information with two or three children working together and helping each other with encyclopedias. They were such loving students. I never once had a discipline problem. No...not one!

My Birthday

I must say a word or two about my birthday. Somehow, someone had found out the date of my birthday and when I came into school on that propitious day there was a huge three-dimensional cake created by a student using construction paper and paints, and placed up on the blackboard. The words underneath were saying...*Happy Birthday Mrs. Guziejka*. A few parents brought in goodies that day toward the end of school; that had been prearranged obviously and they had a bit of a party for me. I was thrilled to have been thought of in that way. That had never happened before in our school and therefore, I was absolutely and totally surprised. I was close to tears!

At Christmas time, needless to say, I did my usual; Christmas art work was displayed on the walls and snowflakes made by the children were pasted on our windows; it looked like a blizzard was going on outside. We also learned songs, both secular and religious...*Frosty the Snowman, Rudolph the Red-Nose Reindeer, Silent Night, Away in a Manger* and many more. I had an upright piano in my room, but it was in very bad shape so I did not use it much; I tried to have it tuned but no one would pay for it. "No money," I was told and I had so little money myself that I could not spare a dime then to have a school piano tuned, which would have amounted possibly to two hundred dollars. It was in horrible shape!

But even without the piano, we had great fun singing. In fact, to celebrate Christmas before the school closed for the holidays, all four classes gathered on the stairs between floors for a singing session; all things considered, they sang relatively well. I had two wonderful years with the students in the Quessy School. The students had become so loving and kind. I believe that if we as adults are warm and loving and kind to children, they will be the same in return. Some teachers, unfortunately, did not agree with me.

For example, my daughter Susan was in the third grade in Dracut at the time I was teaching in Chelmsford. She was a bright girl, but her writing skills had not caught up with her mind yet. Not all skills come together in a young person at the same time. Susan would come home with piles of books, and homework; spelling especially bothered her because she had to write each of about twenty words five or ten times, every night. Then she had to write the full definition of each word from her spelling book, not the simple short one, but the entire long one. This was ridiculous I thought. I did not tell Susan I disapproved, but I did encourage her to do her homework. It all reached a point where she cried, and cried every night. Her handwriting was awful, she was tired at night, and the work was miserable for her. So I decided to meet with Susan's teacher.

When I told Susan's teacher of my concerns, she replied quite boldly, "Mrs. Guziejka, I am preparing my students for college, therefore I must have my class do this work!" I was totally astonished.

"Susan is just a little girl," I said, "only eight years old and reads beautifully, but still has difficulty with writing skills. Her coordination has not caught up yet with her intelligence. She has difficulty writing and is very slow at it since she wants to do well! I don't understand you at all."

Her teacher replied, "That is the assignment for my whole class and I expect them all to do it." And that was the end of the conversation because she walked away and left me standing there, with my mouth agape!

I could never teach like that or be like that. Susan struggled and eventually learned to write, and spell, but it was a nightmarish time for her and she should have been in bed early each night having her mother or father read a bedtime tale to her and giving her love and cuddles, instead of what she was forced to do each week. (Needless to say, she had the cuddles and nighttime stories and love and hugs from her parents anyway!)

⚜︎ ⚜︎ ⚜︎

But back to my stories about the Quessy School. The school building was in the country and we had a huge piece of wide-open land in the back of the school. A marvelous skating area was created which was used in the winter and my sixth grade students who owned skates brought them and skated for fifteen minutes every day, coming in refreshed and looking for more projects.

During my second year at the school we had a new teacher for one of the sixth grade classes. Her name was Janice Vaughan. We 'car pooled' together. Actually, I had the car and drove and she rode with me. No money was exchanged since both of us made so little in those days and this was Janice's first year of teaching. I said nothing to her about giving me money for the rides, but at the end of the year she gave me a lovely copper pitcher. She knew I loved copper and brass and antiques. I treasure it to this day and think of her.

Janice was a beautiful young woman; she had won the Miss Maine contest. (I'm not definitely sure if that was the state but I am almost certain I am correct). She was in the Miss America contest also but did not win that one. She had a stunning face, a lovely figure, neither too this nor too that, and a gorgeous, full head of naturally blond hair. The children loved her. During our rides back and forth to school, she enjoyed asking me how to do one thing or another in regards to teaching certain classes and I certainly was thrilled and honored to tell her.

Janice got married after her first year in Chelmsford, (which was my second year of teaching there). I could not attend the wedding for one reason or another, the cost of traveling to Maine being one of them; and she was then going to teach in Maine after the wedding.

However, while returning home from their honeymoon Janice and her husband were involved in a car accident and Janice was killed outright!

To this day I remember reading about her death in our local newspaper. It was such a shock to me, and all I could think of was how her mother and new husband must be feeling! Thank God school had ended! It was the summertime…therefore I did not have to face the children she had taught although I was not sure if any of them would know about the tragic accident either. It was such a sad time! I still have the little copper pot Janice gave me sitting on my mantle…and I remember her fondly!

Building Our House

I might have stayed much longer at the school in Chelmsford since I loved my school and classes, but I became pregnant with our second child, so I retired in the summer of 1959 and Eric was born the following January 21, 1960. Eric was a big and beautiful baby boy with a great disposition and wonderful ways. He caught everyone's attention and I felt blessed. Now I had my two children, next I would have a new house and third, I did not have to work!

In the meantime, my husband Ed had bought a book titled: *How to Build a House*, and in the fall of 1957, he began building our house on land we had bought in Dracut. He worked on it part time, of course, since he had another job. But he finished it, enough to be habitable and fairly comfortable, for us to move into. So on August 21, 1959, my new baby grand piano was delivered to the house, and on August 22, 1959, with the help of many friends, we moved ourselves into the house 'lock, stock and barrel' as the saying goes.

We proceeded in a cavalcade of cars, one following the other with all our belongings stacked in and on and above each car. We resembled a parade, it seemed, through the city of Lowell, up Central Street, onto Prescott Street and then on to Bridge Street until we were in Dracut. Dracut was not at all far from my mother's home in the city, possibly five miles at the most. We continued on up to Dracut and up our high hill, called *Old Marsh Hill Road*, to our shingled Cape home and my beautiful ebony baby grand piano sitting all alone at the end of the long living room.

It was a momentous day for me and I will never forget any part of it. It was a marvelous day full of happiness, sunshine and wonderful friends and family. Our house became almost fully habitable and partly decorated by many people in the one day. Of course, there was a lot more finish work to be done inside the house, but we were able to sleep in it the first night and to eat in it as well thanks to the wonderful friends who brought all types of food and drink along with boundless and cheerful energy!

I had given my notice to Mr. Rivard, the superintendent in Chelmsford in the spring of 1959, since I thought I would not teach again until the children were grown up and in school. *Wrong!*

Who could have dreamed of all the negative things that occurred in our lives after we moved into our home in Dracut? I certainly had not. I do not clearly remember the dates, but sometime after Eric was born, Ed hurt his back at work. It was much more than a mere muscle strain, and Ed was in a lot of pain. When we went to the doctor, he told us, "You have to be operated on immediately, if not sooner!"

I looked at the doctor and issued a most surprised, "What? What did you say?"

"I said," the doctor continued, "Ed has to be hospitalized now and have surgery. If he does not have surgery quickly, the disc in his back will rupture and go into the blood stream and he will die. It could happen tonight, tomorrow or whenever…we just do not know when."

We were both young, and knew very little about doctors and surgeries. All I knew was that I did not want my husband to die. Ed was also horribly scared after hearing the doctor's words. So, of course, he entered the hospital the next day. *Sadly…he has never been well since!*

All was horrible, awful…words cannot describe the feelings, the agony and the worry we both went through. After that initial surgery and a few more painful years, he had to have another surgery with a different doctor. Another disc was removed; he now had two discs gone forever from his spine! Ed was in so much pain continuously that he could never return to work after this second surgery. Then a few more years went by, and we found a famous back surgeon in Danvers. He said that Ed had to have a fusion done to his back. Ed was in the Danvers Hospital the entire three months of one summer! Then more years went by and Ed was forced to have that fusion, 'torn down' in a Boston hospital. Ed was never able to return to work. Ed's problems with his spine have been difficult for Ed and me, he has awful and never ending pain, but we are still together and still love one another.

I will not dwell on or go into minute details and facts, but you may rest assured it was painful for him in all ways and painful for me in all other ways. Ultimately, many years later, Ed attended a Pain Unit for three months to learn to live with pain. He went back two more times to the same Pain Unit, for shorter stays. Since then, as a result of their work with him, he has learned to live with his pain as well as possible. The result was that he had no more surgeries, no more pain clinics, no more pain pills, even to this day. You see he had become dependent on the pain pills, which made all his agony much, much worse...we learned to live one day at a time.

"Oh, how full of briars is this working day world.
When sorrows come, they come not in single spies but in battalions."

Hamlet
—Shakespeare

Chapter 13
Nashua, New Hampshire School District

In the summer of 1960, I realized I needed a job since Ed would not be working for a *little* while, (I thought then it would be a little while). Strangely enough, when I had given up hope of Ed going back to work, and the bills were piling up higher and higher, the telephone rang one day. I answered it and a lady's voice said, "Hello, Mary?"

"Yes… this is Mary."

"This is Anne…Anne Shugrue…how are you?"

"Anne, for goodness sakes, I have not heard from you for what seems like ages. Where are you calling from and are you teaching?"

I was so excited to hear her melodious voice that I began to tremble. Anne had a beautiful singing voice, as I recalled from college days and was quite attractive.

"I am teaching…I am in Nashua, N.H. and I just love my job! I am calling to ask if you would like to work in Nashua as a music teacher. There is an opening and you would love it here. Everyone is so nice and friendly," she replied.

"Work in Nashua?" I said.

Actually I was a bit dumbfounded. First of all, I liked Anne very much but had not heard from her or spoken to her in years, so of course I was a bit puzzled. Also, who put her on my trail and how did she know I needed a job?

She rattled on with great excitement in her voice, "Yes, there is a music specialist job opening in the elementary schools and I thought I would tell you about it. Nashua is a lovely place to work and I would speak for you if you were interested. I thought I would call you before they went looking around for anyone else since the job opening was just announced today."

I was absolutely astounded and floored! I quickly replied with a resounding, "Yes! I would…I would like that very much! Tell me what I should do first."

"I will set up an interview for you. Are you teaching now?"

"Oh, no, Anne, not at all…I had a baby a short while ago…in January, so naturally I had to take time off from working."

Of course, instead of just taking time off, I thought I had left teaching for the time being, thinking I would stay home with the baby for a few years. (As you may recall, I had resigned from Chelmsford.) But then, Ed became sick and now I really needed a job!

"Actually, I am quite desperate for a job," I told Anne, "but didn't seem to know where to start looking actually. I am so glad you called, I'm excited!"

I could not believe my luck. It was like manna from heaven. I went for the interview with Anne; she sang my praises while I was standing with her and the superintendent. Then while he and I talked alone, she waited for me in the hallway. I was hired immediately and after the interview, while she and I were in the hallway, we did a little bit of a dance. We were like two children singing Ring Around the Rosy, holding hands and smiling broadly while singing. We were both so elated!

The pay was low; I still remember the amount. It was $4,500 per year, but it was steady and with some benefits. The drive was only twenty to thirty minutes away from my home to the nearest school in Nashua, N.H. if I drove on the back roads. I was given four schools at which to teach music and they were all far apart from one another. Consequently I did do quite a bit of driving. However, to my complete surprise, a gasoline allowance was provided due to all the driving to and from local schools. All I had to do was hand in the mileage each month and after half a year I would receive what they thought was the proper amount of money based on the amounts I handed in to the office. That part worked out very well.

My schedule took me to the following schools: Temple St. School, Ledge St. School, Amherst School and the Fairgrounds School, two of which were located at the edges of the city. The Temple Street School was situated in the very center of the city and the smaller Amherst School was not too far away from the center of Nashua, but still, required another trek in the car.

I never had a room or office of my own; my office was the trunk of my car and before long it became full to overflowing. To make matters worse, New England's winter weather can be difficult, so, driving from the Ledge Street School to the Amherst School or to the Fairgrounds School in the winter was just awful! On the days where I went straight to a school and stayed there for the day, the drive was manageable. However, on the days where I taught three classes in one building and then had to virtually *fly* to another building to do five more classes…by the end of the day I was ready to fall apart, literally.

The newer and more modern Ledge Street School and the Fairgrounds School were larger, and there were many classes for me to teach. The other two were the oldest schools in town. As I look back, I am not sure how I maintained my smiling countenance, delivered my songs and games and small dramas, and still drove home at the end of each day.

The only school I found easy to reach was the old Temple Street School. It was right in the heart of Nashua. My memories now are exclusively of that poor

Temple Street School. Today, that old and gracious building has disappeared and an elderly housing unit has been put in its place.

I do not have a lot to say about the Nashua schools since I only worked for their system one year. But, I must tell you my Temple Street School memories have stayed in my mind for a long, long time. When I completed my first teaching day at the 'Temple,' all I could think to myself was," Oh dear...oh my goodness...how sad..."

It was a school filled with extremely poor children. My heart broke into little pieces just to look at them, how they were dressed, how forlorn the little ones looked, how they came to school dirty, and possessed no self esteem and little, if any, self worth. I felt so sad for them. I had tears gathering in my eyes as I went through the individual rooms to meet the teachers and the children for the first time. Then and there I determined to help them in any way I could. I could not help any of them financially because I was relatively poor myself, but I could love them. I would sing to them in my own fashion...and teach them to sing...and to dance and to act out songs and stories. Singing, drama and dance can make one happy if only for a brief while...and that was what they seemed to need the most.

The other Nashua schools were larger and located on the outskirts of the city, except for the small Amherst School; the people who lived on the outskirts of Nashua had better jobs I presumed, and consequently earned more money. Although they were not necessarily rich, they were at least capable, it seemed, of feeding their children and dressing them nicely as well as seeing to their schooling, homework and extras. The inner city children came from abject and absolute poverty. I was not in Nashua long before I knew this fact conclusively: some of the parents did nothing for these darling little urchins, if indeed they had two parents or any, for that matter. Some were bunking in with grandparents.

While I taught the children songs, small dramatic skits, and little dances, happiness came flying into my being as I studied their facial expressions. When I saw I was able to bring smiles to their faces it brought a huge smile to mine. I was helping them in my little way to feel and think better. I also read poems to them, in particular to the younger children although, in retrospect, the upper grades also enjoyed dramatizing poems and singing songs pertaining to the poems. My favorite poems were A.A. Milne song/stories about Christopher Robin and Winnie the Pooh. These were two of my favorites for young children and are still my favorites as of today. Some of the poems were set to music, as in:

"They're changing guards at Buckingham Palace
Christopher Robin went down with Alice,
Alice is marrying one of the guards,
A soldier's life is terrible hard,
Says Alice."
(And on and on to the remainder of the verses…)

Another favorite of mine is titled "Vespers":

Little boy kneels at the foot of his bed
Droops on his little hands, little gold head
Hush, hush, whisper who dares,
Christopher Robin is saying his prayers…
(and on and on for several verses)

I remember the younger students kneeling on the floor at their desks, pretending to be Christopher at bedtime. I always found it so remarkable, so wonderful for children, to learn a poem and act it out. I still have all my music in my piano bench and in drawers. They are easily sung and acted out by students in lower grades levels; and if presented correctly by a music teacher they can be used successfully with much older children.

Singing and dramatization will take the children out of themselves. The students in the Temple School were not happy to begin with, but at that age they did not know why or how or even that they were unhappy with themselves. What I taught these children made them feel loved and wanted. I absolutely felt intense affection for these young, sweet and most oftentimes dirty children; they seemed like babies to me and I wished I could take them all home.

Sadly, I do not remember if the school housed children up to the sixth grade or not, since my memories of the older children do not seem to surge forward in my mind right now. I believe it did, but then my schedule was so extremely busy that my biggest and fullest memory is of the poor younger children at the Temple Street School!

I must tell you about one thing that impressed me during that year. The nurse in these buildings rotated school to school as I did; maybe she had fewer schools, but I am not sure. She was a gem, a rare jewel in my eyes. She spent all of autumn and some of her summer, in her spare time, visiting store keepers and business men or women, asking for money for new clothing for the needy children of all ages in the Temple Street School.

One day she took me into a room to show me her collection; the room was absolutely huge, having been the dining room for the Temple Street High School many years ago. All the clothes she had collected were systematically laid out on the long cafeteria tables. All the clothes were new. Either she was given the equivalent in money from different shopkeepers and bought them herself, or the stores donated clothes from their racks or both.

The tables were set up with stacks of clothing and with names on top of each stack. They were all in neat little piles: new winter jackets, new leggings, new boots, new sweaters, new mittens and new shoes and more…I found this to be incredible! These piles of clothes were for Kindergarten and up through grade six. She worked at this project daily after school and evenings throughout the fall.

"I love doing this," she told me. "It makes me feel wonderful all over and most worthwhile. Each year since I started this project my heart only grows fuller!"

I was proud of her and happy for her also. I had never met anyone before who did this type of thing. The nurse said, "I still have more to do. I have more names and I still need more winter clothes for these poor little tykes. No one is going to be cold this winter or hungry, as long as I am alive," she said firmly.

I was amazed at this woman's efforts. She outfitted all the poor, she said, but then…all the little ones in that school were poor; I saw none in September who did not look very poor. I wished I had money to help the nurse…or time and money to help, which would have been the best thing, but it was not to be and she knew that and asked nothing of me.

I had the utmost and deepest respect for Thelma, the nurse, and for all the teachers who worked at the Temple Street School. Their work was not easy but they accomplished as much as possible. Also, I will never forget the faces of the children when they got into their new clothes. I do not remember the date that the families came in with their little ones for the clothing but I am fairly certain it was before Thanksgiving. When the children did receive the clothing, however, there were smiles and glowing faces all over the school. It was wonderful! It was just like an early Christmas…my heart overflowed with love for Thelma and the children!

❧❧❧❧

The Nashua School Board thought the Temple Street school building was the correct size for the elementary age children in that area. I will never understand that! No one considered that the third floor was condemned! I found out about that after being there for a while. All classes were held on the first two floors only. No one was allowed up on the third floor. One could say, "There is nothing wrong with that!" But then, knowing children as well as I do, there was much wrong with it since anyone could get in, walk up the steps, do something they shouldn't and on and on it could go.

The way the Temple Street School, second floor middle section, was built was unusual. There was a large, empty interior space. Once I had worked there for a few weeks I decided I would use that huge space and have the children do folk and square dancing and singing and whatever else I could come up with. I never had a 'Music Room' but then, I could use empty space and call it our music room!

I did not really want to teach in the small and crowded classrooms since the children would not be able to do anything involving movement during my lessons. As it was, I barely had space to walk around a classroom while singing and whatever else I always liked to do while teaching. This wide empty space was most fortuitous for me. It was perfect for what I wanted to do with the children. In the four corners of the large square open area, there were stairways leading up to the condemned part of the building. I used those wonderful stairs in one corner, (never going all the way up to the top, of course,) and the children and I called these stairs 'our stage'.

The students were able to sit at least four, five or six of them on one stair, depending on their ages and thence their sizes since the steps were quite wide. Consequently, in pretending it was a stage we were able to accomplish many creative scenes on these stairs. The children loved to pretend and act out some of the songs.

When we had our Christmas performance I invited the parents to come. The performers stood on the stairs to sing and some small dramas took place in front of the chorus on the floor. Everyone was happy and the children were thrilled. I was over the moon with joy for my little rascals and so were they! There was nary a face without a lovely smile beaming forth as they sang their little songs while performing dramas to the songs.

I often wondered how on earth the wonderful teachers in this school were able to accomplish as much as they did being in this awful, ragged building between the poverty of the children and the paucity of equipment. If the school was lacking so much for music how much were they then lacking for all other subjects? Some days I returned home in wonder and awe at what I saw happen in the Temple Street School and all done in love and devotion to the cause.

One day I happened to walk into one of the first grade classrooms. Evidently one of the little girls was celebrating a birthday. The child was six years old that very day. She was sitting alone on a high stool in front of the class with a golden crown on her head made of cardboard and painted gold…by the teacher, of course. As I walked into the room the teacher came to me and quietly said, "Would you have the class sing the Happy Birthday song for this little girl? Her name is Sarah." Of course I said I would. Then she gave me a book with an unknown birthday song written in it; the children knew it already, I was the one who did not know the song; the song was far different from the common and ordinary "Happy Birthday to you…etc." Therefore, we sang the one from the book first and then our ordinary/typical Happy Birthday song afterwards. The one in the book 'read' like this; it is now singing away in my mind like it was yesterday.

"Sarah's six years old today
Sarah's six years old to-oo-day
And she is so happy in her heart
That she's six year's old to-oo-day!"

This teacher worked very hard to crown each of the children on their birthday. She always had a wrapped up gift for each child, bought with her own money. No one was left out throughout the year. They all looked forward with great anticipation to being either the King or Queen of their day in the classroom.

"To business that we love, we go to with delight"

Antony and Cleopatra
— Shakespeare

Winter finally ended. What a good feeling that was! One spring day I was in the Temple Street School with my little ones on our 'stage.' The children's eyes were focused on me while I was speaking to them; then suddenly I saw all their eyes shift to someplace beyond me, or behind me.

A person had walked in on my class. I turned around to see who had come in and to my utter and complete disbelief the gentleman was a wonderful friend of mine from college days…Al Tatarunis. He had defended me in college against Cyrus Thompson, the man who told me after a concert that I needed to have my hair cut. Al was a marvelous and open guy, very frank to say the least. He recognized me immediately, came over to me at the piano and in his inimitable, unmatchable style quietly questioned me with great amazement and wonder on his face.

"Mary, what in God's name are you doing teaching here?" he loudly whispered.

In utter disbelief, I stared at him and could not believe Al was seeing me teach in this rundown building. The children were all staring at this man; I must have looked pitiful when I replied, "Ed is sick," I murmured, "I needed a job and this position was open."

His next words were, "I am Director of Music in Danvers now." Then… pointing his finger directly at me he most emphatically said, "You are coming to work for me in September!"

I nearly dropped my teeth. He then went on to make the offer more interesting. At the same time all the children on the 'stage' were looking back and forth from him to me trying to figure out who this man was.

Al said, "I will start you off at six thousand dollars a year…does that make you want to come to Danvers?"

I nearly wept and fell into his arms. I always loved Al as a friend and mentor while in college but to have him drop into the Temple Street School, out of the blue, with such an offer was 'heaven-sent!' He had no idea I was working in Nashua since we had lost touch with each other over these eight years. A raise in salary from $4,500 per year to $6,000 per year was a heap of money for me (or for anyone) in 1961. I hugged him in front of the children and whispered in his ear saying, "I will be there, nothing can stop me."

He returned my hug and left…he probably went on home to Danvers since his 'teacher search' was over. I was deliriously happy…and returned to my students who had been waiting patiently for the next song, or drama, or dance!

There is not much more to say about my year in Nashua other than I ended my school year with choruses singing and short dramatizations, but nothing as elaborate and great as I had done in Bedford and Chelmsford. I was sad and sorry that I could not have done more. But then I had so little time and such large numbers of classes it was impossible for me to do more in that one, seemingly short, year! All the driving from one school building to another was also an impediment since it took so much time away from what I knew I should have been doing…teaching students.

While I felt bad about leaving the Nashua schools on the one hand, I was deliriously happy to have a new job that would pay me well! I had to think of my family and not just be loyal to Nashua. I also knew I would enjoy working for Al and be exposed to new developments in the teaching of music. Although the drive to Danvers was a long one each way, the money each year would keep me going.

"Nothing can come of nothing."

King Lear
—Shakespeare

Chapter 14

Teaching in Danvers, Massachusetts

To be or not to be-that is the question.
Whether t'is nobler in the mind to suffer
The slings and arrows of outrageous fortune
Or to take arms against a sea of troubles,
And by opposing end them?

Hamlet
—Shakespeare

My family life is very tied in with Danvers since I was teaching in the Danvers School system when my husband, Ed, had one of his most serious operations and I had two little children at home needing me, and their father.

I will not go into the dates since there are so many, but Ed's first major back surgery, the removal of a disc, happened at the beginning of my year in Nashua. Then, of course, we all assumed he would grow better and return to work. Well, he didn't. He did try working, but his pain was so horrible that he could not keep his job. That meant trips back to the doctor's office.

We were not happy with the results of the first surgery; it was a complete failure, therefore we went looking for another doctor. Also we decided since we lived only about twenty-six miles from Boston that we should see the best neurologist or neurosurgeon Boston hospitals had to offer. Of course we found one who was supposed to have been the "very best," and...like the last one, he said, "*Hmmmn*...we must operate and remove a second disc in your husband's back."

"Oh, no," I cried, "not again!" Then I thought to myself, "How can Ed survive another surgery?" Then, I thought, "How can I possibly survive another one?"

After what felt like hundreds of days in the hospital and hundreds of trips by car for me to go see Ed in the hospital, he finally returned home. We realized later on that he never did grow any better. Meanwhile life was moving forward nevertheless.

Ed could not work, but I did. I was thankful to God that I was young and healthy and had a profession that I loved. Ed stayed home, in and out of bed the whole long day.

I will not go into detail about his situation in this book, they are all written up in his book, titled, *Pain...My Friend* which was published in 2001. Instead I will tell you about our children and my teaching position with Al Tatarunis, the Director of Music in Danvers.

In the fall of 1961, my oldest daughter Susan was a beautiful child of seven with long blond hair and blue eyes, and very bright. Eric was two years old, smart and happy, full of fun and most active. I was blessed. In spite of Ed's problems, I felt blessed by God to have had two such beautiful children and a lovely husband as well.

Susan attended the Dracut Schools and Eric, being a baby, played around on the floor with Grammy and Grampa when they came to Dracut. My mom was usually here every day during the workday week. Eric also played with daddy too, since Ed was home and almost permanently in bed for a long while, but the children always loved to play on his bed with him.

Ed tried to work at a few odd jobs when he thought he was growing better, but nothing worked. People were good and kind, understanding and helpful, but nothing, in spite of all he attempted, would make the pain go away. My mother, when she reached 62 years of age, relinquished her job at Educator Biscuit and centered all her days on us. Later on in those difficult years, instead of having me drive her home or Ed drive her home when he could, she slept at our house in Eric's room. She would come Monday morning early and stay overnight through Thursday evening, returning to Lowell on Friday afternoon after I returned from school.

All was cozy, our children absolutely adored their grandparents and I felt comfortable leaving them with my marvelous mother. To this day, I miss her terribly and think of her often. Dad, on the other hand broke my heart with his alcoholism; his alcoholism came and went, like a chronic disease; it was awful and unfortunately, it did get in the way of a good life for all. This is a child's poem, from a nursery rhyme book, which sums it all up:

> "When he was good, he was very, very good,
> but when he was bad…he was horrid!

The verse came to mind often since it was a favorite nursery rhyme when I was very little. Then, as I grew older and understood more about what was happening with my father, I felt it often applied to him as well.

My dad and Eric grew close during my dad's good times, (and he did have spells with no alcohol that lasted for a long time), but he also had long ones that were horrible. Susan also loved my dad, but maybe not in the same way as boy to man, let us say. However, one must understand, I never stopped loving my dad nor did I ever stop trying to help him. I loved him completely, in spite of his problems.

I worked in the Danvers school system from1961-1968, but I do not remember the exact dates of when I was in certain schools.

The Great Oak School was the first school I observed upon visiting Danvers just after I was hired. Al wanted me to teach in the Great Oak School (as well as other schools I will mention later) and therefore wanted me to watch the music teacher who presently worked at Great Oak. I suppose it was to see how long her classes were, what she accomplished, how she did it and all that type of thing.

The Great Oak School was large compared to the other schools. It was relatively new and housed probably 600 students or more. The music teacher taught eight or ten classes a day! That was absurd, I thought, since no one can teach music education to that many classes per day and hope to achieve anything of value. I had done similar to that in other schools and was hoping that in Danvers, things would be a little different, more progressive. A sinking feeling developed in my stomach.

I watched her teach. "How awful," I muttered to myself! I certainly knew I would *never* teach that way. I sat through one or two days of this, maybe more, and was happy when those days were over.

Granted, the music teacher had large classes, and was always in control, but the students just sat there and did what she wanted them to do in a rather pathetic fashion, not much happiness exuded from their faces. They were well behaved, almost 'de plus,' meaning, 'too much' as one says in French.

First, the teacher sang the song once or twice. Then she had them sing it with her, once or twice, and rarely, if ever talked to them between songs. Then the second song was done the same way, then the third. I believe she 'taught' as many as eight new songs in one lesson. She was quick!

Based on the eight years of teaching experience I already had, I felt the children learned absolutely nothing except to sit still and follow directions. They would never have been able to sing those same songs to me later in the day or the next day. She sang *with* them all the time, meaning…she sang at the same time that they sang. She never even knew if they had learned the songs. I was disgusted, bored, and angry at the way she failed the youngsters. Once I replaced her, I changed everything.

I had one school I especially loved, the Maple Street School on the main street of Danvers. (It is now used as a home for the elderly.) I thoroughly enjoyed the Principal, Bob Tivnan. He was funny, had a great laugh and a wonderful sense of humor; I still see him on occasion and I continue to have a warm spot in my heart for him even now. The other teachers were equally friendly and helpful too, but Jane (Brudzynski) Moroney, Bob Tivnan, Peggy Bright, (whom I called Margaret Smart for fun) and Jean Bouris were closer to me than some of the others. Their congeniality was absolutely par excellence.

During my first two years in Danvers, I also taught at two 'one-room schoolhouses.' They each had a first grade and that was fun for me. Never had I worked in a one-room schoolhouse before; they reminded me of the old Western movies. I had to drive to all my schools and there were quite a few, and again, I was paid for travel; twice a year, I handed in my travel vouchers with the time and miles on it and was faithfully reimbursed.

I also taught at the Wadsworth School, a four-room schoolhouse. The teachers there were much older than I was. They were firm about having the children behave well when I was in their presence, or in the presence of any visitor for that matter. The teachers seemed to be happy with me; I was always on time, the children liked what I did and were well behaved. Consequently, the four ladies seemed to enjoy having me there once each week to work with their children and I too enjoyed being there.

I also taught at two larger schools. One was the Highlands School, near the Wadsworth School, and the other was the Riverside School, which was on the other side of town. I did a fair amount of driving for a few years!

One thing that Al accomplished with the children that I admired and actually loved was 'a cappella' singing. Usually a cappella, (meaning without accompaniment,) is performed by adults. But Al worked hard with sixth, seventh and eighth graders and got them to produce the most beautiful harmonic sounds.

A few times I went to assist him while he taught. Actually, he never needed any help, so I ended up listening, watching, and learning how he developed a large 'a cappella' chorus of nearly a hundred students. I learned so very much throughout those sessions.

Consequently I tried the a cappella singing in the Highlands School with my fifth and sixth grades and we all loved it. It seemed to me to be the best way to have a gorgeous sound come out of children's voices.

I started with the so fa scale….do,re,mi,fa,so,la,ti,do. I taught them how to sing the various scale sounds by themselves, the easiest being the 'thirds' together, as in so and mi (they are a third apart). For example, one half of the class would sing 'mi' while the other half sang 'so' and then, both groups at the same time.

Then when the students were comfortable with two part singing, I added 'do' to those other two notes, which then gave us three part chording. When the children heard how beautiful that sounded they wanted more. Since the two fifth grades and two sixth grades at the Highland School did well and loved the chording sounds, one thing led to another and they were singing lots of three-part music a cappella, (with no accompaniment from me) only my directing with my hands. The children sang beautifully and were proud of their accomplishments as was I! We continued on until I left to go to the Thorpe School several years later.

Why did I not teach 'a cappella' in all my schools? Well, the truth of the matter is this: I had too many schools. So, where certain things were well received by the students in one school, I went on with it. In other schools, the same things did not always work as well for various reasons.

Much of my work depended on the discipline in the room. There were some teachers whose classrooms were near to bedlam constantly, which is a difficult situation for a visiting teacher, or as they were also called, a peripatetic teacher. Also, it is difficult for a music teacher to see students only once a week for thirty minutes and hope to achieve a cappella singing, in particular if there were discipline problems already existing.

Then there were some classrooms where all kinds of wonderful things could happen and did. So much always depended on the overall atmosphere with the children and the teacher in that particular room; some classrooms were awful to be in and some were wonderful and no matter how hard I tried with some of the classes I only succeeded to a degree whereas with others, the attitudes and atmosphere in the individual rooms were wonderful.

What made the biggest difference was whether the classroom teacher was helpful or not and what type of attitude she had towards what I was trying to accomplish. I am sorry to say, some teachers had horrible attitudes, no pleasantries, no encouragement for the children, no desire to have me in the room except to give them time off to go to the teachers' room and smoke or talk or eat. That is the absolute truth…no exaggeration!

As I mentioned earlier, I loved teaching at the Maple Street School in the center of Danvers. So happy in fact that I came up with the idea to have two second-grade classrooms join together and present a musical play *Snow White and the Seven Dwarfs*. The teachers of the classes loved the idea. While the students were *only* second graders they were precocious and loved everything I did with them. When I told them about doing a musical play they went berserk with joy and happiness.

I began work on the project immediately since I was so happy to have these two helpful and lovely teachers working side by side with me. I began by telling the children the story of course, and then went on to teach the songs.

Most of the children knew the *Snow White* story already and they all loved it. I found a beautiful old and colorful book of the story and typed up my own version of the dialogue at home. The children all had an opportunity to read and act out and think of what they wanted to do or be in the play. Finally we had 'try-outs' and the main characters were chosen.

We had a wonderful Snow White who had a pretty voice and sweet acting ability. Grumpy was magnificently grumpy all the time and Doc was absolutely swell! Sneezy was marvelous, he loved to sneeze, (pretend) and Happy had no trouble at all…being happy, that is. I almost forgot to tell you…Dopey was precious! Actually, they all were very happy to be in the play and on the stage. The remainder of the students were the chorus. All students were included.

Our first performance was on the stage on the third floor of the old Maple Street School. We were so well received by the audience that the Principal, Bob Tivnan, was jumping with joy. He literally was…jumping! Suddenly, he came up with a brilliant idea while we were discussing the performance. He pounded his fist on the table and hollered, "We will go *on the road!*"

I said, "I am not really sure what you mean."

He hollered back at me with the same excitement pouring out of his voice and said, "I will hire buses and my secretary will contact the other elementary schools and we will take the whole show by buses to the other schools!" We will be "on the road again"… and thumped his fist on the table!

I was so thrilled, words cannot explain how happy I was to have someone want to work with me in that manner. It would be such an adventure for our second grade classes but also such a great learning experience for the children in the other schools, and that is *most* important!

And so we did…we went on the road…not all in one day of course, the children were too young for that, but we did travel to several elementary schools and all was very well received. I thought the whole idea was outstanding and each night I returned home with a big smile on my face. I was deliriously happy!

❊❊❊

In every school where I taught all holidays were celebrated, such as Columbus Day, Veteran's Day, Thanksgiving, Christmas, Lincoln and Washington's Birthday, Easter, and the last celebration of the year, Memorial Day.

The music teacher was always involved in these celebrations. I loved doing them since they inspired the children to sing better, to love performing, and to know more about history.

One year, when I was preparing the Christmas program for the Great Oak

School, I asked the art teacher, Louis Mangifesti, to help me do something really original, something emotionally moving for the students and the parents. I wanted people in the audience to know how important music, art, and drama are in a school system. I also wanted the children to feel good deep inside themselves, and these art forms will do that very thing!

Louis came up with a magnificent idea. First, the children in the chorus would stand on step-risers, in a semi-circle, wearing red capes and white collars. Then, Louis' idea was to stage a manger scene high and in back of the chorus with a 'see through' piece of material in the front. Lights shining on that material a certain way would give an ethereal effect to the whole scene. The Mother, baby and Joseph, of course, could not move a muscle through all the singing of the Christmas Carols. (The baby Jesus had to be a doll wrapped in swaddling clothes.)

Well, it was truly beautiful, all worked out well. The singing was sweet and pure, some songs were sung in two parts, and others in unison; every child, in all the fourth, fifth and sixth grades, was in the production, no child was omitted.

Then Miss King, the Principal, decided at the end of the simple but beautiful performance, to give a speech. Well, it became a loooong speech, and suddenly and quietly a little girl in the third row vomited all over the children in the second and first rows in front of her. I looked at the students and motioned to them not to move or say a word. I gave them all a *hard stare*! The students were marvelous, with vomit all over their backs in the first two rows, at least six or seven were affected, no one moved.

But…Miss King went on and on and on…until finally I had no choice but to speak with her and ask her to stop talking. The smell by then was creeping forward. Fortunately, she ended her long speech abruptly after I spoke with her, and the poor little girl and the others who were damaged…phew…by what happened, were taken care of by some other teachers or their own parents.

That was the end of our lovely and colossal pantomime. It ended a bit differently from any other I had ever had the pleasure of organizing, but nevertheless it was still beautiful!

I put together so many Christmas programs over the years that they have mostly merged together in my mind as 'one event.' I would have students sing Christmas religious songs, two part harmony, and secular songs in unison with piano accompaniment, and some of the songs with pantomimes and some not.

One group of students was not included however, the small class of eight or ten 'special education' students. They were handicapped children, a combination of mentally, physically and/or both. I had never taught that type of class before that first year in Danvers. However, by the time spring came along I started thinking why could they not have an opportunity to be in a performance?

Therefore, when May came, and it was time for the Memorial Day production to go into full swing, I asked their teacher, Anna, if she would like to have her children participate.

"Of course," she replied enthusiastically. "I would love it!"

I decided to ask a sixth grade boy to memorize Abraham Lincoln's "Four score and seven years ago…" speech and have the class of 'special education students' in a pantomime as statues in the background. But, I wondered, *how*! How could we maneuver all of this, move the students around *and* keep them quietly still like statues.

I contacted Louis Mangifesti, the art teacher, again who said he would love to help with the project. He decided to assemble a small stage on wheels.

The day of the program I played the introduction on the piano to the Battle Hymn of the Republic, my chorus of older children sang, and much to the delight and joy of the audience and a few tears…in rolled the stage Louis had assembled with the 'special education students' on it…on their own stage, so to speak, in a tableau formation!

I will never forget little Diane; she was Betsy Ross and she sat as still as a statue with the flag draped over her body. Diane was thrilled; Diane's mother had made her a Betsy Ross costume with a little white bonnet, the old type with little ruffles all around her face; Diane was so happy. She never moved the whole time she was pretending to be a statue…and what was so remarkable… she pretended she had a needle and thread in her right hand and was frozen in the act of sewing a star on the first flag of our country! The other children were similarly frozen as statues of the famous people they represented. I forget who they were representing unfortunately, but the audience was in tears. I know…I was!

Diane's mother had another little girl, younger than Diane, probably three or four years old and she had the same condition, the same problems as her sister, Diane. One family with two beautiful children who would never walk or talk, that is how bad they were. I felt so sorry for them. But, I must admit, I was happy as a skylark that day about the whole scene, all the 'special education students' performed beautifully…also I had tears in my eyes at seeing how proud, pleased and happy Diane was as were her parents and her sister.

❧ ❧ ❧

At some point in the 1960s, a new Danvers High School had been built and with it a magnificent auditorium. Al and the high school bands and choruses used it often for concerts. But it was open to everyone, so one day Al said, "Mary, why don't you use our high school auditorium for one of your performances?" I nearly fell off my chair.

"I would absolutely love to!" I answered.

"Well, it's yours anytime you want to use it, just let us know the date far ahead of time and we will help you all we can," he replied.

I was thrilled. After spending many years without appropriate places in which to deliver operettas, choruses, or plays, etc. I now had one at my disposal. I went home walking on air and couldn't wait to plan on what we could do to use it.

As time went on several ideas came to my mind. I decided that the students in the Highlands School, the ones that sang so well with the a cappella singing, would be in the show. The following are memories of our first performance in the Danvers High School Auditorium: I remember that we had a Barber Shop Quartet and my boys absolutely loved it. They could not sing in four-part harmony, but they sang in two and three part harmony and were dressed as in that era with ancient looking straw hats on. I also had a couple sing a duet...*Bicycle Built For Two*...with the boy and a girl in old-fashioned costumes sitting on a double-seated, old-fashioned bicycle. The solo parts my children played were done very well and the chorus from the Highlands School sang beautifully.

As a result, we were invited to be a part of another show, and that excited my young performers. To be able to perform with the high school students was a thrill for them and it showed. The High School Band played a few selections and Al's groups of wonderful singers demonstrated their very polished and excellent abilities.

I was nervous, I was shaky and unfortunately I do not remember as much as I would like to remember at this point since I was playing the piano and directing my students as well. My nerves had run amok. Nevertheless, the 'boss' was pleased with the whole affair and the children were thrilled as was the audience...

I enjoyed every year of my tenure in Danvers. But then, in my fifth or sixth year of teaching in Danvers, I was given a new position. A new and very large school had just opened and I was to be the music teacher for the whole large school. I no longer had all the other little schools; I now was the only elementary music teacher in this large building. (Not to confuse you, the reader, but I was *not* in charge of Band or String lessons at all. That was separate).

The Thorpe School seemed huge to me after all my smaller ones. Unfortunately, however, it was situated at the very farthest point in the town of Danvers, which made my daily grind of a drive fifteen minutes longer each way. Meaning, I now drove an hour each way to school and…in heavy, heavy traffic! Also, a new highway, Interstate 93, was under construction at that time and there were always tie-ups and various problems, and many days my journey back home was even longer than an hour.

By this time, my poor husband was always in excruciating pain and most of his days were spent on the bed or in the bed. But I heard, through other people in Danvers, about a new doctor who was supposed to be 'heaven sent' and a wonder at surgeries on people's backs. He even worked at the Olympics during one of the years that I was in Danvers. We were told by many people in Danvers to go see this marvelous doctor. So we did.

I made an appointment and this doctor said that Ed's back was in such bad shape that a bone fusion *must* be had to help him walk better, or to even walk again, since at this point, Ed did not walk much at all. We had a bed in the living room and it was placed just in front of my piano at the far end of the room.

Well, we agreed to the operation and he had the fusion. He spent 80 days, (part of June, all of July and all of August that year) in the Danvers Hospital. It was horrible, that is the only way to describe what he and my family and I went through. I was with him daily, I did not miss one day of going to Danvers all summer and the remainder of the time, when I was not working or visiting with Ed, was spent with my children.

When Ed was about to come home, he was delayed another two weeks due to pneumonia. Can you believe all this? I couldn't! But this is what happened. When I heard he was delayed in coming home for two more weeks I decided to do something for myself. I took my children and the car and went on up to Canada for a few days to be with my most favorite cousin, Margo. She had a poor farm, always with many problems, money being a major factor, but she was always happy, always giving, and had always loved me since early childhood, as far back as I could remember. Our visit together gave me a sorely needed respite for four days!

We returned home, the two children and I, and then Ed came home from the hospital, and school started the day after Ed came home! He was better for a while, but not good. I was tired, and worn out, but nevertheless, I felt it was good to be on a routine once again. The children went to school, my mother still came to our home and slept in Eric's room, all went as well as possible and I drove to my far distant brand new school. I drove with a bit of fear and trepidation the first few days since the school was huge and I would rather have stayed in my past schedule of several smaller schools. I knew almost everyone in all my previous schools and we got along just fine, and all was relatively well. Now, I felt I was starting all over again with new and old teachers and about 800 new students!

I had great difficulty adjusting to the Thorpe School. I missed the closeness and smallness of my other schools, I missed the children I had grown to know so well. The only three or four people I knew at the Thorpe School were Peggy Bright, the dear friend I labeled, 'Margaret Smart' and Bob Tivnan, now the Principal at the new Thorpe school. He was the principal that instigated the Snow White traveling shows and prompted their fame throughout the town. I knew Marion Perry also and she became a wonderful friend, she and her husband John and Janie her daughter. She was a 'specials' teacher who taught students at their homes when they were very ill, or in long-term recovery from an illness.

One winter day during my first year at the Thorpe school, there was a wild snowstorm. Bob suggested to the staff on his loudspeaker that whoever lived far out of town should leave immediately! I gathered my musical stuff, got into my car, started the motor after clearing the windows, turned left to drive up the little incline, turned right and after just a very few yards skidded into a driveway never to come out again that night.

No one would believe me the next few days, but my car actually slid into Marion Perry's driveway. Well, since the car was stuck solidly in snow and the down-slanted driveway was icy, there was no way I was leaving that day. It was only three o'clock in the afternoon by then. As it turns out, her husband called and he could not get out of Salem, MA where he had a barbershop. He slept in the barbershop in a chair!

The snow was bad and the grounds were very slippery. Then I tried to call home so Ed, my mom and our children would not worry about me, but all the lines were down. No calls were going through. After several hours of trying to call home it happened that around eight in the evening, I was able to get a call through to Ed. Then, horrors, I was told Susan's school bus in Dracut had tipped over, gently, fortunately, into a snow bank; no one was hurt and the children were invited into a neighbor's house for hot chocolate drinks while awaiting some one or other to bus them home or pick them up. I felt a massive relief when Ed got to the end of the story and told me all was well and not to worry!

Our dear little son, Eric, was only five years old and in kindergarten. He was delivered to our home that snowy day by a school authority at 5 p.m., many hours later than normal since he was in the morning kindergarten class. All the Dracut roads were blocked until then. I will tell you no more on this except that poor Marion, after hours of nervous anxiety finally found where her daughter Janie was. She and I had a strong drink after we knew where our families were and that all were safe and we toddled to bed early… I was able to go home the next morning around 11a.m. It took that long for the streets to be ready. It was a horrific storm!

❧ ❧ ❧

I was not as happy as I hoped I would be while teaching in the Thorpe School. The teachers, in general, seemed not very friendly, maybe because it was such a large school. The atmosphere seemed colder, less warm, shall we say. That is always a difficult situation for me when one has to teach in someone's room and that particular teacher would rather not have you in her room. I know that was part of the problem. However, as usual, there was *no* music room available for my work, and *no* band and string room available either for the two music teachers who taught strings and band!

Also, my schedule was awful. I would be in the north of the building as far north as one could be and then my next class would be in the south wing, as far south as south could be. I would rush like crazy with a huge rolling table with all my gear on it; homeroom teachers never, ever wanted the itinerant teacher to be late. Heavens! That would be awful. Whereas I understood their reasoning, no one seemed to care about mine, and my problems.

In retrospect, I guess I should have done this or I should have done that, as in…talked with Al or talked with Bob Tivnan, the Principal, but I was, first of all, in utter despair over Ed and the situation at home. Then, the driving on the awful highway that was not finished, coupled with my miserable schedule, really got me 'down.' I just did not seem to have the gumption or the spirit or whatever it would take, to ask for a change of schedule or a place to teach or…or…and anyway, there were no extra rooms available anywhere in the Thorpe School!

Therefore, asking for one would have done absolutely no good for me in that situation. There was no room whatsoever in which they could have placed me!

I tried to avoid some of this misery with a few classes. I took some of the classes occasionally to the cafeteria. The children liked the change as well, but we had to work on the stage with the curtains closed so it was quite stuffy and once again I had to work with an untuned piano.

If it had not been for the lovely married couple, both instrumental music teachers, who were older than I and were so cordial and sweet, and also Peggy Bright and Bob Tivnan with their marvelous senses of humor, it would have been a more horrible year than I felt it was already.

There were a few fun moments of course. One time, I met Bob, the principal, while pushing a large cart on four wheels that usually held books or painting materials or what-have-you. Bob always had a marvelous sense of humor and it popped out of him at this moment. He joined me as I pushed the cart, and insisted that I sit on the cart as he pushed me. And at that moment two little boys from Peggy Bright's first grade room joined us, one of them wearing my pink cardigan sweater I had accidentally left in her room. So while Bob pushed the cart, the two little boys walked in front of the cart, carrying my music books. I felt uncomfortable for a few short moments, as in, "what will the other teachers say if they see me" type of thing, but it was a hoot, I must admit, a fun time…and I decided then and there not to worry about what the other teachers might think!

The boys had broad smiles on their little beautiful faces all the way to my next class. We laughed and smiled the whole way there and sang one of their favorite first grade songs called *Marching to Bombay*. I must say the two little boys looked so darling that I now wish I had a photo of them. There has to be humor somewhere…sometime…I guess. It helped me through that day, for sure!

My memory escapes me as to whether I worked at the Thorpe School one year or two. I know it was no more than two if it was indeed two. All I remember was a whole lot of running around, from one end of the huge building to another, and working hard to keep to my schedule and teach my little ones all the things I always felt they should learn in music class.

We did entertain the parents at school, the older students and I, at Christmas and of course, Memorial Day but I remember nothing else at this point. I know I tried 'this' and tried 'that,' but deep inside I seemed to feel as though I was giving up on everything. It was a most exhausting set up for all specialists, although the physical education teacher always had a large room of his or her own. I was happy for them, but sad for the other teachers who were specialists.

In utter desperation one day, I went to see Al in his office in the high school. It was in the spring. I did not know how to tell him what needed to be told. I was in some respects still shy, not in my teaching, but in other ways. He was in his office working on one thing or another when I arrived.

Al, in his typical and enthusiastic booming voice, said, "Hey, Mary, come on in. Take a seat…" Then he looked at me, puzzled and said, "What's up? Is something wrong?"

I guess my face was crumpling up and getting ready to cry because cry I did. I looked at him and said, with tears streaming down my face, "Oh, Al, I don't know how to tell you…but…but I just cannot work here anymore." My crying was moving along now at a rapid rate. I was terribly embarrassed but I attempted to continue saying, "The drive each way takes…takes… one whole hour." I tried to recover my sanity and then blow my nose as Al handed a box of tissues to me and I added, "Ed is always sick, and I just cannot do the long trip anymore." I did not add 'and the schedule is horrendous!'

Al was wonderful. After we spoke only a few more minutes he said, "I have a friend, his name is Ed Grigoli; he's the Music Director in Andover. I'm going to call him to see if he has an opening."

Al dialed the phone, got through right away to Ed Grigoli and Ed told Al he had an opening for an elementary music teacher and to send me to see him right away.

I was absolutely…taken aback. I found it all so unreal. Was this really happening to me?

Al gave me a hug on my way out and said not to worry. All would be well. I went to see Mr. Grigoli on my way home that day. I learned he wanted me as a music teacher and all I had to do was meet with the Superintendent of Schools in Andover.

Ed Grigoli told me, "Don't worry. I talked with the superintendent and I told him if Al thinks you are a good teacher then I know you are. Now that I have met you, I too would also like to hire you. Just go see the Superintendent tomorrow afternoon at 3:30 PM." By the next day it was all over, I had a new position in the Andover schools starting in September. The ride was only twenty minutes from my home. I felt it was a miracle.

I told Ed and my mom when I got home from school and they were extremely happy for me, of course. Now all I had to do was finish this present school year. I was sorry to leave Danvers, but happy not to have to drive all that way twice a day and I must shamefully admit, I did not miss the Thorpe School at all except for Peggy and Bob and of course, Al and Marion. Jane had already left Danvers. I did especially miss my old school friends and all the children I had grown to love, but on the other hand I was excited. I was so happy it was unbelievable.

> *A happy life consists of*
> *Tranquility of the mind.*
>
> **—Cicero**

Chapter 15

Andover, Massachusetts
Teaching Career

The quality of mercy is not strained
It droppeth as the gentle rain from heaven
Upon the place beneath. It is twice blessed
It blesseth him that gives and him that takes.

The Merchant of Venice
—Shakespeare

It was wonderful to have found another position so easily. I still had never looked for a job; up to that point, they all presented themselves, somehow, to me. How nice! How very, very nice!

I taught in Andover, MA so many years that I will not describe each year since whoever reads this missive might be going, "ho hum, ho hum and then... yawn!" Nevertheless, I will write about some highlights of my career and...there were many in Andover.

At how many schools did I teach while in Andover? I started off with two large schools, the Doherty School, in downtown Andover, and the Sanborn School, which is located behind the Internal Revenue Service building near Route 93; that was the school building closest to my home. Eventually, and for the longest time, (I was in Andover for sixteen years), I had only one school and that was the Sanborn School. At the most I had to teach at three schools in one year, the third being the Shawsheen School, but that did not last long. God was good to me!

The most surprising highlight of those years was that I became pregnant with my youngest and last child, 'Amy Louise.' My older two children, Eric, then nine years old and Susan, fourteen years old, were equally thrilled and, Ed too, of course. Baby Amy was so 'mothered' she was almost 'smothered.'

Once I learned I was pregnant, I had to tell my Director of Music which made me extremely nervous since I had only been teaching for a few months in Andover. I was a bit agitated since this pregnancy was unexpected. I felt the director was not especially happy with my news, but he handled it all well. Meanwhile, I worked until Christmas vacation and then stayed home to have my baby. I was afraid to work until the very end of the pregnancy, thinking something untoward could happen.

Knowledge of having babies, in those days, was not as progressive as compared to today, 2012. Today, many mothers work until the end of their pregnancy, have their babies and go right on back to work. Back then, in the sixties, we did not, since it would be horrible, (the thought at that time) to show the school children that I was expecting a child. Everything, in terms of 'dress' was to keep the baby's haven in the mother's body well hidden.

All went well, I was not fired or 'let go,' and I resumed teaching the following September, although having a baby and working at the same time was a whole lot of work. However, I must admit I was thrilled since I always wanted one more child!

Ed was still very sick, ailing and in bed almost all the time. I had placed a hospital bed in the living room by my piano. He spent the daytime hours there, then he was helped upstairs for the evening, but at least we were all together. My wonderful mother stayed at her home that summer, except when she wanted to come and see our precious baby.

When I returned to teaching in September 1969, I spent three days in the Sanborn School and two days in the Dougherty School each week.

Somehow, I'm not sure when, maybe after I left Dougherty and went to the Sanborn School, I also worked one day a week in the Shawsheen School, a very old building. Miss D. was the principal at that school. I had the great displeasure of having to work in that building for her for a while. She never smiled, never greeted me except with a frown or a smirk, and she was most unpleasant when it came to any requests I had to ask of her. Then, for some reason, things changed. I was no longer required to teach in the Shawsheen School and I must say, I was happy to leave. The principal was a difficult person, did not really want me there, and was unhappy with me all the time! Maybe she asked for me to be transferred, and if that is the case, I will be indebted to her for life.

Eventually I became a full time music teacher at the Sanborn School and what a difference that made! I would like to say that I finally had my own music room...but...I cannot. I had to teach in each of the rooms found in the three wings of the building, but...teaching in one building, although without a music room, was still far superior to teaching hither and yon across the whole town as I had done in Danvers and in Nashua!

Picture, if you will, a capital letter 'E'. The Sanborn School was built somewhat like that. There were three 'wings' that led off from the main corridor to the left if you peered at it from the front door of the school. In the first wing the classes consisted of two kindergartens that held two classes in the morning and two classes in the afternoon, plus three first-grade classes and three second-grade classes. The second wing housed the third and fourth graders plus one room for speech classes and another small room in which teachers could eat their lunches in privacy. The third wing held the fifth and sixth graders and a generously sized library.

On the right of the main corridor and at the end, was the gymnasium and if one imagines walking up from the gym toward the beginning of the corridor at the front door, on the left hand side was the dining room and kitchen. Wonder upon wonders, that relatively large dining area had a *stage* at the end of the room! I stood in awe and with great pleasure spreading around my being since

I would be able to produce shows for and with the children; the stage even had nice curtains.

After a while, since I had no room of my own, I often took my classes to the cafeteria/auditorium (cafetorium), and had them sit on the steps that ran full length across the front of the stage. I had a piano there most of the time, so all worked out rather well for teaching music. When the piano was not there, as sometimes happened, I then had to engage help to move it back down to the cafetorium. The stairs in front of the stage always made me think of our 'step singing' in front of our Lowell State Teachers College, which had been held each year at graduation.

The piano was in the cafetorium almost all the time, so you can imagine what a relief it was on the days when I could use that space to teach a class (meaning I did not have to teach in front of teachers who were trying to do their paper work in their own rooms. Also it afforded me much more space in which to work with the children.) There were some slots of time when the cafetorium was not being used at all, and that was when I could go in and either teach songs and two part singing and/or dancing, yes...folk or square dancing. Plus a few years later I acquired some *Orff* Instruments and used them in the cafetorium. I was thrilled with that and made use of it whenever I could. If I was not using it, the physical education teacher, Dave Huston, used the space. He was a great teacher who worked with youngsters who had many differing types of handicaps.

A microphone was also available for use for a show or lectures, but then, I never allowed my children to use a microphone, whether in speaking or singing during any of my productions. I always felt, and still do today, that the 'mike' spoils the truly beautiful and pure sounds of the children's singing or talking voices.

The principal's office, secretary's office cum reception room, and the nurse's office were to the right of the front door upon entering the school, and in between the cafetorium and principal's office, there was a huge closet with chairs.

That stuffy, small, dark closet with chairs was where the band teachers had to work with their students. "Oh, my goodness," I thought to myself, "I am so extremely happy I do not have to teach band or strings in a closet." I would have died, shut up in that room all the time, so I guess I was lucky in the sense that I could at least use each classroom *and* the cafetorium.

Whenever chairs were stacked in the hallway near the double doors and screeching sounds came from behind the doors, we knew that band lessons were being held. Not the whole band, but group lessons on brass, i.e. trumpets, trombones, French horns and the baritone and bass horns; some groups learned reed instruments, i.e. clarinets, flutes, soprano, tenor and bass clarinets…then the string teacher also taught in the closet on other days that it was free. There was no air in there and no windows at all…it was awful from my point of view! They managed nicely it seemed but I personally could not have done it. I do not like dark and closed in places, crowded and noisy as well as no air!

I was amazed when I discovered that in each 'wing' of the school a piano was available, and a nice piano at that. They were usually situated at the end of each wing, against the wall, and somewhat out of the way of the students. In total there were three pianos and relatively new ones, not old clunkers! They were small upright pianos, almost as high as my chin, and in good shape. Since there were three pianos for me to use and no other teacher ever wanted the use of any of them, (most teachers could not play piano, so therefore would never try to have a sing-a-long with their children), the pianos stayed in excellent condition.

I did discover that they all needed tuning. Pianos rightly need tuning two or three times a year, but sadly, that had not happened in the past. Luckily, the school pianos performed relatively well without that, but I insisted on having them tuned at the beginning of my stay at the Sanborn School and the Director of Music complied with my wishes.

Each time I needed to use a piano, I had to push it from class to class. I was fairly strong for a forty-year old woman, but not strong enough to move the piano from room to room. Therefore, I carefully chose boys I thought would be able to help me; they were most cooperative and helpful and did not 'fool around' either. Nor would I have allowed that to happen. A falling piano can be quite dangerous. Sometimes the girls asked to help and I let them and all went well.

There was a time though when one of the men teachers decided to have the 'guys' in his room, twelve-year-olds, fetch the piano from down the hallway so they could have some music without the music teacher being present. The boys moved the piano to their classroom, and then as the male teacher watched, the boys gave a healthy, hefty push from the keyboard side and down the piano went, on its back and on the toes of one of the boys! Thankfully, it flattened the toes of his leather shoes and not his foot or leg or ankle. I had just turned the corner of the hallway when the piano crashed onto the floor! I was sorry for the boy, but fortunately he was not seriously injured. However, I thought it was rather stupid for a healthy grown male to send the boys down the long hall to fetch a cumbersome and dangerous object like an upright piano and, with no supervision. That was the second time a piano was pushed over, falling on the floor, in front of me!

❊ ❊ ❊

I did my usual fun songs, story songs, dramatizations, and then began my a cappella work when I felt the children were comfortable with me and I with them. Later on, the folk and square dancing began. The younger students learned folk dancing. The third graders to the sixth graders learned the Ed Durlacher square dances. All of the square dances were presented on records in those days, and all arranged and called by Mr. Durlacher. I was fortunate to have his complete set of records. I also had a relatively good record player and that was a huge help. Mind you, I had to *move* all this apparatus from room to room, so I had one of those large rolling metal tables and not to forget, the necessary piano to be moved as well. It was a quite an event, moving from class to class, but somehow I worked around certain obstacles and eventually I was able to make it a little easier than in the beginning. All went well.

I will not go year to year in my recital of facts but I will hop from one success story to another, or maybe some not as successful, as I see them come to life in my mind; I felt I had several great years in promoting lovely singing and great acting and dancing with the students. I feel I was able to build the students' self -esteem, and that was the most important thing as far as I was concerned.

I loved putting on 'shows' of any kind that were suitable for the children. With all this wonderful equipment at my disposal and some…I say, *some*…co-operative teachers, I did shows such as *Amahl and the Night Visitors, Hansel and Gretel, Oliver!, HMS Pinafore,* and *The Mikado* plus we put on square and folk dance festivals out on the pavement in back of the third wing.

I had the assistance of loyal and loving friends, who enjoyed working with me and loved the children…most importantly they liked my work with the children. Dick Valle was the physical education teacher, younger than I by about fifteen years, but cooperative and open for all kinds of suggestions and worked with me all the sixteen years I was in Andover.

Jeani Pendergrass, the librarian, who arrived my second year in Andover, was invaluable with anything I attempted to do. She was not only a marvelous resource person, she also loved acting and singing and shared her talents. She performed in theatricals for years with an adult organization in or around Cambridge. She was a fountain of information and helped me, and the students, in so many ways.

Susan Rogers, the fourth-grade teacher or fifth-grade teacher, depending on the year, was cooperative all the time with whatever I wanted to do with her class, and wonderfully so. She was always ready for something new and different for the students! We are still close friends. The other two fourth-grade teachers and I also worked well together, Mary Durant and Carol Redmond. They were always helpful and cooperative with anything I could do to help their students learn. Also, Bonnie Browning, a third-grade teacher helped me produce *Hansel and Gretel*.

There were many other teachers whose names I cannot remember now who were also helpful. Then, there were teachers who never helped, and actually seemed to disapprove, or become angry with me when the shows were going into final rehearsals. I tried not to let it get me down.

I could do the rehearsals for the older children's productions after school. However, at some point many shows had to be rehearsed during the school day and that was what some teachers did not like, having their regular class schedules interrupted.

Initially, Mr. Normandy, the principal at the Sanborn School, told me he wanted a small program performed each month for the whole school, and from different grade levels throughout the school. The program was to be informative focusing on historical figures, such as Christopher Columbus in October, Abraham Lincoln and George Washington in February, and of course, Christmas in December and on and on… We also presented other programs, the names of which I cannot recall now.

The principal's plan worked well for the first two or three years I was at Sanborn School. After a while though, I needed a change. Too much of the same year after year is awful for the students and the audience, and dreadful for me, the teacher. However, to my pleasure and satisfaction, Mr. Normandy was cooperative and pleased with my productions, so he did not mind changing the schedule around each year after that.

The Wizard of OZ

The *Wizard of OZ* was my first production at the Sanborn School. I thought all grade levels would enjoy it, the younger ones by being in the audience while the fifth and sixth graders performed.

The student who was Dorothy sang her solos beautifully. A student played Toto, the dog and was quite a character. He was dressed in a dog costume and walked on stage on his hands and knees. Initially, that boy was extremely shy and had many problems finding or keeping friends, as I recall. The part of Toto was wonderful for him, and at the end of the performance, he felt very proud of himself. That was what I wanted to have happen. He seemed to gain inches in height and also felt so very good about himself!

The students portraying the tin woodman, the scarecrow, the cowardly lion and the witch were excellent actors and/or singers. The songs were all sung beautifully and the singing and acting was really quite good. All went well.

I had been able to acquire the music for the songs separately from the text. (I still have the music book. All the pages have come apart, but I paper clipped them together the last time I saw them. They are, to this day, in my desk downstairs). The script I either found separately at that time or wrote much of it myself. Never mind. We made no money on the show, therefore we broke no copyright laws. It was a beautiful performance, and all the parents loved the *Wizard of OZ*, as did the children.

What does a performance do for children? Why is this type of teaching so very important? My answer is simple and to the point. It gives the children involved a massive feeling of self worth. It allows a shy child to become someone else. I was shy as a child, and I can still to this day, as old as I am, remember my many presentations on stage…one of which was called:

THE ADMIRAL'S GHOST
by Alfred Noyes

I'll tell you a tale tonight
which a seaman told to me,
with eyes that gleamed in the lanthorn light
And a voice as low as the sea.

You could almost hear the stars
Twinkling up in the sky,
And the old wind woke and moaned in the spars
And the same old waves went by

Singing the same old song
As ages and ages ago,
While he froze my blood in that deep-sea night
With the things he seemed to know.

The poem goes on for several more verses; I loved it as a child, dramatized it on stage and have never forgotten the feelings I had that night. It was a long poem, but I learned it, acted it out, and loved it. I was about the same age as the children who were in my *Wizard of OZ* production. I was terribly shy and withdrawn, but then, wonderful things happened to me when I made dramatic or musical presentations. My musical presentations and drama performances as a child helped me be what I am today; they carried me through many years of success with children. I could witness the growth of self-assurance in my students whenever we had these performances. They became sure of themselves, proud of their successes and consequently happier children!

Amahl and the Night Visitors

Amahl and the Night Visitors, by Gian Carlo Menotti, was new to me when I had my oldest child, Susan. She was about five or six years old when it was performed on the television for the first time. Whenever I knew the opera was going to be shown on television at Christmas time, I had my children sit and watch it with me. Susan learned quickly and was able to sing some little sections such as Amahl's part, "*Mother, Mother, Mother come with me, I want to be sure that you see what I see.*" I answered her as the Mother in the opera did, "*What is the matter with you now, what is all this fuss about?*" Susan then sang, "*there is a King outside the door…*" and on and on we went. She knew practically the whole opera. This 'touches' my heart as I write about this particular performance with Susan! Before the holidays were over I bought the music book and the record. I knew then that I wanted to introduce it to my students while at the same time teaching my own children the gorgeously simple, beautiful and tender opera!

I happened to have a special child in the fourth grade that year. I had her in class from the second grade to the sixth. She had been a star singer since she arrived in the second grade. Her voice was gorgeous and true to pitch…her voice had vibrato and she had poise and acting ability, all of which came to her naturally. The child's name was Laura Need and now she is an M.D. living near Boston.

Susan Rogers' fourth grade class was the one I chose to learn the opera for presentation. Now, in no way could a class at that age learn a whole opera, therefore I shortened it to fit their abilities. I had another extremely brilliant child and she played the role of the Mother. Her name was Brenda Mesler and she also had a lovely singing voice, and strangely enough, she too is an M.D. today!

Laura played the part of Amahl, and Brenda played the part of the Mother and their voices, as young as they were, carried nicely into the audience. All worked out well and the two girls balanced each other to perfection. The other students had average voices, not necessarily suited to singing opera, so I decided we would have a 'talking' and 'sung' opera. I edited the opera in certain areas as I deemed necessary, but since it was originally made for young children, it did not require much editing. Amahl and the mother sang their parts and the Kings and villagers spoke their parts, except for the chorus song, which they sang in unison. When it was time for the villagers to dance and sing for the Kings, they did and they loved it.

Our Kings were spectacular; we had three Kings and all were good, but one stood out a little more than the others. He happened to be a black boy, so of course, he played the role of the Black King. The kings were dressed in fabulous costumes. The mother's of the students who sewed and put the costumes together did a fine job and all were thrilled with the end results.

Laura, (Amahl) loved to sing and act. That was obvious to me from the first time I met her in the second grade. Therefore, after she was chosen to be Amahl this is what she did.

In the opera, Amahl is a poor, crippled young boy, who had to use one crutch all the time; his bad leg was rolled up in rags and held in place by twine. The crutch was a plain old, staunch, sturdy, thick, knobby stick, with old ragged cushioning tied together with twine or rope. Well, Laura with the help of her brother, made her own crutch and every morning she dressed like Amahl, and practiced walking with her crutch on her way to and from school. The first time I saw her in that manner was in the corridor as she was heading for her classroom in the second wing. I was absolutely, delightfully, totally impressed! I still see her in my mind's eye as she hobbled down the corridor. That morning when she arrived with the crutch and the bound up bad leg everyone in the corridor stared at her in wonder and amazement. I had taught some wonderful children in my time but none quite as artful and inventive as Laura.

It was easy to decorate the stage for the production since Amahl and his mother lived in a barn with just a few old chairs and a beat up table. Mother and child slept on the floor in the hay. The beginning of the opera and then the sleeping scene, and the middle and ending of the opera were performed on the stage. However, the Kings processed up the middle aisle of the audience, as well as the dancers and singers later on as in the real opera…with their helpers carrying goods for the King.

The 'opera' was performed…beautifully! It was as top drawer as any fourth grade could ever have made it and *more*! The audience was thrilled. There was not a dry eye among some of the parents and in particular Laura's and Brenda's parents. Mine were a little moist also. Mrs. Need, Laura's mother, cried and sniffled as she said, "This should have been recorded!" But, in those days the school had no recording equipment, unfortunately.

I was more than happy; I was thrilled. I still watch the opera every Christmas and all I can think of is the fourth graders dramatizing *Amahl and the Night Visitors*…singing, acting, performing beautifully and delivering a lovely message!

Summer School

The summer following Amy's birth, my mother was able to be with my family and I was able to take a summer school position in Andover. The extra money was helpful to our family, and I enjoyed the challenge.

The Summer School Program was held at the new Bancroft School, which had just been built that year. It was built somewhat like a castle, and it had 'all open classrooms,' meaning no walls, which I still, to this day, dislike intensely. But that did not bother me in the summer school job.

The school had an auditorium, similar to the one in the Sanborn School, but much nicer and newer, which I loved using. It also had a very fine stage and piano and being summer, there were no interruptions from other classes.

That summer, instead of producing just one musical, I tried something different, which I thought would appeal to the individual students with their likes and dislikes. We performed excerpts from children's shows and also some ballet since we had two sisters who excelled in ballet. I also had one student, the superintendent's son, Kenneth Seifert, who had the potential of being a fine boy soprano singer. We performed a few short skits from the Charlie Brown musical and I chose "Let's Go Fly a Kite" for him to sing and dramatize a bit. He acted and sang the part well.

The two sisters wanted to create their own ballet, and I suggested they dance to Mozart's *Eine Kleine Nacht Music*. They created their own ballet steps to fit the music. They loved the music, and choreographed their own pirouettes and dance steps. All developed beautifully.

Along with the different acts, and I have mentioned only a few, the students and I planned how the stage should look during this song, or that dance or that routine. They were included in making decisions with me, which was good for their minds. Instead of having them follow directions all the time, I gave them decisions to make. I had probably about thirty children and all thirty children at one time or another did an individual act, and also sang in the chorus. They just slipped in and slipped out of the chorus to perform their individual pieces of music and were superb all the way.

For example, during a solo from *Charlie Brown*, the chorus sang a few "Charlie Brown" songs. Charlie Brown himself sang some solos. Then a few skits taken from the musical were also acted out.

That summer, I wanted the children to choose what they wanted to do. Some wanted to learn to paint scenery, and yes, of course, it would be a little rough and ragged around the edges, but they were students ranging from five to twelve-years old. The thing that was most important was that they were doing, deciding, and deciphering what needed to be done, delivered or developed to and for each scene.

A highlight of the summer for me was working with a student, named Bobby Cammett, who lived in Andover and was quite handicapped. He had been born with hydrocephalus and encephalitis and was in a wheelchair. (At that time, it was predicted he might only live to be about fourteen years old. But he is now 53 years old and doing so well that he is absolutely amazing!)

I went to Bobby's house before the summer school classes started. I had not as yet met his mother or father but I knocked on the door and told them who I was. I was invited in to sit down and meet Bobby. I told them I wanted Bobby to join my summer theater group.

"Well," his mother replied "there is no way I can bring him there." After many minutes of back and forth conversation with me telling her how good it would be for him, and Mrs. Cammett saying she could not possibly bring him down the ten or twelve steep stairs at their house each morning, and then bring him back up later, I ended by telling her, "I will do it. I will be happy to come by each morning and bring him down the stairs; I will help you do it and I will take him with me and you will be so pleased at what he will accomplish; I am positive Bobby will enjoy the four weeks experience."

Mrs. Cammett said an absolute, "No!" I then said quickly "I will be here Monday morning to fetch Bobby," and left.

Monday morning Mrs. Cammett was at the Bancroft school with Bobby, much to my surprise and great pleasure, and she said to me roughly, "You put me to shame, I could not allow you to do what I should be doing,"…or words to that effect. That was about forty-five years ago. Bobby came every day to summer school and he loved it. And we are still dear and close friends, although his parents, sadly, have passed on at this point. Bobby is also a great actor even now and loves Shakespeare!

I had chosen a lovely piece of music for him to dramatize. It was titled *The Lamplighter*. At that point Bobby could, with slow and deliberate effort, walk across the stage with braces on his legs and with crutches. The scenery was perfect and the pantomime by Bobby was absolutely beautiful. There was not a dry eye in the audience.

All went so well that when the next summer school production was held, he was there. Meanwhile, the Cammett family had moved to a ranch house on Lovejoy Road in Andover so Bobby would have no stairs to face every time he wanted to go out. The house was also in a section of town that would allow him to attend the Sanborn School where I was teaching.

When Bobby was in the sixth grade his teacher directed and produced an abridged play of Shakespeare's *Hamlet*. This was part of their English and History studies. Bobby played the part of Hamlet then and he was great. His voice had changed at that point; he was absolutely a Basso profundo; he could no longer walk, but he could stand. It was when he delivered the lines in *Hamlet* that I knew he would be great as Fagin in *Oliver!*, the musical that I was planning to produce during Summer School.

Oliver!

After the second summer school performance at the Bancroft School, I decided, since our Sanborn School had no auditorium other than the cafetorium and stage to request permission to use the new and gorgeously well-equipped West School Auditorium. Permission was granted and this made our play acting far more exciting; all our future presentations were absolutely brilliant! Parents and students were thrilled. And I was able to use the same auditorium for my future productions.

There were five solos in *Oliver!* for Fagin. I told Bobby he could learn all five or any of them he wanted, if five would be too many, four or three would be just as good. Guess what he did? He learned all five. He was marvelous in the musical!

I had to reconfigure the musical a bit, since in the play or movie, Fagin runs around quickly, sprints from here to there singing or talking or scolding all the little 'boys' who were living with him in the attic room of an empty building… which obviously Bobby could not do. I decided that Bobby would 'stand'; while he 'stood', the waifs did the running around or changing of places while they sang songs. We figured out how Bobby could sing and act by standing, propped against something. But…the audience would not notice that; it all went so smoothly and the little waifs in *Oliver!* ran or walked around him, or sat at his feet when he sat for a while on a barrel or something of that sort that fit the scene. Our staging was set up the opposite of the musical or movie, but it worked for me, and it worked for Bobby. That was all that mattered.

I become really agitated when I am directing a play or musical. I act out each part so the students can see what I want. I can become most vociferous,

Bobby Cammett as Fagin during "Oliver!" rehearsal

Bobby Cammett as Fagin during the production of "Oliver!"

so, for example, Fagin, (Bobby) would imitate me. The students themselves always enjoyed my displays of anger, or pleasure, meaning any of the character's parts, etc. However, one day, little Anne Marie, who was about seven-years-old, came to me, crying and pleading with me, "Please, Mrs. Guziejka, don't scold Bobby anymore. It makes me so sad." Being so young, she did not quite understand what or why I was hollering at Fagin, (Bobby). She was truly upset, until one of the helping parents took her aside and soothed her and made her understand that I was not angry with Bobby, just teaching him how to act, how to holler, how to have inflections in his voice…etc.

Another amusing incident during the rehearsals of *Oliver!* involved a student, Paul, who was supposed to yell 'stop thief' during the play. I wanted him to yell 'Stop thief, stop thief' with great feeling while pointing his arm to the left, at the alleged 'thief.' I had to work with Paul extensively to get him to perform his part convincingly. At that point in the play, Fagin (Bobby) was propped up in back of the curtains where the two curtains met to be ready for the following scene. Well, during one rehearsal, I was working with Paul and his yelling of 'stop thief.' He did it once, poorly; a second time getting better; then a third time with me 'hollering' at him as I usually did when directing my actors.

Well, Paul finally put more oomph into his part and flung his arm out with such a force as the thief ran away, that it swung to the left and hit the curtain… hard, which he was not supposed to do. He knocked Bobby, who was behind the curtain, over and onto the floor with a good loud thud!

Everyone scurried to pull back the curtain and there we found Bobby, stretched out flat on the floor on his back. Paul looked as though he was about to cry, and then bent over to help Bobby, but Bobby yelled most emphatically: *"Don't touch me...don't touch me...you have done enough damage already!"* With utter relief, I could see by the smirk on Bobby's face that he was not hurt; he was chuckling a bit as he gave that last command, and somehow, we helped Bobby to get up.

On the night of the production, there was not a 'dry eye,' in the house after the show was finished. Sean Callahan, who was Oliver, sang the emotional, poignant and tear-jerking solo called, 'Where is Love' in a simply 'lovely' way, with sobbing and tears at the end of the song. All five of Bobby's solos were showstoppers. I loved Bobby's rendition of 'Reviewing the Situation.' Bobby's father was crying and blubbering and sniffing into his large handkerchief, and I could understand why. Everyone stood and clapped heartily for the success of Fagin and his five solos; Oliver and all 'Fagin's boys' and the other actors received accolades from the audience. The applause seemed to go on forever. That is one show I will never forget! I guess it is safe for me to assume...the whole performance was a success.

❧ ❧ ❧

In the meantime, in addition to my musical work with school students, life at home was keeping me busy. My husband Ed would have good spells and then bad spells with his back problems. He eventually ended up having a fourth surgery in Boston. The other surgeries, we were told, had done him more harm than good. Therefore the fusion had to be 'torn down.'

If I thought we had bad times before, I was wrong, it was worse now since this fourth surgery made everything very painful for him; he had such a long recovery that the only way I can describe it all now is to say he never really recovered from any of the four surgeries. They left their indelible mark on him and his horrible memories have never fully left him.

What finally did the trick? What made Ed 'turn around' so that he would be able to live a better life? He went into a pain unit thanks to Dr. Hank Everett from Andover. He was a psychiatrist and somehow it was arranged that we would attend his group meetings at the Lowell General Hospital. How that arrangement was made I cannot remember. During some of these sessions Dr. Everett could see Ed was not improving. Ed had become quite addicted to pain pills. Dr. Everett suggested Ed enter a Pain Unit in Woburn, which was located about a half hour from Dracut. The stay in the pain unit was the best thing that ever could have happened to Ed, and after three months, Ed began to seem a little better, nay…a whole lot better, although there were occasional setbacks, no question of that.

He re-entered the pain unit two more times, but those were for shorter spells of time, six weeks instead of three months. After these sessions I saw a major change in Ed. It is not to say that the pain went away, or disappeared… poof…up into the atmosphere, …but Ed learned to deal with the pain better… and better. He stopped taking pain pills of any kind.

> *As we advance in life,*
> *it becomes more*
> *and more difficult,*
> *but in fighting the difficulties*
> *the inmost strength of the heart is developed.*
>
> **—*Vincent Van Gogh***

By my fourth or fifth year at the Sanborn School my students were always looking forward to the next production. School would open in September and the very first thing the children would ask me would be: "Mrs. G…what show will we put on this year?"…or "Mrs. G. are you sure we will be able to have another musical this year? What will the name of the new musical be?"

I absolutely loved my work and my love for it rubbed off on the students. I always believed that was the mark of a good teacher. If a person is teaching something they do not enjoy, then it all forms a film on the enjoyment and the understanding of whatever it is the children are trying to learn. I have seen some children's shows that were absolutely abominable. I swore whenever I put on a show, the students would love it as much as I did and that would be the only way they and I would be successful.

H.M.S. Pinafore

When we produced Gilbert and Sullivan's *H.M.S. Pinafore*, all the male characters wore sailors' costume with their funny hats, which was typical of British Navy uniforms one hundred or more years ago. The girls' solos and costumes were lovely; the girls wore hoop type gowns…again, representing ladies of England at that time.

Mary Guziejka rehearsing with students

The Captain of the Pinafore and the famous Admiral performed beautifully, in character all the time, and their solos were spectacular. It was marvelous seeing the important Admiral walking sedately in full costume down the center aisle of the auditorium, holding his saber and singing with the chorus and also singing solo.

I have masses of eight-by-ten photos of the Sanborn production down in the storage chest in the cellar and I dragged them all up here to the computer room to make everything a trifle more clear to my memory. Unfortunately, although the pictures are great, it still does not bring back the names of the children. Having taught so many students for so very many years, their names are more than a little hazy now.

In 1977, Ed and I had the great pleasure of staying in the Savoy Hotel in London, England. While there we discovered much information about Mr. Gilbert and Mr. Sullivan, composers of so many famous operettas. It seems one of them lived at the hotel and as a result their musicals were performed at the Savoy Hotel Theatre. I attended a musical at that very theatre at one time. Small sections of the original scores and manuscripts for the Gilbert and Sullivan operettas are framed and hanging on the walls in the Savoy Hotel. I was so impressed to be able to have seen a little of the original scripts and music.

The Mikado

Later, I produced Gilbert and Sullivan's *The Mikado* with the Sanborn school students. It is about the Japanese and their customs, but all the writing was a spoof, a comedy, and with some 'comical' sadness. The operetta was a gigantic success as far as the students and their families and I were concerned.

Laura Need, who had portrayed Amahl when she was in the fourth grade, played the lead in *The Mikado* and was a 'smashing' success once again! The audience was delighted when she and two other girls sang, 'Three Little Girls From School Are We.' The three girls were in authentic kimonos and using authentic Japanese fans. Even their hair was done up in the fashion of that time in Japan.

The fathers of some of the students in Sanborn School were making business trips to Japan. When they learned of our desire to produce *The Mikado*, they brought back kimonos and other Japanese artifacts. One family, the Ziggenbein family, presented me with a Japanese kimono to wear the night of the performance. I will never forget them, their generosity and their many kindnesses. I taught all their five children at the Sanborn School.

The boys in the chorus of *The Mikado* looked spectacular. They all wore the same color of jacket which was a bright green color, and patterned after a short kimono, with sashes tied around their waists. Their trousers were black and with wide legs ending at calf length. They wore no shoes and that was the best part for the boys. They loved that. That may have been their best moments in the play, running around with 'sabers' (made in the art department from cardboard) and barefoot!

The whole show was successful…I was proud and so very pleased with… and for…my students. Their faces were shining and they all seemed to stand a little taller after the show ended. I received several bouquets of flowers from the children and loved them, but the best present for me was their performance and how well they acted, staying in their Japanese character the whole way through and thoroughly enjoying every bit of the experience.

Square and Folk Dancing

Not all children can 'star' in a show, nor do all children want to do the same as everyone else, but I have not as yet met any child through my fifty years of

*Scott Elliot (above) as
Lord High Executioner
in* The Mikado

*In photo at right
Dennis Hardcastle*

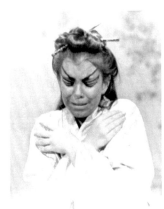

*Laura Need as Yum-Yum
in* The Mikado

teaching who did not enjoy 'Square Dancing and Folk Dancing.' I started square dancing in Andover with the third graders. I had a wonderful set of record albums put together and 'called' by Ed Durlacher. Every record was gauged to follow one another from easy to more difficult. Record #1 introduced the 'calls' and then on it went. I had six records and both sides had square dancing.

At the very beginning of the record, Mr. Durlacher explained the calls and movements for each call. After the classes learned one, they did not need to listen to his directions each time they danced it. The dance flowed naturally as he 'called' the steps. Third graders started with album one, and fourth and fifth-graders started with a review of album one, and then progressed to album two. The fifth and sixth graders learned all the steps provided by all the records. I taught the square dancing classes about once a month, or more often if all worked out well with the students I was teaching. Then, if the students were really good and asked nicely, at the end of another lesson we would fit in more dancing.

The younger students learned how to dance simple Folk Dances from around the world and they were adorable. They loved it. I loved it also, and all of us were happy.

As a result of all this folk and square dancing, towards the end of each school year we had a 'Sanbarn Dance Festival'…(please note, it was not spelled 'Sanborn' but 'Sanbarn') the children liked that particular spoof.

Why 'Sanbarn?' Because the area outside the third wing of the school building was made to look like the outside of a barn. The art teacher was outstanding and had real life sized figures decorating the 'barn.' The children loved decorating the 'barn,' and each year it became more intricate with three dimensional animals and haystacks placed hither and yon around the dancing area.

Mothers and fathers and relatives attended the 'Sanbarn' Dance Festival. They were encouraged to dress the part if they wished and all were invited to dance at certain times but many were shy and afraid and did not. However, some parents willingly tried to learn and several of them dressed for the part, and had great fun dancing or being shown *how* to dance, by their children. And each year the pleasure grew; the students loved the festival and the costumes. It was a successful venture that carried on each year I was there.

Pleasure in the job
Puts perfection in the work.

—Aristotle

A 'Moving' Event with a 'Special' Class

There was only one area in which I was NOT satisfied with my square dance/folk dance program. I had not yet included the 'handicapped class'. This class was new to the Sanborn School in the mid '70s. It consisted of approximately ten boys, ranging in ages from ten to almost eighteen years old. All of them were confined to wheelchairs and most of them had difficulty talking although they all seemed to have good hearing. The boys always brightened up immediately when I came into their room for a music class.

Because of my success with all the other students in square dancing and folk dancing classes I found myself puzzling about how to manage 'dancing' with the handicapped boys. "Why can't I have the handicapped boys dance also?" I kept asking myself. An idea burgeoned quickly in my mind while walking down the corridor and I found myself, 'off to the races!' I approached my dear friend, and fellow teacher, Susan Rogers, (she taught fifth grade at that time) and I shared my thoughts with her. My plan was to have her boy students push the handicapped students in their wheelchairs through the square dance movements while the girls in her class would take turns being the wheelchair bound students' partners. Susan responded enthusiastically to my idea and said, "Let's do it!"

Therefore, over the next few weeks I held several square dance lessons with the handicapped students and Susan Rogers' students in the cafetorium. It was an emotionally 'moving' sight to see. Both groups of students enjoyed the dance classes immensely, mistakes and all, as witnessed by their faces. I can still see in my mind the pleasure exuding from the students' faces, handicapped students and non-handicapped as well, as they all worked together on this project.

The dancing classes were going so well that after a few weeks of practice I decided to have the students perform for their parents and their parents' friends. I arranged for them to sit in chairs on the stage so they would be comfortable while watching the square dancing moves on the cafetorium floor below.

After the students performed the few dances they had learned, one could see tears in the eyes of their parents and friends. Happiness was absolutely glowing on the faces of their boys in the wheelchairs as well as in the faces of the 'helper' students from Susan Rogers' class. I was absolutely thrilled! When the dancing came to an end, we all returned to the classroom of the handicapped boys for refreshments of cake, cookies, and ice cream provided by their teacher. *Everyone* basked in the afterglow of happiness of a dancing experience well shared.

That afternoon was an event that will linger in my heart forever!

London, England

My dear friend, Mary Ellen, was always trying to help us in many ways, and one night in the mid 1970s she called on the telephone with a plan that absolutely floored me. She said, "Mary, listen to this…Ray and I are going to London for seven days with two other friends and also we are bringing two of our boys. We want you to come with us. Bring your mom and the kids and we'll have a great time." She added, "I will make all the arrangements for you!"

"Mary Ellen, how on earth could I possibly afford to do that," I replied. I was ecstatic about the invitation but much to my sorrow, not at all positive we could afford that type of travel.

"Everything in London, and all over England, is in a deep depression and the fares and hotel rooms are very inexpensive," Mary Ellen explained. "The tourist agencies are absolutely crying for people to come, they need the money so badly. You can do it…see if you can!"

I thought about it briefly and then told her I would call her back with an answer.

By then, my father had died, and Amy was almost six-years-old. Susan was in college, taking courses, but Eric was 14-years-old and would come along with Amy, of course. I had never before traveled abroad. I thought to myself, "I would love to do it. But how?" I decided that first I would talk with my mother and Ed.

My mother said she would pay Amy's fare and hers. I would only have to pay for Eric's and Ed's and my own. Ed was not working, but was well enough to travel and stay in a hotel. The fare for the airplane was so unbelievably inexpensive, and, to make matters even more unbelievable and better, the price included the costs of a first class hotel as well. It was the Royal Horse Guard Hotel with a view of the Thames! Needless to say, we all went, all ten of us, five of them and five of us. I was deliriously happy!

We took two trips over February school vacations (we loved the first time so much, all of us, that we traveled to London the following year as well). We stayed at the Royal Horse Guard Hotel, and absolutely loved it. It was old, fancy, and well decorated in great English style of the old days. Nothing was in the least bit modern, which I dearly loved. The hotel faced the River Thames; it was centrally located and near Buckingham Palace; Trafalgar Square was a five-minute walk away and Westminster Cathedral and the House of Parliament and Big Ben were also within easy walking distances. We were also in walking distance to the Tower of London. We missed absolutely nothing of great importance in London that week. Somehow, we were able to squeeze in visits to the British Museum and the British Art Museum which was across the street from St. Martin's of the Fields, and which I still, to this day, dearly love!

During our second trip to London, halfway through the week we took a plane to Paris, France and spent three or four days visiting the L'Arch de Triomphe, the famous Art Museum and the famous Boulevards while seeing artistic works too numerous to count. All was outstanding and amazing for Ed and me. My mother was thrilled, and with good reason, since her family came from Normandy, France, and her maiden name was Leclerc. We walked down the

Mary Guziejka, husband Ed, Eric and Amy in Paris, France

Leclerc Boulevard in Paris; the monument there was named after General Leclerc who was my mother's first cousin and an important figure in World War II. The lovely statue of General Leclerc is at a roundabout on the boulevard. My mother was so quietly happy and so absorbed in everything she saw that she had a perpetual smile on her face and her blue eyes twinkled all the time.

In 1977 we returned to London for a week once again, and stayed at the famous Savoy Hotel. But, this time, we went without my mother and children. We were three couples. My mother was very happy that we were going back and offered to stay with all the children at our home. We did more touring in London and also took bus tours further afield to see Stonehenge, Dorchester Cathedral, Winchester Cathedral and other famous places almost too numerous to mention. I was in seventh heaven every time I went to London or Paris!

Those wonderful trips abroad had kept me dwelling constantly on the idea of living abroad…but thinking…it was "*all but a dream, too sweet to be substantial*", a quotation from Shakespeare. But then, I wanted to do something special for me! I had taught music and other subjects to hundreds of children for so many years and had been under such emotional strain at times, that I began to feel my life was at a 'dead end'…yes, so much so that I wrote the following letter to myself at that time, obviously under great distress!

Dead end. My life is at a dead end. "Mrs. Guziejka, your mouth is smiling but your eyes are sad," said Jennifer, one of my first grade students. My music lessons are growing stale. They are no longer good. I'm singing while I'm teaching, but my mind cuts out, shuts off like an electric power outage. I find I don't know where my thoughts were or where my mind left off…where it has gone, or is going.

Trudging through the hallways of school, pushing my piano or hauling my cart, my life grows heavier each day, ponderous and weighty. Everything in my school day is déjà vu. I see my own figure clearly down the hallway turning a corner with a piano while knowing full well I am at the opposite end of the same hallway rushing to get to a room, pushing and pulling with all my force so as not to be late for the next teacher who is always unpleasant when I finally slink into the room.

The room is always too hot, stifling; color is gone; everything is dark. I am falling into a hole; joy is gone. Songs and children are all that survive and they too are slipping away. Schedules are set up so that music specialists move from classroom to classroom. We have five minutes to move from one classroom to another, regardless of where the next classroom is located. It could be next door to the room I'm in, or two or three hallways away. Doesn't matter to the principal. It is all the same. While moving to the classrooms, I must push a cabinet-sized piano. Along with that I must have books and musical toys, rhythm instruments to teach the children about beat and rhythm. I must move all and everything within five minutes. Sometimes I have the help of eager fifth or sixth grade students, but they want to move quickly and often spill everything over, dropping it all on the floor. Occasionally, the piano itself falls over.

*Burn out. That is the word. **Burn out.** People talk of it, people com-*

plain of it, but I am in it. I live it daily and I am the loser. I must change, move, quit, stop, leave, die…anything, everything, something must happen. All is gone…everything is dark, I am falling into a hole. Joy has disappeared.

After the full realization of burn out…after seeing myself clearly, after the knowledge of the depressive way I was living fully came clearer to me, I began to search for a course of action. This did not come as a bolt out of the blue; it did not come as a vision' but come it did! A thought, a gleam, an idea, a hope, a prayer, not one, but all five of these took shape. I looked at my husband in bed, an invalid. I saw my children in a hideous situation with a drudge as a mother who no longer smiled. I saw a home I was struggling to hold on to.

❧ ❧ ❧

After returning from our last trip abroad, I met a teacher at one of our many teachers' meetings from another school in town, not from the Sanborn School. She had been away on a sabbatical and had worked in a school in England. It was exciting listening to the recounting of her tale. I personally did not want to teach, I wanted to study, I told her.

With much enthusiasm, and her voice, seemingly rising up an octave, she said, "What is holding you back? You can apply for a sabbatical, get a loan on your home for secondary expenses, and rent your house while you're gone. That's easy. That's what I did," and, then she added, "I feel like a new woman now."

"Also," she went on to say, "I absolutely loved living and working in England. There is nothing to match it here and I know you will feel the same way once you are there. It is the very best thing I ever did for myself!" She ended with, "Try it and if you have difficulty, feel nervous, and/or just want to talk, call me on the telephone."

I imagined taking all of my family somewhere: my husband and my three children, but I was not too sure of where the money would come from. I did dream, I must say. I had worked hard and steadily for twenty-five years. Night after night, my mind went back and forth thinking about applying for a sabbatical leave, meaning I could attend school in London or wherever they would have me!

I was amazed at myself, thinking I could do something of this nature…live abroad, study abroad, see and learn new things…my family and me. Of course, I would never go off and leave any of them, although Susan was in college at this time and certainly old enough to leave in the states.

I was amazed also for even thinking I could swing such a project…or even attempt to do something of this scope and nature. The biggest question was, would the Town of Andover grant me a sabbatical with pay, or even consider granting a sabbatical to a music teacher?

I fretted and worried and worried and fretted, as is my want…and finally found courage somewhere to write a letter and accept whatever the inevitable would be.

All caution thrown aside, I wrote a letter to the Superintendent of Andover Schools. That was the hardest job of my entire life…to this day I recall the gaping black hole into which I had to drop this one-paragraph letter which could change the course of my life. I trembled at the mailbox, I couldn't breathe for a few moments, gasping and palpitating. I thought and searched my mind and heart. I knew my strength. I knew once the letter was in the box I would pursue my plan since I was too proud to do otherwise, and I also knew I could not fail… so I dropped the letter in the box.

I am telling you all of this because after being 'set free in my mind,' so to speak, my mind was soaring…absolutely flying all over the place with my new idea, due to the previous three trips to London and one to France. I felt I had a gem of an idea, and then it became what I felt was a brilliant idea. I weighed everything in my mind, back and forth, back and forth, as in… should I? Could I? Must I? I mulled my ideas over, day and night, worried about this and that, and then, finally, went on to explore them since I fully realized that the worst thing that could happen would be a refusal from Dr. Seifert, the Andover school superintendent, and the School Board.

I decided I would write to the University of London and two other universities in England, one in the south and one up north, to study for my Masters' Degree. I did not really know where to start, so I wrote letters and sent them out to the universities for information. I then wrote the letter to my superintendent requesting a sabbatical. I was a nervous wreck; an absolute bundle of nerves is the only way I can describe it.

Questions…questions…questions soared into my mind. What would I do with my house for that year? I knew I would have to rent it. Where could I borrow money to support us for the year? How would I do it? I was so scared; I was scared of being accepted and scared not to be… it was almost unimaginable for me considering my background and my nature and my family! As time went on, I wrote more letters and talked to more people.

I sent out all my letters and references to three universities in England and then waited…and waited…and waited, while I continued to teach school. Finally, in the spring, I cannot remember which month, I wrote again and received a reply from the University of London. The letter said they were waiting for a letter stating I had been granted a sabbatical. I went to our superintendent and he said similarly, "We are waiting to hear if you have been accepted at one of the schools."

I felt this was all so stupid. So, I asked Dr. Seifert, our superintendent to, "Please, send a letter to the University of London stating you are willing to give me a sabbatical!" He did, and finally, after much fingernail chewing and looking at calendars after teaching all day, the acceptance came through. I had been accepted into all three Universities, but I chose to go to the University of London since there is so much to see and learn there, in the school itself, as well as in London proper. I really and truly wanted to live in London!

I am rather proud of the fact that I always wanted to succeed or achieve on my own. When I went to the bank for a secondary loan on our house I was trembling all over. My only mistake, in retrospect, was that I should have asked for a few thousand dollars more. With the amount of money I requested we played it close to the edge, but I only realized that much later.

We rented our home almost immediately. We were lucky. I saw an ad in the *Lowell Sun* stating a man and his wife in California were looking to rent a house for one year since they were coming here to the University of Lowell on sabbatical. What a stroke of luck and what a coincidence! I called them on the telephone that very night and it was done. They sent a deposit for two months in advance.

All I had to do now was pull myself back down to the ground since I thought I had flown up to heaven. The only things left to be finished were to decide what to do with items in my home that I wanted stored, pay up all our bills, and pack our suitcases and leave. Yes, I was still teaching all this time, and you can almost imagine the energy I was expending, between teaching, flying in the air mentally, and doing all this paper work and phone calling etc.

All was arranged: my mother would come to see us with Eric at the end of September for one month. Eric would continue working at his job until then, since he had graduated from high school and needed money also. Ed and I assumed we would have found a house to rent by that time! Susan would spend six weeks with us at Christmas time since that is how long she would be out of her college for the holidays.

We would leave on the fifth of August to give us time to find a place to live and to register Amy in a school. She was nine years old at that time. And last but not least, as they say…to begin my studies at the University of London, England! I was riding on a cloud, soaring through the heavens. I was so happy!

BON VOYAGE!

Chapter 16
London Sabbatical

"Strong reasons make strong actions."

King John
—Shakespeare

W e're off to see the wizard, no…not the wizard of oz…but off to *London*… London, England! I was so elated that the song kept going through my mind over and over again. Wheeeee!

We left…with bag and baggage and nuts and bolts, with all in our home in the ready for the tenants we had never met *and*…we were on the plane! It was happening; I was in a complete daze and fog while saying my sad and tearful goodbyes to my mother and Susan and Eric; I think I cried all the way to London. At least I had Amy and Ed with me. That was a big help. In case you have *not* noticed, I am most emotional *most* of the time!

We never did meet the people who were moving into our home when leaving for London or upon our return. They arrived after we left and left before we returned home once again. Fortunately for us someone helped us with that issue, a friend became a 'meeter/greeter' and all went well.

Bed and Breakfast

The first thing we did after arriving in London was to go to a 'Bed and Breakfast,' meaning a home away from home. We felt fortunate in finding this particular one, it was great, just what we needed and hoped for. The landlord and lady were warm, lovely and most helpful the entire time we inhabited their lovely dwelling. We learned about this place from Colin Evans, a musician in London to whom I was introduced by Paul Gayzagian, my treasured musician friend from the University of Lowell. The B and B near Hyde Park was owned by an Irish couple in their forties. (I did not have to ask from where they came since the first sentence they spoke told me they were from Ireland).

They were lovely and most helpful and the husband of the pair had a marvelous sense of humor. It is good he had that sense of humor since he had to lug all our bags up about three or more flights of stairs. It seemed to me that he was up and down at least ten times since we had so many bags due to the fact that we were staying for a year. My nerves were hither and yon in my mind and body. I had not slept a wink on the flight from Boston to London. I was so absolutely, thoroughly excited and therefore wide-awake throughout the whole trip; it was incredible. *And*…here we were…in London, at Hyde Park, and I was still wide eyed with joy and happiness.

After we settled in, we decided to go for a walk to scout the area around the B and B, hoping it was near a place we would recognize from our previous three trips to London. Voilà…after much walking…we found we were around the corner from Hyde Park! So exciting for me! Amy was happy as a lark to be out of the plane and therefore spent much of her time doing cartwheels on the grass in Hyde Park; that was her year for cartwheels no matter where we were, and what we were doing. If there was grass available, Amy performed cartwheels!

When I was not meeting or talking on the telephone with our friend, Colin, to discuss where to live in a more permanent place than the B and B, we went to Hyde Park for Amy, who at that time of her life, was practicing her gymnastics. She did all kinds of gyrations in Hyde Park and seemed to be very happy!

Colin also introduced us to a great swimming pool in a club that served lovely dinners. The pool was great and I took absolute advantage of it the *one* time I was there. I was a good swimmer so I swam a mile in no time, and Amy was also a good swimmer…actually the three of us were. That was one sport Ed could do beautifully, even after all his surgeries. But the cost of using the pool and club was prohibitive for us, consequently we never returned to it again.

The following day was spent in and around Trafalgar Square seeing the National Gallery, and then, down the street to Westminster Abbey and the Parliament buildings, all of which reassured us we were really in London. Then, after all our touring, I settled down in earnest to find a home in which to live.

Finding a dwelling for a year was difficult I must admit. The B and B had the funniest, most peculiar, telephone room in the world! The room was *not* a real telephone booth, no…it was a small room, a *very* small room, and the phone had a short cord, and no seat was to be found anywhere. It was a pay telephone so I had to have dozens of English coins with me to make each call.

I had amassed piles of newspapers and adverts (adverts…English slang for advertisements) for places to rent and I made what seemed like dozens of telephone calls to many 'estate agents' meaning 'real estate offices and salespersons' at their offices or homes. I placed my first call and then I realized the cord was not long enough, so I had to kneel on my knees, all the while turning my neck upwards to the telephone that had a short cord. I became so exhausted while making the calls that I decided to kneel on the floor with the phone in my hand. You would have bent over in two and laughed out loud if you could have seen me trying to kneel on the floor and talk on a phone that was inches above my mouth! Never to be deterred…I carried on! It took three or four days to find a place to live.

At one point we decided to answer a newspaper add that *seemed* interesting. The owners of the B and B told us where to go; we hired a taxi. When we arrived at our destination the driver let us out and then left us…and we discovered almost immediately that it was a horrible place. I could never have lived there, nor could I have had Amy live there and go to school. It was filthy to begin with, and crowded with many people of all mixtures and cultures; all of them seemed poor and mostly all were dirty, albeit friendly. While I felt very bad for them, there was no way that I could have lived in that area for one night, let alone for a year. We left quickly.

After three or four days of being closeted on the floor in the telephone room, with our B and B allowance running out, I was beginning to get discouraged! I kept trying to think of how I could get some help. Then I remembered! It came to me seemingly in a flash…the lovely Savoy Hotel and Martin Mauel, who worked on the fifth floor of the Savoy; this was where we had stayed the last time we visited London with Mary Ellen.

I called Martin at the Savoy Hotel from the B and B telephone room. Kneeling on the floor, straining my neck upwards, I told him who I was and all about my dilemma. Fortunately for us, he remembered me. In his German accented English Martin said, "Not to worry, Mary…Martin will help you! Martin will help you! I will help you find a place to live!" And…he did. He called a friend of his who was a real estate person in a lovely borough about thirty minutes by train outside of London, toward the east. I was elated and slept fairly well that night.

The next day Martin called and directed us to South Croydon and a house at Robin's Court, Birdhurst Road. I loved the names! We took a train almost immediately after his call, and again we were fortunate to meet friendly and helpful people. We were on the train platform in South Croydon trying to figure out how to find the street where the apartment was, when a charming young lady with a broad and beautiful smile walked over to us and said, "Let me help you. I could not help overhearing a few of your remarks. My name is Vera Kasey and I live here, right near Robin's Court." She then put out her hand to shake hands with the three of us.

I could have hugged and kissed her then and there! Vera was a delightful person. She evidently was not in a hurry since she walked with us up to the house. It was a three story house; small, but most adequate with four identical adjoining apartments. Kenneth Shoesmith was the owner and he was waiting to show us around. Thanks to Vera and Mr. Shoesmith, we were settled into the narrow, furnished, three-story house a few days later. I think we were only in London at the B and B between five to seven days.

Fortunately, the apartment was furnished, well…somewhat furnished. It was equipped with pieces of furniture for us to live in with relative comfort! The house was simple and plain, it was one of five apartments attached to one another in a row; all were three stories high and all looked exactly alike. There is a special name for that type of house there and I cannot remember it…but I think they are called 'Row Houses' here.

The first floor had a hallway with stairs going up to the second floor, then a few feet straight ahead was a very, very small kitchen, and a counter that divided the room so that it left us with a dining area. It was small but adequate for our needs. Outside the back kitchen door was a small backyard, or a 'green' as they call it in England. "Amy could play, and do back flips" I mused, "and have friends over to visit."

Beside the front door and to the left there was a garage. The garage door was closed but we went in to inspect it from the front hallway while looking at the downstairs rooms. We never owned a car in England that year, (we could never have afforded one) but used the garage for the washing machine and dryer and storage of suitcases. Fortunately for us, the washer and dryer were there, and their use came with part of the rent. That was a huge relief for me.

The second floor had a living room with a couch and two stuffed chairs with two lamps for reading…a bathroom and one small but adequate bedroom, and the third floor had two bedrooms, our bigger one, and Amy's small bedroom plus another bathroom. None of the rooms were big or spacious but more than adequate for our needs at this time and the furniture would be just fine also. Each bedroom also had a bureau and bed and night table.

"Hmmmn," I said to myself, "this is perfect for us. Amy will be next to us at night, and when Eric comes, he can sleep in the second floor bedroom. When Susan visits, well…we'll work it out then; we always have the couch that opens up and there is always the floor for Eric and Amy if necessary."

"We'll take it," I told Mr. Shoesmith. We quickly did the paper work and made the rent payment (three months advance rent).

Then, luckily for us, the lady we met at the railroad station, Vera Kasey, became an invaluable friend. She brought home cooked meals to us until we were settled, and then some. It all depended on what she was cooking and if she wanted to see us and had time off from work, etc. (She worked in a chemical laboratory in inner London). She also had a daughter who was about five years old, four years or so younger than Amy. Amy and Neif, (pronounced Neave)…

Amy Guziejka and Neif Kasey, daughter of Vera, in London, 1978

played almost daily. We went on many day trips together; Vera showed us around in the first few months probably more than anyone else. We found the English people to be friendly, helpful, thoughtful and kind. I cannot say enough about how good everyone was to us that whole entire year. It was an unbelievable year of friendship, music and travel!

❧❧❧

Once we had moved into our apartment, we had to take care of some paperwork in downtown Croydon, a city of 300,000 people, including filling out forms telling people why we were there, getting some shots and enrolling Amy in the local school system. Amy had been relatively school phobic at home, and she was afraid to start school in England. What transpired the day before she was to enter school did not help matters either.

My mother and Eric were planning to join us in early September, Eric to spend the year with us, and my mother to visit for a month. Eric was 18-years-old and had graduated from high school in June before we left for England in August. Eric was always a hard worker and had a full-time job as a waiter, and had two other jobs (one at a drugstore one day a week, and another part-time job in the mail room at the post office). He was trying to earn as much money as possible because he was looking forward to coming to stay with us in England. After we left, he lived with my mother in Lowell until it was time for them to join us.

The night before he and my mother were to fly out of Boston to London, Eric was cheerfully walking home from work. He was two doors away from my mother's house, when five young men jumped him and severely beat him. As if that was no bad enough, this happened in front of a gas station, but the men who worked in the station only stood by and watched! *Yes! stood and watched!*

We never really knew why Eric was attacked, we assume it was for his money, but he was a mess. The police were called and Eric was taken to the hospital. My brother helped by going to the hospital to see Eric and taking care of the hospital affairs. Eric had been beaten around the head and face. He was all blood, cuts and terrible bruises. My mother was frantic of course. My brother called us from Lowell (it was the middle of the night for us in England) to tell us what happened. We did not sleep a wink the rest of the night. And Amy was to start school in the morning.

Fortunately Eric's injuries were not severe enough to stop him from coming to London. We met their plane at Heathrow the next day. I spotted Eric and mom at a distance, before they went through customs. It was a horrible sight… Mom and Eric each in wheelchairs! (A week before they were to come to London, Mom had fallen and broken her wrist. Her arm was in a sling). I broke away from Ed and dashed to the nearby ladies room, sobbing all the way. Sitting on the throne behind closed doors, 'I cried my eyes out' as they say! I could not believe how those awful guys had hurt Eric. My brother had told me his face was swollen and bruised but I never dreamed he would look as he did when he arrived. Also, one of the 'animals' had bitten him…Eric had a hole in his neck!

I left the ladies room as soon as I could pull myself together. Oh, my, what a sad/happy time! We took them home and tried to make them as comfortable as possible. We waited on them constantly, trying to help them feel better somehow but sadly, only the passing of time could help both of them and us.

❧ ❧ ❧

Back to Amy: she was supposed to start school that morning. After receiving the telephone call from my brother telling us about the attack on Eric, Amy did not sleep at all. She was always a poor sleeper but this was her worst night yet. The next morning when we accompanied Amy to school, she looked like a poor, white, 'orphan of the storm' as we sat in the principal's office. The principal, Mr. Kilty, was most understanding and reassuring and I liked him instantly; but I did not feel reassured about Amy, knowing her shyness, her constant feelings of insecurity in her young life, and her obvious worries about what had happened to her brother.

Mrs. Rabinowitz was Amy's teacher. She stood there with her arms folded the morning we brought Amy in to school. With one finger on her cheek and the other arm across her waist, she assessed Amy and said, "An American!" and added, "tsk,tsk, tsk!" I looked askance at her and then she said to me, "She doesn't look very promising…" I was floored with that remark. Being a teacher myself, I was absolutely stricken and stymied by her words…and…*all* this was said in front of Amy. However, some magic must have occurred later because Mrs. Rabinowitz turned out to be a wonderful teacher in many respects. Amy grew to like her after a while and Amy's year in school went quite well.

(Amy tended to have hiccups when she was nervous…and it was Mrs. Rabinowitz that delivered Amy from her hiccups. I will have to ask Amy to explain fully how that happened as I was not there but it had to do with Amy lying down on the floor…and the rest I do not know)

In the meantime though, all that day while Amy was in school, I fretted about her and I fretted about Eric and mom, alternatively crying, and then, after the crying ceased, worrying while waiting to go to Heathrow. We arrived back at our Birdhurst residence with Eric and mom and waited anxiously for Amy to come home from school. Much to our surprise and delight, she arrived with a huge smile on her face and six or eight new girl friends. The children all thought Amy was wonderful, they clustered around her and one of them said, "She talks funny!" It was the cutest sight I had ever seen and Amy reveled in it. I was happy for Amy and quite relieved!

Amy learned to play the recorder that year and sang in the chorus at Christmas time. In the spring the school put on the musical *Oliver!*, (my most favorite musical for children), but it was performed by older students, so Amy was not able to be in it. We all went to see *Oliver!* though and it was superb! The show however, ran for three nights, which I felt was a bit too much for the children. Their singing voices, although sweet and lovely and on pitch, were overtaxed. At that age, singing voices should not be used to excess.

The staging however was quite clever. Someone had designed the staging so that the audience benches and seats were built 'up' and the audience could look 'down' on the children who were performing. Therefore the voices of the children were better heard, and the quality of the singing and acting was beautifully produced. In my opinion, that is the way all stages should be built.

So, even though she could not be in *Oliver!*, Amy did have many opportunities to do other performances with her recorder and singing during the school year. Whenever she was with us in our apartment one could always find her by hearing a little melody being played somewhere on her recorder. Being a musician myself, I was always so pleased to hear her play it.

It was through Amy's school in England that I learned about the Harvest Festival. This was a wonderful event celebrated, as far as I knew, in all the schools in England. It was exactly what the name implies, toward the end of October, once the harvest was brought in, a festival was held to thank God for all the good things in life, meaning food and friendship.

I discovered this by accident. I wanted to be involved at Amy's school, but since my own course of study at the University of London would be beginning in October, I could not be a full-time volunteer. However, the Harvest Festival required the help of parents because the students would visit 'shut-in' people, bringing food and other items to people who could not easily get out, or who were elderly.

On the day of the Harvest Festival that October I was free and able to participate. I went to Amy's school early. I was in time for the blessing of the goods and to hear the minister of the nearby church speak to the children in a loving and positive way and administer a blessing to the audience. Mr. Kilty then spoke to all of the audience before the choir sang a few hymns.

At the edge of the stage there were three steps that ran the length of the stage, and these stairs were lined with 'goods'. They were not just baked goods but all kinds of items that could be used by someone who had little or no money or was elderly. Each basket had a name on it and was filled with food and a gift or two, such as a scarf for cold weather or boots or sweater, whatever that person required.

The prayers, speeches and hymns were lovely, and then the big moment came for the children. We were divided into groups. I was assigned to a group with Amy and her friends. I was given a map. The group of five or six children under my care had the goodies in the baskets to give to the recipients. Then we all walked to the homes assigned to us, following the map.

The children were eager to show me the way to all the homes, and I found myself quite enthused with this whole affair. As we walked the children chit chatted back and forth mostly trying to tell Amy and me what was going to happen. It was certainly a sweet and loving time.

One home we visited stands out most in my mind. The children and I walked quite a way before we came to this home. When we arrived we found an elderly man sitting on a chair on the stoop, the top landing that is, waiting and waiting. When he saw us coming down the street he was suddenly extremely cheerful, joyful, beckoning and virtually jumping out of his chair. The children were equally as happy to see him. They seemed to know who he was! One stood beside him with an arm around his shoulder, another stood on the other side next to him and the others sat on the steps at his feet. I found out very quickly... they were waiting to hear his stories. We visited and listened to this man's stories of the war and the war battles, the stories were probably about World War I, he seemed that old. We listened, all of us, attentively for at least half an hour or more.

Then it was time to go. He was in tears, not crying and sniffling, mind you, but as we left, two big tears ran down his cheeks. He thanked us and then thanked us again many times as we prepared to leave. He also pumped my arm up and down several times while trying to shake hands with me and thank me as we were leaving. All the children received great big hugs, as I recall! He must have been in his eighties and I am not sure now how many battles or wars he was in but he told wonderful stories. I was beginning to feel tears coming on also, but I knew we had to leave! We had to carry on to the next house and then the next and the next....

I do not remember quite how many people we visited that day, but it was a full day and a lovely and wonderful thing for these children to do. Most importantly, they learned a strong and deep lesson, which was caring for each other and most especially, to care for the less fortunate! I do feel that these children will keep this in their hearts and memories when they are adults and continue to pass on the good feelings and the selflessness that showed all through that day. I was so thrilled to have been a part of it.

I brought this event home and shared it with my Sanborn School in Andover, Mass. I started it the following year at Thanksgiving time and I titled it: "The Harvest Festival!" And I am thrilled to tell you that the Harvest Festival in Andover is still continuing, thirty-three years later, carrying on each year, and bringing much happiness with it to older and disabled people of Andover. May it be ever thus!

Queen Elizabeth

I was told by one of the adults at Amy's school that if and when the Queen and her entourage ever had to pass in the direction of any school, someone would notify the schools involved. Then when the time came for her entourage to pass by the school or schools, the school children would line up outside, her motorcade would slow to a crawl, and the Queen would wave to the children and they would smile, throw confetti or wave flags.

When I learned about this, I was anxious for my sake, and for Amy's, to participate. I was fortunate to be available the day the Queen was scheduled to drive by. At the appointed time, we toddled excitedly down the road to the main street. The children lined up on the edge of the sidewalk and started waving their flags immediately although Her Royal Highness had not arrived! They were talking a mile a minute, and were so happy to be able to see the Queen. They could hardly wait!

Well…we waited, waited and waited, longer than I expected. First, the children stood and looked down to the right, all bending at the waist to see if she was coming. After a while the children all sat on the curbing, and then they stood and then they sat again. Well, after what seemed like hours, finally someone issued a warning in a very loud and dramatic voice…"Her Majesty the Queen is arriving, the Queen is coming, everyone stand and wave your flags."

The children stood…expectantly…excitedly…flags poised to wave…everything grew quiet…the Queen, her Majesty herself, was about to arrive! Well, she must have been very late for wherever she was going because her motorcade went by 'lickety split and with a *whoosh!*' her hand doing its usual sideways up and down wave, and her profile showing just a tiny bit. The motorcade *never* slowed down, just roared away up the street quicker than one could blink an eye…almost! The children grew quiet, nothing more was said…well, she is the Queen and these things can happen! We all turned around and traipsed back up to our school!

I did see her, I must admit, but unless the children's eyes were exactly on the correct spot, they would have missed her completely. That was my 'seeing the Queen' episode!

Eric and the Savoy

I had hoped that Eric would continue his education while in England. We visited two schools for him, but the prices were absolutely way beyond what we could afford. We discussed it, but Eric told me, "Mom, I really don't want to go to school. I would rather work and we cannot afford it anyway!" Eric was always practical and knew the situation we were in. He was just happy to be with us and in London. Since Eric did not feel comfortable about attending a school of higher education at this time of his life, we dropped our plans.

However, he did want to find employment. But how? He was not British, and we weren't sure where to start. Then, I remembered my friend Martin from

Eric Guziejka's senior high school portrait

the Savoy Hotel. I called him again and he said in a booming voice with its German accent: "Not to worry Mary…Martin will find him a job."

"But how?" I said incredulously, "How can you find him a job, just like that?"

Martin reassured me by saying, "Martin find him a job. You send Eric to me tomorrow. I find him a job, a good job!"

We agreed on a time to meet and Eric went down to the Savoy Hotel and came home a few hours later. "Mom," he said excitedly, "I'm going to be a waiter at the Savoy Hotel!" And he became quite a good waiter. He worked days, and occasional evenings, which led to an interesting event for him

Most of the waiters at the Savoy were Italian, Greek, or Spanish and none of them were tall. Eric however was six-feet four inches tall, and with his fair complexion and height, he stood out from the crowd and was open and friendly with everyone. The other waiters used to tease him about his height, and his American accent. But Eric laughed along with them and they all got along well.

One evening, after Eric had worked at the Savoy for a few months, a special party was being held in a room on the ground floor of the Savoy overlooking the Thames. A waiter approached Eric and said, "Look over there. Did you know there are two kings and three princes standing over there?"

Needless to say, Eric was stunned. Here he was, just out of high school from a small town in the States, and he had never seen *one* king or prince, let alone several in the same room. The waiter suggested Eric wait on them, and handed Eric a tray full of special drinks. Eric nodded and hastily obliged.

When he presented the drinks to the gentlemen one inquired, "Well young man, and where are you from?"

"I'm from Dracut, Massachusetts sir, in the United States of America," he replied.

"Well then," the king or prince asked, Eric was not sure of the person's title, 'what *are* you doing here…at the Savoy Hotel…and in England?"

Eric told them about his mother going to school at the University of London, which led to more questions and a longer conversation. He learned that he was talking with King Olaf and his son from Norway, the other King and his son were from Sweden, and the fifth person was Queen Elizabeth's husband, Prince Phillip.

One thing led to another, and Eric stood and talked with the kings and princes for thirty to forty minutes. He was so excited and exhilarated that when he came home to South Croydon after three a.m. he ran home from the train, galloped noisily up the two flights of stairs, and burst into our bedroom bellowing, "Mom, Dad, Mom, Dad…wake up, wake up! I had a drink with two kings and three princes tonight!"

I sat bolt upright and said, "What?"

Eric repeated, "I had a drink tonight with two kings and three princes and we talked together; the Duke of Edinburgh, the Queen's husband, and I talked for about half an hour or more! He wanted to know where I was from, how I happened to be working at the Savoy Hotel and then asked what my mother was studying at the University of London."

By then, Ed and I were wide-awake and listened enthusiastically to his tale. We were all absolutely astonished, but thrilled with the opportunity that had 'fallen' into Eric's lap!

About four a.m. Ed and I went back to sleep. However, I'm not sure if Eric ever slept that night. The next day at work however, Eric was gently reprimanded and told that he was a 'waiter' and therefore not supposed to enter into conversation with any of the patrons of the hotel, especially *royalty*! Fortunately, Eric's boss was understanding of the situation though, and Eric was not fired or punished in any other way.

Later that year, Eric had an opportunity to work at another hotel, the name of which slips my mind right now, to learn special ways to mix drinks. I'm not sure how long he attended this 'school,' perhaps a couple of weeks, but the management of that hotel took a liking to Eric…loved his work and personality… so the hotel invited us, Eric's parents, to come for dinner and drinks as their guests.

We were thrilled. We dressed for the occasion, not that we had many fancy clothes, but we were presentable. We took the train to Paddington Station. Then I said to Ed, "Ed, this is such an unusual and important event, don't you think we should take a taxi to the hotel restaurant and 'arrive in style?' Otherwise my feet will be killing me from the walk, and I'm certain we'll look worn out."

I'm sure I had a pleading look in my eyes, and I also knew that Ed's back problems made it painful for him to walk long distances. So we decided then and there to splurge on the expense of a taxi.

When we arrived, we met the owners and were shown to our table, one of the best in the house. Our meal was served, then a small orchestra appeared at our table. The musicians were all dressed like our own George Washington and friends…in white wigs with a pigtail, white stockings to their knee trousers and black patent leather slip on shoes with a buckle top. They played lovely chamber music the entire time we were there. I must admit, the lovely feelings from that evening stayed with me for a long while. What a fascinating life I had fallen into!

My Mom

My mother did not fare at all well during her month long trip to see us. She developed pneumonia and was bedridden. Fortunately, we were able to take her to an English doctor and he saw no need to hospitalize her. He said she would do well at home in bed. We all took good care of her, and the doctor even came to the house several times. (They did house visits in England then). In spite of all that, we all had many laughs and good times together. She was an

Mary's mother and Eric

absolutely lovable person at all times!

Since Mom was sick Vera brought her mother, who was near to my mother's age, to visit. After a few days had gone by and she seemed to be better, one new English friend after another came to say hello, bringing little gifts to her. Then the days seemed to fly by and finally she was feeling totally better. As you may recall, we had already taken her to London for a week in 1974, and then to London and Paris in 1975. She did not feel the need to go back into London, and did not seem to mind missing out on all the other famous places of interest that our new friend Vera was busily showing us. But one day, when she felt much better she agreed to go to Westminster Abbey…and she did enjoy herself. She was feeling much better and for that, I was supremely happy!

My mother was also able to venture forth on a trip to Brighton, planned by Vera We went by train to Brighton to see the ocean, and also a large castle previously owned by Queen Victoria. It was gorgeous! We sat on the sand in the sun at the beach and enjoyed a sumptuous 'Vera' picnic. Eric, Amy and Neave also came on that trip, and we have a few nice photographs of that occasion. One in particular that I love was taken on the railroad platform, with all of us huddled around a bench with my mother looking radiantly happy.

I cried buckets seeing my mother off at Heathrow airport at the end of that month. Back into the ladies room I went, to howl a bit more and then to wash my face and emerge, ready to face the world. The month had gone by so quickly. However, once mom arrived home and was met by my brother at the airport, I received a phone call saying she was fine. My mother was quite deaf so whenever she called or I called, my brother, or Susan, had to be next to the telephone translating for her, but she was fairly used to that. She was the most wonderful person in the world and I still miss her, as old as I am now. She lived to be almost 92 years old, short of one month, and was relatively well all that time until her last bout of pneumonia. Yes! It was one more bout of pneumonia that finally called her to her just reward!

Amy Lost?

Amy never slept well as a child. But when we moved to South Croydon, she started sleeping a good continuous night's sleep. I do not know what magic took over, what could have caused it, but she finally was able to sleep through the night, which was quite a relief for us. I was in seventh heaven and Ed was happy also.

One time, a strange thing did happen, however. We woke one morning and Ed said, "Did Amy come into our room last night?"

"No," I replied and then asked, "Did you see her last night?"

"No, I didn't," he replied. Then he turned and went into Amy's room, which was next to ours. He returned to our room and said, "She's not in her room." I then murmured out loud to myself, "I wonder where she is."

Normally, Amy and her poor sleeping habits would have brought her to our room to crawl in bed between us, if for some reason something bothered her.

I rose up and clambered fumblingly out of bed, put on my slippers and looked in her room. Then I went downstairs and looked around, none of which took long since the apartment was so small.

"Not here, Ed," I hollered upstairs. I was now beginning to grow frantic! We both went into all our small rooms on all three floors and could not find her anywhere. At this point we were now nervous. I even looked in the garage where the washer and dryer are placed…no luck there either…and then I opened the back door and peered out onto the long and narrow plot of grass that was fenced in. She was definitely not there. Anxiety was crawling into my being!

I was beginning to think something horrible had happened, as in someone had kidnapped her. Again Ed and I scoured the few rooms again. Then, Ed had to go to the bathroom to take a 'leak,' as he called it. Next to the toilet on the third floor, there was a large bathtub and our dirty laundry was piled in there waiting to be washed. (We had no clothes hamper, and since we took showers in the second floor bathroom, it was there, in the bathtub on the third floor, that we decided to collect our dirty laundry.)

As Ed was sitting on the 'throne' (he always called the toilet seat 'the throne') trying desperately to figure out where Amy could have been, an arm appeared from under the dirty clothing. He was stunned. He looked again and suddenly up rose a figure draped in our dirty laundry. It was *Amy*!

Hard to believe but for some reason, Amy had wandered in and fallen asleep in the bathtub and must have been cold. Being cold, she must have snuggled deeper into the sheets and towels and clothes that were going to be washed that very day, Saturday. Ed called to me in a loud voice, and I flew upstairs wondering what had happened. I found Amy in the bathtub, half awake and half asleep not knowing what was going on around her. I walked her back to her bed and she returned to dreamland to sleep for a little while longer, not fully knowing what had happened.

Ed and I just hugged each other not knowing what to say. I started to blubber on his chest since at that last minute after the frantic search around our small quarters we had begun to panic…yes, *panic*. I was ready to call the police. Had the police arrived and found Amy submerged under dirty clothes in the bathtub it would have been an unspeakable and unthinkable embarrassment! "All's well that ends well," Shakespeare once said. Amy was safe and sound and that was all that mattered!

Laundry Lost?

Our washer and dryer were in the garage in the front of the apartment, next to the front door and hallway leading to the kitchen. There certainly was no room for the washer and dryer to be put inside the apartment, the kitchen being so very small and the dining area not much larger. Being new in the apartment, many things went wrong and many little items were lost or misplaced several times. It really takes a while to get used to anything new... like where are my shoes? Or where are my pants? Then it became, where is my laundry?

There had been a car parked in front of our apartment for a few days. It was parked there seemingly for no reason, since no house was across the street from us. There were plenty of parking spaces to be used, but for some reason this car, suspiciously, I thought, was parked outside and opposite our garage door. I was very careful with Amy and also very careful about locking doors and the like.

One day I had washed our clothes and about an hour later, I went to put them in the dryer. But...when I went to take them *out* of the washer, they were not there. I looked in the dryer, thinking maybe I had forgotten and had already put them in the dryer, "Hmmm," I said to myself, "No clothes there." I then looked one more time in the washing machine. Still, no wet clothes in there.

I then went to see Ed who was on the third floor reading. "I cannot find our laundry Ed, our wet laundry, that is."

Ed, looking puzzled replied, "What do you mean, you cannot find our laundry? It has to be in the washing machine, where else could our laundry have gone?" He never likes to be interrupted while reading.

I snapped back with a louder voice than usual, "I don't know, which is why I came to ask you. Maybe you hung it out on the clothes lines out back?" Of course, I didn't believe Ed would do that, since... number one, that would be the last thing he would think of doing, and number two, he was reading on the third floor.

Ed said, "Mary, don't be silly, you washed the clothes, didn't you?" Ed started to get up now.

I replied, testily with, "Of course I did, what did you think I would do with the dirty laundry if not wash it?"

He then got a little sharp with me and said, "I'll go look in the washing machine myself..." I followed him down the two flights of stairs thinking... "He feels I am making a mountain out of a molehill, I am sure."

We both went into the garage; he opened the door of the washing machine.

He looked inside and declared, "Mary, you must have dried them and forgotten!"

I answered quickly, growing angrier by the minute and declared, "Ed, I looked in the dryer, and anyway, what makes you think I am so stupid as to not remember that I already dried them?" He looked inside the washer one more time and the wet clothes were still not there. He next looked into the dryer and the clothes were not there either.

Then he walked around and around the garage, thinking and thinking and finally he said something about the car in front. "Why is that car sitting in front of our apartment? That car has been here every day this week!" He asked that of no one in particular, just kind of muttered it out loud to himself.

I started to grow more anxious so we talked back and forth about what to do. "Let's go look upstairs," Ed said, "maybe you forgot to bring down the clothes." With utter disgust and anger I shouted, "Of course I remembered to bring down the clothes, I washed them already. I have just not dried them yet!"

He went outside, looked at the car, came back into the garage and then… we both looked at each other, still not knowing what to do nor where the pile of wet clothes were hiding. I was contemplating calling the police. But then… why or how would anyone want to come into our garage and remove what was in the washing machine? None of this made sense to me. None of the children, Amy and friends, were inside the house, so I knew they could not be playing a joke on me. Nevertheless, I began to grow nervous and anxious.

"Suppose Ed is correct," I ruminated, "and maybe someone is playing a practical joke on us, or wanting to steal something from us, not that we had much to steal." At that point I was virtually 'chewing my cud.'

Just as I was about to place a phone call to the police, I decided to go back into the garage *one more time* to have another look in the washer. This would be about the fifth time I had searched the washing machine with my eyes and hand. "I will do it one more time," I said aloud to no one.

I put my hand inside the washing machine… it was a small, low machine that opened in the front, I had to be down on my knees to be able to look into it… I was virtually inside of it with my head bumping the inside rim…when I saw something stuck up at the top. I put my hand up there and lo and behold, I found all our laundry…all of it firmly stuck inside to the *top* of the round wash-tub! In utter amazement and surprise I yelled at Ed: "Come here, quickly!" I made him put his hand inside the wash-tub after I removed mine and he found…yes, the wet laundry stuck to the top of the tub.

Talk about sheer stupidity and embarrassment…all I could mumble, as I sat on the cement floor of the garage, was, "Thank God I did not call the South Croydon Police Department." I was mortified, abashed, and absolutely red-faced as I pulled out the wet clothes and quietly put them into the dryer to dry.

I meekly looked out the garage window after the dryer had started and noticed the car was not there…it was gone and it never returned again after that day!

University of London Graduate School

And now finally…to the real reason any of us were in England at all at this point. It was to be my first day of school. I went up to Ed, rather meekly, hands folded as in prayer and head down…saying, "Will you take me to school the first day?"

He looked at me in complete surprise and loudly yelled, "*What?*"

I quietly stated, one more time, "I am so nervous, I feel…I feel worse than Amy did on her first day. Please, please, come in to London with me?"

Of course, he had no choice, did he? He came with me and then returned to South Croydon. At this point we had both become well acquainted with the train systems and the two stations, Victoria Station and the other near Trafalgar Square called Paddington Station. He would have no problem finding his way home nor would I, but I was quite nervous about going in to school on the first day and keenly felt that I needed moral support.

It was not the travel into London that made me nervous, it was the first day of school that worried me. I had to find the building, the rooms, and meet a whole lot of people…I was an emotional wreck for a while. Although once the initial introductions were over, as in: "I am from…where are you from?…what do you teach?…how many children in your classrooms?…oh, you teach high school band!," etc.…I felt most comfortable. Since we were all teachers, regardless of what country we were from, we talked endlessly once we got to know each other. I grew to love the other teachers, now my fellow classmates, they were so sincere and earnest and…enjoyed my 'funny' accent! My face was aching on that first day from smiling all the time.

The University of London offered a one-year Master's Degree program in Education that attracted students from all over the world, as well as many students from the London area. Most of them were individuals who had already been teaching for several years, just as I had, so we were older and had a lot in common. There were maybe 75 to 80 of us meeting on that first day for orientation to the program.

The large group was broken down into their areas of education specialty such as literature, math, science, music, etc. There were a few people in the group who were school administrators, and they had a special course of study as well.

In the beginning, I was puzzled about why we were being divided into smaller groups for classes, etc., but as I understood how the program would allow us to focus on our specific educational interests, I was thrilled. Actually, I prefer to be in smaller groups of people.

I was grouped with five other teachers specializing in music education. We five attended the music education classes together. However, a major purpose of the program was to visit and observe music classes as they were taught at schools in and around London. We were given a long list of schools in the greater London area that had agreed with the University of London to allow us to observe classes. Each student chose the schools he/she wanted to visit based on his/her area of specialty. For instance, as an elementary school music teacher, I wanted to observe music classes at elementary schools. There were a couple of men in our group of music teachers, and they were more interested in and observed high school music classes.

So, over the course of the school year, I grew to know Ros, Sonia, Trevor and Allistair quite well. Professor Mutrie, who could not have been more pleasant and informative, supervised us. I was the only American in this group. The other four music teacher/students lived in boroughs or villages within a thirty or so mile radius of inner London. The five of us met for a few classroom periods per week, but spent most of our time visiting other schools and observing classes. We also attended concerts given by school groups, sometimes on our own and sometimes together.

Occasionally, there would be classes, or special events that required our *entire* class of 75 to 80 graduate students to meet together, and therefore I grew to know other 'students' as well.

At any rate, our group of five music education teachers got along so well that we decided whenever one of us was having a birthday, we would all go out and have dinner in London somewhere, perhaps Chinatown or Trafalgar Square, near the National Gallery of Art. We would share the cost of the birthday person's dinner. We always had a lovely time.

One evening when we were going out for a birthday dinner, Allistair, one of our group of musicians, said to me, "Have you ever ridden on a motorcycle?"

"Only once," I replied, "and I was scared to death and I will never do it again," emphasizing the word, *never*.

Allistair laughed and answered, "Well, you are doing it tonight. I am going to ride you around Trafalgar Square and then over to Chinatown." I must have had a strange expression on my face because he continued, "How many people do you know, at home in the states, who have been driven around Trafalgar Square on a motorcycle?"

I laughed and of course said, "None!"

Not wishing to offend him, (and he didn't seem ready to take *no* for an answer) I went. We mounted the motorcycle, and before he even started the motor I was holding on to him with a vice-like grip. I was gripping so hard I was afraid I would leave an imprint on his chest. Off we went, soaring around Trafalgar Square.

Three times he drove me around Trafalgar Square! (I think he enjoyed making me miserable). Then we drove to the restaurant at which we had agreed to meet in Chinatown. And in the end, I found I was not too scared, at least not as scared as I thought I would be. When it was over I was thrilled to have done it, as silly as that may sound!

"Allistair is a love!" I murmured to myself, "How many of my friends at home could brag about riding around Trafalgar Square on a motorcycle?" I then dismounted with his gentlemanly assistance and walked into the Chinese restaurant to meet our other friends for dinner.

'Cort'ny Fish'

In our larger group of students there was a humorous Australian. His humor was not comparable to anyone else we knew or know even now. His name was Brian...Brian Courtenay...and as he said in his droll way, "Ye'll niver forget it, just think of "Cort'ny fish?'

Brian was about fifty years old or a little more. He told me he worked in Administration but I cannot remember at what level, although I think maybe he was a supervisor of several territories in Australia.

Brian and I became good friends and he wanted to meet my husband. (His wife was back home in Australia with his family while he was in London for the year. She was going to join him for holidays, maybe Christmas and/or spring break but meanwhile, Brian was lonely). Ed and I invited him to dinner at our South Croydon apartment and since the ride back on trains and buses would be difficult, especially if he had imbibed a bit too much, I encouraged him to sleep overnight at our place.

"Of course you're welcome to stay overnight," I told him. "We can make a bed for you in Eric's room since Eric comes home late at night and most of the time flops on the couch, or doesn't even come home, but sleeps at a friend's house."

Brian accepted our invitation. On the agreed upon date, we waited and waited, but for some reason Brian never appeared at Birdhurst Road. I went to school Monday but did not see him. However, a few days later he tracked me down.

"Brian, what on earth happened to you Saturday night?" I asked. "We waited and waited and you never arrived! Are you all right, or were you sick? Why didn't you call me on the telephone?"

We had a telephone, but we could not call out, we could only receive calls. The telephone was part of the rental house, but it would cost us extra to make calls *out* of the house, so since we were 'pinching pennies' during this year, we chose to not take on that expense. Funny arrangement I thought, but it worked for us during the few times we received a call.

Brian replied, " I did a nay have yer telephone number. Guess ah lost it somewhere somehow. But," he added, "I did leave ya a message, I did a nay want ya to worry."

"We received no message anywhere. Where on earth did you leave it?" I told him.

"On the train station wall, where's the people wait for the train to stop in South Croydon…" he replied.

"Brian, don't be silly, how could you have left a message on the wall of the train station?" I said.

He replied, with a large grin on his face, from ear to ear. "You go look, I wrote it on the wall of the station, in big letters so you could'a all found it!"

Brian then went off to class chuckling out loud. I mentioned that to Ed later and he asked me, "Well, did you find a note down at the station when you came home today?"

"I surely did. Come down with me now," I said, "and have a good laugh with me."

Ed whined as usual, "I can't go down now." However, I made him come with me in spite of his protests. It was only a short walk and well worth the effort for there, sure as anything…in *huge* chalk drawn letters, "*Your Aussie friend was here to see you and he could'a nay find you. Why did you nay stay home tonight?*"

It was signed *"Brian!"* including the date and time in equally big letters next to his name!

Of course, one could not help but chuckle over his humor; it was so very different.

So, we rescheduled a time for him to visit us in December near Christmas. This time we met him at the train and he stayed overnight. (We figured that would be a better thing to do considering it was the holidays and if Brian drank too much we would not want him to get lost or hurt himself. He enjoyed his Lager!) After a lovely evening of food, conversation and lots of beer, Brian staggered off to bed in Eric's room on the second floor, and we proceeded to our bedroom on the third floor. Amy had gone to bed in her room earlier in the evening.

Well, in the middle of that night Amy came into our room, hopping mad. "Mom, Dad, wake up, wake up."

We woke, blinking our eyes wondering what on earth was wrong.

Amy continued in a loud and angry voice, "Go downstairs and tell that man to stop singing Christmas carols. I can't sleep."

We listened and, yes indeed, Brian was actually singing Christmas carols. At first we could not figure out why he was singing in full voice at this time of the night. So we went down and approached his bed and discovered he was singing in his sleep!

I was not sure what to do. I had never been in this type of situation before. To this day, I don't remember exactly what happened, but I think Ed went into the bedroom and shook Brian's shoulder a bit and he woke…mumbled, turned over and fell back to sleep, silently this time.

The next morning, we mentioned the singing. Brian told us he always sings in his sleep no matter where he is sleeping and looking quite crestfallen (deliberately I'm sure) he said, "I am'a so sorry." We told him he was forgiven…and we all had a good laugh, except for Amy, and off he went after breakfast, back to London cheerful, whistling and humming, no doubt.

St. Albans Cathedral

Trevor, another man in our small music group, asked me one day, in a very formal fashion, if he and his wife could take Ed, Amy and me to St. Albans Cathedral. Saint Albans was north of London, about a thirty-minute ride by car from London. Trevor had always seemed a bit shy; never talking much when we were together as a group. He said that he wanted to do something 'special' for us. I enthusiastically took him up on his offer.

We would drive there in his car. (I was surprised to learn he had a car because he never drove into school in London. He later told me that it was too expensive to drive all the time, and he and his wife only used the car on weekends. They were both teachers, and not well paid). "We will picnic on the green after arriving at St. Albans," he said. "I know of a very beautiful spot, and I am certain you will love it!"

Well, we did just that, meaning…we loved it! Trevor's car was small, so Amy and I squished into the back with Trevor's wife, and big Ed sat squashed in the front passenger seat while Trevor drove. This was such a treat for me! I was so excited that day I had trouble containing myself. We did not have access to a car the year we were in London, and I missed the freedom to 'get up and go.'

We left early in the morning for St. Albans since we wanted to arrive at noontime. Upon arriving, we climbed up on a knoll overlooking the Cathedral to admire the spectacular view and to eat lunch. I must add, the word, 'spectacular' does not do justice to the view, it was all so very beautiful!

Trevor and his wife cooked our lunch. Since they had invited us on this trip, they insisted we sit on the green and be waited upon! A blanket was laid out on the grass upon which we were to sit and Trevor did the cooking in a miniscule 'cooker' right there on the grassy green knoll overlooking St. Albans. The lunch was hot dogs, rolls and salad plus a desert and a drink. It was really quite generous of our hosts because they were not rich by any means.

After lunch we walked down the grassy slope and toured the inside of the cathedral. We enjoyed the ancient sculptures, old art, and the overall antiquity of the Cathedral! We all said private prayers and farewells before leaving the building.

We then spent an hour or so walking through the town of St. Albans enjoying its beauty and antiquity. So many of the villages are extremely old, so much older than anything in the United States of course. They each have their own distinct personality, and we found no two alike. We had a lovely day together!

Cambridge

Ros, another member of our small music group, lived and worked near Windsor Castle and became quite friendly with us. She was generous with her time and knowledge of England, which she enjoyed sharing with us. I distinctly remember going with her one day to the polling booths while she voted for Margaret Thatcher. What a wonderful choice that turned out to be! I will never forget that day!

Another time she and her husband, Matt, took us to observe *fencing* matches! I had never seen one before, and never dreamed I would see one! Seems Ros' sister-in-law 'fenced.'

One time, Ros, Matt, Amy and I took a trip north to Cambridge and stayed overnight. (Ed did not join us on some of these trips for various reasons, his health, space in the car, or he had something he would rather do).

I loved that trip for two reasons; we visited the Cambridge University campus and also punted on the 'Cam' River. (All of Cambridge, I was told, is the university, meaning there is no separate city, whereas Oxford University is located in the city of Oxford). Cambridge was gorgeous!

I had heard the word 'punting,' and was aware it involved boats and a river, but had never seen it done and certainly had never done it before. A punt is an open, flat bottom boat with squared ends. One person stands and pushes the boat along with a pole. Matt did most of the 'punting,' however, at one point he insisted that I try it, so I did! I have to admit, I was scared to death that we would all fall in the 'Cam' (Cambridge River) when I tried to punt, but we didn't. Matt gave Amy a turn to punt and Amy, for her small size, performed better than I. It's one of my many memories of trips with Ros that I treasure.

❦ ❦ ❦

"Musical training
is a more potent instrument than any other
because rhythm and harmony find their way
into the inward places of the soul."

—Plato

"My major interests and concerns while observing schools in England were: to observe buildings that had 'purpose-built' music Rooms; the type of music which would exist if these rooms were available as in treble choirs, use of Orff instruments and musical drama; also to observe scheduling the days' activities, meaning, time-tabling, and mostly to observe music classes. I needed to know about music scheduling since scheduling music classes at home is horrible, the only thing it means to many of the teachers at home is time off from their class, nothing else....Next...how music fits in to the

*overall picture of the school, how often the children have music per week...
the length of the classes and what equipment is available; and what are the
attitudes of the teaching staff towards the teaching of music in the building."*

The above paragraph is from my Master's Thesis and sums up my goal for
studying at the University of London that year. I was also inspired by the following quote:

*"Bad taste is infectious. While deplorable fashion may not be a serious matter,
since ugly clothes do not injure the health, bad taste in the arts cauterizes the susceptibility
of good taste...We have to get rid of the pedagogic superstition that some sort of diluted
substitute art is good enough for teaching...Nobody should be above writing music for
children: on the contrary, we should strive to become good enough to do so."*

— Zoltan Kodaly, "Children Choruses in Hungarian Musical Review"
1929, p. 81 as quoted by Kenneth Simpson, from *Some Great Music Educators*, published by Novello and Co. Borough Green, Kent, England

I observed many, many classes during my two semesters studying at the
University of London. As in any school system, some music classes I observed
were excellent, but then some were poor, almost horrible, from my point of view.
It brings to mind the nursery rhyme:

*"When she was good, she was very, very good,
and when she was BAD, she was horrid."*

I was interested in certain specific aspects of music education. Therefore
the University of London Music Department sent me to schools in inner and
outer London that would supply me with what I needed and wanted to learn.
Now, I'll share with you observations about the schools as I made them in my
thesis, but I will not categorize them as good, bad or mediocre.

Gorringe Middle School, Morden

The children appeared to live in a low socio-economic family background,
although neatly uniformed as at Rowen High School. The children were younger
since it was a Middle School; they were happy, eager to please, smiled contagiously,
talked easily and enthusiastically, and wanted to sing for me. Two lovely young
eleven-year-old hostesses gave me the grand tour after the headmistress met me.
The group that impressed and excited me the most was the 'low' group; it was obvious that the children were in ability groupings. The teacher was not only lovely
to look at but she was enthusiastic and most exuberant during her work with these

children; her work was geared to make the children comfortable in their learning situations and to become actively involved in it from all angles. The activities and attitudes, which prevailed in their room, told the whole story of the educational process, which was evolving. As a result of my visit and her children's desire to be friendly, their next project was decided upon then and there. It was to be 'stamps from America' as a result of an exchange with children in the Sanborn School, Andover, Massachusetts, which in turn would lead to the discovery of the geography, history, culture and songs from America. I hastened to tell them that America was very large and I lived in only a tiny corner of it."

Rowan High School, Inner London

Rowan high School had 250 girls in attendance. Two music classes were observed; the first of which was turned over to me since the teacher decided the girls would want to ask questions about America. The music teacher floored me with the following words said to me out loud and in front of the students, "They do not like to sing anyhow. They won't sing for me. They are always difficult to handle!" (A teacher should never talk like that about a class in front of the class…I was aghast!) I talked with the students for a while, telling them who I was and from where I came and that I taught music to students at home. When I was finished with my brief talk, their music teacher had them *say…not sing…* the words of two songs from the musical *Oliver!*, which they were studying: "Food, Glorious Food"…and "Consider Yourself at Home." I sat there listening to the class *say* the words to two songs and nothing else! The class said them in an extremely boring style, which is understandable from my point of view. It was horrible for the girls. Rigid control existed in that classroom which in itself would dispel any hope of relaxed and free singing. The teacher never smiled and the girls never smiled except when all of whatever they had to do was over, and then they were allowed to talk to me once again. They and I talked for the remainder of the period and we had a pleasant talk but without any music whatsoever!

East Croyden Junior School

The girls came from poor family backgrounds, although they were neatly uniformed as at the Rowan High School. The children were younger, middle school age; they were smiling, eager to please and anxious to show what they could do in music. The teacher was equally exuberant and had a positive attitude throughout the whole lesson. She loved her work and she geared it to make the children happy, positive about music, and to learn about music in a broader sense. The activities and attitudes which prevailed in the room told the whole story of the educational process which was evolving.

As a result of my visit and her children's desire to be friendly, their next project in this music class was decided upon then and there. It was to be stamps from America, which would come as a result of an exchange of letters with the children at my Sanborn School in Andover, MA. I organized that project with the class and the teacher. That, in turn would lead them to learn about geography, history, culture and music via American folk songs that tell everything one would want to know about the history of America. The whole day in this lovely lady's music class (I stayed for all her classes) was wonderful, inviting, and loving and learning. Children left her room smiling and anxious to return. They also did not want me to leave!

Regina Coeli, Pampisford Road

While visiting Regina Coeli I was able to see and be a part of the development of a recorder consortium for ten and eleven year old children. These lessons were geared to the use of the Orff Instrumentarium and the development of a treble choir. All of these were handled quite capably by Mrs. Jill Lang who also proved to be a boon for providing further observations and field work including:

A Christmas Concert was given by the Regina Coeli school at St. Gertrude's Church in Croydon, December 10, 1978. It was held in the evening and was the Nativity in Pantomime with the currently popular song story of the Nativity titled: *Christmas Jazz* by Benjamin Britten. It was a very new composition for me and quite difficult for the choir.

A Croydon Parish Church Concert that assembled the choirs of ten to fifteen different schools whom, having learned the music in advance at their own respective schools, sang together at the concert. This was a rare opportunity to hear treble voices singing beautifully in a church of this magnitude and antiquity. The sound was absolutely outstanding. There was also a full orchestra of student musicians and other choirs singing together conducted by Inspector Knight.

A rehearsal at the BBC held in February by Douglas Coombes.

A concert at Fairfield Halls consisting of the Early Music Recorder Consortium from Regina Coeli and other assemblages of choirs from many schools in Croydon which filled the large hall to capacity, and…the Band from the St. Giles School. I was most impressed!

The Rehearsal at the BBC

The rehearsal at the BBC was a taping-teaching session directed by Douglas Coombes. He was in the process of making teaching tapes with accompanying teachers' manuals. The tapes would be played on the radio or could be bought by the schools with the manual.

Should a primary grade teacher want to do a music lesson with her class she could:

+ turn on the radio
+ do a follow up lesson from the manual
+ buy the tape-teach form of the program and not use the radio
+ follow up the taped lesson using the manual
+ collect the series to be used in ensuing years with other classes.

The tapes proved to be advantageous to many primary school teachers who wisely recognized the need for music in the every day life of a child.

The National Committee of instruction of the Music Education National Conference, and American association, adopted a position paper in November of 1976 which states in part that, "*music is basic in education, that music, along with the other arts, deserves a prominent position in the curriculum of the elementary and secondary schools, and that the important contributions of music to the aesthetic and cultural objectives of education are more than sufficient to justify that position. At the same time, the Conference recognizes that music can make other contributions to the educational and personal growth of the student and that these ancillary contributions may be highly valued in some communities. The diverse benefits of music instruction will accrue to the students regardless of the motivation that initially led to the inclusion of music in the curriculum and regardless of the relative values placed on the various outcomes.*"

The tapes were a great help to teachers in schools that had no music specialists. All the Junior Schools I observed had music specialists, but hardly any of the Infant Schools were provided with music teachers. Hence, Kodaly's findings that "*children and adults are musically illiterate, since the institution was built from above and only slowly extended downward to the laying of the foundations,*" proved to be more than accurate based on my observations. High schools had music educators, many junior schools had music educators, but hardly any infant schools had any specialists in any area.

Mr. Coombes conducted the taped lesson. The singing was performed by the treble choir from Regina Coeli, a gentleman played the piano (it should have been a harpsichord, I was informed) another gentleman played the celeste, and a very fine singer sang either alone or with the choir. Mr. Coombes delivered the narrations. It was a long, arduous, exciting day for the choir since the taping invariably consisted of many retakes and as is the pattern, when children grow tired and their enthusiasm wanes, the quality of their singing was consequently less than good toward the end of the session.

Some of the children played the instrumental accompaniments, tambourine, drum, triangle and metallophones at designated places in the script. The choir was essentially the teaching class representing the class being taught in the actual situation. Wonderful, was all I could think of as it ended a long time later. I was totally amazed at how well the performers held up and carried on!

St. Giles School, Croydon

This school was especially designed for all kinds of handicapped children, both physically and mentally. I was so impressed that I returned several times to visit and assist in any way possible. (The school was about six miles away from where I lived in South Croydon, but at that time of my life I could easily walk that distance).

The school was housed in a new, modern and 'purpose-built' building. There may have been two hundred or more handicapped children in the school. The building was delightfully spacious, airy and sunny even on a cloudy day, (it seemed). The building burgeoned with positive attitudes and optimism. The music room, swimming pool and the upcoming Christmas Concert were my areas of interest and engaged me the several times I visited.

The children had water therapy daily and since I had been a water safety instructor for many years I found myself dividing my time between the music room and the pool. Needless to say I enjoyed all of the lessons, observing and interacting.

I was especially impressed that St. Giles had a band. I was fascinated by how the band teacher taught mentally and physically handicapped children to play band instruments. I must admit their performance would not measure up to a normal band in a regular school; the children played with a rather 'flat' tone constantly. Nevertheless, one could listen and identify the music. The students were thrilled with their progress and thrilled with themselves and responded beautifully to all the band lessons.

The students, ages about twelve to eighteen, had regular band class hours and also met every day once again for band rehearsals at lunchtime as well. They were rehearsing for several engagements and their happiness burgeoned and blossomed, filling the room whenever they played for someone or some event.

I attended their Christmas Concert. The band played carols, (never quite on pitch, as I recall) and the other school children sang the usual Christmas carols. They had created and pantomimed a nativity scene. The handicapped children performed very well throughout the entire performance. The whole experience was so emotionally moving for me that I will never forget any of the St. Giles school events, children or teachers. They were all wonderful!

Streatham Hill School

At this school I observed the work of Ros Sandorek, one of my fellow classmates in the University of London graduate program. She produced a creative Christmas Concert. The Nativity was the theme and Christmas in other countries was the focus with accompaniments to the singing and dancing by children playing recorders, guitars and piano.

Her program had a flavor of Aston and some methodology of Orff and Kodaly. It was not the typical Christmas concert as have been previously mentioned, but more a teaching situation of learning by doing; it was researching, exploring and experimenting. John Curwen, a music educator, had the foresight in the early 1800s to allow the children to explore and experiment, 'notice and discover.' He valued picturizing, i.e. mental pictures, long before others.

John Curwen said, "More often than not school music has concentrated on the skills of the performance. Even so called 'creative' music is only an extension of directed ensemble performance...of course these skills are important. Performance is an essential musical activity, but it is not the whole of music. Performance is vital and valuable; it should exist, and more performers would come to the surface if and when our schools provide a better understanding of music education for the masses instead of the select few who seem to excel or who are gifted and talented."

The All Farthing Primary School—Wadsworth, London

This school was in an old, old building. I walked around it three times before I found something that looked like a door to enter. On the door was a sign, 'Close door-no heat inside!' I gingerly let myself into the building. The door was difficult to open and even more difficult to shut tightly. And once inside, I found it was indeed *cold*!

Not seeing the office of the headmistress anywhere, I made my way up the stairs, heard some music, found the classroom it was coming from and walked in. There stood an older lady, short and stout. She peered at me puzzled and asked if she could help me.

"I am here to observe the music teacher give some lessons," I said with a smile. She looked askance and flustered.

"I am the music teacher and did not expect anyone to come today. Oh dear," she said, "I must have made a mistake, or someone made a mistake."

I then said, most understandingly, "If you would rather I leave and come back another day, I would certainly be happy to do that very thing."

"Oh no, not at all, oh, dear...oh dear..." she said coming to me and embracing my hand in her two small ones. "You just come with me now and watch my children rehearse for their performance of..." and here, she became most excited, dropped my hand and clapped her hands together and would probably have jumped up and down if she had not been so old, *Ali Baba and the Forty Thieves*.

"You will be no problem at all," she burbled. "Do, do come...come right in here." The lady was quite flustered, but absolutely charming.

She then hastened to bring a rocking chair for me, and then a pillow; somehow a blanket appeared and she wrapped it around me so I would not be cold. Last but not least, she disappeared once again and you will not believe what she had in her hands when she returned! It was a hot water bag, the old fashioned type with hot water inside and a black plug to keep it in. She actually plopped it in my lap as I protested saying, "Oh no, really I do not need all this and certainly not the hot water!"

"You just stay there and enjoy it," she stated in a loud voice with a beatific smile on her face. Then she left me to enjoy the remainder of the day. To be honest with you, the hot water bottle was absolutely wonderful. The school was definitely cold.

She and her students and her husband, who was the pianist, were incredibly sweet and wonderful to me the whole day. We all had lunch together and she refused to let me leave since the grand rehearsal would be going on all afternoon. "You must certainly see that!" she demanded.

Therefore I stayed and watched the rehearsal of *Ali Baba and the Forty Thieves*. It was marvelous; I returned on the evening of the final performance, which thrilled the lovely music teacher. The children were outstanding in their part, performed beautifully and sang like angels.

Inner London School

At this school, the music teacher sat me down to listen to the girls sing. She had an upright piano with its back against the wall. She sat on the bench and never *once*, not even *one time*, did she look at her class of girls after she said 'good morning' to them. Never turning around she would holler at them, "Page 81." The book pages would rustle; she would start playing. How on earth do you suppose they sounded when *some* of them decided to sing? Well, you are correct, they sounded terrible. She played like this for at least 45 minutes, without stopping between songs or ever looking at them When the time was up, the teacher hollered, "You are dismissed!" That was it. That was the whole music lesson. I was absolutely shocked. I had never, ever in my years of teaching seen or heard anything quite so awful. Each week these girls came in quietly, opened their books and waited for a command. Then, like robots, they 'sang' each song and then left.

The teacher came to me after the girls had left the classroom and told me how much she hated teaching, and then asked me if I thought she should go to the USA for a music teacher job. Well, you must know what I *wanted* to say… which of course I couldn't. So I said, "Well, I don't really know, but I must go to another class now. I'm late. Thank you for having me." Leaving as quickly as possible so I would not insult her, I made a hasty retreat!

Duncombe Infant School

Duncombe Infant School was a charming, ILEA (Inner London Educational Association) funded building with its own music teacher, Mrs. Sonia Singham. The children obviously enjoyed being taught by Mrs. Singham who was a joyful and happy person at all times, and the students were happy while she was in the room with them. She had her own music room, (lucky lady) in which to teach, and a full complement of books and instruments available. She also had the full support of Ms. Ofstein, the Headmistress. She and the children made music *sing*!

The above are just a few of the many classroom observations I had the opportunity to witness during the educational portion of my year in London. If the reader is interested in learning more about that work, a complete explanation is in my thesis. Now, I'm going to return to telling about our family's experiences living in London that wonderful year.

❧❧❧

Christmas is coming, the goose is getting fat......
—Traditional Folk Song

Before I knew it, Christmas was upon us, and that meant a vacation from observing classes and taking notes.

I wanted a Christmas tree for Amy, but was not sure where to buy it or how much money it would cost. I was told that they are usually quite expensive. Our neighbor, Gordon Long, was outdoors tending to his grass in the back of our dwellings, so I walked up to him and asked,

"Gordon, could you please advise me where I could buy a small Christmas tree for my little girl?"

"Of course I can, I would *love* to!" he said putting down his garden tools and then wiping his hands, "Ye go to the market down in the city. Now then, if ye want to buy a small and very cheap tree, always walk down to the very end of the market. That is how the market works. The cheapest of everythin' is always at the bottom, way down to the end of the market. That is where you go."

The market was an outdoor street market with many, many stalls and anything you wanted (well, practically anything) one could find at this outdoor market.

Gordon then pointed his finger at me and continued, "Don't ye be afraid to barter them down. Ye can do it. Just stand right up to them and tell them what ye want and how much ye want it for. They'll give you a high price, and ye tell them ye will not pay that much, but ye would pay whatever half the price would be. Ye joost stand your ground and do not give in to them. They will give in to YE!" (Do you think my neighbor had figured out that I was a little shy and reticent when it came to that type of thing? Well, I guess he had, because I was!)

I thanked him very much, found Ed and off we went to the market. I told Amy to stay home, since she had homework to do, but to sit in the window while doing her homework, and watch for us. We would not be long since the market was not far away. Our neighbors, Patch and Gordon, were merely a stone's throw away and she could run over to their house if need be.

Ed and I walked about ten minutes and then proceeded down to the very end of the market exactly as Gordon had instructed. We found a few small and bedraggled trees, and asked for the price. The disheveled man selling the trees looked poor and haggard but was friendly. He knew immediately we were Americans; everyone seemed to identify where we came from when we started talking. He started bartering with us. And while trying to sell us a tree he talked away about the war and how much he loved the Americans…he muttered in a high toned raspy voice, "Eh and fer sure lass, without the Americans the war might still be going on."

I smiled sweetly at the man and told him, "I need the least expensive tree for my little girl since I am studying here in London and do not have much money." With a sly smile on his face he rasped away at me saying, "I will make ye a deal. I will sell it to ye for two pounds, (that was cheap) but ye 'ave to give me a kiss!"

Ed was with me, so I had no fear, and I stood a bit on tiptoe and said, "I will take the tree!" And quick as a cat can blink an eye I kissed him on his cheek; he was so elated and happy that he handed the tree over to me immediately! He got the two pounds for the tree and the kiss and he had a smile on his face from ear to ear as we left him wishing each other a Merry Christmas!

Well, we got home with the tree but realized we had no stand for the tree.

The next day I rapped on Mr. Long's front door. He appeared and questioningly said, "Yes?"

"Mr. Long, I'm sorry to bother you again, but my Christmas tree needs to stand up and I just don't know how to do it. Can you give me an idea that would cost no money? I do not have the money to spend on a tree stand, and thought you might know some little secret I do not know."

He looked at me thoughtfully, probably thinking how stupid I was and then said, in his Scottish accent. "Ye git a boo-ket and ye gather a boonch of stones. Ye put them in the boo-ket and then place the tree in the stones. Ye niver buy a tree stand (He emphasized the word *niver*)….cost too much!"

"Where do I find the stones?" I asked because we were living in the city, not in the country as we did in the states.

He replied once again with much patience and a great deal of drama in his little speech, "Ye go round the streets and whenever there is a loose stone ye pick it up and soon ye have enough for the boo-ket!"

He was right. I went around after dark and collected enough stones for my 'boo-ket.' Guess what? It worked.

I had no problem with decorations for the tree. Amy and her friends had a tree decorating party in our apartment and the tree ended up looking 'smashing.' We had plenty of drawing paper, and the girls and boys across the street and from Amy's school were quite clever and made great, child-like decorations and hung them all around and on the tree. Some were most clever I must say.

I thought the tree was lovely to look at, as did Ed and the children. Susan and Eric were with us for Christmas. Yes, Susan and her friend Beth had arrived to join us. We were all thrilled and excited they were with us. Ed and I had met them at the airport a few days earlier and my three children were almost deliriously happy to be together again. Needless to say, Ed and I were equally happy!

There were not many presents, but we were together, all of us. That was 'present' enough for me! Ed and I did not exchange presents but we wanted to do something special for the children; therefore, we bought tickets for the musical, *Jesus Christ Superstar*. It had just 'come out' and it became a 'smashing' hit overnight in London. The children, including little Amy, went into London alone to see it. (The music is not to my taste and I did not want to spend the money on tickets for Ed and myself). I was not worried about their safety because Susan was 22 and Eric 17, and I trusted them to look after Amy. The children enjoyed the musical tremendously and that was the outcome I had wanted.

We had a severe snowstorm the night before New Year's and everyone in my family thought that was great since it was not something that happens often in London. Then the next day the temperatures rose as high as seventy degrees. We all went out and enjoyed the sun and the snow and the heat, watching the snow melt rapidly.

Susan was with us for about two or three weeks over the holidays and she and Eric hopped around to many places of interest since by then he had gained much knowledge of London and its outlying areas. She, of course, knew only a little. Her only trip to London had been on a Shakespearean school trip from Andover when she was fifteen years old. A friend of hers came along with her this time for a couple of weeks, therefore we did not visit as much as we would have liked with Susan since she and Eric and/or her friend, Beth, were extremely busy.

The Calder Family

The day before January 1, New Year's Day, Ed was stricken with the flu, and was confined to bed with a fever and all that accompanies the flu; consequently, I went to Calder's New Year's Eve party alone, returning home relatively early. Ed did not mind, nor did I. Amy sat up with him on the bed until I came home before midnight and...*all was well!*

The Calder family lived across the street and up the hill from us in South Croydon. We met when we were walking up the street with Amy one day early in our year in England. Mrs. Calder was coming out her front doorway with her children. We greeted each other, chatted and that was the beginning of a wonderful friendship. They were such a lovely family how could you not want to be friends with them? They invited us to see important places. Also we were invited to go to various events when our joint schedules allowed.

One Sunday, Francoise and Hugh Calder invited us to a boat show in one of the boroughs outside of London (I believe it was King's Cross) where there was a gigantic building that could house such an event. Many members of the royalty were supposed to be there that afternoon. Exciting! The place was extremely crowded. We visited display after display of boats and small ships in huge bodies of water...INSIDE...this building. Yes, they were actually in large, man made bodies of water. It was exciting to be at this event and I was also enjoying being with Francoise and Hugh, and, at the same time Amy was happy to be with their children, Michelle, Andre and Alexi. The four always had a great time together.

As we ambled along inside looking at this and looking at that...suddenly... Hugh excitedly proclaimed, "This is what I was looking for. Look!" He pointed up to a huge ship.

The children looked up in the air and were a little puzzled, all trying to see why Hugh was excited.

Hugh said, "That apparatus is called a 'Jackstay.' If a ship is out to sea and something goes wrong, it might start to sink," he continued. "Another ship might be nearby and the 'Jackstay' would be able to save the people who were on the sinking ship! The people on the sinking ship would have a seat in the 'Jackstay.' They would ride, one at a time, across the water due to this pulley and seat, to the other ship. Then they wouldn't drown...and they would all be safe. See how it works?"

The children were staring up at this pulley and rope apparatus trying to figure out how people could be saved by riding on a seat and a length of rope. Hugh continued with, "It rides across the water between the two ships on ropes and pulleys, and the person is pulled, while sitting on a little seat that might resemble a small child's swing seat, across the water and arrives at the opposite ship safe and sound."

Well, once they understood the concept, the children were eager to try it out. But suddenly it seemed, as if out of nowhere, there was a large group of 'royalty' and their friends who wanted to try out the 'Jackstay.' They were all dressed in black afternoon attire and the ladies wore elegant dresses and flowing hats with wide brims while the gentlemen wore their 'top hats' and black suits.

As you can imagine, they got first crack at riding the 'Jackstay' and all the children in the area had to wait in line for their turn. It was amusing watching the royalty as they rode across the small river of water. The two ships were in two huge, bodies of water inside the building (which must give you some idea how large this building was).

After a while our children had their turn. They had watched how the royalty had 'ridden' over the waves, so they knew what to do. (Naturally none of it was like riding across a real ocean), but one by one each child was 'jackstayed' across the water to land in the other ship. I watched Amy very carefully since I was a little nervous about it all. Maybe she wasn't, but I certainly was! She did well, seemed to like it and did not seem scared.

At one point during my sabbatical year in London, Hugh's job required him to work in the Philippines for two weeks. He was encouraged to bring his wife along. However, Francoise said she could not possibly take her three children out of school and would not dream of leaving them alone with the au pair girl they had working for them.

Hating to see a good friend miss a chance to travel, I immediately offered to take the children to my house for the two weeks. (I hadn't paused to think that there was hardly any room for the three of us in our apartment, let alone three more children and the au pair girl).

Francoise and I talked a bit more. She had never been to the Philippines, and was thrilled with my offer.

"I will talk to Hugh about this," she finally told me. A few days later she and Hugh came to see us and said they would like very much for us to mind the children, but, in so doing, we would have to stay in their home. We could enjoy their home, invite company over to visit if we liked, and also have the use of their car. They lived in a three-story brick house with many large rooms. It was a lovely, old house in excellent condition for its age. They also had a second car we could use. Their other car would be left at the airport.

"Oh," I said, "We couldn't do that."

Hugh said, "Of course you can. I will help you bring some of the things you need for two weeks and you just enjoy our home and have a good time while we are gone. In fact, I insist you use our little car."

I was shocked, most pleasantly shocked I must admit, but I was happy. Ed and I both agreed, on the spot, that we would move across the street since we wanted them to have their trip to the Philippines. But also, we would have a car for two weeks and, to make matters even better, we could stretch our legs and live and dine in comfort as opposed to the little apartment in which we were currently living.

The last thing Francoise told me before she and Hugh left for the Philippines was, "Mary, don't let the dog out the front door." After Francoise delivered her edict about the dog, she turned and walked down the stairs, clambered into Hugh's car already loaded with their luggage. I turned to close the door as their car drove away and the little Scotty dog scooted out between my two legs. Oh dear…he's gone!!! I thought I would have a stroke or something equally as serious. The older children went looking for him, I went looking, then Ed went. No luck.

Finally, as I recall, before dark the dog must have become hungry because he came to the front door and whined and scratched to come in. Thank the good Lord. I could have kissed him all over. Just think…I was a nervous wreck all day and now I would be able to sleep that night!

We had a lovely two weeks staying at the Calder's house. As luck would have it, I did not have classes every single day of those weeks, so Ed and I were able to take a few trips with the Calder's youngest child, four-year-old Alexi, while the other children were in school. It was wonderful having the use of their little Renault car.

Winston Churchill's Chartwell

Ed, Alexi and I made several half-day trips, always making sure we were back home before the older children returned from school at approximately 3:30 p.m. We visited here and there and hither and yon outside of London and in the country. As a result, we finally got to see Winston Churchill's home. I was thrilled with the whole place!

The name of Mr. Churchill's country home is Chartwell. Today it is preserved as a memorial to him. (We went back a few more times so that Amy and Eric, could see and enjoy it as we did). While there with Ed and Alexi, I managed to take some time to sit on the bench where Churchill used to sit and contemplate, overlooking the lovely views beyond the pool and the natural waters all around. I thoroughly enjoyed sitting where Winston had sat, lost in my own thoughts and memories.

Chartwell contains many of Winston's personal mementoes: his medals and uniforms, his hats and books, his treasures and trinkets. All are kept where they would have been if Winston were alive. This house, I was told, was built in 1930 and it is set in the heart of Kent with tall trees, smooth lawns and shining lakes.

Churchill once said, "A day away from Chartwell is a day wasted." This quote has been inscribed in the house. There is also a photo of Churchill retiling the bricks at Chartwell (all houses need such work after many years) holding his tile tool in one hand and the ever-present cigar in the other.

Because of my early memories of the war years, Churchill, his voice and his speeches always fascinated me. He was dynamic and his voice was unusual to me, as I was quite young then. We were allowed to walk through all of the rooms of the house in which Churchill and his wife and family lived. I was quite taken with the whole event and that was all thanks to the small car of the Calder's.

The beds in the Calder home were sumptuous and large, and the children all liked one another and got along very well. Next to our diminutive, three decker home for that year, their home was huge and we loved the spaciousness and the décor. The dog and I remained close friends as long as I was on Birdhurst Road and never ran off again.

Hugh and Francoise had a nice time in the Philippines. Although Hugh had to work for some of the time, it was not taxing work and they enjoyed their time together in top class hotels and traveling first class on the airplane.

When the two weeks were over, I was satisfied with myself for having been able to take care of their home and children for them. They were also happy that we felt able to go off in their car to visit famous places…well, a few famous places! We were all pleased with each other and so happy we had friends as nice as they were. It was a great respite for me from school, and such a pleasure to have a car to rumble around in!

After Christmas, my classes at the University of London resumed at the end of January. With great joy and pleasure I set off for Eton College, per invitation, one day after Christmas and I will never forget it. Yes, I was invited to visit Eton College, in the town of Eton, which is situated next to Windsor Castle.

There was an embarrassing episode on my first day at Eton. I was invited to dine with the Masters and the boys in their dining room. I was given a seat at the Head Table! Oh, my goodness, I felt so honored! However, I was so engrossed in talking with all these important men, (there were no women there at all) that I talked and talked. (Anyone who knows me will say, "That is nothing new!")

At some point though I realized, that the boys could not start eating until the Head Table teachers or guests were seated and grace was said and that would not happen until I stopped talking.

"Oh, dear," I said to myself, feeling my face turning red. I glanced around and quickly folded my hands in prayer, as everyone appeared to be doing, and the prayers started! Grace was said and then everyone began to eat lunch.

Well, I started talking again with the gentleman on my right and another on my left. We talked about this and that and everything in the world I could think of since I am what one would call, the 'super friendly' type and I had many questions.

Then again I became aware there was no other noise in the dining hall. I looked up and saw the three long lines of tables where the boys sat; they were as quiet as mice. No one was saying a word. Also, they were all looking my way! Then, it occurred to me. All the boys and all the teachers were waiting for me to finish eating and to stop talking so the Head of Eton College could give a blessing prayer and a dismissal.

Amazingly, there was not a sound or a movement among the boys. I was so embarrassed and surprised once again; absolutely not one small bit of sound was to be heard in the room while they waited for me to stop talking. I stopped talking instantly, apologized, and the Head of Eton said in a booming and polite English accent, "None... is necessary!" I then indicated I had finished eating... thus, the prayer of 'Thanks' was said, and the boys lumbered off to either their next class or outside to do whatever high school boys do after lunch. My face was red hot to the touch, I am sure.

The Headmaster was lovely but the person I became most acquainted with was the Music Director Graham Smallbone. At the end of my last day, the third day of observing Eton boys in many situations, I was invited to visit the music director's home and we sat and talked and talked for several hours... about America and England and teaching music on all levels, of course. What else would two music teachers talk about at that point? He was so lovely and 'down to earth' and seemed to enjoy being in my company. Mr. Smallbone spent at least two hours discussing the students, choirs, classes in music, and his system of rotating the arts schedule every three weeks.

Creative arts, music, drama, design and dance, are taught all day intensively for three weeks at a time to groups of boys and then the schedule rotates and new groups begin. This type of scheduling accommodates all the boys throughout the year, but for those who wish more there are boys' choirs, boys and men's choirs, instrumental lessons and orchestra. Sixty teachers come to Eton College for instruction of orchestra and orchestral accompaniment. "How wonderful!" was all I could say while listening to these amazing facts! The school population consists of 250 boys per year.

I was most interested to learn about a project being performed at Eton by the boys. The Eton College boys 'adopted' families and took care of them throughout the school year. These families were mostly elderly people or handicapped people, families who could no longer do certain things for themselves, as in shopping for groceries, walking to the stores or shoveling or cutting the grass.

Consequently such families or individuals were assigned to the boys, and the boys would take care of them all year. Once or twice a week they would stop to visit the people in their assigned home and ask if there were errands they could do, or, if none, then, they would just go into the house and sit down and talk with the families. I thought that was a wonderful, giving, kind and generous way to teach high school students to be thoughtful, caring, and considerate.

I was so impressed with this project that I wanted to introduce the idea to the Sanborn School in Andover, but knew I could not manage this same type of program in the states since the children in my school were too young. However, this project was also part of my inspiration for the Harvest Festival I introduced to the Sanborn School.

Cecilia Vajda

One of the greatest pleasures I had during my sabbatical in London was the opportunity of meeting and studying with Cecilia Vajda. Cecilia was born in Hungary and wrote many, many books on her theories of teaching children and adults how to read music and sing, solo or in harmony with others, and with no accompaniment necessary or with accompaniment.

She taught with the sol-fa system; the students could 'read' notes in any 'key' by use of the syllables do,re,mi,fa,so,la,ti,do. Yes, those few notes were all that was necessary. With those few notes she used hand signals, a different one for each of the seven notes, for example, 'do' was always signed by a fist whether it was high 'do or low 'do,' since it was the strongest and most necessary note. Another example, which is easily understood, is 'fa'; the sign for 'fa' is a fist but with the thumb pointed down toward the floor. The sol-fa system was a teaching tool to aid youngsters and/or adults to learn to 'read' music and it worked beautifully.

I used this method in Andover constantly after my return, whenever the children and I sang, or learned new songs. I wrote up my final work, my thesis for the University of London, and in it, demonstrated my work with all my school children. They were able to sing two and three-part harmony (music) easily and with understanding. Also, simultaneously, some could accompany themselves on the 'Orff' Instruments developed by Carl Orff. Cecilia Vajda's hand signal method was based on the Zoltan Kodaly way of teaching music, and much knowledge of singing was developed as a result.

I was absolutely ecstatic with the methods and the children's progress and most importantly, their understanding of the music and the sol-fa system. As the students used her method, they understood what was happening and why, and that was the best part of all. When I was a little girl I learned music and loved it, but music was taught then by the rote system, meaning... 'memorize it, but do not understand it...' which was the unwritten or unspoken 'rule of thumb' at that time. Memorize I did, but understand fully, I did not, until I went to college and had some assistance. I was thrilled therefore to learn Cecilia's method which enabled the students to have a greater appreciation of the music.

Cecilia and I became good friends during that year-long course. In fact, she persuaded me to apply for a grant to travel to Hungary to learn more about her teaching methods. I did so when I returned from my sabbatical, but in the early 1980s the school in Hungary was so impoverished that it could not offer me any financial support for travel or living expenses. Naturally, I could not go at that time since we also had very little money here as well, and I would have to bring my family. Unfortunately, that ended what would have been a wonderful adventure for me.

I did manage to attend a couple of her summer courses in England in later years, but that is another story to be told later in this book. After that, our paths never crossed again. We made a few telephone calls, one year to the next, but could never manage to sort out our times and countries, and money to figure out how to get together again. Lack of money was always our biggest obstacle.

I never had the pleasure of being taught by Carl Orff, but Cecilia and other music teachers in England used his music teaching method. The Orff method worked well with children of all ages.

Carl Orff created a series of instruments with removable bars on the tops of varying sized wooden boxes. The children played whichever notes were needed while composing or accompanying a melody or harmonies. Then, they would either leave all the bars on the large wooden box-like containers or take off the ones not needed and using only, for example, as few as two bars, for the beginning of the learning of harmony and melody.

It is impossible for me to explain all his method here without pictures and long detailed explanations, but thanks to Cecilia I became quite proficient at having my own Andover students work with their solo singing voices and the Orff Instruments after my return home. They created their own individual musical melodies and also their harmonies for accompaniments. The children wrote their own melodies on staves with two, three or four part Orff accompaniments and many, with words. Some students worked in groups of five, some preferred groups of two, or three… they made their own choices. We used Japanese Haiku as a base for their songs, and melodies and harmonies. We eventually performed their work for their parents and the event was a great success.

The children loved performing in the show. It allowed them to demonstrate all they had learned. They also made individual tapes and each child left school that year with their own book of melodies and harmonies, some with words and some without. When we put on a show using Japanese fables and haiku, many students performed in tableaux depicting the story in the melodies. The whole event was a massive feat, well done, and inspiring, besides being quite novel.

Colin Evans

I owe much to Colin Evans. I met him when he was a director of music in a very large district in London. He was a hard worker, and a great musician who worked untiringly while teaching music to children and he continues to do so now, living in Thailand and writing original compositions for children to play!

My good friend, Paul Gayzagian, a Professor of Music at my college in Lowell, had met Colin previously. Paul introduced us via mail. After settling down in South Croydon I got in touch with Colin. He arranged for us to meet in London. While in London with him he escorted me around to visit his schools to observe what the students were doing in music and how they were learning. I was extremely impressed with all I experienced. Some of what I saw was almost unbelievable.

The lesson that absolutely floored me the most was a violin lesson going on in the first grade. *Yes!* The entire first grade performed, not just the brilliant ones. The first grade violinists were taught that music has 'form' and they learned the 'form' as well as notes and bowing. The little ones walked to the 'form' of the music they were playing. They had small violins in their hands and were playing while they walked. Older college age students were on hand to keep the instruments tuned.

The children were playing a piece of music that consisted of four lines of music. The form of the piece of music was A, B, C, D, and each time the first line ended the melody did not stop, but the children, while playing the tune, turned and walked in the other direction, demonstrating 'form': for example, the beginning of the 'form' was on 'A' and at the end of the first line of music, 'B' arrived and at the first note of 'B' the children turned around, did not miss a note or beat, and walked to the 'C' part of the form. The next one was 'D' again, and when 'D' arrived, they turned and went back the other way, walking all the time, never missing a note or a beat.

I was absolutely amazed. Students in the first grades in Andover, MA could not possibly do anything like that at this time. This method in London had been started at the beginning of the first grade and all children had violins and many helpers. This was a novel way to teach as far as I was concerned, but the best part of it was that it worked. It was also a great learning tool for the college age music students who were helping the children tune their instruments. Their playing was absolutely outstanding and to be performed by children as young as six years old was amazing!

Colin took me around to many other schools in his directorship area; I learned so much from all these people. I kept copious notes on all I saw and where I went and what was accomplished or not accomplished… and, in my estimation, I must say England does keep beautiful music flowing…all around the world and all the time.

Colin is still a good friend, now retired and writing music for children of all ages while living in Thailand. Once in a while I hear from him. He was so very helpful and so good to me; one time we went to meet his parents in Wales at their home. They were such lovely people; we spent a long and joyous day together!

Diary Excerpts

I thought at this point in my story it would be interesting to include some of the excerpts from my diary. It was not a great diary, not like that of some famous authors; it was a tired woman's diary, but here and there were some interesting entries I'd like to share.

JANUARY 13, 1979

"Today when the blossoms all cling to the vine, I'll taste your strawberries, I'll drink your sweet wine, a million tomorrows will all pass away..."

Happiness exuded from me...I heard from my pal Jeanie Pendergrass from home. I realize now how much I depend on my special friends from home.

Amy goes to see *Dick Whittington*, the play...tonight, while Eric and Susan and I go back into London to see *Once Upon A Catholic!*

Added extra: I also introduced myself to the Admiral of the British Navy at the Boat Show. He had gold braid up to his elbow.

He said, "Have the Brits been good to you?"

I answered, "Oh, Yes!"

He then asked, "Have *you* been good to the Brits?" I then snuggled up to him and said, as he put his arm around my shoulders..."*Oh...yes!!!*"

JANUARY 14, 1979

Today was one of my depression days. Every once in a while it hits me for no apparent reason except for guilt and worry over my mom, my dearest mom; I am always burdened with guilt, and have been, it seems, my entire life. I'm here and she is home, virtually alone...when I reread yesterday's page of this diary and saw how happy I was, how much real enjoyment I have been having, I cannot then fully understand why these next two days I am or was so depressed. My depression was so bad for those next two days, (written on third day) that I had all I could do to hold back floods of tears that really wanted to stay with me all day.

JANUARY 15, 1979

Rail strike again...everything around here, on differing days, strikes...one day it is bread, another day, the busses, another and another and then, the rail-road again on the third day. Everything that could strike…struck! All of them on varying days all through the winter months.

Today was more of yesterday. I could not get my mother out of my mind. I felt I was not fulfilling my duties to her. I felt the pleasures I would be having here, constant every day ones, I should be having at home…with mother as well as my family. Also meaning Susan, whom we had to leave behind at college.

I should have *made* myself go to school in London today, that is what I wanted most to do and I did not do it. Now my determination has waned. I missed two great days in which I should have been in classes…now I am even more upset.

JANUARY 22, 1979

Fully assured I would be organized and attend all lectures I started out again on this day. I went on the bus number 68. I was trying to save money, since the bus is always cheaper than the train but slower and not as direct. After a short while, the bus broke down. At least it seemed to have broken down. I was then told by the bus driver to take another bus, number 69. It did not take long for me to realize that one did not go where it was supposed to go. Therefore, I once again disembarked and looked around, totally lost, of course, for another bus to at least carry me somewhere near the college. On and on and on this went for a total of four buses and four fares later, (with an eye to saving money ha!) I finally ended the journey at Westminster and was unbelievably deposited in the midst of a strikers' demonstration! Yes, there seemed to be hundreds of men milling and merging all around me and almost as many, it appeared, of the mounted po-lice men waiting for something terrible to happen. (I soon learned many awful things happen during these trying times!) Amy had no school due to the strike, which I did not know having left before her time to leave for school in the morn-ing. In utter frustration and puzzlement I eventually gave up trying to get to the college, it was still far away from where I was and I had become, once again, ex-hausted. I realized I could not walk that far at this point of borderline hysteria and not knowing the way, at the same time.

I then walked diagonally across the street heading towards Westminster Abbey and then I went into the private room on the right, after one enters the huge front doorway. It was closed up in glass on one side, with a glass door to allow those inside who want to have silence during their meditation. I knelt down and prayed a bit; then, sat down and relaxed trying to think what to do next. I meditated, if you will! Yes, that was a relief, and I rested while sitting at the altar for quite a while.

I decided to explore the Abbey while I was there, alone and no pressure since I could not go on to classes...by now they had started and the first ones were about finished, of that I was certain! I was walking slowly down the right hand side of the huge and beautiful Abbey when I met...unbelievably, Margo and Ed and Amy who had come to London to work on some brass rubbings! What a shock and surprise I had! I was totally flummoxed! (Since I was to have been in classes all day I did not remember they would be in London at Westminster!?! I was a mess, literally a mass of confusion!)

We removed ourselves eventually from the Abbey after many brass rubbings, and also from the strikers. After I had rested a bit Margo and I walked to Harrods while Ed and Amy went home. It was a long walk, but something I had always wanted to do. I was totally aghast at the prices in Harrods.

We arrived home, once again, and I was worn out, headachy and totally exhausted, but so happy we were in England and having these experiences and that I could share them with 'ma cousine, Margo!'

JANUARY 23, 1979

Meeting with Mrs. Pugh, administrator U. London...Cancelled! No meeting...Railroad strike...no classes in London...snowstorm...worst winter here since 1962.

Eric stayed home that day...his day off.

We went to a Pub for lunch again, in the snow, and then went to school (Amy's school was in session today unlike London) to meet Amy, Michelle, Andre, Paul and Samantha. They were all enjoying a snowball fight. They had a wonderful time playing in the snow.

In retrospect ...at home...the enjoyment in the children's faces while playing in the snow...throwing snowballs, rolling in it...is something, which is taken for granted in New England. I loved watching Amy, Dylan, Paul Chapman and Andre and Michelle and Samantha as they all somehow wended their way home by jumping on and rolling off of piles of snowdrifts. The usual ten-minute walk lasted 45 minutes on this day and the children all arrived home happy and soaking wet and totally enthralled with the day and themselves. Eric and I looked on from afar and smiled all the time.

MARCH 14, 1979

Observation of another school in London…(no name given in diary)

Music teacher was a picture of disillusionment suffering from agonies of no money, no future, poor job, Headmaster *weak*…ineffectual, no extras put into Music Program from ILEA (Inner London Education Authority).

"Nothing…nothing…nothing"….she said!

Very old building…smelly Loos…(bathrooms) same ones for teachers as for children…salaries four thousand pounds per year, max! (That would amount to, roughly, 8 thousand dollars a year)

MARCH 18, 1979

Barbican Station: Ed and I went to the London Museum with all the children, Alexi the youngest and the other two Calder children and Amy. Mary Ellen, also, since she was the 'au pair' girl and then we bussed to McDonald's for supper.

Cost for the day with free museum entrance was 15 pounds and that included train fares and tube for all of us plus McDonald's, although Ed and I did not eat then, only the children.

Horrible scene occurred on the way home in the train to South Croydon. Actually a fistfight almost occurred with a 'drunk' who was annoyed because our darling little Alexi was crying. He came over to us and called Alexi a swine, this beautiful three year old child, and then proceeded to call Ed other words… all the other awful words he could think of for not controlling this child we had with us. He yelled at Ed and told Ed to *"Beat the kid up!!! that will make him stop crying!"* Finally, a conductor came over and removed the man from our presence. The children and I were all scared and Ed also at that point!

JUNE 1, 1979

Day in Chipstead with Joy

Go to Reigate… Leave home 11:30

Amy to play at Calder's

We met Joy and Pooh (Charles) at the train station near their home. We lunched at the Well Inn. We had walked by it on the 'Beating of the Bounds day' and that is where we met the other half of the 'Walking' group and the Rector. We had mince (hamburg) pie and onion for 90 pence, full plate and quite good.

Pringles then brought us to Nagles' house and had a picture of us taken behind the *Iron spider gate*! We then entered the old cottage, which dated back to 1500 or so…quaint…low ceilings. I was thrilled to be in a house as old as that.

We went on to Reigate and then to the Chipstead Church for a 'rubbing' of Lucy Roper. I did one rubbing (picture), which was not as good as I would have liked and then did another, which was better, at least for *me*! Ed rubbed one in black and white also. We returned home by 8 PM and now I ache from the rubbing efforts. Charles drove us to our South Croydon home, thank the good Lord since, as usual, I was terribly exhausted. The ride home is always a treat since we usually always take a train to go to Chipstead. I ache today from all the efforts …hard to do a 'rubbing', I discovered!

JUNE 11, 1979

(*Oliver!* show by the Park Hill School: Amy's school put on the musical *Oliver!* which I have directed many times but in a slightly smaller way.)

Diary says:

Dress Rehearsal 1:30

Also, the show ran for three nights, (which I think is far too many performances for that age group and their young singing voices!)

Voices were extremely good as I expected albeit tired (and there is nothing that upsets me more than a tired child's voice. That should not happen!) by the second and third night.

Acting by the main characters was generally good

Scenery was excellent

Children actors performed on the floor while the audience sat up on differing levels… (I always wished I could have that type of staging for my children's performances at home…the audience can then see the performance better but mainly, the children's singing voices or adult voices, all sound far superior when performed in that manner.)

Major character voices were suffering a bit from fatigue…whole show was very long for that age level also.

Fagin was excellent, but his tired voice was quite apparent.

✿ ✿ ✿

Not only did I have an excellent experience learning more about music education and related topics while studying in England, but living there for a year gave us the wonderful opportunity to explore London and its environs, and occasionally travel farther afield. Carol Grey and her husband Ed, a bus driver, and their daughter Debbie, who became a good friend of Amy's, were instrumental in helping us make those longer trips.

And of course there were other people, some of whom I've already mentioned such as Francoise and Hugh, and Vera and her daughter Nieve, as well as fellow graduate students Trevor, Roz and Sonia who made our yearlong stay in England absolutely wonderful. As I said many times and will repeat again, the English could not have been nicer or kinder to us. I have a great love and respect in my heart for all the people I met that year on sabbatical!

Hampton Court

Carol Grey and her husband invited us to a picnic with them at Hampton Court...one of the homes of King Henry VIII. We might not have gotten to this famous place without them since it required traveling by car, and we had none. We felt privileged to have been invited. Lunches were prepared and off the six of us went, Carol, Ed and their daughter Debbie, and Ed, Amy and I.

In my mind's eye I still see all of us on the grass at a large park eating our lunch before entering the grounds and exploring Hampton Court Castle. The rooms were enormous, the grounds were lovely, and we were even allowed to go on down to the huge kitchens in the castle that supplied the food and drink for the myriad of gatherings and parties offered by the King to his cohorts.

Because traveling was so difficult in the time of King Henry VIII, when people came or went to visit, their stay was usually for a long time, as in several months at a time. This required a host to have plenty of room and resources to accommodate guests, and their entourage of friends, bodyguards, servants, etc. for a long stay.

The statement that has stayed with me the longest, in reference to Hampton Court and King Henry VIII with his six wives is the following, "divorced, beheaded, died, divorced, beheaded, survived!" The children from Amy's school taught that to me to help me remember the order of the six wives of Henry the VIII.

Hampton Court, I was told, had the first indoor tennis courts. When I learned during the tour that Henry VIII played tennis on the same day that his second wife, Anne Boleyn, was beheaded, I almost went into shock! What horrible and despicable behavior!

Well, we saw those tennis courts. As I peered at the tennis courts a mental image of Ann Boleyn being beheaded at the Tower of London while he played tennis in his Hampton Court has stayed in my mind forever. But in addition to the tennis courts, we saw many rooms with large fireplaces and walls decorated with large paintings of royal family members or exquisite scenery. The dining room was enormous and set so beautifully; it was absolutely precious and priceless to look at.

Outside the court and all around the grounds lovely gardens existed. In one area there was a maze of evergreen trees, all the same kind, and the same height. It was most confusing and arranged of course for one to enter and become disoriented and thence...be lost! I would not go in, but Amy and Debbie and Debbie's dad, Ed, had a glorious time in the maze trying to find each other and/or the way out. They all stayed in the maze for what seemed forever...before they found their way out again. We have photographs somewhere in my closets or cupboards of all these events, but I have not hauled them out yet. I certainly have fond memories of those times however!

Dartmouth

Paul Gayzagian, my kind professor from Lowell State Teachers' College, introduced me to Ken Rockett. Mr. Rockett had hoped I would attend Dartmouth College in England, where he was a professor, for their Master's Program. But of course, I chose London.

Ken never forgot us in spite of my choice. He and his wife invited us to spend a few days with them down near Dartmouth, which is near the channel. We did, and we all had a lovely time. They were delightful people, well informed and most generous as virtually all the English were with whom we came in contact. Then, after two days and a night with them they offered us the use of their trailer home for another time when we felt we could come again. I was absolutely flabbergasted. It would mean we could explore the Dartmouth area and there would be no cost, as there would have been had we slept in a hotel. They kindly and generously went one step further and chose what they thought was the best view and nicest countryside and the greatest bay over-looking the channel.

The dates were fixed for some time in the spring and off we went. Eric took time off from work to come with us also...and for that...I was thrilled. So Amy and Eric sat in the back seat of our rented car and tussled and teased and tossed each other around, and Ed and I sat in the front. (I loved hearing them play together.)

Ken had made a detailed map with directions for us to reach his home and pointed out places we might like to visit along the way. At one point, and I love this one, we had to drive the car onto a ferry and be ferried across to be able to arrive at our destination. When we arrived at their home, Ken and his wife fed us and put us to bed and then, the next day drove with us to their trailer. We found that Ken and spouse had lugged their trailer to the spot they thought was the best in the Devon area, which is down in the south. We spent almost a week there, sleeping and eating breakfast in the trailer and driving off from that spot to visit all the surrounding areas.

The trailer was so small, that for four of us, with Ed and Eric being large and tall men, it was absolutely funny. We found we had to leave the door to the trailer ajar at night to make room for Eric's feet. I can still see my son's feet hanging out of the trailer door at night. Thank goodness the weather was warm!

We toured all of Dartmoor, saw the wild ponies and went in and out of quaint villages, ate, slept and admired all there was to see. All in all, it was a lovely family time, and it was not costly except for the car rental and petrol, as the English call gasoline, and the food we would have to buy no matter where we were. Eric cooked up a few steaks for us at one time on the grill that was provided in the trailer.

Cousin Margo

Margo is my first cousin from my mother's family. Her mother was my mother's much older sister. Therefore, Marguerite, her correct name, was fifteen years older than I. Consequently, because of my many trips to Sherbrooke in my early childhood and then later as an adult, we became as close as an older sister and younger sister could be. I never had a 'sister' so I truly loved her and still do now. When I was six years old, she was twenty-one, and she thought I was the cutest and greatest little one of all times. We behaved with each other the way I dreamed and hoped sisters would. As I grew older I loved her more and more. She is still with us, but unfortunately she now has Alzheimer's disease and in its fifth stage, which I feel is the worst stage. She also lives far away; seems far although it didn't when I was a little girl. I always called her frequently on the telephone but now she does not seem able to talk with me.

While we lived in South Croydon I made her promise she would come to England to see us because she had never traveled outside of Canada. Her husband, Gerry, had died a while back and Margo, 65, was living alone. She said she would come and I insisted she stay for three weeks at the very least, which she did. I knew that when I was busy with my classes, she and Ed could visit around and I also knew she loved Amy and that the relationship was most reciprocal.

Margo always had a desire to go to Scotland, especially since her loving husband, Gerry, had died. She wanted to see where her husband was born and had lived. It was very important to her, so I told her I would help her get to Scotland when she came to England.

The big day arrived, we met Margo at the airport and hugged and hollered and hugged some more and just had a wonderful and loving time at Heathrow! Then we were off to South Croydon and the three weeks were like a whirlwind for all of us.

One weekend we rented a car. (Margo generously paid for the rental, knowing how little money we had that year). We brought her to see many places we had already seen but *not* in the city of London. (One would be foolish, especially being American having always driven on the other side of the road, to take a car anywhere into London. We only used a car in the countryside to see the castles and the beaches.) She was so excited all the time. Eric, or Amy and Ed kindly took her into London on days I had to go to classes.

Recession, Strikes, Terrorism

I have not yet mentioned that during the year we were in England, the country was in the grip of a deep economic recession. As a result there was great strife and many strikes that slowed and even shut down transportation systems at times. Terrorists even planted a bomb in a car in a garage of the House of Commons. A member of the house had gotten into his car, driven it up the incline just a few feet, and then, was blown to smithereens!

The event occurred on the day I was walking to classes because no busses were running due to the strikes. I came upon the scene shortly after the explosion occurred. I was so upset and terrified upon arriving on this scene that I had great difficulty in believing that I was actually seeing what I saw! How does one relate the horror attached to such a scene as that one! I began to have difficulty breathing and believing that I was actually witnessing anything of that ilk. I stiffened upon seeing the car in bits and pieces. The police were there by then, but there were ladies shrieking or crying and running around. Although I was not actually a witness to the bomb exploding, I saw more than enough for my gentle nature.

I had all I could do to stay together and carry on somehow to Westminster

Abbey, a few yards up the street from the House of Commons garage. Feeling utterly down, fearful and discouraged I decided to go into the meditation room in the Abbey, which is on the right hand side after one enters the front door. I went in, said my thoughts and prayers and after a while, pulled myself together.

I then decided to walk down one corridor in the cathedral while meditating on all I had experienced, and as I walked I looked to the right. There was a passageway there. Who did I see but my husband Ed, my little girl, Amy and my wonderful cousin, Margo! After I boohooed in their arms a bit, they explained to me that they had decided to come in and do brass rubbings while I was at my University and attending lectures or whatever. God was good, they missed being near the explosion!

✴ ✴ ✴

The time came for Margo to go to Scotland to see where her husband Gerry came from. However, I could not go with her due to my classes at the college, but then she said, "Oh, Ma-reee"...with an emphasis on the second syllable...as in "eee" since she was French Canadian and one could hear it in her speech. "I can go by myself. I would not want you to miss classes and Amy needs you here also," she told me.

She was right of course, but I did help her purchase her tickets for the train to Scotland. By the time the day came for her to leave on her trip the trains were running on diminished schedules due to the strike. Also, to make matters worse, one never knew the time the train or trains were coming or going. Hundreds of people every day hovered around our East Croydon Railroad Station to see how they could get a train that would take them to work in London.

Margo and I went down to board the train at East Croydon, (the major trains did not go to South Croydon), and everything was different. People were behaving differently and there was a huge...I mean...*very huge* mob of people trying to get a seat or even stand while on the trains. I started to be very nervous!

No trains were coming...we waited and waited...none came for the longest time. We were growing more and more agitated since Margo, after getting on this train had to get over to King's Cross station on the other side of London to go to Scotland from there. Her tickets had already been bought and paid for, but that was before the strike!

All I could think was, "Oh, what will we do? If it is bad here, it will be bad all over London at all the train stations. Should we go back home or carry on?"

A train finally arrived and hundreds of people ran, and shoved, and pushed, and some got in and some did not. Margo was pushed and shoved into the train by the crowd and I was left on the walkway as the train started to leave. Then suddenly, in horror, I realized I had Margo's train ticket to Scotland in my purse! There she was, somewhere in a train to London with no ticket for Scotland, but she had her luggage!

I really did not know what to do, I paced and paced and waited anxiously for another train. Eventually, and I don't know how much later, one did arrive and the pushing mob was on once again. I got to Victoria Station somehow and looked all over for Margo thinking she might have waited there for me to arrive, but I could not find her!

I took a taxi to King's Cross, I felt that was the only way to go, and I hurried up to the platform, which I found by going up one of the escalators. The train was there, hissing and steaming and everyone was in their seats, ready to leave.

I told the conductor my problem and he was understandingly sympathetic but said to me, "I am so sorry Miss, I cannot hold the train any longer...we must leave in five more minutes."

"Ohhh," I murmured aloud, "now what shall I do?" I asked the conductor. "I have her ticket here in my hand."

"I am truly sorry Miss. I just cannot wait another minute, since the time never waits for anyone, the clock just keeps going."

I was so anxious I was about ready to bite my nails. I was holding Margo's ticket upright in my right hand, positioned between the train and conductor and the escalator. Suddenly I saw a pair of anxious, nay, not just anxious, but very scared eyes coming up. They showed first on the escalator, and then I saw her shoulders and then her full body arrived! The expression in her eyes told the whole story in one glance! *fear and fright*!

I screamed "*Margo*" loudly above the noise of the engine and yelled quickly, "Don't say a word, here are your tickets...walk up those steps...*now*." I literally pushed her up and into the train car with her bag, yelling goodbye as she stood hanging on to the long handle bar with the conductor next to her. Her facial expression was one of a fright beyond belief, not understanding fully what was happening, her eyes were as huge as saucers. I hollered at her as loud as I could, as the train pulled away, "Have a good time and don't lose your tickets!" I last saw her on the moving train hanging on to the railing and the conductor...who was trying his best to be helpful to her!

The train was gone...and I was weak all over. It took a few minutes for me to make myself start moving again and carry on to my University of London classes.

I heard from Margo on the phone later that night, a very short "May-reee I am here and I am fine." Then we disconnected as she remembered neither of us had much money to spare. Not many days had gone by though when I received another frantic call from my dearest 'cousine.' The terror of the night before was still well ensconced in her voice as she recounted a story beyond my imagination.

It seems Margo was in bed in the hotel reading a book before sleeping when the fire alarm went off and screaming and yelling started. The hotel seemed to be on fire. All the guests, in their nightgowns and bathrobes or whatever, were scrambling, trying desperately to get out of the hotel as fast as possible. Margo, of course, was trembling and tense while recounting this horrible story to me. She cried and boo-hooed on the telephone, "I am coming home, I want to come home tomorrow, May-ree, can you tell me what to do?"

I said, "Margo, listen carefully please. When you get to Victoria Station take a train to East Croydon, and then take a taxi and come right home." She could never have managed in her state of mind to change trains at East Croydon and get on the South Croydon train, so I told her to take a taxi and forget the cost!

She was home the next evening and recounted to us, in her ever delightful high pitched and most agitated voice, what happened. "I was in bed, May-reee, and it was about eleven o'clock, when I heard a noise, a terrible noise. There was a party going on somewhere and they were all military men in uniforms, and they were all drunk." Margo most definitely emphasized the word, *drunk!* "Yes, all of them were very drunk. Then, May-reee, what they did next was so very awful! I was so frightened. It seems they went in and around the hotel and pulled fire alarms and then the hotel emptied as everyone was screaming and hollering, 'Let us out...let us out'...and all of us were in our night clothes..." and Margo continued hysterically...yelling, "But May-ree...*there was no fire!*"

"What? What do you mean there was no fire?" I asked.

Margo went on to state in her still fearful and upset voice, "The drunken idiots pulled false alarms. All of the alarms went off, ringing and ringing and the drunken fools stood outside enjoying the rushing of the scared people; they were laughing drunkenly at the fright, pointing at us all and screeching at us in our nightgowns and pajamas. We were in our nightgowns and robes while coming out of the hotel...Yes! In our nightclothes! We were all scared to death!"

We all hugged and kissed Margo, in our attempt to calm her and quiet her down and then gave her some hot chocolate and put her to bed. The next morning she said in a most definite voice, "I am *not* going anywhere else unless I am with you or your family until I go home! I am too old now and I do not want to travel alone anymore. I was so scared, May-reee, you cannot imagine!" And in her inimitable style she issued a decree, "And that is that!"

The Pringles

While I was studying at the University of London, Ed went to a school for adults at Coombe Cliff near our home, where he met a lady who became a friend of ours for life. Joy Pringle was her name. Joy taught a class, *Speaking With Confidence,* which Ed thought would be interesting, so he signed up and attended the course.

The first time I met Joy was in the winter. Ed had taken me over to Coombe Cliff to introduce me to 'Mrs. Pringle.' I will never forget how she was dressed. She wore a long plaid and pleated skirt which fell a little above the ankles, a pair of high leather boots and of course a top to match. She had hair almost down to her knees, yet she was not young by any means, being then, at least in her

Joy Pringle with Mary Guziejka in England

early sixties. I was fascinated with her and her way of speaking. We talked a while and she then said, in her most proper English style, "Ohhh, (in a high nasal tone) you must come to our home when the bad weather is over, in the spring, to see my flowers and we will have tea in the garden." I thanked her profusely and being so fascinated with her, I was hopeful she would not forget to invite us again with a definite date!

As was promised, she kept her word and one day, she invited us to visit her. It was spring and plants and flowers were in beautiful bud. We had a most delightful visit. Her lovely and erudite husband, Charles, joined us, along with their two dogs. The most wonderful friendship developed after that day. Joy and I were like sisters from that time on (especially when we learned we shared the same birthday, May 9!)

She worked with Ed on his English and his delivery of the language. I don't think she succeeded too much with him, but she certainly enjoyed him as much as he enjoyed her, they teased each other constantly, he in his American style and she in her proper, very proper, British style! Nevertheless, we got along famously and in time, after I returned home, she and Charles came to spend three weeks with us and the friendship grew from there. Actually they came to see us twice or thrice in Massachusetts.

So, between their trips to us, our trips to visit them, and living together often, we became like family. We visited many wonderful scenic and historical places together. Also, since she and Charles had both been members of the services during World War II, they had unusual and exciting stories to tell all the time.

I must end this paragraph by telling you Joy had a very special and unique job with the British Military at the start of World War II. She was a message decoder…amazing…and was based up on the east coast in England, almost into Scotland! Thus, to make all this most loving and kind and dear, and oh, so meaningful to me, I will quote once again…

> *I can no answer make*
> *But thanks and thanks*
> *And ever thanks*
>
> **Twelfth Night**
> **—Shakespeare**

Excursions

Our family went on so many trips during our year in England, that to list them all now would be impossible. However, I will do my best to highlight *some* of them. We covered the top to the bottom of England, a little bit of Scotland, we visited Edinburgh, and the mid and northern half of Wales and a week in Ireland, the three of us together. Some of the time we were with Joy and Charles, other times, just my little family and sometimes Eric, too, would have time off from work, so then we were four.

After we had settled into our home in South Croydon in the year 1978-1979 we took a trip to Scotland to see the annual 'Tatoo.' It was magnificent. I loved Edinburgh, Scotland and always hoped to return to it, but sadly, I could not. There is only so much one can do in a year and I certainly did more than I ever in my life expected to do. 'Tatoo' came from the word 'tap toe,' which described the movements the musicians made while marching. Through a hundred or more years, and probably due to the Scottish accent, the term for these annual festivities became, 'Tatto.'

Bagpipe bands come from all over the world to parade and play. We had been told by our new friends we should *never* miss the 'Tatoo' so we took a train trip to Edinburgh, (we traveled First Class, which was marvelous, and I decided there was nothing else like it.) We had a grand time visiting Edinburgh and seeing the famous ruins and castles.

The weather was cool for the end of August and the first of September since Scotland is far north; it was so cold that we had to drop into a store and buy ourselves something warm to put over our outer garments. Amy and I each bought a woolen cape and Ed probably bought a sweater. We felt much more comfortable then, although, at the 'Tatoo,' we could have used a lap blanket for the three of us.

We found the 'Tatoo' to be fascinating, exciting and unusual...and loved it and every part of old Edinburgh. One group in particular that we loved was the program put on by Chinese women. The Chinese were precision marchers and performed all types of fancy steps and exquisite patterns while they marched and performed. They put on a dazzling and spectacularly breathtaking performance. I do not remember the other groups as well as I remember the Chinese, but nevertheless, all the groups were most sensational. We were so happy to have attended such a grand and unusual event.

❋ ❋ ❋

Ed's favorite spot in England was **Stonehenge**, introduced to us by Charles and Joy. The boulders are absolutely enormous and tradition or legend claims they were somehow brought down from upper England or Wales, but how? One might ask how that could happen, since no group of men could possibly move them easily, they were so enormous. But their formation has a legend attached and it was most interesting. Truth or legend, how does one truly know? Needless to say, we visited several times, always bringing a friend or two from home to see it. I believe Eric also took our daughter Susan to see Stonehenge. She favored it among all the historical places, just as we did.

To quote from a booklet called, *A Guide to Young People*, "Stonehenge is the most famous prehistoric temple in Europe and is visited each year by a quarter of a million people." Now, this little booklet dates back to 1978-1979 so I would assume that the number of visitors has grown considerably. The booklet continues, "Stonehenge #1 was built during the Neolithic period or, New Stone age, about 2200 B.C. It had three-construction periods back then and the third and final was rebuilt about 1300 B.C. The total weight of the stones is certainly more than 100 tons, and not found where they were placed. The authorities are fairly certain that the stones were brought by river from 130 miles North. About eighty stones were moved." The sources feel they were boated down on the Bristol Channel from Prescelly Mountains.

Why did Stonehenge exist? It was a temple…plain and simple, a prehistoric temple, and because it has so many unusual features it was most probably a religious center of special importance. No historians have yet been able to find what kind of gods were worshipped by its builders or what kind of ceremonies were held.

❋ ❋ ❋

I feel I want to list a few more places we visited while in the British Isles; I will start with The Vale of the White Horse. The White Horse is a delightfully large, profile type, image carved on a hillside, from Roman days. It is a lovely place to spend a Sunday afternoon taking a hike to visit it and the surrounding area. The image of the white horse was carved into the side of a mountain *hundreds* of years ago.

We visited one of Charles Dickens' homes, he had so many houses it seemed. We had already visited about four of them with one being up along the north coast of England; it was located on the Seaside and I believe it was called

Broadstairs; that was absolutely delightful since it had many of his possessions still in it. We also visited every Roman ruin anywhere nearby where the Pringles lived and even further afield. Joy and Charles were deeply involved with anything from Roman times and/or any historical ruins and knew so much about them; their knowledge and intelligence put me to shame, I felt I knew so little!

❧ ❧ ❧

One day we found ourselves visiting the Jane Austen home. (I have read all her books several times.) It was a far ride from the Pringle's home, so Ed opted not to go. Joy and Charles and I explored Jane Austen's little home and marveled at how she was able to write and be so successful at her young age, in a little home, with only 'hair pens' and a tiny table on which to write which Jane herself had positioned by a small window…"so she could look out at the people passing by" to quote Jane. Jane died at a very young age, sadly, and her monument is in the capacious Winchester Cathedral amidst all the notables of that era and before. Many learned scholars are still attempting to understand why Jane was buried there and several reasons have come to the forefront and many agree that since her home was in the 'close' she should be buried in the Winchester Cathedral.

After visiting Austen's home and after a copious lunch, we were all feeling a bit sleepy when Joy said to Charles, "Dah-ling…pull over, dee-ah…at the hay field…Mary and I will lie down in the hay and take a snooze."

Charles replied with, "Yes, of course, dah-ling."

Guess what we did? I was so surprised. Joy took a blanket she had stored in the car and said to me in her darling but officious voice, "Come, Mary, we will find a spot to snooze a bit. Charles will nap in the car sitting up." Charles did just that very thing!

I followed her, we climbed a fence, walked several feet away from the road, and then she spread out her blanket; the tall hay was surrounding us so no one could possibly see us if they were passing by. She then plopped down on the hay, I followed suit, and we both napped for about twenty minutes. "Amazing," I said to myself as I stared at the gorgeous blue sky and white clouds, "I would never have done this at home."

❧ ❧ ❧

Ed and the Pringles and I visited Thomas Hardy's home twice, down near Dorchester, but the first time we went we found it closed because it was Holy

Week. So we went back another time with the Pringles. I always found Thomas Hardy to be a prolific and superb writer, therefore I was thrilled to have the opportunity to see his home. It is a place *not* to be missed if you, the reader, are someone who loves reading his books. I loved his home, his garden and his tales. Therefore, in my own garden at home in Dracut I have planted one of his favorite flowers, the lupine.

The following summer as my sabbatical year ended, Joy enticed us to come back to see her, which we did for a week or more and then she gave us the keys to her thatched cottage in Blewbury. That was so unusual, such a surprise and so very exciting for the three of us. Amy, Ed and I spent one week in Blewbury visiting all over the village itself and in the outlying towns as well, which were all beautiful.

However, as generous as Joy always was she was also very frugal. How, you may ask? The only amount of money we had to pay to use the cottage was three dollars for the week for the use of the electricity and the gas! She was an amazing friend and of course we were glad to be able to pay her.

The first morning, after spending the night at Blewbury, we heard a light knocking at the door. A child about Amy's age was standing there and asked me if my little girl could come out to play. Of course I answered with a smile on my face and said, "*Yes!*" This little girl also had a horse. Before we knew it Amy was riding a horse.

I wondered how the little girl knew we were even there? The horse field was right across from Joy's cottage, which was called, Nottingham Fee, (Fee stands for the word 'field') so it stands to reason the little girl saw us come in the day before to spend our week. Amy was in her glory and the two girls had a wonderful time together when we were not out touring the village and environs.

One cannot, in a brief account, put across to the reader exactly how charmingly lovely the village of Blewbury was then and still is today. The villagers have respectfully kept the whole village virtually the same, almost exactly as it was about four hundred years ago. Ed, Amy and I loved every aspect of what we saw, including the different thatched cottages, and the neighbors and how friendly they were.

When our son, Eric, married a few years later, he and his bride, Kelly, decided to go to England for their honeymoon so I arranged for them to have a week in the thatched cottage of Nottingham Fee in Blewbury; it was our gift to them. They were thrilled with it. Also, thanks to Joy I was able to introduce them to a few other events, as in the Shakespeare 'open air' theatre near Dorset situated on a cliff of sorts. I believe they attended a Shakespearean play.

Kenneth Graham, author of *Wind in the Willows*, also lived in Blewbury at one time, not far from Nottingham Fee. Joy made me promise that I would go to see his house, and although no one was allowed inside, there was a sign on the house designating it as his home.

Knowing we were going home relatively soon, we were determined to visit several famous historical sites. English friends would always say to me in their delightful accent, "What? Mary, you have not seen this? Well, you absolutely have to. We will drive you there over the weekend if you are not already tied up with someone else."

Or someone else would say, "You must see this...you absolutely cannot go home without having been to..."

Therefore, with a long list of places to see and valid reasons why we should not miss seeing it, off we went on our own part of the time, and the remainder of the time with seasoned Brits. We toured London for a few weeks in June until we thought we would drop. Many times we brought Amy with us, or Susan, when she was there, or Eric when he had time off. We also saw a few fine musicals and shows in London, since once in a while Eric would be given free tickets from someone when he worked at the Savoy Hotel. Many of the 'greats' in London would either eat at the Savoy or live there until this 'musical' or that 'play/drama' was finished. If they were directors or others, such as coaches or dramatists or electric light people, anyone who worked on or in a drama, for example, and had grown to like Eric, a gift of a pair of tickets would be handed to him.

If I happened to be in London for half a day or finished classes early in the afternoon, I would often go on a search for this old place or that Roman ruin somewhere...hither and yon around London all by myself. One day I was gazing at Big Ben, thinking, "shall I try to go in or not try to go in?" Then I saw the House of Lords and the House of Commons. I decided I would rather go into the House of Lords. I loved Big Ben but more from the outside to hear the chiming bells rather than to go into it. A long time ago it was a prison with cells, I was told, and very dark inside with not much air. The 'inside' was definitely *not* for me!

I then carried on and went into The House of Lords! Why did I make that decision? I decided simply because the House of Commons had a line that snaked down the street and all around the corner. I surely did not want to stand in a line that long. The line of people was so long it might have taken two hours to just get into the House of Commons. Instead, I could almost walk right in to the House of Lords, there was not much of a line. Therefore, I spent at least two or three hours inside the House of Lords, sitting and listening and listening some more. I could hear and understand and I found it all fascinating. It was rather droll the way some of the men in the House of Lords talked to each other. They were most respectful to one another unlike some of our meetings in the U.S.A. today! To this day I cannot tell you exactly what I heard, this happened such a long time ago, but there is no question of it being a most wondrous event for little me who hailed from Massachusetts!

✹✹✹

Another time we took Amy to the famous Madame Toussaud's Wax Museum up by King's Cross station in London. I have a photo of Amy, shyly standing next to the wax…almost real looking…figure of Judy Garland. Amy, Ed, and I loved Madame Toussaud's. So many famous people were represented and looked as though they could start talking with you if you gazed at their wax figures long enough. We saw the whole Royal Family; Henry VIII and all his wives; and many famous politicians. Of course, whenever we had people visiting we had to return to many of these favorite places, in particular this one. We became well acquainted with the underground transport, affectionately called 'the tube' and buses and walking, and walking and walking! (We walked out of all our shoes except the one pair we used in which to return home.)

We went into Westminster Abbey often, whenever any company came or whenever we wanted to see it again on our own. It is filled with religion but also filled with historical burial spots for famous people, artists, poets, and statesmen. It also has the burning flame, as you walk in the front entryway, for the 'unknown soldier' which is impressive.

Also at Westminster Abbey, amongst all the wonderful people who are recognized throughout history and are proudly buried in Westminster Abbey, there is also a dear and quiet small room shut off from the remainder of the Abbey by large glass doors. That room is simply for silent prayer. I have never seen anyone in there when I wanted to go in, which was nice for me. One may also light a candle to the memory of the person for whom you pray. I went there whenever I could just to meditate, to think and thank God, and pray for my little family and this wonderful opportunity that had come my way.

❧ ❧ ❧

We always took people to see the Changing of the Guard at Buckingham Palace. Also, another favorite was The National Gallery in Trafalgar Square. I saw all the paintings and rooms many times, and my favorites were all the Impressionists. Not to say I did not treasure all art, but I did love sitting and looking, and absorbing the paintings of all the famous impressionists.

There were times when classes ended at the University of London and I still had time to sit somewhere and reflect, or pray or try to absorb all that was entering my mind, my body and my spirit. I would just sit in the area of my favorite paintings and absorb, breathing a few sighs and saying a few prayers of thanks.

If you are at the front doorway of the National Gallery of Art, looking across the street to the left you can see St. Martin's of the Fields Church. The church was well known for feeding the poor a long, long time ago, and is still doing so now. People who have little money could afford to eat at St. Martin's of the Fields, since the price for a meal was very low, and the food was exceptionally good. We ate in the basement of the church quite often when we were in the city.

We also attended services upstairs in the lovely old church since the atmosphere was wonderful and the singing was absolutely charming. Some evenings the concert consisted of symphonies by famous orchestras; they were great and free, so we went there many times! Each time we went we tried to buy a small item from the gift shop downstairs since all profits are used to help the poor.

We also visited St. Paul's Cathedral that the famous Christopher Wren designed. One day I asked what turned out to be a stupid question. I had not done much thinking. I was with Joy and Charles and I kept looking around for the famous Christopher Wren burial spot and memorial. Much to my surprise, his tomb is the Cathedral itself, I was told. He did not need a special place under the first floor as all others did or here and there on the main floor or upstairs. He had designed the Cathedral and that was his memorial.

The Cathedral is overwhelmingly beautiful both inside and out. While visiting with Joy and Charles another day, Ed stayed in the second balcony with Joy, since she felt she could not climb any higher. Charles and I went to the tippety-top; it was a bit frightening as I do not like great heights, but I would not have missed that for the world...we enjoyed a massively, beautiful view. I must say, the climb was a long, scary one, but we went slowly.

Other times we rented a car and toured a bit here and there with our visitors. For example, Sue and Bob Rogers came to be with us for a week or so, and

Terry and George came. (Terry is another music teacher who lives in Andover but worked in the city of Lawrence.) We had so little money then that thankfully all our visitors from home were happy to pay for the rental of the car, either half or all of the price.

❧ ❧ ❧

Joy and Charles offered their home to us for two more weeks before we returned to the States, since they would be away those last two weeks of our stay in England. That was startlingly generous of them. I truly wanted to accept, but I knew, deep in my heart, it was time to go home. We had to leave this heavenly world in England at some point, so why add another two weeks on to the whole thing when we would still have to go home no matter what? We also had run out of money and we were all three of us on our last pair of shoes…need I go on? Eric was able to stay a few more months, until November, as he continued his job at the Savoy Hotel. Since he would not have a home to live in once we left, a friend offered him a bedroom until Eric's visa ran out.

The year was 'priceless' and I do not refer here to money. This sabbatical and the study of music in the English schools was the best thing I had ever done for me, and consequently, for my family. I felt restored…it gave me a new look at myself as in where I wanted to improve in my career, and what I wanted to change. It readied me to go home and work on my projects in my music classes in order to write my thesis for the University of London.

I had made so many dear, dear friends, I went home with mixed emotions, loving England as much as I did and yet at the same time, missing my mother and my daughter Susan terribly. I was more than happy about going home for those two reasons. Life always seems to be a contradiction; it would certainly be different once we arrived home.

As I sit down to write this autobiography of…Mary and my family, my music adventures, and all my memories, I do nothing but thank God each and every day and will for the remainder of my life for all that has come my way. They were…and still are tried, tested, and true treasures…the vicissitudes of my life!

"So long as men can breathe and eyes can see,
So long lives this, and this gives life to thee…"

Sonnet 18
—Shakespeare

Chapter 17
Return to the States

All the world is a play
And all the men and women are merely players
They have their exits and entrances
And one man in his time plays many parts.

As You Like It
—Shakespeare

In August 1979 we returned home with a *whoopee,* and a 'wonderful to be home feeling' and were met with celebrations from those who missed us; family, number one, and then good friends, all of whom were anxious to hear about my education at University of London and what we saw and what we did. Most importantly though, I was reunited with my mother and Susan. Susan had not come back to England in the spring as we had hoped. Money for her and for us was too tight at that time. My mother did not make a second trip to England as I had hoped and wished. Her age and poor health held her back.

Eric did not return home with us in August. His working papers for England were good until the end of November, so he waited until Thanksgiving to return. And by then, he and his buddy, Tommy, had concocted a plan whereby they would go to Texas and work on a ship out of Galveston. As it happened, Tommy had to change his plans, but Eric chose to stay in Texas without him and work.

He called on the phone one day, excitedly saying, "Mom, I have a job in a restaurant, and love it here. Texas is great, the weather is hot and all the people are very friendly. Would you mind if I stayed in Austin for a while to try it out? I really love it here!"

I could hear the excitement in his voice as he talked and by then he was almost twenty years old. "You had better call me on the telephone once a week to tell me how you are…or else I will come down and look for you," I told him emphatically. He promised he would and he kept his word.

He had loved his work in England at the Savoy Hotel; consequently he continued to work at restaurants in Austin. Soon he was appointed a manager of one, and then met a lovely young woman, Kelly, who became the love of his life. They married and in several years they began making plans to open their own restaurant. The plans never quite worked out, but other things did and to this day he and Kelly are happy and productive. They have two lovely children, a boy and girl, all grown up now. Michael is a senior at the University of California now (2012) and Kim is attending night classes with a plan to attend full time in the near future. Ed and I are extremely proud of them both!

❧❧❧

I returned to my former teaching position at Sanborn School in September. Amy came with me. She had been miserable in the Dracut schools before we went to England. I applied and received permission from the Superintendent in Andover for her to attend school in that town. Amy was thrilled. She left every morning in the car with me and spent her day at my school. She acquired some lovely friends and did quite well in school for those two years at Sanborn. She was in the Sanborn School for the fifth and sixth grades and was involved in my project for the thesis required by the University of London.

Mom returned to her former schedule of staying at our house Monday through Friday to help with the household chores. I could tell she was happy we were back in the States again. It showed all over in her face and actions.

When I returned to the Sanborn School I taught the usual singing, dancing, musicals, plays and the like. However, I added the Kodaly method of using hand signs which I had learned in England: Do, re, mi, fa, sol, la, ti, Do...as in, high Do and low Do...which were demonstrated by a closed fist...fa, for example was a closed fist with the thumb pointing downward, ti, next to high Do was a fist and the index finger pointing upwards...there was a symbol for each note.

I had grown to love working with the 'hand signs' while studying in England since the children responded to them immediately and with great pleasure. When using the Kodaly hand signs one can play games in the air with the hand signs, therefore the children followed the signs vocally as I produced the hand signals; they sang what my hand sign indicated.

In the beginning I sang with the children while making the hand signs and they repeated my hand signs. Then, in time, they sang alone following my hand signs. I played games with easy two-part music, for example, having half the room sing one tone for four beats while the other half sang four different quarter notes at the same time. Voilà! Two part music! It was so pretty, all sounded so lovely, with those young voices singing two-part music 'a cappella'... (meaning no accompaniment.) The children loved it, felt successful, and I was thrilled.

The children found they could easily sing simple two part harmony and not just by rote...but with understanding. The word 'understanding' is the important word here. I worked hard at it with them, making it fun at the same time, and they responded quickly and loved the beautiful sounds they made.

One day, while poking around in an old closet at the Sanborn School looking for anything that might make my classes more appealing to the students, I found some ORFF instruments. I had no idea they were there! I pulled them out and began using them with my students, who loved them. Then and there I decided what my thesis for the University of London, England would center on. It would be about my teaching methods coupled with the success of the Kodaly and Orff Methods and Drama.

I needed to hand in a 'paper' to the University of London Music Education Department in order to receive my diploma no later than three years after I had finished my course work. Well my 'paper' eventually grew to at least 300 pages. It was a book. It was accepted and now it resides in the University of London Library of Music section! I am thrilled, even to this day, to think I can go there any day and find it along with the work of other 'Masters.'

How to begin the whole project was the part that stymied me. "How to start, what shall I do, and how shall I do it?" These were the questions soaring around in my brain for two years after I returned from the University of London. Meanwhile, I attended to my daily classes teaching the two-part or three-part singing method using the Kodaly hand signs.

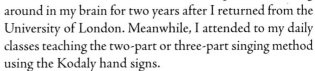

I was in a quandary though as to when, how and where I could teach all the music, drama and dance since I did not have a music room. But then, fate was on my side for a change! On my third year back at the Sanborn School, I acquired my own music room. That was a huge and wonderful beginning for me. For some reason, enrollment must have been down and a room was made available to me at my school; the Principal and Superintendent knew I wanted and needed a room, as I had been pestering them about this for many years. I also petitioned for some added help a few hours per week listing the reasons why and that too was granted. *Hallelujah!* That lady was Anita Duffy, a lovely musical lady, who offered to help me in my classes two hours a day and was paid a substitute's salary!

By the standards of a purposely-built music room, mine was sub-standard since it was far too small. However, since this was the first time in my 28 years of teaching I had EVER had a music room, I was in heaven. So, relative to nothing…I had everything! I had step risers for singing, stacking chairs, three tables, and a collection of Orff instruments and an upright piano. I also had an expensive Sony record player with a separate tape recorder to connect to the unit. (It kept blowing fuses so it was not of much use until we were forced to use it toward the end of the Unit and only then did someone see to its repair!)

The room itself was at the end of the third wing of the building; it had wide, long and big windows on two sides. That was a great boon to me. The room proved to be bright and airy at all times due to the huge windows. Even though by music standards the room was small, we had space...glorious space, in which to move around the room to music...unencumbered.

Previously, when I worked at the Sanborn School, or any other school, I traveled to all the rooms and buildings pushing pianos and equipment. Therefore, I was exhausted before half of the day was over. This year, I felt as though I had died and gone to Heaven. With a room of my own it meant the students would come to me, instead of me going to their rooms. When we became busy and totally involved with a project, many of the children would ask to come in to my classroom before school or after school or during part of our lunchtime to practice on the instruments or make their own melodies. I never denied any of them the pleasure of working on their own music outside of class time. I was always there with them, even if I had to eat my lunch in the room at the same time. The children were lovely and well behaved, and the Orff instruments sounded soft and soothing with golden tones issuing forth to my ears. I was deliriously happy!

I also had more energy since I did not travel room-to-room carrying equipment and pushing my piano. Also, I never put the instruments away in closets at the end of the day; they were always available to the students. As opposed to the past, when I lost much valuable teaching time in a year by carrying, lugging, pushing, and becoming situated, I thought this school year would be 'a piece of cake' by comparison. I was anxious to produce musically literate children in our Sanborn School, so I looked forward to using my own room with the instruments easily accessible, and most importantly, the privacy my own room afforded me.

As a result I decided to focus my thesis on the use of the Orff instruments and the Kodaly Method with my fourth, fifth and sixth grade students. Third graders were involved also but in a different way. They were still a little too young for all I intended to accomplish that year, nevertheless they were part of the project but on a more elementary level. I did not neglect my students in Kindergarten, first and second grades; they and I carried on as usual and even the little ones started learning the hand signals and sang beautifully in their fine soprano voices.

Once I'd decided to use the Kodaly hand signals and Orff instruments, I chose Japanese and Oriental music to study. You may ask "Why"? In other words, why the Orient as opposed to...say...cowboy music from our West or the classics? The answer is fairly simple. I greatly enjoy the sound of Oriental music. Also, the Oriental scale has only FIVE tones in it, while the Western music scale has seven tones, two of them being half tones, making it harder for the students to harmonize.

A complete explanation about the differences in the Oriental versus Western scale would require a book in and of itself. Let me explain this much though: the five tone Oriental scale is easier for children because no dissonances could ever occur and the children could more easily compose their own music by using this 'pentatonic scale.' It leaves out the dissonant notes, which is why it only has five tones. One can never really make a mistake, harmonically speaking, when using it while either singing or accompanying a song.

Also while in England, I had had the great pleasure of observing some Japanese children being taught very elementary words in the English language at the home of their tutor, Joy Pringle in Chipstead, Surrey, England. She taught Speech, Writing and English at the Adult Education Center in South Croydon where we lived while on sabbatical. At that time, schools in England required that the non-British children have private English lessons for two years before being allowed to attend the English schools. The Japanese children and their mothers worked diligently to learn English.

Mrs. Pringle had told them I was a musician and that I would love to hear some children's songs and they enthusiastically complied. As I listened to the fragile melodies that floated in the air as the women and their children sang the children's simple songs in their native tongue, many ideas flooded and roared through my mind. Our own language has a harder and harsher sound whereas the Oriental language is soft, like a bell tinkling or a bird singing or a wind gently blowing past your window. As I sat and listened to these ladies I knew I wanted to incorporate these sounds into my teaching when I returned to the Sanborn School.

Then, I was asked to sing a song in English. I sang easy ones for their little children such as, *Where is Thumbkin*, and *Itsy Bitsy Spider*, both of which employ finger play, which the little ones loved. This small display of mine seemed to leave the Japanese children quite enthralled by their success. As a result of this visit, when I returned to the States, Joy Pringle had the mothers of the Japanese children send messages to the children of the Sanborn School in Andover, Mass. These messages contained simple Japanese words and phrases with their translations and also stories of customs and festivals. Also I had asked them to send some authentic children's songs from Japan in their original language and they did. I was in awe of these Japanese ladies, truly impressed by their generosity, their kindness and their awareness of the importance of music in their children's lives.

By combining the Kodaly hand signs and the Carl Orff instruments with the study of Oriental music, I hoped to make the coming school year at the Sanborn the best ever for the students in music class. Before school started I gathered a collection of Oriental books. I went to Cambridge to the Harvard Coop. I came home with arms full of catalogues, picture books, calendars, and storybooks focusing on the Orient. I also purchased a variety of prints and posters showing ladies in traditional kimonos; villages and places of great heritage in Japan; Buddha; Japanese screens; nature scenes and more.

There were several fathers of students in my classes who traveled to China or Japan on business, so when word got out to the parents that we were studying the Orient, they brought home artifacts from China or the Orient to help us decorate our music room. Fans of all shapes came pouring in, some of which turned out to be 'antique' as well. We had lanterns of all sorts, and Oriental dolls in such a number that at final count we had over fifty dolls propped up around the music room. There was also an assortment of airline travel brochures and menus, lacquered boxes, an eight-foot long windsock which was intended to be a kite, books on haiku and cassette tapes of the Japanese language. Within a month, the music room resembled a conglomerate of Japanese festivals. Also, we were able to take turns wearing Japanese Kimonos and 'Happy' Coats that had been given to us by parents.

For me, Mary Music, (a title given to me by my students, since my last name was difficult to pronounce!) there was nothing more delightful than to see students working assiduously and diligently in groups together, dressed in oversized Happy Coats and Kimonos. They were allowed to 'dress' the part as they worked on the pentatonic scale and on the xylophones; naturally all of this depended on the type of lesson and on a particular day; but the wearing of costumes I allowed all the time.

We did have some articles that proved to be more popular with the younger students. One was a straw coolie hat. (I have such a hat hanging to this day in my sunroom.) The other article was a beautiful silky, dark blue jacket, with a gorgeous fiery red dragon embossed all over the back of the jacket. My own personal favorite was an ice blue kimono embroidered all over in silver with an ice blue OBI (sash).

Costumes, when worn by a person, child or adult, give one a feeling of being someone else, a feeling of importance while hidden, and a feeling of ease while singing or acting. Consequently, I found 'problem' students, ceased to be problems. That was especially helpful for my two second-grade classes, because there were several 'problem' students at that time.

My primary goal was to teach young children to 'read' music; secondly, for them to understand it, and third, to sing the notes they could read and most of all, to enjoy what they were able to sing by reading the notes. (The usual approach to teaching music at an elementary level was simply 'rote' learning. The teacher would sing a line of music; the students would repeat it, and so on until the song was completed. There was no real understanding of the piece of music itself.) My secondary goal was to have students accompany their songs using the Orff instruments. Playing and singing their own songs, I felt, would give them a better understanding of music and also, most importantly, a feeling of success.

The Orff instruments were xylophones and metallophones with removable bars. In the beginning, students would remove all but one or two bars (simply lift them off and place them gently on the floor) leaving perhaps only the high C or low C to play along with a song. As the students became familiar with the notes and patterns, we would put more bars on the instruments. A simple repeated pattern of two or three notes can be played repeatedly as an accompaniment to a gentle and simple song. That pattern is called an ostinato. Any age student can play and feel genuine success afterwards, simply because one can never make a mistake. That usually makes the student want to learn more!

The first step was to show students how I composed some poems and songs and some accompaniments that could be played on the Orff instruments by any one of the children from fourth grade up. I composed little songs using the five-tone scale and the accompaniments I wrote for the Orff instruments. They were easy and simple and each of them told a story of the Orient.

When the students arrived in class they were assigned different instruments. I did that because so many students would choose a favorite instrument and not want to learn or share or work with a different instrument. To begin, I taught them my newly composed songs, for example, 'Springtime's Come and Winter Now Is Gone'…or 'Tannabata'….or…'Nighttime Fishing a Yoi Yoi' or 'Lift The Blinds… Let sunshine in… long shadows will be cast against the walls…'

The students learned to compose HAIKU, Japanese poetry, to use as words to a song. Haiku is a Japanese "poem" with three lines; five syllables in the first line, seven syllables in the second, then five more syllables in the last. Haiku is not a rhyming poem, but it always speaks of beauty, the weather, clouds, love, caring, etc. The children composed their own Haikus and then set them to music using the Orff instruments. I could see the self esteem increase in the students; they loved their melodies, their Haiku poems and playing the instruments. They worked in small groups with one child on the bass xylophone; one on the alto xylophone; and one on the soprano xylophone and/or metallophone, soprano, alto and bass as well, and drums. The size of the groups was determined by which instruments would be best for their Haikus.

Below are some examples of Haiku composed by younger students:

Friendly clouds above
Grass blowing in the cool rain
Swish, swish, swish, swish swish
—Tommy, seven-years-old

Puddle to puddle
Crickets playfully jumping
Happy rainy day.
—Jimmy, seven-years-old

At the end of that school year, ALL of the students' original compositions (words and notations) were collected and copied and put together in a booklet for each student to take home and have forever. They also each had a tape recording of their melodies and their groups playing on the Orff instruments to accompany the songs. The students especially loved the tapes because they were the ones playing their own melodies and harmonies. Each student was able to 'read' ALL the music in the booklet (that is what they had learned) and so could play or sing any of the original songs without the help of a teacher.

During the yearlong study of the Orient, I had the good fortune to have several guest speakers visit the music classes. The first speaker that autumn was Michael Byrne, who had lived in Hokkaido, Japan for a year. He was a guidance counselor at the Sanborn School. He was also a fountain of knowledge and eager to share it with the students. He illustrated his talks with slides and Japanese artifacts. The students loved listening to Mr. Byrne, and he always answered all of their questions.

Charles Mitsakos, Assistant Superintendent of schools in Andover, was another excellent speaker. He had toured Japan as an educator on a grant to assist in setting up the JISEA,(Japanese Institute for Social and Economic Affairs.) This 'Institute' encourages other educators to travel to Japan for the purpose of studying and sharing information. He had much information to offer the children, but most of all about Tokyo, the capital of the country, and Kyoto, the center of cultural life in Japan. I was so elated all I could think was, "How great, to have this mass of information here in Andover from both of these teachers, and…right at my fingertips."

The students were most interested in hearing about Japanese schools and family life. They were fascinated by photos of the Japanese students in uniforms and surprised to learn that all the students were required to study English in addition to Japanese. Also, Japanese students were required to take an active part in keeping their school clean and attended school five and a half days a week. The slides also showed a classroom of students who, when finished with their work, clasped their hands behind them and waited for the teacher to give the next lesson or order. The Japanese believe that hands that are not idle and free to roam will not get into mischief.

The slides and lectures about Japanese family life, especially the emphasis on courtesy to each other and guests, also interested our students. Dr. Mitsakos had slides of a typical Japanese home with 'paper thin' sliding walls, the bedding, and of a mother serving food to all her family and then eating last and alone.

He also had numerous slides of the beautiful shrines, pagodas and gardens in Japan as well as of fans, umbrellas, screens and other numerous works of art. In 1980, before computers were so widely available, Dr. Mitsakos slides were a wonderful resource for my class.

Our third visitor was Kashiko Nagasugi, a young lady from Kobe, Japan. She was an exchange student studying at Andover High School. The students fell in love with her immediately. She had a charming manner, a lovely smile and a great 'giggle' whenever something funny arose. Kashiko arrived wearing a gorgeous kimono and the slippers that accompany it and spent most of the day with us. I invited another music teacher from the Bancroft School to come with two of her classes since I was very sure they too would learn from this lecture, although they were not participating in my year long Oriental venture. Kashiko shared numerous stories and photos with the classes and we could have listened to her for weeks I'm sure. She did come back another time to visit with our Sanborn students. She was so well liked, kind, amusing and extremely gentle, that I am sure many students still have some memories of Kashiko tucked away in their minds.

Joyce Chen Chinese Restaurant

In order to broaden the children's experience, I arranged for all the students in the upper grades to go to the famous Joyce Chen Chinese restaurant in Boston.

I wrote to Joyce Chen early in the year about my music project and what I was hoping to accomplish. She agreed to help out to the point that when we were there, she was dressed in her native costume and helped her staff serve our meal. She explained to the students about the food, how to use chopsticks, and other customs in China. We were seated at five tables, yet she made sure each student could see and hear her. She demonstrated the use of kitchen items and table scarves and she had many photographs to share. She also let some of the students touch her clothing and brought in dolls and other small items found in a Chinese home for the children to examine. The students listened attentively while she talked and I was proud of them.

In order for all the upper class students to participate in a meal at Joyce Chen's Chinese restaurant, we had to make three trips into Boston's Chinatown. The bus was full for each of those three trips. At the end of one of those trips, the sweetest thing happened. Joyce Chen stood near the doorway to say "goodbye and thank you for coming" to each of the children and Chris Workman, a sixth grade boy, happened to be first in line. Joyce Chen was short, almost the same height as Chris. When he went to say good-bye, he put his arms up and gave her a big hug, which she returned! Therefore, each and every boy in line did the same thing without a moment's hesitation. It was a dear and sweet moment, and I wished I had had my camera with me. I could never have planned this to happen; it was just one of those loving and significant events in the life of a teacher.

Oriental Expressions

All our work and studies about the Orient and pentatonic music scales culminated in an 'Oriental Expressions' performance written and directed by me in the spring of 1983. A chorus of 100 children stood on step risers on the left side of the stage. The Orff instruments, xylophones, metallaphones, and basses were lined up along the front of the step-risers while the musicians for each instrument would be kneeling on pads behind the instruments. They accompanied the chorus when it sang.

On the opposite side of the stage was a bed with a little boy sleeping. The center of the stage was reserved for Japanese pantomimes and Box Plays (an old custom of Japan where a small drama was literally performed in a 'box') with curtains opening and closing for the different scenes.

The program opened with a boy in the bed having a dream saying, "I just do not understand what Mrs. Guziejka keeps saying and what she wants us to do. She keeps saying, 'the Pentatonic Scale, the Pentatonic scale' and I don't understand it. I just do not understand what she means."

At that point, the pentatonic scale appeared on the stage (six boys in black costumes and each with one large note—*do, re, mi, sol, la, do*—attached to their costume). These 'notes' talked to the boy in the bed and sang acappella to demonstrate harmony in the pentatonic scale.

Following the explanation, the boy jumped out of bed and exclaimed, "I know what she means now. I know the pentatonic scale and I can sing it, I know I can..." The boys who represented the notes of the pentatonic scale invited him to sing with them, and all seven boys sang a song I had composed about the

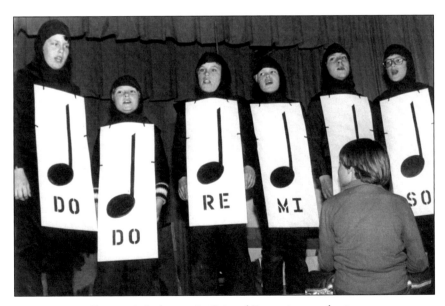

Pentatonic Scale notes in Oriental Expressions production

pentatonic scale in beautiful a cappella three-part harmony! The boys each had a solo and eventually all sang again in three-part harmony. It was a great opening; the audience loved it and I loved it!

The remainder of the play involved pantomimes and 'box plays' that came to life in the boy's dreams. We had narrators telling about customs in Japan and the chorus sang complimentary songs accompanied by the students playing the Orff instruments. One of the pantomimes was particularly outstanding: 'Nagara River at Gishu.' The curtain opened on a scene of fishermen in a boat. Not one of the students moved AT ALL during the scene, not even their eyes, because I had assigned each one of them a spot to stare at so they would look like they were statues. They held their poses while the chorus sang songs in the three-part harmony I had composed to go with the scenes.

Students pantomiming Japanese fishermen

After several of the songs and the 'two plays in the box' were finished (my daughter, Amy, acted in one of the plays in the box with Marcia, her friend,) there was a surprise for the audience. The entire third grade (two classes of approximately 60 children) appeared in the body of a dragon. The leader of the dragon body wore the head, and the fabric of the body was long enough to cover the entire two third grade classes. It snaked through the audience while the music played as our chorus sang.

The Sanborn School art teacher, Jim Bachelder, had helped students to create the dragon's head and body. In fact, when he learned of my plans to focus our musical studies on the Orient for most of the year, he decided to focus on Japanese art in his classes. The students' artwork was beautiful and included Japanese screens that graced our hallways. Visitors always had something interesting to look at that year when they entered the school.

During the intermission of the play, slides were shown on the stage to the tape-recorded accompaniment of original music composed by the fifth and sixth grade students. Toward the end of the performance there was a parade of Tannabata trees carried by individual students through the audience. All the trees had been constructed in art classes throughout the year. The art teacher and I collaborated beautifully the entire year!

The whole show was wonderful and seemingly enjoyed by all, except one man. I can still see him in my mind as he stood in the audience and said loudly, "This is the worst mess that I have ever seen in my life! It stinks!" And then after a few more awful words…he grabbed his daughter and stormed out the door. I was upset, not for myself so much, but in fear some children would have heard him. Unfortunately, his own child heard since she was standing next to him. I am sure she was absolutely heart broken after what her father said and did. My heart ached for her.

My husband and Mrs. Pringle, the writer from England, and her husband Charles, who were visiting us for three weeks, were furious about the whole incident as were other parents who witnessed this man's explosive temper. I am guessing he may have been inebriated, which might explain but does not excuse his bad manners. It was a sad way to end a fabulous evening and most particularly for his little girl!

However, I was exceedingly thrilled that the 'Oriental Expressions' program was written up in the Croydon Newspaper in England. Mrs. Pringle wrote up a wonderful report for the newspaper in the city where Ed and I had lived while I was on sabbatical in England.

Following the 'Oriental Expressions' program, the fifth and sixth grade students recorded their self-composed songs and harmonies at a seminary not too far from the Sanborn School. I wanted each student to have a recording of the music he/she had made during the year. We went to the seminary because they had the necessary recording equipment. With the permission of the students' parents, small groups of students went to the seminary after school to make the recordings. Sanborn School reading specialist Sheilagh LaMontaigne and my husband and a few parents helped with this massive project. Therefore, each student had his own personal tape recording of ALL the original songs and accompaniments as well as a booklet with a copy of each of their original compositions. We were even able to include photos from the performance of 'Oriental Expressions.' It was quite a year!

> *Rain has fallen*
> *And a rainbow has just formed*
> *The storm is over.*

> **—Julie Develis, 11 years old**

An Anthem of Peace

At some point during the years after I returned from my London sabbatical I began to compose many melodies using the pentatonic scale. Also, Poland was in the news for the battles it was having while trying to gain its freedom, and I was moved to compose a poem about freedom. I titled it, *An Anthem of Peace*, subtitled *A Polish Anthem*.

An Anthem of Peace

In liberty be free
Be free to form a choice
In liberty be free
Be free with heart and voice

With heart and voice we firmly sing
A song of love to this the King
Of peace and brotherhood
Praise God let all rejoice

In peace and in unity
We march along
With brotherhood nurturing
We sing out strong

It's freedom's call
For one and all
Then mankind will live again
Will live again!

At this time in my life, I can't remember exactly which came first to my mind, the poem or the melody I composed to accompany it, but I worked on it at home many, many evenings to the point where it became a bit of an addiction.

Eventually, I was satisfied with the melody, but I needed someone to harmonize it for me and develop music for the piano and band. I did not feel I had the musical knowledge and skill to do that properly. I decided to call Colin Evans, my musician friend in England who had been such a help to me.

"I would be glad to do it. Just send it along Mary and we will come up with something good!" I was thrilled with his reply and quickly said, "Oh, Colin, it will be in tomorrow's mail!" Well it was, and he did compose the accompaniment

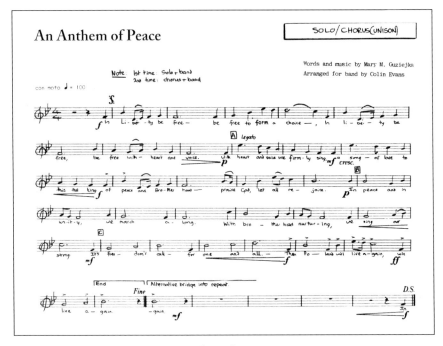

Anthem of Peace

to my melody. Then, using his accompaniment for piano, he wrote a complete score for band. I was not very adept at composing scores for band, therefore I was quite excited!

As a result, I decided to see if a music company would publish the song. I sent it to ten publishing companies and nine of them sent back FORM letters stating simply that they liked it but could not use it now. The tenth one sent a personal letter explaining that in order for any publisher to publish my *Anthem of Peace*, I would have had to send in nine more original pieces to be published

Anthem of Peace, first page as scored by Colin Evans.
(Complete version of the score printed in Appendix)

to make it worth their while financially. This gentleman obviously knew I had never done this before...and he could not have been nicer. I called him on the telephone a few times and we talked and he suggested what I could do. He was very sweet and understanding and filled with ideas. I was disappointed, but kept on sending my anthem hither and yon.

In the meantime, word about my anthem was spreading in Andover and at my alma mater, Lowell State Teachers College. The band members of an undergraduate class played the anthem and I attended the performance with a large group of family and friends. As a result, a reporter from the *Lowell Sun* newspaper interviewed me and wrote an article about me and the *Anthem of Peace* that covered nearly a full page of the newspaper.

> **An Anthem of Peace**
>
> Tuesday, March 30, 1982
> 4:00 p.m.
>
> University of Lowell
> Durgin Hall Lowell, Ma.

> **You are cordially invited to attend an Open Recording Session of**
>
> **A Polish Anthem**
>
> Mary Beakey Guziejka
> Music & lyrics
> Music Specialist—Andover Public Schools
>
> Colin Evans
> arranger
> co-ordinator of music
> City of London & Tower Hamlets, England

Then, it spread from there. I found myself attending different churches in Lowell where the choruses sang my anthem using Colin Evan's four-part vocal harmony accompanied by his piano arrangement. My anthem was also sung in several churches in Andover. Everett Collins, the music director at an Andover church, had his choir sing my *Anthem of Peace* in church and invited me as a guest. The four-part harmony was so beautiful it gave me shivers up and down my spine. Then at the end of the performance he asked me to stand and nod and bow…I was thrilled, I had a hot face and I wanted to hug Everett, but that was not quite the time and place.

Another performance I remember was on the 4th of July in Andover. The Town Band was seated in an old-fashioned band stand in the park. I will never forget that memorable day! Each time I happen to drive by the old-fashioned band stand now I recall the band playing, along with *America* and the *Star Spangled Banner*… **my** *Anthem of Peace.*

I even sent a copy to Luciano Pavorotti and to my amazement he personally answered with a lovely note of congratulations and wishes for my success written on his notepaper, which had a photo of him on the front cover. (I still have it here somewhere in my assortment of 'precious junque'!)

I also sent one to our President in Washington D.C. at that time. All I received was a stock, pre-printed 'thank you' in acknowledgement. I was disappointed in a way, but not really surprised at the impersonal reply.

Unfortunately, my *Anthem* never did become published for whatever reasons. Maybe I was not assertive enough, since I was so very busy at school working on the 'Oriental Expressions' production.

But most satisfying of all for me, was when the children in my Sanborn School asked at the start of each class, "Please Mrs. Guziejka, could we sing your anthem first?" Who could ask for more?

"And these our lives,
Exempt from public haunt
Find books in running brooks,
sermons in stone,
And good in everything."

As You Like It
—Shakespeare

At some point during these years back in Andover, I began thinking about how much I had enjoyed our year in England. Ed had also enjoyed the experience and wanted to live abroad again. I remembered the Broe sisters, Barbara and Ginny, who were a year ahead of me in high school and college. After they had graduated from college in 1951, they went to work for the Department of Defense Dependent Schools, DODDS, which had just begun operating some schools for students of military families on bases outside of our country.

I decided that was something I would be interested in doing. I thought then was as good a time as any to change jobs and live abroad for several reasons. One, and a most important one, was "more money," and another was the interest and excitement we all found while living and studying abroad our one year in England. Traveling and living overseas broadens the horizons, no question of that. I also felt it would be not only a major education for me but for my entire family, and most especially Amy, who would be in high school. Also, since my husband could not work at all due to his health issues there was little money coming in to our home.

I sent for an application, but told no one about my plans except Ed. Hard to believe now as I write this memoir, but I was afraid I was too old and would not be hired. With fear and great trepidation I began the long process of submitting the application. Meanwhile, I continued to work in Andover.

However, during the third year of teaching at the Sanborn School after my sabbatical, things began to change. The school district had a new Director of Music who seemed to take a dislike to me. I had always worked hard and accomplished much but for some reason she decided she wanted me to leave or change jobs or teach only part-time.

One day while teaching a first grade music class, she decided to observe my teaching methods. She came in *one* day, then the *second day*, and then *each* day during the whole week, which is stringently against our teacher's contract. As a result I became quite nervous. She was not friendly while doing these observations, as she had been in the recent past. I could not imagine why she was doing this. Usually we were observed twice a year, two classes, at the most, maybe three classes, and of course, 'written up,' meaning critiqued based on the observations and given a 'grade.'

The next week I was called into the principal's office for a meeting. The principal said she had decided she would 'let me' go to work two afternoons at the Bancroft School, which was on the other side of Andover. I left her office completely flummoxed, trying to understand and figure out how I could accomplish such a thing since my regular teaching schedule was quite full.

Before this was resolved, I was called in to confer with the Director of Music. She told me (and I have *never* forgotten these words,) "Mary, I feel you are too old to teach a full day now." I was aghast at that remark, absolutely dumbfounded, amazed. I was only fifty years old. I exclaimed loudly, "What?" She repeated, "I feel you must either retire because of your age, or just teach all the Kindergartens throughout Andover in the mornings and only work a half day."

The next remark was the 'icing on the cake' as far as I was concerned. She stupidly said, "Also, Mary, you must understand, I can hire two teachers out of college for the same price we are paying you here in Andover. Therefore, I would like you to know I intend to hire *two* new teachers from the University of Lowell College of Music." I was so shocked and stunned I absolutely did not know what to say or do.

I was not the sort of person to argue with anyone, much less argue with a superior. The music director and I did talk, but by then I had become a nervous wreck. I eventually left her office not knowing what to do, or where to go, or how to start. I was angry, I can tell you that. I was very angry. I was also in tears, crying all the way home.

The next day I went to see the principal again about my meeting with the music director. She was no help at all with that problem. Also, she still felt I should go to the Bancroft school two afternoons a week to teach starting immediately, not next year.

She could not understand why I found a problem with teaching at the Bancroft School. "After all," she said, "you like to teach music."

I sat rigidly in my chair facing her. I asked, "When will I eat my lunch?" And then I continued with, "How will I be able to work a full day here each day of the week and go there on two afternoons as well?"

The next sentence from the principal has never left my memory. She said, "You can eat a sandwich while you are driving."

She went on to say, "Mary, shorten the times for some of your classes here, then figure out a way to eat while you are driving to the Bancroft School."

I had grown terribly angry; I sat on the edge of my chair and felt as stiff as a board; I faced her with great animosity. I then tried to be firm but did not succeed, and tremblingly I said, "How could that be done? The school is on the other side of the town and one has to go through downtown traffic to get there." I was almost whimpering and deep inside myself, I was annoyed at the way I was handling this conversation.

"You hold the wheel with one hand and eat your sandwich with another!" the principal growled at me. She was not teasing, she never teased…she was absolutely serious.

In all my years of teaching I had never, ever…come across such a person, and been subjected to such utter stupidity. Somehow, I walked out of her office still maintaining my dignity until I saw Dick Valle in the hallway. He was the physical education teacher with whom I had worked closely for years, i.e. with the children in folk and square dancing in his gym. He had also been a big help when I was producing the musical shows with the students. He was wonderful and always there to help.

He looked at me closely and asked, "Hey Mary, what's wrong?" I had tears in my eyes and before I knew it he was holding me in his arms as I cried on his shoulder right there in the hallway. Between tears, and trembling, I told him, "The principal wants me to teach two afternoons at the Bancroft School and eat my lunch on the way over there. She said to hold my sandwich by one hand and the steering wheel by the other!" By now I was sniffling. Meanwhile he had guided me down to his office in the gymnasium, where we could talk.

Dick repeated most firmly, "She can't do that to you, the contract will not allow it. You have to have a lunch period just like all the other teachers." Dick was a strong member of the union! He then added, while patting me on the shoulder, "Don't worry, Mary, I will talk about it to the Union President. The Union will not allow it."

I was a member of the Union, and knew Dick to be a wonderful teacher and a great friend. I eventually was able to pull myself together knowing he would act on this issue immediately. I am not sure how I got home that day, however. Dick was the kind of friend who always volunteered to help me through thick or thin and always kept his word!

Within the next day or two Dick had a report from the union and told me, "Mary, you'll have to work while the issue is going on. You will have to drive to the Bancroft school, eating your lunch somehow, while the case is being considered. I am so very sorry." He put his arm around my shoulder to comfort me. Once again, I was totally dumbfounded. I knew this was not Dick's fault, but then, how could anything like that be a rule anywhere? In my opinion the issue should have been acted on immediately, but then, who was I…only a lowly music teacher.

Well, I managed somehow, when one has to, one does… but meanwhile I felt quite depressed, and the Union was not able to get the issue resolved quickly since it seemed the Principal and Director of Music kept putting off the meeting. They had the power to do that I was told. Also, my Union friends said I had to 'work the issue' while it was going on. I must admit, I was miserable for many reasons. I had been a good teacher, an honest and hard worker for sixteen years in Andover, and yet, I was being 'dumped on' by these two women. I was in such a dither the whole time it was almost unimaginable. I felt as though I was trembling internally as I taught. I tried to be as good as usual with the children, but I must admit, I had a very hard time.

However, at the same time, I was waiting to hear whether I would be accepted by DODDS as a music teacher. I had told DODDS I would go anywhere in the world to teach. I did not want to be fussy. I had been told most new applicants chose Germany first, over all the other places in the world so they could work in and travel around Europe. I thought I might have a better chance to be accepted if I did not list any preferences.

On April 28, 1984, which happens to be my mother's birthday, our mailman, who knew we were looking for something special from the government, came rushing to our door yelling, "You got a letter, you got a letter from the government." I will never forget the look on his face. He was absolutely joyous for me. Then overcome with the excitement of it all he yelled, "I was stationed in Okinawa, when I was in the service…I was stationed in Okinawa…"

I tore open the letter there in the kitchen with Ed, and another friend who happened to be visiting, plus the mailman standing around, and I almost fainted on the spot. Inside was my acceptance with my posting location. "I am going to be stationed in Okinawa!" I shouted.

The mailman looked aghast and tremblingly said, "I didn't open it, I didn't open it, honest I didn't!" as he backed out of the kitchen, afraid we thought he had read the letter. I quickly reassured him I thought no such thing, it was just a natural coincidence. I was 'beside myself' with joy and happiness! I called my family, but told absolutely no friends from school, no one at all.

✹ ✹ ✹

The meeting with the Union, the Principal, the Superintendent and the Music Department Head and me, was finally held the last week of school, probably the second or third to last day of that final week. The entire 'grievance' was torn up in front of the two women. All their complaints against me (and there were quite a few by then) were all destroyed. The Superintendent seemed quite pleased and needless to say, I was relieved and happy. He himself tore the pages into shreds in front of the two administrators while they sat there with 'humiliated and angry' faces.

By then, the school year had ended for the students but we teachers still had two more work days for 'clean up' and end of year meetings. At lunchtime the final day I took a spoon, and tapped the table hard. That was the way that all the 'important' teachers made announcements. I was never a 'spoon tapper,' but I decided that day I would give it a try.

All the teachers stopped talking and looked around to see who was tapping. I was standing while tapping so they did not have far to look. I then announced that I was leaving and moving to Japan to work in Okinawa for the Department of Defense Dependent Schools. One teacher, who always seemed to feel that she knew more than anyone else, hollered out from her seat in a most sarcastic fashion with a huge false smile on her face, "Okinawa is **not** in Japan…you're not going to Japan."

I replied to all one more time and in a ladylike fashion, "Yes, I am going to be teaching in Japan." At that point, a loyal friend stood up and said loudly to the group, "Okinawa is now part of Japan, and has been since the war..." Silence then reigned for a few moments. All was quiet! Then, my lovely and ever faithful true friends became loudly jubilant, all rising from their chairs to hug or kiss or compliment me while wishing me good luck and great fortune. They emphasized that they and the school would miss me.

My DODDS contract ended my career at Sanborn School in Andover. Except for the problem I mentioned during my last year in Andover, I absolutely enjoyed the faculty. Generally speaking, I had made lovely friends of some teachers as well as students and their parents. I enjoyed my sixteen years of teaching in Andover to the fullest! Some of the parents of my students had been wonderful to me, and were most supportive of everything I did...for and with their children. I was sad to be leaving them, but deliriously happy to have been accepted by DODDS.

The Superintendent and I had one more last talk in his office. He congratulated me, but insisted that I sign a contract for a one or two year leave of absence. I truly felt I did not need one, but he convinced me to take it anyway to make certain this career abroad was what I wanted. He was being practical and I was happy for that...so I signed the papers and left singing and humming and smiling!

After the first seven months in Japan, I knew from the bottom of my heart I would never return to Sanborn or Andover or teach anywhere again in the States. I wrote a letter to the Superintendent of Schools in Andover informing him that I was extremely happy overseas and all set to stay where I was, with the Department of Defense Dependent Schools, until my retirement was decided upon by me!

> *Time shall unfold what plaited cunning hides*
> *Who covers faults at last shame them derides*
> *Well may you prosper!*
>
> **King Lear Act 1, Scene 1**
> **—Shakespeare**

Chapter 18
Okinawa

When to the sessions of sweet silent thought
I summon up remembrance of things gone by

Sonnet xxx
—Shakespeare

Okinawa! "How on earth did I ever arrive here?" I said to myself in utter disbelief, knowing full well how, but in a far reaching corner of my mind, I was still puzzled and perplexed and overwhelmed at the fact that I had arrived in Okinawa, Japan, so far away from home and…about to work for DODDS!

Ed and Amy and I exited from the military plane and like one of the Popes (I believe it was Pope John Paul) I almost threw myself on the ground to kiss the earth below the wing of the plane. After 28 hours in a plane from Fairbanks, Alaska, I thought I was going to go out of my mind before reaching terra firma! I still see myself wanting to kneel on the ground and embrace the dirt on the tarmac! I also wanted to thank God we had arrived in Okinawa safely, and for helping me accomplish this major feat, towards which I had worked unfailingly for a long while.

I restrained myself with the greatest of effort; I did not kiss the tarmac, and did the best I could to walk upright into the airplane hanger and then on to whatever else was to come after that. However…hysterical giggles seemed to want to surge forward from my throat and mouth! It was finally the end of what had been a long journey, (not just the almost 28 hour plane ride from Alaska to Okinawa) but the entire process of applying to teach overseas.

Why Okinawa? Well, as I mentioned earlier, I wanted to have the best possible chance to be hired by DODDS. I decided it would behoove me to say I would take any position available in my line of work. (I discovered later that most teachers do not want to go to Okinawa.) Anywhere they would send me would be fine.

I was interviewed at the Lexington, MA Military Air Base in the late winter of 1983 by a gentleman who was the principal of a DODDS school in Spain. (He was so nice to me in the interview I began to hope I would work for him). I prepared thoroughly for the interview bringing with me a portfolio of photographs from my musical productions as well as letters of congratulations from the Andover superintendent and assistant superintendent of schools, as well as letters from parents and other people who had worked with me over the years.

My interview was scheduled to be a half-hour long, but we ended up discussing music and teaching and all for an hour and a half. None of that bothered me, actually the longer I was there, the closer I was to being hired…I hoped. I had no idea during the interview of how much time had gone by, but when I left him, he seemed quite pleased and I felt more confident. I went out into the waiting room and discovered that several other disgruntled people were also waiting for interviews and one of them let me know his feelings.

"You were in there too long! Didn't you know other people were waiting their turn?" he said gruffly.

I was taken aback by his comment. It was the interviewing principal who had led the discussion and allowed it go on for so long. That was not my fault. I looked at the group, a bit embarrassed, and mumbled, "Oh, dear, I am so sorry, he did not dismiss me, and I could not just get up and leave!"

They did not look at me again, and I repeated, "I am sorry," and quickly scurried out of the room heading for home. The man's gruff comments did not upset me though as they might have in the past. Instead, I felt relatively confident. All the way home from the Air Force Base I kept thinking, "He would not have kept me in his office for such a long time had he not liked what I had to say about the school children. And my music teaching...he seemed to like all that I taught! He would have politely dismissed me nearer to the beginning of the interview if he did not like it."

❊ ❊ ❊

As you can imagine, I was elated to receive the good news by mail in late April 1984. The next few months are a blur in my memory at this point. I finished my teaching at Sanborn School in Andover, but did not share my news until the very end of the school year.

But I was busy at home making plans for leaving. Our family had to go through all sorts of medical exams and tests at the Air Force base in Lexington. We 'packed out' as the military calls it; some of our goods went into storage, and some went with us, not on our plane but later on a special ship that takes cargo of that sort. We were not allowed to ship many of our goods to Okinawa. I am not sure why. Maybe the reason was because of money; maybe the country of Japan posted a limit on poundage. (I never could really discover the reason why, but transferring, as we ultimately did, five times during the sixteen years I taught overseas, I discovered the poundage allowed was different at each move and for each country.)

The most difficult part of moving possessions was finding a home for my ebony baby grand piano. One day I was talking with my friend Grace and mentioned my problem. "Mary, I will baby sit your lovely piano. I would love to have it in my home!" Grace played on her own old upright piano nearly every day, but

I had never thought of asking her if she would like my piano in her home. All worked out well, her husband Dana arrived a few days before our departure with a friend or two and a truck. They moved the piano and my 'baby grand' had a lovely home, was practiced on almost daily and tuned each year as long as I lived/worked overseas. She was thrilled and I was equally content knowing all would be well.

And then there was my 82-year-old mother. Several times I begged her to come live with us in Okinawa. She would be considered a family member by the government who would pay for her transportation and give her a food allowance. I was thrilled, but she refused to go to Okinawa with us.

Even the day before we left, I was almost down on my knees pleading with my mother to join us in this adventure. Finally, she exploded at me (which was unusual for her), "I don't want to die in Japan. When the time comes, I want to die here!" I did not ask her again, and I eventually realized she had made the right decision for herself.

❧ ❧ ❧

Our medical work and packing completed, our hugs and kisses and crying finished, we left. Oh my, that was horribly difficult! I can still see, to this day, my daughter Susan standing outside my mother's apartment, crying her eyes out. My mother stayed inside and probably cried, but she would never let herself cry in front of anyone. Leaving my mother at her age and Susan, my oldest daughter, was the hardest thing I had ever done to them and myself in my whole life. But maintaining my sanity and earning some money were both big issues for me at that time. Money was a major issue since Ed had not worked for many years, and would never be able to work again because of his medical problems. Teachers were not well paid at that time, and the expenses kept mounting up.

❧ ❧ ❧

We flew from Massachusetts to an Air Force base in California in a non-military plane. Prior to leaving home, we had been told about our 'perks' by an earnest and excited young woman who worked in the military offices in Bedford, Mass. (She was new on the job and eager to help us.) She explained we could stay in a hotel for a week in California and see all the sights in San Francisco and the government would pick up all the cost.

With great excitement in my voice I said, "*All* the cost?"

She answered sweetly while nodding her head, "Yes, all the cost. Don't worry about a thing. Just enjoy yourselves. It will be so nice," she said, "for you to travel around and see many places and things you always wanted to see before, and… since you have never before been to California…" then she went on as I eagerly listened, "*And* remember," she said pointing her finger at me, "our government will pay *all* your travel expenses."

Well, we did see the sights and sounds of San Francisco and had a wonderful time. San Francisco is a glorious city to visit. We rode the trolley cars, visited the Market Place, the Golden Gate Bridge, and Long Wharf. We hired a car and visited Big Sur and the Redwood Forest where we could walk through trees. I absolutely loved San Francisco and would thoroughly enjoy seeing it again.

Unfortunately, after landing in Okinawa and applying for my travel reimbursement, I learned the woman at the Bedford military base had been wrong about the government covering all our expenses in San Francisco, much to my dismay! It seems she was new in the office, and either misunderstood or thought she was being helpful. Whatever, I learned *nothing* was paid for except the flight! No hotel for a week was paid, no trips were paid, no food, *nothing*! We had submitted a claim with many pages and receipts and all that was necessary, only to find out that all the money we spent on sleeping, eating and traveling, would not be reimbursed! The lady in the office in Okinawa said, "I am sorry but we are only authorized to pay expenses for your family up to twenty-four hours before boarding your flight to Okinawa, and, of course, your flight tickets!"

My face fell down to my toes as I stood there. I had a few moments of panic. We left the States with very little money since there were many items to be taken care of with our moving expenses, repairs to our house, and the like. As I said above, we had been told, in all sincerity, that we could spend a week in San Francisco and *all* expenses would be paid. Now, as my heart sank, I was not at all sure how we were going to manage without the expected reimbursement! We *never* would have stayed a week in an expensive hotel and spent as much money sightseeing had we known; the young lady at the Bedford air base office had made a major mistake! Her last words to us were, "Have a great time!"

Fortunately, there was a female lawyer in the office who overheard my story. She felt very bad about the whole affair and took it upon herself to help us with our affairs. We did not know she would look into the case. She did not say anything because she was not sure she would be successful in getting us reimbursed for our expenses, but she felt bad for us and thought that the fault lay with the military in not properly training the girl who had helped us in the Bedford, Massachusetts office prior to our leaving.

Many months after we had been in Okinawa and I had almost given up hope of retrieving any of the money, we received a check in the mail for most of our expenses in San Francisco. Oh joyful day! Once it was all settled we met with the lawyer who had taken on our case unbeknownst to us. She was as happy as a lark and told us so. Ed and I hugged her and thanked her profusely many times! As we walked out of her office, I felt like I was walking on a cloud!

❧ ❧ ❧

From California, we were to fly to Fairbanks, Alaska, to board a military plane to Okinawa. For some reason the plane to Alaska was delayed for at least 12 hours. Amy, our 14-year-old daughter was still upset about being uprooted from her home and forced to go with us to Okinawa. She was sad and soulful looking and would not talk with anyone or do anything except sit and stare into space. My heart ached for her, but I did not know what to do.

There were many other military families in the airport's waiting area. At some point, a young man came up to us and asked if he could speak with me privately. I went off with him alone.

"I know that girl is your daughter and I feel very bad for her, she seems so unhappy. Would you allow me to sit and talk with her?" He was so nice and earnest, I mulled over his offer. I knew how miserable Amy was and so I decided it might help her to have a new friend.

"I know what she is going through. I went through the same thing with my family once. I come from a military family and we traveled all over and I just did not want to go with them when I was her age," he added. I immediately gave this polite young Air Force man permission to speak to Amy. He told me he was eighteen years old and on his first assignment and it happened to be Okinawa.

They started talking. Amy seemed reluctant at first and then, the next thing we heard, after several minutes, was Amy...giggling. Then after another little while, I could hear more giggles, then more, then she and the young man walked around the waiting area; due to the delay one could not just sit and sit and sit. It seemed, if only temporarily, she was having a pleasurable time with this polite young man. After a while, when Amy had gone to the ladies' room I asked him how he was able to make her laugh and seem so much happier. He replied rather sheepishly, "I told her some dirty jokes!"

❧ ❧ ❧

We eventually arrived in Fairbanks, and there boarded another plane for our 24-plus hour ride to Okinawa. Amy wanted the window seat; Ed needed the aisle seat, which left me in the middle seat again! On the military plane there was even less legroom than on a commercial flight. Once the plane was underway, and I could get up from my seat, I think I 'walked' to Okinawa. I paced miles and miles up and down the huge, long plane while everyone else slept. I was too keyed up to be able to sleep, and besides there was not much room in my seat with the overflow of arms and legs from Ed and Amy on either side.

During my walk, I discovered the hostesses had an area in the plane where they could take turns either sleeping or just resting. There were two sets of bunk beds and a long, ceiling to floor, dark cloth to be drawn to cover them from prying eyes (like mine) while they were sleeping. I was so naïve about flying in those days I had no idea that bunk beds would be available for these long trips. I was happy the hostesses had an opportunity to sleep or at least rest, on a sojourn such as this one, one that went on forever, it seemed. Well…I felt it went on forever!

The hostesses were quite nice. A couple of them talked and talked with me, asking "Where was I going, what was I going to do and where had I come from and what made me make this decision to go so far away from home?" which helped pass the time. When I could no longer walk from utter fatigue I crawled over my husband's sleeping body, ensconced myself in the middle seat, but truly, could not sleep. I could not close my eyes for one minute during that long flight! Excitement, anticipation and middle seat discomfort caused me to be awake for the whole ride to the Okinawa airport!

*"If music be the food
of love, play on"*

**Twelfth Night
—Shakespeare**

We were met at the Okinawa airport by a 'meeter greeter.' Her name was Carol Cook and she taught first grade at the Bob Hope Primary School where I was to be positioned. I was extremely grateful to have her help since I was so exhausted I thought my mind had left me for good. I could hardly walk, let alone think since we had had virtually no sleep for almost three days. I absolutely could not think at that moment.

She explained it was her responsibility to see us through the next four or five days of our entrance to Okinawa, the school and billeting and all that goes with it. I must say she did an excellent job. She delivered us, with our tons of baggage, to the beautiful Hotel Hilton. The next three or four days with her were all a whirr and a blur as she led me around, somewhat like a mother with a dim witted child! I was extremely grateful to have her with us because of all the 'red tape', meaning all the offices we had to find and all the questions to answer and all the forms to fill out. "Thank God for Carol," was all I could think of over and over again.

Okinawa and the Hotel Hilton were absolutely gorgeous. The hotel was situated at the top of a hill, on the narrowest part of the island, only two miles wide, from the Pacific side to the East China Sea side. Fortunately, we had two rooms (one for us and one for Amy) with balconies that overlooked each side. I still could not actually believe we were in Okinawa, Japan; we had arrived, we were here and we were SAFE. All I could do was look around and stare and pinch myself, and tell myself I had made it, I am in Japan, I had a new job and *All would be well!*

The Okinawan people were polite, cordial, welcoming, and smiling all the time. On entering the hotel for the first time we were met with warm and cordial bows by everyone. I loved it. We slept for what seemed like hours after we arrived.

Then sometime the next day, (I knew we had not slept enough) Carol Cook tapped on the door and off she and I went to more offices to fill out more papers. The paper work, seemingly, went on forever! Eventually it was finished and we, all the new teachers, (I was not the only one), were shown to our individual schools.

Amy had to sign up at her school also, the Kubasaki High School, which was not on the base where I would be teaching. It was on another base further away. I do not remember how many bases there were on Okinawa but there were several. Amy took a bus trip each day from the hotel and later from our home and became acquainted with many high school students and eventually, began to enjoy herself!

❦ ❦ ❦

The young Japanese ladies who worked in the offices of the hotel were in native dress. To me, they were fascinating. They had lilting high voices, and would greet us with a lovely bow and 'konnichiwa.' Then, we were taught to say, 'O-hi-o Gazaimas' and bow while saying it, which was in response to their initial greeting. As we became more familiar with the greetings we added, 'doh itaschi machite!'

We stayed in the Hilton Hotel for more than three months. *Yes*, I was going to work every day from the fancy Hilton Hotel. Housing was scarce and we were on a year's waiting list to be eligible for a military housing unit. Every morning upon waking I had to pinch myself to make sure that I was really in Japan, and I was about to go to school and teach children to love music!

During our stay there, we discovered the owner of the hotel was from Lowell, Massachusetts where my husband and I were born and brought up! We learned the man had even attended Keith Academy in Lowell, where my husband attended high school. We never met the owner, although I did try to find him. I wrote a letter to him but never received an answer. I was told he had married a Japanese lady. His father had been in the scrap metal business during World War II and his company reclaimed masses of metal debris left on the Pacific Ocean floor from the ferocious battles. The business prospered, and he was able to buy the Hilton Hotel property years later.

Bob Hope Primary School

Bob Hope was revered by the Okinawans for all the good work he had done for the people on the island. The Japanese fought against and almost annihilated all the Okinawans; after a time, the Americans rescued those that were left and that is where Bob Hope entered the picture. He visited each year with his troupe of performers and raised money for the poor people who were left without homes after the war. He also lifted the morale of the Americans who were stationed there during the war and certainly aided the Okinawans who were left homeless up and down the island.

The Bob Hope Primary School is where I was assigned to teach. It was huge, larger than any school I had ever worked in. The second school near us, on the same large plot of land and built in the same style and equally as large, was the Amelia Earhart School. The schools held approximately a thousand children each, from kindergarten through third grade in the Bob Hope School, and fourth through sixth grades in the Amelia Earhart School. The students were all from military families or families connected with the military in other ways.

I had classes of thirty children, six classes a day, all day long and I only saw them for music one period a week. My room was in a wing that jutted out in the back of the very large, square building; the 'wing' was like a large, fat finger built outside of the big building and beyond my room was the Gym. All of this was towards the back of the major building. (It was a long walk to the ladies room that was in the main building, but thankfully on the first floor!)

I only had time in my schedule to teach first, second and third graders, no time for kindergarteners, (once in a while I would be able to invite a kindergarten class to come in and share music with a first grade; that was appreciated by the kindergarten teachers.) Such a full schedule was hard for the teachers and I felt sorry for the students. My classes were forty-five minutes long, which is too long for first and second graders, they were too young, but we managed…since I could be most inventive when the need arose.

❊ ❊ ❊

In the DODDS organization one makes friends quickly who often prove helpful and loving through the years. (Even now that I have been retired for eleven years, a few of us keep in touch with one another.) They all helped me to pull my way through the beginning and the remainder of my time abroad. Most of these people had been with DODDS for a long while and therefore knew how difficult it was for families to adjust easily or quickly to another country and its language and its customs. One always needs a support team and in Okinawa I found one.

Shortly after the school year began, the teachers at the Bob Hope School organized a day at the beach for all the teachers of the military schools in Okinawa. There was to be a picnic, boating and swimming. I knew no one at that point and hesitantly, I looked at the stranger who invited me to go and I said, "Yes…I would love to go to the picnic." Well, how else would I become acquainted with all these new people? The veteran teachers arranged for a large boat and the food and everything else one can imagine needing for such an outing.

I asked Ed and Amy to join me. But Ed said, "Mary, my back hurts, I'm too tired and I could not stand being in the sun all that time!" Okinawa's sun is wonderful, but relentless! Amy, who was still grumpy and exhausted from the entire move muttered, "I don't want to go, Mom! You go without me." Amy never usually refused a trip to the beach, but this time she did. So I went on the outing by myself.

Somehow, I found my way to the boat, but do not ask me how since I don't remember. Probably some of the teachers from my school met me at the hotel. I know I went on a boat ride in a large Okinawan fishing boat, but after that, I only remember sand, sea, surf, exhaustion and…Madonna.

At some point, I wandered away from the big group. I ambled along on the sand alone and either I saw Madonna Russo first, sitting in the water, or she saw me first. It does not matter, since she invited me to sit down in the water with her. She was also new to Okinawa and did not have any friends yet either.

Mary G. right, Madonna Russo, center, and another friend enjoying an Okinawa beach

The two of us sat there on a small island in the shallows of the Pacific Ocean talking and talking and talking about her, about me…about our jobs and our families and how she happened to teach in Panama before coming to Okinawa and on and on! We have been good friends ever since. Madonna and I have not stopped talking yet, although she is in Minnesota and I am in New England! We talk on the telephone now and again, no sand, sea or surf for us at this time. She, being much younger than I, as most of the teachers were, is still working in a school in Minnesota.

While in Okinawa, she and I became walking buddies, we both loved to walk miles in the evening on the base and also traveling buddies and over time, even though she moved away and I moved somewhere else, ours has remained a loving and happy friendship!

"Shall I compare thee to a summer's day?
Thou art more lovely, more temperate…

Sonnet XV111
—Shakespeare

❧❧❧

"I talk in order to understand;
I teach in order to learn…"

—Robert Frost

After the shock of so many classes and their length wore off, plus the facing of such a large and full schedule, I decided I had to do something about this whole teaching mess. All my younger students in the States only had thirty-minute classes per day. It is too difficult for children that young to sit in class for a long time, and pay attention to one type of lesson. (It was also difficult for me, the teacher, since I needed change as well.)

I could not sing all day for all those hours and hope to teach the students anything, or worse, I would fall apart and so would they. Therefore,I became inventive. I decided that I had to do some dancing and singing. I had brought my favorite recordings of folk dancing and square dancing. I also decided we would sing and act out the songs, or pantomime to the music, as befitting the words of the songs. On a regular day, before starting what I called my bigger projects, I divided the class time into two portions; fifteen or so minutes for folk dancing, and the other thirty minutes or less, would be devoted to learning how to sing.

On several occasions I had a television rolled in. The school had a few of them on wheels, and I showed pertinent sections of the movies *Sound of Music*, the *Wizard of Oz* and *Heidi*. I also used my favorite Kodaly hand signals to better the tone quality in their singing, and some instruments to demonstrate the rhythm and beat found in all music. One cannot have one without the other. (We did not have any Orff Instruments at that time in Okinawa, which was sad.)

It was difficult teaching at first, not knowing names, and having so many students all day long with no breaks except lunch (and the occasional bathroom break when I could find someone to supervise my class for a few minutes.) However, the children seemed to love me and I loved them, so there was no problem there. Since we all got along so well together and the class singing, after a while, was beginning to sound glorious to me, I decided we must do a musical show! I decided I would start with the second graders and produce the *Wizard of Oz*.

Wizard of Oz

I played around with many options in my mind for a few nights about how I could involve as many students as possible in the production. There were about 360 children in the second grades alone. I decided I would teach the songs to all the students in the second grade. It took much time after school as well as during school. However, the children loved the *Wizard of Oz* story and their singing and acting improved and they learned how to work in large groups.

I discovered quickly that the children in the Bob Hope Primary School loved all the songs I taught them and thus, sang them very well. They also were all 'finding' their singing voices. Some children just sing almost automatically while others who may never, ever hear singing in their homes, or for whatever other reasons, have to be taught to sing and to sing on pitch. I told the second graders about my plan to put on the play *The Wizard of Oz* for their parents and friends. They were thrilled, quite excited about the whole idea.

The next problem was to decide how to fairly choose students for the speaking parts. I sent letters home explaining everything to all the parents. To have a speaking part, the student had to be able to stay after school for at least two afternoons a week in the early part of the rehearsal, and almost daily the week before the show went on. There were no late buses, so a parent would have to be able to pick up their child after school. Since some students had to take the bus home, this limited the tryout pool.

The drama tryouts came and went, and the parts were given out and…no second grader was left out of the production. All were either in the chorus or in one of the speaking/singing roles, and all worked out beautifully. I had never before worked with such a large group of children to stage a musical. We had, roughly, three hundred and thirty children in the *Wizard of Oz* production and all went well! I was delighted at their understanding of the performance and their pride in the overall production!

One of the major 'hurdles' to overcome was deciding on the student to play Dorothy. Two identical twins, Heidi and Becky, tried out for the role. Both were good actresses and sang beautifully. My brain worked overtime deciding which one to choose and how to make both happy with the decision. Then, I came up with what I thought was a brilliant solution…I decided to have them both play Dorothy. One would perform for the first half of the show and one for the second and they were not to tell anyone, it was to be a big surprise! (I could never tell the two girls apart myself. Keeping this secret from their parents may have been the most fun of all, until we got to the costume part and then, of course, they had to explain what was about to happen in the show!)

Wizard of Oz production, Okinawa, Japan

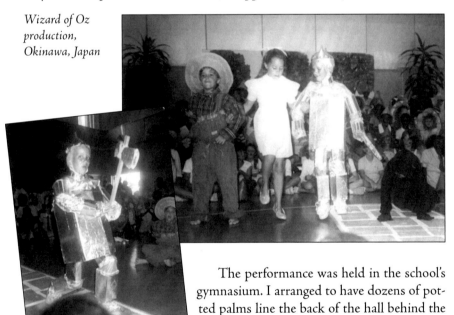

The performance was held in the school's gymnasium. I arranged to have dozens of potted palms line the back of the hall behind the audience. The first Dorothy was to sing and act and when she reached the end of the yellow brick road at one point in the script, about halfway through the performance, she then would spin around and hide in a group of palms! Then the second Dorothy would come out of hiding and continue on as if nothing unusual had happened. The two girls playing Dorothy were totally indistinguishable, one from the other!

Becky and Heidi had on identical clothing, their hair was the same, their voices were absolutely beautiful and identical and their acting was indistinguishable from one to the other! No one would know the shift had been made unless it was a teacher helping out in the back of the hall or their parents.

At the end of the show there was tremendous applause and when it died down, I introduced the actors. I started with the lesser parts first, with each actor bowing while I played music appropriate to their roles on the piano.

Then it was time to reveal the secret. "Will Dorothy come out and take a bow?" The audience went wild. Dorothy sweetly skipped out as I played my accompaniment and she curtsied to the audience. Then, when the audience calmed down I said, "Will the other Dorothy come out and take a bow?" The audience looked puzzled. I played the entrance music once again, and out came the other twin from behind the tall potted palm trees to the front of the gym. There they stood, both Dorothy's, holding hands and as identical as could be, smiling from ear to ear! The audience went wild. It was such a lovely and beautiful night, and I was proud as punch!

The production could not have happened without the help of many of the parents and the art teacher at the school all of whom sewed costumes, painted scenery and did whatever else was needed to help put on such a large musical. They were exceedingly generous at all times and showed much appreciation to me for all I was doing for their children. They were always available to help me for the three years I worked in Okinawa! The military families were the best; helpful, grateful and always available when I needed someone.

It is so very important to have students feel good about themselves. I wanted all the students to have as many loving and different experiences as I could possibly give them. All of these experiences contributed positively to the children's inner feelings about themselves. To this day I still believe that if a child feels *good*, about him or herself…via the mediums of music, art and physical education, the day-to-day learning in the normal classroom will move along as well and at a great pace!

> *"As we advance in life, it becomes more difficult,*
> *but in fighting the difficulties*
> *the inmost strength of the heart is developed"*
>
> **—Vincent Van Gogh**

Korea

If all the year were playing holidays
To sport would be as tedious as to work;
But when they seldom come, they
Wishe'd for—come!

Henry the Fourth
—Shakespeare

When the two-week Christmas break arrived during our first year in Okinawa, I was ready for it. I had talked with other teachers who had traveled extensively, and decided since I had such a small budget, that we would go to Korea.

"Why Korea?" some teacher friends asked, "My goodness, there are other more exciting places!" Well, for one, we could travel to Korea on a 'space available' basis, meaning Ed, Amy and I would only have to pay ten dollars each for a ride on a military plane if there was space available. (I cannot remember if we paid $10 each way or for a round trip.) Other teachers had praised the advantages of 'space available' flights for saving money. The option sounded good to me, but I had a lot to learn!

I was intrigued by everything about Seoul, Korea at that time because we could stay in a military-owned hotel at very little cost and we could fly to Seoul so inexpensively. At that time, Seoul had a population of about eight million people. I have since learned from a friend who teaches at a private school in Korea, that the city's population is almost eleven million people. The underground rail system in the city comes and goes at an average rate of one every three to five minutes all day and night. Amazing!

The other factor that attracted us to Korea was the opportunity to visit the DMZ, 'demilitarized zone'. Many teachers at my school in Okinawa had talked about it and told us what an interesting area it was.

Our trip to Seoul, Korea was on a military medical flight. It was comfortable enough, but unusual because there were not many seats, and those were faced backwards to accommodate the sick and wounded soldiers in their beds. However, the plane was spotlessly clean and the military nurses were wonderfully nice to us 'civilians.'

Since I had only been working for DODDS for four months, we were relative novices at traveling elsewhere for vacations. I am not sure how we got to the military hotel where we were staying. It must have been by taxi. I was a bit numb with the excitement of actually being able to travel to Korea.

The hotel was great. It was big and comfortable, just the same as if we were home in Boston. The doorman for the hotel was unusual though. He must have been seven feet tall. He was certainly the largest man I had ever seen. He wore a tall, black, all fur hat; the hat itself had to be at least twelve inches high. He also wore a long and heavy overcoat, a fancy one with shiny buckles, and high boots on his feet. The hat was the kind you would see worn by the guards at Buckingham Palace. He was polite, and most caring, but never smiled. He was just intent on doing his business.

We had a nice room for the three of us with a television. We unpacked, rested a bit and then started out for a place called *Itewan Street*. Everyone we knew on the base had told us that we, '*absolutely must*' go to Itewan Street first thing upon our arrival. It was a famous shopping area where everything was at least sixty to seventy percent cheaper than in the USA or on our base or anywhere in the world.

Our teenage daughter, Amy, was with us, and as many of you know, teenagers can be stubborn. Although I told her it would be cold in Seoul, she would *not* dress warmly. Well, you guessed it. She froze. We had to keep going into the stores on Itewan Street to let her warm up. The stores were tiny, narrow and long from front to back.

The first store we went into had an oil heater in the center of the narrow long room. Two Korean girls came forward, and seeing Amy was so cold, they smilingly and quickly led her to a chair in front of the little bitty stove with a wood or coal fire and encouraged Amy to sit. That was all the heat they had in their long narrow room.

None of the girls spoke English but they knew Amy was suffering from the cold. One girl quickly stooped down and undid Amy's shoes, (Amy would not wear boots) and the Korean clerk held Amy's feet in her hands until they were warm. It was a touching scene, but I did not take a picture since I thought Amy would be uncomfortable with that. They brought clothes for Amy to try on and boots and mittens. To this day I do not remember what or if we bought her anything, but Amy was smiling broadly and sheepishly the whole time.

Each and every little shop we went into all the sales clerks came forward and tried to entice Amy to either sit and warm herself or talk to them. They were lovely and it was a beautiful sight to behold. I think Amy's height and her long blond hair with loose curls appealed to the shorter Korean shop girls with their straight black hair. The girls just seemed to love Amy everywhere we went.

One day we went to see what turned out to be the Korean Cultural Center. We did not know we were in a Cultural Center, although all the native Koreans were dressed in gorgeous garb, all colors, and robes and head pieces and the like, but, we still had no idea where we were. It was an outstanding old village in the heart of the city of Seoul.

We took some photos and while doing all this searching and seeking and picture taking, a beautifully bedecked young man came forward, bowed low and said the few words he could in English asking to have his picture taken with Amy.

"She is so beautiful, she is so beautiful," he kept saying in his halting English. Amy was shy and giggly at the time but did agree to have her photo taken with him. Later that day, after seeing all we felt we could manage, we took a taxi back to the hotel. We bowed politely to our doorman, the same huge man with the tall black furry hat, and went on to our room.

As was Amy's custom at that time, she flicked on the television the minute she went into the room while we were hanging up coats and things. She was sitting on the foot of her bed with the television just inches away from her, and… the first person she saw was the man who nicely asked to have his picture taken with Amy! Yes! It was the same man. The English translation at the bottom of the screen told us this man was the star of a movie that was being filmed at the Cultural Center!

Amy was absolutely non-plussed. So were Ed and I! We were all excited. Amy watched the whole bit that was on television, it was not the entire movie, but sections of it. I felt they were probably advertising the film! I still cherish the memory of that afternoon and its events to this day.

The DMZ

Ed, Amy and I were able to obtain passes to enter the heavily regulated Demilitarized Zone in Korea. Since I worked directly for our government, we were allowed many, or most, of the same privileges as the military. Therefore, visiting the DMZ was *high* on our list of what we felt and knew was important to see and learn. All who lived in the northern section of Korea, for example, were Communists. The South Koreans on the other hand were all democratic and definitely not wanting Communism or war. Ed and I were both intrigued by the history and we felt Amy would learn much about any place we traveled or visited.

The border separating the two sections of Korea was established in 1953 (the year Ed and I were married) at the end of the Korean War as a barrier between North and South Korea. It is located at the narrowest strip of land in Korea and extends from the Sea of Japan on the East to the Yellow Sea on the west. North Koreans were barred from entering South Korea, and vice versa.

This was one place we did not want to ignore; it had so much history attached to it. We had to see it ourselves. The desk clerk at our military hotel helped us find a taxi-driver to take us on the four-hour round trip to and from the zone. The taxi driver was kind and friendly and explained in his halting English many facets of the DMZ while we drove along. He also pointed out some weird structures made of cement and placed along the highway at seemingly regular distances one from the other. The taxi driver said the huge, box-like cement structures were hiding ammunition of all kinds, i.e. machine guns, bombs etc., although to my eyes they looked like nothing in particular and seemingly had no purpose or reason for being there. There were so many all the way to the border that I lost count.

I cannot recount exactly what the driver said since his English was not such that he could explain things to us in great detail. But, we gathered that South Koreans were going to be able to either set off some kind of bombs toward North Korea and/or whatever one can imagine if the North Koreans unexpectedly attacked South Korea. I am a bit lost on that information since I have never been in a war or seen any of these military launchers or whatever and I am also quite happy to be able to say I haven't!

We happily carried on in the taxi for two hours when we arrived at a pair of huge iron gates. At this point our taxi driver let us out, and told us he would wait for us there. I must have been feeling a bit apprehensive at this point, because I had hoped he would be able to come into the DMZ with us. But that was absolutely against the rules. He wished us luck and thanked us for being Americans and able to enter the area. He and South Korean natives lived in hope of no more war. I thought that anyone who spoke about the DMZ with such prayerful fervor in his voice must have been through some difficult times in the past. We did find him again after we came out of the gates much later, patiently waiting to drive us back to our hotel!

How awful to have war going on around you all the time! We did feel quite honored to have this opportunity to enter the DMZ, which was strictly regulated and open only to U.S. Military. The tour of duty for these military men was for a year at a time only, no longer, and I would imagine that was because it was a difficult, and a most arduous and unsafe life plus, extremely cold all winter.

We were given directions by the guard at the gates of the DMZ after he looked at our papers and directed us to certain buildings. These buildings he told us were where the signings of the famous treaties took place in or around 1952. The following information is taken from my notes and also from information on my computer:

DMZ—Korean Demilitarized Zone: "The military demarcation line (MDL) of separation between the belligerent sides at the close of the Korean War is North Korea's boundary with South Korea. The demilitarized Zone (DMZ) extends for just a little over 1 mile on either side of the MDL. Both the North and the South Korean Governments hold that the MDL is only a temporary administrative line, not a permanent border.

The DMZ is an area of land encompassing a 4 kilometers wide strip of land straddling the 151 mile long MDL. The 27th of July 1953 Armistice Agreement established the DMZ along the approximate line of ground contact between the opposing forces at the time the truce ended the Korean War.

The opposing sides agreed but through all these years North Korea has broken the treaty many times in the air, on the sea and on land and many North Koreans infiltrated and also committed violations at sea and in the air and also infiltrated armed agents along South Korea's extensive coastline and outlying islands. It is in this DMZ area where most violations have taken place."

We also visited the 'Bridge of No Return.' In 1953 this bridge was used to return prisoners of war on both sides who were allowed to make a free choice as to whether they would return to their place of origin or not. As we walked along the pathway in that area, all I could think was, "How grim!"

We walked freely around the U.S.A. side of the DMZ and said "hello" and "how are you" to many soldiers from the U.S. Army. The men who were there had not really, to our knowledge, been out of this area for a long time. At one point, a military truck went by carrying many soldiers. When the driver saw Amy, our beautiful daughter, walking with Ed and me, it came to a full screeching stop. There were whistles, many calls of "Hi and hello and where did you come from?" Amy blushed, beaming her beautiful smile and waved at the soldiers. We all waved and smiled as they drove away and wished them Godspeed and Good Luck! Fortunately, we did have an opportunity to talk to a few soldiers, although, not many since they all seemed to be on duty. Ed shook hands with one or two young men and offered his words of praise telling them, "We are so proud of you, keep up the good work!" They also seemed to enjoy hearing the little accolades and better yet, seeing us.

We left the DMZ thinking how sad the whole situation was. I would have been terrified all the time had I lived there. Also, how terribly difficult it must have been to live in South Korea, or even in North Korea, if you were a common, everyday type of person trying hard to live peacefully and earn a living and raise a family!

The year we visited the DMZ was 1984. I am writing this in 2011 and the conflict is still going on in Korea; there is still much fear and constant worry about when the next bomb will come down on Seoul or anywhere in South Korea and wipe out several thousand people. We returned home to Okinawa with most sober thoughts in our minds…extremely pleased we had been able to see and absorb all this history, but at the same time, so unhappy for the citizens who must live in fear constantly.,

It was on our trip back to Okinawa from Korea that we learned about the disadvantages of traveling on 'space available' flights. When we arrived at the airport on our scheduled day of departure, we were herded with a few other military people onto a very large plane…a cargo plane. What did I know about cargo planes? Very little, except that they must have carried cargo from base to base.

We discovered the few 'seats' there were ran up and down the side of the walls of the plane; fortunately there were not many of us traveling. And the seats were not anything like conventional, individual seats, but rather a firm type of netting. Our bodies sort of spilled over onto other people on each side of us as we sat there. Ed and I put Amy in the middle between the two of us. Eventually the plane started its engines and they roared loudly all the way to our next destination. We had been given head phones as we entered the massive plane to block some of the noise but they did not seem to help very much.

Finally the plane took off and as we flew up into the air we noticed that instead of growing warmer in the plane, since it was freezing cold to begin with, it grew…colder! Yes, and then the cold became even colder to the point where I felt I had blue lips and blue hands. We were absolutely freezing as we sat huddled close together. Most of our two bodies spilled over onto Amy in an attempt to keep her warm, or at least a little bit warmer.

There was a man next to me on my right. He was wearing a leather type jacket and he was very cold as well. After we were in the air for a while he and I talked about the cold and I asked if we would still be alive when we arrived in Okinawa! He suggested we all let each others bodies warm each other, if you can imagine what I mean. At his suggestion we all turned sideways a bit and I hugged my body on his, as Amy hugged mine and Ed hugged Amy's and so forth…that way we all gained more heat than if we sat and faced forward into the cargo plane. (He must have traveled like this before, I thought.) After a while, the backside of the person at the end of our huddle was cold, so the man suggested we all shift our bodies to face the opposite direction. This went on for a very, very long time considering the fact that we had three other bases at which to stop before landing in Okinawa.

The cold was virtually intolerable but then another surprise came our way during the flight. There were no bathrooms on the plane. If one had to 'relieve oneself' one then had to disengage oneself from the long line of turning and freezing bodies and go behind a long, flapping curtain a few feet away. There you could urinate into a pail, and…with everyone else seated and staring. "*No thank you,*" I said to myself after watching a few men use it. I don't think I could have if I had had to, nor did Amy or Ed!

Eventually we arrived in Okinawa and again I felt like prostrating myself onto the warm Okinawan ground to give it great big kisses. Yes, it was a cheap flight but costly in 'cold' bodies. I think it took a few days for us to warm up in the Okinawan sun but thankfully our apartment on the base was warm as Ed and I snuggled up in bed together after long and hot showers!

🌿 🌿 🌿

It was not until we had been living in Okinawa for almost four months that we were finally able to move out of the hotel. It took that long for us to find a small house in Okinawa to rent. (There was still no apartment available for us on the military base.)

The old and decrepit looking house had an Okinawan charm to it and being the only one available we rented it. What a nightmare it was after we were in it for a while! The insects took over…there was one whose name I forget…it was green and like a small snake that roamed the walls of the house. *Argh!* Then, I was told to let it stay, not to kill it since it kills the other insects that were bound to enter the old and poorly built house. *Argh!*

We had a lovely view in the distance of the Pacific Ocean, from the back of our house. That was nice, and while the house had a special Okinawan charm, it wore off after we were in it for a while, actually, a very short while, and the *damp* set in through the winter. Okinawan winters are not cold, but they are undoubtedly damp! January through April we saw no sunshine, so the 'damp' stayed and stayed.

After a few months I developed a severe case of asthma. The American military doctor told me, "Mrs. Guziejka, you must find another house to live in somehow." But before I was able to do that, I developed pneumonia, no hospitalization, thank goodness, but pneumonia nonetheless.

After recovering, I went to the American military housing authority to plead my case. To make a long story short, they were most kind and understanding and found for us a clean, brand new place on the SeaBee Base a few miles from the Kadena Base where my school was situated. I was so lucky. We got moved! The new apartment was spotlessly clean, most American, as opposed to Okinawan. There were four apartments in one building. Each apartment had an upper and lower level. We even had grass outside our back windows, but, sadly, no view of the Pacific. Well, one cannot have everything, I said to myself!

I found I was only about two or three miles away from my Bob Hope School, and that was marvelous! A young lady, Nancy, and her husband, Jim, and their two little boys, who lived next door in an identical apartment, were equally lovely. They were friendly, gracious and generous with their time and anything else one can think of in their attempt to make us comfortable and feel right at home. I have not had pneumonia since! Thank the good Lord!

❧ ❧ ❧

As part of the DODDS contract, we were allowed to return home for several weeks each summer. The cost of this trip was covered by the military. After my first year of teaching in Okinawa, Amy and I decided to go home in June, immediately after school ended. (Ed stayed in Okinawa because the travel was too tiring for him). We spent time with my son Eric in Texas, and then time with my daughter Susan in New Hampshire and my mother in Lowell, Massachusetts. We had missed each other so very much through the year.

On our way back to the States though, Amy and I stopped in Hawaii for a week. We met up with my good DODDS friend Madonna at the military-owned Hale Koa Hotel. The price of the military hotel was quite affordable compared to the commercial hotels, and it was just as lovely.

After we settled in and rested up a bit from the flight, Madonna and some other DODDS teachers who were traveling back to the States, decided we would visit Hawaii's Polynesian Cultural Center. There, villages were assembled for display and study. Their history went a long way back. Every small Polynesian village in that area of the Pacific was fully represented on the island of Waikiki with lovely native people in their local dress, huts, tents, fireplaces, and foods of all sorts; the area itself is huge. I was thoroughly impressed since I had never been to Hawaii before. We also visited the huge volcano that I had seen from my hotel room window. And of course we spent time on the gorgeous white sand beaches with absolutely outstanding waves crashing in on us!

In addition, I toured the Pearl Harbor Memorial area in Hawaii where American ships had been attacked on December 7, 1941. I was ten-years-old in 1941, and still remember now how terrifying the attack was at the time. The tour included a short boat ride to a spot where one of the American ships is still submerged underwater. It was a moving sight that made me feel shaky, even though it had been forty years since the event.

⁂

Madonna had a friend, a doctor in the military who worked at the hospital in Waikiki. He offered to drive a small group of us around the island. He took us to see the huge waves on the other side of the island. They were unbelievably gigantic! It was almost impossible to believe that waves could indeed soar that high into the atmosphere! They are located in the area of Kailua!

We also attended a Hawaiian Luau where we ate native food and watched the dancers. Amy and I loved it. The Hawaiian dancers performed beautifully! We have a great photo taken of us…two or three teachers from our group along with Amy and me and a few native dancers. Delightful!

The doctor also took us to a huge military vessel, and we were allowed to visit it first hand! This was the first time I had ever seen one of this type and up close. I was quite excited! We were allowed to visit inside all the important rooms and the decks, and also…the surgery, which I remember quite well!

Then it was time to leave Hawaii and board our flight to the States for our two-month visit with our family. We all cried buckets at arriving, holding on fast and hard to one another…and also upon leaving, since the eight weeks we were home seemed to move along at a rapid rate.

Second Year in Okinawa

To business that we love
We rise betime and go to't with delight.

Antony and Cleopatra
—Shakespeare

Difficult, it is, to know where to start regarding our second year 'stay' in Okinawa. So much to see, so much to do and my mind kept saying, "Where do we start?" I knew I had to 'start' with my teaching, and make plans for the new academic year in Okinawa.

I knew I also wanted, nay, *craved* to see more of the island and friends, and also to travel further afield if at all possible! Therefore, Ed and Amy and I went to many places, observed many varied events, attended cultural situations, walked all over Okinawa (it seemed) and traveled to many other countries or islands while living there...as many as were possible that I could fit around my teaching responsibilities.

Mary setting off on adventure during one of her many trips while working in Okinawa.

The children in my classes that second year were different and yet the same. Approximately half of them had moved on because their father or mother was transferred by the military. However, as many military families as were transferred *out* of Okinawa, *many more* new families came in! I still had what I called *huge* classes of darling students, little busy-bodies, what else could one expect with five, six, seven or eight year olds?

I braced myself once again and

continued in the pattern I had developed the year before, teaching song, dance and drama. The second year of teaching in a school is always better than the first. I had some of the same students from the year before, although many new ones had moved in! In the beginning, I never knew whether I was 'coming or going' or 'who was on first' as they say!

❋ ❋ ❋

Early in that second year, I was approached by a second grade teacher at the school about helping her with a Polish play. The school was planning an open house event for the students' parents where each class would put on an 'international' demonstration of some sort.

The teacher was from Poland and had taught her students a few Christmas words in Polish. They loved learning them because they sounded funny. She decided to do a skit about Poland and asked for my help. I said I would love to be involved, so off we went.

I knew a few Christmas carols in the Polish language and my husband Ed helped me when I got stuck with some of the words. They were comparable to our old English Christmas carols. It happened that the three Polish songs I knew were the ones Ed and this teacher also knew from childhood.

I wrote a skit based on the carols. The teacher and the students loved it. The skit was in English of course, but there were Polish words thrown in such as 'dobje' (good); 'tesshikur ederem' (thank you); and others I have now forgotten.

The skit was cute and sweet, if I do say so myself, and went over very well with the parents. It was performed several times during the day depending on the flow of the audience at the open house. When a group of five or ten adults gathered around our area, the children started over and performed once again. Of the many, many exhibits presented that day in the school's huge dining room, ours was the only musical skit!

Observing Okinawan Schools

During one of our general teacher's meetings at the Bob Hope School, we were told there were opportunities for us to visit and observe classes at the Japanese schools on the island. I jumped at the invitation. What a wonderful opportunity to gain more knowledge about teaching practices and customs. I stressed to the person arranging the tours that I wanted to observe music classes and also, other non-music classes. I wanted to expand my knowledge of Okinawa since I was teaching and living here!

The Okinawan schools, as all other schools in Japan, were managed and directed by the Japanese government. All the money for the buildings and supplies for the schools came directly from the Japanese government; that meant the curriculum was the same throughout the country, and all schools had an equal share of benefits and resources, unlike our schools in the United States.

I visited four schools and was thoroughly impressed. Why? All Japanese schools are the same, whether in a rich or poor area of the country. The director of each school makes certain that nothing wavers from the government instructions, no matter what province they are in, whether the province is rich or very poor.

All schools were built alike and taught in the same fashion. Upon entering the front door of any school, a visitor would find the walls on either side of the hallway lined with little cubicles, each holding a pair of shoes that the children took off as they entered the school. This enabled the children to change into a soft, felt like type of slipper. (Keeps the floors clean, doesn't it? And teaches the children to be tidy as well.)

Also, each music room was simply outstanding, built and designed beautifully to benefit the teacher while she teaches music to all. (As compared to schools in the States. I never had a music room until my last two years in Andover.) The teacher stood down on the floor with two baby grand pianos. I say 'down' since all the children sat up above the teacher, with desks and chairs on levels and in a gradual incline, positioned properly for singing and teaching. It was a large room. Each child could see the teacher and the teacher could see each child, which was an excellent seating arrangement. Also, the acoustics in the room were marvelous as well.

Each child had his or her own desk. When the desk was opened at the top, there was…surprise, surprise…a keyboard inside with two octaves! This keyboard resembled a shortened piano keyboard encompassing middle C and then continuing up and on to two octaves above. Each child also had his or her own recorder; a flute-like instrument made of wood or plastic, and held in front, not to the side. It is much simpler than a flute but with a very nice sound nevertheless.

The Okinawan children learned to sing, to perform, and to actually read and sing the notes for the music, which would be played on their two octave pianos. They were capable of singing in a lovely fashion and could play recorders as well and consequently, could read the music easily. Unfortunately, I could not say that about any of the schools at which I taught in or observed in the USA.

Behind the two pianos, there was a solid glass divider, and on the other side a soundproofed recording room. I never, ever in all my years of teaching had anything like this at all with which to work. The Japanese students could go into that room when it was their time to record their songs or their piano playing or whatever else came their way, no matter what age or grade level they were. It is always so very beneficial for the children to hear what they have learned! I was so amazed! The recording room was far better than any I had ever seen in recording studios at home!

The school had set up a 'roaming reporter' program. A sixth grader was chosen each week to interview students on the playground at recess or lunch break. Every sixth grader had a turn as a 'roaming reporter.' It worked a bit like 'amateur antics' since the students interviewed by the reporter could sing, or answer whatever the reporter asked them. It was fascinating and amazing to me!

The Okinawans also had a system whereby one grade looked after another at lunchtime and recess. In essence, the students were responsible for each other and themselves. When it was time to eat, some students from a sixth grade for example, were chosen each week to be responsible to help the first graders. They made certain that the little ones washed their hands before eating, and that all was cleaned up in their eating area after eating. The helpers also watched all the younger students as they brushed their teeth, which I found amazing; to make sure no one forgot to brush and to ascertain that the brushing was done properly.

One other amazing thing I saw was first-grade students in the physical education class walking on stilts. Absolutely...I saw it with my own eyes. It was marvelous to see. Somewhere in my many albums I have pictures of this. They wore their little white caps with a visor while doing it. All children wore uniforms and the uniform also consisted of a cap for all the boys and I do not remember what the girls wore for their heads. The children were sweet, beautiful and precious, and most polite and friendly.

I was also fascinated with the work done in the kindergartens. The kindergarten students helped their teachers to raise chickens, roosters and other animals. They took care of them with the teachers' help of course. They learned how to be good and kind to the animals. If a child learns to be good and kind to animals, I feel certain it will help them be kind and good to each other as well...and that is so necessary. Kindergarten students only attended school for a half a day, but there were two shifts. I was so impressed with the little ones as they gathered their eggs in the morning; they were darling and as sweet as could be dressed in their traditional Okinawan/Japanese attire.

I visited three other schools while in Okinawa, but all were much the same as the one described above.

The Sound of Music

During my second year of teaching music, I decided to produce another musical as I had done with the *Wizard of Oz* the year before. The second graders of that production were now in the third grade and felt they were…ahem, 'professionals.' They exuded such confidence.

I chose *The Sound of Music*. I had a videotape of the movie at home, and I spent several Sunday afternoons watching the tape, selecting scenes and songs appropriate for the students to perform. I wrote my own script for the students based on the songs. It worked! Julie Andrews would have loved it. Even as I type this manuscript, I have photos of different scenes from this production beside me. What wonderful memories!

The musical was performed in the gymnasium and I had the help and co-operation of many parents to sew and put together whatever costumes were needed. The nuns looked incredibly good in their costumes. All the students in the third grades had a part in the production, either in the choir, or as an actor. Some children do not want to do more than sing in a chorus. Some children are quite shy and unsure, and are exquisitely happy to be in the chorus and not speak out alone. Then there are some students who want the lead parts and only try for the lead parts.

The 'Doe a Dear' along with 'Raindrops on Roses' songs were probably the 'standout' hits of our production. The students seemed to love to sing the cute and funny song about the nun…"She climbs a tree and scrapes her knee, her dress has got a tear, she whistles on her way to work and…warbles on the stair… and underneath her wimple there are curlers in her hair…" etc. from the song, 'How Do You Solve a Problem like Maria?'

The show ended with the outstanding song, 'Climb every Mountain!'

All went supremely well! I was thrilled with the performance! Better still, I was thrilled with how the students felt about themselves. They were so good and happy and extremely proud of their accomplishments. The most wonderful thing a child can have happen to him or herself, is to be in a situation where he or she feels good about himself, or herself; music, poetry and dance and drama do that for children. *The arts feed the soul!*

This 'meal' then carries over into their other classes and with their other teachers. It is contagious. I have seen it happen over and over again during my fifty years of teaching. Producing a musical takes a great amount of effort and caring, but the process always worked beautifully for the children and for me.

Wonderful, wonderful, and
Wonderful, wonderful, wonderful!

As You Like It
—Shakespeare

Tokyo for Thanksgiving

Life in Okinawa was not 'all work and no play' for me. My family and friends and I traveled whenever we could. Madonna and her friends showed us the way, many, many times. She and her friends went to this place or that place or this country or that country or all over Okinawa. We saw this gorgeous view or this calm and lovely beach area and on and on ad infinitum. The three of us, Ed and Amy and myself went with Madonna and Netty for a few days to Tokyo over the Thanksgiving holiday that second year.

We were excited when we left for Tokyo! I knew very little about the big and famous city, other than the airport. We checked into the New Sano, a military hotel, therefore the prices were quite inexpensive as compared to the regular hotels.

While we ladies registered at the desk, Ed wandered around the fairly small lobby looking things over. He saw a gambling machine, one where you put in a quarter and then pull an arm on the machine and little round things roll around in a window and sometimes people win money.

Ed had never gambled before, (neither had I) but when he saw it, he wandered up to the machine and casually put in a quarter. Suddenly, all the bells and whistles in the foyer of the hotel let go. Everything seemed to ring out loud. He was so stunned he did not know what was happening, and then many, many quarters fell out and landed all over the floor, rolling this way and that with everyone scrambling to help him pick them up.

He had a shy expression on his face and also looked most embarrassed! He always had trouble bending as a result of all his surgeries on his back and could not easily pick up the coins but everyone around was eager to help him! He won about eighty dollars in quarters! We were never able to make certain how many because they rolled around everywhere and everyone in the lobby was bending and fetching and laughing and giggling at Ed who looked astounded, and embarrassed, to say the least!

After checking in and picking up quarters, we went to our rooms, unpacked and set out to see the city. We went on an underground rail ride, like the subways that we have in Boston. The only difference is that in Tokyo, they had what are called 'pushers.' The carriages would be so full, that the 'pusher' would have a narrow, long, smooth board, maybe eight feet long, and the 'pusher' would hold the board and gently *push* into the train car all the people who were still trying to enter the car. He would use the wooden board and gently shove the people who needed to enter that particular car, which then made those who always wanted to stand at the doorway in order to exit first, move to the far right and far left of the cars. Yes, we were pushed. I will never forget it. Of course, no one was ever hurt, we were just pushed into place, which caused my claustrophobia to rise to a new height! I had always wanted to know how the 'pushers' worked and now I do!

We also went to Disney World. *Yes*!!! They had one in a very large area on the outskirts of Tokyo! It was fairly new at that time. Amy was not too happy with that. She said, in a low and dismal voice, "I could never go Disney World at home but I have to come here, to Japan, to see one!" No smiles issued forth from her either. She was still having a difficult time adjusting to her move from home.

I had never been to any other Disney World; so all was new to me. At one point I saw groups of young girls and young men dressed in the clothing of the Civil War days, mid 1860, let us say. They all wore something different and quite nice; they were wearing the typical hoop skirts and bonnets and no two were dressed alike, but something struck me as being not quite right. I kept thinking, "What is different, what is out of place with this scene?"

Then, suddenly, I knew. The blond wigs on the Japanese girls just did not fit their faces. When you put a blond, curly wig on a young Japanese lady something looks askew. Once I figured out what made everything different and a bit odd, I am afraid I had to smile, and smile broadly I did. But they were very friendly, bowing and laughing and enjoying being 'Americans' in the Civil War era!

According to friends of mine who had visited Disneyland in the States, the Japanese Disney World was quite small by comparison. There were many rides, roller coasters, and other similar concessions as at home, but the place was definitely not huge. It did not seem to 'go on forever.' Everyone in our group enjoyed the various rides; Madonna and Nettie were always lovely to Amy, teasing, talking and doing things with her whenever it fit the situation. I think Amy enjoyed the rides, but I did not want to ask her.

By the way, I *never* go on any kind of ride…too nervous and I just do not like them. I had a couple of bad experiences as a small child in Canada. Some of my Canadian cousins felt I would grow used to the roller coaster ride if they made me take it. Therefore, they just about forced me on to the rides and when they ended I was as white as a sheet and trembling all over. I swore to myself I would never take another carnival ride again, and that was that!

I loved the Tokyo Zoo, which was really more park-like than zoo-like. The animals were not in cages, but in large fenced in spaces that reflected their natural habitat as much as possible. We saw a panda bear but unfortunately, he did not wake up to have his picture taken, he just snored and slept on top of a pole on a round board. In my photographs he looks like a huge round ball of black and white, and I never saw his face, no matter how much I talked to him.

While we were looking at the panda, a group of lovely Japanese school students came into our view and Madonna and I went over to see the children. They were very friendly, and smiling and they all wanted us to take their pictures, and then they wanted us to be in the pictures with them. They numbered between ten and twenty children of around ten, eleven and twelve years old. No English words were used but their pantomimes told the story. They were so beautiful. All had black hair and bangs, boys and girls alike, and all in uniform, looking splendid, happy, sweet and lovely. They were most polite! I think smart looking school uniforms are great, I wish we had them in the United States as the Japanese children and Okinawan children do. I loved wearing a uniform as a child in grades five through eight and then again, through high school. We all looked the same, so therefore I never had to worry about how I looked or what I wore.

While at the park a young family of four, a father and mother and a baby and a small child, asked politely, after they bowed, if I would have a picture taken of them with me. Of course I acquiesced and was proud and happy to be asked by them. I had no name or address to which to send a copy of the photo, I could not talk to them in their language, but they wanted it for me to have and keep. That was so very sweet!

We went into the famous Tokyo Department Store, but of course, I have forgotten its name. We had lunch up on the top floor surrounded with windows, which gave us what looked like a view of the Tokyo world. It was beautiful! We shopped of course, and ate out, and kept ourselves very busy since we only had three days to enjoy the ambience of Tokyo. Amy and Ed went home earlier than we did, but Madonna and I stayed to see the *Nutcracker Suite* ballet put on by a professional group. Amy did not want to see it at that time.

I was surprised that the main dancers were Europeans; but the chorus dancers were Japanese ballerinas. Again, the differences in their bodies and ours stood out quite distinctly to me. I needed some time to get used to seeing the Japanese girls do the ballet steps that I was used to seeing done by Europeans and Americans. The Japanese girls were much shorter, and none of them seemed to have the long and straight legs found on the ballerinas in the USA. However, it was lovely, and a very nice but unusual performance; Madonna and I were pleased we attended. We took a later plane home that night; the trip from Tokyo to Okinawa was approximately a two-hour ride that was not the least bit stressful.

Mabuni Hill

One Sunday after Christmas during our second year in Okinawa, Ed and I went for a ride around the island. Okinawa is a long, slim, snake-like island surrounded by ocean, the Pacific on one side and the East China Sea on the other. The views were always tremendous. We drove until we came upon an area that had many, many monuments high up on a cliff overlooking the Pacific Ocean. We walked around looking at each of them. Not being able to read what was written on them we nevertheless enjoyed ourselves and loved the individual monuments. Some of them were quite huge and all of them were very beautiful. We were quite sure that we might have been in a cemetery but then we had no way of knowing for certain.

After we had been walking around awhile, two older ladies came humbly forward and started bowing down to us. They bowed down very low, mentioning some words that sounded a little like English, but not quite. Eventually, after a few moments, one lady said, bowing low once again, "We so solly, we so solly," (some Japanese had difficulty pronouncing 'r,' so the word 'sorry' then became 'solly,) and gestured at the monuments. The other lady did much the same and then the first lady tried to explain where we were and why the monuments were there. Eventually, in her broken English and much kanji, it came to us that we were standing on Mabuni Hill, where a ghastly, horrific battle occurred during World War II.

These little ladies, in their seventies and from mainland Japan, looking small, poor and humble, were apologizing to us, bowing and bending and weeping, for all the murders and killings that occurred on this very spot where we were standing! I found these to be the most poignant, heartrending and piteous moments during my entire 17 years living overseas. (When I got back to the base, I learned that two hundred thousand people perished in that lengthy and bloody battle.)

It seems there are 47 'prefectures' (comparable to our 'states') in Japan. Each prefecture, by order of the government of Japan, since World War II ended, has to take groups of people by bus and plane to make amends at this massive, monumental area where thousands of Okinawans, Americans and Japanese were killed. The Japanese come and pray and leave flowers and messages. The whole scene was so moving we all four were in tears and in each others arms, together. We had to stoop way down to hug the little ladies, who, as you know, had nothing whatsoever to do with the war, absolutely *nothing*…but their government was the culprit!

At the time that battle took place I was only about ten or twelve years old; I knew something awful was happening, but never really had it sink in to the depths of my soul as it did on that eventful day in Okinawa. We also learned the Japanese (during WWII) were terrible to the Okinawans. Thousands were tortured and killed, and also thousands of Americans were killed in the battles. Because of the torturous treatment they suffered at the hands of the Japanese, we were told Okinawans *will never* consider themselves to be Japanese. We were told several times by many Okinawans in our three years of residing and working in Okinawa that they *are not Japanese!* They are Okinawans!

I think of the annual trips taken by the Japanese delegation from each prefecture in mainland Japan as a touching and loving tribute to the poor people who died mercilessly. We must also remember today's Japanese are not the murderers and nor did they begin and pursue the battles that happened at that time. This is Peace Prayer Park and may it ever remain so.

"My heart is heavy
My age is weak
Grief would have tears
And sorrow bids me speak…"

All's Well That End's Well
—Shakespeare

Our Last Year in Okinawa

"To business that we love we rise betime
And go to with delight"

Antony and Cleopatra
—Shakespeare

At the time I began teaching my third year in Okinawa, I did not know this would be our last year in Okinawa. However, when information about transfers was distributed in the early winter of that year, I decided to apply for a transfer because although I loved being in Okinawa, I needed to see more of the world.

It was during that last year in Okinawa that I decided to produce the musical *Oliver!* with the third grade students. However, I did not want to use the school gymnasium again. I woke up one morning with what I thought was a brilliant idea. I decided to ask to use the Base Theatre for the show *Oliver!* I found the theatre, explained to the man in charge who I was and why I wanted to use the theatre and voilà, it was granted to me! No cost either. What a fabulous man…I was thrilled. "The children will be absolutely 'over the moon with delight,' (one of my favorite sayings) at being able to perform in a real theatre, just thrilled, I know they will," I thought to myself.

I was able to have a piano placed on the floor below the stage. I then decided I would have many, many step-risers on the floor in front of the stage so all the students in the chorus could see and be seen throughout the whole performance. The students portraying the main characters would perform on the stage. *All* the three hundred plus students in the eleven third grade classes learned all the songs I considered most pertinent to the show. (Since I was working with non-professional eight and nine-year old children, I shortened the show and left out all the love scenes and love songs. There was no way we could have performed the entire three-hour show!)

The third-graders' singing voices were sweet and lovely and I would be the last one to want to ruin them by overdoing the singing and acting. I had taught many of them from the year before and the one before that; although probably half of them had transferred in from elsewhere, there were still enough children who had my previous training in vocal production to make the songs sound beautiful.

The little boy who played Oliver was wonderful, a very good actor with a beautiful boy soprano voice. At that age boys and girls generally sound similar but I did not have one boy or girl whose voice could compare with this one. He was a fabulous boy soprano singer! When he sang Oliver's famous, "Where Is Love" there was hardly a dry eye in the theatre.

Also, the boy playing Fagin was outstanding; he loved the 'little boys' and was amazingly funny. The street urchins (all Fagin's 'boys') put all their hearts and souls into the performance. They stayed in character all the time and sang and acted to perfection!

The masses of children (orphans in the show) entered from the back of the theatre and came streaming down all the aisles on cue, not in a formation, but the way boys would enter if they were street boys and hooligans, not caring what others thought, while I played music for their entrance. (The show was already ten or fifteen minutes underway before it was time for these masses of children to enter from the back of the theatre and stream down the aisles to the stage.)

They played that part really well; it was a sight to behold! The 'boys' (girls were playing the parts of boys as well) entered singing and cheering. There were so many of them that it seemed like children came out of nowhere and everywhere! Amazingly good, they sang the whole while! Down the aisles they came and up into their places on the 'step risers' that had been placed all the way across the floor in front of the stage! The 'boys' were not in a formal arrangement on the step risers. They either stood, or slouched, or draped over the steps...whatever way I had assigned to them. We had borrowed step risers from all the other military schools on Okinawa, so we had at least ten or twelve sets of step-risers on the floor in front of the stage. This gave each child the feeling that he or she was 'on stage' and always a part of the show.

The Artful Dodger was wonderful. His is an outstanding part, even more than Oliver's role. Oliver must be sweet all the time, but the Artful Dodger could let go and be a naughty boy. His singing voice was pure like a bell and his acting was superb. Naturally, I was quite pleased with the whole affair. The Artful Dodger was a boy in the script, but Pam Spencer acted the part of the boy, although she was a girl. She was a wonderful actress and singer and only a third grader; I hope, today, she has continued on with her career as such!

Following the performance, an announcer from the local military station came by the next day to interview me for Okinawa Television. At one point he asked how I could take on such a production, manage so many children and have it performed so perfectly. I was a bit nervous, having never been interviewed

Mary and one of Oliver's 'gang' in Okinawa

for television before, but I thought I answered well enough. I explained to him it was a 'love/hate relationship' for me. I loved the children and the play and seeing them perform, but, it was a huge amount of work nevertheless!

Fortunately I had lots of parents who helped paint scenery, make costumes, do programs and hold cue cards and such. Also, the art teacher joined in wholeheartedly and was a tremendous help. But still it was an enormous and diffi-cult task to put such a large show together with so many young children. I had never di-rected a performance before that had such a large and wide scope.

However, the performance was a success and there were compliments galore from the parents. (Many asked what I planned to do the following year.) All the parents seemed to understand the complexity and think highly of what the children and I had accomplished.

The principal of the school awarded a cash bonus to me at the very end of that school year for my "wonderful work with the children of the Bob Hope School!" I was thrilled and felt pleased and proud and grateful that all worked out as well as it did.

Be that as it may, the Assistant Principal did not think the way the Principal did. The day after the interview aired on the military television, the portly Assistant Principal entered my room at the end of the day after the students had left, banging my door and with a mad scowl on his face. He was furious! I was non-plussed.

He looked down at me, hollered and almost spit in my mouth, saying,

"Mary, how could you possibly say those awful words on public television about our children?" He then went on to criticize me soundly for my 'love-hate relationship' remark. He let fly a few more sentences that were quite derogatory and then slammed the door once again as he left. After I recovered from his criticisms (I was in a state of shock,) I realized he had no idea of what was meant by the term 'a love/hate relationship.' But…I had to let it go; I felt there was no point in holding on to anger when I knew I had done a terrific piece of work with these children, who would never forget being 'on stage.' Of that I was most certain!

And besides, the following article appeared in the local military newspaper, so I felt certain that the Assistant Principal was alone in his opinion.

"THIS WEEK ON OKINAWA"
May 31–June 7, 1987
BOB HOPE PRIMARY SCHOOL
3RD GRADE CLASSES PRESENT "OLIVER"

"The superb performance of "Oliver" on May 14 at the Keystone Theatre reflects the hard work of many students, parents, teachers and other community members. The presentation was adapted and directed by Mary Guziejka, music teacher at Bob Hope Primary School. It was adapted from the musical OLIVER written by Lionel Bart based on the novel, OLIVER TWIST by Charles Dickens, 1835.

"Oliver" is the story of an orphan, born in a workhouse north of London to a Mother whose name was not known. In writing this novel Dickens exposes the workhouses and the city conditions that led the children of the poor into crime.

Work began on "Oliver" in February and continued until the May 13 and 14 performances. Many children practiced 2 nights a week after school. Approximately 249 children participated and all children had an opportunity to try out for speaking and solo parts. Ms Guziejka said she considered quality of voice but also determination of students to capture the particular character.

The play opens in the Work House with the orphans. Joseph Carouselle, the Principal at Bob Hope, dons a chef's hat and apron and lends a hand while stirring the "gruel" during this scene while the chorus sings "Food Glorious Food". Then Mr. Bumble, the Parish beadle, brings Oliver before the governors who decide to sell Oliver because he has asked for more food. Oliver is then sold to Mr. Sowerberry, a coffin maker and finds life hard and decides to run away. On the streets he meets Dodger who introduces Oliver to the miserly old Fagin who lives in London who in turn gives

Oliver a place to sleep. The next day, Dodger and Charley Bates go with Oliver to pick Mr. Brownlow's pocket and Oliver gets caught. The Mr. Jessop declares Oliver is innocent and takes Oliver home with him. In the streets all the sellers come through selling their wares, which include sweet red roses, ripe strawberries, and milk. The play ends with Fagin suggesting he and his gang go to the South of France and reminds Oliver to "CONSIDER YOURSELF ONE Of US!!!

"Many others contributed hours to help make the production possible. Ms. Margaret Alber, Art teacher at Bob Hope helped with the flats and worked with the 3rd grade children while painting scenery. Mrs. Gerry Muller created calligraphy signs and also helped with the painting of the flats. Ms. Debbie Watson spent hours collecting and keeping track of props. The Arts and Crafts Center provided portrait pictures of some of the main characters and then the pictures adorned the front bulletin board at Bob Hope before the performance.

Mrs. Guziejka played the piano accompaniment and directed the entire production. After the production was over she said, "Children, you were wonderful!!! If I had buttons on they would be popping off; I am so proud of you! Now when you go to see a play you will know how much work, courage and patience goes into a production." These words are typical of the praise and love that emanate from Mrs. Guziejka. She has long been associated with the arts.

In 1982 Mrs. Guziejka composed for the piano, AN ANTHEM OF PEACE or a POLISH ANTHEM (second title). She sent copies to Luciano Pavarotti and the Pope among other people and received favorable replies from both of them.

Mrs. Guziejka has been teaching music to children for thirty-five years and she has served Bob Hope Primary School well for the past three years. Other productions here included Hansel and Gretel, the Wizard of Oz and The Sound of Music.

She hopes to continue teaching many more years and her immediate future plans include teaching next year at the DODDS Schools in Izmir, Turkey where she will be teaching Grades K-12.

Our community has been fortunate to have such a dedicated Music Teacher in our midst. Mrs. Guziejka feels that performances such as "Oliver" help build self-esteem in children and help make children sensitive to the feelings of other people. Mrs. Guziejka contributes her success to her Mom and Dad, her piano teacher, Anna Scannell and her drama coach, Louise Dunn. She has demonstrated clearly, here at Bob Hope Primary School, how one person can make a difference and what a difference she has made in the lives of her students! She has truly made music live in the hearts of all."

Musical training is a more potent
Instrument than any other
because rhythm and harmony find their
Way in to the inward places of the soul"

—Plato

Adventures While Living in Okinawa

One of the many advantages of teaching with DODDS was the opportunity to travel and learn more about the country and area where we were stationed. It was one of the 'perks' Ed and I thoroughly enjoyed and took advantage of as often as possible when I was not busy teaching. One day we went to the rice fields. We parked our car and walked around in the area, just exploring the rice paddies with great interest since they are something one would never see at home in Dracut, Mass. Eventually, some Okinawan ladies spied us and began smiling and talking amongst each other while waving their hands at us. They were sitting in rocking chairs on a porch, ostensibly enjoying some time off from labor. We smiled and waved back at them and they came to greet us, inviting us up onto their long and narrow porch. They were a working class type of people and most friendly. Due to their charming and persuasive gestures we stepped up onto the porch and sat down at their invitation.

We tried to talk with them. I knew about ten words in kanji. They knew about the same amount in English. Despite that we all got along smashingly well, had some tea with them, did much smiling and bowing and enjoyed just being together for an hour or so. We employed much drama, and hand and arm movements, I must say! Madonna had come with us that day, which made the visit a bit easier. Their thatched cottage was absolutely charming; however, it was definitely not one I would want to live in, having grown used to American amenities. They all sat on the floor and slept on the floor and ate on the floor. Naturally, they had cloth covers where it was necessary and some stuffing inside some cushioning. We have some nice photographs of the ladies on the porch, and I remember the day vividly. I hope their memories are equally as nice as ours!

✼✼✼

One day, early in our stay in Okinawa while we were still living in the hotel, Ed and I took a walk down the street. We walked by a large vegetable garden where an Okinawan man was working. I said, "Konnichiwa." (Japanese for 'Good afternoon.') The man answered me with the same word, thinking I could speak Japanese. Then, when he found that was all I knew except for smiling prettily at him we found this man to be far more conversant in English than the ladies I mentioned in the previous vignette. Not totally fluent but able to manage quite well.

Eventually, after a few minutes of talk he invited us to join him at his home, which was just a short way up the street, to drink a cup of tea! He was not truly a farmer, but he had a plot of land on which to grow some of his favorite foods. We went to his home and he had us step up into his long room, which made me think of a long porch that had been made into a room. His wife came to the door, did not sit down, but bowed and smiled and smiled and bowed once more, and then went to make tea (chai). She was not at all fluent in English, unfortunately. The tea came in, she poured for us and then left, and we sat, sipping tea and comfortably talking with this gentleman who had been a high-ranking officer in the Japanese Army at one time. I believe it had to have been during World War II considering his age, but I forbore asking him. Seemed too embarrassing a question to ask. His whole long and screened in room was lined with large and framed photographs of the officers with whom he worked during World War II…presumably. The large, framed photos went up as high as the ceilings and along one side of the long and narrow room where there was no screening.

We must have conversed for about an hour with topics concerning our military, their military, and what his rank was and what his duties were during the war, when we decided it was time to courteously take our leave. As we stood, the officer, now civilian, offered to show us the inside of his home downstairs. We accepted with pleasure of course!

Amazingly, those rooms were not western looking like the porch/room. The room we stepped up and into was Japanese style. While we were looking around and admiring all, I noticed a very low table on the floor, not in the center but not too far from the stairs which went up to the next level; the table had a covering, as in a table cloth over it that ended while draping the floor. I assumed that was where he and his wife had their tea, Japanese style, sitting on the floor on a cushion or on their legs while kneeling on a cushion. However, at one corner of the table I could see some black hair sticking out. With great excitement in my voice, I said, "Oh, you have a dog or cat lying under your table!"

The man, bowing and bending and happily beaming from ear to ear, hands in his opposite sleeves, replied, "Oh, no, that is my daughter! She is sleeping under the table!" He bent over and removed the cloth from the low table with one hand, while giggling and covering his mouth with his other hand, leaving the cloth draped on the tatami mats, which covered the floor. I was absolutely embarrassed, as was the daughter. The man, having pulled off the covering left the daughter to do whatever she had to do while in that embarrassing situation. She scrambled out from under the low table and bowed, then backed away, and bowed and bowed once again, backing away all the while, and then ran upstairs as fast as possible to her room!

The man, hands folded, head moving up and down slightly, and smiling broadly, said, "She is always cold upstairs in the winter and since there is an electric heater under this table she comes down in the night when she is cold and finishes her sleep here."

I was absolutely embarrassed as was his daughter. The man just smiled, laughed a bit, actually, and said, "Not to worry. We find her sleeping everywhere!"

Naha

One day we visited Naha, the capital of Okinawa. We were told by other Americans to go into a certain department store since it had whatever one needed for clothing; I do not remember the name of the store. When we arrived, we parked the car, walked around and eventually found the department store. (We found it difficult to keep track of all the names, which were all written in Kanji. We could read nothing. Artistically speaking, Kanji is flowing and lovely much of the time but definitely unreadable for an American unless they learned it well ahead of time!)

When we got into the department store, I had the most interesting experience. In the women's department, I found I was sought after by several young Okinawan clerks who wanted to help me: find clothes for me, find shoes for me, Okinawan sandals, that is, and do anything they could possibly do for me. I would have to say they went a little 'cuckoo' over me. I *never* had so much attention before this in my life! It became a little comical after a while, but, oh… so sweet.

They brought forward arms full of kimonos, along with everything else that goes with them. I wish I could remember all the names. The 'obi' was the sash. Before I could blink an eye, before I even knew what they were going to do, they were dressing me in the most beautiful kimonos, with sashes, and were parading me around for the other clerks in the store to see. I was a bit embarrassed I must confess, but not wanting them to think I did not like them, nor wanting them to feel I was rude, or they were rude, I let them parade me here and there, and I became a *star* attraction!

Well…no, I did not buy a kimono or anything else; I could not at that point afford anything at all, having not yet been reimbursed for the expenses we incurred traveling to Okinawa. I felt sorry I could not buy anything, for their sakes, but they seemed fine with the whole process.

Ed certainly had a marvelous time, laughing and chuckling away at my embarrassment and also liking the way I looked. Then we were directed to go to the food bars. Well…while there we received virtually everything, free…clerks were flocking to feed us. Samples were coming at us from all quarters. All was amazing! I could not eat anything they gave us, well… I could eat the rice cakes and things like that, but I am not able to manage raw fish at all! Ed was brave and did eat some. But then, Ed can eat anything and loves everything.

The whole afternoon was just an example of how lovely the Okinawan people were, and still are today; of that I am positive!

Botanical Gardens

The Botanical Gardens were not very far from our home on the Seabee Base. We had heard so very much about the gardens that one day we drove over to see what fascinated all the teachers at school. Ed and I love gardens and our curiosity is boundless, therefore we had to go see it.

After arriving, we were directed to drive into a particular area. We did and then ended up in back of a bus, which had probably come from a hotel. All the Japanese in the bus were dressed up beautifully, what we would call 'Sunday best' in the USA. We could not help but see all of them as they delicately stepped down onto the pavement, one by one, from the bus. They were most dignified and talking softly. The bus had stopped by the front entrance and we were stopped exactly behind the bus near the ticket office. Then, on the right side of our car, we saw the Men's Room and the Ladies Room.

Well, the bus ahead was just about empty when an old man crept out of it. He tottered around, looking here and there. Ed and I could not figure out where he was going, he did not go to the Men's Room nor did he buy any tickets, but we waited patiently in any case, not wanting to hit him with our car. Strangely, however, he seemed to be headed for our car, while all we were doing was waiting in line to buy tickets and then park our car.

Puzzled, I said to Ed, " I wonder where he's going? He looks like he is coming here to see us."

I had looked at Ed when I said that, then returned my gaze to the old man, who was 'dressed to the nines' in a suit; a coat, shirt and tie and trousers, all to match. Much to my horror at that moment, as he stood between our front windshield and the rear of the bus, sideways, he unzipped his pants, pulled his penis out of his pants and urinated fully on the ground in front of our car, splashing all around his body.

"Ed, I cannot believe what I am seeing," I whispered as I put my hand to my mouth and stifled a giggle. "I can't either," said Ed.

We both found it a bit unusual considering the type of people around the bus all dressed in such high style, as was this elderly man, and who were also paying a high fee for the visit to the Gardens. The old man finished what he was doing, took care of his penis, zipped up his pants and wandered over to the booth to buy his ticket...and...that was that!

※ ※ ※

One summer, as we teachers were all preparing to take our annual home leave, Christine, a good friend of ours who worked at my school and knew Ed would be staying in Okinawa that summer while she was going on home, called and asked him a favor.

"Ed, would you mind very much going to my house once a week and driving my car around the base or wherever you feel like driving it? The humidity here and the heat in the summer is so intense that if it is not driven a bit each week, the battery will die and the car will just not work at all when I return home," she explained.

"I would be more than happy to help you with your car while you are gone," Ed replied. Christine was absolutely ecstatic. I guessed that she had to buy a new battery for her car each year. Her car was not new and that might have been part of the reason.

Faithfully that summer Ed drove the car weekly, checked everything out, put gas in, and waited for all of us to return home at the close of summer.

One day, before I had returned to Okinawa, the phone rang in our apartment. Ed answered.

"Ed, something seems wrong with my car. Could you come over for a few minutes and help me decide what to do?" Christine asked. "I'll be right over," he replied.

Ed met her at her house, went over to the car, took her keys, and got in. He tried to start the car a few times, and nothing happened. He decided then to try jumpstarting her car—hooking wires from his car battery to hers. It still would not start. He removed the wires, closed the hood with a bang and suddenly, *the whole motor in Charlotte's car fell out landing on the ground beneath her car!*

At that point, the matter 'fell out of his hands' and Ed went back to our apartment on the base. To this day we're still not sure what became of the car.

Chinese Restaurant

Some of the teachers I worked with had been in Okinawa since shortly after World War II ended. (At that time they lived in barracks and commuted to school daily in an army truck. The school was in another military building; the Bob Hope School had not yet been built.) These teachers were well experienced in places to see, restaurants at which to eat, and other things to do, especially pertaining to the beaches, the beautiful waters and scuba diving. I decided I did not want to learn how to scuba dive, I just wanted to swim by myself, but I was happy for the many teachers who did. These gals all wanted to see all the varieties of fish found in these waters. The fish were so beautiful; they seemed to be all colors of the rainbow.

The veteran teachers in particular recommended one restaurant to us. We were told we **had** to eat at a Chinese restaurant, which was located 'on the economy,' meaning not on the base, but directly outside one of the military gates. Therefore it was easy to find!

One day Ed and I went to this restaurant. There was no one in it, and it only had about three, or at the most, four tables with chairs. So we sat and looked at the menu which we had trouble reading. It was almost all in Kanji!

An elderly Chinese man came forward as he heard the door open and close and he came to take our order. We were smiling and pointing to the pictures on the menu and he was bowing and smiling in return and then again, bowing even more profusely after we stopped bowing.

We gave him our order and after he wrote it down, he took off his apron, said nothing to us since he could not speak English and left the building. We sat there in complete surprise and wonder, not knowing exactly what was happening. After looking out the window and discussing the issue, Ed said, "Maybe we should leave?"

"No I don't think so; let's give it a little more time. Maybe he remembered something he had to do," I replied.

Time passed…it seemed long, but then, it may not have been more than ten or fifteen minutes when the Chinese man came in with bags of groceries in his arms. He disappeared into what presumably was the kitchen.

Within a short while he appeared with plates of steaming food that he put in front of us. Since all rooms and walls were open and his stove and utensils were nearby within eyeshot, we could see that he had been busy cooking. He had concocted our meals, and over they came to us piping hot! They were marvelous, a great taste and we certainly knew they were fresh!

Evidently he had gone out to a store to buy all the foods he needed with which to cook! We were amazed when we figured it all out. Unfortunately, he could not tell us since we did not understand Chinese.

We ate our meals and bowed and thanked him and of course, gave him a big tip! Off we went to tell the girls who had told us to go there. They laughed at our surprise since they knew all of this from past experiences. Then Madonna said, "He serves the best food on the island and he always goes out to buy everything needed for each order!" That was certainly a treat and a surprise. I never in my 'eating out' life ever saw that happen before and will most likely, never see it again!

A Grandmother and her Grandson

One short and powerful memory still lives with me today. Ed and I had been told we had to see an Okinawan doctor for some reason or another. Neither of us can remember exactly why. We needed some type of Okinawan medical certificate I believe. We were told which one to see and what time, so we set off to find the street.

We eventually arrived to find a large crowd of people waiting outside to enter the doctor's small and decrepit looking building. That was a bit of a shock for us, since we were used to doctor's practices in America. We were dismayed to think we might have to stand there for what could be an hour or two. The temperature was in the low 100s; nothing was comfortable since there was nowhere to sit; Ed could not really stand that long and nor did I want to bake to death even though nothing at all was wrong with me!

In a quandary we continued standing trying to figure out how to handle our situation when we looked over casually to one side and saw a most unusual sight. A boy of about twelve years old, obviously a very strong boy, was slowly trudging, down a hill toward the doctor's small building with a large and delicate burden on his back.

I tugged on Ed's arm saying, "Ed, look, look what's coming down the hill." The boy was carrying an old lady, seemingly very ill. She was actually across the boy's back…'piggy-back' fashion, and her head bounced above his shoulders with each step he took. Her eyes were closed. She had thin white hair tied back in a knot on her head. Her arms were clasped around his neck and chest, and her legs slung around the front of his body while his arms held them up somehow. Goodness only knows how far he may have walked with her…I wanted to cry at the sadness of this sight.

I stared in utter disbelief for what felt like many minutes and decided then and there, I did not have many problems at all. At almost the same moment, or a minute or two after, an Okinawan from the doctor's office came to us and led us in, since we were Americans from the military I guess, and we were given some sort of document. There had been no need for us to stand outside waiting in the crowd.

By then sweat was pouring off of us like rivulets, we were absolutely drenched in perspiration; we were also most relieved but quite ashamed that we had been able to go in before everyone else and especially before this boy with his grandmother. The crowd passed no outward or untoward judgment on us that we could see. All were still smiling and nodding at us as, bowing their heads to us as usual. As we left the small building, the Okinawans separated to make way for us to pass through their ranks. Then we saw the boy was still there… patiently waiting…in the crowd…holding his sick grandmother up on his back…piggy-back fashion…a sight I will never…ever…forget.

Rope-Tugging Contest

Paul Truesdell, the reporter from the Okinawan Military Base newspaper, invited Ed to go to many varied and sundry events during the three years we were living in Okinawa. Ed did not work, therefore he had plenty of time on his hands while I worked, and he was always ready to go to whatever the event was and wherever it was. The two men got along just fine and Paul will never know what a service he did for my husband in befriending him and taking him along when he went out to cover stories. The island was so small that the traveling was not a big factor in Ed's decisions. Everything was close by it seemed.

One end of the rope in the rope tugging contest.

One such event was an annual rope-tugging contest held between two neighboring towns. It was a long, established tradition known in English as 'The Big Tug of War.' Ed accompanied Paul while he reported on the event. I was unable to go because I was teaching.

The rope was about a quarter of a mile long. Ed was fascinated to watch the rope being made with branches fastened onto male and female ropes weighing more than two pounds. (Since I was not there, to this day I cannot quite figure out how the leaves in bundles helped the rope tugging festival, although from the photos I have seen the branches were like 'arms' sticking out of the rope and helped with the pulling.)

The young people involved in tugging the rope wore samurai costumes and enjoyed themselves to the fullest. Ed was given the opportunity to 'tug' as he held on to one of the 'arms' that protruded out of the main body of the huge rope. The rope was suspended from a tree. At each end of the rope was a loop that was going to be meeting up with the other town's loop. One was supposed to be 'female' while the other was 'male.' When the loops got together the question was which loop would get up on top of the other first.

Both villages were moving their ropes with the loop ends. The men fought each other to see which one would get their loop on top of the other. Once that was accomplished a big log went into the hole of the loop in order to hold the loops together. It was only after that happened that the famous *Tug of War* began! There was a line and the people on both sides had to pull and pull until the stronger side pulled the rope over the special finishing line.

Ed talked about the famous tug of war for days. He still, today, maybe twenty-four years later can see it in his mind. It was so very colorful! One must keep in mind all the Okinawans, and there were hundreds of them watching or pulling the 'ropes,' were in native dress as well. The whole affair was spectacular!

Hong Kong, Christmas 1985

During our second year in Okinawa we chose to go to Hong Kong for one week during our Christmas break. Amy, Ed and I went by ourselves, no group tour this time. I really wanted Amy to learn about and appreciate the differences and the startling beauty in all these countries.

Teresa, an art teacher friend of mine from Andover, had met a delightful Chinese man while he was studying at the University in Lowell, Massachusetts. She dated him a few times. He invited her to Hong Kong after he finished college, but she never did visit him. She did however write to him and gave him our names and where we would be staying while in Hong Kong.

When we arrived and were shown to our rooms in our Hong Kong hotel, we found a big bouquet of flowers in a vase from Qin, (pronounced "chin") and an unusually large box of chocolates. A letter accompanied the gifts giving us his name and telephone number and offering to show us around. He was young, most knowledgeable, well traveled, and spoke English fluently; therefore we saw more wonderful sites than we would have dreamed of seeing on our own. He took us to one place that we would never have seen without him, an area north of Kowloon known as the 'New Territories.'

A Chinese man from Hong Kong had spent many years in Montreal, Canada earlier in the century. When he came home, he settled in the 'New Territories' and built dozens of houses just like you would see in Montreal.

"This looks like Canada, like the little boroughs outside of Montreal," I exclaimed to Ed as we entered the area. "Why it looks just like Quebec where my cousins live!" I was shocked, but pleased. Qin explained the history of the area to us, and how the Chinese gentleman had been so enamored of his experience in Canada that he decided to recreate a portion of it in the 'New Territories.' The trip brought back many pleasant memories of my childhood experiences.

We thanked Qin profusely when he returned us to our hotel. He could not have been lovelier!

Another day we went up Victoria Peak, named after Queen Victoria in England since England ruled Hong Kong for a long time. The cable car ride up the mountain to the Peak was a bit terrifying for me, but the scenery along the way was beautiful. Once at the top of the mountain, we left the cable car behind and walked. The view was spectacular, with water all around us and gorgeous views of other small islands and their mountains.

The Peak area itself is large and broad and spreads out into forests with lots of wildlife. It is a mecca for birdwatchers. Also, the Peak was where many of Hong Kong's most affluent residents lived. As a tourist, I would have liked to spend more time there, but could not, because there were many other places to see. Always too much to do in a short period of time when one travels it seems.

One thing that amazed me in the city of Hong Kong itself were the many, many tall apartment buildings. I counted thirty floors on one apartment building. I read a statistic that said, "Residential high rise apartments contribute to the Kowloon district's density of 165,000 persons per square *kilometer*," (that's less than a square mile.) That was in the 1980s; it staggers me to think what the figure might be now.

At any rate, the apartments towered around and over each other, and many of the apartment dwellers hang their clothes out to dry on lines between the apartment buildings because the people could not afford clothes dryers. We were able to chat with a few residents of the apartments who could speak some English. They told us that as many as nine to twelve people might live together in a small three or four room apartment. Amazing!

On the whole though, Hong Kong was more beautiful than I expected and I enjoyed every minute of our trip. We walked and walked and rode boats and ate and met people and shopped a bit. We had previously arranged to meet DODDS friends from Okinawa since many teachers and their families visited Hong Kong at Christmas. We ate dinners with different teachers almost every night. And one evening we thoroughly enjoyed a boat ride from the island of Hong Kong to Kowloon! The boat was a two-tiered ferry named "The Star Ferry." The cost was as low as ten cents, or less, each way at that time. One cannot find any good price like that in today's world and especially here in the USA!

When it came to shopping, we also found prices were quite low on premium goods. I was able to afford a custom-made leather jacket, expertly made out of a lovely leather just for me. I still have the jacket, but don't wear it all that often now because of our unpredictable New England weather. So now I just look at it in the downstairs closet occasionally and remember the trip and the fittings at the tailor shop. *Sigh*!

I feel it is important to note that China resumed sovereignty over Hong Kong in 1997, on July 1 I believe, ending 156 years of British rule.

Southeast Asia Tour, Christmas 1986

The following Christmas, our third year in Okinawa, we decided to go on a small group tour of Southeast Asia organized by a friend of mine. During the two weeks we were to visit Taipei, Taiwan; Kuala Lumpur; Bangkok, Thailand; Singapore, then spend the last five days of the tour in Hong Kong. I only knew a few of the people on the tour in the beginning. However, it was a charming group of people and a few days into the tour we had all become fast friends!

Our sixteen-year-old daughter Amy, being a typical teenager, did *not* want to go on this trip. She wanted to stay in Okinawa with her friends. But I would not allow that. I did not want her to miss out on this wonderful chance to see so many countries. Well, Amy was glum and complaining when we arrived at the airport for the trip. Again, as in Alaska so many years ago, a young military man who had noticed Amy and her 'unhappiness' while we were waiting to board the plane, approached me. "It looks like your daughter doesn't want to take this trip," he said to me.

"You're right, she doesn't want to be going with us at all," I replied.

"Would you mind if I talked with her?" he asked politely.

"Not at all. That would be just fine," I told him.

"Before this trip is over, she will have a good time!" he countered.

"What do you mean?" I asked.

"You'll see," is all he would tell me.

He was traveling with two other young military men, all charming and handsome, and about eighteen or nineteen years old I judged. When we boarded the plane, Ed and I sat together and Amy was in a row by herself. The young man sat in the seat next to her. Within minutes after take off, I could hear Amy giggling, and she seemed to giggle all the way to Taiwan, our first stop. Through-out the trip, the young men accompanied us on the tours, and when it was time to take photos, they would join Amy and say: "Mrs. Guziejka, take a picture of Amy having an *awful* time in Taiwan," or Kuala Lumpur, Bangkok, Singapore,

Amy having an 'awful' time during her Southeast Asian trip.

or wherever…and of course, Amy laughed and giggled her way through all the countries we visited.

Our time in Taipei was short, just an afternoon, evening and the next morning. That evening I noticed that the light seemed very low everywhere we went. We had to squint to read the menus or signs. I also noticed that almost every Taiwanese person wore glasses. I've always wondered if there was a connection between the two, the dimly lit buildings and poor eyesight.

The following morning we visited a massive monument to Chiang Kai Shek, a political and military leader in 20th century China. There were many sets of stairs leading up to the monument on all sides. At this point, Ed was briefly separated from our group. He had gone around a corner to study something that interested him. Everything was lovely and quiet. Ed rounded the corner by himself, and not seeing our group, started to climb the snow-white steps of the monument by himself—not another person was on the steps.

Well, the moment Ed set foot on the stairs, the Taiwanese Military Band came marching out to pay their daily tribute to Chiang Kai Shek. It looked as though the band was playing in honor of Ed's entrance. Ed looked up, saw our group and joined us. He did his best to act dignified under the circumstances, but it was a bit of an embarrassment for him.

Next, our group visited the Sun Yat-sen Memorial Hall. He was the first provisional president when the Republic of China was founded in 1912. The hall was extraordinary, filled with displays, photos and descriptions of Sun's life and the revolution he led. Later during this same tour, we had the opportunity to motor up the Pearl River outside of Macau and visit the birthplace of Sun Yat-sen. The home was kept in mint condition, representing the way it was when he was a child. It was fascinating, and wonderful to visit the two sites during the same tour.

Kuala Lumpur

My memories of Kuala Lumpur are vague. I mostly remember the hotel where we stayed two nights. The hallway in the lobby was open and soared several stories high. They had an extremely tall Christmas tree gracing that area. It seemed to fill the entire area and was decorated with lights of all colors. It was one of the most magnificent Christmas trees I had ever seen.

I remember visiting a few villages and noticing that the people were very gentle and sweet. At a gift shop Ed bought some pewter napkin rings with a three dimensional object on each ring representing our astrological signs. I am Taurus, the Bull, so my napkin ring had small bull on top. Ed had a dragon on his ring, and Amy's had a rooster. These lovely little pewter items are sitting here on top of my desk as I write this memoir. Such wonderful memories!

Thailand

Thailand's 'floating market' fascinated me. The only way to visit it is to get into a boat yourself. Farmers, fishermen and small craftsmen all had boats in the river where they lived and sold their goods, so they did not have to rent space in a building. They were all relatively poor, thence their resources were limited. The scene was charming, but unusual, and I wondered how the families would manage any small children on the boats, while the parents were busy selling to customers. I learned soon enough when I saw children tied to the boat with long ropes so they would not fall off the boat, or could be easily pulled back in from the water if they did.

The river was crowded with boats of all sizes from small to quite large. It was not easy to navigate among the boats as they were moving all about, but our boat captain did quite well. The people were all friendly, and did not seem upset if we did not buy something. I will never forget that day at the 'floating market,' it was so vastly different from anything I had ever seen before in my entire life!

We also attended a special program in a large tent in Thailand that showcased folk dances and other customs of the country. I cannot remember well enough to describe the show in detail now, but every performer was outstanding in his skill. There were some 'sword swallowers' and some snake-handlers, who demonstrated and performed with the snakes. My favorites though were the many ethnic dances and music.

While in Thailand we also visited the 'Gold Market' as had been recommended by so many of my fellow DODDS teachers. I must confess, I had never seen so much real gold hanging on chains or thread or string in all my life. Each separate 'stand' had its own display and there seemed to be countless stands with myriad displays of gold. I bought three necklaces; one each for my daughters Amy and Susan and one for me. I also bought Panda Bear gold coins to hang on the chains.

The weather everywhere we went in Thailand was super, i.e. hot, hot and hot, and no rain. One of the days in Bangkok some of the younger teachers on the tour decided to go for a day trip to a beach and they invited Amy to go with them; Ed and I were very pleased for her and thence, able to do our own thing, which was to stay in the hotel and nap! Trips of this ilk are exhausting, and I found I always needed some kind of a respite in the middle of a journey!

Singapore

Singapore was more modern than Thailand, and the people seemed richer in some respects. The city was made up of three major nationalities, British, Chinese and Muslims. Often they wore the clothing most associated with their heritage, the Muslims in long robes and turbans, the Chinese in Oriental clothing and the British in what I considered 'modern clothing.'

Despite Singapore's modernity and relative wealth, we had to smile when we entered an elevator in one of the tall buildings. On the back wall of the elevator was posted a sign in large black letters which read: '**Do NOT Urinate in this Elevator.**' That is exactly what the sign read! We all smiled for quite a while after reading that sign and of course…heeded the words!

We also had the opportunity to ride in a rickshaw. Amy was in one by herself and Ed and I in another, the rickshaws only had room for two in each, so off we went, zipping in and out of traffic all across the major roads of the city on our way to our destination. The rickshaws are no longer 'pulled' by running

*In Singapore:
Mary in a rickshaw.
Amy with snake.*

men as they were years ago. Now rickshaws are designed to accommodate a bicycle in front, and young men ride the bicycle and whizz in and out of traffic with the passengers seated in the back. Much more efficient!

Also in Singapore, men would stand on the street in certain areas and entice tourists to let them wrap a large snake around their shoulders and neck. Amy was convinced by someone, (no names to be mentioned here...) to have a snake on her shoulders; I am not sure if she thought it was 'such a great opportunity' as it slithered around her shoulder and then back into its owners hands! As I watched the whole process all I could think was, "I'm glad it is not me...I might become hysterical!"

Amy also rode on an elephant! I have photographs of both of these 'once in a lifetime' occurrences! I am not convinced as to how much Amy enjoyed all these experiences, but being a good sport, she acquiesced and I took my usual snapshots! Fortunately for Amy, the three very polite and most thoughtful young military men almost became part of our family during the tour. Throughout most of the photo opportunities, the three would jump forward quickly and pose around Amy who was of course, giggling, as all four of them had their pictures taken by me. They are, I must say, charming and sweet pictures, even to this day! We had many laughs all the way through this trip, and also, most importantly, we all learned so very much!

Hong Kong

Our Southeast Asian trip ended in Hong Kong where Ed, Amy and I had spent the previous Christmas. We were delighted to take another trip on the Star Ferry from Hong Kong to Kowloon. The double-decker 'water bus' ran twenty-four hours a day, seven days a week. The upper deck of the ferry was white, with white life preservers lined up all along the middle of the long, oval boat. The lower deck of the ferry was green.

There were large doors on each end of the ship, which allowed the boat to never waste time turning around when it reached port for passengers, vehicles and cargo to unload. Ed, Amy and I took several trips on the Star Ferry just to enjoy the ambience, the people, and certainly the enormously gorgeous views of Kowloon and Hong Kong Island. When one is tired from many trips to differing countries and miles of travel…the Star Ferry ride can calm the mind and body. It did wonders for tired bodies and minds like Ed's and mine. I cannot speak for Amy since she was only sixteen years old and sixteen year olds do not grow tired as we do. But we enjoyed the relaxing luxury of those 'water bus' rides.

Mainland China

Ed and I wanted to see more of mainland China, but we only had one day to do that. We were told the best way was to take a ferry to Macau, a small island about an hour and a half from Hong Kong. There, we could board a tourist bus that would carry us alongside the Pearl River. It was on this trip that we visited another home of the famous Sun Yat-sen.

When we reached Macau, we had about an hour before we had to board the tour bus. Therefore, we took that time to visit the famous façade of St. Paul's Church. The remains of the Church of St. Paul is one of the top tourist attractions in Macau, China. Built in 1602, the church features a spectacular stone facade. Although the body of the church burnt down in 1835, its stone facade managed to survive the devastation.

I feel so privileged to have seen the façade of St. Paul's Church, and yes, only the whole entire front is still standing, nothing else. That huge façade is seemingly untouched by time, and without anything, absolutely nothing, to support it; it just stands there at the top of a small hill by itself!

One climbs a series of long steep steps to reach the façade. The façade itself is fancy and elegant and of very Roman Catholic origin. While we were there, a

Mary in front of facade of St. Paul's Church in Macau, China

Chinese man explained to us that the church must have had bad 'feng shui' meaning 'bad luck or bad genes' to have suffered the fate that it did.

On the bus trip along the Pearl River we saw farmers using buffaloes and plows to cultivate their land. I also saw many men and buffalos and oftentimes, just men, plowing with different types of home made plows. It tore at my heart to see them working so hard. The plows were shaped somewhat like large, rusty looking scissors to open wedges in the rutty fields. The Chinese farmers were dressed in rags and bent over from all the arduous work that is involved with farming in such an ancient manner.

We also stopped to visit one of the towns. That town was so incredibly poor, my heart ached at the way the people lived their lives. I dared not think of what their homes/houses were like, how they were maintained or how they were built and how many people lived in one or two rooms. If in sumptuous Hong Kong the apartments of three or four rooms held seven to nine or more people, I could only imagine how many people lived in these humble little houses and how miserably these farmers slept. The whole scene was so very sad, yet the people were carrying on and seeking customers and smiling timidly.

We then traveled on to another place that seemed like a town but not like any I had seen before. There were 'stores' (and I call them 'stores' advisedly) up and down the main street. But the 'stores' consisted of little more than men sitting on the unpaved ground with sewing machines at their sides while working for customers. Some tailors hemmed, some repaired, some put on buttons and the like. Other people were selling food or candy or fruit while sitting or squatting on the sidewalks of the main street. To me, this scene was sadder than seeing the people selling their wares on boats in Bangkok.

After walking quite a way up the main street, I noticed a few old men walking and holding on to something, which was not discernable to me at first. As we got closer I realized they held birdcages with one or two little birds in each cage. They were holding the cages in the air as they ambled up and down the main street while happily talking to friends who were doing the same. It appeared to us that the old men were taking their birds out for a walk...*but*...while in their cages. Some men were already sitting, (I assume they had already 'walked' their birds) on a few old chairs by the wall and others were walking toward us or in front of us joining the men who were sitting or moving on. That was certainly one of the most fascinating and most unusual things I had ever seen. We all smiled and nodded to each other as we walked on by, and we found that they and their birds were most polite!

Our next stop was at a restaurant for lunch. I was a little afraid to eat the food having just seen what I described above. Fortunately the restaurant was clean and nice with tablecloths and mirrors and other fancy decorations. The food was good, although I only ate a little cooked rice (my digestive system is easily upset). However, the only Chinese in the restaurant were the wait staff. They were proud to be working there, because the restaurant was reserved only for foreigners, no Chinese were allowed to eat there. That left me feeling rather sad for the natives. Then when I saw where they *were* allowed to eat, which was quite a way off and up the street, I felt worse; it was a ramshackle horrible looking little place where they were allowed to buy little snacks.

After lunch, we visited around the area for an hour or so and then boarded our bus to visit one of the homes of Sun Yat-sen. It was quite small and the image that stays in my mind to this day is his bed with a canopy over it. It also had lovely curtains tied back on each post, but available to be drawn shut to protect the sleeper from drafts or flying insects, most likely. What was most amazing to me though was what his head rested on all night...a block of wood.

"How could one sleep with one's head resting on a block of wood?" I wondered. But the embroidered blankets and curtains were absolutely lovely. The accoutrements were rich and lovely looking but scarce. It was a humble home but rich at the same time in its orderliness and tidiness. I believe it was one of his childhood homes but then that is only a guess and a feeling. There were booklets and brochures for the visitor to take, telling much of Sun Yat-sen's history but I cannot find mine!

We arrived in Hong Kong from Macau in time for a late, light supper. Amy had gone on to Okinawa before us with a couple of ladies from our group who left a day early in order to celebrate the New Year at 'home.' Amy was to stay with friends (she did not want to miss being with her high school classmates on New Year's Eve in Okinawa, Japan!) We returned the next day, arriving in Okinawa on New Year's night from a most successful and noteworthy voyage. The whole trip was long and tiring, but…endlessly interesting. It was a wonderful experience and a trip I will never forget!

The countries we had visited I had always read about but never dreamed I would ever be able to see them in person. To be physically there…exploring the countries' landscapes and observing the customs and seeing the styles and most of all enjoying communicating with the natives was almost unbelievable! I cannot help but thank God and my parents for all those wonderful opportunities!

Leaving Okinawa

I have had people say to me, "Well, if you loved Okinawa so much why did you leave?

My three years in the primary school in Okinawa were wonderful, but I had always wanted to see more of this magnificent world and if I did not transfer soon I would never be able to follow my desires. One never grows younger, one only grows older and I was bordering on 'old' when I started to work for DODDS!

So, when the transfer papers had been passed out at the school earlier in the year, I listed my three choices, the last one of which was Izmir, Turkey because I had seen there was an opening there. I forget now what my first choice had been, or even the second.

When I finally saw the paperwork later in the year, which said *yes* to a transfer to *Izmir, Turkey*…I was elated! The news left me with incredible feelings that seem difficult to describe here and now. I raced home after school to tell Ed and Amy my news. I stormed in through the front door, yelling and waving the paper work, "We're going to Turkey, we're going to Turkey!"

Ed was upstairs lying down and he yelled back, "What did you say?"

Trying to holler while rushing upstairs and completely out of breath, I exclaimed, "Oh, Ed, Ed, you won't believe this...I can't believe it myself...I am being transferred to Izmir, Turkey!"

Ed then became excited and hollered, "Let me see the paper work, I can't believe this is happening..." I bounced onto our bed, Amy was nowhere around, probably had not yet returned from school, and I hollered with as much excitement as my whole being could control and sustain!

Still hollering rapidly as though Ed were deaf I went on with, "We are moving from Okinawa after school ends! And...I am going to teach high school band as well as elementary school music. What do you think of that?" Having spoken of teaching high school band my voice seemed to raise another octave. Maybe all the neighbors could hear but it was of no matter...I was happy!

All kinds of feelings and reactions then came into play. We were both hugging each other and laughing and crying at the same time. I tried to calm down a bit but decided I didn't want to calm down at all since this type of thing does not happen often. We were hugging and holding, eager to leave and yet loving where we were. What a quandary...I loved being in Okinawa but looked forward to living in Izmir, Turkey!!

I was qualified to teach High School Band but had never had the opportunity to do so before. I decided I would accept the job, the transfer and the challenge, and move to Izmir. Such a feeling of elation and fright I had at the same time! When school ended that year, we had to pack up our house and say goodbye to the friends we had made in the last three years. That was difficult to do, but after spending some time with DODDS teachers, I had learned how inventive they were, and I felt we would meet again one day. And surprisingly to us (since we were novices to this way of life), our DODDS friends *did* keep in touch with us, and we saw many of them during the next few years. More on those stories later.

In the meantime, I learned not everyone was as keen about exploring the world as I was. On the last day of school, I decided to see the children off on their busses. (The homeroom teacher always escorted their students to the busses. Since I did not have a homeroom, this was not one of my regular duties, but I decided I wanted to say 'so long, farewell, auf weiderzein, goodbye' one last time as the students departed.)

As I crossed the first floor corridor, a teacher, who was coming down from the second floor with her class, leaned over the railing and hollered at me, "Mary, I hear you got a transfer."

"Yes," I hollered back, while looking up at her with a huge smile on my face.

"Where are you going to teach next year?" she hollered back.

"I'm going to Izmir, Turkey," I replied with an even broader smile.

With deep disgust emanating from her face and voice she replied, "You'll hate it there." And that was that. I was left in the hallway with a complete feeling of puzzlement. That was her way, evidently, of saying 'bon voyage/goodbye' to me; a charming person, I must admit! I had never known her well, but I do not ever recall seeing her with a smile on her face at school. To this day it is a mystery to me why some people will stay in a particular job for years if they dislike it so much. She, as I found out during my three years of working with her class, obviously disliked teaching. Why then…stay…since that behavior affects children so negatively? I never could understand this, and yet I saw so much of it through all my fifty years of teaching. I, for one, loved all I did with children no matter where I was working.

Actually, that teacher was the exception to the rule. During my three years of working for DODDS, usually whenever anyone received a transfer, no matter where they were going to teach next, everyone was very happy for the person, saying, "We'll miss you but we're happy for you!"

For example, one day I was at the Officer's Club when I happened to meet a kindergarten teacher in the ladies room. Although I did not know her well, she seemed to have a positive and humorous outlook on life. When she saw me she gave me a big smile, said hello, then went into an empty stall.

I was waiting to enter the next empty stall, when a five-year-old girl entered the ladies room. She was cute and comical as only a five-year-old can be. Suddenly, to my amazement, I saw her kneel down on the floor in front of the 'stall' where the kindergarten teacher was. She bent over a bit more and then peeked under the toilet door; looking up and inside of the toilet stall, she hollered excitedly with her squeaky little voice, "Miss Smith, I knew that was you sitting there. I could tell by your shoes!"

The child stayed there for a moment or two, perhaps receiving some reply, which I could not hear. The girl then got up, brushed herself off and left the ladies room. When the teacher finally came out of the stall, she was 'laughing her head off.'

"I have had many things happen to me since teaching kindergarten but this one 'takes the cake'!" she said to me. I had to give her credit, maintaining such a good sense of humor about the incident. We chuckled about the incongruousness of the situation, and the charming and open innocence of little children. As we left the ladies room, she wished me 'Bonne Chance' on my new job, then called out in a loud and laughing voice as she rounded the corner away from me, "You will love teaching in Turkey, I know, I have been there."

By May of 1987 Amy had officially graduated from Kubasaki High School and had decided to go home to live with our daughter Susan and her husband John. After taking a bit of a break, Amy planned to find a job for the summer, then start school at a junior college in Concord, N.H. in September. Ed and I also went home to the states for a month or so that summer to visit our family and friends whom we had not seen in a year.

Then, it was off to Izmir, and a whole new set of adventures!

But if the while I think on thee dear friend,
All losses are restored and sorrows end...

Sonnet xxx
—Shakespeare

Chapter 19
Izmir, Turkey

When to the sessions of sweet silent thought
I summon up remembrance of things past....

Sonnet xxx
—Shakespeare

'Around the World in Eighty Days'
Well...half 'way 'round

The summer of 1987 was incredibly busy with packing up to leave Okinawa and then moving to Turkey in August. We attended a few 'going away' parties and visited some of our favorite places on Okinawa. We had become close to a number of people and it was heart wrenching to say goodbye. Would I ever be able to come back to Okinawa? (Doubtful then and probably never...now!)

Sad/happy is the only way to describe our feelings. Ed enjoyed Okinawa as much as I; although he was not able to teach or work he nevertheless had made many friends and connections who had shown him all around Okinawa. Ed would especially miss Paul Truesdell, the roving reporter for the military newspaper who had included Ed on many of his assignments. However, the prospect of going home, seeing my mother, son and two daughters again, and then starting over in a new school and teaching *band* for the first time in my career left me beaming from ear to ear.

All my DODDS experiences hold wonderful remembrances, all mostly good, some funny, and some, the kind one wonders at afterward. I hope I can hold onto all my memories always. Many things went wrong, but many things went well. It was a hard time, it was an easy time, it was a rough time, it was a seamless time; and living in Izmir was, of course, more different than Okinawa and more different than anything I had ever experienced in my whole life. But then, each and every country is vastly unusual, one from the other. Therefore, I am now anxious to tell you all about Izmir, Turkey, about the 'before,' the 'during' and the 'after!'

※ ※ ※

The military allows its employees to make 'rest stops' when moving from one base to another. Therefore, Ed and I planned a Hawaiian stopover for a few days. I had been to Hawaii before, but this was Ed's first visit to the lovely islands. When he visited Pearl Harbor, he was emotionally moved. Ed and his five brothers had all been in the service during World War II. Ed was in the Navy, but did not see any 'action' because the war ended before he completed basic training.

However, Ed's brother Stanley had been stationed in Hawaii throughout the war, but fortunately was not on a ship in the port on December 7, 1941. Another brother, Henry, served as a paratrooper and participated in the Normandy Beach invasion and other famous battles during World War II. The other brothers served in other military divisions all over the world. Thank the good Lord, they ALL survived.

Once in the states we visited our son Eric and his wife Kelly in Texas, our daughters Susan and Amy in New Hampshire, and my mother in Lowell. Before we knew it, our six weeks of home leave was over and we were on our way to Izmir, Turkey. Leaving my family grew harder and harder each summer, but the rewards and benefits for me, and my family…could not be ignored either…and I also loved my job.

As I mentioned earlier, the military allows rest stops for its employees moving from one base to another. Therefore, it was a whirlwind of travel for us that summer. From Okinawa, to Hawaii, to Texas, to New Hampshire, then Massachusetts, then England, Germany and finally Izmir.

After visiting family and friends in Massachusetts, we flew to London, England to visit our good friends Joy and Charles Pringle. We always enjoyed our visits with them in the small village of Chipstead.

From London, we flew to Frankfurt, Germany. There we met and visited with Barbara Bennett. She had attended Lowell State Teachers College and majored in music education, but was about five years older than I. I had heard from other teacher friends that Barbara was teaching overseas, working for our government. Therefore, I acquired her address from our college and then wrote her a letter informing her we were coming to Frankfurt, and would like to meet her.

Barbara was a long time employee of DODDS, had married a German gentleman, and to the best of my knowledge she had spent most of her teaching career in Germany. I vaguely recalled she had come back to the Lowell State Teachers College in Lowell years ago to talk about DODDS, but I had not attended her talk because at that time I was not interested in working overseas. By the time we met up, Barbara had become the Supervisor of all the DODDS music education teachers in northern Germany. Germany was a big country with many American military bases, so she had a good size job on her plate.

Barbara met us at the military hotel in Frankfurt where we were staying. Over the next couple of days she took us to Heidelberg and several other interesting sites. My memories are a little vague as to exactly what we did those two days, but she was most kind in her hospitality as she showed us around.

The other two days we had in Germany we were on our own. Germany's big cities were quite modern since most of them had suffered extensive bombing damage during World War II and had been rebuilt. However, the German countryside was still filled with old, quaint villages. One day we took a boat ride on the Rhine River. The daylong trip stopped at little villages all along the river. At each stop we got off the boat and walked around the villages and enjoyed their quaint atmosphere. In a village where we had stopped for lunch, we met some Oriental girls who were visiting Germany. We ate lunch together and had the most interesting conversations, especially when they learned we had lived in Okinawa. They themselves were from mainland Japan. The whole day was lovely, as were the little German villages and the friendly German people who lived there.

Nothing can come of nothing...

King Lear
—Shakespeare

Finally we left Germany and flew on to Turkey. We arrived, but NOT in Izmir and not at a new and modern airport. Instead we debarked into a tiny, dark, dingy, dirty building somewhere outside the city proper. This 'airport' had no discernable system of organization. We could not read any of the signs because they were *all* in Turkish. We anxiously searched around this miserable mess of an airport for our 'meeter/greeter,' dodging hens and roosters who were preening and pecking all around, leaving piles of feces all over the floor. We had to watch carefully where we walked!

In time, we found our luggage, but never found a 'meeter/greeter' as we'd had in Okinawa when we first arrived. We waited and waited thinking perhaps the person was late or lost. Finally, when we were the only ones left in the small dirty airport it seemed, aside from the hens and roosters, we decided no one was going to meet us, and we had to find our own way to Izmir. "Oh dear," was all I could think..."oh dear!"

No one spoke English and all I could say in Turkish was 'Mirhaba' (hello) and 'teshikure ederim' (thank you), but somehow we found a taxi to take us to Izmir. We gave the driver the name of our military hotel. He drove us to Izmir and then drove around and around the area of our hotel, stopping, seemingly, to ask directions. (Of course, at that time we didn't know he was driving around our hotel, since all the signs were in Turkish).

Whoever he spoke with when he stopped got a big laugh out of whatever he was saying. All the conversations were in Turkish of course, so we had no idea what was being said. After the exchange of words, he would climb back in the car, hunch his shoulders up in the air, lift his two hands, palms upright, as though he knew nothing, and then drive off with us again.

I kept telling him the name of the hotel but he seemed vague about it. Finally, after he drove around the center of the city three more times we became suspicious since he seemed to be enjoying himself immensely, (too much, if you were to ask me then) at our expense. We told him to stop on the main street, which faces the Izmir Bay; we got out with our luggage; and paid him a whopping fee. Fortunately, we discovered the military hotel was just up the street and some friendly young Turks helped Ed and me with our luggage. Evidently the taxi man thought he would play us for fools and then in turn, earn more money. Unfortunately for our wallets, he succeeded.

At the military-sponsored hotel, called The Kordon Hotel, we were shown to our room after checking in. Although the room had a nice view of the bay, it was smaller than 'small.' It was almost a hovel, and the standards of cleanliness were quite lax. After living there for a few days I found I kept getting sick to my stomach (always a weak spot of mine). After a couple of weeks had gone by, I got up the courage to speak to the principal at my new school, Harvey Getz, and asked if the military would pay for us to stay in a hotel other than the specified military hotel.

"Yes, of course! No problem with that," he told me. I was so relieved. We moved to the Izmir Palais Hotel, across the street from the Kordon Hotel, but still facing the bay. We were given a larger, much cleaner room that also faced the bay. We still had a 'room with a view!' The Aegean Sea flowed into the Izmir Bay and consequently there were many vessels ranging from huge ships and tankers to small rowboats crossing the bay all day. The view of the sky, the clouds, the water and the overall changing scene was lovely! Once, when we were in our apartment, Ed counted 54 different types of sailing vessels in the bay.

At any rate, we ended up staying at the Palais Hotel for several months while we searched for an apartment; a task which turned out to be more difficult than we had imagined.

In the summer before we moved to Turkey, I visited with Teresa, a fellow teacher at the Sanborn School in Andover. While I was in Okinawa, Teresa had been teaching in Izmir. She gave up her job with DODDS though because her mother had become quite ill. While we were chatting I told her we were going to have to find an apartment in Izmir since there was no military base housing available as there had been in Okinawa.

"Oh, do ask Mrs. Z," Teresa said with a big smile, "she would be so happy to help you find an apartment. She was such a great help to me when I arrived!"

Mrs. Z taught one of the fourth grades, and because of Teresa's insistence, I asked her if she could help us find an apartment. We went with her one afternoon to see an estate agent and to look at an apartment. To our utter amazement and surprise Mrs. Z was cross, grumpy, and hard to get along with during our first interview with the Turkish real estate agent. I became so upset and embarrassed at having asked her to help us when obviously she did not want to do it at all, that I told her, "Thank you very much Mrs. Z. I think we have an apartment already. You will not have to go with us again."

Mrs. Z grunted, no smile, no asking of where the apartment was located, nothing…just a grunt! I will never forget Teresa's final words to us as we left for Turkey, "Contact Mrs. Z. She speaks Turkish fluently and would *love* to help you!" *Wrong!*

We eventually did find an apartment on our own. (A 'meeter/greeter' as

View of the bay from our apartment balcony in Izmir, Turkey.

we'd had in Okinawa never did come forth. The DODDS teachers in Turkey seemed grumpy and cross, and not nearly as helpful at that time.) The apartment we finally found on our own was on the bir inci Kordon, (meaning the first street, which faces the bay) and that apartment became ours for the remainder of the years we stayed in Izmir.

❧ ❧ ❧

During our first evening in Izmir, when we were still at the Kordon hotel, after unpacking, Ed and I decided to take a walk to find the elementary school where I'd be working. It was supposed to be near the hotel. As we were walking we met an American high school boy, (it was easy to tell the difference between American boys and Turkish boys.) I stopped him; told him who we were and asked if he could direct us to the school.

The boy, Mike, was a student at the military high school. He walked us to the schools; pointing out which one was the elementary and which one the high school. We did not go into the buildings as they were closed for the night, but at least I knew how to get there the next day when I had to report to work.

After leaving Mike, we continued to walk around Izmir for a while. We found it was not clean, tidy and nice like Okinawa. Unfortunately, there were beggars sitting, or squatting on the sidewalks with their backs to the walls of the buildings. I always felt as though I should feed them and give them clothing. I saw a young woman with only one leg, sitting on the ground begging for money or food!! I still, to this day see her face, her lack of good clothing, her hunger and *one leg*!

❧ ❧ ❧

The elementary school where my music room was located was a refurbished old tobacco warehouse. The building seemed older than old. My classroom was on the fifth floor of the building. I had to climb black wrought iron stairs all the way because there were no elevators. (And knowing Turkey as I do now, I'm not sure I would have felt safe riding a Turkish elevator.)

When I entered my classroom, one of the first things I noticed was the windows had bars on them. (As it turned out, all the building's windows had bars. In later years, the bars were removed from some windows, but never from mine. In the beginning I felt as though I was teaching in a jail!) The room did appear clean with what looked like new white acoustical cork tiles on all the walls,-a very important feature for a band classroom. It was not a large room, and certainly not glamorous, but in spite of the barred windows I was certain I could manage.

Down the hall and on the same side as the band classroom, there was a small, inadequate auditorium. But then...it was better than nothing and, after all was said and done, it was a small school, especially compared to my school in Okinawa.

After finding my classroom, I was shown the offices where I had to fill out what seemed an endless amount of paperwork! (If there is one thing the military likes...it is paperwork.)

The high school was in a small building around the corner and just a few yards away from the elementary school. That building (which had *not* been an old tobacco warehouse) was too small to house the 'extra' classes such as band, home economics and physical education for the high school students. The seventh through twelfth graders had to climb the steep iron stairs carrying their books and instruments to my classroom on the fifth floor for their band lessons.

All in all, everything in both school buildings was small, inadequately located, and difficult to deal with as a teacher. (The bathrooms especially left a lot to be desired.) But on the other hand, I loved teaching in Izmir and thoroughly enjoyed what I was doing in spite of all its problems, and we all learned... the students and me. Yes, I learned vast amounts before my time was finished and had a good time doing it!

The enrollment at the high school was considerably smaller than the elementary school. Although no one ever told me specifically, I think many military parents thought that an education at the Izmir military high school would not be as good for their children as an education in the states. However, after being in Izmir a while I felt those parents were wrong. Study and travel overseas offers many major opportunities not available in the states. I felt, after a very short while, that when our high school students graduated and went home to the States they would have an education that would rival anything in the USA.

☙❧ ☙❧ ☙❧

During my last few days in Okinawa I was surprised to receive a letter from Izmir, Turkey. I opened it quickly curious to know who in the world would be writing to me from Izmir. It turned out to be from the band teacher I was to replace. As I read the letter, horror filled my being. The more I read, the worse it got! The whole letter was disgusting; it was all about the 'awful' students, 'the hateful kids' who despised band classes, their poor attitudes, and the broken down, rotten instruments and anything else he could name that was negative.

He despised Turkey and the school and anything connected with it and wondered why on earth anyone would want to choose a place like that to live and work. He also said I was foolish to even consider teaching in Izmir and other sentences that were so degrading to Izmir and DODDS that I will not repeat them here. I wish now that I had kept the letter. Instead, I was so disgusted with it I tore it up into tiny pieces and threw it into the trash.

Therefore, it is no wonder that when I began teaching high school band that year I only had sixteen students in the class. One of them was Mike, the young man we had met our first night in Izmir. It was a relief to know at least one student. He played the drums. I was determined to change the 'negative' attitude of the students towards band class, and I'm proud to say that by the end of my seven years in Izmir about 50, or almost three-quarters of the junior and senior high school students were either in beginner or advanced band.

> *I talk in order to teach;*
> *I teach in order to learn*
>
> **—Robert Frost**

However, it was not easy in the beginning to win the students over. When I first met my sixteen band students they all seemed sullen and bored…but then why not, after having that man as a teacher for a year or two I would have been sullen also! I sensed immediately how disillusioned they were and how they were probably only in the band because their parents did not want them to drop out.

I took them into my confidence and involved them in the decision making process about the work we would do, especially about having more concerts during the school year. And I suggested that we absolutely *should* have *uniforms*. Gradually, each day the band students became more and more interested and seemingly excited, not too much but…a little, about the prospect of concerts and band jackets and the like! Each day two or three students would 'perk up,' look more interested in what I was saying, and based on the behavior of those two or three students, two or three days later, a few more students started to show more interest in the class. Nothing happened overnight, but somehow after a few weeks the students began to smile, talk with me, *and*…to practice a little.

Mary Guziejka and Izmir High School Band students in uniforms

They especially seemed excited about the band 'uniforms.' The uniform ended up consisting of a tailored blazer, worn with white shirts, black trousers and bow ties. The main decision to be made was what color the jacket should be. We discussed it in class. The Turkish flag is solid red with a white crescent moon and a white star. We talked about the importance of the color red in Turkish culture. I told them that wearing red would honor Turkey, our host country so to speak. And so it was decided the jackets would be red.

Who paid for the jackets? The parents of the students in the band raised the money somehow; they all seemed quite excited that I was in Izmir working with their children and seemed willing to help with any project I suggested. I wrote many letters to the students' parents about what was needed and they were most cooperative.

We had the jackets tailored in Konak, a famous market place in Izmir. I had become friendly with the home economics teacher at the school, Joann Cobanli. She agreed to help me with the project of fitting the students (she was always kind and generous with her time and talent). She spoke more Turkish than I did, and so was able to communicate with the tailor better than I could. We went to Konak with three or four students at a time to make sure each student had as much individual attention as possible. Sometimes, parents of students went along with us. The entire experience was great fun, and once they had the jackets and we dressed in our 'uniforms' a time or two, I noticed the students were sitting up a bit straighter and I swear I could hear a distinct improvement in the sound coming from the band. We wore our 'uniforms,' red jacket, white shirt, black trousers and either a black or a red bow tie each time we gave a concert.

> *To business that we love*
> *We rise be'time*
> *And go to with delight!*
>
> **Antony and Cleopatra**
> **—Shakespeare**

This is not to say that the band improved overnight. They had learned very little in the previous two years and they needed to learn to read notes and play scales. But they worked harder and began to improve.

The school had a new principal that year, having arrived the same time as I. I soon learned that this principal, Harvey Getz, played the saxophone. One day I asked him if he would mind playing with the advanced band class when he had time. He responded enthusiastically, checked his schedule, and joined us as often as possible, sometimes several days a week. (The band met daily).

When he came into our room, I noticed the students sat up a little straighter. We gave him the music we were working on and he played well, but perhaps a bit too loud. The saxophone section sounded good, but after a few days, one of the girls in the saxophone section came to me after everyone else had left the class and said, "Mrs. Guziejka, do you think it would be okay to ask the Principal not to play so loud? We (meaning the three other saxophonists) cannot hear what we are playing because he is so loud!"

She was a nice girl and I knew she was not trying to be rude, just being honest. Mr. Getz played his heart out all the time, as though he was the only one in the room. The whole episode was rather sweet and funny; she did not want to insult him, and yet, she was having an awful time trying to play since he was too *loud!* When one plays in a group one has to listen to the group, not play as though you are a solo performer.

It was a difficult situation and I was not sure how to handle it, but luck came my way. The principal began to grow busy…busy with this or busy with that, whatever principals have to do and for quite a while he was unable to join us in the class. Whenever he did manage though, the saxophone section sighed and smiled at each other, but welcomed him into the room warmly each time he returned after that episode.

At this point I need to share with you another problem I had shortly after arriving at the school. The school owned more than 70 band instruments, but I found them flung all together in a small, dusty classroom closet. They were all in horrible condition. Some were broken and none of them had had any annual maintenance. I was flummoxed at first. How could I expect students to learn to play an instrument well if it was in such poor condition?

I called Gary Bogle, the Music Coordinator for the Mediterranean Region of DODDS as soon as I could. I introduced myself (I learned he was stationed outside of Madrid, Spain) and we had a long talk about the instruments, the students and my concerns (that this was my first time teaching high school band).

Gary was more than generous with his time and he helped me immensely. He had some new instruments sent to our school immediately and advised me where I could send the broken ones for repair. I felt quite happy at that point since I had never worked with anyone else who was as thoughtful and kind and productive except for my supervisor Al Tatarunis. in Danvers! I was immensely grateful for Gary's advice and help; his undying love of his job affected me greatly through my seven plus years in Izmir.

The custodian diligently took over the shipping of the broken instruments to be repaired. He made many, many trips up and down the five flights of stairs for me and methodically marked, packaged, and mailed them to the repair facility. The instruments were not all sent out at the same time since there were so many of them. But in due time they were all sent off, and when they each returned, they were beautiful and quite functional. That was absolutely thrilling!

Elementary School Classes

There is pansies,
Them's for thoughts

Hamlet
—Shakespeare

Whenever I think of my elementary school students, I equate their beautiful young faces with flowers. The more you 'water' them with time and understanding, the brighter they become. Have you ever noticed how happy everyone is when singing? The happiness seems to develop within the child almost automatically.

My goal has always been to teach children *how* to sing, with an understanding of the music so that they will continue to enjoy music and singing for the remainder of their lives. I would never, ever want a child to walk away from a music class saying they hated to sing. As I've mentioned before, I constantly used the Kodaly hand signals in all my music classes. The hand signs designate in the air where the sounds, (notes) go, as in 'up, down, or stay on the same level etc.' This helps to create a lovely tone quality to the children's voices and constantly increases their ability to understand the 'how' of music.

I also incorporate drama with the singing. I ask students to act out the words of the song while singing. This gives the children more confidence to sing. I also use dance. Children love to dance and a dancer always enjoys singing. In addition, I have students draw pictures of the songs. Children love to draw, color and paint and also absolutely love picturing what they are singing.

We had music books filled with songs; I taught the children by rote, meaning by memory, but following in a book at the same time. I sang, they 'framed' the phrases of music from second grade upwards, (meaning one finger of one hand at the beginning of a line or phrase, and one finger from other hand at the other end of the same line or phrase.) Within time they knew many, many things about following the directions in which the notes move, meaning up, down or stay the same, for starters. I rarely used the piano as accompaniment, and when I did it was only after they could sing the song with lovely intonation. Why? Well, the tone quality of the children's voices invariably is much better, more pure, and superior sounding when learned or sung by the child's voice without accompaniment.

I did not use music books with the kindergarten and first grade students so I had their complete and undivided attention. Sometimes I had to work hard to keep their attention, but dancing or acting out songs helped immensely. I can, in all honesty, say the students left happily when we were finished and returned the next time humming or asking, "Can we do this song first, Mrs. G?" or "Can we do a dance first, Mrs. G.?" If all in the world were as happy as kindergarteners and first and second graders, it would truly be a lovely world.

I only saw each elementary school class one 40-minute period per week, unlike the high school band students with whom I worked daily. That was not a large amount of time; nevertheless I felt some tiny miracles did happen in the years that I worked with the younger students. Dramatization makes a child live outside of himself and take on another role, meaning another role in life, and no matter how small, this is important. It could have been 'Higgeldy piggeldy my black hen' or 'Jumping Joan' or 'Humpty Dumpty' or 'Marching to Bombay' (a special favorite with kindergarteners and first graders.)

I was especially rewarded when the sixth graders got into the habit of singing a Christmas carol on the way to my class each day during the holiday season. The carol was one I had composed at the special request of a friend I had recently met in Turkey. Buck was writing a children's book about the 'Tasmanian' bush (he was a native of Tasmania) and he asked me to compose 'The Bush Christmas Carol.' Written in the key of 'C' and in 4/4 time, I taught it to the sixth grade class that first year in Izmir, and they took to it immediately. I'm not sure, but I believe the teacher of the class they were in before they reported to my music class encouraged them to start singing the carol as they were leaving to come to my class. It was the sweetest thing a class could have done for me. The lyrics to the carol are as follows with the first stanza being repeated at the end:

The Bush Christmas Carol
—Mary Guziejka

Are there any words to be said by me
That can best describe to you the joy I see
In the world around me that I hold so fine?
All the world is yours and mine.

All the trees and leaves and mountains
All the skies and seas and blue,
All the birds and rainbows, friendships
And our family,
I love you!

We did not do any big dramas with the elementary school children in Izmir, except during one of the years when the upper grades performed the musical, *Oliver!*, and I opened the tryouts to upper elementary age children. However, everyone, no matter what age they are, likes to show someone or tell someone what they have accomplished and my students were no different. Therefore, we always had Christmas concerts for parents where the students in all grades dramatized Christmas scenes, with pantomime and song.

I also wanted to let the students demonstrate their folk and square dancing skills to the parents, but we had no playground or other space large enough to hold all the children and their parents. I spoke to the principal about my desire and he was a gem. He obtained permission for us to occasionally use the Bayrakli Park, which was an area a few miles away from our downtown school. The US Military had many offices and repair shops at Bayrakli; it was like a base, but not officially, as I interpreted it, although I could be in error on that one.

In time, we chose a date for our first event at Bayrakli Park. I called for volunteers, and the parents came in droves. A letter had gone home to parents informing them of the time and place and asking if the children could come dressed with some little piece of clothing or hat or whatever that would represent Square Dancing, or 'a hoe down'. As it turned out, many families had lived in Texas or other southern states and were well aware of how to dress the children for a 'hoe down'. Therefore, when the day finally arrived for the dance, the children were costumed beautifully. In addition, many parents came to watch and to dance with their children. Parents also organized refreshments for the event, and set up tables with drinks and home made sweets. The event was great fun, and became an annual program at Bayrakli.

Also during my first year in Izmir, there was an event in the spring that turned out so well, I wrote a story about it which was published in a music magazine in Massachusetts. I was not paid for the publication, but that was of little importance to me. The fact that I was actually published was the important issue. I will let the story speak for itself.

YAKAKOY
by Mary M. Guziejka

'Yakakoy' sang and danced its way into my vocabulary one day in March while the principal and I were talking. We were seated around a table in his basement office. I was trying hard not to focus my attention on the various ankles parading by *his windows. Our discussion centred upon his concern for our elementary school children and their lack of exercise. A wiry sort of man, he seemed to be plugged into an electric circuit much of the time. Great energy poured out of his voice and body, his arms and hands flailing in the air as though he was swatting a fly. He bellowed loudly, "Izmir elementary school has no playground! Who ever heard of such a thing? A school without a place for children to play, and we have to live with it. Well! I'm going to do something about it. I'm taking the children on a volksmarch. All of them!" He slapped his hand on the table, saying, "And… I'm going to do it now. We are going to hike in YAKAKOY!"*

The name of the village fascinated me. I ran it around on the back of my tongue for a few seconds. It pulsated. Yakakoy, Yakakoy, I thought. What a great rhythm, and so pleasurable to pronounce! I felt a thump, thump, thump, in my chest. My heart beat a little faster. My mind sifted rapidly through ideas of how my high school band and I might participate. With a rush of words I exploded loudly with, "What a marvellous idea! We'll have a concert, an old fashion outdoor band concert!"

Mr. Getz sat there staring at me, his eyes growing bigger and bigger, his arms stretched out across the whole table, palms flat.

"The children will love it," I continued, "I just know they will. The young ones can listen and the older ones will play." More words bubbled out of my mouth as I added, "And a picnic while they listen to the music. Yes, we'll have a picnic!"

Mr. Getz jumped up from the table, knocked over his chair, arms flailing in the air and yelled, "What a wonderful idea! Let's do it!"

The Izmir American Band is under my direction and I would embrace any new idea to motivate my high school students to practice. I would walk miles. I would climb mountains. I would go on a volksmarch! Having an outdoor band concert in the little village of Yakakoy seemed absolutely perfect.

The following Saturday, the principal, my husband Ed, with his always present camera, and I went to inspect the village which is located a few miles outside of Izmir, Turkey. We paced the road, set the course, and gauged the miles. We found Yakakoy to be charming. On the outskirts of the village we found an honest to goodness real Roman road with round, ancient cobblestones. The stones shone in the sun, giving off a warm, yellowish glow. Then to my pleasure and surprise a well -preserved, arched Roman bridge appeared at the end of the road, and spanned a stream of clear, bubbling, singing water. I was thrilled.

"Oh, Ed. Look!" I grabbed his camera arm and pumped it up and down. "The children can play over and under the ancient ruins. It's like they were built yesterday.

Our school children have an opportunity in Turkey that is second to none anywhere else in the world." The pitch of my voice was rising. "This is where civilisation began!" My excitement grew by the minute. Ed kept snapping photos.

He calmly walked on alone downstream, composing his pictures while I treaded carefully on the cobblestones. (I don't know why, but he's always calm whenever I'm excited.) I clambered onto the Roman bridge and sat a while in the ever-present Aegean sun, absorbing the past and the present as they collided in my mind. Two thousand years have gone by and here I am, preparing American children to descend upon these memories. Unbelievable!

Leaving my daydreams behind on the bridge, I hurried to find Ed and we continued our trek to the village. Our principal, an inveterate runner, was miles ahead of us. Never mind. We had much to see, and a slow pace was just what was needed that Saturday afternoon.

We saw small, whitewashed, old square houses, built of crumbly white stones, low to the ground with red wavy tiled roofs. 'Click, click', went the camera. The houses were sometimes walled in or jammed together for friendship and security. They huddled into one another reminding me of childhood playing card houses, leaning one onto the other as if too much wind would blow them over.

Donkeys, camels, hens and chickens lived in close proximity with the villagers. I noticed hens and chickens lived INSIDE and OUTSIDE the houses as well. Some were perched on stoops while others stalked proudly and haughtily around Yakakoy.

"Oh, Ed," I cried, "Maybe you can photograph some camels or donkeys for me while we're here." Ed knew of my love for animal pictures. My album is filled with them. An assenting grunt came back as a reply. He had the superior camera.

While climbing the hilly, winding road, my eyes embraced the gorgeous, white puffy clouds, gentle rolling fields, orchards, groves, hillocks and purple mountains far off in the distance. One can breathe in Yakakoy! To my complete delight, I found that Yakakoy has what we all crave: serenity, peace and charm.

"Oh, Ed!" I cried, "It's not a city and it's hardly a town. Why...it's just right!"

In sharp contrast, Izmir is an overpopulated city, dirty, grimy, and polluted, in the water and in the air although natural beauty surrounds Izmir with mountains and sea. It is gorgeous if one can overlook anything that was touched by man. Our school building is an old tobacco warehouse with barred windows, sandwiched between a children's clinic and hospital, a factory and an empty building forever awaiting a tenant. Izmir is where we live and go to school. We also have no playground...

There was so much to see as we approached the heart of the village; the mosque *with its minaret, and the cay (tea) house which contained the only television to be found in the village; houses crowded quixotically around the mosque and a little one room schoolhouse, which sat across the road.*

I poked Ed excitedly and hollered above the wind. We were high up and the wind was strong. "Look, Ed, the cay house has a courtyard. That will be our stage. It's at least five feet above the road and our small children can sit facing the stage with their backs to the schoolhouse." My eyes darted from one house to the other, and I smiled at the village children who dared to peek out at me. My mind pressed forward impulsively forming the plan for the day of the Volksmarch.

"Of course it has a courtyard," Ed replied smugly, looking as though I had no brains at all. "No one in the Mediterranean would sit inside to drink tea when they can sit outside in the sun." Straight-backed wooden chairs and benches, polished by time, marked the simplicity of the courtyard. The chairs were smooth and shiny as satin from years of use. They would hold our musicians.

The principal, Ed and I drank our cay in the courtyard and planned our attack. We would separate the children into two groups, since the grateful Izmir Sultan Band students were excused from classes for the day! The younger children would arrive early by buses and tour, visit and play games and have a 'walk' up the high hill to listen to the band concert. The High School Band would arrive later in uniform (no jackets, too hot) and with instruments, presenting themselves at the 'stage' area.

The big day finally arrived after much preparation, and here we were, in the gorgeous sun with our beautiful children and our High School Band, which was dropped off closer to the Cay House so as to avoid carrying and lugging all their instruments.

Teachers, chaperones, Ed and the principal and I were also walking. The air was clear, brisk and fresh. The wind was blowing, birds were singing, and the earth was real; it was the colour of vibrant, red clay. Everyone in the school wore Turkey's colour, which was our school colour. Red! It was a gorgeous day!

Teachers smiled, children squealed with delight. High-pitched voices filled the air. None of the villagers knew we were coming. "They will certainly be surprised," I said happily to no one in particular as I plodded along.

We finally reached the turn off point for the younger children to leave the older group. The primary children moved off with the kite carrying adults toward the Roman road and bridge. The other one hundred and fifty children kept going, rushing forward, and interrupting the tranquil existence around us. Time raced ahead as they walked past points of interest. Pine groves caught our attention as village women sat on their haunches diligently sorting and collecting cones: wonderfully edible nuts hide in these cones. A cemetery sat still in the middle of our rushing pace giving evidence of its age; tombstones topped with turbans, a silent testimony of days gone by. I looked at my eager and enthusiastic young children and knew they were about ready to stop. They kept asking, "Are we almost there? Are we almost there?" They yearned for the cay house as it meant a time to eat and be entertained. This was the halfway point of their march.

A loud and explosive cheer issued forth from the front of the long, red, snaking line. We were there. The last hill was conquered. We rounded the bend and the wind smacked us in the face. We had arrived!

At the same time, luckily, the band students and instruments arrived in their school bus, since it was impossible for them to walk the whole route carrying all their instruments and music. They were quickly dispatched (it was a small band of about eleven students at that point) to the 'stage' area outside the cay house by the wonderfully reliable band parents who helped me every step of the way.

The first people we saw at the top of the hill were women. They were bundled and swaddled in layers of cloth causing them to appear fat and flowing in the wind. Their heads were covered with scarves but their faces were showing. Many were sitting on mounds of earth, apparently resting at the noon hour. A few were standing, quietly talking. They greeted us with, "Hoz gildenez, hoz gildenez," (meaning…welcome) shy smiles and waves. The women nodded approval at Ed's picture taking as he showed them his camera with an expectant look on his face. A small group of men sitting in the courtyard of the cay house, but not too near the women, appraised the situation. They saw the band students with their instruments, and gestured for us to come up and sit. The only communication between us was positive and welcoming body language.

The principal and three of our teachers were invited to sit on chairs at 'stage' left. Murmuring and bowing went on at length until all were seated. On 'stage' right some of the men from the village sat quietly; their heads covered with turbans, moustached and with brown faces, which seemed almost black. A few others sat in a row behind the musicians. The band was arranged in two rows across the middle of the 'stage.'

I saw instantly that my position would be tenuous. Oh, dear! The only place left for me to stand was on the edge of the 'stage' since I had to be in front of the students to direct the band. Never mind. I have been in more precarious positions before. I dismissed my worry. I can do it, I mused. The chaperones, Ed, still snapping pictures, and our audience, the school children, were settled below me across the road. All sat.

I stood, in a red jogging suit, tuning the eleven musicians. Then, with the audience quiet and instruments ready, my baton moved to signal the start of the first piece.

Suddenly, as my baton lifted for the students to start playing, a loud, cacophonous, continuous wailing tore from the tall, turreted minaret, exploding in our ears. My baton froze in mid-air. The minaret abutted the cay house. I immediately realised what was happening and glared at my band students, praying for them to be respectful throughout the call to prayer. No one moved a muscle. It finally finished. I pulled my anxious self together, took a deep breath and resumed our starting position once again.

The wind continued to blow but we were prepared. Always ready is my motto. We had colourful spring clothespins to hold our music on the music stands. I began to conduct with one hand while holding the music stand with the other. My left foot anchored the music stand in place. The wind was strong. We opened our concert with 'Alexander's Ragtime Band,' which never fails to make people move to the music. I licked my lips anxiously, and went on to a more serious rendition of a 'Chorale and Canon.' Then came the foot tapping, 'An American Folk Fantasy', ('Around her neck she wore a yeller ribbon...etc.') always exciting to play anytime, followed by the great dignity of 'The Masterpiece Theatre Theme Song.'

The band was doing well. The audience was clapping wildly and the Turks were smiling broadly. Relief flooded my body. Success was within our reach. Once again I found myself trying hard to breathe and smile at the same time. I was nervous.

This is such an auspicious occasion I thought; we really should play 'Alexander's Ragtime Band' one more time. The audience liked it so much the first time and I knew the band loved it. The Izmir Sultan Band members were watching me. Every eye was on me. They responded to my signal. 'Alexander's Ragtime Band' began again. We were well past the introduction, and my baton was flying with pleasure. I was smiling from ear to ear. I could feel it. My face was beginning to ache. Oh joy!

Suddenly, I noticed the band students' eyeballs had left their music and were peering to their left while still playing. Oh, my! To the right and over my shoulder, I caught a glimpse of a Cecil B. Demille unrehearsed spectacular!

Excitedly, my baton moved faster, while my foot remained glued to the music stand. My left hand gripped the music that was being forced to flutter over the rainbow of clothespins. All my body contorted to see better while directing, and to my complete surprise, an ageless, brown faced, turbaned Turk, astride a donkey, appeared, leading not one, not two, but three huge, gorgeously ugly, dignified camels. YES! The whole caravan trudged sedately and majestically through our audience of children, as the little ones scrambled on their bottoms to quickly remove themselves from the camels' hooves!

The moustachioed turbanned leader never looked left or right but moved straight ahead. The big beasts plodded in absolute time to the tune of, 'Come on along, come on along, I'm the leader of the band…' The camels never missed a beat! The band members, not able to speak, with instruments thrust into their mouths, had eyes popping out of their heads; their eyes registered utter amazement and disbelief at the sight. Our little children were smilingly speechless. These magnificent beasts were only a hand's touch away from our children. They looked like gigantic, thorny balled, brown porcupines rolling along. Their day's load of brush was baled onto them completely encircling their bodies, many feet in diameter, leaving only appendages to the view. The villager on the donkey gave us no notice. Looking straight ahead, with great detachment and aplomb, he plodded on with his day's work as usual, disappearing down the hill, around the bend, and out of sight.

It was a National Geographic Award picture, but a grown man cried…Ed. He was out of film.

❊❊❊

I was always looking for occasions for my students to perform for an audience, whether it was another class of students, a small group, or a larger audience. We had a Parent Teacher Organization (PTO) at our school that had monthly meetings for parents. Unfortunately, for whatever reasons, not many parents attended these meetings.

The PTO scheduled a dentist to talk to parents about dental hygiene for students. A PTO member had heard about the square dancing I was teaching the students, and asked me if I would arrange for a small group of students to put on a square dance demonstration for the PTO meeting. This might encourage more parents to attend the PTO meeting. I was still fairly new in Izmir and, not wanting to step on anyone's toes, I only asked two teachers if they would like their classes to participate in the program. I would need the teachers' help to keep the students organized before and after the square dance performance.

Well, word got around amongst the teachers. Consequently, another teacher came and asked if her class could dance also, and then another approached me, (word got around fast it seemed) and then, yet another. Of course, I said 'yes' to each teacher as long as they promised to attend the meeting that night to help me keep order. We had a first grade class, a third grade class and fifth and sixth grade classes perform that night. About 100 students in all participated. Parents attended the PTO meeting in droves!

The evening of the meeting, the dentist told me his talk would last only twenty minutes. "Well," muttered I to myself, "that's not too long." So I answered to the dentist with a big smile, saying, "That would be just fine, just the right amount of time."

With the help of the other teachers, I figured I could get the students lined up and organized and ready to wait until the dentist finished his talk, then we would enter the gym and do our dances. A double line of children stood in the hallway on the first floor of the school, and another double line of students sat on the stairs leading to the second floor.

The only problem was, the dentist *never* stopped talking (at least it seemed he didn't!) We were hovering in the hallways with about one hundred children who were fast losing steam, becoming nervous and fidgety and needing to go to the bathroom, etc. I was finally able to get hold of a PTO officer and nicely, but firmly, informed her she had to do something *fast*! She understood immediately and she did. She whispered to the dentist and he seemed totally shocked, he had talked forty-five minutes and had not realized the time; he apologized profusely to the audience, and departed, leaving us to move on to our part of the program.

By then, I was a bit afraid of how the children would do with their dances because of the long, long wait, but I should not have been. They were so happy to get out of the hallways and stairways that they quickly formed into their sets, first graders danced alone, meaning just their class, then the second graders and then the older grades. They all danced beautifully and enjoyed it immensely. The parents loved it. However, I was worn out with apprehension, anxiety and waiting! When I arrived home, I flopped onto the bed and that was the end of me for the evening.

Little did I dream what was to come 'down the pike.' The next day a teacher climbed two flights of stairs to my classroom. That was a lot of climbing; she was not in great condition being an extremely large person. She walked into my classroom; the door had been left ajar; and since there happened to be a chair just a few feet away from the open doorway, she plunked herself down and then…let me know in no uncertain terms how she felt. She claimed I deliberately left her class out of the PTO performance and that she would *never…ever* forget what I did to her and her class!

I was totally taken aback. I was aghast, actually, and could not believe what I heard her say. Not all the classes were invited to be there; several other classes did not dance and no other teacher seemed the least bit disturbed. I only chose two fifth grade classes to dance initially since the PTO members asked if I would, and the teachers of the other two or more classes had specifically asked to be included.

I was shocked and could say nothing comprehensible to the teacher who was breathing heavily in the chair in my room. While I stood there trying to find the correct words to make the situation better, she rose as quickly as she could, albeit, slowly, from the student desk, turned her back and plodded out of the room in great anger. Mrs. Z. never forgot the incident either and let me know about it again six years later at another event!

❧ ❧ ❧

During my second year of teaching in Izmir I learned that in the summer of 1989, a Movement/Dance workshop for schoolteachers was going to be held in Germany. Having used dance in my elementary classes for years, and always anxious to learn more, I applied for the program.

As part of the application process, I had to write an essay about how I had used movement/dance already and why I wanted to learn more.

I've included a copy of that essay here, because I think it sums up my feelings about the importance of including 'fine arts' in a school's curriculum. My application was accepted and I attended the week-long seminar held in Bad Kissingen, Germany in August 1989.

Not many weeks went by during my first year of teaching after graduation from college and becoming officially a music teacher before I realized that folk dancing should be an integral part of a music program. I found a need for variety and physical activity in my music curriculum during the school day, no matter how little; my students needed the same. Therefore, I introduced folk dancing and square dancing to my general music classes. My classes flourished. Children sang more beautifully, danced more enthusiastically and enjoyed every moment while interacting with one another in a nicer, more considerate and friendlier way than ever before. They gained in poise and confidence and most importantly, but hardly ever thought of then, movement relieved stress. Children smiled. Those who may have felt they were without friends, had opportunities to exchange dance patterns with one another, i.e. clap, stamp, turn, swing, bow, dos-i-dos, inside, outside, line dance, circle dance. Those with handicaps joined in, instead of watching. This all took place more than thirty years ago. Since then, dancing has been firmly incorporated into my teaching program.

I never let one year go by without including dancing in all forms, to lesser or greater degree, depending on the school, the place, or space.

My own knowledge increased by attending Folk and Square Dancing groups in Bedford, Massachusetts (my first teaching position). Since then I have taught myself by means of classes, In-service courses, friends, children and dance festivals. I have constantly sought knowledge of movement and dance. I know its value...I have proven it through the years. It has a strong place in education. It makes one feel good about oneself, which is sorely needed and most especially these days. When children feel good about themselves they then have no desire to fail, instead they strive to succeed, not only in music, but in all subject areas. It has a far-reaching effect. The smallest, most elemental of dances done by any age child succeeds in bringing smiles, producing rhythm, mixing groups of children and clustering of friends: success, success, success to all and often.

One year a 'problem' group of sixth grades dwelled in my building in Andover, Massachusetts. I then decided to begin a peer group, teaching program. The sixth grade problem class took on the task of teaching the primary children how to dance. Of course, it was introduced through my leadership and enthusiasm. The project produced instantaneous success. The most effort I expended was in the planning and guiding and most importantly my positive attitude toward it. My attitude was always one that expected much, all the time, from all the children and done with great enthusiasm. The little children loved dancing with the older ones and/or each other and the older ones felt great pride in the success they saw during their dances. It brought tears to my eyes. All children want to learn and all children want to be 'good.' Many have just never learned how. Music and dancing can pave the way with little effort and large results.

A few years later I worked with ten severely disabled boys. Just seeing them for the first time almost broke my heart. Their teacher and I decided to have the boys 'square dance' for the 'Mother's Day" luncheon. This involved a group of fifth grade girls from Susan R's. class who became the partners and her fifth grade boys who were the 'pushers' of the wheel chairs. The luncheon for the parents would follow the dance demonstrations. None of the boys could speak intelligibly but they could smile and laugh and attempt to 'clap hands.' We placed the mothers of the disabled boys up on the stage to better see their sons dance with the girls and boys of the fifth grade. One square had to have four wheel chair boys and four girl partners and four fifth grade boys to push the wheel chairs in time to the music. Also, all our children were in costume, i.e. overalls and bandanas on the boys and peasant skirts and blouses on the girls. There was not a dry eye during the presentation of the dances to the parents and nor will the handicapped boys ever forget their square dances.

How else could sensitivity be taught in a better form to fifth graders and with so much pleasure? The audience was clapping and sniffing and wiping eyes all throughout. The boys in the wheel chairs wore broad and beautiful smiles, accompanied by their bandanas and overalls and cowboy accoutrements and the little girl partners in their peasant skirts and blouses were just lovely, with their full smiles and the overall knowledge that they were helping someone!

Besides the traditional folk dances and square dances I have dabbled in creative dance using appropriate classical pieces of music. I will list a few of the most successful pieces of music here: The Carnival of Animals by Saint Saens, The Viennese Clock, Mozart's Eine Kleine Nacht Music, The Snow by Debussy, Air Gai by Gluck, (which became a huge favorite) and many others. Most of our classical music usually tells a story and therefore it can be told, written or danced or painted on paper or canvas. A little handicapped boy of about ten years old, Bobby C. essayed painting some pictures of a donkey, in various forms of movement, to the music of The Little White Donkey by Ibert. It was eventually drawn and painted and photographed into slides for a slide tape presentation. He was able to 'draw' his dance while others in the class 'danced' theirs.

Dance and movement establishes the beat and improves coordination in children. A dancing child is a confident child; a confident child is a happy child; a happy child is a singing child. A singing child is one who strives to succeed. Music, song and dance can accomplish all these wonders in a child.

For sixteen years in Andover, Massachusetts I was privileged to work with a wonderful physical education teacher in an elementary school building. His name was Dick Valle. His square dance program usually only lasted for one month while my dance program was ongoing throughout the year intermingled with other musical efforts. Consequently we joined forces and worked together. First of all, I usually taught small group classes, as in one class at a time; with the two of us intermingling we could manage more classes more often. The accommodating principal allowed for schedule changes after we explained our project. Together we taught large group classes in the gymnasium, which gave us time to teach more classes more often. Since I never, at that time, ever had my own classroom for music I found doubling up with Dick and his classes to be wonderful for my teaching methods and desires, and for the children. I normally always had to teach with the home-room teacher in her room which was not always the best situation for her or for me at times or for the children. Our

joint classes culminated on Memorial Day weekend with the entire school partici-
pating in our annual Square and Folk Dance Festival with parents watching. The
parents brought their own chairs and food and sun umbrellas, and everything hap-
pened out of doors! All the children absolutely loved dressing in the costumes of square
dancers and the whole affair was one hundred percent successful from my point of
view and also from the point of view of the physical education teacher, Dick Valle,
and the many parents who attended and helped out along the way.

I have a fondness for dance having recognized its value and need for our children.
All teachers need to be renewed as well, and I am no different. All my big and suc-
cessful projects renewed my spirit and forced me to carry on with more. Seeing the
happiness on the children's faces was absolutely satisfying for me.

I started a dance/movement program here after my arrival in Izmir and will
continue to teach dancing this year and in the future for however long that may be.
I am constantly seeking new ways to enhance my existing program and to improve
my teaching style.

Thank you very much for considering me as a candidate for the
Movement/Dance class to be held in Bad Kissingen, Germany, August 1989.

I was accepted. I attended the class! Sadly, however, the class was poorly organized and managed; not worth the time. The only redeeming quality of the situation was the chance to explore Bad Kissingen, Germany during our free time.

❋❋❋

One day during my first year in Izmir, the home economics teacher, Joann,
and I were talking. She was a marvelous teacher, we shared the same 'philosophy'
about teaching students, and we had become good friends.

"I would like to have the students model their clothing," she told me.

"That is a wonderful idea," I replied enthusiastically, "You have a modeling
show and my band will play the music. The band can play the background music
while your students model their hand made creations, and then the band can
play at intermission, or alone before the show starts, or all three!"

A huge smile enveloped her face, which let me know immediately that she
thought the idea to be a good one! We talked it all over, tossed it around a bit,
and finally came up with a plan. My students, as in any student situation, needed
a reason to play, needed to show off their skills in order to improve and polish
those musical skills. Therefore, the more events at which they could play, the
better they would play in the future…and then, the more they would like what

they were doing. We all need to have 'un raison d'etre' in life, especially my Junior/Senior High School Band.

Joann then told her plan to the students in her high school Home Economics class; the girls were thrilled, and believe it or not, so were the boys! She always seemed to have a few boys in her home economics class. They liked to cook, for one, and some of them enjoyed designing their own clothes. Some of their designs were silly, funny or quite serious, actually. Now the boys did not, could not, would not want…to make suits of clothing at that age, but some made vests, and others made various and sundry items they thought necessary and good to wear. The girls were no problem at all and found many different items that could be made and that they would model.

It all worked beautifully, the modeling all went off rather well. The students were super, they walked out to the audience, turned around here and there to show the clothing at different angles, and then walked back and forth once again in front of the audience to the background music being played by my little band. In general the students seemed very pleased. The audience consisted of their parents, siblings and friends.

After the modeling and the band performance ended, the students in the Home Economics class who were in the cooking and baking end of their studies, (not in the sewing), provided home made treats they had prepared. Joann and I were actually quite thrilled about the whole affair, and, as a matter of fact, backstage, where no one could see us, we were jumping up and down for joy like two high school chums!

✼ ✼ ✼

One day the father of one of my band students, Mr. Kolbet, asked me, "Would it be possible for me to come into your band class and try to help my son or any of the others who might need help?"

I replied with a resounding, "I would *love* to have you come to band class however often you can find the time to play and you may sit next to your son if that is what you wish." He then smiled and said he would be in whenever he could find the time off from his job and also would love to help whichever student might need help, not only his son.

The father talked to his boss in the military and arranged somehow to attend several band classes a week. The band improved a bit each day he was there by the example he set. We got to know each other well and one day I asked, "Mr.

Kolbet, would you tell me if there is some way we could have other military members come in as volunteers in the band class as you do?"

Mr. Kolbet replied with, "Why don't you go across the street and up around the corner to the Commander's Office and talk with him. The Commander is a fine man and probably could work something out with the bosses of other guys who play instruments."

I should have thought of that myself, but I was still learning about high schools and the military and commanders. Mr. Kolbet showed me where to go and what to do and off I went after school one day. I was not nervous because I had developed more emotional strength in the short time I had been in Izmir.

I met with the Commander and he thought I had a smashing idea. He said he would also give the men or women who offered to help with the band a bonus, which would consist of extra merit credits. Therefore all who volunteered would receive some meritorious remarks, which would appear on their military records. I thought to myself, "What a great idea and what a nice man!"

Wonder of wonders, I had ten volunteers come to me within a few days. Some had no instruments, but by then many of my repaired or new instruments had arrived so we were 'set to roll' as they say in the military. The ten volunteers could not all come at the same time, so they came to me whenever they could. Naturally, it all depended on the work they were doing at that time for their commanding officers.

Whenever any of them came in to play in our high school band, my students would perk up, sit up tall and straight and try their best to sound like the instrumental people sitting next to them. We never knew, the band and I, when anyone would arrive, which made the process more amusing for me, as I watched the expressions on the students' faces and saw the students sit up straight and tall whenever any volunteer arrived. I loved the whole procedure!

Only one boy gave me trouble. One day, he acted up while we were playing. He was slumped down in his chair and had his feet up on the chair in front of him. Next to him sat a great big soldier, sitting straight as an arrow beside this boy and also playing the trumpet. This soldier took his right elbow, and...never missing a beat in the music...bent over a bit and jabbed the student in the left side; that boy shot up out of his chair and sat perfectly straight for the remainder of the class. I pretended I saw nothing happen. It tickled my funny bone, as the saying goes, but I noticed the boy never slumped anymore, at least not when the soldiers were in the classroom!

It was this same student though, who disappeared from my sight one day while I was directing the band. Yes, just vanished out of sight. Fortunately we were not performing before an audience when this little episode happened. While directing, I edged my way over toward my left side, and although I might have stopped directing in the proper way, the band still continued to play. I found my student…argh! He was lying down on the floor with his feet on his chair while attempting to play his trumpet. That was his deliberate attempt to gain attention, of that I was sure. I was furious but, of course, smiled and with great authority, said, "Sit back up on your chair this minute and meet with me when the class ends." Well, he certainly moved fast, I must say. I cannot say I cured him of anything, but his behavior did grow a trifle better.

He and I met after class and he let out his frustrations, which I could tolerate since I understood where he was coming from in his agony. The student hollered at me saying, "I hate being here, I hate playing in the band and I hate my trumpet most of all!" With that last statement he ended up rushing out of the door and kicking and throwing his trumpet down all the five flights of stairs. I could hear the thump and the bang and then more thump, thump, thump and more banging as the poor instrument fell and careened down those awful five flights of metal stairs! The student got rid of his anger I must say! After that little scene he did improve somewhat and today he is a delightful young man with a loving family and a great job!

🌿🌿🌿

I would like to stress, again…how very beneficial it is for students to practice or play an instrument while sitting next to an adult who is talented in his instrumental field. It is most helpful when an instrumentalist, especially a child who is learning how to play, sits next to a musician who has a marvelous tone emitting from his instrument. The child, or even an adult playing, will virtually…automatically and almost unknowingly, begin to emulate the sound of the fine instrumentalist sitting next to him or her.

As time went on, there were more and more opportunities for our high school band to play in concerts and competitions outside of Izmir. One of these involved flying to a base in Adana, Turkey near the borders of Iran and Iraq. I was a bit nervous while traveling with a large group of high school students to such a 'volatile' area, but I decided the 'powers that be' would never allow students to travel to that area if there was going to be any real danger to them.

In what became an annual affair, the band students and I flew from Izmir, to Ankara,and then, on to Adana where we met up with band students from two other military bases. We were there for three days of classes, rehearsals and concerts with each other. The students slept in homes of parents of the Adana High School band.

At the end of our very long and full days of practicing in the Adana High School, I was totally exhausted! I believe much of my fatigue was derived from nerves…anxiety…as in, would my high school students behave? Would they get in trouble? Would they play well enough? That thought was with me always. I had overseen the lunches for my students in the high school lunchroom and the practice sessions at night as well as all the practices for the morning and afternoon sessions. When I finally got to bed each night, I must admit I was so tired I did not know how I could possibly manage the next day, but I did.

When we were returning home from Adana, my high school band students had bought themselves all kinds of candies and chips and other sweets and drinks in the airport…you name it, they had it! We boarded the plane, and as I was looking around for a place to sit, a young, and very tall Southern airman came over to me and took charge. I knew he was a southerner the moment he opened his mouth to speak to me. He might have seen I was tired, or decided with that large bunch of kids, I would need help.

"Ma'am," he said with a distinct Southern drawl, "ya'll sit in this here seat and have yourself a good sleep. I will look after all your kids, not to worry yourself about them. They'll be fine." The gentleman then tucked me into a seat, put away my extra things, as in my carry on luggage, and strapped me into my seat!

I think he was at least six feet five inches tall and also quite thin, a bit bent over at the shoulders, and with sandy colored, wavy hair. The best part of all was that he could not have been sweeter to me; therefore I sat where he told me, although I thought perhaps I should be sitting nearer to my students on the off chance that one of them needed me for one thing or another. Another soldier, a lieutenant, was sitting next to me reading a book, a very quiet young man. He was not paying any attention to us, the attendant that is, or to me, the tired teacher, which was fine with me. I wanted to sleep!

"Thank you, oh thank you so very much," I muttered, "and yes, I am quite exhausted, now that you mention it!"

"Ya'll just go on and have yourself a nice little nap," he reiterated once again handing me a pillow. This airman was so very kind and thoughtful, I almost cried. I felt tears floating around in my eyes. The other young man and I were seated in the front section of the plane and our seats were sideways. Oddly, from my way of thinking, there were three seats facing the side of the plane, and three in back of us facing the other side of the plane. Then, as I looked toward the back of the plane, I could see all the seats; they were situated as one would normally find them, two on either side of the plane facing forward.

The motor of the plane was running. Being so totally fatigued, I must have fallen asleep immediately, with my head bouncing to and fro I suppose. How long I slept I will never know. Suddenly, the military man next to me on my left nudged me once; then he waited a bit and nudged me a second time with his right elbow. I could hear his voice, in my semi wakeful condition at that moment, saying, "Lady, lady, wake up, wake up, all your kids are throwing up! Lady, can you hear me, I said all your kids are sick!"

I could not pull myself out of my sleepy grogginess, but I managed a growling type of mumble, "Oh…no…" I then paused only for two seconds or so and said to him in my gravelly, sleepy voice, "the steward said not to worry, he will take care of them", and I immediately fell back into a deep and sound slumber

When I finally woke a little while later, and pulled my thoughts together, I looked over to my right where all the band students were seated and to my surprise I noticed they were all white faced, every last one of them, and all looking very ill. They also seemed to have something in their hands, like a bag. It was difficult for me to see at that distance, having just awakened. After a few more seconds I realized they were bags, paper bags it seemed. I believe they are called, 'throw up bags.' Nary a smile issued from any of the band students as I looked at them. They were, all of them it seemed, snow white in the face, with a tinge of green showing through! My amazement and dismay were very real. How could I have done that? I felt then, that I should not have slept; I should have gone to them and helped them out. To this day I cannot believe I fell asleep at that time. But then, a little voice inside my head said, "Good for you, Mary, the steward took care of everything. What you did was a smart move on your part."

At that point the steward saw I was awake and came loping right over to my seat. Yes, tall southerners do lope along when they walk. "They's all right Ma'am, don't ya'll get up, stay right where you are. They's all just having a little air sickness from having eaten too much candy and junk and we's having awful turbulence today. Not to worry, just ya'll go back to sleep again."

And…guess what? I did. I promptly fell asleep once again. I had no idea I would be so fatigued from the whole time in Adana, i.e. the teaching/directing all day, the final big concert at the end of all the work and seeing to the children. Consequently, after hearing his soothing words, I just faded out immediately and went back to sleep! I will never, ever, forget my tall, southern, lanky helpmate. He was just wonderful...to me and to my students!

We disembarked at Ankara, the capital city of Turkey, and the students lolled around quietly in the airport, looking very pale, no one talking until they quietly boarded our plane to Izmir for takeoff. That was a very short trip relatively speaking, it probably lasted an hour or less. We landed and they were then met by their parents and were off my hands completely. The students had performed beautifully in all areas, as in sleeping in other homes, practicing hard, and playing beautifully. I was extremely proud of all of them at that moment; I was also glad to be home and hoping they all felt better on the 'morrow! The whole event was successful and once I had finished with this first adventure, I knew that the other concerts (one each year) would be much easier for me to manage.

❧ ❧ ❧

However, fatigue overall was catching up to me. One day in the hallway of the elementary school I ran into Gil F., a high school teacher. We began talking and soon he sensed that I was quite fatigued.

"Mary, you sound absolutely worn out, exhausted" he said to me, then added, "Have you thought yet about swimming in Cleopatra's waters?"

I thought he might be teasing me. "Well, no," I replied, "I haven't. Where are they and are they really Cleopatra's waters?"

He nodded gravely and added, "I'd like to take you there. You look so worn down and tired, I think the pools would help you."

Well, I did need something to perk me up; I was feeling bedraggled. He said he swam nearly every day and would be happy to drive me. I smilingly accepted his offer. He asked if Ed would like to join us.

I called Ed from school. "Mary," he told me, "you go with Gil, find out where the pool is, how to get there and you and I will go another day. I am too tired to do anything right now other than lie on the bed and sleep or read." I had guessed that Ed would not want to go, but I wanted to ask since he enjoyed swimming and the activity was good for his semi-destroyed back/spine.

That afternoon, when classes were over, Gil and I got into his car and he drove me to my apartment. I gathered a towel, bathing suit, and cap etc. and off we went. The waters of Cleopatra were a few miles outside of Izmir, along the coastal road and not too hard for me to find later. Upon our arrival Gil showed me around the entire complex. I was quite taken aback by the whole place knowing how many thousands of years ago these hot and healing waters existed and that Cleopatra actually swam here herself.

Gil and I swam in the newer, more modern large circular indoor pool. We swam laps as much as was possible in a perfectly round pool, back and forth forever it seemed, but it did not matter. It was uplifting and I was pleased to have a friend who cared so much about my feelings, physically and mentally, and introduced me to this most unusual place. Gil enjoyed swimming as much as I. Needless to say Ed and I went many more times to swim in Cleopatra's waters before my teaching days were over in Izmir!

❧ ❧ ❧

Back to school and band trips: another time, on a return trip from Adana, the band and I boarded the plane; I made myself comfortable and then slept so soundly that when I woke I *thought* we were near to Ankara. To my utter amazement, I discovered after a few minutes that we had not yet left the ground at Adana, and I must have slept for an hour or more. You see…the airplane motors were deceiving; they had kept the airplane motors running all the time that I slept, therefore…I assumed we were up in the air when in truth, we had not yet departed!

On this occasion we were having difficulty with Turkish authorities and for the life of me I never understood why. After being on board for an hour or more, I was informed that we had to disembark. Empty the plane was the order! We were herded into the airport and the students lolled around for another two hours or more, either lying on the floor, hanging off of the seats upside down, leaning against cupboards, and going to the bathrooms! They were all over the place…but, thankfully, none of them ever caused any trouble or problems. Actually, in retrospect, they never did cause any problems!

We finally received permission to board again and take off. However, the Turkish authorities must have suspected we had some spies with us, because they were most serious the whole time, inspecting the music cases, which were inside the plane where we sat, and the suitcases, which were in the 'hold' of the plane. They also questioned all of us, yes, all the students too. Nevertheless, I understood their reasons to be careful because the Kurds lived not far from Adana. The Adana Air Base was much nearer to the fighting and battles than the other bases in Turkey. The city of Adana was home to the USA's largest air base in Turkey. The base had a huge school, many teachers and all the extras and a very large enrollment. I, by then, was happy being in my own little school in Izmir and not the least bit sorry that I was not working in Adana; they were too close to the Kurds as far as I was concerned!

The students and I did finally arrive home with no other problems during the flight and layover, but we were about five hours late for the parents to pick up their children. However, all being from military families, they were used to that type of delay. No one scolded me, the parents were fully aware of the happenings since they had received telephone calls from our Commander's Office.

✹ ✹ ✹

As I mentioned earlier, our bands, advanced and beginner, made the annual trip to Adana to rehearse and perform with the school bands from other bases. In the beginning, the trips were only for three days, but that was hardly enough time to get much accomplished, so I convinced the regional music director to expand the trip to five days—a full week. It was sensational!

In addition, the adult band volunteers were able to accompany me on some of these trips. The volunteers were an enormous help with the students in all the bands! I usually had a different group helping me on each trip, sometimes only one or two, and one time as many as ten. It all depended on whether their commanding officers could give the military members time off from their normal duties.

The annual trips to Adana became easier for me because of their help. The volunteers helped with the band in many ways, especially in giving individual groups special attention when rehearsing. I could tell the adults, "This section in the band needs help here, or there, or that section is lacking balance, or too few trombones today," and they would fill the gap. These adults were absolutely wonderful! They always wanted to accompany me on any trip or play in any concert if they could possibly arrange the time off with their superior officers.

There was a woman adult volunteer who was not in the military herself, but was married to a military man. Donna was wonderful at transposing music into other 'keys' as in B flat or E flat or A flat, when necessary. I must admit I was not at all clever in transposing. I could do it but it would take me many hours. Donna just sat and zipped away at it on the computer while I taught the lessons to the band. I was so relieved when she first offered this type of assistance that I could have hugged her to death or cried on her shoulders. She was a great help to me, as were all the adult military volunteers. The band accomplished wonders as a result of their constant assistance and devotion.

❧ ❧ ❧

One year when we were about to leave on one of these annual trips to Adana, an officer came to our school that morning. He came upstairs to the band room to inform me that there would be a casket on board our plane and probably in full view of the students! There would be a dead body in the casket. I groaned at his words! Would my students be able to cope with this sad affair? I questioned my ability to share this information with them. Could I do it delicately and truthfully? Then the officer left me alone to deal with the situation.

I made a quick decision; this was *not* going to stay with me alone! I shot down the five flights of iron stairs like a bullet after the officer left and grabbed the principal and told him he must talk with me *now*! (We had a new principal at that time, Harvey had left and Terry E. had taken his place! This was now my third year in Turkey.) He and I went into his office; I explained the story and he was also totally nonplussed, dumbfounded might explain it all a bit better. I looked at my watch and realized I only had a few more minutes before all the band members returned from stowing their instruments on the busses, and would troop back up the five circular flights of metal stairs to the classroom for last minute instructions before we left.

Terry, my voluble principle, exploded, and in a very loud voice said, "I have *never... ever...* had this happen before!" And then he paced around his office groaning.

My voice grew louder and my nerves were ready to explode, "Well, it is happening now, Terry, so tell me, please…what shall I do?"

The principal grew frantic and in a rather loud voice with his arms gesticulating in the air and his hands stiffened into fists, he roared, "Mary, you must know that because of the other schools involved and the airplane bookings we cannot change any of our dates at this point. It is far too late. We have to go ahead with it."

I edged him along further with my voice also growing louder; I strongly felt *he* should handle this situation. "But Terry, what shall we do *now?* Will you tell them? Will you tell the students...or will I?"

Terry groaned aloud, sat in his chair for at least five seconds, then stood up and said despairingly, uttering each word in a slow and despondent manner, "I'm coming upstairs with you...I will tell them." And off we went, both of us, up the five flights of steel stairs.

Actually, it all went well despite his agony and my worry. The students were dignified about the whole affair, a bit subdued and quiet; they had much respect for the whole sad and necessary trip. I was quite proud of them. At first we were told the casket had to be in sight of the students in the back of the plane, therefore I informed the students ahead of time. But when we arrived at the airport and boarded the plane, no casket was to be seen. All the students, carrying their instruments, trooped on board, quiet as mice. I was so proud of them! As they walked to their seats, their eyes seemed to be looking and searching discreetly in the plane for the body or the casket or whatever they thought they would see and much to my satisfaction and *relief,* the casket was *not* in sight. Evidently a place was found in back of the plane or in the underbelly of the plane and all was taken care of before we arrived at the airport. Nevertheless, the students stayed quietly respectful through the whole flight. I was so relieved to see their humble and subdued behavior, and so proud of all of them at the same time, I could have hugged them all! My students were growing physically but also, growing emotionally and intellectually with each concert and each trip we took. I was enormously proud of each and every one of them!

Graduation Ceremony

Traditionally, the graduation for the DODDS Izmir High School was held at Ephesus, an ancient Greek city, and later a major Roman city, near Izmir. Ephesus did not mean much to me until I moved to Izmir. I had studied about all the ruins in Turkey and Greece back in Keith Hall, but then, you may rest assured that was a very long time ago and the true significance of Ephesus was not in my mind then.

Ephesus was one of the more important sites of ancient ruins in Turkey partly since Saint Paul delivered his famous speech to the Ephesians there and was also imprisoned at Ephesus for quite a while.

The graduation was usually held in front of the ancient Celsus library at Ephesus. The remaining ruins of the Celsus Library consisted of a two 'tiered' front, or, as one might call it in America, a double decker front…there is none other of its kind anywhere in the world I am told. It was absolutely grand and glorious to behold! Ed and I both remembered having seen a photo of 'Ephesus' in our high school history books.

The ancient city of Ephesus had much to offer, but I will list only a few of its marvelous qualities at this time. It had an amphitheater, which was absolutely huge. This amphitheater is allegedly one of the largest in the ancient world, probably holding twenty-five thousand people at one time. Another smaller, much smaller, amphitheater existed in another part of the ancient city, which was all the way to the other side of Ephesus and towards the way out of the ancient city. We were told that the smaller one might have been used for the politicians: senators and the like, to meet and talk and vote. And of course, there were the Celsus library ruins, where the high school traditionally held its graduations. In addition there was a market place and countless tombs and memorials to the many famous Romans.

Not only were ancient important ruins preserved, but also the more mundane, but necessary, aspects of ancient life. In particular, I'm referring to toilets for men. Just down the street from the Celsus library and on the way to the small amphitheater there was a large square area, bordered by a ledge at about

Oldest daughter Susan standing in front of ancient toilets in Ephesus, Turkey; in the background Ephesus library facade.

seat height. This ledge had thirty or forty oval holes.Men could sit on the holes and 'do their business' while talking with one another. There were no dividers or individual stalls. It was absolutely unusual and almost unbelievable to me! In the center of this space was a large water fountain, no doubt used for cleansing.

❄❄❄

At any rate, as the time approached for the graduation that first year I was in Turkey, the principal informed us there was an ongoing argument between the Mayor of Selcuk in Ephesus and the caretaker of the Celsus library ruins! Consequently we were told that our school was *not* going to be allowed to use the famous library for the staging and backdrop at graduation. None of the authorities at the school knew exactly why. Since this was the end of my first year of teaching in Izmir I was quite disappointed. "Sadly," I murmured inwardly, "another time will have to suffice."

Nothing could be done as a result of the argument and denial between the mayor and the other dignitary in charge, so we were forced to have our graduation in another ancient ruin that was called, in today's language, Bergama, but in the ancient language identified as Pergamon.

Pergamon was, and still is, a most respected ancient ruin on the other side of Izmir. It may not have the reputed dignity of Ephesus for reasons beyond my ken. Pergamon was located many miles away in the opposite direction from our school therefore, not near Ephesus at all. (Ephesus being toward the south and Bergama, or Pergamon, being toward the west.) Many people felt it was not of the same importance as Ephesus since the Celsus library in Ephesus had the *only* two-storied ancient structure. None of the other ancient ruins and libraries possessed such dignity or had the same scope or depth, (according to researchers).

The amphitheater we were scheduled to use in Pergamon for the graduation was quite small, although there was a much larger one in the area as well. Ed and I went to see the larger amphitheater and we came to the conclusion that it would not be as safe to use for our graduation. It appeared very crumbly in spots, and at the same time it was unimaginably steep, so steep that if one tripped and tumbled there would be serious outcomes from that kind of tumble. If one happened to stumble and fall, nothing would be available to hold onto or to support a falling body such as banisters or the like.

However, Ed and I took some time to sit (most carefully) on the last row of stones at the top of the amphitheater. The view of the surrounding area was gorgeous! We sat there and let our imaginations soar back to those days after Christ's time imagining incredibly different scenes of their civilization.

There was another area on the way to a small amphitheater in Pergamon, called the Aesclepion. Essentially, it was a building constructed like a tunnel, walls on both sides and a ceiling connecting them. This long, tall, narrow tunnel had many large square openings in the top. The tunnel-like building was beautifully finished inside. We learned that people would enter the tunnel, proceed to a pre-assigned opening in the ceiling above them, then pour out all their 'problems' to a person standing/sitting above the opening. This I guessed was the ancient precursor to our modern-day appointments with psychologists. Only in this situation, the 'patient' never saw the face of their 'doctor,' only heard the voice.

After the confession or statements of their problems were finished, the patient listened to the 'words of wisdom' coming from the person above the opening. Following that, the patient walked out of the tunnel to recline on a relatively large stone area semi covered by lovely, warm and flowing water. The patient could gaze at the lovely pools of water listening to the soft and flowing gurgling sounds, contemplating the quiet and peaceful scenery. The patient would seemingly be at peace with himself. (You notice I only spoke of men in this situation…women were not allowed to participate in this practice. Women held no important place in the lives of men at that time, except in the brothel of which there were many.)

But let us go back to that first year's graduation ceremony, held at Pergamon instead of Ephesus. *Pomp and Circumstance* rang out beautifully from the band at the beginning of the program when the graduates processed out onto the Roman staging below, and to the right of where the band was sitting. Then representatives from our U.S. military came forward with a most impressive 'Posting of the Colors.' Immediately following that, our band played the *Turkish National Anthem* and then the *Star Spangled Banner*; that was standard protocol. Ed and I were always impressed when our American Military 'posted the colors' before the anthems were played and sung. It was quite emotional for us and never ceased to be, no matter how often we witnessed the ceremony. I suppose it was because we were in a foreign country so far away from 'home.'

Following the posting of the colors, there were speeches and then the diplomas were handed out to the small class of about twenty graduates. The graduation ceremony ended with my own original composition for band entitled, *An*

Mary leading the Izmir High School Band
during the high school graduation ceremony at Pergamon

Anthem of Peace. I stood a little taller each time it was played by the band picturing how impressive the ceremony was, and in this most unusual, to me at that time, country of Turkey!

The band was marvelous, albeit extremely nervous. Being my first year as a band teacher and remembering how the previous teacher performed, it was no wonder they were nervous. We had three volunteers playing with us. One was my first military man volunteer, whose son played in the band. The other two were instrumentalists from a Turkish high school who came to our school one day and meekly and politely, asked to come play with the band on occasion. Of course, I welcomed them completely! They were a marvelous addition to the band; they were a bit older and had been playing longer in their Turkish school. They set a great example for my students, I must say! I believe these two young men played with the band for at least two years! I have no idea even now, how these high school boys found our school and band and offered to play with us. None! Evidently, they had no band to join but loved to play their instruments!

All in all, we played quite respectfully considering we were a very small group of instrumentalists. I have a framed photograph of that small band sitting on the stone steps of the small stone amphitheater a little to the right of the stage. The photograph shows me directing the band as the graduates come in to receive their diplomas. It was June 1988.

After the graduation was finished I praised all my band members, telling them that they sounded like professionals! I was so proud of them! I was just enthralled by my first graduation, held in an ancient ruin but, most importantly, the band sounded good which, of course, led the students to feel good about themselves. That was the main issue as far as I was concerned!

> *When you work you are a*
> *Flute through whose heart*
> *the whispering of the hours*
> *turns to music....And what is it*
> *To work with love? It is to*
> *weave cloth with threads drawn*
> *From your heart, even as if*
> *Your beloved were to wear that cloth.*
>
> **—Author unknown**

Christmas in Rome

During our first year in Izmir, Ed and I decided to spend our Christmas break in Rome. We also wanted our youngest daughter, Amy, to join us since she had never been to Italy.

In the meantime, we happened to meet Buck and Joan Emberg; a couple our age. They had each gone through a divorce with their respective spouses sometime back, then met and married each other. Collectively, they had eight grown children between them (he had four and she had four). When we met them, they were teaching for the University of Maryland as part of the DODDS program. (As I learned later, the University of Michigan and the University of California and perhaps a couple of other universities, sponsored classes on bases for military personnel who wanted to continue their college studies).

Buck and Joan were such good fun to be with, and when the two men, Buck and Ed, were together it became a laugh a minute. One night we invited them to our apartment for dinner, one thing led to another during our conversations and we happened to tell them about Amy, and how we missed her terribly and wished she were here.

We explained how she was trying to find her way at home, meaning, what she wanted to study while in a small college in New Hampshire. Buck bellowed at that point, but then, he always spoke rather loudly, and most emphatically said, "Why don't you bring her here?" Joan added, "We would love to have her in our classes."

I responded with a doubtful remark, "First of all, I never dreamed I could do that since I am not really in the military."

Joan said, "You can bring Amy here to live with you and attend our classes with the University of Maryland. We would love to meet her and have her in class. And…you are 'with the military' since you work for them."

I replied, rather hesitantly, letting Joan's statement wallow around in my mind for a few seconds, "Amy is not too sure of herself. She doesn't really know what she wants to do with herself in college or out of college, therefore she is a bit reticent." I also added, "She seems to lack confidence in herself and yet I know she is quite capable."

Buck bellowed at me once again and said, in his typical fashion, pointing his finger at me all the time, "You tell her I said to get over here for Christmas break and she can then start in our classes right away in January. If she is not sure of herself, she certainly will be before I am finished with her!" I can still hear his loud voice resonating in my head after all these twenty and more years have gone by.

Now the motors in my mind started to turn. I cogitated, I hemmed and hawed, and tried to figure out how we could convince Amy to come back 'home' with us to Turkey; how we could entice her to live with us in Izmir. So I took the bull by the horns, as they say, and I called her on our phone and talked and talked; I told her about Buck and Joan, what they said and how she would love being taught by them. I then told Amy, "There is never a dull moment with Buck, I assure you! He is a fantastic teacher and Joan is in charge of the library and research."

I was not sure of any other subjects she taught at that time since Buck had done much of the talking. I continued with, "The fee is wonderfully low, minimal, if any; the teachers are great people, the two we know, that is, and the classes are small. All the students are military people. Besides all that, we will meet you in *Rome!*"

In a small, small voice Amy hesitatingly replied, "Mom, can I call you back before I make the decision?"

I am sure Amy could not answer me immediately because of her anxiety. Many things had gone wrong for her; she was not extremely happy in her present college. Also she lived in a small apartment with a friend but that was not working out well either. Nothing seemed to be 'coming together' for Amy while she was in New Hampshire—it seemed to me!

Amy called back in a day or two and said, most pleadingly I thought, "Mom, can I come to Izmir?" I cried, Ed cried…we were both so happy as we hollered, "*Yes!!!*" into the telephone.

Rome, Italy

So, we began planning our Christmas trip to Rome. We intended to spend two weeks touring with Madonna who at that time had moved to Gaeta, which was just south of Rome. Amy knew Madonna well and liked her very much while living in Okinawa. Madonna booked rooms for all of us in an ancient small, square old building, which had been converted into a tiny hotel. It was originally a small home. It had only four rooms to rent, but the backside of the building was built right on to the ancient wall that encircled the Vatican! Madonna had sent a photograph to us. The house looked like it was groping and hanging on to the Vatican wall, it was so ancient. I had never seen anything like this before!

We were thrilled with everything…Amy was coming, we were delighted to be going to Rome, and Madonna had taken care of everything for us. She was such a dear, sweet person. I can never, even now, thank her enough.

Ed was so excited to see Amy, that when she finally came through the gateway at the airport in Rome he yelled *"Amy"* in a very loud voice and then, once again, *"**Amy!**"* in an even louder voice! He startled me as well as the people around us! Ed is usually a quiet person and would normally never do anything like that in an airport, but this was his daughter and he let it all out. She saw him coming and heard him hollering at her. They just about jumped into each other's arms!

How incongruous that loving reunion was! There were guards in the airport standing on high platforms with machine guns in their hands pointing at the crowd, ready to let go if and when… And there we all were, hugging and kissing and thrilled to have Amy with us. The whole thing was a bit bizarre to us, such a loving reunion watched over by gun carrying men. We took Amy to our hotel, and she slept and slept and talked and talked for two days. I would say she was happy to be 'home' with us.

Madonna and the gentleman friend who accompanied her arrived after the first two days and stayed in the same hotel. To my great pleasure and excitement I learned Madonna had been able to acquire, for all of us, tickets for the Midnight Mass with Pope John Paul!

Our tickets were close to the front, but in the *back* of the Altar. At first I was disappointed, to be so close, but in the back instead of in the front. However, I had been told before I left Izmir, "…whatever movements, words or chants the Pope makes during the Christmas Service, they are all repeated by *him* at the back of the altar." That turned out to be true, and so we got to see the Pope up close and it was a wonderful experience.

While at that Midnight Mass, I noticed in the front and on the left of us a group of nuns. They were from Quebec, Canada, and singing Christmas carols in French. Guess what I did? Yes, I crossed the aisle. I saluted the nuns with French phrases as in, "Joyeux Noel, mes Soeurs," and in a little while "d'ou viens tu?" and they seemed delighted I had come across the aisle and thence they proceeded to make room for me. We all sang the carols in French together as I had done as a little child at home in Lowell in the French school. (The organist in the Vatican was playing songs from many nationalities to fit the occasion after the Midnight Mass.) I was thrilled and the nuns were pleased to meet me and told me so, after the Mass. We all spoke in French! These nuns had come from Canada simply to be at the Christmas services. They were extremely excited and happy to tell me all their plans! We all hugged each other right there in the Vatican at Midnight Mass!

Christmas day arrived and Amy, Ed and I stood out under the Pope's balcony in front of the beautiful building where Mass had been said the night before. Because our hotel was a part of the ancient wall around the Vatican, we had an excellent spot in which to stand while the Pope gave his Christmas blessing. All the other people who had come for the blessing, and there were thousands, were far away from the Pope. I could have almost touched him, except that his balcony was a floor above the walkway where we stood. We were twice blessed it seems. I was extremely happy and deliriously excited. The only missing element was the remainder of my family, Susan, her husband John, and Eric and Kelly and their children and my mother. They were all either too busy or not well enough to have made the trip to Rome that year.

We spent a wonderful two weeks traveling inside Rome on foot with

Madonna. She knew how to get around Rome relatively well since Madonna taught at the DODDS School in Gaeta, not too far from Rome, and is a devout Catholic. We also traveled outside of Rome in Madonna's car with her gentleman friend from the states. We saw all that Madonna could take us to see in our short space of time!

She drove us to see Mount Vesuvius, and the ancient city of Pompeii, only to find, sadly, that Pompeii was closed so we could not go inside the area. I did discover that Pompeii is a big area! I was quite disappointed and, in fact, two more times in the two other years we traveled to Rome, we went to Pompeii and still could never go inside. I was told that was just happenstance! Disappointing, to say the least, at least it was for me!

But then, in Rome at Christmas, we went wild visiting all the other famous places…the Vatican with Michelangelo's Pietà for example. (The Pietà is simply gorgeous, a wonderful work of art!) After visiting the Vatican Museum, we went to the 'The Spanish Steps,' which are called *Piazza di Spagna*. We have lovely photographs of Amy and me in front of the Trevi Fountain, the Pantheon and the Castel Sant'Angelo! The Pantheon, and The Coliseum were absolutely remarkable as well! However, I was so excited about all that I saw I now find it difficult at this moment to decide which place I may have preferred over another. All the great works of art and history left me almost speechless, this being our first trip to Rome. We did not see 'David' on that excursion, but we did manage to see 'David' on another visit!

What a wonderful way to start the New Year!

❋ ❋ ❋

Then, it was back to Izmir. Ed and I were thrilled to have Amy with us once again for a while. We introduced her to Buck and Joan one night at dinner and they convinced her to take University of Maryland courses with them. Ed and I were absolutely delighted; Amy would live with us again with the cost being almost negligible as compared to when she was in New Hampshire. More importantly, she had two great teachers who would look after her and see that she got the correct knowledge and information and guidance as to what she might want to study while there to prepare her for her future.

She attended University of Maryland classes for three semesters, I believe, or four, (I am not quite sure right now), under the auspices of DODDS. She had Buck and Joan for teachers, plus a couple of others whom I didn't know.

She did very well scholastically and certainly gained in assurance of herself. She no longer thought less of herself. She felt good about her classes and seemed to like all the people she met.

In the time Amy was with us, we took her on innumerable trips. I could not accompany Ed and Amy on some of them since I had to teach and rehearse for many band concerts. By the middle of my second year in Turkey, the band had grown in size and it was scheduled to play for ten different functions at Christmas time. With every concert each member of the band improved; they were eager and thrilled and loved playing for others and of course, being excused from their usual classes! I was absolutely beside myself with joy at their continual progress! I figured by spring the band would be outstanding. I wished I could have the man who wrote that nasty, sarcastic letter to me before I arrived in Turkey hear the band now! However, with his attitude he would have found fault anyway I am sure.

Moscow and Leningrad

During her second year with us, Ed and Amy joined a small church group on a trip to Moscow and Leningrad in early December of 1988. We learned about it from a man who lived in our building, Jack, who was a lot of fun to be with. He kept everyone jumping with jokes and stories and new ideas all the time. I liked him very much; Amy said he was the 'life of the party' during the trip to Russia.

They returned home with many stories, but one in particular touched me deeply. While en route from Moscow to Leningrad, they were stranded for many hours at an airport because there was so much snow. There were many people in the airport; Amy and Ed's Izmir group of probably ten or so people; and then a large group of girls *not* from Ed and Amy's group, maybe fifty or more were all stranded together. Well, our friend, Jack, got everyone talking with each other. As it so happened, they discovered the girls were from the Philippines and had no proper clothing or shoes for that type of weather, only little thin sandals, and, it seemed that they were going to work up north in Siberia, (slave labor we called it). Amy felt so bad for these little girls since most were small and were very young and with no proper and caring adults to watch over them...and certainly no appropriate clothing for this kind of weather. They were younger than Amy, certainly, around fifteen or sixteen years old.

Amy had taken a small radio with her on this trip; some of the Philipino girls noticed it since Amy presumably had it to her ear. They showed great interest in seeing and knowing what this 'thing' was. Amy, who is always thoughtful and sweet, decided to show the radio to the girls, meaning let them listen for a few moments. Before Amy knew what was happening, all the girls had lined up politely and patiently, without a murmur, waiting to listen. Amy kindly let each girl listen…and they were thrilled!

After that, Jack decided since the girls were from the Philippines they would never have known what snow was, or what one could do with snow or, better still, how to make a snowman or have a snowball fight! So he hailed to them to come, waving his arms around in the airport to all fifty or so little girls, designating, 'Follow me!' And… of course, they did; they all followed him out to the snow to play. Not Ed of course, with his health problems he could not go out of doors to participate in the snow scene, although…he could watch them all. Amy went with Jack, and a few other Americans, to help the Philippine girls learn how to play with snow. All had many laughs with Amy showing them how to make snowmen and Jack beside her all the time putting in his two cents worth, throwing snowballs at them and showing them how to throw them back at him, and enjoying the whole affair immensely. I imagine the Philipino girls found the experience interesting, but probably got quite cold. But under the circumstances, not much could be done to avoid that.

That particularly pleasurable time had to come to an end, as all good things must. Amy, Ed and the group of Americans from Izmir proceeded to Leningrad while the Philippine girls disappeared, quietly…vanished, at the Leningrad airport as though they never existed, never to be seen by Ed and Amy again!

> *The quality of mercy is not strained*
> *It droppeth like the gentle rain from heaven.*
> *It is twice blessed*
> *It blesseth him that gives*
> *And him that takes.*
>
> **Merchant of Venice**
> **—Shakespeare**

Egypt

Shortly after the Russian trip with Ed, Amy and I decided to go to Egypt over the Christmas break in December 1988. A group of our friends organized the trip. Ed did not join us this time. Too many trips were hard on him considering his back pain and other health problems.

When the plane landed in Cairo, our luggage supposedly went out to the small bus waiting to take us to the hotel. When we arrived at the hotel, my luggage was missing. An oily, toothless, dirty taxi man, leering at me, said he would drive me back to the airport to pick up my luggage. He had very little English language capabilities, but he made his purpose known nonetheless. His friend came along also. I hesitated to go alone with them, but I had very little choice. It was obvious to me that Amy was terribly tired, therefore, off I went leaving her in our room.

The ride was not pleasant, I was frightened; the two dubious looking men sat in the front seat doing nothing more than leering at me, the driver peering into his rear-view mirror and the other looking over his shoulder. I found my luggage sitting, waiting to be picked up; it was all by itself on a very dirty sidewalk that was filled with tobacco and spit! Anyone could have walked off with it, and I was left with a feeling that this may have been preplanned. I picked up my luggage, and they drove me back to the hotel. When the taxi finally reached the hotel, I paid handsomely, tipped liberally and dashed in with my luggage!

The next day around noon we visited the National Egyptian Museum. To my surprise, we found it was absolutely *huge*! There was so much to see and it was such a large place that we would have had to spend a week doing nothing more than studying the ancient artifacts in that museum. It was a marvelous place to begin a tour, to say the very least, but with only a week before school was to resume we had little time to spare to accomplish what had been planned for us on our Egyptian itinerary. All was set up ahead of time at a travel agent's office in Turkey. We often found too much was included on most of the trips planned for us by agencies. It proved to be almost impossible to see all that was arranged for us in the small number of days we had.

As we were wandering around the museum, looking at various and sundry relics of the past and studying this and that, a strange thing happened. The guards in the museum were Egyptian men, wearing long robes, with long flapping sleeves and gun belts strapped around their waists. Suddenly, they extended their arms straight out in front of them and clapped, not as you would if your were applauding, but instead one loud clap all at the same time. Then, the clap was repeated every few seconds. The claps could be heard throughout the museum. It seemed to be a signal for something. Then, we noticed everyone leaving the museum…so the claps must have been a signal to empty the museum. But why? Then we looked at a clock on the wall, and realized it was noon, so it must have been their lunchtime. Up until then, our small group of ten or twelve from Izmir had felt somewhat frightened by the clapping, but once we realized what was happening, we calmly left the museum ourselves. We had lunch and finished our museum tour after. It was certainly the strangest way of emptying a museum that I had ever seen!

Mary and Amy in front of Egyptian Sphinx

Following our museum visit, we went to see the famous statue of the Sphinx on the outskirts of Cairo. It is located along with three pyramids. Because of photos I had seen over the years, I'd always assumed that the Sphinx and pyramids stood alone in a vast desert. *Wrong!* The city of Cairo had grown to such an extent over the years that the Sphinx and pyramids are not in a distant desert, but are just fifty yards or less from nearby apartments. When we arrived I was absolutely shocked to see the city virtually nestling on top of the pyramids!

Tourists were allowed to go inside the pyramids. Some of the teachers took the tour. Our high school secretary, Arlene, told me she had to enter on hands and knees and crawl inside a long, low tunnel for several minutes to reach the inside of the pyramid. Once fully inside, Arlene said you could stand upright and examine the insides of the pyramid. I decided *not* to go inside a pyramid because I'm claustrophobic. Amy did not go in either. Picturing myself crawling along on my hands and knees for ten or more minutes left me with absolutely no desire to see the insides of *any* pyramid, I can assure you!

However, it was not easy waiting outside the pyramids for our fellow tour members. Camel drivers who were fascinated by Amy's blonde hair constantly approached Amy and me. The dark and dirty Egyptian camel drivers leered at us and one driver even asked if he could 'buy' Amy. The men made our group nervous and Amy and I remained close…very close…to each other.

After our first day in Cairo, the tour itinerary called for our group to fly to a region below the famous Aswan Dam. From there, we would travel north to Cairo, visiting famous sites along the way. We flew in a small plane and arrived at our hotel late that night. We were offered some kind of supper, but the food looked most unappetizing. Actually, it was disgusting…greasy cold soups with fatty pieces of meat which, if they were not beef, were probably camel! I became nauseous just looking at the food. Amy and I opted to forego the meal.

It was around midnight when Amy and I, hungry and tired, finally reached our room in the dingy, dirty hotel. You can imagine our utter dismay when we walked into our room and found the bed occupied! A scrawny, skeletal-like, man was asleep in what was supposed to be our bed. He was filthy dirty and smelled beyond belief. Amy and I were both horrified, but Amy's adrenalin must have kicked in. My twenty-year old daughter approached the bed and shook the man, but he could not seem to wake up. He had on a dirty, white piece of grimy sheeting and sported an equally dirty, long, thin beard and mustache. He could not hold his eyes open for long. He looked at her and they closed again. At that point, Amy grabbed him by his robe, dragged him out of bed, and flung him into the corridor, yelling at him the entire time. He probably never really knew what happened to him!

Then, tired and worn out, we marched back down to the reception desk to demand a different room for the night. There were none available we learned. Well, could we at least get a clean set of sheets? Some sheets were provided us, but we had to change the bed ourselves. Once made, we fell exhausted into the bed…but sleep did not come easily for me that night.

The following morning, with only a few hours of restless sleep, Amy and I looked at the food being offered for our breakfast and could not eat again…it looked too horrible. Then our tour group boarded buses for the trip to Aswan Dam. We hoped we could find something we could eat later that day. The trip was wearing on both of us!

During our drive to the Aswan Dam, I saw many, many camels being herded in large groups from Sudan (south of Egypt) to Cairo. I was told they were being taken to the market. The scene was like something out of a movie for me…seeing the camels and the drivers and knowing they would be walking through many miles of desert. It was a most unusual and wonderful sight, but…very humbling!

Following our tour of the Aswan Dam we visited the Abu Simbel temples. The twin temples were originally carved out of the mountainside during the reign of Pharaoh Ramses II in the 13th century BC, as a lasting monument to himself and his queen Nefertiti, to commemorate his alleged victory at the Battle of Kadesh, and to intimidate his Nubian neighbors. However, the complex was relocated in its entirety in 1968, on an artificial hill made from a domed structure, high above the Aswan High Dam reservoir. The relocation of the temples was necessary to avoid their being submerged during the creation of Lake Nasser, the massive artificial water reservoir formed after the building of the Aswan Dam on the Nile River. It was amazing to see what had been done. I don't think I ever would have known the temple had been moved if I had not been told. What an incredible feat!

The drive from the Aswan Dam to the Abu Simbel temples was long and there were no bathroom facilities available. At one point, our vehicle stopped at sand dunes. Those in need of relief disappeared behind a dune for a few minutes. It was not something I could do however. All I could picture was stooping to urinate and probably dousing myself with my own liquid. I held on for what seemed like forever until we arrived at Abu Simbel. There we found only shanties with holes for urinating and defecating, but for me that was better than a sand dune!

After I had 'relieved' myself and could walk comfortably, I thoroughly enjoyed touring the temple. It is generally considered the grandest and most beautiful of the temples commissioned during the reign of Ramesses II, and one of the most beautiful in Egypt.

Four colossal 65-foot tall statues of the pharaoh Ramesses II decorate the facade of the temple, which is 114 feet wide. The colossal statues were sculpted directly from the rock in which the temple was located before it was moved.

From the Abu Simbel temple, our group went on to Luxor to view the remains of Thebes, Ancient Egypt's New Kingdom capital. A mile or so north is the Karnak Temple, a stupendous complex built over 1300 years. Across the river are the amazing tombs and mortuary temples of the Theban Necropolis. All the tombs and monuments were imposing, inspiring and stimulating, but soon I began to feel overwhelmed. There was so much to see and comprehend and we were moving so quickly without much sleep and even less to eat.

I believe I relaxed the most on a slow boat ride up the Nile to the Valley of the Kings and Queens. It was then that I fell in love with the feluccas, a traditional wooden sailing boat used in protected water. Our tour was not actually on a felucca, but I thoroughly enjoyed gazing at them sailing up and down the Nile as we proceeded in our motorized boat. They have only one, beautifully shaped sail and they look peaceful and serene moving up and down the Nile.

Eventually we arrived back in Cairo and were taken to the market place. It was busy, dismal, dirty and teeming with people. The sellers virtually force themselves on tourists, entreating you to buy whatever wares they were offering. I was not comfortable and held on fiercely to the bag around my waist that held my money. I could not wait to leave. Yet, despite the crush of people and pushy vendors, I did end up buying a couple of souvenirs that I thought were unusual and unique. One item was a small wooden window similar to what one would find in a house. There was a board attached to the back to 'close' the window and within its thick frame there were animal bones. It fascinated me and now stands on a shelf in my sunroom with other copper and brass artifacts from Turkey. The other item I purchased was a large tin lantern with hand-punched designs on all sides. It is designed to hold a candle and therefore emit a lovely light for hours.

On the whole, the Egypt trip was a whirlwind of experience for me and our small group of friends. It was a difficult trip due to the crowds, the dirt, and the poverty Amy and I witnessed throughout the trip. So far it has been my only trip to Egypt. (If I were ever able to go again, I would certainly stay in first class hotels and sail down the Nile on one of the magnificent feluccas). I was happy to have visited Egypt, but deliriously happy to get back 'home' to Turkey.

We arrived home on New Year's Day. (We had celebrated New Year's Eve about five in the evening in a nice restaurant near the Cairo airport since we would be in the air at midnight). Our flight back to Izmir was short and insignificant thank God. Amy and I were glad to have a long and cleansing shower and sleep in our own beds when we arrived home quite late that night...*Ahhh!*

Scrooge and Charlie Brown

I've talked extensively about working with the high school band in Izmir, which was a wonderful and new experience for me. However, having that new responsibility did not lessen my desire to have the high school students participate in a musical. So, after my first full school year in Izmir I decided we should perform *Scrooge*. My memory is a bit hazy, but I believe it was in December 1988. (The weather is so unvarying in Izmir, not really any seasons as we are used to in New England, that memories of special weather conditions do not attach themselves to particular events. It was always sunny, warm and warmer throughout the year).

Producing the *Scrooge* musical was a massive amount of work, but by my second year I had gotten to know many people who were able and willing to help with the project. Joann Cobanli, the home economics teacher at the high school helped with the costumes. The art teacher and her students did a wonderful job with the scenery and props under extremely difficult circumstances. The only place we had to perform that first year was in a small military movie theater. The movie screen could not be removed from the center of the stage, therefore that left us with very little space in which to work.

For example, Scrooge needed a full size bed for the dream scenes, but there was not enough space on the stage for a full size bed. The art teacher worked with the 'shop' teacher and designed a bed that appeared long and regular size to the audience, but was actually quite short. The 'shop' teacher followed instructions perfectly and the bed worked wonderfully. The actor playing Scrooge curled up in the small bed while sleeping, and the audience never knew the difference.

The high school students acted and sang beautifully. Dan Tougas was the perfect Scrooge; mean and nasty in the beginning. A girl was made up to look like a boy and played the role of Tiny Tim, which was easy enough to do since she was a small seventh grader. Dan's sister, Sarah, played the part of one of the ghosts and did a magnificent job, as well as the other actors, whose names I cannot seem to remember now.

All went so well that I felt the musical was sensational. I knew then that I could manage to have another musical next year, which I did.

The following year we decided to perform *You're a Good Man, Charlie Brown*. Students who had performed in *Scrooge* the year before, tried out again, which is what often happens when students have had a good experience performing. In addition, many other high school students came forward wanting to be in this musical, having seen the previous one and knowing how much fun it had been for those in it. Again, we performed on that awful stage at the military movie theatre. Yes, the very narrow one! There are times in life when one has to 'make do.'

The students who had performed the year before gained more confidence

Sarah Tougas, top row left, as Lucy in Charlie Brown.
Her brother, Daniel Tougas, as Linus standing below her.
Darren Fast, bottom left, as Charlie Brown. Aylin Guvenc, center.
Mark Duncanson, far right.

in themselves and were even better this time around in their acting/singing. Sarah Tougas, who had played a ghost in *Scrooge*, was Lucy in *Charlie Brown*. At this time, I don't remember the names of all the students who played the other major characters. I do know there was a new student in the high school, Darren Fast, who tried out for *Charlie Brown*. He auditioned for the lead role, acting and singing beautifully, and he won it. I was so pleased!

I must confess, I have great joy in my heart when I witness individuals who truly want to perform and who work hard during rehearsals and who succeed; they carry this success with them all through their lives. I have some marvelous eight by ten photos of the show. A parent or friend took the snaps while the play was on and gave me a whole set of eight by ten photographs as a surprise and a present!

The best part about working overseas with the military was this: no matter where I happened to be or what I was doing with any of the students, the military personnel were generous with their time helping with whatever I asked. They were always 'great' and 'grateful' to me at the same time. Anything I needed for costumes or sets, the parents constantly worked to see that we had it, whether they had to make it or buy it or borrow it from someone or somewhere!

All of this extra work was exhausting of course. The musical productions were worked on after a day of regular classes. But then I always felt that if one kept fit physically one could not help but do well at work, since one would feel so uplifted by exercise. I walked anywhere from four to six miles each day along the coast on the great sidewalk overlooking the Izmir Bay. I think it was this exercise that gave me the stamina to meet all my obligations at the school.

Daughter Susan's Diagnosis

On December 19, 1989, as we were into our third year living in Turkey, I had a call from my daughter Susan in the states. For a brief second fear flashed through me. Susan had suffered many health problems over the years. We had taken her to many doctors, but no one could figure out what was causing her health problems. I cannot adequately describe her symptoms at this point, except to say she was always not feeling well. There was something wrong with her every few weeks or months it seemed, and usually different symptoms each time.

However, Susan carried on with her life as best she could. She attended Henniker College studying botany, met John who became her husband, and studied and worked when her health allowed.

She was calling that day to say she had been diagnosed with MS…Multiple Sclerosis. The horrible disease was the cause of all her health problems over the years and was incurable.

Susan was hysterical while trying to talk on the phone and Ed and I were shocked and dismayed. When we finally pulled ourselves together, we made arrangements for her to come visit us as soon as possible.

She arrived in Izmir on January 14, 1990. She stayed with us for ten days and during that time we cried and hugged and hugged and cried. (Amy was still with us then). The four of us discussed Susan's plight; we talked about cures, of which there were none. We talked about her future. We kept assuring her she would be able to manage and still finish her schooling; find work and continue with her life. We vowed to help her any way possible.

After a few days, we all recovered enough from the shock of her news to show Susan around Izmir. I showed her my school; introduced her to teachers and friends; brought her to the market places; enjoyed the lovely beaches along the Aegean Sea. All in all, we were as happy as we could be under the circumstances. The days flew by, and soon her visit was over and she returned to the states.

She did graduate from college a few years later. Unfortunately I was unable to attend the ceremony, but my mother, brother, and good friends from Andover did. By then, Susan had to spend much of her time in a wheelchair. The day of the graduation though, she insisted on walking across the stage to accept her diploma. I was told she received a standing ovation. I was sad that I was not able to attend the graduation myself, but my family and friends sent me numerous photos, and Susan and I talked on the phone that day. I was so proud of her!

1990 Persian Gulf War

In early August of 1990 Iraqi troops invaded Kuwait. The action was internationally condemned and soon there was a war that involved the United States. Iraq borders Turkey on its southeast border. Terrorists sympathizing with the Iraqis' targeted American facilities in Turkey with random bomb attacks. Within months of hostilities breaking out, all the Americans who were visiting, but not working, in Turkey were told to leave as soon as possible. Amy had been visiting us over the Christmas break in 1990. (We were now in our third year of living/working in Turkey). We sent her home as soon as possible. The next morning brought the horrors of war too close for comfort. The following story I wrote after an event Ed and I experienced in January 1991.

BOMBED OUT OF BED

"London Bridge is falling down,
Falling down, falling down,
London Bridge is falling down,
My fair lady."

I was lying in bed in that delicious state between awake and asleep when a ter-rifying noise roared into my consciousness with a horrific sound of crashing and vi-brations! Our apartment shook and trembled waking me with a violent start as the full force of the impact tossed my body hard on to Ed's, covering him largely from head to toe; glass from our huge blown out sliding windows smashed and landed all around us on the bed, and the floor! The building actually reverberated causing glass to fly this way and that. As the building shook and the glass flew and the sound still reechoed in my head, all I could do was scream like a maniac... hollering, "We've been hit! We've been hit! Ed, we've been hit!!!"

In a frightening flash my mind saw bombs dropping from planes as I trembled from head to toe. Still on top of Ed's body we grasped each other and held on tightly, as life became very precious, with each moment seeming like a long hour. Suddenly, screaming violently into Ed's ear, I yelled, "Ed! We're going to die!!!! We're going to die, I know we're going to die!!!" I clung to him with fear and horror believing at that moment bombs were dropping around us from airplanes flying overhead. I could see them so vividly in my mind and even now, as I write this story, I still see the bombs falling! I never, ever, thought it might be terrorist bombs!

My mind was working so fast: "I must be wrong. I have to be wrong, this can't be happening to us!" But then...I knew we were two weeks into the Persian Gulf War and Turkey borders Iraq in the southeast, so maybe the planes were coming here and over our apartment."

Ed kept yelling to me in his loud and grating voice while trying forcibly to remove me from his body, "Let go...let go of me so I can close the rouladins," (a special type of interior window covering in our apartment).

With all his might, Ed bumbled out of bed, his legs tangled in the sheets...pulling my body with him since I held on to him like a vice grip. The small word 'scared' could not describe the terror...yes, the terror...I was feeling in those moments! Quickly, Ed removed my hands and their grip on his body, and pushed me aside, *slid into his slippers, rushed through the shattered glass to the windows and instantly pulled the rouladins shut.*

I was close behind Ed, hanging on to the back of his pajama top, gripping it like a vice and with no slippers on my feet as I treaded through the shattered glass! Ed turned to me sharply, startling me with a roar, screaming in a voice I had never heard him use before, "Don't come over here! Don't come here… watch out for the glass! Stay behind me!"

So, I did what I do best in emergencies…I did exactly the opposite, I bumbled around in the broken glass like an idiot, hanging on to his shirt until he forced me to let go. Ed turned around and wrenched my hands loose from him; after he disengaged himself from me I stood stupidly by, watching…dumbfounded…shell-shocked! A barbarous and vicious terror was forcing me to become a maniac.

After the rouladins were closed, I quickly followed Ed, once again like a robot, by hanging on to his pajama shirt; we somehow managed to steer ourselves through the broken window panes and into Amy's bedroom, which was next to ours. We were horrified at what we saw! Shards of glass covered the twin beds; I recall vividly how they punctured the covers on the bed, and stood up in the air like icicles. Had Amy been in the bed she would have been punctured all over her body! At this realization, a stupid, silly sort of sound bubbled up from my chest and out of my mouth, I was hysterically screeching, "Amy's safe, Amy's safe…she's not in her bed!"

We had been able to get a seat for Amy on a plane in Istanbul the night before, which was bound for the USA. She left on the very last American plane to fly out of Istanbul for some time!

Ed yanked down the rouladins in Amy's room and then physically pushed and guided me the few short steps down the hallway into the bathroom, which was across from our bedroom. I had been standing stupidly, riveted to the spot in Amy's room. Again, I could not seem to function for some reason unknown to me at that time. My mind seemed blank…terrified…raw! I could not think.

The bathroom became a semi-dark haven as Ed closed the door and I squished down on the side of the washing machine, collapsing onto the floor. Ed then sat on the toilet; he had to do what one usually does first thing in the morning. Some things never change…therefore, he went about his business, despite the war. I was too frigid with fright to be able to function in that fashion.

I then pulled my frightened self up a bit, sitting straighter, still leaning my back on the washing machine. It felt good, like a protection. The machine was cool and held me in an upright position but my head slumped down almost between my knees which were folded and up close to my body; I was able to see, my eyes felt round as saucers as I wrapped my arms around my knees. I knew that was what one would do if in a plane crash!

By this point I was borderline hysterical! I was breathing hard and shivering, with unusual sensations fluttering in my chest. Emotionally hallucinating, I saw that the bathroom gave an aura of being warm and comforting. It had a yellowish glow, like the sun. There were no windows in the bathroom and the dim light was still on. How long would the light stay on, I wondered?

Petrified and panic stricken...words cannot describe how frightened I was... thoughts flew rapidly through my mind: "Surely another bomb was going to come this way and hit the building full force." I was convinced that one more explosion would plunge us into greater depths of darkness and despair and total destruction. "How many more planes were above us, how many more bombs would be dropped?" I asked myself.

"Oh, God," I implored, wailing like a banshee, "What shall we do, what shall we do?" and dropped my head once again down on my knees and just wept...utterly and hopelessly wept...the fright was unreal. Suddenly, after letting myself flow into my tears, my mind cleared a little and I started to think out loud...to Ed...to no one...to myself?

"I can still see," as I peered around the bathroom, "and I can sit here for today and then maybe I can begin to think rationally."

I didn't know what to expect and time was standing still. A few seconds felt like an eternity as Ed and I sat...waiting and waiting. Straining to hear, but hearing nothing; tense to the point of breaking into little pieces.

Suddenly, something prompted me to move, to get up, to do something, but I didn't know what. Ed was still sitting on the only seat in the room, not knowing what to do either...I somehow crawled a bit and then boosted myself up from the floor, opening the bathroom door just a tiny crack, slowly, slowly...I had no idea how much time had gone by. Was it ten minutes, an hour... two hours? All time had stopped and all my 'thinking' seemed to be out of proportion.

Then, through the open door, I heard people's voices chaotically calling and yelling. Their sounds came through the broken windows. I imagined an ambulance racing through the streets of Izmir, sirens wailing. I actually thought, nay... KNEW...I heard sirens. I even SAW...literally saw, in my mind, BOMBS DROPPING FROM PLANES! Terror engulfed me completely once again and I shut the door tightly and hung on to it. Still hanging on to the bathroom door, I started to babble in my high-pitched anguished voice, shrieking, "Ed, Code Delta! Code Delta! WE'RE IN CODE DELTA…I KNOW WE ARE IN CODE DELTA."

Ed once again assumed control of the situation, raised himself up off of the toilet seat, and ordered me to get dressed. We would have to leave the protection of the dim bathroom.

"Mary," he yelled, "get dressed in case we have to evacuate quickly, put some clothes on"…and since I did not move, he yelled again with a great and startling force, "NOW!" Startled, I visibly jumped forward letting go of the door.

Like a disconnected thought floating in the air, I remember thinking how orderly Ed's mind was. I grabbed a jacket hanging on the bedroom door hook, which was only about four feet from our protective bathroom door, and quickly threw it over my red jogging suit, which had become nightly sleeping attire since it was always so cold in the apartment in January.

Ed barked at me once again, and groaned, his voice sounding like wood cracking, once he noticed what I was doing, "Don't put a jacket over your pajamas! Put your clothes on!"

By now he had become quite loud and was physically pushing, or shoving me to-wards the closet. I then noticed he was already out of his pajamas.

"When did he put his clothes on?" I muttered to myself, while standing in the doorway of our bedroom looking Ed up and down, wondering where his pajamas were. I felt numb and dumb once again, all over. Muddled and moving mechanically, I scurried like a scared squirrel from the closet to the chest of drawers and back to the closet still expecting bombs to drop from the sky. My chest hurt with the pain of breath-ing and my eyes felt bigger than my face and I could not stand looking towards Amy's bedroom door every time we had to be in the hallway. Somehow I dressed myself but I don't know how I did it or what I put on.

Clothes on, Ed hurriedly directed me by my shoulders to the kitchen, down the narrow hallway, to call Jerry; he is our CPO friend who lived two floors below us. Then I realized, smiling to myself and thinking, "Civilian Personnel Officers know all the answers." Well, I always felt they did. He was very smart and also a great friend of ours. "He will tell us what to do. I know he will…I just know it…"

Muttering to myself I turned around and seemingly raced down the hallway to the kitchen with Ed following; the kitchen was only a few yards past the bathroom. Also, a boon…each apartment kitchen had a phone, which we could use to connect with other apartments.

Breathlessly, I punched Jerry's number on the kitchen phone. He answered with a shaking voice and before I could say a word, he yelled at me, "Are you all right? Mary, are you all right?"

I stammered that we were and I was able to bawl out loud to him on the phone, "Jerry, I'm so scared, what shall we do?"

He howled back at me saying, "I called Security Police."

With those words, small as they were, I felt a small measure of relief fill my mind and body. Someone knew what to do! I replaced the phone and almost smiled, and without even thinking, I hung up on him. I can still see myself standing in the kitchen, leaning against the wall while holding the phone in its cradle, afraid to move for fear I would fall.

I then yelled at Ed, telling him, "Security police will be here at any moment then we'll know what's happening." Of course, it never occurred to me that security police would have dozens of other calls to make or receive and would never arrive for hours!

Suddenly, that small measure of false security made my mind begin to clear. I felt more rational and found myself worrying about friends who might not have heard the bombs or worse; friends who might have been hit or hurt by the bombs! Should I call people to warn them?

A shattering thought then pushed everything else aside and again, my fear rose up and I screamed to Ed, "Maybe bombs are dropping in other parts of the city and we can't hear them! I rushed to the front of the apartment with Ed following me, which I never should have done. Not wanting to get too close to the huge floor to ceiling windows that fronted our apartment, I cautiously peered out at the bay.

I was startled. Surprised! I thought…"How weird!" Positions had reversed; everything was normal there as I looked out the window of our seventh floor apartment.

"Ed," I yelled once again, speaking rapidly, "everything looks fine out here, people are walking back and forth and talking, as though nothing has happened not running or hiding either. Why? I don't understand… I just don't understand why people are walking and talking as though nothing has happened."

Then, as I peeked out on the bay once again, my fear still high in my mind, I thought of Ruth. She's also a teacher and lives only a few buildings down from us on the left hand side. Feeling like a stark and raving crazy lady I whispered, to no one in particular, not sure where Ed was at that moment, "I must call Ruth, I must call Ruth…"

We had a phone that connected us to the outside world in addition to the kitchen phone; I literally flew back to the small hallway by the doorway to the outside phone, fumbling for the teachers' telephone emergency directory fearing the worse. Ruth's voice was strong and brisk when she answered, "There's no damage to my apartment."

"No damage?" I yelled at her. Puzzled! How could my apartment be so damaged when she had none and was only three doors away from our apartment building. She also still sounded normal, unlike me, Mary, the music teacher, who was beginning to feel like a lunatic. A rapid thought stormed through my head and out of my mouth as I screamed, "Were we the only ones whose apartment was bombed?" Without waiting for an answer, I then yelled,

"What are you going to do, Ruth?"

She replied in a cool fashion, unlike me in my terror, "I'm going to school."

Horrified at her words and demeanor, I screamed through the phone, "You're going to school with bombs dropping all around us?"

"We have to go in, the kids are coming today and they are probably already there and they will need us under these circumstances…"Ruth replied in her same fashion.

I then howled firmly and definitively, "I may HAVE to go in today, but I don't have to go NOW…"and in complete panic once again I dropped the receiver onto the floor.

The confusion in my mind was growing and the fear had not lessened. Ed started yelling, "Call Terry! Call Terry! He's your principal, your head of command; he's your leader! He will tell you what to do…"

I pushed more buttons and Terry answered quickly. He must have heard the explosions since he lives just beyond Ruth, but still in close proximity to us. In my frantic and erratic voice, trying to be coherent, I told him what happened to us and asked him what to do…

His voice rang in my ear, "How should I know? I don't know what to tell you. I'VE NEVER BEEN BOMBED BEFORE!"

Shocked, I laughed shakily, and then, stupidly trying to joke but not succeeding…I wailed at him saying, "You're our leader, Terry, you must know. I need some leadership and I need it NOW!"

At that, we briefly laughed hysterically together, and then his voice blasted into the phone once again, "I don't know any more than you…!"

I groaned out loud and dropped the receiver onto the telephone table, but then, it fell onto the floor and lay there…just looking at me!

Hardly comforted, my gnawing dilemma was whether to go to school or not. I knew the American children were helpless and, according to the clock, had already arrived at our school; they could not be left alone with the guards on the busses, they needed hugs and love and protection.

BUT, I too was scared and I did not want to go!

I bellowed at Ed, "Call Joann, call Joann, she'll know what to do!" I did not want to touch the phone again! He grabbed the phone unceremoniously and called Joann…he was about to ask her what she was going to do and what I should do and to tell her to be cautious when another shattering explosion occurred outside her home! Ed could hear the blast on the phone. Hysteria enveloped us once again.

He yelled in his loudest voice, for all to hear, "Another bomb blast," Ed screamed, "another bomb blast…Mary, call Jerry," Ed yelled…"NOW…so he won't go out."

That did it! I was babbling again. My voice was foreign to me…saying all kinds of words…fear wrapped itself around me like a cloak. Ed and I grabbed each other and held on like glue…I made a decision, and in my worn out raspy voice I stated, "I AM NOT leaving my apartment!"

Within one moment, the raspy brrrp,brrrp,brrrp of the kitchen phone startled us once again. "Jerry" I mumbled, "it has to be Jerry".

I left Ed's arms and moved quickly from the hallway phone to the kitchen phone and picked it up to find it was indeed Jerry.

He yelled at me saying, "I have to leave for work…"

I hollered back, "You can't go, another bomb went off."

"I HAVE to leave for work. I have orders to report to work in ANY emergency."

"But Jerry," I wailed once again, "a bomb has gone off at the Cultural Center." In total hysteria I retold the whole bomb story: "Jerry, we…we…were trying to talk to Joann about school and the kids and what to do, when…when…another bomb went off by the Principal's office at the Turkish Cultural Center." Jerry's only answer was a moan and a groan as he dropped the receiver onto the floor…

Within forty-five minutes from the start of this whole mess a call came from the principal's office via Ruth, a branch of our 'telephone tree' to say terrorist bombs were set off throughout the city and that the bombs were not launched by missiles from Iraq. We were in 'Code Delta' and Code Delta means, STAY IN! That was that!

Information poured into everyone's homes all day. The final count of bombs was three. The first was in back of our apartment building aimed at the U.S. Military storage depot but…instead, blew out our windows and frightened us all to death! The second blast was at the French Embassy, which destroyed five cars, blew out many windows in nearby apartments and left the surrounding buildings charred as well. That area was a mess for a very long time since there was so much damage. The last bomb went off at 7:20 a.m. at the Turkish American Association building, familiarly called the TAA: it damaged windows and some of the building itself. The TAA was diagonally across from our high school and on a direct route for all of us who walked to work.

We were told later that our teacher friend, Tom, who was walking to school near the TAA at the time of the blast, suffered from the impact. For thirty minutes after the explosion Tom could not talk, the fright was paralyzing; he could not utter one word. Several days after the blast had descended upon him, he was still trying to recover emotionally.

Meanwhile, the principal, Terry, went to the high school despite what was happening since he was under orders to do so. There, he met two other couples. Three were teachers and one a secretary, (the wife of one of the teachers). All five had arrived virtually together at the school office minutes before the TAA bomb exploded; as its powerful blast reechoed around the area John Taylor maniacally yelled to everyone, "Hit the deck! Hit the deck"!

They all sprawled onto the floor, John falling on his knees in prayer fashion and the others burrowing under furniture and most especially into the kneeholes of the large desks in the office. Fear of the unknown is horrifying! What did it hit? Who was hit? Is this the last bomb? Will there be another in a minute? Where will it explode next? Thoughts of this nature ran through their heads constantly without letup as they hid in their respective hiding places.

The remainder of my day was a blur and whirr of telephone calls and the cleaning up of shards of glass. I did nothing but answer phones...if the kitchen telephone did not ring, the outside telephone rang. Often, they both rang together. Kind and inquiring friends called; the calls were from those not affected by the bomb blasts. Then our doorbell started pealing...

A Turkish man was yelling, "Lady, lady, glass, glass!"

I grabbed Ed's sleeve once again...my voice went up another octave as I continued whining and wailing, "Maybe they're not really glass men, maybe they're here to hurt us! Terrorists disguise themselves well; what should we do? Should we let them in?"

Ed looked out of the small peephole implanted in all the doors in Turkey, and we saw a group of Turks standing patiently holding an enormous, long and wide, sheet of glass, waiting to be let into our apartment. I breathed a sigh of relief. I felt faint! The owner of the apartment building must have sent them over.

Turks came and went with enormous sheets of glass and repair tools all afternoon it seemed, back and forth and up and down; we were on the seventh floor and none of the glass sheets could fit into our tiny box-like elevators, so up and down the seven flights of stairs they traveled much of the afternoon. None of the laboring Turks spoke

English, therefore we had to figure out what to do with them and what they were going to do with us. With great anxiety we had to determine, each time the bell rang, whether they were friend or foe. Fear hovered around my head constantly...all day! Every time the doorbell rang I had difficulty breathing...

After the workmen finally left many hours later I wandered into our shattered, slovenly and semi-repaired bedroom hearing something familiar out on the street in the back where the first bomb exploded; hammer hammer hammer, pound pound pound...hammer hammer hammer, pound pound pound...

I groaned loudly and thought out loud..."life goes on in Turkey despite bombs." The carpenters were at work somewhere in back of our apartment just as though nothing had happened. The street cleaners were out cleaning up after the bombs and damage, and the average everyday life of the Turks was continuing as usual.

All Americans and ONLY Americans were ordered to stay in. The terrorists were not trying to dispose of the Turks, oh no, they were looking for someone else... us...the Americans! Tears started to stream down my face and in my mind I heard the song:

> *"Build them up and tear them down,*
> *tear them down, tear them down,*
> *build them up and tear them down,*
> *my fair lady..."*

Following the bombing incident, we received orders not to leave our apartment for seven days. My depression deepened, and I was afraid it would never leave me. During that week however, my friend Yvonne, who was not employed by the military, was able to visit me. We talked about what was going on. I told her how terrible I felt and shared my fear that I would never 'come out' of the depression.

"Mary, what you are going through is not unnatural, just don't worry about those feelings and in a short time they will leave you," Yvonne told me. She gazed at me with a serene smile and continued, "Go with them, Mary, do not fight those feelings you are having now, they will leave you bit by bit, a little at a time, but they will leave! The depression will disappear."

Yvonne was correct. She and her husband and three children had lived through a period of bombings and terrorist attacks in Egypt in 1981, following the assassination of Anwar Sadat. At one point, following a terrorist attack near where they lived, Yvonne rushed to the private school her children attended and found the entire school population hiding under the seats of the school's auditorium. She had lived through a time of great unrest and terrorist activity. It was wonderful to hear her reassuring words following the bombing we experienced.

Eventually classes at our Izmir school resumed. However, in order to avoid establishing a pattern of activity that might allow the terrorists to plan more destructive actions against Americans, school began at a different time each day. Each morning everyone in the school (teachers, parents of students, etc.) received a call stating what time the school day would start. Sometimes it was as early as 7 a.m. and other days as late as 10 a.m.

In addition, all the teachers were ordered to walk to school and to *never* take the same route twice in a row. Anything to make sure we did not establish a pattern a terrorist could predict. I must admit, this was all extremely frightening for me, but I followed orders daily. I found myself looking over my shoulder all the time. However, I did discover that after a few days I had grown more used to it and the whole affair did not bother me quite as much as it had in the beginning.

As Yvonne had predicted, my depression faded away before our week of being confined to the apartment was over. Then it seemed I became accustomed to the daily change of school hours. Once I had grown used to that, all became… well, certainly not normal, but relatively normal, or, I guess I could say, normal for that time!

My elementary classes became very small since many military parents decided to send their children back to the States to live with relatives. Some of the high school students were sent home as well, but nevertheless, I still had a good size band.

I do not remember exactly how long the war lasted and how long we lived under those war conditions; it was many months, but not a full year. Unfortunately, there were more bombings throughout Turkey, including several more in Izmir.

Prior to the war, my friend Sharon Boling and I often walked on the sidewalk up and down the Izmir Bay in the evening. We would walk up to six miles talking and enjoying the lovely views as we unwound from the day. After the war began though, American women were not allowed to walk on the street without a male escort. Sharon and I did not want to give up our walks, so Sharon's husband, Larry, a tall, sturdy Oklahoman, accompanied us, walking a few paces behind us all the time.

One evening, Ed and I had invited Larry and Sharon to our apartment for a light supper of soup and sandwiches after our walk. As we sat at the table talking, laughing, and eating, a bomb exploded near our apartment. Our building shook and fear gripped me like a vice. I began to tremble all over. The explosion was so loud it seemed to be right next to our apartment. All of us jumped up from the table and rushed out onto the balcony to see what had happened.

Then, in a state of absolute terror, I remembered instructions from the military, and screamed loudly, "Ed...Sharon...Larry, we're not supposed to be on the balcony!" We had been warned *never, ever* go out on the balcony if we heard bombs exploding or bullets fired. Snipers could be waiting to shoot anyone who appeared outside.

We all retreated quickly back into the apartment, shut the doors with a bang and closed the drapes. We all felt foolish. But we had seen where the smoke and fire were coming from, about three doors down on the right from us.

Suddenly Ed yelled, "That explosion was at Gretta's apartment building! She's alone over there. I'm going to see if she's all right!"

"You are *not* going over there!" I replied forcefully. "You are *not* going out. I won't let you. It's too dangerous!" I continued, becoming wild with fear.

"I'm going anyway. Heino is away...Gretta has no one with her," he responded as he glared at me. "I'm going to the bathroom first, then I'm going over to see if she's all right...and don't try to stop me from helping her!" Ed turned quickly and hurried down our hallway to the bathroom.

Within a minute or two he came back up the hallway, zipping his pants, when *another bomb blast* occurred. It sounded like it came from the same direction as the earlier one. Our building rocked back and forth, everything in the room shook, the pictures on the wall swayed. I went white with fear and could not speak.

Ed looked at the three of us sitting in the living room, sank down in a chair, and murmured, "I won't be going over to Gretta's."

We could hear sirens and commotion in the street for several hours after the second blast. We learned later from the police that the second blast had killed one of the terrorists. Something went wrong with the bomb, and it ended up exploding in the hands of the terrorist. He was killed, but the force threw his body under the framework of a car on the street.

The intended target for the bomb was the office of General Motors on the ground floor of the building just a few doors down from our apartment. The upper floors included the apartment where Gretta lived. The General Motors offices were severely damaged, and one of the employees was killed. The apartments above were shaken, but did not suffer major damage, and no one was injured.

When we checked on Gretta later, she told us that following the bombing, Turkish police had hammered loudly on her apartment door with their fists or guns. Gretta opened the door a crack. A Turkish police officer pointed at her and hollered, "YOU...you go down and move your car!" Evidently, the body of the dead terrorist had ended up under Gretta's car!

Gretta told us she left the police by the door and looked out the window, saw the body under her car, and returned to the door telling the officers, "I am not going out there to move my car!" Then, in her heavy German accent she bellowed at the officer, "YOU will do it for me! Here are the KEYS! I am staying right here!!!"

The police moved her car. It seems Ed need not have worried about Gretta! This tough German woman knew how take care of herself!

❧❧❧

There were no more bombings near our apartment building, but one could not get away from the effects of terrorism. During this time I attended a week long workshop for DODDS music teachers in Adana. I had been hoping we would stay on the military base in the city. I would have felt safer. Instead we were housed in a nice hotel in the center of Adana.

My nerves were not helped any when the hotel busboy, who was showing me to my room, told me that the day before I arrived, two young people had been killed on the sidewalk right below my window. I looked out the window of my second floor room and saw bloodstains and outlines of the pools of blood on the ground below. The young busboy said the police had no idea, clues or evidence about why they had been killed. I was horrified; feeling sorry for the victims, but also nervous for myself. The terrorism was so rampant, could I be shot at any time?

Somehow I managed to make it through the week of workshops. Fortunately, there was a male music teacher (not from Izmir) attending the conference and staying at the same hotel. He and I walked the few blocks together each day from the hotel to the military bus that would take us to the classes on the base.

During the workshop sessions, we teachers were able to get our minds off the war and terrorist attacks as we discussed music education and teaching techniques. We practiced 'teaching' on each other and had many laughs. However, at the end of the day, I still had to walk around the bloodstains near the front door of the hotel.

❧ ❧ ❧

As I mentioned before, following that initial bombing, the military had ordered all Americans to vary their routines going to and from work everyday. There was one rather high-ranking military officer in Izmir though who refused to follow those orders for some reason. He insisted on going to and from his office every day along the same route while wearing his military uniform. To this day I don't know why he wasn't reprimanded and told to comply with orders by a more senior officer. Maybe they were all too busy with other things.

One day, as he approached his apartment block coming home from work, there were three or four Turkish men loitering around the entryway to his building. Why the officer did not 'take notice' of them I do not know. The officer entered the building and took the elevator to the seventh floor. The Turkish men joined him on the elevator and got off at his floor, and attacked him in the hallway. They severely beat him on his head, face and body, thought he was dead, then fled down the stairs.

The officer was not dead though, and somehow he managed to get up and chase them down the stairs. They escaped however, and the officer collapsed on the ground outside where someone found him and took him to the hospital. He was sent to the States where he underwent extensive surgeries, including plastic surgeries to his face.

What was most unusual though was that this officer returned to Izmir a year or so later. At a large meeting of all military and military-related personnel, this man stood up in front of the group and apologized. Yes! He apologized profusely for his stupidity and stubbornness in not following orders. He hoped we would learn from his experience and never behave as he had. The officer had indeed behaved poorly a year earlier, but it took great courage for him to apologize to us all and I do believe we all learned a serious and sobering lesson from him that day!

No act of kindness,
no matter how small,
Is ever wasted!

—Aesop

❧ ❧ ❧

Eventually the Persian Gulf War came to an end and we all felt we could begin again. I felt so blessed to have the students that I had and the helpers… i.e. parents and a few teachers, who so willingly supported me in my musical projects. I have always felt drama, music, art, dance and other creative endeavors helped students feel good about themselves and encouraged them do better in their regular school studies.

As the Persian War hostilities began to subside in the late spring of 1991, our lives and school routines became more normal. In addition, the argument between the mayor of Selcuck in Ephesus and the caretaker of the Celsus library ruins was finally resolved. Our high school seniors could resume the tradition of having their graduation ceremonies in front of the ancient two-story ruins of the Celsus library.

Ephesus

According to information from Wikipedia, the library of Celsus is an ancient Roman building built in honor of the Roman Senator Tiberius Julius Celsus Polemaeanus (completed in 135 AD) by Celsus' son, Gaius Julius Aquila. Celsus paid for the construction of the library with his own personal wealth. The library was built to store 12,000 scrolls and to serve as a monumental tomb for Celsus. He is buried in a sarcophagus beneath the library, in the main entrance which is both a crypt containing his sarcophagus and a sepulchral monument to him. It was unusual to be buried within a library or even within city limits, so this was a special honor for Celsus.

The building is important as it is one of few remaining examples of an ancient Roman-influenced library. It also shows that public libraries were built not only in Rome itself, but throughout the Roman Empire. The interior of the library and all its books were destroyed by fire in the devastating earthquake that struck the city in 262. Only the facade survived. The facade was completely destroyed by a later earthquake sometime around 375 AD.

In a massive restoration conducted sometime later, the front façade was rebuilt, and now serves as a prime example of Roman public architecture. The edifice is a single hall that faces east toward the morning sun, as Vitruvius advised, to benefit early risers. The library is built on a platform, with nine steps the full width of the building leading up to three front entrances. The center entrance is larger than the two flanking ones, and all are adorned with windows above them. Flanking the entrances are four pairs of Ionic columns elevated on pedestals. A set of Corinthian columns stands directly above the first set, adding to the height of the building. The pairs of columns on the second level frame the windows as the columns on the first level frame the doors, and they also create niches that would have housed statues. It is thought there may have been a third set of columns, but today there are only two registers of columns.

What a marvelous setting for a high school graduation! The Izmir high school band played *Pomp and Circumstance* by Elgar as the twenty or so seniors processed from behind the ancient library's pillars down the steps and to the folding chairs set up for them below. Appearing one by one in their red graduation caps and gowns, each student stepped down carefully onto the enormous stones and boulders, some of which were quite difficult to navigate, while holding on to their caps in the slight breeze from the Mediterranean as the audience clapped.

Once the graduates were in place there was the 'Trooping of the Colors,' always a moving ceremony, especially for Americans so far from home. The color guard brought out the American flag, the Turkish flag, and another flag, which

Mary standing in front of the Celsus Library facade at Ephesus during a visit in 2005. The entrance to the old market place can be seen on the right side of the photo.

I believe represented the regiment. After those flags were presented, the guards stepped back into a perfectly straight line and our band played the *Turkish National Anthem* and then the *American National Anthem*. Following those pieces, the special guard turned at a loudly issued order by the Head Trooper and the group then marched off in the shortest, and most precise, resounding, marching steps I have ever seen or heard...to disappear behind the Agora (the ancient market place).

Then there were speeches by the President of the class, the Principal of the school, and a congressman from Washington, either a Senator, or Representative, or someone in a similar category. John Taylor, the teacher and mentor to the senior class at our high school also spoke; he always brought smiles to the faces of the graduates as he recounted anecdotes about their high school years. He had also been a teacher in Izmir for countless years and knew all the graduates well!

Eventually the graduates received their diplomas. As each graduate's name was called, the young person stood up and gingerly made his or her way to the podium to receive the diploma. The students had to watch their steps carefully as they walked across the stones.

After the diplomas were handed out the color guard returned to take away the flags with their precise marching steps and formation. Then it was time for the graduates to 'recess' and they did so while the band played my *Anthem of Peace*. With their brilliant red robes flapping in the breeze and huge smiles on their faces, they stepped in time to the music and disappeared behind the Celsus library's ancient columns.

Then, if one listened carefully, one could discern huge cries and hollers and screams erupting from behind the pillars. The *graduates!* Along with the screams and hollering one could also see square red caps sailing in the air. Then, several girls from the high school band came surging forward and gave me big bear hugs. The boys in the band shyly looked on, and then, slowly came forward to join the happy group. The entire affair was heavenly, a rewarding success on all levels. I was thrilled, 'tickled pink,' and giving thanks to the 'powers that be' to have granted me such a wondrous experience.

The memories of those graduation ceremonies are among my favorites.

Oh wonderful, wonderful,
And most wonderful, wonderful!

As You Like It
—Shakespeare

Audree and Bill

Audree lived three doors down from us in Izmir and was an English teacher in our high school. She had also worked for DODDS in Spain for many years. While in Spain, she had met Bill, a teacher/professor with a university, similar to our friends Buck and Joan. Audree and Bill married, and eventually Bill was transferred to the Adana Air Base in Turkey. However, there were no DODDS openings for Audree in Adana, so she ended up working for DODDS in Izmir. Bill worked in Adana during the week and traveled 'home' to Audree in Izmir on weekends, a fifteen-hour drive, one-way!

Audree and I became good friends and spent lots of time together. Occasionally on a Friday, or if either one of us had a 'hard' day at work, we would go to Izmir's best hotel and have a drink and sit and giggle in what we came to call 'the green room.' That was not its official name, but Audree and I liked to call it that because the large, long window-filled room overflowed with potted plants that gave it a beautiful atmosphere.

Other times, Audree and I would visit each other in our apartments. One evening when she was visiting she said, "Let me give you a key to my apartment."

"What on earth for?" I replied.

"In case I lose my key…then I can go to you and ask you for the spare," she said with her usual smile.

"Well"…I thought to myself, "what a great idea. I never would have thought of that!" I looked at Audree and declared, "You are so smart, Audree, I am the one that should have thought of that."

Another day I was at Audree's apartment visiting and we began talking about the balconies on our apartments. We each lived on the seventh floor of our buildings and we each had front and back balconies. The back balcony view was dismal, but the front balcony had a lovely view of the Izmir Bay and the many and varied vessels that went to and fro.

"Bill and I like to sit out here at night to look at the water and have a drink and a snack before bedtime," she told me.

I thought that was rather nice but said, "My husband will never sit out on the balcony for some reason unknown to me, and therefore I sit out there alone. I certainly do not enjoy my balcony quite as much as you do, Audree, although the views are exquisite, I must say!" Then, after a few more words on the subject I excused myself; I was quite tired from a long and active day in school, and went along home.

That night after I had gotten into my pajamas, and Ed and I were reading in bed we heard a knock on the door, then someone repeatedly ringing the doorbell. I got out of bed and ran down the hallway wondering who on earth was coming to visit at that time of the night. I opened the door, and to my surprise, I found a man standing there, and with a lovely English accent he said, "Ma'am, I do believe your friend is in trouble."

I obviously did not have any idea as to what or to whom he was referring, as I stood behind the front door, trying to hide my robe and pajamas.

"She is waving her arms and yelling and yelling over her balcony, and with the noise on the street in the background, all I could understand was your address," he continued.

I was extremely puzzled since the only one I knew well enough to call to me would be Audree, but I had just left her a short while ago and she was fine.

"She keeps saying something about a key...a key," he added.

"Whoops," I thought, "Audree must be locked in or out or something."

"Where is she hollering from?" I asked of the gentleman.

"A man and a woman, from their front balcony...both of them are hollering and saying your address and something about a key...that is all I could understand with the noise on the street being so very loud. They are hollering from their balcony, very high up." (Audree and I each lived on the seventh floor of our apartment buildings.)

Puzzled, I put on my shoes and tossed a coat over my pajamas, told Ed what was happening, and got the key to Audree's apartment. I was a bit nervous about going out in the street in my pajamas with a strange Englishman, but he seemed honest enough. He walked with me over to Audree's apartment three buildings away.

"There they are, look..." the man said to me, "see them hanging over the balcony railing?"

I looked up and sure enough, there they were, both Audree and Bill. Bill was shrieking and waving his arms, *Bring up the key!!!! Bring up the key!!!*

All I could think was, "My goodness...they must be locked out on the balcony!" The gentleman and I rushed up to their seventh floor apartment in the elevator. I ran to their apartment and used the key to let us in.

Then I was met with the most amusing site! Audree and Bill with arms straight up, high over their heads, their faces and bodies plastered on the glass doors and clad in their nightclothes, were hollering, "Open the doors, open the doors."

"Their balcony doors should have opened into their living room just as mine do," I thought to myself, "but obviously, for some reason they did not." Audree and Bill continued yelling, "We're locked out, we're locked out!!! Open the door, open the door!"

I presumed it was with the same set of keys I had, so I tried the keys in that lock, and finally succeeded in opening the door and they tumbled into my arms...well Audree did, I can't remember about Bill.

Well, as you can imagine, there was a lot of hugging and crying and explaining. Evidently the door had locked automatically after Audree and Bill had gone out on the balcony with their food and drink to enjoy the views of the bay. Then, when it was bedtime, they could not open the sliding glass doors. That's when they began to shout at passersby on the street below. They were extremely grateful to the English gentleman for following through on their plea for help. He left shortly after he determined that all was well. Audree and I had many good laughs about the incident over the years.

As long as I'm talking about balconies, there was another custom I enjoyed watching while living in Izmir. Even in the 1980s there were still street peddlers who offered their wares such as pots and pans, food, bottles of oil, or spices, up and down the residential streets of Izmir. More than once I saw a Turkish woman living in an apartment above the ground floor lower a covered basket to a peddler on the street below, all the while haggling over the price of whatever goods were being offered/bought. Once an agreement was reached, the peddler filled the basket with goods, the woman pulled it back up to her window, then lowered the basket back down with the agreed payment. It was swift, accurate and fun to watch!

Verona, Italy

I always loved opera but never did attend many for one major reason: they were expensive. However, I do vividly remember seeing *The Barber of Seville* with my mother in Lowell when I was quite young!

After I had been teaching in Izmir several years, I somehow learned about a weeklong educational course on opera offered each summer in Verona, Italy. The DODDS system encourages its teachers to take educational courses, and will pay for the cost of the course if it is relevant to the teacher's specialty.

I obtained more information about the course, requirements, costs, etc. I filled out an application and presented it to my principal. In due time, my request to take the course was granted. Hurrah!

Meanwhile, I had called my friend Madonna who was teaching with DODDS in Italy. I talked her into taking the course with me. Madonna is not a music student or music teacher and was not certain if this was what she wanted to do, but nevertheless, she agreed. (She still thanks me when we speak, on rare occasions since she lives in Minnesota now, about encouraging her to take this course of study.)

And so in the summer of 1991, Madonna and I met in Verona, Italy. We boarded in a Catholic home for priests and brothers who supplemented their income by renting their rooms to visitors. Because they were the rooms of Catholic brothers, the rooms were more than simple, they were absolutely Spartan! However, they were immaculately clean and the Catholic brothers were quite welcoming and provided us whatever we needed during our stay. There were about eight or ten students of this opera course staying at the 'religious' home when Madonna and I were there, including several young Americans.

Our schedule included morning classes about opera in general, and then more specifically about the four operas we would attend. I enjoyed studying the music of the operas, the meaning of the words, and discussing the music of each. As well as treasuring the moments at the opera, I also loved the visits and the traveling we were able to squeeze in after classes and before the musical affairs in the evenings.

The operas we attended were *Turandot, Aida, La Gioconda* and *Zorba il Greco. Aida* is performed every summer to please the public since it is so very much loved and in demand. The operas are performed outdoors in an ancient Roman amphitheatre built in 30AD. Think of a rather less battered version of the Colosseum in Rome and you have a picture of the Arena di Verona. The Arena was conceived as a stadium for the games and the circuses with which the Roman government kept the people happy. The Arena has survived remarkably intact. The original white and pink limestone cladding disappeared sometime after the earthquake of 1117. It largely destroyed the outer ring of the Arena di Verona, leaving only a small portion near the entrance. It is a spectacular site.

The first opera we attended there was *La Gioconda*. I followed one young man from our group, and Madonna followed me. I asked him where he was going and he replied, "Oh… I am going to rent two pillows."

I was puzzled of course and asked, "Why do you want two pillows?"

He must have thought I was rather dumb, but he answered sweetly with, "The seats and backs of this old stadium are all solid stone and after a while I cannot stand sitting there any longer, so…I rent pillows."

Obviously this was not his first time attending the opera in Verona. I thought about this pillow business for only a moment and then edged my way into the line bringing Madonna with me. We left with one pillow each since the concierge was running short of pillows, but the next night, like our friend, the handsome young man, we each rented two pillows!

Of the operas we saw, *Turandot* and *Aida* were my favorites. I did not enjoy *La Giocanda* as much, but it was interesting. The final performance we saw was *Zorba il Greco*, not really an opera at all, but a combination of Greek folk dancing and singing.

Turandot was magnificent. The two lead female singers in *Turandot* were from New York City. Somehow, the idea popped into my head that evening and I said to my group, "Wouldn't it be nice to say hello to the ladies from New York? We could probably go backstage and find them before they leave." (At this point unfortunately, I do not remember their names.)

"That is a great idea Mary," our group leader replied enthusiastically.

Not everyone in our group cared to do so. Madonna and I, the young man who taught us about renting pillows and his girlfriend, and our instructor all went off together. I knew there had to be changing rooms somewhere. We climbed over the stone seats and wended our way endlessly towards the stage area until I felt we had to be near the dressing rooms. Then I saw doors with the stars' names on them and knew we were in the correct place. Well, as it turned out, we had arrived at their dressing rooms before they did.

I saw the two ladies and without any hesitation, enthusiastically approached them with my two arms thrown up high in a clear effort to embrace the lead singer. My enthusiasm was palpable. At the same time I hollered, (I don't know where my voice came from, it seemed so loud at the time and I had not meant to holler) "We are here from the United States, and you were just so wonder-ful…we had to come back and tell you!"

Both…one and then the other opera star hugged me graciously and with much openness and affection to their hugs and words, meaning, they were not at all annoyed with the invasion of their privacy, and then the other few friends in our group followed my suit. We had a splendid short talk of about five min-utes or so. After congratulating the ladies and thanking them profusely once again, we left them to relax and change from their costumes and make-up. Most probably the next thing on their agenda would be to fall into their beds since such ambitious performances are always quite strenuous, and most tiring! My friends and the director of the class and I were quite thrilled about the whole affair. It topped off our evening and home we went to our little monks' cells to fall into bed.

Aside from studying and seeing the operas in person, there was a bit of time each afternoon to visit the villages around Verona. Madonna and I became friendly with several other Americans taking the opera course; the young man who taught us about the pillows and his girlfriend; and another couple stationed in Italy near Cinque Terre. He worked for the military as an underwater diver and she was a teacher for DODDS. Our intrepid group of six poured through pages of travel folders and maps of the area, and made plans to visit a few villages over the next few days in the time we had between classes ending in the afternoon and before our late suppertime.

Each afternoon we drove to a village or small town we had agreed to visit. We parked the car, and walked around to explore. We walked what felt like miles, in and out of churches and other interesting sites over the next few days. I loved seeing one particular church in Padua along with Saint Anthony's tomb that was inside the church.

We continued on like this any afternoon we had time, visiting village after village…visiting the churches…oohing and ahhing at every turn, and then on to another village. One particular day was extremely hot, and we were growing exhausted. Suddenly one of our group noted, "We seem to be the only ones walking through the towns, I wonder why?"

And indeed, there was not one person, not one soul, walking on the streets in these villages except for six, foot sore, weary, drained Americans. Then the light dawned in my heat-bedraggled mind, and I muttered sluggishly to the group, "Italians are smart, they are all in bed…this is *siesta* time!"

Our group groaned in recognition. Feeling utterly stupid, we realized that no one who lives in Italy, and most especially in the summer, is ever out walking in such intense heat as we were at that moment! Indefatigable pack of people that we were…we all looked absolutely silly and sheepish as we realized what we had been doing. We had a great many guffaws over the whole thing, but decided we too should escape the heat.

We went back to find our car which was parked, God only knew where, and then on to the Franciscan Priory, once again, exhausted, but with enough strength left in us to shower and rest before dinner was served and then…the opera!

Joy, gentle friends! Joy, and fresh days of love
Accompany your hearts!

A Midsummer Night's Dream,
—Shakespeare

Izmir Hilton Hotel Grand Opening

In the late fall of 1991, the Hilton Hotel chain finished constructing its new hotel in downtown Izmir. Prior to its construction, no building could be

taller than eight stories, because of the danger of earthquakes in the region. But in the mid-1980s, Hilton had filed plans for a 32-story hotel. Permission to build was granted by the Izmir authorities because the building was specifically designed to withstand earthquake tremors.

As you can imagine, the opening of this magnificent structure was a major event in the city of Izmir. I was particularly pleased because my high school band was invited to perform during the opening ceremonies, which would include a visit from the president of Turkey, Turgut Ozal.

The students were thrilled with the invitation. To be asked to play for the Izmir Hilton Hotel opening was honor enough, but to know that the nation's president might see them

Plaque presented to Mary by parents of Izmer High School Band students

also…well, how often does that happen in the life of a high school student? The band students practiced like never before. They got their red jackets cleaned and their trousers pressed…their shirts were spotless and they wore their black ties to be formal. Their behavior was marvelous, could not have been better. They were absolutely…unerringly…*super*!

The day of the grand opening arrived and we got to the hotel before 10 a.m. The hotel management set us up on the first floor in a moderate sized open area that faced the main hallway of the new hotel. Visitors touring the hotel had to walk by us. Sometimes visitors would stop and listen to the band for several minutes.

The band played all day on a schedule of 30-minutes of playing; followed by a 30-minute break. They were marvelous. Not one student misbehaved even in the slightest way and no one played any tricks on anyone either. What I found most amusing was their eyes. I could see their eyes leave the pages of music off and on throughout the day (usually at times when they were familiar with the music they were playing). They were searching for the President of Turkey, looking for him to go by…constantly! It was the cutest and sweetest thing I ever witnessed as I conducted the band!

The President did go by while the band was playing, but unfortunately he did not stop to listen to the band, so only a few students caught a glimpse of him. I was hoping he would stop, if only for a minute, and at least wave his hand. Someone in charge explained later that the President had arrived late and had other venues to attend, therefore, could not stop and converse with the students.

Despite that minor disappointment, the students in the band had a wonderfully exciting day. At the end of our performances, the manager of the hotel personally thanked the students and praised their playing and dignified behavior. Then he gave each student a small gift bag that included an Izmir Hilton Hotel t-shirt, a free pass to the game room in the hotel, and a certificate for a free ice-cream sundae at the hotel's restaurant.

At the end of the day, they all went home with their proud parents and big smiles on their faces. At some point or another while preparing to leave the hotel, I could hear different students exclaim loudly and with great excitement, "Mom, Dad, I saw the Turkish President!" Who am I to dispute all that? I went home totally exhausted, but oh, so happy!

Oliver!

In the fall of 1992, I felt it was time to stage another musical. This time I decided we would do *Oliver!*, the musical I had already directed at Sanborn School and in Okinawa. I opened up the tryouts to the fourth, fifth, and sixth graders as well as the high school students.

Terry Emerson, the School Principal performs with students in 'Oliver!'

And joy of joys, we did not have to perform on the military movie stage. The Turkish American Association (TAA) offered the use of their stage and whatever other equipment we might need. I was 'blown away' by their offer. The prospect of being able to perform on a larger stage with no obstructions made my heart palpitate with delight. In addition, the audience would be seated comfortably in regular theater seats.

I had a marvelous 'Oliver' a boy from the fourth grade and the very best 'Artful Dodger' also from the fourth grade. They acted and sang solos in boy soprano voices using the pure and ringing tones of unchanged voices! Unfortunately I do not remember the names of the actors at this point, but their performances were exemplary! Twenty years later I can picture the *Oliver!* cast in my mind! When the show ended I was left floating with happiness!

We only had one performance since it was all just too, too massive a production for me to work at for more than one evening with my overall schedule being as busy as it was. It was also hard on the students as well since many of the older ones were also in the band, and busy performing at various functions whenever I could fit them in.

The audience gave a standing ovation as the actors took their bows. When the clapping finally died down I began to walk to the doors of the auditorium, nodding and speaking, while accepting loving remarks from parents about the students' performances. I finally reached the back of the auditorium.

I was standing just inside the large double exit doors saying goodnight and hugging the performers as they left. I loved seeing their delight and pride in what they had accomplished. I also shook hands with parents who thanked me for what I had done for their children in the musical. Suddenly...a queer and most unusual thing happened. I knew I was standing still but at the same time I was moving. I looked down at the floor in front of my feet...the floor was moving, but...I wasn't...the floor was!!!

A military man was rushing forward as I was trying to think, and he started yelling in his loudest voice, "OUT, OUT, EVERYBODY OUT!" I looked at him, stupidly puzzled and not understanding why the floor was moving and why he was yelling.

He grabbed me by both arms, stared into my face and yelled sharply at me, "Mrs. G., **Get out of here...now...we're having an earthquake!!!**" "OUT...OUT," he kept yelling as he turned me around and shoved me forward and out through the doors. Everything seemed to be falling apart in that one brief moment when the floor started moving. Parents were screaming, children were crying with fright, men in uniform were trying to move the crowd out...and...there we were...in the middle of an horrific earthquake!

To this day I'm still not sure how I got out. It was chaos...teachers and parents were trying to sort out the young crying children while helping them to find their parents. Panic was showing itself in the crowd...some of the parents were rushing home and away from the TAA with their children. Others were distressed and running back and forth looking for their children. Everything was chaos. I eventually got out and onto the sidewalk where I happened to look up and over some rooftops. I was looking at the new Hilton Hotel...and horror, absolute horror, struck my soul!

The Hilton Hotel was swaying, yes, actually swaying back and forth. It was a 32-story tall hotel; the only building in Izmir that was over eight stories high; obviously, one could not help but notice it. But...it was specifically built so as not to fall in the event of an earthquake. It is beyond my comprehension to explain to you how engineers and builders did that. However, it did not fall or collapse but it swayed, back and forth and back and forth and everyone around me looked at it; we were all frozen on the spot, mesmerized, and thoroughly frightened…as in, "what would happen if it fell?" It was swaying back and forth like a swing…once the crowd saw this giant edifice swinging back and forth, the screaming and rushing and pushing of mothers and fathers and children gained momentum. It was an unbelievable sight to behold! I was supremely glad that I was not on the top floor having dinner, which many of us had done in the past year because the food and views were excellent.

I rapidly looked around once more, seeking out any children who might not have found their parents and unfortunately I found one little girl crying her eyes out. Terror, fright and panic filled the entire atmosphere.

"Come here, my little one," I said softly as I stooped down and gathered her up against me; this child was a tiny one. I held her in my arms saying, "Let me hold you tight." She held on to me as though she was going to die, clutching and grabbing me and my clothing.

Panic stricken I said, "Tell me, where are your parents? Did they come to see you in the show?" hugging and caressing her at the same time. She could not stop crying to answer me then, but did finally after a few minutes of cuddling and holding.

"I don't know…I don't know…I just want to go home, Mrs. G. I just want to go home…" she said. I held her as the huge crowd was dispersing in terror. Then I suddenly looked up and over her head. I saw a couple staggering up the street. They were totally drunk! They were her parents. Anger filled my body! They swayed and walked with a crazy gait and came over to me and asked in their drunken voices where their child was. Their voices were slurring and their walk was staggering. They were absolutely inebriated!

I replied, in a cold fashion, "She's here, crying in my arms, waiting for you to come for her." No comforting words were said to her, they just took her by the hand and staggered home with her between them. I felt so sorry for that child. Not one loving word was said to this child, as her parents fell over each other while trying to walk. To this day as I write this part of my memoirs, I can still, in my mind, see the hotel swaying and me bent over the child, holding her in my arms while she 'cried her eyes out' from fright.

I hated to let her go. But then, at that point there was very little I could do. The Hilton was swaying; people were crying; many parents were still looking for their children; military personnel were hollering directions. On and on it went for what seemed like forever! Those awful people were that beautiful little girl's parents. I was wild with anger at them and disgusted because I could do nothing else under the circumstances. However, I told the story to the principal several days later and gave him the child's name. He told me not to worry; he would make her case known to the guidance counselor. After that it was out of my hands.

❧❧❧

Eventually, when all the people had dispersed, and it seemed no more shocks were coming, (how little I knew) Ed and I walked, (staggered would be a better word) back to our apartment. We saw cars by the hundreds trying to drive out of the city and moving, *when* they moved, at a snail's pace. The Turks knew more than we did, having lived there for so long and having been through so many earthquakes; they knew enough to leave the city. I never thought of that until after my dull and shattered mind realized why there was a traffic jam!

There were traffic jams all over and cars filled with people. And there I was. The late hour, fatigue and shock of the earthquake having caught up with me, all I wanted was to go home to bed. Imagine my surprise when we arrived at our building to see all our neighbors standing on the sidewalk. Having never been in an earthquake before, I was not familiar with the notion of 'aftershocks.' How discouraged I was to learn we should not go into our home, our apartment, our haven with a bed, since aftershocks could bring the building down! All I could do at that point was groan…and groan again!

To go to bed, was what I sorely wanted to do, I did not want to stay outside on the sidewalk. Hence, I headed for the seawall in order to sit and rest my weary bones!

"For heaven's sake, don't sit on the sea wall," someone hollered at me as I walked in that direction. "Another tremor could send giant waves over the seawalls and we would never survive!"

With that comment, we all moved away from the walls, but then, the buildings would have fallen on us as well, if another tremor came! The whole event was a total nightmare, the likes of which I had never experienced in my life! We had no place to sit, no place to sleep, and no car at our disposal, and, if there had been one, we could not leave the city due to the horrendous traffic jams all around us!

After standing around, or should I say…staggering around, until about *three a.m.* I felt I was about to die standing up.

"Ed", I sobbed, "Let's take a chance and go upstairs to our apartment. I can't stand up anymore and I will not sit on the filthy pavement." Simpering like a child, I cried, boohooed and the like…saying, "I need to sleep, I am ready to pass out."

I was ready to bawl like the little girl in my arms earlier. In utter agony I wailed out loud…"I have to lie down, I have no choice…I must lie down." By then all others in the area had left, I had no idea where they went, and we were the only ones remaining, or…should I say, wandering around, waiting for another tremor. Ed finally agreed and up we went to our apartment.

We did not use the elevator because that was absolutely verboten; therefore we dragged our bodies up the seven flights of stairs, fell onto the bed and slept until…whenever! I don't remember at this point if school was cancelled the next day or not. It must have been but I have no memory at all of the days following *Oliver!* and the earthquake. None!

I did learn several weeks later that the principal of our school had a horrifying experience during the earthquake. It seems that he, his wife and an out of country guest decided as soon as *Oliver!* ended they would leave the auditorium and head over to the new Hilton Hotel for a meal and a couple of drinks. He wanted to be seated at a table on the top floor overlooking the great views of Izmir and not have to greet and talk with the parents in the audience. I knew the principal had attended the musical because I had seen him there. I was not aware that he left with his guests just before the curtain calls.

Well, they were up on the top floor of the Hilton when the quake struck. At that point, they discovered elevators did not work, which meant they had to *walk* down thirty-two flights of stairs. The principal's wife evidently went berserk, and could not function. She had to be carried down all those floors! Yes, carried down…thirty-two flights of stairs while out of her mind with fear! I felt so bad when I heard about it later; considering the quake and the condition she was in, it must have been horrible for her and for him!

All of this experience left me stupefied for several days. But, God was with us, and no aftershocks hit our apartment. We were so fortunate I thanked God every day for the longest time and I pray *never* to be in another earthquake again.

The earthquake was on November 6, 1992. The damage all over Izmir was extensive; we were told later that some sections of Izmir were much worse than others and some, not damaged at all. The most crippling damage in Izmir was the area between our apartment block and the school, and mostly in the older and smaller buildings as I recall. We were left with cracks in the living room and bedroom wall here and there, but no huge devastating damage to our apartment or any of our possessions. I don't recall any people reported as killed. Within a week or two, life began to carry on more or less as normal again. During the weeks before the Christmas break, the high school band had several concerts and they performed beautifully at each. I was extremely proud of the students, and thankful to all the parents and other military personnel who helped us all so much.

One day after school, when things had begun to settle down, one parent/friend came to me and said, in reference to our show *Oliver!*, and the earthquake…"Mary, whenever you put on a show you always go out with a bang…!"

Christmas in Germany

Helen Kennedy had invited us to spend our 1992 Christmas holiday with her in a village outside of Butzbach, Germany. I had met Helen the first year I taught in Izmir. The following year she transferred with DODDS to teach in northern Japan, then sometime in the next year or two she moved with DODDS to Germany. We had enjoyed each other's company that first year, so we always kept in touch.

Helen met us at the Butzbach airport and drove us to the village where she was living, named 'Lich Eberstadt' (Little Village). It was delightful to be in Germany again. I had enjoyed our brief visit to the country in 1987 when we were first traveling to Izmir. I looked forward to seeing more of it on this trip.

On Christmas Eve Helen took us to the home of her friend Manfried where we had a small dinner and sang carols. Manfried lived in a modest house with Mai Ying, and their two young children. They were a most generous couple however. They had opened their home to two refugees from Georgia (which had just celebrated its independence from Soviet Russia). One of them was Oleg, a 35-year-old doctor who had been forced to leave his wife and three children behind in Georgia. The other was Robert, a 21-year-old artist. (Mai Ying was an artist also).

The evening turned out to be quite emotionally moving for me. I played Christmas carols on the piano and everyone sang along in German or English. Our means of communication were somewhat limited since none of the nine of us shared any *one* language. We smiled a lot, pantomimed, bowed to each other, and smiled some more. I loved hearing the carols sung in German, but when they could, some of them insisted on singing in English to prove that they could. It was all a bit comical and there were many laughs shared by us all. But at times I was also almost blinded by tears…tears of joy and sadness thinking about *who* we all were, *where* we were, and *how* we had all come together at seemingly the last minute for this beautiful sharing of a peaceful tradition on Christmas Eve. It is an evening I will never forget!

As I recall this episode now for my memoirs, I wonder how these people are and if the refugees were ever able to enjoy a more 'normal' life. Ed and I certainly learned a great lesson from them all.

Eventually, it came time for us to leave this celebration to attend Christmas Eve services in a church in Butzbach. The Lutheran church there dated back to 1600 (incredible for me to comprehend). The steeple with its 'onion' shaped top reflected the 'eastern' influence of that ancient time. The inside of the church was white washed and trimmed beautifully with dark-stained wood. There was a large Moravian star hanging from the vaulted roof. Helen had introduced us to the minister the day before, and he had graciously invited us to attend the midnight services.

It was a small congregation, only sixty or seventy people, but they filled the small church. Strangely though, none of them made eye contact with us or greeted us in any way. It was an unusual experience for me because ever since joining DODDS, wherever we traveled people had been extremely friendly. There was no cheeriness or exchange of Christmas greetings, except with the minister and his daughter, whom we had also met the day before. As we traveled around Germany with Helen, we found the 'cold indifference' of the general German population was the rule rather than the exception.

Christmas morning we had a sumptuous breakfast at Helen's apartment, then the three of us, Helen, Ed and I, packed our bags and drove to Obperfraundorf. My good friend Madonna from DODDS in Okinawa was working at the Hohenfelds U.S. military base in Germany. She had a small apartment in the city. She always went home to Minnesota at Christmas to be with her mother, so she had invited us to stay in her apartment while we were visiting Germany with Helen.

"How will we get in?" I had asked her on the phone in Izmir before we left.

"I'll leave the key in the mailbox," she said.

"Is that safe Madonna?" I replied.

She chuckled and said, "No one steals anything here. Isn't that amazing?"

It certainly was, I thought to myself. We could never have done that in Turkey. Chalk up another difference between Turkish and German culture.

The trip from Helen's apartment to Madonna's was several hours by car. When we arrived in the small picturesque German village, the temperature was just above zero *Fahrenheit*! We found the key to her apartment right where she said we would, in the mailbox in front of the house. We quickly let ourselves into her darling attic apartment on the third floor of the building.

Her apartment faced an old Catholic church. As a result, we heard a lot of bell ringing and saw many people coming and going over the next few days. As I gazed out her attic window all I could think was how extremely lovely everything was. There was a cemetery right next to the church, and each grave had a lighted red candle on it the entire time we were visiting. On the day after our arrival, I observed a special custom of the parish. The children cleaned the graveyard carrying away boughs and twigs; went in to the church for service; then came back out with their parents to pray again at the graves. What a respectful and loving custom for the children to learn. I couldn't help thinking, "Why don't we Americans do sweet and loving things like that with our children?"

We toured the village and traveled to Regensburg and Augsburg. Augsburg was the home of Leopold Mozart, the father of Amadeus Mozart. As a musician, I was fascinated to see Leopold's grave. We attended a wonderful service at the magnificent old cathedral in Regensburg. The cities both had histories stretching back to medieval times and it was quite fortunate that they were not destroyed during World War II.

On Sunday, we visited Wertingen, about two hours from Obperfrandorf. Our friend Heino whom we'd met in Izmir had invited us there. He and his companion Gretta had lived three doors down from us, and Ed and Heino had become good friends. He was a filmmaker and had been filming a story in Africa.

He had become ill with liver cancer though, and so was now in Germany living with his brother Franz and his brother's wife, Marlice. They are both doctors, so it made sense for Heino to recover at their home following his cancer surgery. When Heino learned we were coming to Germany for the Christmas holidays, he insisted we come to dinner at his brother's house and invited Helen also.

They prepared a sumptuous lunch of fresh trout. Unfortunately, I am allergic to fish and could not eat it. I apologized to Marlice, but she just looked at me in a hard, unsmiling fashion and removed my plate of fish. I ate all the vegetables and other odds and ends on the table, but Marlice continued to seem quite 'put out' as they say, by my refusal to eat the fish.

The Christmas tree in their home was huge and had *real* candles on it, as in ones with a real flame. Because I was fascinated, Heino actually lit the candles for me on the tree. I was fascinated and in awe! I could never imagine lighting real candles on a Christmas tree inside my house. I would most likely burn the house down! I can't remember now how long Heino allowed the candles to remain lit, because we left soon after the luncheon.

It grows dark early at that time of the year, and we were not familiar with the roads in the area and did not want to get lost returning to Madonna's apartment. In explaining our need to leave so early to our hosts, I said, "We don't really know our way home," (meaning Madonna's apartment). But then I looked at Ed and Helen thoughtfully and asked, "Come to think of it…just where is home?"

As you must have ascertained by now, we did, in time, find our way home to Madonna's apartment after visiting Heino. We went to bed and got up the next day for another journey. Ed and I were still freezing, I was perpetually *blue* it seemed. I felt there was a permanent hump on my back from hunching up in my leather sheep-lined coat during this trip to Germany. Of course, I've always had some trouble staying warm, but Ed and I had lived for the last nine years in semi-tropical or tropical climates (Okinawa, Izmir), so our bodies were not used to that German winter cold.

Czechoslovakia

The next morning we said good-bye to Madonna's apartment and drove to Karlovy Vary in Czechoslovakia. We spent four nights and days there. It is referred to as a 'Kur Bad' town, which translated into English means 'curing thermal baths.' When the Germans had occupied the city during World War II, they called it 'Karlsbad.'

The city is in a valley with a river running through the middle of the city. It was a long and narrow river, with ducks, geese and swans swimming freely, and with walkways and park benches available on either side of the river. I was fascinated to see the river running directly through the center of the city.

The few hotels there were high up on the main road and famous for having huge bathing pools on their roofs, outdoors, in which people could bathe all winter in the steaming hot water. When the weather is extremely cold, as it was when we were there, steam rises from the hotel rooftops. It was an awesome sight. I spent so much time gazing at the steam rising to the heavens that I developed a kink in my neck, but it was too pretty not to look!

Besides the 'cure' aspect of the city, Karlovy Vary is also famous for its delicate and lovely crystal and its equally beautiful porcelain, which Americans buy in huge quantities, their prices being relatively low. I bought six, long stemmed wine glasses for Amy and six more for us, for our home. I don't usually buy much when I travel since it is usually so costly to travel, but these lovely and delicate glasses I could not leave behind. I found that the German stores in Czech Republic fascinated me more than the Czech stores. German stores are very, very beautiful!

Czechoslovakia had been under Communist rule for 50 years and was a poor, struggling country, trying to make a 'come-back' at the time we visited. We saw many signs of restoration work being done and there were buildings with architecture that reflected opulence of older times, with lots of gingerbread cut out type woodwork on buildings downtown. One could close ones eyes and imagine Victorian ladies parading the parkways and columned walkways through Karlovy Vary in better times.

It was purely a coincidence, but we were in the city on January 1, 1993, the official day that Czechoslovakia was peacefully dissolved by parliament into two completely independent countries: the Czech Republic and the Slovak Republic. That was an absolutely awesome experience, the flags were waving, people were sauntering happily up and down… all looked so lovely and *peace* reigned!

The next morning we left Karlovy Vary. Our original plans had been to travel on to Prague, but we were too fatigued, and so decided to return to Germany. (Fortunately, I was able to see Prague with Charlotte Miles at another time…it was so very beautiful and being a musician, I must admit that in the classical sense it was the most musical of all the cities I ever visited.)

On our way back to Butzbach, we stopped in Bamberg, a city dating back to medieval times. After touring around a bit, Ed and I decided to have lunch in a small, pub-like restaurant. (Helen was not with us at that moment, having had other errands to tend to). The restaurant was so small we were seated at a table with another couple that looked to be approximately our ages. The couple was reserved, and did not look up at us as we sat down, typical behavior for most Germans. However, I smiled at them. Ed decided he liked the look of the food the gentleman was eating, so I asked the woman if she could tell us what it was. As it turned out, her English was rather good, enough so that we could understand what she said. Her husband could understand English but could not speak it.

She helped us with our food order, and by then the 'ice was broken' as they say. We had a delightful conversation during which we learned they lived in East Berlin and were in Bamberg to visit their son. They had lived in Berlin through World War II and the building of the 'wall' that divided the city into East and West Berlin. She had been a professor of Russian, but was no longer working because Russian professors were not needed. Her husband had been a philosophy professor, but when he turned fifty years old, he was considered too old to work. At that time he worked occasionally teaching driver education.

Imagine my delight when I discovered she too was a musician and played the piano. I told her about my ebony baby grand piano in the United States, the make, model and sound it produced. I was heartbroken to hear her baby grand piano had been destroyed when their house was bombed during World War II. By the end of our conversation, Ed and I both felt so sorry for them. They were such a nice couple, gentle, polite, well educated, yet they had so little hope for their future in terms of working and money. It made both Ed and me reflect on how fortunate we have been and still are, by accident of birth, to have been brought up in a democratic system. For all the good and/or bad it has, it beats all other systems.

Eventually we all had to leave one another. I realize I will never, ever see them again, but I will never forget them either. I hope they are faring better at this time. Maybe they are, at this moment as I write my story, living with their son and doing a bit better emotionally and financially.

Ed and Helen and I then drove back to Butzbach, and Ed and I flew home to Izmir on January 3, 1993, pleasantly exhausted from our German trip.

❄❄❄

When I returned to school after our Christmas break, I received a notice that a drama competition was going to be held in Ankara, Turkey (the nation's capital) in the spring. Sponsored by some American organization (I don't remember exactly who now) the contest was open to any interested DODDS high schools in the Mediterranean area.

"Hmmm...how exciting!" I said to myself and could hardly wait to tell my high school students about the project. At that time, I did not have access to many drama scripts, but I did own a book of plays that included the script of *Riders to the Sea*, a small one-act play by John Synge. I discussed it with the high school students, and even though there was only one male role in the play, the remainder were women, the students were anxious to work on the play.

Daniel Tougas, who had been Scrooge in my musical some years before, won the role of the son Bartley. His sister, Sarah Tougas, who had played a ghost in *Scrooge* and played Lucy in *Charlie Brown*, won the role of the mother; Hope Conkle played the grandmother and six other girls were sisters or villagers. The play is set in Northern Ireland in a small fishing village. The mother has already lost her husband, father-in-law and five sons to the sea. She is reluctant to let her last son sail to a nearby island to sell a horse for fear she will lose him as well.

Daniel performed that small role as the son very well, but then spent the remainder of the play on the stage as a soaking-wet dead body (that of a recently drowned brother), which was carried into the home by the women of the village. It was a serious and sad play, but the students seemed to enjoy the challenge of performing the serious roles. (And they had some fun too, mostly behind stage when the girls had to pour a bucket of water on Dan when it was time for him to be the 'wet/dead body' on stage).

Rehearsals went well, although we did have a bit of trouble with the 'keening', which was the crying and wailing the women did when it was announced in the play that the last son had also been killed at sea. The girls thought their own 'keening' sounded a bit false. Then one of the actresses, Susan Casey, suggested, "Mrs. Guziejka, why don't we sing a sad tune instead of trying to cry, which sounds so awful and false?"

I was delighted with her suggestion (and wondered why I hadn't thought of that myself). I gave the girls three notes in a minor key to sing over and over again as they swayed in rhythm to the music while kneeling. There were no words, they only sang the sound of 'oh' in those three notes, and the sad sound floated out over the audience.

Finally, it was time to compete. The students and I traveled to Ankara with a few parent chaperones. The plays were all performed in one day in front of a group of three judges from the United States (who were not employed by the military schools). Our group did quite well I thought. The students had 'stayed in character' throughout the play and I was very pleased with their performance. The judges wrote comments about each play, but the winner was not to be announced until the next day.

The following morning there was a brunch for all of us at the military base where the competition was held. After we had all eaten, the lead judge of the competition got up and made some remarks before announcing the winners of the competition.

"I have acted in plays myself, and been the judge for many drama contests, but never in my career have I run into any play like this one. It was very well done and performed to perfection," she said. She continued on with the favorable comments for several minutes, and all of us in the room were wondering exactly which play she was talking about.

Finally she said, "Will Mrs. Guziejka please stand?"

I nearly fell over, I felt so faint. To this day I'm not sure how I made it to the judge's table to receive the trophy, but obviously I did somehow. She asked all the students who had been in *Riders to the Sea* to stand, and went on to praise and congratulate them. They were overjoyed, but also a bit shy. I was so proud of them I felt I would burst!

When the ceremony was finally over and we were back in a room by ourselves, the screaming and yelling and talking began and went on for some time. I enjoyed seeing the students so happy. I wish I could have frozen that moment and taken it home to keep forever.

We returned to Izmir with the silver cup and were met by a group of proud and happy parents as well as the principal and assistant principal and other friends. The trophy was placed in the high school's display case and to this day I have fond memories of that sad, but intriguing play, *Riders to the Sea*, by Synge.

"T'is the mind
that makes the body RICH!"

The Taming of the Shrew
—Shakespeare

Later that year, I took another trip to Ankara, but this time with the high school band students for a week of rehearsals with students from other high school bands in the region, which ended with a concert where they all performed together. All the rehearsals and special workshops took place at the military base located about an hour outside of Ankara. The students who had traveled to Ankara for the week were assigned to stay with U.S. military families living in the city. They traveled to and from the base on school buses. The teachers from the high schools stayed at hotels in Ankara, and usually took taxis out to the base each day.

The week of rehearsals finally ended, the concert was performed in the evening and all went well. Gary Bogle, the music education supervisor for DODDS in the Mediterranean District, and I happened to be staying in the same hotel, so when the concert was over he suggested we share a taxi back to the hotel. I was delighted because it was late, I was exhausted, and I did not particularly care to travel into Ankara alone at night.

Well, Gary tried to get a taxi, but none were available. We waited for a while, and finally decided to board one of the school buses carrying students back to their 'temporary' families in the city of Ankara. I recognized some of my Izmir students and there were students from other high schools in the region on the bus as well.

"Mary, as soon as we see a taxi, I'll wave it down," Gary told me. "We don't really want to be on the bus all the way back into the city with these kids. We deserve a little peace and quiet after the busy week we've had."

I nodded in agreement, then looked at Gary and said, "Not to worry Gary, I'll be fine."

The students on the bus were 'letting off steam' after their long week of rehearsals and then the concert. Girls and boys were giggling and screaming in the back of the bus. Gary and I peered out the window as we approached each taxi stop, but we never saw any taxis. "The taxis are usually always in abundance and always available," I muttered to Gary, "but there don't seem to be any now. What do you suppose is happening? Somehow, the streets don't seem to look normal."

The bus stopped occasionally to let students off at the homes where they were staying. But, as we got closer and closer to the city, the bus kept going slower and slower. The streets were mobbed with people everywhere. The Turkish bus driver spoke no English, so he could not explain what was going on. Finally, the crowd grew so thick, that the bus came to a full stop in the street. Gary and I were becoming worried and anxious.

As I looked out of the bus nervously wondering what we were going to do, I saw the most unbelievable sight. "Gary, did you just see what I saw?" I asked fearfully.

"Oh my God," Gary replied. Turkish men were jumping from the eighth floor of some of the buildings, that is from the top of the building. Some landed in nets, others landed on cars, and others landed on the ground itself, and I'm sure were severely injured, if not killed.

Gary and I both saw this happening and then we panicked. Words cannot describe the shock that came over us! That we could be witnessing such awful scenes was unbelievable, but worse yet, it was happening in front of the twelve year old girls still on the bus. Some of the girls began to cry while some were screaming, "Mrs. Guziejka, Mrs. Guziejka, what will we do, what will we do…?"

Then on the other side of the road we saw a dump truck filled with men in the back. We watched in horror as the driver of the truck raised the dump portion as high as possible and then slammed it down as quickly as possible to the seeming delight of the men in back. They all bounced up and down and up and down and then rolled out of the back of the dump truck and onto the ground! I am sure they were drunk! Then they would try to get up and back into the dump truck to do it all over again. Incredible!

By then it was dark. "I'm scared," I told Gary.

"You're not alone," he replied. "I think I'm more frightened than you right now."

More and more seemingly drunken men gathered round the bus. The bus driver took his hands off the wheel and shrugged his shoulders indicating there was no more that he could do. The men outside the bus were yelling, laughing and leering at us in the bus. Then, they began rocking the bus back and forth.

"We have to get *out* of this bus right now," Gary hollered over the crying, screaming girls inside the bus and the yelling, shouting men outside. "*Open the doors,*" Gary yelled at the driver, "*we have to get off! We have to get these little girls off the bus!*" he yelled again.

The bus had stopped, the driver opened the doors and Gary yelled at all of us: "*Don't let go of each other, hang on tight…follow us, hold onto each other and get off the bus!*"

We got out of the bus as quickly as we could and began to move away, and within a few seconds I looked back and saw the bus being *pushed* over onto its side. I grabbed Gary and hollered at him, "Gary, Gary, look, oh my God…we got out just in time…the bus is on its side. We could have all been hurt!"

We all stood there for a moment stupefied. The girls were crying and clinging to each other. All I could think of was what if we'd remained in the bus, what would we have done then? The noise around us was deafening. "Gary, what shall we do…what shall we do?" I yelled, hoping he could hear me.

"Follow me. Do what I'm doing," he yelled. He then had each girl hold on to one another like a chain. They had their two arms around each other's waist. We snaked through the crowd somehow in this manner. As we struggled to find a way out of the crush of thousands of people we saw more dump trucks 'dumping' people and more men jumping off the tops of eight story buildings. I was terrified and wondering how in the world people could indulge in behavior like that.

We continued snaking through the crowd for what seemed hours. We came across a Turkish policeman. He had no control over the crowds at all, but spoke at least enough English to give us directions to our hotel. Fortunately, the girls we were leading lived with American military families not far from the hotel. We somehow managed to deliver each one safely to the appropriate home.

It wasn't until two a.m. that Gary and I finally arrived at our hotel. We sank into the nearest chairs in the lobby, which was quite empty. "I'm ordering drinks for the two of us," Gary said.

"Gary, I don't drink anymore," I told him.

"You are tonight!" he replied firmly. And I did.

After sharing our drinks and a bit of hysterical laughter about our evening, we went off to our own rooms for a few hours sleep.

The next morning, when we gathered with all the students to board buses for the trip home to Izmir, we learned that many of them had been through a similar ordeal to ours. What had caused this street rioting in Ankara? We were told that the Turkish soccer team had beaten the Spanish soccer team in some important match in Spain! Gary and I groaned. The exhausted students, many of them with faces as white as sheets, were lying about on their duffel bags which were all over the grassy areas, and each other, waiting to board the bus. It was a long quiet ride back to Izmir that day. Everyone slept…except for Gary and me!

❧❧❧

And with that, I'll finish my recounting of teaching related experiences in Turkey. There were other interesting and rewarding adventures with students and the high school band, but now I'd like to take time to highlight a few other non-school related trips we took while in Turkey.

Ed and I thoroughly enjoyed my experiences while working for DODDS because we met so many people who had traveled extensively all over the world. They were all kind and helpful to us as we explored the countries around us. They would suggest places we should travel and things to see, and even better yet, at times they invited us to join them on trips or excursions. We were so fortunate.

Our first holiday when we initially arrived in Izmir was Labor Day. Two other teachers invited us to join their families on a sailboat they had rented for the three-day weekend. There were at least eight of us on what turned out to be a rather small boat. There was little room to move around, so we mostly sat and read while soaking up the Mediterranean sun and occasionally going for a swim off the side of the boat. It was all a new and unusual experience for us, but somewhat relaxing after our summer of packing, moving, traveling and looking for a place to live.

However, the four-hour bus ride back and forth to Izmir was challenging for Ed and myself. The buses were filled with Turkish peasants who brought their live chickens and even a sheep or two on the bus. The rides were noisy and the smells were putrid. It had been an interesting weekend, but once back in our hotel in Izmir, Ed and I decided that bus rides and sailing, and sleeping in a tiny cramped vessel for several nights was just a bit too difficult for us physically and mentally.

Joann, the home economics teacher at the DODDS Izmir high school, and her Turkish husband owned a home on the Aegean Sea about 30 miles from Izmir. She hosted an annual party for teachers at her home. Over time, Ed and I became good friends with her and her husband, and we spent many lovely days at her beach home during the seven years we lived in Turkey.

I absolutely loved swimming in the Aegean Sea, or sunbathing while gazing at the lovely, calm water. We would swim and eat and eat and swim again. Occasionally, Ed and I spent the night with them at their home and we always had a wonderful time laughing and visiting. Joann sometimes took me to the markets near their beach home, which I always enjoyed. She spoke a little Turkish and had been to the market often enough to know which vendors were honest and which ones had the best vegetables or other goods she was looking for. There was never a dull moment when we spent time with Joann and her husband.

❄❄❄

It was Joann who introduced us to Evelyn and Homer Kalcas, a delightful couple with whom we became good friends while in Izmir. They were an older couple. Evelyn was an author of several books about Turkey. She had moved from Australia to Turkey when she was young and traveled extensively across the country until she met Homer, married him and settled down. For many years they lived in Istanbul, on the Asian side of the Bosphorus. Evelyn liked to proclaim, *"Homer and I sleep in Asia and work in Europe,"* meaning, they slept in Istanbul, (Asia) and crossed the Bosphorus on the bridge daily to Europe; he taught school on the other side of the bridge while she wrote books, most likely in her home in Istanbul, but then, knowing Evelyn as well as we did, she might have sat on the top of a mountain and written a book; she was lovely, brilliant, unusual and awe inspiring!

The huge bridge that spanned the Bosphorus in Istanbul took people from one continent to another daily. It was fascinating for me to think about going to work in one continent and living in another. I came from little Massachusetts and Evelyn originated from huge Australia, and somehow, somewhere, met Homer who lived in a little place that was part of Greece and then became Turkey due to wars and repossession. They were all mixed up as to who, where and what, but were delightful 'story tellers' with many experiences to share from their long and unusual lives, to both Ed and me who were enthusiastic listeners. Also, Evelyn helped Ed in the writing of his book, *Pain-My Friend*.

She and Homer made a delightfully mismatched pair! She was gruff and loud, but not exactly boisterous, most intelligent, and made her presence known; he was the very opposite…quiet, friendly, informative and intelligent, but unlike Evelyn, very humble. He and I loved to sit together in the back seat of the car and talk while our spouses drove on to the next 'whatever' and loudly enjoyed each other! Someone took a photo of Homer and me sitting together on a bench; it is a very sweet representation of the two of us and I will always treasure it.

Evelyn directed us to any place in Turkey that we wanted to visit and many we had not asked to visit. I did not grow to know them as well as Ed did, since he did not work, and Homer and Evelyn were retired. (I seemed to work all the time, late afternoons and some evenings, which left little time for traveling.) Nevertheless, I was happy for them and in particular pleased that Ed had friends with whom to share his travel stories.

On some Saturdays, when I did not work, we took Evelyn and Homer out for a ride. I do not know exactly where we went at times, since we let Evelyn choose where to go or what she felt we should see. We went to many Turkish villages and I loved seeing all the everyday happenings of these people since they were most unusual.

One day the four of us were driving along, and I said to Ed, "Oh, Ed, look at the ladies on the donkeys. I wonder if they would let me take a picture of them?" I was always hesitant about taking photos since I never wanted to offend any of the natives or cause them to be upset with me.

Evelyn, bellowed fiercely at Ed, "Stop the car! Mary, you go out and ask them if they would like their picture taken!"

As soon as Ed stopped the car, I got out, gestured, smilingly said 'hello' and showed my camera to the ladies. They nodded in return which told me they would not mind having their picture taken. I took one or two photos of them on their donkeys, and bowed; they seemed delighted, and I went back to the car.

I still had my right foot on the ground and only my left foot in the car when suddenly Ed started to drive; I screamed loudly and then screamed again! "Ed, stop the car, stop the car...you ran over my heel."

I then cried again, "Oh, Ed. *Ohhh...!* Ed, it hurts so much, I think it's bro-ken...why did you do that? *Ohhh.*" I was almost crying but did not want to give in to it with Evelyn and Homer there. Well, poor Ed was scolded severely by Evelyn who was trying to tell him to stop the car and simultaneously asking him why he did this to me. I can see it now in my mind; naturally it was an accident, Homer felt terrible, Ed felt worse, but...my heel felt awful. It had tire markings on it for several weeks. Fortunately for me and for my high school bands, it did not break!

Homer and Evelyn were elderly when we met them and we had only known them for a short time when Homer fell down the stairs in his apartment build-ing. Stairs in Izmir apartments were horrible, metal spiral staircases that were easy to trip on. Homer was in the hospital for a week or two, but never fully re-covered and died there. We were all devastated by his death.

After Homer's death Ed was wonderful to Evelyn; he helped her go to the bank, and carry her groceries to and from the car. (Evelyn never owned a car.) He drove her here and there as needed; in return, she directed us when we trav-eled. She sat in the front, while I sat in the back as usual, but sadly, without Homer... and she told Ed the best route to take to anywhere we had not been or had not seen. She would say in her loud, domineering voice, "Well, you *should* go here, and *why haven't you gone there before this?*

Evelyn claimed that when she first moved from Australia to Turkey she traveled across and up and down the entire breadth and depth of Turkey, walking most of the time. She said she occasionally boarded a bus that was going in her direction. I never did learn exactly how she managed in terms of supporting herself during this time. She must have saved money, or worked occasionally during her trek across the country. Once she settled down with Homer, she wrote several books, and we own a copy of each one.

Unfortunately, after Homer died, Evelyn's health got worse to the point that she eventually ended up in a nursing home in Istanbul. A friend of mine from Izmir kept in touch with her though and said that Evelyn managed to be the 'boss' of the nursing home until she died sometime in her late nineties. Ed and I miss her, but cherish all our memories of Evelyn.

Istanbul

While on our first Thanksgiving break in Turkey, we arranged to meet my friend Madonna in Istanbul. She and I had met in Okinawa, but now she was working and living in Gaeta, Italy.

While there, we visited the Blue Mosque with its six minarets. It is one of my favorite sites to visit because it is so beautiful. Before entering the mosque, visitors must remove their shoes and place them in one of numerous box/like shelves covering a wall. Ed and I did so, then walked inside in our stocking feet and marveled at the brilliant blue hand-painted tiles covering the interior of the mosque. As we gazed at the gorgeous surroundings, Ed suddenly grabbed my arm.

"Mary…Mary…my sneakers," he whispered in terror to me, "we have to go back and get them…all our money is zippered into the compartment of my sneakers."

"Oh no, I forgot about that," I responded a bit fearfully.

Ed's sneakers had a secret compartment where we placed *most* of our money to avoid having our pockets picked, which happens quite often in Turkey, no matter how careful one tries to be. Ed grabbed my shoulders, turned me around and pushed me through the groups of people entering the mosque. "We **have** to go back and get them!" he said in a loud whisper.

"But then, we won't be able to finish seeing the mosque," I argued quietly. "To come back in, we'll have to stand in that long line and pay again."

"I have seen enough," Ed replied angrily, **not** whispering. "It is the money that concerns me now. Move!"

And so, I let myself be guided all the way back to the entrance against the flow of the hundreds of other tourists. He retrieved my shoes and his sneakers, then we pushed our way out through the people crowding the entrance. It was a mess getting out. However, I was happy we got to see the gorgeous mosque at least for a short time. I was able to notice as I was hurriedly making my way back to the entrance that there were many men praying on the main floor of the building. I asked someone where all the women were. I was reminded that in the mosques, women and men must be separated and the women were only allowed in a hidden balcony somewhere upstairs. I kept thinking 'how awful!'

Fortunately, I was able to tour the Blue Mosque more thoroughly a few years later when we visited Istanbul again. During that trip I also had the pleasure of seeing the Ayasofya, a gorgeous church built in 537AD. Known as the Church of the Divine Wisdom; in 1953, it was converted into a museum. Ayasofya's wide, flat dome was an amazing engineering feat for the sixth century, and architects still study the building's many innovations.

It is a fantastic place to visit. The treasures there are far too numerous to list here, but I found it to be an absolutely 'mind boggling' place of worship with numerous treasures reflecting the building's use over the centuries by the Muslim and Christian faiths.

Next we toured the Topkapi Palace in Istanbul. Built in the 1400s' for the Ottoman Sultans, the palace was bedecked with colorful tiles and jewels *everywhere*! Then we visited the Dolmabahce Palace, facing the Bosphorus strait, and the famous Obelisk of Thutmose III that is nearby. Carved from pink granite, it was originally erected at the Temple of Karnak in Luxor during the reign of Tuthmosis III in about 1490 BC. Theodosius had the obelisk cut into three pieces and brought to Constantinople. Only the top section survives, and it stands today where Theodosius placed it, on a marble pedestal. The obelisk has survived nearly 3,500 years in astonishingly good condition.

The Galata Tower in Istanbul is one of the city's most striking landmarks. It is a nine-story cone-capped cylinder that dominates the skyline and affords a panoramic vista of Old Istanbul and the Bosphorus. There is a restaurant and nightclub on the top floors. One evening Ed, Madonna and I went to dinner there. Following our delightful meal, belly dancers performed for everyone. They wore very little and danced vigorously, and sat on the laps of different gentlemen in the audience. Well, one of them danced her way over to our table and sat on Ed's lap. The expression on Ed's face was so hilarious that we all had a great laugh. I often wondered if it was discomfort or sheer enjoyment! *Hmmmn!* That was absolutely the funniest thing I had ever seen happen to my husband!

Earlier in the evening, when we first arrived for dinner, Madonna spotted other DODDS teachers she knew from Gaeta, Italy in the dining room. She went over to say hello to them and then rejoined us. After the belly dancing ended, she asked if we would like to meet the other teachers, and we told her 'of course!' We went over to their table, we were introduced, chairs were brought for us and we sat and proceeded to talk with each other for some time.

One of the women shared a story I remember to this day. She was an older teacher, short, heavy and seemingly, from her demeanor, very bossy. Her voice was sharp and very distinct.

"I am very, very careful about my money when I travel," she told us. "I *do not* want to be robbed." None of us disagreed with her about that. "I have to tell you though about one time when Frank and I were on our way to a wedding," she continued, her voice growing louder and higher in pitch as she talked.

"It was hot where we were traveling and there was no air conditioning in our car so the windows were open. Since we had been robbed once before in a car, I decided I would **not** be robbed a second time, so I decided I would tuck my purse between our two seats," she explained excitedly with her voice rising in pitch.

"And, I told myself over and over again that if anyone reached into the car for my purse, I would take my two hands," she folded them into fists, "and beat the living daylights out of the head and back of the robber!" Then she demonstrated, much to our delight, her fists pounding up and down in the air on the imaginary creature.

"Well, we had stopped at a light in heavy traffic that hot day on the way to the wedding," the woman continued. "Suddenly, a hand came in…" she paused, "and crossed over my chest and grabbed my purse! I was just about to beat him on the back," she said, once again demonstrating to the group with all her might by putting her arms and fists higher in the air, "when *I wet my pants!*"

Our group screamed with delight (and maybe a little sympathy). "Did you manage to get to the wedding?" someone asked. "Did you go back home to change your clothes?" another inquired.

And in her high shrieking voice she stated most emphatically, "Yes…I most certainly did. We went home, I changed my clothes and we went to the wedding. I was *not* going to let that man stop me from going to the wedding of a good friend!"

❧ ❧ ❧

A few years later we returned to Istanbul once again with our good friend, Jerry, who lived underneath our apartment on the sixth floor. He wanted to have his car while visiting in Istanbul, so we traveled on a ship that transported cars as well. It was a ship that was frequently docked a few yards from our apartment in Izmir. We boarded with great excitement, got settled into our separate rooms, met up on deck and then…the ship left the harbor. We were off…stayed overnight on the ship, and sailed into Istanbul the next evening like a distant relative of the Royal Family of England! I felt so good about it. The weather was perfect, the sun was glorious and the two men were funny together, as usual, so there were many laughs to be had amongst the three of us.

A friend of ours whom we had met in Izmir before she moved to Istanbul loaned us her apartment for a week. (She had gone on a business trip somewhere else). We revisited many of the famous sites we had previously seen, including the Blue Mosque, the Hayja Sophia and the Tower where the belly dancers were. And this time we were able to visit the markets, which I thoroughly enjoyed. The assortment of goods is vast, and the personalities of the Turks manning all the stalls are absolutely delightful…delightfully different than any other markets I had visited. We were also able to take a day cruise on the Straits of Bosphorous, which we had never done before. I loved it!

Jerry drove his car back to Izmir so we could stop along the way at historic sites, including Troy. I was actually a bit disappointed with Troy compared to the numerous other ruins I had visited. Since my childhood I had been fascinated by the story of the Trojan horse.

I believe there were probably ten layers of the city of Troy, meaning when one city (layer) decayed, or was torn apart by war and age, another was built on the first site. Then on the second site, the same thing would occur and on and on up to nine or ten destroyed layers of Troy having been built and ruined, again…either by man or age or both! Remnants of stone houses were all crumbled away with only a small portion staying together that might remotely resemble what could have been a 'stone house' of sorts.

The second part that was a disappointment for me was the famous Trojan horse in which numerous Greek soldiers hid in order to trick the Trojans. The Greeks had been trying valiantly to trap and destroy all the Trojans for years. (Many still, to this day, dislike one another fiercely, which I discovered when I made a trip to Greece and went into the BX. In Greece, I ended up hearing 'dislike' bordering on 'hate' dropping from the lips of an old man working at the cash register because I worked in Turkey!)

After ten years of fighting, the Greeks finally withdrew from Troy, but left a gigantic wooden horse outside the walls of the city. The Trojans found it, were curious, as one would imagine…as to what it was and how it got there, so they hauled it inside the walls of the city leaving it there for the night. At dawn, the trap door inside the horse opened and Greek soldiers hiding inside came out and opened the gates of the city from the inside, allowing other soldiers hidden outside the gates, to come in and decimate the Trojans and the city!

Of course, the original Trojan horse no longer exists, but a replica has been reconstructed. When I finally saw it, I was disappointed. I felt that it looked too modern. Visitors could enter the Trojan horse, but with my claustrophobia, I could not bring myself to do that.

The drive back to Izmir normally takes about twelve hours. But we turned it into a three-day trip while stopping at the many places of interest along the way. Jerry, an avid and excellent photographer, needed time, to decide what to 'shoot' and where to go; therefore we stayed in different hotels for two nights so as not to miss anything while on our way home to Izmir! We all agreed that it was a marvelous trip and an excellent way to travel, cruising to Istanbul then driving home.

Honoring the Dead at Gallipoli

One spring while in Turkey, we were able to join in the annual pilgrimage taken by some members of the English military to the island of Gallipoli in the Straits of the Dardanelles. The trip by bus and then boat, stopped at many of the World War I battlefields in that area. There were heavy casualties on both sides as the Irish, British and French fought to invade Turkey. They not only had to fight the Turks, but also the Germans who joined the war and sided with the Turks. I had never learned that in high school, and therefore was quite amazed to hear that the Turks and the Germans fought the British and other countries during that war. The invasion failed. But a submarine was used in this battle and at one site we saw the submarine from that period that had been saved and maintained for visitors.

As we stopped at each battlefield, we honored the dead by praying. I had never studied much about World War I in high school or college, therefore everything I learned was surprising to me. I do remember that one of my uncles on my father's side of the family fought in World War I. He slept in the trenches and was gassed by the enemy and never fully recovered. He was a nice man as I recall, and it was sad for me as a young child to see him suffering all those years later.

There were brief memorial services at each of the burial sites; we learned so very much that day and felt such sorrow! Obviously, many were killed since the burial grounds seemed to be endless as we walked from one end of one burial ground to the other. The war was...as all wars are...devastating!

The trip was emotionally moving and different from other voyages, to say the least, but the scenery was lovely. We were blessed with marvelously warm and inviting sunshine. The most beautiful and natural highlight of those memories were the grounds on which we walked. They were filled with carpets of flowers...red poppies! They blossom naturally at that time each year, all of which must be why we used to celebrate 'Poppy Day' here in USA while I was a child. 'Poppy Day', was later changed to Memorial Day, which memorializes all war veterans and not just the ones at Gallipoli or World War I.

Pamukkale

Pamukkale, meaning "cotton castle" in Turkish, is a natural site in the Denizli Province in southwestern Turkey. The city contains hot springs flowing out and over boulders and over the years created numerous terraces of soft white limestone. We visited there many times over the years while living in Turkey. People have been bathing in its pools for thousands of years. This huge and beautiful area is probably one of the most unusual sites I have ever seen. I was really taken aback. We stayed overnight in Pamukkale and swam in the waters... that was exciting and made me deliriously happy. One would like to just linger there all day, gazing and relaxing while looking at the beautiful stone portraits the flowing water has made over the years! The area is now a World Heritage Site.

The ancient Greco-Roman city of Hierapolis was built on top of the springs. I remembered studying about Hierapolis when I was in the eighth grade at the French School, and *now*...unbelievably so, I was there and sleeping in it, and also soaking in its wonderful waters! All the DODDS teachers took their guests to visit Pamukkale, no one ever misses seeing it when they come to Izmir, the area is extremely gorgeous, and the water is sublimely soothing.

My most memorable visit is one I made with Ed, Amy and Mark, a new teacher at our Izmir school. We stayed in a hotel where the doors of our rooms opened to a pool of hot water only six feet away. The water came from one of the seventeen hot springs in the area and was about 91 degrees Fahrenheit. We swam and floated in our pool just like the Roman soldiers had done eons ago. The heat of the water relaxed us so that when Amy and I returned to our room, we readied ourselves for bed, although it was early evening. (Ed slept in another room with Mark) We were talking as she lay on her bed, and in the middle of a word she fell asleep and slept for twelve hours. She was indeed relaxed!

I had the opportunity to visit Pamukkale once again about five years ago while I was visiting Joann. We stayed there for two nights in a lovely hotel and spent our days relaxing by and in the water. While there, we noticed many long man made ditches. I think they were built so people could take advantage of the warm mineral waters without having to pay a hotel to use its pools. I also noticed that the 'hotel' we had stayed in many years ago with Amy and Mark, was no longer used as a hotel. Instead it was a government-operated building with souvenirs, stalls, and information booths and bathrooms.

Cappadocia

One year in Turkey, after school ended for the year, Ed, Madonna and I spent two weeks traveling to and in and around Cappadocia, a fascinating region in central Turkey. It is a high plateau area pierced by volcanic peaks with unique geological, historic and cultural features. It is best known for its moon-like landscape with underground cities, cave churches and 'fairy chimney' rock formations that were turned into houses in many cases.

The area has been occupied since prehistoric times, but is especially famous today because the early Christians sought refuge there when they were being persecuted by Romans after the death of Christ. These Christians sailed from Jerusalem to Turkey and hid out in the Cappadocia area. There they found the 'fairy chimneys'…tall, narrow spires of rock formed from ancient volcanoes.

The outer layer of the 'fairy chimneys' was an erosion resistant sand colored rock. Beneath that layer was a softer rock that could be easily dug out. Men went to work and emptied out the insides and left the firm outer surface as a protecting wall. Homes were then made for people to live inside these 'fairy chimneys.' They looked a bit like a gigantic upside down ice cream cone. And usually on top there was a stone of the harder volcanic rock that looked like a beret sitting on top of the column. We saw one that was tall enough to hold a six-story apartment building in it, and people were actually living in it

There is no way I could possibly adequately describe the different types of 'fairy chimneys'; many were in groupings. There were very tall, fat ones, and some very low to the ground. Some were in clusters all over, every place you looked and no two cones or 'fairy chimneys' were alike, even their 'beret' type tops differed. It was the most fascinating thing we had ever seen. They all looked, to my eyes, like huge and enormous clusters, which were actually growing out of the ground, and getting taller and bigger each year; but, no, that was not happening and these groupings seemingly went on forever. Many miles of many clusters of them existed millions of years ago and are still there waiting to be seen or lived in today.

There was also an underground city in case marauders arrived to remove the natives from where they were. Remember, the people who escaped and ended up here in Cappadocia were early Christians living in a Muslim country to escape from being killed in Jerusalem. They must have lived in constant fear.

I went down into the underground city…scary…and not enough good air for me. After going down two levels, and seeing where the cows and chickens were kept and where the people lived, I had no desire to go down further as I have a claustrophobic problem and down two levels instead of four or five was absolutely enough for me. The oxygen came from a hole in the roof that carried down to the bottom. If I were a scientist I would be able to explain better about the air in the underground, but at the moment this is the best I can do.

Ed would not go in with me, but Madonna did. It was all most incredible. The people who lived there lived in close proximity to their cows, chickens, and each other. While there, I read that there was a period where they could not leave the underground city for some forty days because there were invaders looking to kill them.

Now, many of the 'fairy chimneys' are used as churches and contain wonderful original paintings inside of them on their soft walls. To me that was absolutely incredibly hard to believe…but true! We went into several of them and observed the lovely wall paintings. We stood in awe, there in Cappadocia, at the age and magnificence of the art.

In the villages around the area, there were communal ovens outdoors where the women baked their bread. The women wore flowing, tattered dresses, but seemed quite happy and willing to show us their homes. We thanked them profusely and went into a few. Talk about a different way of living, I have now seen them all! We had our cameras and of course, I asked them if they would mind if we took their pictures; I could not speak their language but I did much smiling and nodding and showing of the camera and they all wanted to be in our pictures. They were actually very sweet people!

While in the Cappadocia area we went to visit a school and happened onto a ceremony which we guessed might have been a graduation. The school authorities and all the children were outside doing their routine dances and it was most impressive. They encouraged us to take many photos and I did, of course. I would not have missed that for the world. Their dances are not at all like our folk dancing and square dancing; theirs were mostly done in long lines and joining of hands and circles…so it was a treat and a great pleasure for me!

Cappadocia was a marvel in many ways; the people had very little but were most generous and loved having us there. What more could one ask for? It was nothing like a busy city or active town; it was just slow and easy and absolutely warm and friendly. I just loved the concept of the communal ovens outside of the 'houses' where all the ladies met and baked their breads and chatted the whole day away!

※ ※ ※

In September 1993, the high school band was busier than ever and I had already lined up our Christmas performance schedule. I was pleased and 'proud as punch' of the boys and girls in the band and the way it had grown and improved over the years.

At that time, I went down one flight of stairs to Joann's home economics room to enjoy lunch with her and other teachers, or perhaps some of Joann's non-teacher friends. Each day brought in different people and interesting conversations.

Over time though it seemed no one involved me in conversations and I felt I could not hear what was being said. They did not look at me and I felt they were all whispering and not inviting me to be part of the conversation. I could not understand why this was happening and I began to feel bad and not enjoy the lunches.

Then one day Joann floored me when she said, "Mary, you absolutely must go to a doctor to get your hearing checked!"

"There is absolutely *nothing* wrong with my hearing," I retorted angrily. "Why do you say that?"

Then, most kindly, but firmly, Joann said, "You don't seem to hear anything anyone says. You also constantly ask people to repeat things."

"I beg...your...pardon," I muttered, "no one even *talks* to me lately for some unknown reason!"

"Mary, something is wrong with your hearing. I feel you should go to the doctor and have your hearing checked!" Joann answered firmly. She also seemed to be a bit irritated with me and I was very upset. Crying is a thing I can do too easily and I did not want to cry in front of her or anyone, so I packed up my lunch detritus and left. (Politely, however, since I would never leave any other way.)

But the lunchtime experience of feeling isolated happened again and again. Finally, I went to the military clinic to see a doctor. He checked my ears and my hearing most carefully, and wrote out an order for me to go to a specialist in Adana, on the American military base. Oh, dear, another flight, but, then, I smiled and thought, without students, hmm...and no cost hmmm...! Maybe that trip will not be too bad!

The hearing doctor in Adana had nothing good or positive to say about my hearing.

"What?" I asked, "what did you say?" after he examined me.

"Mrs. Guziejka, you are deaf and there is nothing that can be done about it," he replied.

"What do you mean?" I asked angrily.

"Just as I said," he continued. "You have lost a considerable amount of hearing."

I was absolutely devastated...I just could not understand how I could be deaf and if so, why? How could this have happened to me?

I saw another hearing specialist that same day in Adana and had more tests, which also confirmed that I had a hearing loss and nothing could fix the problem. I was totally crestfallen. I had gone alone to Adana, Ed was home, and I felt so forlorn...I just could not believe this was happening to me since I always had superior hearing...actually, very keen hearing all my life. I was sick at heart and all alone!

I absolutely had to go back to work in spite of what all those doctors were saying. The anger within me was rife. Therefore, I went back to the military doctor in Izmir and brought him all the necessary papers. As he studied them I said, "I must go back to my students, doctor...I absolutely cannot miss one more day of school! I have many concerts to prepare for!"

The doctor, ignoring my last remark, said, "Tomorrow you will be teaching, and a sound engineer will go to your room."

"A sound engineer? Whatever for?" I replied.

"To find out what is causing your deafness and whether you should continue to work at this type of job or not!" he patiently explained to me.

"Oh, God," I prayed to myself, "don't let this happen to me, please! I just cannot believe this is happening!"

The doctor picked up the phone and made the necessary arrangements immediately. The next morning a sergeant arrived with a tripod and some kind of attachment on the top of it. To this day, I still can see the sergeant with his tripod. When my first band class arrived, he proceeded to tell me to have the bands play just as I usually do, and then said, "Please, ma'am, do nothing differently than you usually do daily."

I directed the band, they played, and meanwhile the students had no idea what was happening. It was just another day in the lives of my band students. We were beginning our Christmas music!

All the time they played I was aware of peculiar sounds in my head, sounds that should not have been there and they appeared more obvious to me when the bands stopped playing. I had no idea what was causing that. I had a very strange feeling in my head and unfortunately this was not the first time this had happened. No...not the first...much to my acute and keen sadness!

At one point, the engineer stood up straight since he had had to stoop a little to read the mechanism he peered into. He then removed his earphones and put both his hands over his ears. The expression on his face was most appalling. After the children left he came to me and most politely said, "Ma'am, you've got a big problem in this room!" He then packed up his gear and left immediately; he left me wondering what was going to happen next!

I received another phone call and was told to report to the doctor the next day. Dragging my feet and with a huge lump of sorrow in my chest, I did as I was told.

The doctor, looking kindly, but most seriously at me said, "I have read the reports; the sergeant brought them over immediately." He looked up at me again and rather seriously, I thought, continued with, "You will not be returning to work."

I was appalled! I sat bolt upright when I heard his words and was close to tears when I almost screeched at him saying rapidly, "I have to go back to work,

I have ten concerts for the holidays and the little ones have to rehearse their Christmas songs for the manger scene!"

Oh, dear…the tears had started to come, slowly, very slowly at that point. My lips were quivering when he once again said most firmly, "I will not allow you to teach one more band class. Not one! You are *not* to go into your classroom again!"

Then, I cried in earnest, the tears flowing down my cheeks as fast as they could, "Doctor, you have to let me, you cannot do that, I cannot leave the students when we have so much to do."

I carried on much more in earnest, hoping to convince him of something… although I knew not what exactly…"I also have a Band Festival in April," my voice was rising… louder and very high pitched, "several high schools are coming, and the band *must* play at the graduation in June at Ephesus! I will stop after school ends in June! I promise I will stop.

The doctor replied…once again most patiently, "Mary, your hearing is so bad that if you return to the room with your band playing, you will be absolutely, totally deaf in a very short time, like in a few days or a few weeks. Also," he added in a most definite tone of voice, "if you return to teach in that classroom with the bands I will wash my hands of you and your case."

He was nice enough, not loud and hurting, but firm and definite and seemed to know what he was doing. However, I simply could not let my bands stop, give up, so to speak, I could not let them down. A flood of tears left my eyes washing my face once again, and I did not even think of embarrassment at that point. I just cried and cried, sobbed, and hiccupped as well.

He left his desk and came over to me patting me on the shoulder, and quietly said he understood my sorrow, but firmly stated for the last time, "If you go back into that room and perform with the band students, I will not be responsible for your case any longer. You and I will be all through from tomorrow on. Also, you will be totally deaf in a very, very short while and I know you would not want that to happen!"

Still weeping, and borderline hysterical, I went through two or three of his clean hankies and I muttered, "No"…as a hiccup issued forth and then another bit of crying came forward while I begged one more time of the doctor, "Can I at least go into school and explain why I am leaving and why we cannot play anymore? I must say my goodbyes. I cannot just leave the children without an explanation…"

"Yes," he said, "I will allow you to go in tomorrow, but you are *not* to touch an instrument or *hear* one played. That is an order!"

He also seemed to feel very bad…he then put his arm around my shoulder after I stood up and he walked me out to the main door, "Remember," he said, "you may teach at an elementary level since there would be no band noises… children have small and non invasive singing voices. Their voices will not hurt your hearing problems. You will still be able to continue teaching, but it will have to be somewhere else." Hardly consoled by anything at that moment, I mumbled goodbye and thank you and left him at the door.

❈❈❈

Downcast hardly describes how I felt. I went on home to our seventh floor apartment; Ed was shocked to see me, and then when I told him what was going to happen he held me for a long time in his arms trying to console me but I was absolutely inconsolable.

After my weeping ceased, I said to Ed, "Now I know why I kept hearing sounds that were not there…I heard a whistling sound in that great and huge hayfield Evelyn took us to see a while back. I thought I kept hearing the 'silence' since the area was so still and beautiful, but I was *not* hearing silence I was hearing the deafness in my ears."

Ed was at a loss for words and I…I was absolutely heartbroken! Even today, eighteen years later, I still hear noises that no one else hears and they are loud and horrible! We held each other again for a long time and then, finally, I had to pull myself together and make a plan to see my two principals. Although, I am most certain my doctor at the base had already called Mr. Emerson to inform him of my dilemma and the school's problem!

I eventually learned what had caused my hearing loss. Remember how clean and beautiful the band room was when I first arrived? It had lovely white walls. Well, it appeared clean and beautiful because the sound proofing tiles had been freshly painted white. That was lovely of course, but the paint destroyed their sound proofing qualities. I had been teaching band class all those years with unabsorbed sounds hammering away at my eardrums.

"What to do, what to do…where would I go, where would they send me and in the middle of the school year at that…" was in my mind constantly and "how…how can I disappoint my own students like this?"

I returned to school the next day, December 1, and said my sad and sorrowful goodbyes to all my students. What an awful time that was! I was then put on a 'paid leave' until a job opened up elsewhere in DODDS.

I called home after my last doctor's visit and my children, Amy and Susan and Eric, felt genuinely bad and tried to console me as we talked on the phone. My mother, who was deaf herself, told me I was strong and I would manage. Whenever we talked about a problem, Mom *always* left me with a feeling of marching on out to battle knowing full well that I would win the war!

Ed and I decided to call Joy, our good friend in England. After I told her what was happening she said firmly, "Dahling…You come he-ah for your holidays. That is an order!" With no hesitation, Ed and I went off to Chipstead village for Christmas. We lived with Joy and Charles in their lovely home for the two-week holiday. She and I went over all my problems and the information behind the problems; I think we wore out the issues; both she and Charles felt very heavyhearted for me. Joy was always loving, a remarkable lady and a most wonderful friend. (At this writing, unfortunately, my dear friend has passed on, died just a few months ago! I am heartbroken!) Charles and Ed were equally consoling, both of them having seen much of my work in the past, Ed in particular, of course and they also knew how much the school and students and bands meant to me.

We returned to Izmir after spending Christmas at Joy and Charles' home. I tried to be active somehow in Izmir. But, I was so upset that I could not work, and…I did not feel like sight seeing anymore. I was just too sad. Where would I go for my new job? Where would DODDS send me? Those questions kept me preoccupied. The other thing that worried me constantly was how much more would my hearing deteriorate.

The two doctors had told me I could teach elementary music only, that small children's voices would not be invasive, and would not hurt my hearing nor cause it to worsen. That statement gave me a little relief but I still was not allowed to teach in my Izmir school since a substitute had taken my place already!

Three weeks went by, slowly, slowly…and on the fourth week I was informed DODDS had a permanent replacement for me in Izmir, and that I was, in turn, going to replace this particular teacher, a lady, who taught in La Maddalena. I would be in her school, and she in mine.

Her school was on an island in the Mediterranean above the northern tip of Sardinia, facing Corsica, and belonging to Italy. When I heard this news I was certainly pleased about it, but I cannot truthfully say I was happy. I had reached a pinnacle of success in Izmir with the bands and now I was knocked off the pinnacle…I would never teach high school band again. But then, I could still teach elementary school children whose voices were 'not invasive' so said the hearing doctor.

On February 1, 1994, Ed and I moved to La Maddalena, an island as small as the head of a pin on a map, situated between Sardinia and Corsica. It was one of those happy/sad moments in our lives.

And these our lives
Exempt from public haunt
Find tongues in trees, books in running brooks
Sermons in stones
And good in everything.

As You Like It
—Shakespeare

Chapter 20
La Maddelana, Italy

*"The course of true love
never did run smooth..."*

**A Midsummer Night's Dream
—Shakespeare**

In order to go to La Maddelana from Turkey we had to take a ship from Izmir, travel on the Aegean Sea and cruise on up to Venice, Italy via the Adriatic Sea. I had to force myself to not think about what I was leaving, but to think about a new and exciting future. Not easily done under my newly discovered 'deaf' circumstances, but I worked at it steadily. The whole trip was quite romantic and something that I never dreamed would happen in my lifetime. Ed even took a photograph of me in the prow of the ship, as we sailed into Venice. I had on my new white ski jacket and if I must say so myself, the photograph is striking.

We slept on the ship for three nights. One night I had what I thought were horrific, shocking nightmares, until I discovered, a few minutes later, these 'nightmares' were actually happening. The ocean was rough, the boat was pitching up and slamming down and rolling and then doing the same all over again. I woke to the sounds of a lady screaming violently as the ship was dipping up and down. I clung to Ed for dear life. I was afraid the ship would sink and we would drown. It was a most frightening ordeal! I have no idea how long the rough seas lasted, but eventually they calmed down.

The ship docked, three days later, on the outskirts of Venice. The day was beautiful, the sun was shining and I felt like a queen as the ship approached the magnificence of Venice. Ed snapped another photo of me while leaning on the ship's railing with Venice in the background a few minutes before we sailed into port. This was an occasion I shall never forget.

We had been invited to stay with Cara Allen and her

Arriving in port of Venice, Italy from Izmir, Turkey.

husband in a town outside of Venice for a couple of days. I had met her when she worked for DODDS in Izmir. Her husband was in the military and was transferred to Italy, so she was now teaching second grade at a DODDS school near Verona, Italy. When the ship docked, we found our car, squeezed our luggage into the 'full to the brim' car and drove off the gangplank and to Cara's home. I don't remember much about our long trip to her home, but...we found it. They were overjoyed to see us when we finally arrived and we virtually fell into their arms when they met us at their door!

After a brief rest, they took us around to see the general area where they lived in Italy. Unfortunately, I do not remember the name of the town. It was charming; all of the Italian towns were charming from my perspective. The next day, on our own, Ed and I went up into the Lake District for dinner while viewing the magnificent surroundings. Cara and her husband had to work during the day, but met us for dinner in the Lake District that night, which was lovely. We only stayed two nights with Cara and her husband; we did not want to be in the way while they were still busy working and, of course, we were also anxious to move along to my new assignment.

After our brief visit with Cara and her husband, Ed and I talked about our options. We decided we would drive to the port of Civitevecchia northwest of Rome. From Civitevecchia, we would sail to the island of Sardinia, and from Sardinia, sail to La Maddalena! Our route from Venice to Civitevecchia took us through the ancient city of Sienna where we spent the night in a lovely small hotel.

Sienna is famous for horse races which are held in the city's central piazza, a tradition that began in medieval times. The races are still conducted annually on July 2 and August 16 and draw huge crowds to the center of the city. The large oval stone racetrack is covered with a layer of dirt, but the race is still dangerous for both horse and rider. Ed and I were not there when the races were being held, but it is such a famous part of the city's culture that we made sure we toured the area.

Around the central racetrack are old, old stone houses. Everything in Sienna seemed to be built in stone, not only the buildings, small or large, but all the streets! They were all made of the same sand colored stone. I was mesmerized with the whole area and could picture in my mind the famous horse races. The horses race furiously around the oval center of the small city with their shod hooves clattering in everyone's ears while tromping on the stones!

The old churches built of stone were also beautiful and fascinating, as was the history of Sienna. After slogging through the city we then eventually found a small restaurant, which seemed clean and nice; we enjoyed our meal then returned to our hotel.

Later that evening I came down with symptoms of food poisoning—extreme vomiting and diarrhea. I was in such a bad condition, that on my second day of suffering these symptoms, the hotel sent for a doctor to come to my room. The doctor was a beautiful Italian lady who spoke English with a lovely accent. She was a welcome sight to my sickly eyes.

She gave me a medicine that she said would help my condition. "If by midnight tonight all is not better, then an ambulance will pick you up and take you to the hospital," she told me with great pity and understanding. At that point, I felt so terribly ill that I was afraid I was going to die.

However, that evening the vomiting and diarrhea stopped and by midnight I was feeling much better. Giant waves of relief flooded through my mind and body. I had been on the verge of panic! I had never in my life gone through anything that severe before. I lost about ten pounds in the few days I was forced to stay in bed to recuperate. The doctor came one more time to check on me, and charged us nothing…absolutely nothing! No money was involved since I was a foreigner in their country, she told me. After examining me thoroughly, she declared I could continue on our trip to La Maddalena. Amazing—-no cost to us at all!

Ed and I drove to the port of Civitevecchia (which means 'Old City') and boarded the overnight ferry to Sardinia. Then, Ed became ill with food poisoning! I had to drag myself out of bed at midnight to find the ship doctor. He was most unpleasant, seemingly drunk and not happy to be awakened at that hour. I cannot remember what, if anything, he gave to Ed, but we did go back to sleep at some point as the ship sailed on.

When we arrived at Sardinia the next morning both of us were barely able to walk and felt awful all over! What a way to begin a new job, was all I could think of at that time! Fortunately, we did manage to drive ourselves to Olbia in Sardinia. At that port, we drove our car onto another ship, which took us on the twenty-minute ride to the island of La Maddalena.

Because my illness in Sienna had delayed our arrival in La Maddalena for a couple of days, I had called the principal of my new school to let her know what was happening. She and her husband met us at the ferry after we docked and cried out in voices filled with enthusiasm, despite our white faced, haggard looks, saying, "Welcome to La Maddalena!" (I am not sure now what kind of a smile and answer she received in return but I did the best I could under the circumstances!)

"Now, get your things together," she said while clapping her hands, "we want to take you to your hotel and then after you are settled we will drive you around the island to see the sights, and then… take you out to supper!" I groaned inwardly and then proceeded to tell them that we had both been very ill and could not eat or stay up very long; she had no clue as to what would be appropriate under those circumstances. As it turned out I was able to convince her that Ed would have to stay in the hotel but that I could go with them for a light supper. That pleased both of them. But…I felt absolutely awful, trying hard all the time not to show it to them by keeping a smile on my face. I did not enjoy my light supper, sadly, and I could not wait to get back to the hotel to fall into bed.

After two or three days Ed and I recuperated and we went to find my new school. It was situated way up on the very tip of the island. I had learned earlier that La Maddelena is six kms. in length and one km. in width. When we arrived at the top we found all was extremely different and charming with the gorgeous sea surrounding us just about everywhere we looked. Someone, I cannot remember who, probably one of the teachers, pointed out a house one could see while at the top of the island in which the famous Garibaldi lived; Garibaldi was a national leader of Italy at one time. La Maddalena was certainly charming, but very small.

Charlotte Miles and Christine Deischer, two lovely and caring teachers I met at the school on my first day, were the most helpful and wonderful people on the island and I cannot thank them enough for helping us become settled. Thanks to Christine, we were able to find temporary quarters consisting of two rooms. She lived upstairs in the complex and discovered there were two rooms available for us for immediate occupancy so in we moved. We spent several weeks in the tiny two room furnishings while all our worldly goods stayed in storage as usual! Meanwhile, I had started teaching, singing with the children, and doing my usual activities with Kindergarten through eighth grade. As soon as school ended each day, Ed and I would read all the advertisements in the newspaper for apartments and then start off in our car to look for them.

Because La Madd was such a small island, we did not have trouble finding our way around, but it was not easy to find an available apartment. Some of the newer and younger teachers who came in August six months after I had arrived with Ed, opted to live on Sardinia and come to work by ferry boat every morning and go home again the same way in the afternoon, in order to work at our school. That would have been a real chore for me, boarding the boat, parking the car in the boat, then a twenty minute boat ride and then the drive up the mountainous road to the school. I could not have faced that daily trip at all and felt so very relieved when we found an apartment.

I do clearly remember one of the first times we drove around La Mad, looking for the school.

"You read the map and tell me which way to go," Ed told me as we got into our car.

"Uh, huh," I replied...and started pouring over the map while he drove. The speed limit was very low, maybe 35 miles an hour or a little less because the island was so small. But map reading is not my forte. We drove along the main road as I kept studying the map trying to figure out where to turn.

Then, at some point, Ed stopped the car and looked at the map himself. He realized, much to our mirth, we had already been around the whole island and I was still looking at the map trying to figure out where to go. I did say earlier it was a VERY small island. It seems we had circled the lower part of the island without realizing this and had never found the streets or ways to go up the mountainous terrain to the school. We had a good laugh at ourselves. We then started all over again, with Ed reading the map first, and eventually found our way to school.

The apartment we finally rented was not wonderful, but it was adequate. We entered what seemed to be the ground floor with a kitchen and living room, and two small bedrooms and a bathroom between the two bedrooms. The whole little place had the shape of a square box. The building was situated on a cliff and it was not until after we signed a lease with the apartment owner that we learned a bar and restaurant were situated below our apartment on the cliff side of the building, just below our bedrooms. Not a quiet place to sleep I assure you. How on earth could we have been so...*dumb?*

However, La Maddalena itself was gorgeous. The scenery, serenity and solitude of the beaches surrounding us were wonderful. The mountainous terrain was covered with trees and the sky above was a beautiful blue dotted with puffy clouds. The color of the water changed depending on which direction you were looking. There were inlets and bays around the whole island. In time, we found if you did not like swimming in one little inlet, you could just move your things across the street and there was another inlet waiting for you with the wind going in an opposite direction from the first inlet. All, in that respect, worked out well.

I wish I could say the same for the school in which I taught. After completing the almost endless paper work that took a couple of days, I was able to begin teaching. That was when I learned I had no music room! I had to teach music in the children's regular classrooms, which I had done before and knew I could do again. But the school was overcrowded, especially in the sixth grades and above. There were thirty or forty students in each class, and while I was there, more students arrived. We later learned that there had been a mistake made in the Washington Pentagon offices. The military men assigned to our base were not supposed to be sent with their families, but somewhere in the chain of command, the orders had not been changed, and so more and more military men *and* their families moved to La Madd.

My heart went out to the homeroom teachers who were teaching in such overcrowded conditions and to the students themselves. It was also extremely difficult to teach music under such circumstances. No piano, no Orff instruments, no room to get up and move. I myself often felt crushed up against the chalkboard as I talked, or tried to talk...or sang, or tried to sing...in order to teach the children.

And then, there were other issues, such as the one I encountered with a fourth grade teacher in this school. When I entered the class for the first time I introduced myself to the teacher and the students. I talked to them from the front of the classroom and told them what we would be doing for the remainder of the year. Then the classroom door loudly banged open and slammed shut.

"Miss T., can I buy a soda?" a voice yelled loudly.

"Of course you can," Miss T. replied equally loud, "help yourself."

A refrigerator door banged open and shut and then the classroom door slammed loudly as the student left the room with his soda.

All of the students in the class had been distracted by this interruption, consequently I had to work to regain their attention.

Then, the door banged open again, and the scene was repeated. Over the next forty-five minutes, the same thing happened again and again. It was horrible. I could not keep the attention of the students since they were more interested in seeing who was coming in to buy a 'soda.' I was not able to teach anything!

The same thing happened the following week when I came to teach that particular fourth grade class. I was furious, but not sure how to handle the situation because I had already sensed I would not get much support from the school administration. So, since the weather was warm and nice, I decided to take the students outside and use the wide steps in front of the school as my classroom, and teach the students square and folk dancing.

It had always been my practice to have my folk/square dancing records with me wherever I taught. Over the years I had learned that when I encountered a 'problem' teaching music to students for whatever reason (overcrowding, behavior problems, etc.) I could often overcome the problem if I got the children moving to music. Obviously, I had a problem with this classroom. Therefore, I carried my record player and records outside. The janitor provided me with the extension cord I needed. I was all set.

The children sat on the long rows of low steps in the gorgeous weather. I told them what we were going to do…and guess what? They were absolutely delighted…and when it was over, they were thrilled! It worked! I decided I was *not* going back to teach in their room ever again. And, I never did! Surprisingly, that fourth-grade teacher never seemed to care what I did with her class or where I went or what I taught!

I had told her what I was going to do with her students before I moved the class outdoors. It was then I asked her why children of all ages were coming into her room to buy sodas.

"I am collecting money to have all the cats on the island spayed!" she told me while standing with her fists on her hips. "Therefore, I sell soda to the children in the school. They are allowed to come into my room whenever they are thirsty; all the other teachers are fine with it."

Now, I am also a humanitarian, but I could never put the needs of stray cats before the needs of my students. I could not believe what I was hearing, but evidently the principal did not have a problem with her practice, because *nothing* changed while I worked in that building.

Of course, not all the teachers had little use for music in the classroom. The second grade teacher, Charlotte Miles, was a charmer and a whiz at everything. We became good friends. Every single morning she put on a recording of children's songs. The songs were part of the Music Book Series I used in my teaching. Whenever I walked by her room, the first thing in the morning, the record was playing and the children were singing. That was not done in any of the other La Madd classes, and I had never seen it done anywhere else I taught, except in

Nashua, NH years ago, in the first grade at the Temple Street School.

There, a first grade teacher did the same thing. Whenever I walked into her first grade classroom for my class, music was playing in anticipation of my arrival. As time went on, I learned that she started the day, every morning, with a music lesson. At that time, the town was extremely poor and those children had very little music in their lives, so they loved everything that involved them in music.

I enjoyed teaching in Charlotte's class since the children were able to sing and enjoyed anything I did with them, including folk dances. They were enthusiastic whenever I entered their room for music class. They were a loving reflection of their classroom teacher!

After a week or two of teaching in classrooms, I met with the principal and told her that I needed room outside of classrooms to work with the students in music. She offered to let me use the stage in the auditorium/gymnasium. When I checked it out however, I found it was not going to be a workable solution. Physical education classes would be going on in the gymnasium while I tried to teach music on the stage. Heavy curtains would be closed between the stage and the gym, making the stage dark and stuffy and very unpleasant. With noisy P.E. classes going on beyond the curtains, I knew it would be impossible to keep the students' attention on music lessons. So I came up with another plan.

> *To business that we love*
> *We rise betimes*
> *And go to with delight.*
>
> **Antony and Cleopatra**
> **—Shakespeare**

Because the weather in La Maddelena was almost always perfect, the steps in front of the building became my classroom for grades four, five and six. I taught the primary grade students in their homeroom classes because they were eager to learn anything I offered, and most of my teaching was done by *rote*. I sang; they listened; they copied my voice. We played singing games and we also danced. Also, because they were smaller, there was a bit more room in their classes for them to move around occasionally.

All was working out fairly well, however, I felt the students still needed a 'project' to work on. Children need a goal, something to look forward to, as much as adults do. Our DODDS' school had an Italian woman who was a liaison between our school and the Italian school system. She was a lovely lady who spoke English very well. I asked her if students from one of the Italian schools on the island would be interested in coming to watch our students give a folk/square dancing demonstration. They could watch the dancing for a while then they would be invited to dance with our students and learn the steps themselves.

Well, the woman was so pleased and excited by the suggestion, that she immediately helped me make all the arrangements. On the appointed day, the custodians helped me set up everything we needed on the school playground. Two Italian teachers brought the students from their two classes to our school.

My fourth-grade students performed their dances, then they taught the Italian students some of the steps. The Italian students learned rapidly and began to love the dancing. They became eager, exhilarated and most excited. The Italian teachers and parents had kindly brought over goodies to eat and drink, as had some of the parents of my students. All in all it was a wonderful experience for everyone. In addition to learning folk dancing, the students from the two different cultures learned how to get along with each other. The experience was so well received, that we had a similar gathering a few months later. I was elated! And because it had worked so well with the fourth graders, I repeated the event with the older grades as well. I felt I was satisfying *some* of my students' music needs.

❧❧❧

It was late March of that year when I received a dreaded phone call from home. My 92-year-old mother had pneumonia. At that age, pneumonia is almost always fatal. My brother told me to come home. I was so sad. I cried quietly, it seemed, all the way home on the plane. I hoped my presence would bolster her spirits and help her fight the pneumonia. For a week or so after I arrived she did perk up and seemed to be getting better. Then her condition worsened.

We had to place her in a nursing home. She was mostly unconscious all the time. There was nothing more the doctor could do for her at that stage. I held her in my arms and talked to her. I think she heard, although she could not acknowledge anything I said. After three weeks, I finally had to leave to return to work. Ed and I returned to La Madd, and within a week Mom died in her sleep. The tears come to me now as I write this almost sixteen years later.

> *Farewell, thou art too dear*
> *for my possessing...*
>
> **Sonnet 87**
> **—Shakespeare**

I did not go back home for the funeral, as I could not face it; the death, the very long trip; all my energy was spent. I had three days off from working. I made myself stay right where I was, in our room, (I could not face anyone) and in bed most of the time.

Ed was a prince. He talked with me, read to me, and soothed me as much as possible. Time heals somehow and I finally had to go back to work. But...I do not think time will ever heal the loss of my mother...I had always done the best I could for her, and she, for her family...and that is all one can expect...

> *What's gone*
> *And what's past help*
> *Should be past grief*
>
> **The Winter's Tale**
> **—Shakespeare**

By then, the school year was almost over. I worked another two months in the same situation and found it most difficult due to circumstances beyond my control. There were bright times and lovely times also, therefore, I must not dwell on the negative. The air was wonderful, the skies were always blue, I never saw or felt rain, and the children were becoming charming and lovely to be with, even looking forward to my arrival in their classrooms, and yes, the older students also!

When the summer came, Ed and I went home again to Massachusetts to visit our daughters, Susan and Amy, and other friends. After a few weeks, we traveled to Texas to visit my son Eric and his family. We together mourned the loss of 'Mom' or 'Grammy.' It was a sad summer for us all.

> *My heart is heavy*
> *My age is weak,*
> *Grief would have tears*
> *And sorrow bids me speak*
>
> **All's Well That Ends Well**
> **—Shakespeare**

✣ ✣ ✣

Upon returning to La Maddalena in the fall, I learned that more changes had been made in the school to accommodate the growing number of students. The kindergarten, first and second grade classes had been moved into two houses next to the school. The houses had been emptied of their military residents and those classes, books, equipment and all were moved into the empty houses, along with the nurse's office. Everything was a mess and a jumble and one hardly knew for a few weeks where one would be next time one got up in the morning. I worked with the students in those two houses as well as the students in the main school building for several weeks.

Two of the third and fourth grade classes were housed in yet another building. The rooms assigned to the two classes were far too small and overly crowded; none of my specialties could be performed well in those two rooms. The building also housed the non-commissioned officer's club. I was allowed to use the NCO space to teach those classes because it had much more room than their classrooms. However, the club was essentially a *bar*, and the room always reeked of cigarette smoke and alcohol. Not the most pleasant of rooms in which to teach!

I decided to teach the operetta Hansel and Gretel to both of these classes knowing full well it would help the children and also help me with some of the grief I still felt due to my mom's passing. I decided we would perform the operetta for Christmas. I was absolutely sure they would do well, because I felt good about it all. If a teacher is bored, does not enjoy her work, then, so too, will the children be bored and will not enjoy what is put in front of them. I enjoyed immensely conducting bands and directing musicals and plays, and of course, the inimitable square and folk dancing and last and the most important…singing! I just knew Hansel and Gretel would work and the children would love performing in it.

Since I only saw the children once a week I needed all that time, meaning September through December, to do the amount of work it would take to have a good performance. The students and the two lovely teachers who worked with them, were extremely happy to hear of my plans, and looked forward to seeing me every week. Both the third and fourth grade classes in that building would be in the operetta. The other fourth grade teacher and her class were still in the main building!

There was always room for everyone in my musical productions, unlike some music teachers I have seen who only used the very best students in performances. This type of teaching *might* be acceptable in high schools I felt, but not with younger children.

Then…surprise…surprise I was given a small room in the main building all to myself. It had been the teachers' lunchroom. It was small, but adequate. I had step risers installed since there was not enough room for chairs, tables or desks. The fifth, sixth, seventh and eighth graders met me in that room for music lessons, one class at a time. This arrangement worked 100 percent better with those students rather than trying to teach them in their crowded classrooms. The students loved the step risers and so did I!

As a result, I chose to have a Christmas concert for parents featuring *all* my upper grade students (6th, 7th and 8th) and possibly more grades, depending on how and where the concert would take place. They learned to sing some of the Christmas songs in two-part harmony. The two part or three part harmony made a big impression on students that age and they felt proud and good about themselves when they mastered simple tunes in harmony. They loved hearing themselves sing and as time went on I was thrilled with their improved behavior and musical skills.

I realized we might not learn too many songs for this Christmas concert, but I felt that by next year, they should be wonderful! I used my Kodaly approach and the Orff instruments of which I had only two, but we used them when appropriate. My spirits were beginning to lift, I had a room, of sorts, privacy, and I had most of the children looking forward to performing in a Christmas concert.

We all have to have a goal in life, whether in art, music, dancing, or just plain living, day to day. I know that only too well and in particular, now that I am older and not teaching anything at all anymore, I still need a goal. I have my piano, which I practice daily, I swim laps, half a mile every other day when possible, I try to walk a mile or two in between those two days, and now I am writing. I love writing! I have always loved writing i.e. a few poems, a few songs and a few stories! Now I am writing about my life! Strangely enough, however, I love the whole process!

❧ ❧ ❧

Aside from all that was taking place at work, Ed and I were able to travel around the Italian countryside with Charlotte Miles and Christine Deischer, fellow teachers at the DODDS school in La Maddelena. Sardinia was only a twenty-minute boat ride from La Maddalena, therefore we visited the island on several occasions. One trip involved taking the ferry (with our car) to Sardinia, just south of La Maddalena. We also saw Garibaldi's house on a very small island next to La Madd. Garibaldi was a famous Italian in the early 1800s. He was a military officer, then became a political figure in his later years. Italians consider him a national hero.

In Sardinia we saw ancient structures called NURAGHE. The name 'nuraghe' derives from the word 'nur' meaning 'hollow heap.' The earliest form of nuraghi were 'corridor nuraghi' and from the outside resembled a pile of rock, but the insides had been removed to make a habitation area. The tops of the mounds looked to me like huge, rounded thumbs. There's hardly anything written to let us know exactly what they were used for except a single paragraph by the Romans referring to how difficult it was to win a battle with people who had managed to get inside a nuraghe and were ready to defend it. The Sardinian people have great respect for the Nuraghes; they are an important aspect of their culture.

We also saw giant cork trees. I was so stunned! In all my life it never occurred to me to wonder where 'cork' came from. Did you know that every nine years cork is stripped from the bottom half of the bark of trees? There were huge stands of the trees all over Sardinia. This remarkable tree has a bark that is unique. The cork bark can be harvested from the tree allowing new bark to grow in its place without killing or damaging the trees. This makes every tree a renewable source of raw material. The cork is harvested (peeled) from each tree time after time. The first harvest of the cork bark occurs approximately 20 years after a sapling is planted. I was most impressed and took many pictures of the stripped bark trees. I have far more respect for cork now than I ever had before in my life!

There was so much to see but so little time in which to see everything. We attended a festival in Oristano, Sardinia. Called La Sartiglia, it is a sort of medieval tournament with knights wearing fabulous costumes and white androgynous masks. Their horses are decorated with flowers and there is a contest among the knights. Tin stars with holes in the middle are hung from a ribbon over the street near the Cathedral. A masked knight gallops on his horse at break-neck speed down the street and aims his sword at the small hole in the center of the star. This was absolutely so different, so unusual...we had never, ever seen a festival like this before.

Not only were the men in costumes but everyone was; all the families partake in this festival. The wives and the children and grandparents were all in costumes of that period! They also all participated in the festival; the ladies cook and serve a special type of food everyone enjoyed. We were very welcomed by the natives and the whole affair was most impressive.

While traveling throughout Sardinia we visited very old churches and towns! We also met some extremely old people; one lady had to have been one hundred years old. I watched in great amazement as she, completely covered in a long black shroud, walked nimbly up and down the high hills, and quickly too, I might add. Walking like that was probably why she had lived to such a ripe old age.

Sardinia is also famous for its natural stone/rock formations, which occurred during numerous earthquakes many eons ago. I cannot even give an approximate guess as to how many years back these earthquakes occurred… however, the natural formations on and around the beaches and up the mountains were spectacular! Of my two favorite natural formations one was on La Madd and the other Sardinia. As you approached La Madd by boat, there were rocks, huge boulders, on the mountainside that looked like a polar bear walking down the mountain. Up close one could not see it at all in the same manner or shape but…from a distance it was most definitely a bear rushing down the mountainside. My other favorite natural rock formation was on Sardinia and looked like an elephant. Sadly for me, we never did go as far as the end of the island of Sardinia, since we ran out of time! And…there was so much more to see!

During the Thanksgiving break that year, Charlotte, Christine, Ed and I went back to mainland Italy for several days. We took Charlotte's car on the ferry to Naples. She needed new tires, and she could not purchase them on La Maddalena. Once we found the BX and got her tires, we left Naples because it is a huge, overcrowded city and most definitely not what we wanted to see at that time.

We drove down the coast of Italy, and once again stopped at the ancient city of Pompeii. It was closed again! Each of the three times Ed and I had tried to see Pompeii, it was closed for one reason or another. That was all right, I figured there was a reason we were not meant to see it and I did not mind. Actually, I never tried to see it again. We had explored many, many ancient cities in Turkey, so I managed to squelch my disappointment by looking up at the great

Mt. Vesuvius.

We drove on down the very beautiful Amalfi coastline of Italy and found a lovely place near Sorrento to spend the night, not modern at all, but very homey and most Italian, which was what we all wanted. Once we settled in, we three women took a boat ride to the Isle of Capri. (Ed stayed at the hotel to rest his back). As a young girl, I had been quite fond of the popular song Isle of Capri... and now here I was...on the island itself! We walked around and explored a bit; Capri, being a small island took little time for us to see all that was of interest.

We then got in line to take a rowboat to visit the famous Blue Grotto. It is a popular site for tourists; the entrance to the grotto is small, in fact, everyone in the rowboat must lie on their backs to clear the entranceway. Once we got to the site, we had to wait our turn in a line of rowboats. In one of the boats ahead of us, a very fat man leaned over for some reason. As he did so, he accidentally toppled into the water.

Somehow, the men in the boat from which he fell were able to hoist this huge man back into the boat. He was dripping wet from stem to stern, still, he valiantly continued on with his trip inside the shrine of the Blue Grotto. I guess he did not have much choice. We tried hard not to laugh when we discovered he did not hurt himself, but then, it was a bit embarrassing for him to say the least. I did feel sorry considering his embarrassment and discomfort, however.

When finally it was our boat's turn to enter the cave, we all laid down in the bottom of the boat and saw the natural rock formation of the opening. The inside of the cave/shrine was almost spooky but oh, so nice and so very beautiful! We saw the famous statue of the Madonna in the cave and all was most exciting and very 'moving' emotionally!

I could have stayed on the Isle of Capri forever! Everywhere one looked, gorgeous sunshine flooded the entire area, the beautiful sea and all the lovely houses along the coastline! None of it reminded me of our coastline here in New England! It was all most definitely Italian and extremely inviting.

The next day, we began traveling back up the coast of Italy so we could return to La Maddalena.

We took another side-trip on our way to the ship that would take us to La Madd, one that made me happy and sad. During World War II my Canadian cousin Adrian Becotte was in the battle at the top of Monte Cassino. He was a in a tank that was hit and he was killed outright and buried in a cemetery there. No one in his family had ever been able to visit his gravesite in that cemetery.

They could not afford to make the trip to Italy.

When my friend Charlotte was planning this trip, she told me, "Mary, you told me about your cousin, and his death…therefore, I figured out a way to go to the cemetery he is in. We could take our trip to the coastline, stay a while and on the way back to the ship, take a side trip to Monte Cassino and find your cousin's grave."

I was absolutely elated. You see I loved Adrian when I was a young girl of three or four years old. He used to give me piggyback rides and toss me up in the air. He was in uniform even then. Today, my childhood memory of Adrian and our relationship is still clear in my mind, and he still has two sisters living in Sherbrooke, Quebec. His elder sister, Margo, was most dear to me, and almost 80 years old at that time. She is now 95 years old but has Alzheimer's. She is still a very dear lady to me however!

Prior to the trip, I wrote to our English friends Joy and Charles asking for their help in finding my cousin's gravesite. Charles wrote to the people in charge of The Commonwealth War Graves, and obtained for me all the information I needed to find Adrian's grave. I was deeply pleased and felt 'my cup runneth over.'

We left Sorrento early the next morning to give us as much time in the cemetery as possible. Unfortunately though, we had trouble finding the cemetery on Italy's back roads. When we finally arrived, we saw a sign listing the cemetery's hours and realized it was going to close in twenty minutes.

"Oh dear," I said to Charlotte, "do you think we will ever find the grave before the gates close?"

Charlotte, ever resourceful, said hurriedly, "Ed, you take that direction," she pointed to the right. "Christine, you take that direction, on the left, and I will go to the north, and Mary you go to the south."

We all took off at a run, except for Ed, who could hardly walk, let alone run! As we searched, we noticed Ed was waving his hands at us from a distance. He had found the grave and when we got there he had a bit of a smirk on his face. Men!

The grave was inscribed with Adrian's name, date of birth and death and a poem from Adrian's mother, who was my aunt. Ed took at least eight or ten pictures of me at the grave from different angles. He also got a good close-up shot of the poem on the stone from Adrian's mother. Before long, we heard the cemetery caretaker hollering at us to let us know they were closing the gates. We had to leave…right away. I must say the whole affair was emotionally devastating for me. Never in my life had I imagined I would be able to visit Monte Casino and read about my cousin's valor and his mother's prayer to him written in the gravestone. I was soulfully ecstatic, to say the least!

The next day when we were home in La Maddalena, I called my cousin, Margo, Adrian's sister, in Canada. After she said hello I hurriedly told her what we had done and she screeched, yelling, "Oh, Maryyyyyy…." and then hung up on me! Well, knowing how emotional my cousin could be, I was not hurt, just worried about her. The next day she called and apologized, saying she was so overcome she did not know what to do or what to say. She was most appreciative and will be grateful, always…so wonderful to me, as a child and as an adult. We later sent her copies of the photos Ed had taken and she was thrilled to receive them.

❦ ❦ ❦

Another time that fall, Charlotte, Christine and I had to attend a special meeting of DODDS teachers in Florence, Italy. We took a plane from Sardinia to Florence. I also was to be inaugurated into the Phi Beta Kappa group. I was not overly excited and thrilled, but I was pleased in my heart to have been asked. Something, however, came along to stop the process later on. Sadly, I never did become a Phi Beta Kappa member! I always seemed to be in the wrong place at the wrong time. Charlotte and Christine, who were already Phi Beta Kappa members, had plans to nominate me, but for a variety of reasons their plans did not work out. I was a bit disappointed, but then, considering what happened in the near future, I would have had very little time to think about the Phi Beta Kappa or even mourn the loss.

While in Florence, we stayed at the home of another DODDS teacher with whom I had worked while in Okinawa. I can still see us that first night there… four older adults, three of us in our beds and pajamas, and the hostess sitting on the foot of one of the beds. We were roaring with laughter at each other's comical DODDS stories because there were many; when one travels around continuously as we all had been doing, one is bound to meet up with hysterically funny situations! We laughed almost the entire evening until it was time to close our eyes. I had not laughed like that in a very long time!

What I enjoyed most about this last trip to Florence, Italy were the restaurants, the people and the scenery. I had already been to Florence twice before, and on this trip we had no time to visit any museums or the like, but it was nice to see a little more of the city as we drove through Florence on the way to our meetings, since it is so beautiful everywhere.

When I arrived home from Florence, Ed was angry. Not at me, but at the restaurant below our four room apartment! It seems they had decided the night before to renovate the place during the middle of night when no customers were around. Ed was awake the whole night; the men were drunk and hammering and gales of laughter seemed to rip through the ceiling, Ed said; the noise was incredibly bad.

The next day we went to the military Housing Office and reported the situation, but got nowhere with the problem, so we determined we would look for another place to live. Sadly, for us, housing was scarce on the little island. I could have lived across the water in Sardinia on the coast but the prospects of rising early to take a boat, and with a car, did not appeal to me one single bit. We were stuck, as Ed would say, between a rock and a hard spot.

The front yard of our apartment was the back yard of the restaurant. All the restaurant's filthy garbage barrels were placed near or beside our front door and each night the piles grew larger and larger and spilled out of the barrels and STUNK! When we were looking at the apartment originally, evidently the landlord made an effort to hide the garbage at that time. And the topography of the land was such that we could not see the restaurant's sign from the front of the apartment when we had originally viewed it. It just looked like we were alone on the end of the plot of land. I also took a series of pictures of our 'lovely front garden,' to show to the military Housing Office. They are funny to look at now, but they were not at all funny then! I was never sure which was worse, the garbage at the front door or the noise coming up through the ceilings!

But as it turned out, our apartment 'problems' were soon resolved in a way that I never anticipated.

I was well into working with my third and fourth grade students on the *Hansel and Gretel* operetta and the fifth, sixth, seventh and eighth grade students on their songs for the Christmas concert. We were planning to perform all of this on the same evening on the stage in the school gymnasium. I had my own classroom and was beginning to find great happiness in the La Madd School. I had a small room in which to teach. The children and I got along famously and I loved Italy when…Edna Brauer came upon the scene. She was the director of DODDS for Italy, and maybe more, I was not sure. I had met her once before, although I must say, meeting someone and 'knowing' the person is not the same.

One day in early December, I met Edna Brauer in the hallway of our school between classes. She put her arms around me, gave me a huge hug and a pat and told me she hoped all was well and that I was enjoying teaching at La Madd.

"Yes, all is moving along nicely now," I replied. "I am more used to everything and I am enjoying being here." Then, I left her and went on to my classes and where she went, I did not know.

> *Double... double...*
> *toil and trouble*
> *Fire burn and*
> *cauldron bubble.*
>
> **Macbeth**
> **—Shakespeare**

The next day, I was called into the principal's office. When my last class of the day was over I went to the office. Usually our school principal was friendly; if not the best administrator, she was at least very friendly...always. Edna Brauer was with her in her office. They were seated at a large round table, looking serious and not smiling at all. I was immediately perplexed.

"Mary, do sit down over there," the principal said, pointing at the only chair across the table from them. I sat. I was still smiling at that point, since I always felt I was an extremely friendly person, but neither of the other two women returned the smile. They were very somber.

Edna Brauer started the conversation by stating firmly, "Mary, you are all done here."

I did not know what she meant. I sat there for what seemed like a long minute and then said, "I am sorry, but I don't understand what you are saying."

"We have no room for you here in this school," she replied. "You are all through!"

I almost fell off my chair and said, "What did you say?"

"You no longer have a job here anymore," Edna replied sharply, with no further explanation.

I looked at the principal but she said nothing; nor did she smile or look encouraging.

Briefly I thought to myself, "I wonder where that super friendly lady is, who gave me the big bear hug yesterday?"

Pulling myself together I anxiously asked, "I do wish you would explain what has happened. Do you not like my work? Have I done something wrong?"

"We have no room for you anymore," the principal replied. "There are too many children here so you have to leave. The art teacher will be leaving also."

Boom! Just like that...no words of...'this is the saddest thing I have done in a long time'...or, 'I am sad you have to leave, or I hope you understand'...'or I will place you elsewhere'...nothing!

"I...I...just do not understand," I muttered...and continued on with, "I have an operetta being presented in two weeks, and a choir of all fifth, sixth, seventh and eighth grade students singing Christmas songs. How can I leave now? The children need me!"

"You have to leave now and that is all there is to it," Edna stated one more time and in a most officious tone of voice, no smiles, no words of, 'I am so sorry,' no explanation...*nothing*!

Then, I became angry! "You can't disappoint the children like that!" I said. "What will I tell them and what have I done that was so wrong?"

"Nothing, Mary," the principal replied. "We have to get rid of, or let two teachers go, and you and the art teachers are the two who have to leave."

At that point, the superintendent took the paper work and did not hand it to me politely, but rudely tossed it across the table.

Then, trying to hold back tears, I asked Edna, "Where will you send me?"

"I have no position available in which to place you; you will have to find your own," Edna answered coldly.

That statement left me simply aghast. I had never been treated like this before and certainly DODDS would not do this to me. My record was flawless... I just could not understand what was happening. My mind was shouting in quiet anguish at that point saying, "What will I do?"

They then stood up and left, the meeting was over and I was sitting there at the huge round table like a dumbfounded fool. All alone!

Seeing them leave made me angry and sorrowful all at once. I grabbed my paperwork and left out of one door after they closed the other door. I went to Charlotte. Whereas one part of me could understand the situation to a degree, the other part of me was screaming inwardly in anger at the way it was presented, the manner in which I was treated, and as well, no position to go to and no advice as to how, when or where to work after our Christmas holiday ended.

Oh, how full of briers is this working day world…

As You Like It
—Shakespeare

Charlotte was amazed and horrified by my news, but then she began thinking rapidly. She had a great mind and had worked for DODDS for many, many years longer than I had. Charlotte bristled and sputtered; said a few words I will not repeat; then hauled my trembling body along the hallway, "Come with me and we will see what is posted on the bulletin board!"

All this time there was a board hanging somewhere with openings for teachers in DODDS but I never knew it existed let alone know where it was hanging. After we found the bulletin board Charlotte discovered, much to my surprise, an opening somewhere in England.

As tears streamed down my cheeks I asked, "Charlotte, is it up to me to call for the job?"

"Why no, not usually," she replied, and added with a determined air, "but we can do it now if we have to. I will place the call."

She was most firm about this, thank the good Lord…because by then I was, what is known as…'a basket case!'

Charlotte put the call through. After a very long time she finally reached the proper person, talked a few minutes with whoever answered the telephone, and then handed the phone to me. I then spoke with the supervisor of the DODDS area in England whose name escapes me now. He told me he would look into the problem, and not to worry, he was sure I would have a job since there happened to be an opening for a music specialist at a school just outside of London. It was called The West Ruislip Elementary School.

God was with me, as was Charlotte. Almost immediately the gentleman returned our call and stated there was indeed an opening in the West Ruislip School, near London, England. Then there were several more phone calls that afternoon between me and the West Ruislip principal and the DODDS England supervisor and finally, I was all set.

The West Ruislip Elementary School was approximately twenty miles west of London and toward Oxford, I was informed! I was weak all over when I heard the news. I had not planned to leave La Madd, but then…I had always wanted to teach for DODDS in England. My new posting sort of fell into my lap. I was happy, in a happy/sad sort of way, since I had just gotten started with my children at La Madd and now I felt like I was deceiving them by leaving. I also felt like I was coming in to London through the back door, but then, I had a job!

I was notified that in order to collect my normal salary I must report to the West Ruislip Elementary School the last day of school before the holidays, which was December 22nd! If I could not do that I would then have to wait until sometime in the new year to collect my salary.

I was weak all over. I thought I had better sit down. While sitting, I called Ed, and he was overjoyed for me! He said, "I guess I had better start packing again!" Then he groaned.

Meanwhile, I still had to do something with the Christmas program and I had only a little time left. I had to leave, almost immediately. I felt inside myself that I was falling apart in little pieces…daily! I decided to go ahead with my plans for the performance of *Hansel and Gretel*. It would mean having it performed earlier than planned, but I thought it could be done.

Sadly, I had to drop the plans for the older students, meaning they could not sing at the Christmas program. No time was left for me to prepare both groups to be ready for an earlier performance date. My heart broke for the disappointment I seemingly dumped onto the older students, but there was no help for it. I was told to leave on a certain day and that was an order! I believe I left on or around the 5th of December.

❧ ❧ ❧

The evening for the *Hansel and Gretel* performance finally arrived. The gymnasium was full; I had recovered from the scare of losing my position. Therefore, I was ready, and raring to go!

The children performed beautifully; their singing and acting was absolutely wonderful. That fact helped me much more than anyone can possibly know at that point in my life. I was totally thrilled with their performance, their costumes, with the help from a team of parents, and the scenery done by the art teacher.

After the performance, when the clapping for the students had died down. I decided I must say goodbye to my lovely parent audience and explain why I was leaving so hastily and not returning in January. (I was extremely nervous at that point).

I came out in front of the audience of parents, they were still clapping, and I waited for the applause to die down. Then I started talking to them since I needed to tell the parents I was leaving, but I did not mention any of the negative issues surrounding my transfer.

After that I thanked them profusely for all they had done for me, told them their children were all lovely and wished them a Merry Christmas! Surprise upon surprise…they all stood up while clapping for me one more time!

And then…I could not believe my eyes…the parents all formed a long line and each and everyone of them thanked me individually for what I had done for their children since my arrival and to tell me they wished I could stay, but then, hoped I would enjoy my new posting. Many had short vignettes to recount of the few events that occurred here under my tutelage, as in the dancing with the Italian children and the like! I was almost speechless. But, of course, I had to tell them I had no choice in the matter. Since they were also all military people they understood readily but nevertheless, were not very happy about the decision for me to move.

I was quite stunned by what was happening. The line of people went more than halfway around the entire gymnasium…that had never, ever happened after any of the other musicals I produced. I was aghast, thrilled and near tears. One gentleman, a sailor, told me, "In all my years of living here, and I have been here fifteen years with my family, we have never had anyone teach music, drama and dance to the children the way you have. Never! I wish you were not leaving, but at the same time my family and I wish you much happiness." He gave me a big hug!

I was hugged by many of the parents and children as the long line went by. By the time it was over, I was just about in tears. It was growing late, the children were tired and I was exhausted as well. I said goodbye to my last set of parents and children and turned to tackle the last step in any production, i.e. 'clean-up.'

I was shocked! My good friends and parents who had helped me set up the scenery that inevitably accompanies a musical play had been cleaning up all the sets and the detritus that accompanies a show with many participants. I had nothing else to do but to thank them with tears and hugs and goodbyes. Then… I went on home and flopped into bed, shedding a few tears of sadness and happiness…and thought about facing what was coming next.

Things won are done,
Joy's soul lies in the doing.

Troilus and Cressida
—Shakespeare

The following day, my last day at school, two of the younger teachers came to me as I was in the process of cleaning up my music room, packing my books and instruments, and saying farewells to the teachers and the students in their classrooms.

"You know, Mary, what you did last night was very wrong. I did not approve of that at all. Those people should never have been made to line up like that," said one of the two and then brusquely walked away.

The other one stayed behind and said in a most officious manner "I have never seen anything like that before. You should be ashamed of yourself, looking for praise in that manner," and then walked away.

Of this above all, to thine own self be true
And it shall follow as the night, the day,
Thou cans't not then be false to any man.

Hamlet
—Shakespeare

Ed and I moved into a hotel the next day and the transfer process started all over again. I sighed and with all my mixed feelings, tried very hard to be happy about moving to England. This was the dream that I had since I first started teaching for DODDS!

Obviously, we did not have to look for another apartment in La Madd… that was great. We no longer had to listen to the trashy noises down in the bar room. Nor would we have to face their many barrels of garbage daily at the 'front door' of our apartment! But, there were many things I would miss…certainly the beauty of this little bitty island and the few friends we had made, and most of all Christine and Charlotte!

After several days of completing military paperwork related to the transfer, it was time for Ed and me to board the ship that would take us (and our car in the hold!) first to Corsica and then to France. The ferry was scheduled to leave early that morning, about 6 a.m. Just as we had boarded the ship, I looked over the railing and saw three women entering the docking area. I looked and stared and said to Ed, "Who do you think would be coming to the ship at this hour?"

He looked, but did not see them. Then, as the group got closer, I recognized who they were and yanked on Ed's arm hollering, "I think it's Charlotte, and she has Robbie and Christine with her. Oh, Ed, how lovely of them to do this for us."

My good friends from La Madd school had come to say a last good bye! They brought so much pleasure to us that morning, just by taking time to give us a simple farewell! I ran down and off the ship and hugged and kissed them one last time, then scurried back on board and threw more kisses at Charlotte, Robbie and Christine while watching them grow smaller and smaller as our ship sailed out of sight!

After awhile, Ed and I settled in to the ship. We would be riding overnight to get to France. The military had given us several days to reach my new job, so we were planning to drive leisurely through France for a few days, stopping at night at wherever we were, then continuing on the next day until we reached the coast of the English channel.

The boat ride was great, so lovely to see the receding landscape and watch for the new one to appear. Sunset was absolutely beautiful! The water was gorgeous, not rough, and all went well. After sleeping overnight in the second ship, (yes, we had to change ships once) we arrived in France and our car was hauled out of its "berth." We entered it and off we went.

The trip from La Madd had been smooth and uneventful. I was in the throes of ambiguity, sad about having to leave La Maddalena and yet, excited about living and working outside of London! I had always wanted to live in England again, after that one year in 1978-1979, and now, here I was, going back again, after having almost given up on that possibility. It sort of 'fell into my lap' shall we say. Maybe it was destiny! But then, on the other hand I did not want to leave La Madd in the way I had been forced to…that was most disturbing to say the least!

We traveled leisurely; in the first place we had never been to this area of France before, and did not know where we were going. We had visited Paris and Normandy and other places in that general area, but never on the route we were driving now. We looked at the beautiful countryside as we went along; we were mixed emotions of sad and somber and then, of serious excitement. Eventually we arrived at the English Channel on the coast.

We had a room in a hotel in Boulogne, France. After resting for a while in our room we realized we were hungry, famished actually, so we asked the clerk at the desk which restaurant he would recommend. I don't remember the name of the restaurant, but I do know it was a Chinese restaurant only a few yards up and across the street from our hotel.

We saw two dining rooms as we entered. The room on the right side seemed to be having a private party; one large table was occupied and the sounds were merry. We went into the empty room on the left side of the front door. Our waiter was an older Chinese man and he was charming and polite! We ordered our favorite Chinese food and then the Chinese waiter lingered a bit. I like to talk to everyone, especially anyone from a foreign country. Therefore, I took a few moments to talk with him when we had finished eating and were awaiting desert.

He spoke to us of his homeland, and family from China; we then told him we had been to Hong Kong three times, and to Macau and thence, up the Pearl River. "Ohhhh," he said, "so nice, so nice you could go!" As he spoke to us he bowed frequently and smiled profusely with his hands crossed across his waist and tucked into his wide sleeves.

I then added to my Pearl River story by saying, "We went inland, following the Pearl River, but not in a boat; we were on a bus, following along side the Pearl River." He nodded and smiled and bowed again and repeated the motions once more and then smiled again asking, "Where you from, please, may I ask?"

"My parents were from Poland, but our home is in America; we are here for my wife's work as a teacher for the U.S. government," Ed replied. The Chinese man continued to bow and smile throughout our conversation.

"My parents' families were from France, England and Ireland originally, and then they moved to Canada and later, when my parents married in Sherbrooke, Quebec, that very same day...my father and mother moved to the United States," I added.

"Ah," he said, "you speak French?" nodding his head, up and down, and up and down.

"Yes, I speak French a little, I understand it well, but do not speak it as well as I would like," I said.

"Would you please...to come with me," our waiter said, bowing three or four times with his hands still in his sleeves, "to the next room where there is a party. I would like to introduce you to the people. They are from France, Poland, and Germany."

Well, since Ed and I are always sociable, off we went with this lovely, polite Chinese man to be introduced to the group in the next room.

The most incredible party was taking place. Having listened to the general sounds from a distance, we thought it was probably a party being given by a business, or something of that sort. *Not at all!* We were introduced to the group. There were two adults from Poland, one adult from Germany and one from

France. The adults were holding a Christmas party for a group of young retarded adults who lived in a French 'home for retarded adults' in Boulogne.

The leader of the group spoke English, asked us to join him and introduced us. There were eight to twelve retarded adults and then the caretakers from other countries and us. The atmosphere was quite congenial. The young adult caretakers were happy to have us join them.

Ed spoke in Polish to the young Pole saying, "Jak tam whystko," which meant, "How are you?" in Polish. Two of the girls taking care of the group were from Poland, spoke fluent Polish and limited French, no English. One man was from Germany, and spoke relatively good English. There was also a lady from France who loved hearing me try to speak French with her. Most of them had halting and limited English but enough to get by in this situation.

All the retarded adults spoke French. I then spoke my limited French as in, "Bon soir, mes amis, oui, je parle francais, un peu, mais je comprend plus mieux que je parle!" when appropriate and we all became quite close that evening. The young adults smiled and laughed and some nodded their heads in understanding. This particular school hires mature professionals who want to donate their time to live and work for a year with the retarded adults. The caretakers told us that they were using this time to help others and to 'find themselves.' They all seemed to be loving and caring. We were all speaking and talking and the sounds coming from three different languages being spoken were quite enjoyable.

For some reason, the subject of music came up, and I said, "I am a music teacher…je suis une maitresse d'ecole pour le gouvernment des Etats Unis et je m'enseigne la musique a les enfants. Leurs parents sont tout dans le Militaire." Suddenly, the French lady remembered to invite the Chinese owner to come join us for singing and he brought his family with him. Everyone was so very happy!

I started by having all of us sing Christmas carols in French that I remembered from my French studies in school. The handicapped adults were thrilled. They were smiling and trying to sing with me. Ed then sang his Polish Christmas carols which I also knew since I taught Polish carols in my schools in Andover, MA. Ed was in seventh heaven, as the expression goes, singing his Polish carols with the two young people from Poland. They also coaxed Ed to talk with them in Polish and he tried his best, but used his hands most of the time rather than his mouth. He was funny, since he could not always remember all the words in Polish. The German man also sang a few carols in German, which I did not know, but those who knew them sang along in German.

All in all, it was emotionally moving. The farewells took at least half an hour, as we all hugged and held each other before we parted. We will never see each other again, no names or addresses were exchanged, but Ed and I will never...ever...forget that most moving incident in Boulogne, France, in a Chinese restaurant with a lovely Chinese family and a group of French retarded adults with their four caretakers from Germany, France and Poland! All those different countries, customs and cultures and languages and each and everyone taking time to love and care for one another was just sweet and lovely! As I write this I feel shivers running up and down in my body and great warmth in my heart. Ed and I felt very privileged to have experienced an evening like that.

The following morning we drove our car onto the ferry to cross the English Channel. We landed in Dover, England, got into our car, and drove off to Canterbury. We spent two full days there, staying in a lovely bed and breakfast, and exploring the town at our leisure. We had been to Canterbury before, so it was wonderful to visit favorite familiar places again, as well as explore the area further.

Finally, we left Canterbury and drove on the 'back' roads through lovely and peaceful villages until lunchtime. Then after lunch in a small village, we checked the time and the map and decided that in order to reach West Ruislip in time to pick up my check, we would have to travel more quickly. So we got onto England's Route 25, and traveled at what seemed breakneck speed.

We arrived at the West Ruislip Elementary School at about three p.m. I picked up my check and met a few teachers. I sighed and took a deep breath... a new and different chapter, once again, had opened in my life of teaching music for U.S. government schools!

I talk in order to understand;
I teach in order to learn.

—Robert Frost

Chapter 21
West Ruislip, England

"To be or not be or not to be,
that is the question,
Whether t'is nobler in the mind
To suffer the slings and arrows of outrageous fortune
Or to take arms against a sea of troubles
And by opposing end them.........."

Hamlet
—Shakespeare

How glorious it was to be back in England again! After stopping at the West Ruislip School, Ed and I checked into a hotel near Heathrow Airport and stayed there for the Christmas holidays. Joy and Charles lived about 30 miles away in Chipstead, therefore we were able to spend much of our holiday time with them.

Once the holidays ended we moved into another hotel closer to the school. I started to work, and then after school every day, Ed and I looked for a house to rent. He did most of the driving, including driving me to and from school everyday since I was not used to driving on the 'opposite' side of the road. The first few times I tried, I broke into nervous sweats. The fact that I was unfamiliar with the area, that we did not have a home yet, and we had to drive on what seemed the 'wrong' side of the road, made me glad I had Ed there to do the driving. He seemed to take to driving on the 'wrong' side like a 'duck to water!' Thank heaven!

We eventually rented a house in Beaconsfield, about 12 miles from the West Ruislip School, and about 30 miles from London proper. Quaint country villages surrounded us. We enjoyed the countryside, but it was still easy to travel into London because the trains in England are good, fast and on time. We could be in London by train in thirty minutes after leaving home…just long enough to rest one's toes and read the newspaper.

The names of some the towns in that area were interesting such as Gerrards Cross, or Stoke Poges. I was told those names came about ages ago when for instance a Mr. Stoke married a Miss Poges and they settled in a particular area and a village grew up over time. I heard two theories for the Gerrards Cross village name. One was based on a Mr. Gerrard marrying a Miss Cross. The other theory was that there was a horrible, cruel man named 'Jarret' who ruled the area with a large sword that looked like a 'Cross.' Over time, 'Jarret' evolved into 'Gerrard', but the 'Cross' remained the same. I prefer the initial explanation to the latter one, but both are interesting none-the-less.

It was wonderful to be settled in Beaconsfield (pronounced 'Bekonsfield,' with a short e vowel sound). We had moved so often during the last year that I was in a state of confusion, my head was whirling. Ed and I both remarked later how surprised we were that we survived it all, but nevertheless, survive we did!

After the holidays, school resumed. I learned I would have my own room for teaching. I was in 'seventh heaven.' I got to my room with its piano, but found I had NO classes. Yes, no classes! I spoke to the principal several times about when I would start teaching, and she always told me, "We'll wait until the semester break and then you can start up."

Well, semester break was a month away! I never did understand the principal's reasoning for this, but as you might imagine, the classroom teachers were not too happy with the situation. They wondered why I was just 'hanging around' so to speak, and I had no answer for them. I did keep myself busy preparing my room; finding desks, chairs, music books, having the piano tuned. But once that was organized, there was little for me to do but sit in the classroom all day.

One day I got into a conversation with Gene, who was one of the teachers. I asked him if I could have his fifth grade class come in for music once in a while since the principal had no schedule for me yet. He was delighted with the offer and began making time in his schedule for his class to have music lessons.

I then approached a few other teachers with the same offer, and they accepted. They were delighted to have some 'free' time during the school day to catch up on the endless grading of papers, lesson planning, etc. Things were slowly working out, and eventually the principal came up with a schedule that had me teaching all the classes in the school on a regular basis.

It was February 1995 by then, and I had discovered there had not been a music teacher in that school for several years. I really wanted the students to love music, so I decided after much deliberation to have the students in the fourth, fifth and sixth grades perform the musical *Oliver!*

The older students were thrilled with the story of Oliver, the music and the costumes. We worked on the musical during each class period once a week. Then we had rehearsals after school three afternoons a week. Our performance was scheduled for late April. There was a lot of work to be done.

However fortune smiled on me. I met Carol Rupp. Her husband taught third grade at the school. She herself had taught at the school in the past, but a series of illnesses had led her to retire from her own classroom. However, she continued to volunteer in her husband's class and with other projects in the school as needed. She loved the idea of producing a musical, and she agreed to help with costumes and scenery. I also had the support and help from a number of parents of students. I could not have done this without their help.

During the last week, before the presentation of *Oliver*, we had rehearsals every day after school. I did not work with the entire cast every day, but with pairs or singles or small groups, depending on where the weak parts were and which songs or which parts of the drama needed strengthening.

The performance was wonderful. The gymnasium/auditorium was filled with parents and friends of the students. The boys in the roles of Fagin, Oliver, and the Artful Dodger sang and acted beautifully. The students in the smaller roles were also excellent. And the giant groups of Fagin's 'boys' (a combination of girls and boys dressed in fantastic rags) were great and stayed 'in character' at all times. The applause at the end of the show was marvelous and continuous as each 'star' came back on the stage for a bow. I was grinning from ear to ear; the children and parents were equally as happy judging from the look on their faces and their great big smiles!

I was extremely proud of the students and their efforts. They felt good about themselves because of the work they had done in getting this show ready for a performance; the happy and loving feelings could be seen in their faces, attitudes, and behaviors! They all worked hard to understand the plot, the sadness, the happiness, the music, and to memorize lines and to learn songs and speeches; all of the fourth, fifth and sixth grade students were involved in some way; not one student was left out!

The next day, the reading specialist at our school came to me. She had a huge smile on her face, but with a secretive air she whispered softly in my ear,

Students singing with 'real Oliver' (second from left) in West Ruislip, England.

"Would you like to have the 'real Oliver' from London come here and perform for the children?"

I was flabbergasted. A professional production of *Oliver* happened to be on stage in London at that time. Maybe it had been playing for a few months, but I had not seen the advertisements since I had been so busy with school and house hunting. I had not yet had the chance to go into London proper to see any shows.

"Absolutely! Of course I would…but how…?" I responded eagerly.

"Listen," she interrupted, "I have a book salesman here with me now, in my classroom, and he is staying, coincidentally, in a Bed and Breakfast with the star of the real *Oliver* and his two parents. Since they are the only ones at breakfast every morning, my book salesman and 'Oliver' and his parents have become acquainted."

"Really?" I exclaimed. "How could you possibly bring him here to our school?"

"I have ways," the reading specialist said and smiled at me most cunningly.

"Tell me, tell me…what are they, what are your ways?" I implored.

"My book salesman," she said calmly and enunciating clearly, "talks with the parents and their son at breakfast every morning. They eat together every day and have formed a bit of a friendship. The boy plays the part of Oliver on stage in London! The book salesman wants me to purchase certain reading books for the school. Therefore, as a favor, I will talk him into asking the boy's parents to allow their son to come here and perform for our children."

"But how?" I was so agitated I could hardly be still. "I would think it would be costly."

"The book company will pay for it," she replied. "You'll see, just you wait and see!" Smiling confidently, she turned on her heel and sauntered away.

The next day she came to me and said, "It is all arranged, no worry about the money, and he will be here for the whole day on Thursday."

"I can't believe this is happening!!!" I hollered flailing my arms in the air. "The *real* Oliver from the London stage will be here for *all* our children?" I can become quite excited about happenings like this and especially something that will affect students in such a positive way!

"That is correct!" she said. Then pointing her finger at me and emphasizing each and every word she added, "You may depend on it!"

And off she went down the corridor with a huge smile of satisfaction on her face, leaving me with my mouth agape and stunned with the surprise!

My mind was in a whirl as I started thinking how to handle this situation. Hmmmn! The real 'Oliver' would sing his solos and I knew he would bring a tape accompaniment so I did not have to worry about my piano playing and especially without a rehearsal.

Then I hit upon an idea! I was beside myself with glee over the whole thing. I would have all the students from *our* Oliver sit and listen, along with all the other school children, no costumes, that would be far too much work... and then, at the end... I would announce to our audience that our children were then going to sing for the 'real Oliver.' (We kept calling him the 'real Oliver' since we did not know his name at first and the children liked it so well that it stuck, and stayed with us all the time.)

❧ ❧ ❧

Two days later, the 'real Oliver' arrived at West Ruislip Elementary School. The young boy was absolutely charming. I was totally smitten with his English accent and his way of speaking to me. He was a normal and typical boy with a darling personality. He was a child of about twelve but looked like he was ten years old due to his size. In order to look the part of a poor, unkempt boy who lived in a dismal orphanage, he had to keep his blonde hair semi-long with bangs.

The 'real Oliver' and I stood by the piano in the front of the gym room/cum auditorium, while the students filed in to take their seats on the floor. We were talking over what he was about to do on stage when he asked in his beautifully accented voice, "When it is time for me to sing 'Where Is Love', Mrs. Guziejka...would you like me to cry and sob at the end of the song as I do on stage in the show?"

"Absolutely! Please...make certain you put all the crying and acting into all your songs, my students would love it and they will also learn from you what a real professional does," I told him. With that, I patted him on the shoulder and he went on up to the stage. His father started the tape recorder and yes, he did sob a few times during the song 'Where is Love' and we all loved it. He sang all his solo numbers! Oliver's performance was superb! I shall never forget it!

Then came *our* surprise for the 'real Oliver.' Once he had finished his solos, I brought him down to sit with the other students while my fourth, fifth and sixth graders went on the stage. I had worked with them the last two days brushing up on the song 'Consider Yourself at Home' which we hoped would make the 'real Oliver' happy.

They sang the song beautifully and used all the choreography I had taught them. When the song was over, our Artful Dodger and Oliver went into the audience and took the 'real Oliver' by the hands and invited him to come sing with them on the stage. To be able to sing with the 'star' of a London show was so unbelievably exciting for the chorus…and for me!

It seemed a bit of a shock and surprise for the 'real Oliver,' but when my two students pulled him to his feet, he did not resist. He got up and joined the group with no hesitation whatsoever! He was on stage again between the boys and girls who had been the stars of our *Oliver!* He seemed to love what he was doing, and whenever MY choreography was being used, he watched our students closely and then within one or two minutes he was able to join right in with them. That really tickled me since I am no professional dancer and never thought my choreography to be as good as the dancing which would be found in a professional stage show, but he certainly liked it and performed very well. He was most definitely a quick learner.

He and they all had a wonderful time, as did the audience. All the songs, except for one or two more adult ones that I had not included, were sung by all of the cast and the 'real Oliver.' He and our cast of seemingly hundreds, but really only eighty children had a great time as one could tell by the smile on his face and the smiles on all the children's faces. The audience and all our students and teachers were ecstatic.

Suddenly, it was over and I felt exhausted due to the nervous pressure I am sure; we had sung all the songs and I turned to look at the Principal who was up at the back of the auditorium. She looked at me and gestured with her hands… it was a gesture that said, plainly, "more, more, do it over again." Both hands were going round and round each other…as if to say continue or do one more!

I groaned inwardly and played 'Consider Yourself At Home' one last time and that was that! The applause was marvelous. Many parents had come for this momentous occasion and were standing up in the back and around the sides of the auditorium to see and hear the little boy from the London *Oliver!* and our own children too! But now, it was over and I was absolutely drained of energy. I could not have played one more song! Yet… I was *soooooooo happy!*

Once the performing was over the 'real Oliver's' father, who had accompanied his son to our school, said that he and his son could spend some time there in the school if we wished. I invited them to lunch in the children's cafeteria and he accepted. I asked if he could spend the remainder of the day also, and the father was definitely in no hurry to leave. He replied with, "We would love to stay all day!"

All the older children were clamoring for 'Oliver' to be in their rooms…so we divided up and tried to even out the time 'Oliver' could be in each classroom, with preference given to the older students. There was just not enough time left in the day to make 'Oliver's' visits equal for all the classes and the younger students did not exactly grasp the significance of his visit.

The first 'class' he attended was an extended recess for all the performers. That was sorely needed. During the remainder of the school day, I hosted 'Oliver's' father and showed him around the school. Then he told me about his life with his wife and son in Northern England and in London.

While talking with 'Oliver's' father outside during the extended recess, I scanned the entire area where the students were playing and I observed that 'Oliver' was quite happy. He had become a real little boy once again and went off to be with the others as though they had all known one another all their lives.

I listened to his father's stories about what it was like to have a son be a star on stage in London's West End. He smiled rather broadly and told me that he and his wife were both musicians and their joint music studio was in the North of England. They both love music and this darling little boy was their only child. We did promise to communicate once again, but nothing ever developed from it unfortunately. The 'real Oliver' did write a thank you note later and also included a photograph of himself, which tickled me. I placed it on our bulletin board for all the children to see whenever they came into the music room. I was so…so…happy for the students…and…for me!

Ed had taken many pictures of the show during our evening performance and then many more when the day performance was put on with the 'real Oliver' for which I was profoundly happy. They eventually ended up on bulletin boards in my classroom, reminding the students daily of what had happened during the year and how successful they were. After a few more shows, I created, with the help of a most artistic parent, a huge bulletin board in the hallway outside of the music room. Almost every day, small groups of students clustered around the photos and talked about the event, then happily went on to their seats in my room to see what was to happen next.

Ed and I decided to see the professional production of *Oliver* in London's West End Theatre. The young boy was great in his role. When he sang 'Where is Love,' I was in tears! I tried to visit the 'real Oliver' backstage that evening to give him copies of photos from when he visited our school. However, I received a negative, but most polite reply after knocking on the door, "We are sorry

Madam, be we cannot allow you or anyone to come into the rooms backstage." Crestfallen, I gave the man at the dressing room door the envelope of photos, along with my heartfelt thank you letter. I felt bad... but then, I understood. I never did see the child again...

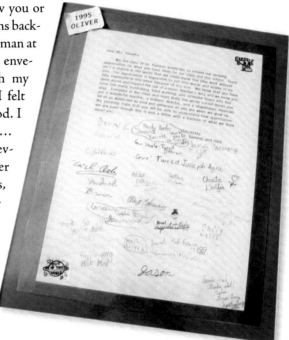

I was deeply moved several days later when a letter from the fifth-grade class, composed, typed and individually signed by each student, was presented to me. They had labeled, matted and framed it. To this day it is a dear memento that brings back wonderful memories.

Dear Mrs. Guziejka,

We the class of Dr. Ramirez would like to extend our undying appreciation for what you have done for our class and this school. There isn't a chance in the world that we could have made this play work without you. Our appreciation is impossible to put into words and unable to be fully expressed in this letter because of its size. We know that you have gone above and beyond all of a music teacher's duty and we know you have put many frustrating, hard working and stressful hours into this play. Everyone in the class and most likely the whole school thinks you are a wonderful teacher, a brilliant director, and a stupendous musician. All of us would like to be as kind and generous as you are when we grow up. We sincerely hope that you are able to understand how appreciative we are even though this is just a letter with a fraction of what we think about you.

   Sincerely,

   Dr. Ramirez and class

And these our lives exempt from public haunt find tongues in trees,
books in running brooks and good in everything...
As You Like It
—Shakespeare

Poland

Shortly after that, the school year in England came to an end. Ed's parents had emigrated from Poland when they were in their late teens. We did not know a lot about their history, but knew that they had grown up in a farming community—Ed's father on a farm, and Ed's mother in an orphanage near there. So, we decided to take a two-week trip to Poland once classes had ended and before we returned to the states to visit family over the summer.

Ed was the next to the youngest of eight children in his family, six boys and two girls. In the spring of 1995, while I was teaching music classes and producing *Oliver*, Ed wrote to Mitchell, one of his brothers in the states and obtained the names and addresses of some of Ed's father's relatives who were still living in Poland. Mitchell and his wife had occasionally sent *care* packages to these distant relatives in Poland. Aside from that, there had been little communication among the branches of those families, and no one in Ed's family had ever visited Poland. Ed was excited to see the farm where his father had grown up.

We flew into Warsaw and stayed at a lovely hotel in the heart of the city. The morning following our arrival we hailed a taxi and asked the driver to take us to the historical sites in the city. The driver, who spoke some English, seemed excited that we were Americans. Fortunately Ed could understand Polish and Ed would tell me what the driver was explaining to him. One of the places he drove us to was the Vistula River where the Russian army had invaded Poland during World War II. We walked with him to the edge of the river as he told Ed about the battle and the loss of lives and damage done during that time. He was a thoughtful guide and anxious to tell us how grateful he was for the wonderful help the Americans gave the Poles during World War II.

We then went on to the 'Old Town' section of Warsaw. Established in the 13th century, the 'Old Town' had been systematically destroyed by German bombings at the end of World War II. Nothing was left! However, following the war, the Polish people meticulously rebuilt that portion of the city based on the memories of survivors, photographs, etc. As many of the original bricks were reused as possible and the rubble was sifted for reusable decorative elements, which were reinserted into their original places.

This new/old town was charming, graceful, and all totally intact, as though no destruction had ever taken place. It was almost identical in its new form to what existed before the bombings. The buildings appeared old and were old and so realistic for that period of time that if one had a magnifying glass it would be difficult to tell where the old ended and the new began. Nothing had ever impressed me quite as much as this 'Old Town'! The Poles are proud of their reconstruction. UNESCO has listed 'Old Town' as a World Heritage Site and I saw the plaque proclaiming it 'an outstanding example of near-total reconstruction of a span of history covering the 13th to the 20th century.'

As we wandered around 'Old Town', we came to an area where young men and women dressed in native costumes were performing Polish folk dances. I was mesmerized and could have stayed forever. There were tables and chairs set out here and there around the square. We bought some ice cream and were invited to join some Europeans and Americans at their tables as we all enjoyed our ice cream and shared stories about where we were from, what we did, etc. The afternoon was bright and sunny, the Polish dance music and costumes were delightful, and the people with whom we sat were smiling, talkative and interesting. All was well!

We also got in touch with Heino and Gretta, our friends from Izmir, Turkey, who had moved to Warsaw recently. Heino, who had battled cancer, was retired now, so he offered to drive us around Warsaw and to Zelazowa Wola, Chopin's birthplace about 30 miles west of Warsaw. His wife Gretta had to work that day, so she was unable to accompany us.

Chopin had been a favorite composer of mine since I was fourteen years old, so to visit his birthplace fulfilled a childhood dream. It was wonderful, and most satisfying and a great experience for me…who almost always has a tear or two cascading down my cheeks during the renditions of some of Chopin's piano solos. It was the treat of a lifetime!

The village is on the banks of the Utrata River and is known for its picturesque landscape, including numerous winding streams surrounded by willows and hills. The inside of Chopin's home is open for tours. It was quite old, but comfortable and well preserved considering the thousands of people who visit there annually. Several pianos were housed in one of the rooms and against the wall. I was never sure why there were so many *old* pianos but then…no matter, it was all delightful!

A park where tables and chairs are set up in a random fashion surrounds the home. Visitors can purchase a beverage or snack and sit outside and enjoy the scenery and listen to recordings of Chopin's works broadcast on speakers throughout the area. One could just sit and spend the entire day in the lovely air and atmosphere and surroundings of the Frederic Chopin home listening to his music. And…many people did sit outside…listening and listening! We stayed as long as possible, but eventually we had to return to Warsaw.

Next it was time to visit Ed's distant relatives. Ed's father had grown up in the farming village of Bialystock on the southeastern border of Poland. Unfortunately, we don't know much about their early history. Whereas Ed's father, Floryan, grew up on the farm in Bialystock, Ed's mother grew up in the orphanage. When, where and how did they meet? Why did they leave Poland? What was life like back then? They would never talk about any of that except to say that they came to the United States on a ship. In fact, Ed's mother never spoke any English. We always assumed that their younger lives had been hard and as far as they were concerned, the 'less said, the better.'

Heino offered to drive us to Bialystock, about two hours southeast of Warsaw. Originally, plans called for just Heino, Ed and myself to go see Ed's family, but then for some reason, at the last minute, Gretta decided she was able to make the trip also. I certainly did not mind that, except for some reason that afternoon she was quite 'cool' to me as we sat in the backseat. Heino and Ed were in the front of the car, talking about 'everything.' I tried talking with Gretta, chatting away as I usually do, but she did not respond. So after awhile, I stopped talking. With Gretta, unlike other friends, I never knew where I 'stood' in terms of friendship; some days she was distant and cold, and sometimes she was a little warmer.

In time, we arrived at Ed's father's old farmhouse. An older woman was living at the farm. She and three of her grown children and two or three of *their* children (high school/college age) greeted us. The older woman just smiled, but did not talk. The sons tried to talk to us, but Ed's Polish is rusty and they knew very little English. One of the teenage girls seemed to know some English and she translated as best she could.

We were ushered into a small, square, modest, living room. The room seemed not to have been used much at all, meaning it was obviously their 'best' room. Ed's mother had had a similar room at her home in Lowell that was the same, always closed off and used only briefly when someone came to visit. There were old albums of photos on the table waiting for our viewing.

Heino, Gretta and I just sat and watched for the most part as Ed looked at the photos and did his best to understand what they were telling him in Polish and a bit of English. Ed shared some of the more significant photos with me. At this point, I don't really remember anything specific except they were his distant relatives. Once we finished looking at the photos, we moved on to the next room, a large, long dining room. As we passed through a small hallway on the way to that room, one of the women opened a door in the hallway to proudly display what must have been a relatively new bathroom. The ladies were so sweet as they presented it to us and so proud to have a bathroom in the house. Previously they had only an 'outhouse.' It made me want to weep that they were so proud of what I would have taken for granted.

I had by now begun to sort out the identities and understand the relationships of some of the people there. The husband of the older woman had died. She was the mother of two sons and one daughter. The wives of the sons were with us, along with their children (the older woman's grandchildren). I was never sure whether the one daughter never married, or whether she had been married and her husband had died. However, she was the most gregariously friendly of the group and seemed delighted that we were there. She tried hard to communicate in English. There was another middle aged woman with us the whole time and it seems she was from the other side of the family, but I could never understand to whom she was related although she had known Ed's mother in the orphanage. She spoke a little more English than any of the other adults.

The home was spotlessly clean and relatively nice, but so poor. We spent the better part of the day with them, essentially partaking of one meal lasting most of day. I noticed that the table in their dining/sitting room must have always held at least twelve people every day and then I saw that many more 'leaves' could be added when necessary. I assumed that most of their lives revolved around this area of the home.

Only one thing was bothering me, and that was Gretta. All afternoon she had a stone cold look on her face that told me she hated having to sit there. She had known what was in store I thought, that we would be visiting Ed's relatives and *not* shopping. I never knew why she had decided to join us on the trip. She pouted all afternoon, but I could do nothing about it, so I tried to ignore her and sat back while watching Ed enjoy his first, and probably last, visit with members of his extended family.

Towards the end of the afternoon, they asked us to stay overnight saying, "We have an indoor bathroom now." We declined however since we already had plans to take a train from Warsaw to Cracow the next morning. I was touched by their sincere generosity. We said our goodbyes, expressing the best way possible our joy and happiness at having met them and spending the afternoon in their home.

Then we got into the car, Ed in the front seat with Heino, and me in the back seat with Gretta. At that point she turned to me and blasted away at me in English telling me how angry and upset she was. She said she had no idea of what the afternoon was going to be like. Had she known....!!!! Then, like a child, she swung her body around, turned her back on me and looked out the window all the way back to Warsaw. I did not argue back, no point in it I thought to myself, and never was I a fighter like that in any case. She stayed in stony silence in that rigid position the whole way to Warsaw, which was at best, a drive of two hours, and she *never* said a word or moved an inch.

When we finally got back to the hotel, we tumbled our weary bodies out of Heino's car and thanked him profusely for taking us to see Ed's family, and for the other trips he had taken us on earlier in the week. He had been so lovely and generous with his time. Because we were leaving for Cracow the next morning, I was not sure we would ever see him again.

As it turns out though, once we returned from Cracow and on our last night in Warsaw before flying back to England, Heino invited us to supper at his house. He was a good cook and we had a delicious meal. Gretta was not particularly friendly, but at the end of the evening I 'turned the other cheek', gave her a hug and a sincere thank you for everything. She was so stunned it showed in her face. She knew not what to do or say, so she stormed away into another room of her house! Heino said nothing about her to us, but he told us he loved us, gave both of us big bear hugs, and wished us well, safe traveling and much happiness in England.

Auschwitz

"The weight of this sad time we must obey...speak what we feel, not what we ought to say...the oldest have borne most; we that are young, shall never see so much nor live so long."

King Lear
—Shakespeare

The morning after the visit to Ed's family, we boarded a train for Krakow (Polish spelling). The train ride was lovely and then we took a taxi to our hotel in the center of the city. That taxi driver was so sweet, he asked me to take a picture of him and Ed next to his taxi. We registered and then were shown to our rooms and spent some time resting. Our main goal while in Krakow was to visit the Auschwitz complex and the Jasna Gora Monastery, home to the Black Madonna of Czestochowa.

After dinner at the hotel that evening, Ed and I went to the front desk to ask about tours to the concentration camps of Auschwitz and the monastery. We learned from the lady at the desk that there were many tours available, but you had to take a separate bus tour to each site. (There was no bus tour that visited both sites on the same tour as they were about an hour or more from each other). Each tour took at least four hours on separate days.

Ed groaned quietly (long, slow trips in crowded buses exhausted him because of his chronic back pain) and left me to figure out what to do and went on up to our room. The lady at the desk spoke English well enough, so I didn't need his help translating.

"I think the bus tour is too expensive and it takes almost a whole day to visit each site and we don't have much time. Is there any other way we could visit these two places in one day?" I asked her.

"There is a hotel down the street in the center of Krakow," she told me slowly since her English was somewhat limited, "that has drivers. Any of them would love to take you in their private car."

I shuddered inside because we were on a limited budget. "Won't that be terribly expensive?" I asked.

"Oh no, no," she replied sweetly, "I don't think so. That way, you can go to the two places in one day and the cost will be less than two days on a bus. Also, the buses are always crowded with many people visiting these two famous areas and you would be much more comfortable in a touring car."

"What a lovely lady," I thought…I mulled this over and knowing how tired Ed and I were, I felt certain this was just the solution we wanted.

Excitedly I asked, "How do I find this hotel?"

"Just go out this front door and walk to the right, then at the corner turn right, walk a few yards straight ahead and you will see the hotel…it is a nice place and they are most helpful."

I thanked her profusely and hustled right on down to the hotel never stopping to tell Ed what I was doing. He was resting and I was sure he would never notice the time anyway!

I found the hotel right away. It was situated just before the marvelous 'square.' I could see the beautiful church with the twin towers, both different and each at a different height from the other. I found a driver very easily just inside the lobby of the other hotel. I talked briefly with him in English and he quoted a price to me that did turn out to be less than what the two buses would have cost us. The lady at our hotel was correct in all she told me. This driver would charge a small amount for a journey of one day and we could see everything we had planned on seeing in one day and more comfortably as well. I sealed the deal.

"I vill be at your Hotel at 10 a.m. vaiting for you in mine car and ve vill go to Auswitch and Our Lady of Chestahova and you vill have a good time!" he told me in his heavily accented voice. He was excited about the trip!

I beamed at him and said, "That is perfect, just right for us." We shook hands and off I went to our hotel, although I wanted very much to shop in that beautiful and bountiful huge square nearby. But Ed would be anxious if I was gone too long and I wanted to share my good news. He was most happy with all I told him and we both fell into bed after our dinner and slept soundly until the next morning when we rose in time for breakfast.

We were ready to go in the morning, and although our driver was early at the hotel, he did not rush us at all. We went out to his car in the front of our hotel. I decided to have Ed sit in the front seat since he could converse a little in Polish and also see better through the windshield of the car. I could relax in the back and enjoy all of the scenery as well. I made myself comfortable and remained seated calmly in the back for the whole day.

"Me…Stachu," the driver said thumping his chest with his right hand as he started up the car. Ed replied, also thumping his chest, "Me, Edju…"

As I sat in the back seat I watched the two men trying to talk with each other. I found it almost comical watching them struggle for the correct words in either language. Ed's hands moved all over the place in the air as he tried to speak Polish. They talked on and on for a while as Stachu drove his car and then, the strangest thing happened.

Stachu stopped the car on the side of the country road, got out, and rushed around to the back of the car. Ed and I thought he must have had to go to the bathroom. He slammed the trunk door shut and quickly came back to the front seat of his taxi holding in his hands a large photograph album. He made himself comfortable in the front seat once again and then opened his album. Inside the cover it said, "to Stachu with great appreciation, from Steven Spielberg and family."

The driver started talking with great excitement and pointed rapidly and excitedly to his chest..."Me, Stachu...was body guard and driver for Steve Spielberg and his family," and then thumped his chest one more time, repeating, "Me...Stachu!" "Me...Stachu...his driver, all the time, all the time...he was here...Mr. Spielberg...making movie!" His English was definitely halting, but good enough for us to understand what he said.

He was obviously so proud he could have popped the buttons off of his chest, if he had had any buttons. He went on to the first picture, and not wanting to be left out since I was sitting in the back seat, I leaned forward and hung over the two front seats trying to see what was in his precious album. Stachu said, pointing rapidly and tapping several times on the photo while he spoke, "Picture...me and Steve Spielberg," then he would look up at both of us while a delightful and happy smile filled his whole face awaiting our reactions. Of course we praised him and told him we were happy to see this wonderful picture. He then turned to the next photo, still hammering on the next picture with his pointing finger...

"Me and Steve Spielberg and Mrs. 'lady' Spielberg!"

He was so excited I wished I could have captured it on moving film. He turned another big page, still pointing, "Here...Mr. and Mrs. Steve Spielberg and all children!" Again, his excitement grew with each picture. His smile seemed wider and his gestures, wider still with pure love and excitement.

"Now, you see Mr. and Mrs. Spielberg, and family, and friends," and he would turn to another page and on and on through each page of his precious album he went, filling us with information. I was sure the Spielbergs had been in Krakow for many months making the movie and quite possibly a year, since the making of a movie is not accomplished quickly. Our driver Stachu was with them every minute of the day and night it seemed. No wonder he was excited. I would have been also!

We went through every eight by ten inch photograph on each page of this precious and huge album until we saw and learned about the whole thing. We missed nothing of Stachu's whole time with Mr. Spielberg! When he was finished he gently took his precious album to the back of the car and placed it in the trunk again and off we went to Auschwitz. I smiled and nodded through the whole parable as I could not speak in his language at all except to say "jinculia" which means "thank you"!

The album was obviously a gift the driver treasured and since Ed was Polish, Stachu was clearly enjoying using some of his English and much of his Polish on

Ed. Ed was in 'seventh heaven' sitting in the front seat listening to Stachu's stories in halting English and Polish. I was happy for both of them and most content in the back seat watching and listening to all of this repartee. I decided I would really have to see the movie *Schindler's List* once we got home, after knowing the Speilberg's almost intimately; well…not really intimately, but I felt I did!

Not long after, we arrived at Auschwitz. Stachu stayed with his car and Ed and I set off to tour the concentration camp, mostly on our own because the whole place was so horrific we could not imagine 'chatting' with other people in an official group tour.

The first thing we saw when we entered the area was the famous sign, (the sign had been stolen not too long ago but was recently recovered) printed in German, *arbeit macht frei* meaning; *Work sets you free*. How incongruous! **What a bold lie!**

A long and sorrowful, "*Ohhhh!*" was all I could muster as we entered the camp beyond this famous sign at the gate. All was more horrible, much more horrific than I could ever have imagined. It was all so unbelievably sad…yes, we knew it had all happened, but here it was now, and right in front of us. All the starch was snatched right out of us as we passed through the gateway and looked around.

We entered some barracks. Eight inch by ten inch photographs in black frames were hanging in perfect precision along all the walls of some of the barracks with the names of the dead people printed neatly underneath the photos. Ed pronounced all of the names, which would have been a bit difficult for me since the names were all in Polish. Many of these names Ed knew from attending the Polish School while living in the Polish Parish in Lowell. They would have been the older relatives of the people currently in Ed's Parish Church. This was profoundly sad.

I remember vividly as a child of maybe ten or twelve years seeing similar photos in the Lowell Sun newspaper. I will never forget those photographs of the thin, skeletal like, unclothed dead bodies with legs protruding every which way out of a mountainous pile of bodies.

The horrible past came streaming back to me. Here we were seeing all this once again. We saw other appalling pictures of the hundreds of thousands of emaciated people barely able to stand, no clothes, just standing and staring with an empty look at whoever took the pictures. I was becoming sicker by the moment, just looking at all of these.

We entered another building where we saw huge containers with hundreds of pairs of eyeglasses. We also saw large barrels filled with…hairpieces, yes…hair from scalps of prisoners…cut off before they entered the gas chamber! To this day I still can see a large…thick and long…yellow braid taken from some young woman's head while on her way to her death.

As a young and naïve child in the 1940s I could not understand all those photos I had seen in the newspaper. I had to ask my mother what it all meant. But I will never forget the horror I felt when I first learned about Auschwitz. And now…now that I have seen it for myself some forty to fifty years later, I will *never…ever…*forget any part of our visitation to Auschwitz. All was beyond belief, and to think this happened in our allegedly civilized lifetime was beyond the pale…

We entered more barracks where the prisoners were kept. They did not sleep in comfortable quarters. There were rows and rows of bunk beds. The bunk beds were stacked one over the other, in some places five beds high or maybe six. It seemed that the prisoners had hardly any room to breathe while they slept. And, then we were shown the ovens in which the prisoners were burned or gassed to death!

The whole tour ate away at us emotionally. We said our own individual prayers as we walked through the barracks and by the photographs. Death was lurking everywhere one turned. Birkenau, another camp nearby was no different than Auschwitz; they were together, virtually next to one another. We were satisfied that we finally saw this horrific killing site, but we were sad the whole time we were there.

I was so disturbed and upset while there that I almost wished we had not gone to see it, but…I am not sorry we did. Does that make any sense? I feel it was important to see the site in person and learn what happened when Hitler massacred the Jews. Somehow, those of us who have seen this evidence of massacre must insure that such a mass extermination would *never…ever happen again!* The scenes I witnessed on this occasion will never leave my mind!

We also saw where some individuals were shot and killed at the 'Firing Wall' also called 'The Wall of Executions.' We were told that fresh flowers are placed every day at the wall by various and sundry people who wish to do a little something for the dead, or maybe… for their own peace of mind also!

These camps were not ONLY where hundreds of people were put to death each day; inside the camp, for those who lived, there was a constant struggle for life and to retain human dignity. They had little food or clothing. The Jewish prisoners were forced to empty the gas chambers and to burn the corpses. Then, ironically, each group of Jewish prisoners who emptied the gas chambers were killed after a few months since they witnessed the crimes and needed to be 'done away with' so as not to be able to report the killings later. One report I read estimated that about 1.5 million people were executed in the concentration camps.

At the end of our tour we watched an old and short movie report, something that was shown when I was about fourteen years old in the movie theatres at home. (And yes, I remembered having seen it as a young teenager! It was an overview of what we had just seen at Auschwitz, and all I remembered is the showing of the bodies, lumps and piles of bare naked thin, skinny bodies…and hair and eyeglasses and ovens.) And then on our way out of this theatre at Auschwitz we saw again the huge heaps of eyeglasses and in another large bin, the hairpieces. The hairpieces made me so ill physically I wanted to vomit… truly, it was a horrible spectacle.

Then it was time for us to leave. I could not stay another minute longer. I was feeling ill. The bus tours of Auschwitz stay as long as four hours. I was more than content to have stayed only two hours…

Also, I must add here, a quote from Shakespeare's Richard of Gloucester speech:

> *Now is the Winter of our discontent*
> *Made glorious summer by this son of York.*
> *And all the clouds that loured upon our house*
> *In the deep bosom of the ocean buried*
> *Now are our brows bound with victorious wreaths.*

Jasna Gora Monastery

After touring the camps, we found Stachu who had been on the lookout for us, and he took us to the Jasna Gora Monastery, an hour or so north of the concentration camps. The monastery is home to a painting known as 'The Black Madonna of Czestochowa.' According to legend, it was painted by Luke, the Evangelist, on a tabletop built by Jesus himself. St. Helen, mother of Emperor Constantine, and a collector of Christian relics in the Holy Land later discovered the icon. The icon was then enshrined in the Imperial City of Constantinople, according to the legend, where it remained for five hundred years. (St. Helen was also responsible for bringing to Rome the staircase, which Jesus Christ was touted to have climbed to see Pontius Pilate. I felt privileged to have seen that staircase in Rome while on another trip, with the blood stains of Jesus still on the stairs in differing spots.)

The painting of the Black Madonna eventually arrived in Poland in 1382. The icon had been attacked several times over the course of many years; the face of the Virgin was slashed and the icon was left in a puddle of blood and mud during one battle, but then rescued. It seems the church and icon went through many fierce battles through the centuries including World War II when the Germans took over Poland and Hitler forbade its viewing.

Fortunately, it has survived and pilgrimages are made constantly by groups from all over the world to see this famous icon. The icon itself, as I remember, is kept in darkness except for one hour a day when it is unveiled and people can see it in full…in the church. We were there for the unveiling time, thanks to our loyal and noble Stachu. It was an emotional time, and we were certainly so pleased to see the famous 'Black Madonna of Czestochowa.'

Following that, Stachu drove us back to our hotel where we said warm, loyal, loving and most grateful goodbyes. Big hugs went around amongst all three of us several times as we thanked him for being so wonderful to us! And in my mind's eye I can still see his car pulling away from us at the curbing…

Krakow Market Square

Thanks to the excellent service of Stachu and his taxi, the day before, we now had an extra day to explore Krakow itself. The next day, after a good night's sleep and a huge Polish breakfast in the hotel we went to the famous Cloth Hall in Market Square; toured St. Mary's Church; St. Floryan's Gate; and the Czartoryski Museum.

Ed's father's first name was Floryan, so seeing Floryan's Gate was of particular interest to us. It was a large tower in what had once been a great protective rampart around Krakow. First built in the early 1300s it marks the beginning of Krakow's Royal Road upon which many processions of kings and queens and other historic figures took place over the centuries.

That day was sunny and warm and many artists sat around in the area painting and displaying their art for sale. We stopped a while to admire Floryan's Gate and all the art exhibits. We attempted to study all the paintings but that would have taken a vast amount of time, therefore, we glanced at all and studied, so to speak, a few that had become favorites of ours. The day was like a Christmas Day…I felt as a child feels when he receives a few toys and does not know which toy to play with first; the child then goes from one to the other and back again all day long. I love original paintings!

It was at the Czartoryski Art Museum, near our hotel, that I had the opportunity to see an original Leonardo da Vinci painting, titled 'The Lady with the Ermine.' I had been looking forward to seeing it for some time. The museum was surprisingly small, but it held numerous treasures in addition to the da Vinci painting.

No picture taking was allowed in the museum. None! That was the first sign we saw after entering the tiny museum. Ed hastily put his little camera away in an inner pocket! Then we saw a caretaker, an older man in charge of the museum. Ed started talking in Polish to this elderly gentleman, his skills having improved during our visit. He talked quite well with the old man, actually. I was quite impressed with Ed and his ability to communicate in Polish.

Not understanding anything at all that they were saying, I wandered off and gazed for quite a while at Da Vinci's 'The Lady with the Ermine.' Then, the next thing I knew the elderly gentleman came over and insisted, in his Polish language, that Ed take a picture of me standing in front of that same painting. He knew full well that Ed had a camera in his pocket. I was shocked, since the signs all over the little museum insisted, *No Photography*…but then, being so happily surprised, I smiled for the camera. It turned out to be a lovely picture of the 'Lady and the Ermine' and me…*Mary*! I must say, he was a nice old man and obviously wanted to give us something to take back home. Such a lovely memory!

The Museum being so small, we went through the remainder of it in a very short while. There were some other paintings equally as important, although not by da Vinci. However, my mind was so focused on da Vinci that it took awhile to grasp that the museum had some paintings by Rembrandt. They were residing all alone in their own room. Although I found Rembrandt's paintings to be impressive I did find that all of them tended to be dark overall. I personally prefer lighter and brighter colors so, Rembrandt was not high up on my list of favorite artists!

St. Mary's Church was a short walk down the street from the small Czartoyski Art Museum; the church was just opposite one side of the famous, long and beautiful 'Cloth Hall.' Speaking of which I must add, in order to see all that was in the Cloth Hall one would need a month's holiday. It was definitely long and large and most attractively filled with beautiful hand made, home made goods and other merchandise just as lovely! We did our best, racing through, since we were a bit short of time. We loved it, and it was oh…so packed with splendid things to buy and filled with people, plus it was almost as long as the huge 'square' itself.

St. Mary's Church was most unusual and we could not understand, for a moment, what was so different about it, but then we paid more attention to the two towers on the outside. One was quite a bit shorter than the other and the designs of the tops of the towers were totally different.

It took me a while to find out why, but find out…we did! The original St. Mary's Church was built in 1397. However the towers were added in the 1500s. The church's two towers, as I said before were of differing heights and, as well, there is quite a legend attached to the building of the towers and the heights of the towers.

The following is what we learned: once the decision was made to add two towers to the body of the church, two brothers embarked on the task. When the elder realized that his tower was much shorter, he murdered his brother out of envy. The legend goes on to say, that secret forces completed the construction of the tower in the name of the murdered brother. Whatever came to pass, the murderer was wracked with remorse: on the day when the church was to be consecrated, he pierced his heart with the same knife he used to kill his brother, and dropped dead from the top of his tower to the ground below. Therefore, the steeples are as thus: one short and one tall tower.

To this day, there is a lone trumpeter in the taller tower who plays the 'Hejnal Mariacki' every hour on the hour. The plaintive tune breaks off in midstream to commemorate the 13th century trumpeter, who was shot in the throat while sounding the alarm before the Mongol attack on the city. It is amazing. Everything stops in the surrounding area as people listen to that lone trumpeter in the taller tower, playing his lonesome notes and then abruptly stops…at… one assumes, the point where the lone trumpeter of years ago was killed by an arrow in the throat.

Our last day in Krakow also happened to be our 40th anniversary. We celebrated with a lovely dinner at the famous Wierzynek Restaurant. The waiter somehow found out it was our anniversary. Consequently, all the attention came to the American couple visiting while sharing their anniversary with the Poles… the dinner and evening in that restaurant turned out to be fun and most special since almost everyone in the restaurant came to us to shake hands and congratulate us. It was a memorable evening. I believe Ed's ability to speak Polish and his generally happy mien brought us all together with the waiters. Since the restaurant was almost empty, I am certain that also helped.

After that delightful and happy anniversary dinner we sauntered back to our hotel which was just a short walk around the corner. We had to pack our suitcases to go home, wherever it was at that point. I muttered to Ed while packing, "Ed, where is our home?" He replied, "Some days…lately…I'm not too sure!"

Following that lovely trip to Poland, we spent a month to six weeks of the summer with our family in the states. Of course, we had rented out our home in Dracut for all the years I worked in DODDS. So, when we came back to visit family and friends for a few weeks every summer, we had no place of our own to stay. We managed however, with the graciousness of my good friend Susan Rogers, a dear and close teacher friend from Sanborn School in Andover, MA and her husband Bob. They were extremely kind and generous each summer when we 'piled in on them'. Other good friends were also generous with their time and homes, but most importantly we saw Eric and Kelly and children at their home, and Susan and Amy as much as possible at their apartments…and all was well.

England, Year Two

School started again at the West Ruislip School. The previous school year had ended well. Therefore, I was pretty sure all would be equally as fine this year. I discovered after teaching so many years that a good attitude can take you far.

The production of *Oliver!* had been such a smashing hit with the students that one of the first questions the children asked when classes resumed were, "What play will we do this year, Mrs. G?"

"Will it be another musical like last year's *Oliver*, Mrs. Guziejka?" another student chimed in.

"Mrs. G., can we all be in the operetta again like in *Oliver!*?" a third child eagerly asked.

"You will all be in it and you will be just as wonderful in this year's operetta as you were in last year's operetta," I answered. They all smiled contentedly and we went on with our music lesson.

But before I could begin working on producing operettas with the students,

I had to start driving myself to school from our apartment in Gerrard's Cross. As I've mentioned before, driving on the 'other side' of the road was not easy for me. Ed had been great about getting me to and from school the previous semester, but I could not depend on him forever.

After practicing with Ed on back roads quite a few times I realized that the time had come and I must drive myself to school alone.

"I am driving today, you do not have to rush your breakfast," I said to Ed one morning.

"What? You're driving?" he said in great surprise.

"Yes, I think I'm ready and I promise, I will drive slowly and carefully," I assured him.

"Well, if you really think so. Remember, I don't mind driving you today," Ed replied dubiously.

"No," I said, "I have to start some time and today is as good a time as any for me to drive."

Off I went, confident and happy. A few minutes went by; I felt self assured and unafraid and my driving was fine for a few miles. That made me feel all the better. Then, I came to a round-a-bout…(here we call it a rotary) and confidently went to the right…*wrong!*

I slammed my foot on my brakes barely missing a smash-up with a tiny English school bus filled with young students! I nearly fainted. I had braked quickly and the lady bus driver had braked even more quickly. Needless to say she was absolutely furious. She clambered out of the bus and I felt if she could have hit me she would have.

"I…am so sorry…I thought…I thought I was driving around the rotary the correct way…" I said in a whimpering voice. Tears were starting to flow freely down my face. Then I saw Gene Jenkis, the fifth grade teacher at my school, who I previously noticed had been in back of me most of the way. He put his arm around my shoulders and led me back to my car. The irate and furious English school bus driver drove away with her children.

"Follow me to school," Gene said firmly. Of course, at that point, I was so nervous and so weepy all I could do was follow him to school like a robot. I was also thoroughly embarrassed to have had him see me in that predicament.

We arrived at the school fence. He parked, on the road by the curb, (on the opposite side of course) and then got out of his car. He calmly walked over to me and put his left arm around my shoulders, I had gotten out of my car by then, and he looked me squarely in the face and said…nicely, "Starting tomorrow, I am driving you to school …every morning!" And…he did!

Daughter Susan's Visit

It was during this second year in England that our oldest daughter Susan came to visit us. She had Multiple Sclerosis (finally diagnosed seven or eight years earlier) and was not getting better. She had been to England at least twice before. Once, when she was a high school student almost 20 years earlier, she had taken a trip with her Shakespeare class. (How we found the money to send her on that trip, I'm not sure; most likely my mother contributed a few dollars.) At any rate, Susan had a wonderful trip and learned so much with her class about Shakespeare and England.

Then, when I was taking my sabbatical year in England, she visited us during her Christmas break from college. Now that we were living in England again, she expressed a desire to visit once more. We were not sure how she would manage it though, given her deteriorating health. She was semi-wheelchair bound at the time. Her husband John could only take a couple of weeks off from work, not the full six weeks she wanted to be with us. But Susan was brave and determined, and somehow she managed to fly from Boston to England alone.

Ed and I were delighted. She was able to spend six weeks with us in the Beaconsfield house. Her condition varied considerably from day to day at this point. Sometimes she could walk around with few problems, and other times she could not walk at all. But she had her wheelchair with her at all times.

I of course had to teach school while she was here, but was able to take a few days off here and there to take her on special trips with Ed. On the weekends of course we traveled to as many of the places she wanted to see as we could. And a few times she and Ed went out on daylong train tours.

I have a lovely photograph of Susan in front of the famous 'Crooked House' near Windsor Castle. That was one of her favorite places to visit—-she also loved watching the swans in the moat outside the castle. There were at least fifty of them swimming around and going after the bits of food tourists would throw to them.

After a few weeks, her husband John arrived and we made a few more trips together into London since John could push the wheelchair with Susan even better than Ed or I could. We had our favorite sites: Trafalgar Square, St. Martin's of the Fields church, Buckingham Palace, Big Ben, Westminster Abbey, the

Tower of London, the art galleries. We loved them all and we never tired of seeing them it seemed.

> *Wisely and slow, they stumble that run fast…*
>
> ### Romeo and Juliet
> ### —Shakespeare

Then John and Susan expressed a desire to go to Scotland for a few days on their own by train. We helped them make arrangements for a trip that was to last four days. We saw them off, and they had a wonderful time seeing sites she had always wanted to see.

Everything had gone 'without a hitch' until they were returning home by train. While in the process of boarding, the conductor said, "Sorry ma'am but you will have to leave your wheelchair here at the entrance, you cannot bring it to your seat."

Well, that was a bit upsetting for Susan, since she never knew at what moment she would need it, or when she could or could not stand or walk.

"Suppose I have to go to the Ladies Room?" she asked the conductor.

"Your husband will have to bring the chair to you Ma'am and then bring it back here," he politely answered.

Well, they did as they were told. The hours went by and all was well until the train came to a station stop. People came in and out of the train as usual and then the train started up. John and Susan were looking out the window at the people going by here and there, then Susan said with great anxiety in her voice, "John!" while grabbing his arm and shaking it.

"John, look there, that looks like my wheelchair rolling by…and there's a man pushing it!" Then she added, more alarmed, "I know that's my wheelchair, see my cushion on the seat?"

John got up in a hurry, but the train had already started moving. Now, what to do…

He found the conductor and told him someone had stolen his wife's wheelchair. The conductor said in his charming English accent, "Oh…dear, that is impossible, why, it is right here…"

The conductor and John looked and then the conductor looked again…but could not find it. The conductor became most frantic with many words of "oh dear, oh dear"… needless to say, Susan and John were also frantic.

By then, several miles had gone by. The only hope they had was that the conductor could call someone at the station to stop this man from stealing the wheelchair.

John and Susan arrived at our home in Beaconsfield with no wheelchair at about 9 p.m. Susan was crying to the point of hysteria, as John was carrying Susan into the house and needless to say, my tears started and then I turned most angry at the same time…at the theft, of course.

I wiped my tears away since they were doing no good at all. John got Susan seated somehow and gave her a drink while I flew to our telephone and started with what seemed an endless series of telephone calls to British Rail! While awaiting their return calls, which did not come soon enough, I made another call, and another. Finally, after several angry, but polite and firm conversations with the British Rail staff, we were left waiting to hear what the outcome was going to be.

At last, a telephone call arrived. It seems three drunken men had taken the wheelchair and were trying to get it into a taxi. Some people at the railroad station thought this rather queer therefore someone in authority at the railroad station stopped the taxi and called the policeman on duty. They then removed the wheelchair and left it safely in the station waiting word from the owner, which, of course, never came since the train had carried them on homeward.

Finally, after several hours, an operator from British Rail called and said, "Mrs. Guziejka, the wheelchair will arrive at….such and such a station." I forget now the name of the station.

"But that is sixty miles west of our home. How do you expect us to retrieve it?" I asked after I calmed myself down. It was well after midnight at this point.

"Oh…we will have it put into a taxi cab and it will be delivered to your door and at no expense to you," she answered politely. "The chair should be at your home in a little more than an hour."

Indeed it was. At about one o'clock in the morning, as we were all sitting around waiting for the ring of the doorbell, Susan…my poor Susan, was an emotional and physical mess, totally distraught, feeling ill, but wanting to wait up to see her chair. She had to make certain the chair would work correctly for her to use it after all it had been through.

Finally, the doorbell sounded. It was the chair. The taxi man brought it up the stairs, pillow and all and placed it gently into the foyer of our house. We thanked him profusely, he would take no money, since British Rail was paying his services, but Ed insisted on a generous tip. We were all happy, silly happy from exhaustion, and then I looked at Susan and saw how weary she was. Fatigue for an M.S. victim is not good. Off to bed we trod, up the stairs and over the walkway on the second floor... off went Mary to bed while John put Susan to bed...I was the only one who had to get up at an early hour in the morning. Not sure if I slept at all that night, but, nevertheless, I had to go to school and happily start singing with all my cherubs.

Apart from the wheelchair incident, Susan did have a wonderful time, and she never forgot the visit. She mentioned how much she enjoyed the trip frequently in future conversations and thanked us profusely for helping her make it happen.

My bounty is as boundless as the sea,
My love as deep; the more I give to thee,
The more I have, for both are infinite.

Romeo and Juliet
—Shakespeare

Not long after Susan and John returned home, I received a call from a lawyer while I was at school. Having *no* idea what it could be about, I did not feel like talking on the phone in front of the students. I asked another teacher to watch my class and 'flew' to the office to use the phone there.

"Hmmn, Mrs. Guziejka, I am Mr. Neaves from the Bank of England...and I have called to inform you that you must move. You must vacate your Beaconsfield dwelling and as soon as possible, I am sorry to say," the caller said politely in his lovely English accent. There was no explanation about why, just, "Sorry, but you must move out of the Beaconsfield house as soon as possible." And that was that.

I called Ed; the thought of moving again almost made me have a nervous breakdown in my classroom! We had not yet been in this house for eight months! But...I held on to my nerves, kept them in place. I spoke to the principal at our school and she gave me the name of a lawyer who helped U.S. government employees in situations like this. I set up an appointment for that afternoon after school.

I told the lawyer what had happened. He in turn called the Bank of England, and we learned that although the owners of our house in Beaconsfield collected their rent monthly from us they had *not* been using it to pay the mortgage.

The bank was going to repossess the house. The banker was polite, understanding and nice, as was my lawyer, but then, as they both said, the bank was not in the business of renting houses, so therefore, there was no choice. We had to move. Then the bank would sell the house to someone else to recoup its losses.

Now, the Beaconsfield house had been far from perfect. In fact there were major problems with the kitchen. One day not too long before the phone call from the bank, Ed and I had been sitting in the sunroom. We heard strange, continuous scratching noises, not loud, coming from the kitchen. I went to investigate and found the upper wall cabinets were inching down from the ceiling. I yelled to Ed and he and I stood there watching as the cabinets slowly slid onto the counter below. We were in shock. Everything was a mess: flour, food stuffs, dishes, toaster, etc. Since our landlord had been so slow to take care of other problems in the past, I groaned inwardly thinking, "this will take some time to be repaired…!"

Then, just a week or two after that, there was the phone call from the bank! Despite the kitchen problem we had grown to enjoy living there. The gardens were beautiful and the sunroom was delightful.

In addition, within a day or so of receiving the eviction notice, I had a doctor's appointment for an annual 'check-up.' It was during this examination that the doctor found a small lump in my breast that would require minor surgery to remove. Well, that news was almost more than I could handle given everything else that was going on.

I went home to our Beaconsfield house and gave Ed the news about the surgery. He groaned aloud! I cried! He held me tightly and reassured me all would be well.

We had to house hunt, we had to move and I had to have surgery and I also had to teach school every day! I felt I was sinking into a trough of despair. Words cannot describe the fear of cancer, then worrying about the work, the horrible amount of work that went into moving. And we still had to find a place to live. I was not sure how I would be able to cope. In the last eighteen months we had moved twice (from Turkey, to Italy, to England) and I was not sure I could handle another move.

I called the school office and told them I needed a few days off for surgery; they would have to supply a substitute teacher. Then, before I went to the hospital, a friend called to tell us that Bill Kilty, a DODDS Inspector of European Schools, was about to retire and would we be interested in renting the house he was living in which was in the next village over from Beaconsfield.

Well, following my minor surgery the next day, Ed drove me to Gerrard's Cross, the next village over, to see Mr. Kilty's house. I don't clearly remember the visit since I was still recovering from the surgery's anesthesia. However, the house was set back from the street and there were large trees and flowerbeds on the grounds. There were enough rooms for us, with an extra bedroom or two. The house was bright and airy with very large floor to ceiling windows in the living room. The semi-oval dining room had windows from the middle of the wall to the ceiling. The only thing I did not care for was that all the walls were painted brown.

I whispered to my husband, "Ed, do you like it?"

"It will all be just fine, and there's a beautiful back garden and also beautiful views of all the gardens on at least three sides of the house," Ed replied,

"Yes, we would like to rent your home, Mr. Kilty," I told the owner.

"Wonderful, wonderful!" Mr. Kilty said, clasping his hands together joyfully. He told us the amount for the rent.

"It is a bit expensive!" I countered, in a mumbling voice, still feeling 'hung over' from the anesthesia.

"DODDS will pay for it, of that I am certain," Mr. Kilty replied.

He should know, I thought, since he had worked for DODDS for many, many years, not only as a teacher but also as an administrator.

I agreed, and looked at Ed, he agreed, and we all shook hands and off I went, home to bed.

Someone helped us find a mover, and my dear friend Carol Rupp helped us to move once again. She had been in DODDS so many years as a teacher, and then as a helper while her husband taught, that nothing seemed to faze her. Carol always had a positive attitude. The day we moved in, over she came to help unwrap and unfurl and carry; she also brought the dinner! She had brought the dinner the night we moved into the Beaconsfield Manse as well.

What a shock I went through that week and the next…eventually, however, things do have a way of working out and I survived. Every day something got put somewhere, although I felt I never knew where anything was for at least a year. I worked, Ed got the meals, as best he could, not being able to find anything in the kitchen for awhile either…and life went on for us in Gerrards' Cross.

However, the brown walls downstairs almost drove us crazy. You see, I love cream and white…my home in Dracut is all cream-colored walls. But, the Kilty's would not allow us to paint the walls any other color while living in their house.

As it turns out, the house itself was somewhat unusual and had quite an interesting history, which we learned about as we lived there. In fact, the history of the house was so unique, it inspired Ed to write an article I am going to include below.

The Dragon House

Looking out the bathroom window one day as I was getting ready to take a shower, I saw three birds, probably some kind of pigeon, walking toward the house on the narrow, ten foot lawn area with trees, bushes and other plants on either side. One of the birds walked on one edge of the lawn area while another was walking on the other edge. The third bird walked up the middle. They were heading towards the house and I imagined the birds were attacking me.

As I watched the attacking birds, I noticed a small white camper stop across the street. The first thing that came to my mind was the place was being cased. Then one woman got out and walked across the street into the wooded area and another woman followed close behind. They seemed to be looking at the birds. Then the ladies appeared to be most interested in our house, they were looking it all over. I had thought maybe they were bird watchers. I turned and continued to get ready for my shower.

The doorbell rang. "What now?" I said to myself and opened the window in the dressing room and shouted, "Hello!" The two women then appeared under my upstairs window. They introduced themselves as Lucy and Betty and asked if they could come inside to talk with me about something special. Lucy apologized for disturbing me and then went on to explain about the house being designed, on the inside, like a dragon and Betty, her friend, wanted to see it so she could write a story about it.

Quickly, I put on my bathrobe and went downstairs to let them in. The excitement on their faces was palpable and I too became excited. But I didn't know why or what for! Lucy explained her mother, Elizabeth Benjamin, was an architect, who had designed the house. Betty wanted to write a story about the house, she said, and it would be helpful if they could come in and see it first hand. Lucy said her mother lives in a borough of London, was in her late eighties, and the house is recorded as a 'listed' house. I was not quite sure what that meant, however.

We walked through the kitchen into the dining room. Looking everything over, Lucy explained how the dining room resembled the head of a dragon. (I hadn't seen that before). Lucy then led us into the living room and told us to face the fireplace. We did. Then she instructed us to turn right and look into the dining area but not focus on the brickwork. The bluish brickwork represented the dragon and it began just to the right of us. As you followed along, one could almost visualize that the windows represented the dragon's teeth. The brickwork takes off again and becomes the wall separating the kitchen from the living room with a fireplace in the center. The bricked wall represented the dragon's body. When you looked towards the door on the left, you could see the stairwell going upstairs.

I was shocked! I could vividly see the dragon's tail. It was going upstairs into my bedroom. My imagination was perfect. For me there was no question about the shape of the dragon.

Lucy said her mother designed the house for an Italian back in 1936. The outside and the inside of the house were supposed to be similar to Mussolini's house in Italy. Her mother decided to design the house to resemble St. George's Dragon due to her love of the unusual and to accommodate what the Italian man wanted.

I gave Lucy my telephone number and told her she was welcome to visit anytime and I also asked her to bring her mother sometime as well. When Lucy and her friend left, I decided to write this experience down, so off I went to my computer that was upstairs. I walked into the computer room and the first thing I saw was a small dragon sitting on the top of my desk.

When we were in Singapore we had bought some pewter symbols, actually they are napkin holders. They were round with the symbol on the top. They were symbols from the Japanese Fortune Calendar; there was a cock for Amy, a curled up sheep for Mary, and a **dragon** for me, Ed! Such a coincidence!

Elizabeth Benjamin, the architect did visit her 'dragon' house. She was delightful and delighted to see the house again. She did not like, however, what had been done to the outside of the house. The outside walls were almost completely covered with wisteria and vines, and surrounded by trees, which we thought were beautiful. There was no sign of anything shining white to symbolize St. George's armor, Elizabeth told us. She showed me a picture of the house without the vines and other plant growth.

She also brought a lovely book, as a gift; with pictures of all the famous people's houses she had designed and had built. So unusual in the early 1900s for a woman to be an architect, and a quite a successful one at that. She was a remarkable lady and here she was visiting me!

Mary had been working the first time Elizabeth and her daughter visited the house, so I asked if they could return again sometime when Mary was home. Mary really wanted to meet this interesting woman. They returned a few weeks later and we had another lovely visit.

Two weeks later a gentleman rang the doorbell. He was a representative of the Twentieth Century Society. This society was founded in 1979 to protect Britain's architecture and design after 1914. "East Wall," the name of the house in which we lived, was on their list. He wanted to know if his society could come and see the house.

I told him about the visits I had had recently with Elizabeth Benjamin and he became quite excited. He thought it would be wonderful if Elizabeth could be at the house at the same time as the members toured the house. I called her then and there, she answered, and accepted the invitation. Unfortunately, she had not checked her calendar prior to accepting the invitation, and a few days later she called back to say she would NOT be able to be there for the tour after all.

July 21, 1996 at 4:30 P.M. a busload of at least forty people came to see the 'dragon house.' What a time we had! I could see that some of the forty could not picture in their minds the house as DRAGON. I had no trouble with it though. The tour group then left.

Several days later, I got a call, from a woman who was in the process of writing a story about Elizabeth Benjamin, (the architect). It was unheard of in the thirties for a woman to do any architectural work, she said. She asked if she could come over with her camera crew and take some video shots of the 'dragon' house.

"Yes, of course you may come!" What else could I say? She said she would be there August 6. They came, and spent four hours filming every inch of the house it seemed. They promised to give me a copy of the tape. I never received it, much to my disappointment. I do have a copy of the published story about Elizabeth Benjamin, however.

One final note, June 5, 1998, Roy Sladen, a professor from Birmingham University came to see the 'dragon house.' He and I had a marvelous visit and

I shared with him all the events we had witnessed about the house since having moved in several years ago.

And here…Ed's story about the 'dragon house' ends.

If all the year were playing holidays,
To sport would be as tedious as to work:
But when they seldom come, they
Wished-for come.

Henry the Fourth
—Shakespeare

HMS Pinafore

I felt I could not live in the land of Gilbert and Sullivan without teaching my students about them and their music. So, I prepared the fourth, fifth, and sixth grades for Gilbert and Sullivan, the year after we performed *Oliver!* I read stories to them about operettas, (the word 'operetta' implies singing AND speaking, as opposed to 'opera' which is only singing); and about Gilbert and Sullivan; then discussed the operetta we were going to perform, the *H.M.S. Pinafore.*

There was a great group of parents who helped me with anything I needed when it came to producing musicals. They loved seeing what their children learned and accomplished with that experience. I met with the parents and told them what the children would be performing and the parents were happy knowing there would be great educational value to it all. In fact, one parent asked if we could do the operetta in a real theatre…instead of in the gym. I jumped at the thought, my heart almost fluttered, thinking maybe we could find a way to rent a theatre.

After more discussion, it was decided that I should look around to see if there was a suitable theatre available for the production. Well, you can imagine my joy when I found an appropriate theatre virtually around the corner from our school. The design was perfect, with a stage and then seats rising up on a slope from the stage. Everyone would be able to see the stage clearly. It was not too large fortunately and the acoustics were marvelous, just right for children's singing and acting voices. I never use microphones with little children's voices. They distort the child's singing voice and are a nuisance as well. The rental cost for rehearsals and the performance was $700.00 or about 1,400 pounds.

I went away from inspecting this theatre with a glow of happiness hovering around me while thinking about using it for *HMS Pinafore*!

The next day I went to the Principal, told her all about it and she also seemed thrilled about the whole idea and said, "Go for it, Mary. That will be great!" She then added though that she would need to discuss this idea at the next teacher's meeting.

The following Monday afternoon at the next teacher's meeting I told the teachers about the plan to produce *HMS Pinafore* with the fourth, fifth and sixth grade students, and to rent the theatre nearby. Well, the idea of renting the theatre did *not* go over well.

"That is a ridiculous amount of money to waste on a child's operetta, I will not hear of it!" one irate teacher bellowed as he jumped out of his chair.

Another teacher friend of his, a woman, stood up and said similarly, "I absolutely agree. I do not approve at all due to the expense. I have never heard of such a thing before!"

A few other teachers murmured in assent, seemingly agreeing. The sad part is, the ones that did approve said nothing, or very little at all.

The Principal then decided that the operetta would be held in the gymnasium instead of the theatre and *that was that*! When the meeting ended, I followed her down to her office. I was quite upset. I saw no harm in what we were doing and decided to defend my position. We sat and talked it all over in detail, and once again, sweetly but firmly, she said, "It is just not fair to spend that amount of money on a single group of children!"

"It is the parents' money we are discussing, not the school's money," I explained to her. "They are willing to pay the cost of renting the theatre. Half of the school children will be in the operetta and the other half will learn about the operetta by watching it; I always prepare the remainder of the children, the younger ones, in advance, as to what they will be watching and learning. Therefore, it cannot possibly be a waste!"

The principal was adamant however, never budged from her decision and therefore…I lost! I walked out as politely as possible and then went home and shared my anger with Ed. He was very good about listening and trying to help by giving suggestions. I was absolutely fuming, I was so angry!

The next day I called my set of parent helpers, we had a meeting, and they decided if that was what the principal wanted, then of course, we would have to go along with it. They had no choice from what I could see.

Then one parent said, "We will have the best theatre possible. You just wait and see, Mrs. Guziejka."

"You lay out what you want for a stage and our husbands will build it for you in the gym," another lady declared. "We will make it as close to wonderful as possible." And they did.

They built three levels of stage, which was necessary for the ship, the *H.M.S. Pinafore*. One level was on the floor, a slightly smaller one elevated and perched on that first one, and then another even smaller one on the very top of the 'ship' for the captain to stand looking out over the sea with his spy glass.

The whole structure eventually was hovering about half way up to the ceiling. Then they painted and made ship-like characteristics and it looked almost real! The mothers put paper up on the walls all around the gym and the paper became "painted waves" and portholes in the proper places and then…voilà! The ship was in the ocean, or, so it would seem to the audience! The parents worked two full weekends, early morning until late evening so as not to interrupt the physical education classes. It was a glorious ship and the waves were enough to make anyone seasick, (not really!) They asked what I had wanted and by george, they gave me what I wanted!

The cast and I worked on the songs and acting during music classes and after school in the gym. The costumes, thanks to Monroe's wife, Carol, who was in charge, were made; the girls had long skirts, with bustles in the back, (oh, they loved their costumes!) and we had English sailor type uniforms of the fashion from the late 1800s for the boys. Carol made old-fashioned collars for the boys on her sewing machine, and then the boys only needed white shirts under the collars plus long black ties, and black pants.

The show went on, all went well and the Admiral and the Captain and the leading ladies could not have been better. They even affected an English accent and their singing was lovely as was the whole entire chorus, ladies and sailors. The student who played Dick Deadeye was marvelous to the point of being a bit frightening, but funny!

I was thrilled. We had no orchestra, I never ever had an orchestra, but I played the piano. When it was all over I thought I would slide off the bench and end up in a puddle on the floor from exhaustion and anxiety.

A few days after the show had ended many of the students who were in the production wrote thank you letters to me. Also some of the teachers of the classes who attended had their students write congratulatory letters, but one letter stands out in my mind and I shall never forget what some of the words were.

The letter was from the student who played the Admiral, who made a gallant and pompous, royal entrance to the ship, entering from the back of the gym and processing down through the audience. Meanwhile the chorus sang the famous song, "Over the bright blue sea…comes Sir Joseph Porter K.C.B. etc." Then, the Admiral of the Navy reached the deck and the chorus stopped singing. He then, proudly looked to the front of the audience, then to the left, and last he looked to the right of the audience in a pompous and majestic manner. With his sword in his scabbard by his side, he sang in a very majestic manner, "I am the monarch of the sea…the ruler of the Queen's Navy…and these are my sisters and my cousins and my aunts…" never missing a note or a word. His singing and acting were absolutely splendid throughout the entire production. He had a lovely voice and for an Admiral, a great and POMPOUS demeanor!

One sentence from his letter, which stands out clearly in my mind, and has for years, was this one:

"Mrs. Guziejka, you gave me wings and helped me fly!!"

This 'Admiral,' this wonderful twelve year old boy…I found out later…had cancer! The parents of the child never mentioned it to anyone hoping that it had disappeared, gone away forever, I imagine. Yes…at the time, when he played the part of the Admiral so successfully, it was in a dormant stage. I was so very saddened and shocked when I heard about the cancer, and now, to this day, as I write my 'memoirs' I still wonder how he is and where he is…is he still with us?

❊❊❊❊

After a couple of years of teaching at the West Ruislip Elementary School, the student population was growing smaller. Not as many military personnel were stationed at the base nearby I suppose. At any rate, I had more time on my hands, so I was asked to be a teacher for TAG (talented and gifted) students. Fortunately, I had taken a two-week course at the University of Connecticut, so I was qualified/certified in that area.

In order to participate in the TAG program students had to be tested and that could take some time. Eventually I had eight students in the TAG program who met with me three times each week. I taught 'music' once a week to each class in the building. I also taught 'enrichment' once a week to each class in the building, and the 'TAG Enrichment' three periods per week, but not to each class and all children, just to a few designated super bright children. They were taken out of their normal classes to come to my special classes for gifted children.

I taught the music classes using the Kodaly Method of hand signals that helped the children produce beautiful sounds with their voices. They learned to sing in two-part and sometimes three-part harmony a cappella (without accompaniment). I prefer that method since I do not find constant accompaniment with a piano helps the children to sing better. Their tone quality does not improve whatsoever when their singing is constantly accompanied by a piano. In many instances where teachers always use recordings or piano to help the singers, the children grow very dependent on these tools and thence cannot sing as well alone or with a lovely musical pitch to their singing voices. The piano is a tool and therefore, before the children use the tool they must learn to sing independently and understand all that is happening.

I decided to take a break from producing musicals of one sort or another, and focus on studying Shakespeare and Charles Dickens with the students. Having already produced the musical *Oliver!* with some of the students, many were already familiar with Dickens and his work. I partnered with Pam Pullman, the Librarian/Media Center Director at the school, and consequently she and I both taught classes that involved projects, i.e. music, acting and watching appropriate films about Charles Dickens. She and I also organized field trips with the fifth and sixth grade classes to visit some of the Charles Dickens houses in and around London.

The most interesting trip we had with the students was to Dickens' Gad's Hill country house in Higham, Kent. Pam made the arrangements, which included an hour and a half bus ride to get there.

On that first day (we made several trips over the course of a few weeks because we wanted to allow all the fifth and sixth graders an opportunity to see this house, but we could only take about 50 students at a time on the bus), the bus driver let us off at the front door of the house and then found a place to park elsewhere.

I stepped forward and rang the doorbell. Waited. Then rang it again. Waited. And rang again. Waited. I began to grow anxious. Were we not expected? This was the day and the time that had been agreed upon.

Finally, an older man opened the door. "Madame," he said in a marvelously deep English accent, "school (ahem) is not in session"...he cleared his throat once again, then murmured, "how can I help you?"

I was confused. We knew Dickens' country home was now a school, but we had received permission and made arrangements to tour the home when school was not in session. I was wondering what had gone wrong, and Pam and I were looking at each other with puzzled expressions, when the older man then smiled, spread out his arms and with a loud and dramatic voice said, "Do, do, doooo come in. Ye are all most welcome."

He waved his arms around some more and continued in an outlandish and dramatic style, "My deahs, all of you, come right in...come right in." Then, slapping his chest with his hand he said, "I will show you around."

We were caught off guard by his change of manner and actions, but we went on in. First, he ushered us into the room that had been Charles Dickens' office (now the office of the headmistress, who was not present).

"Ye moosn't tooch anythin' now, ye just look and be careful and quiet," our tour guide told us. The students, who could only go in a few at a time because the office was so small, followed his instructions carefully and were as 'good as gold,' as the saying goes.

Our guide led us through numerous other rooms in the house, and finally escorted us into what turned out to be a small theatre where Charles Dickens acted out his stories for local audiences. The room was like a long, narrow classroom with a small stage at the far end with curtains.

"Now, ye all be sitten dune and I will go to the stage and show ye how Mr. Dickens acted out his stories," our tour guide told us.

The students were speechless, quite mesmerized by the attitude and speech of our guide. He went up on the stage behind the curtains, then came out and recited/acted out some lines from a Dickens story. The students giggled at his actions, which seemed to please the man no end.

Then he said, "Mr. Dickens luved to hear what the audience would say once he finished his actin' out of the parts, so, ye little ones, can ye guess wot he would do next?" and waved his hands over the audience. None of the students had any idea, nor did I, to be quite honest.

"Ye all watch me now," he continued. He opened the curtain and showed us a sliding door/window type arrangement centered in the back wall. "Mr. Dickens would 'ave the curtain pulled shut when he finished his actin', then he would rush to take off his mask, scarf, or whatever costume/disguise he had been wearin.' Then he would climb out o' the winder, and run round to the front of the 'ouse fast as he could, and join the crowd of people coming out of the small theatre! Yes, he mingled in with them and no one knew who he was."

Then with a giggle, the tour guide asked the students, "Do ye want to know why he did that? Can ye tell me?"

The children had no ideas…they just sat in their seats in amazed silence.

Bending over from the waist and with a wheezy laugh and holding his arms around his chest and sides, the tour guide continued, "Mr. Dickens joined the audience without his costume or disguise so 'e would NOT be recognized and so 'e could HEAR what people were sayin' 'bout his performance. He war a smart guy, warn't he?"

With that the students laughed, and we continued with our tour into the dining room.

"Ye all sit ye dune now and listen here," our tour guide continued. "Mr. Dickens was a-eatin' 'is lunch, when 'e stood up and clutched at his chest…then he moaned and groaned and fell…right SMACK onto the floor."

And as he said 'smack' our guide clutched at his chest, fell to the floor and moaned as a dying man would. As he 'died' he continued on in a somber and dramatic tone as if he were Dickens himself, 'am a 'avin'…a…'eart attack," and then he was quiet, lying there on the floor in the manner he felt Mr. Dickens had. He lay there in silence for a minute or two, then the tour guide jumped up and said, "After a minute or two on the floor, he was dead…'e died just like that!"

The students were stunned and silent at this performance. Pam and I were also surprised, but pleasantly so, we had never expected to have a guide who would bring Dickens so to 'life' for the students. It was an unforgettable performance!

"Do ye 'ave any questions for me now?" the guide asked at the end. By now the students had recovered from their shock and began to ask the man many questions. He had certainly warmed them up to the wonders of Dickens and his life.

Following our tour of Gad's Hill, we went into the town of Higham and toured a Dickens Museum, which I'm told is not in existence presently. I was saddened to learn it was closed because I thought it was a wonderful museum. It featured certain scenes from Dickens' books presented in tableau fashion with lifelike wax figures. In front of each scene was a button to push and a recording of that 'scene' would be heard. The figures were so real I found myself checking the chest of the figures to see if they might be breathing. There were eight to ten of these special tableaux, and the students, Pam and I enjoyed them all!

Then further on in the town we saw the 'Swiss Chalet' the French actor Charles Fechter had given to Dickens in 1864. It was not an entire chalet, but a full size replica of the front and the first and second floor rooms. Dickens had it constructed near his Gad's Hill home, and during the spring and summer months Dickens worked on many of his later works in his study on the top floor of this Swiss chalet, including *A Tale of Two Cities*, *Great Expectations*, *Our Mutual Friend* and the unfinished *The Mystery of Edwin Drood*. Later, in the twentieth century, the chalet was moved to the Dickens Center in town.

Also, while in the town we stopped by the outside of the Restoration House, which Dickens used as the inspiration for Miss Havisham's mansion in the novel *Great Expectations*. What a grand and imposing structure!

Then, having had our fill of Dickens, we walked on to the famous Rochester Castle, which had been built on the site of ancient Roman ruins. We ate a late picnic lunch on the grass outside the castle, then toured the castle itself, that had helped protect England's south-east coast from invasion during the medieval period.

Suddenly it was time to return to West Ruislip! Pam, the students and I were very happy, but oh so tired. The bus ride back to West Ruislip was unbelievably quiet I would say we had a 'crème de la crème day' all in all. And as I mentioned earlier, Pam and I made three more trips back to Gad's Hill over the next few weeks so that every student in the fifth and sixth grades could enjoy learning more about Charles Dickens.

"T'is a far, far better thing than I have ever done..."

A Tale of Two Cities
—Charles Dickens

A Midsummer Night's Dream

In the spring of one year at West Ruislip, I decided to produce Shakespeare's *A Midsummer Night's Dream* play with the schools fifth and sixth grade students.(Actually, *Comedy of Errors* and *A Midsummer Night's Dream* were each performed twice during the last four years I taught in England. I thought these two Shakespeare plays were the most suitable for my students' ages.) I had found an abridged version of the plays that kept Shakespeare's original words, but shortened some of the longer speeches and modified some scenes so that it could be acted by younger people.

The play calls for guards for the King who stand on stage, but do not speak. I had already selected some of the guards, boys who wanted to be involved in the play, wear a costume, but wanted to say absolutely *nothing*! That was fine from my point of view, since I knew they would still experience many facets of the drama, and at the very least become a bit acquainted with Shakespeare. Also, they would then finish the play with good feelings about what they did; of that I was certain.

One day, Rodney, a fifth grader, came to me after all other children had left the room. He was alone and usually never had anyone with him. He never spoke in front of anyone for that matter because he was extremely shy. He spoke hardly one word the whole year. When Rodney would talk to me, which was only once in a great while, he would wait until the room emptied out. Then he would stand close to me if I happened to be sitting at my piano, or my desk and barely whisper into my ear. Obviously, he did not sing either, but pretended a bit for me by mouthing the words when we had singing.

I had been diligently trying to do everything I could think of to make him more comfortable when he talked with me or in front of any of the other students, but I found it to be most difficult. I was gentle with him at all times and never, under any circumstances, would I embarrass him in front of the class.

On one particular day I was sitting on the piano bench when he approached me. He was so close to me that I could feel his breath upon my face. Since I was sitting on the piano bench and he was standing next to me, his head was level with mine. He bent forward, and whispered softly…softly in my ear, "Can I be a guard, Mrs. Guziejka? Can I be a guard for the King in the play?"

"Of course you can be a guard, Rodney!" I said as I turned to him while sitting on my piano bench smiling from ear to ear.

Rodney then muttered rapidly in my ear, and at this point he was almost sitting on my lap so no one else would overhear him although there was no one left in the room, "I don't want to have to say anything…do I have to say anything?"

He seemed quite scared, trembling…but determined…trying in some little way to tell me what his needs were.

"You can be a guard and you will not have to say one single word, Rodney, never…ever…unless you feel you want to." And, I emphasized the word, *you*!

Rodney then stiffened a bit, seemingly in fright, and whispered anxiously… "I have nothing to wear, Mrs. Guziejka…What will I do?"

"Mrs. Rupp will make you a costume, don't worry, and you will look just like all the other guards." A big smile slowly enveloped his face. I was so happy to be able to help Rodney, if only a little. I went home on wings of song!

Daily, at after school rehearsals, Rodney came to take his place in the line up of five to ten guards who took care of the King! We were rehearsing in the gymnasium, which was the only place available to us. Shy Rodney stood stiffly at attention and was obviously at ease with himself, listening carefully to Shakespeare's words, and learning, of course, as a result! He also was seemingly gaining in confidence. Each day that he returned to rehearsal he seemed a tad more comfortable with himself and me and the others.

Then one afternoon a man barged into the gymnasium through the doors at the back of the gym while we were rehearsing and hollered in a loud, crude voice, "Rodney, you *s.o.b.*…. (he did not spell it out, he used all the words!) get your a___ over here right now or I will go down and drag you home by your *blankety blank* hair!" There were a few more words in his awful speech, but I'm not going to repeat them here.

I nearly fell off the piano bench. I didn't know what to do. First of all, I could not imagine anyone doing that…to any of my students and in front of a whole group of youngsters and while the rehearsal was going on. I could not imagine anyone doing this at a rehearsal at all…and most importantly, I could not believe this brute of a man would do this to Rodney, or any child, for that matter.

I quickly looked at Rodney and he appeared to have shrunk in size. He disappeared in a matter of seconds from the line up of guards; he left so quickly I could not even go to him! Rodney scurried rapidly over to that horrible man with his head seemingly down to his toes…dropping his spear and costume as he hustled up to the back of the gymnasium. I was furious and at the same time…so very helpless! I had the whole cast of the play with me. I was quite alone and with no other adults present. I could not leave all of them, and I had no telephone. This whole miserable mess happened so quickly that I could not seem to pull my wits together fast enough to make a difference in Rodney's life. Rodney was gone before I could even decide what to do in a cogent manner. All the students stared at Rodney in quiet disbelief at his humiliation and embarrassment. I could have cried for him right on the spot.

Naturally, I went to the Principal's office as soon as I could find someone to watch the rehearsal for a few minutes and told her about the incident.

I later discovered, after a talk with the principal that the man who had burst into the gym lived with Rodney's mother. She had given written permission for Rodney to stay after school but must have asked this thug to fetch Rodney at the gym, never informing me of what was going to happen, of course. The mother was the one who was supposed to fetch Rodney.

Somehow, things worked out and within a few days Rodney came back to rehearsals, and he was in the play! He was proud as could be and I was also, of him and his performance. He said absolutely nothing, but followed instructions beautifully and had quietly adoring eyes for me whenever he looked at me. He still did not talk much, if any at all, that year.

That summer, Rodney's mother was transferred to another base and Rodney went with her. I never saw him again, but I still have fond memories of him and I hope and pray his life is going well.

That particular production of *A Midsummer Night's Dream*, with Rodney as a soldier, was one of my favorites. I have always especially enjoyed the end of the play when Puck addresses the audience:

> *If we shadows have offended*
> *Think but this and all is mended*
> *That you have but slumbered here*
> *While these visions did appear*
> *And this weak and idle theme*
> *No more yielding than a dream.*
> *Gentles do not reprehend,*
> *If you pardon, we will mend*
> *And, as I am an honest Puck*
> *If we have unearned luck*
> *To 'scape the serpent's tongue*
> *We will make amends 'ere long*
> *Else Puck a liar call.*
> *Give me your hands if we be friend*
> *And Robin will restore amends.*

The sixth grade boy who played the part of Puck delivered the lines perfectly. He descended from the stage into the audience as he gave his speech and exited through the front door of the gymnasium at the conclusion. The audience responded with an uproar of clapping for his performance. I can still see his face in that role, although I cannot, unfortunately, remember his name. **Methinks he was a Great Puck!**

Square Dancing and Folk Dancing

As I've mentioned before, I always incorporated square dancing and folk dancing into my music lessons with students; folk dancing for the younger grades 1-3 and square dancing for grades 4-6. One year while teaching at West Ruislip, I decided to have a 'Mother's Day' and a 'Father's Day' event. The students would invite their mothers to attend one of our regular square dance classes in the gym and then another day would be the fathers' turn to participate.

The event turned out to be even more of a success than I had imagined. Students had a great time teaching the dances, which they knew quite well, to their parents. And when the 50 minute class was over, I had many parents ask me when they could 'do this again?'

I will never forget one of these classes. A father happened to show up on a 'mothers' day. I was a bit puzzled, but he explained to me with his charming Southern accent, "Well, mah wife couldn't come, so I'm pretendin' to be mah son's mother!" He was a tall, black man in uniform and he continued, "Ma'am, this is the greatest. Ah haven't had so many laughs at mahself in a long time! I was the one who had a lot of trouble learnin' all this, not mah son! Mah son had tah teach me how tah do everythin'!"

Well, he certainly stood out in the crowd that day, but we all enjoyed his good nature and sense of humor, and everyone laughed together.

Because the parents asked, each of the grade 4-6 classes had at least three opportunities to ask their parents to come dance with them. I was the happiest teacher ever watching the students dancing with their parents and seeing their self-confidence grow with each step. I felt so blessed.

Finally, we had our annual square dance festival outside, during the afternoon, starting after lunch on the school grounds with all the grades at the same time. The students wore costumes—girls in big, full skirts that flared out as they twirled. The boys with jeans and cowboy shirts and bright neckerchiefs and a few with cowboy hats! The mothers and fathers who were able to attend that day brought lots of good food for refreshments. Even some of the other teachers in the school attended and we all had a wonderful time.

What I most appreciated was this: whenever an extra partner was needed, either a parent would step in and be a partner or an older boy or girl would volunteer to be a partner. These were marvelous examples of 'doing for one another' that I felt certain would carry over in later life with other people or in their own families. At the same time, the students were having a marvelous time and learning the rhythms of the dances from their own country and other countries as well. They radiated happiness, contentment and positive vibrations all afternoon.

On these occasions, I often thought of the words written by Zoltan Kodaly, a famous music education teacher in Hungary whom I've mentioned earlier in this book. He once wrote about teaching and learning music:

"What is the aim of all this long and tiring work? To win 199 competitions? To outshine one's fellow musicians? To obtain fame and renown?

No, it is the bounden duty of the talented to cultivate their talent to the highest degree, to be of as much use as possible to their fellow man. For every person's worth is measured by how much he can help his fellow men and serve his country. Real Art is one of the most powerful forces in the rise of mankind and he who renders it accessible to as many as possible is a benefactor of humanity."

—Zoltan Kodaly, Hungary

Talented and Gifted Class

I was assigned ten students in my TAG (Talented and Gifted) class who met with me three sessions a week for about 45 minutes to an hour each time. (They were dismissed from their regular classrooms to come to my class). It was up to me to develop a 'curriculum' for this group of students and I wracked my brains to decide what I could do with them that was different and at the same time interesting and enjoyable.

Then, in the middle of the night I had a smashing idea; we would study the American legal system. I decided to call one of the lawyers working with our military base and ask for his help. The person I contacted thought it was a wonderful idea and he joined me and helped me teach the basics of American law to the TAG class.

He was great with the children, and they enjoyed coming to the class. Over the weeks, we studied different aspects of the law and the plan was for the students to participate in a 'mock' trial at the end of the year.

There were a few glitches with these TAG sessions. One was the lawyer was busy and could not always attend each class. And, in the beginning, when he did attend, he tended to 'lecture' to the students. He had never taught students that age before so he didn't understand that you could not lecture for a whole period. Students that age have to be active participants or they turn off their minds and almost go to sleep with their eyes open. He and I had talks about that and he improved at each lesson, so that was wonderful!

Another glitch was with one of the students, a boy in the fourth grade who never seemed to remember he was supposed to come to the TAG class. Also this student's regular classroom teacher never reminded the boy when it was time to go the TAG class. Therefore, I had to either call on the inter-school telephone or go for the student and bring him to class. I asked the student's teacher to list on the board the boy's name and time at which he was scheduled to leave the room, but the teacher evidently did not want to, or forgot, and the boy did not remember either.

One day, after several weeks of this behavior, I decided it would be a better lesson learned if I did not do all the 'phoning and fetching' and just let the boy miss the TAG class once. Then, I thought, maybe that would help him learn a lesson and he would remember to come to class the next time. He was a good student and seemingly enjoyed coming to the 'law' class.

Well, shortly after school that day, this boy's classroom teacher cornered me in the corridor and screamed at me for not having 'fetched' the boy for the TAG class. He literally tore me apart verbally, in the main hallway right in front of whoever happened to be walking by and 'laid me out in lavender' as they say in Massachusetts. I quickly decided, since I could not even find the opportunity to say one word to him in my defense, to let it go. I knew, deep in my heart, there was no way to talk with him sensibly at that point. He delivered his horrible oration with his arms flailing in the air, yes, absolutely flying up and down and all around in the open hallway; then he stalked off and up and over to his classroom, talking loudly and to no one in particular.

He won. After that, I had to fetch the boy for each class. I had never, in all my years in West Ruislip, seen a teacher as angry as he was that day and to this day I'm not sure I understand why he was so upset. As far as I was concerned, he should have been helping the student learn responsibility. But these things happen.

At any rate, the class proceeded and ended with the mock trial, with a judge, jury, guilty party and two lawyers. The students appeared to be happy and at the same time understanding and enjoying the sessions. I had them take notes periodically, and as a result of the actual acting out of the trial, I believe they had a good learning experience.

The lawyer and I had hoped to have time to take my students on a trip to a real court. Unfortunately, we just ran out of time because the class had not started until later in the year. But overall it worked well and I was thrilled that the lawyer enjoyed it also. The children learned and were happy at the same time, joyously arriving and leaving each time there was a lesson…except the little boy in the fourth grade. I still had to fetch him at the start of every lesson! But then…he came with a smile and appeared to enjoy our activity fully!

> *This above all—to thine own self be true,*
> *And it must follow as the night the day,*
> *Thou canst not then be false to any man.*

> ### *Hamlet*
> ### *—Shakespeare*

The incident with the TAG class and the fourth grade teacher who could/would not remember to dismiss his student to the class was not the only time I was yelled at by one of the teachers. In order to teach the folk/square dancing classes, I had to obtain permission from the gym teacher to use the gymnasium. It became tedious going in almost weekly to schedule my class times, so one time I asked him if we could come up with a schedule that would work for both of us.

Well, he pulled me apart verbally for this request and he was so angry that he left the room, slammed the door and stormed down the corridor; he left me sitting in his office and never returned while I was there. He never apologized either.

I am not one who can fight or argue with anyone. I become too upset. However, these two unpleasant encounters with fellow teachers did not upset me as much as usual because I thought they were just too ludicrously silly. So, I let it all go…said goodbye to it within me. The following Shakespeare quote however sums up my feelings about both situations:

> *But man, Proud man*
> *Dressed in a little brief authority,*
> *Most ignorant of what he is most assured*
> *His glassy essence like an angry ape,*
> *Plays such fantastic tricks before high heaven*
> *As makes the angels weep*

> ### *Measure for Measure*
> ### *—Shakespeare*

Travel, Travel and More Travel

As I've mentioned before, one of the advantages of working for DODDS were the numerous opportunities to travel. I love history, and England and Europe are certainly full of interesting historical sites. During the six years I worked at the West Ruislip school I took many trips around England and Europe, sometimes with Ed only, sometimes with Ed and friends, sometimes with friends only (Ed's health and back problems often made it difficult for him to travel long distances).

I don't plan to recount here detailed descriptions of the many, many trips we took, but I do want to mention a few of the more special ones.

Pam Pullman the Library and Media Center director at West Ruislip Elementary, approached me one day at school. "Mary, why don't we take the next long weekend and go to Bronte country? I've only been there once and I would love to visit again and show you around. And, I will drive!" (My reputation as a poor driver in England was well known by then).

"Yes, absolutely," I said excitedly as I gave her a hug, "I'd love to visit Bronte country."

And so the next long weekend that came along we drove to Haworth, West Yorkshire, England, home to the Bronte Parsonage Museum. I have long been a fan of the Bronte sisters' novels, so to be able to visit their home and the surrounding village was a delightful treat for me. I immersed myself in looking at all the rooms and furnishings and imagining what the sisters might have done and how they would have lived and worked there.

The area was beautiful, but isolated, even in the 1990s, so I could see how that combination of circumstances could have fueled the Bronte women's literary work. After visiting the parsonage museum, we explored the large church next to the parsonage, but what attracted my attention the most was the large cemetery between the church and the parsonage, and just how close the cemetery was to the front door of the parsonage. There was not more than ten feet between the parsonage and the church, and so graves were literally inches from the parsonage doorstep.

There had been so much demand for the cemetery (so many people died in the mid-nineteenth century) that tombs were placed on top of tombs and there seemed not an inch to spare. The scene astonished/fascinated me. I had seen many cemeteries in my travels, but never one as crowded as this. Bodies were not embalmed in those days to help prevent the spread of disease, and I could not help but wonder if less than sanitary burial conditions could have played a role in the untimely deaths of the Brontes, most of whom died in their twenties. I felt so sad for them all.

After visiting the Bronte homestead, we drove to Leeds Castle nearby. What a beautiful site! I loved walking around the 'top' of the castle and imagining all the battles that may have taken place there as well as enjoying the gorgeous views that day. All in all, it was a lovely weekend with Pam and I am forever grateful to her for sharing it with me.

Poland and Prague

An unexpected phone call from Charlotte Miles, my good friend in La Maddalena, Italy, was the beginning of another wonderful excursion.

"Mary, how about this," Charlotte said, "You show me Poland and I'll show you Prague!"

Ed and I had enjoyed our visit to Poland, but he did not have the energy to go again. I had always wanted to see Prague however.

"You are on. I'm all for it Charlotte. When do you want to go?" I answered.

Within a few weeks, all the necessary arrangements were made. Charlotte flew to London from Italy, then from London we both flew to Warsaw. I showed Charlotte many of the sites I had visited with Ed earlier in Warsaw and then Krakow. We especially enjoyed taking a horse-drawn carriage around Krakow. Such an excellent way to see many, many sites in a relatively short time...so much nicer than a bus or taxi, and much less tiring than walking! I made sure Charlotte saw St. Mary's church with the two towers, one shorter than the other, and the famous 'Floryan's Gate.'

The following day we took a bus to a hotel in the mountains outside of Krakow. There we were escorted to a lovely, large room with floor-to-ceiling windows on one wall. As we admired the view from these windows, a gorgeous double rainbow formed right in front of our eyes! "Charlotte, do you suppose the hotel plans this surprise for all their visitors?" I asked with a smile. She just smiled back.

Once we had settled into our room, we visited several villages that were even farther up in the mountains. As we walked around we marveled at the architecture of the cottages, built of wood with low ceilings and small windows to preserve the warmth in the winter. The cottages all looked alike and reminded me of the toy cottages that came with my brother's railroad set. The villagers were dressed in colorful Polish peasant clothes, and were quite friendly. We ate dinner in a log cabin type restaurant; I will never forget the enormous fireplace there. It was large enough to walk into!

We left Poland by train for Prague, Czechoslovakia. It was an overnight trip, so we rented a small 'cabinet' with two sleeping berths, an upper and a lower. It was a private room with a small sink and chair, but no toilet. The only toilet was down the passage of the train, and shared by everyone in that coach.

Despite this, Charlotte and I were excited about the prospect of sleeping on the train. We boarded, settled in, and then went to bed. Charlotte took the upper bunk and allowed me to sleep in the lower one. We were both asleep when there was a loud banging and thump, thump, thump on our door. I opened the door to find a large Russian guard demanding to see our passports. There was no smile, or excuse me, or any exchange of pleasantries, just a demand to see our passports. I was momentarily flustered, but then found our passports, handed them to him, he glanced at them, grunted and then left.

We went back to sleep, then a little while later, there was another thumping at our door, and another unfriendly guard demanding to see our passports. Again I jumped up and showed him our documents. This happened several times that night, and at one point I glimpsed a funny smile on Charlotte's face.

"Charlotte, what *is* so funny?" I demanded to know.

"I'm glad you're on the lower bunk," she replied.

I looked at her and replied sardonically, "I have a feeling you planned it this way!"

When she began to giggle, I knew I was right. She *knew* we were going to be interrupted at all the border crossings through the night. She laughed the remainder of the night, and before long I was laughing with her. No matter which bunk either of us had been on, there was not to be a peaceful sleep that night!

At this point, I remember few details about our visit to Prague. I do know we stayed and toured only in the old part of the city that is absolutely beautiful. I especially remember the old and lovely churches. There seemed to be one on every corner, and many of them had concerts on a regular basis. We were there for three days and were able to attend a concert in one of the churches. It was absolutely beautiful!

I especially enjoyed the ancient clock in the center of Prague's Old Town Square. The clock dates back to the fifteenth century and still tells accurate time to this day. Its most striking feature though was the arrangement of figures representing Christ and his twelve apostles that can be seen every hour on the hour. It was fascinating.

I had the pleasure of taking another trip with Charlotte a couple of years later. She came again from La Maddalena to visit with her mother in England. Ed and I joined them and we drove up to Chester, a 2,000 year old city north-west of London near the border of Wales. The city has a castle and wall surrounding it. We thoroughly enjoyed touring the castle and reading about the history of Chester as a Roman settlement so long ago. Then we took in the views of the city from atop a portion of the two miles of wall that surround it. It was all so beautiful and vastly different.

Blewbury

I have many fond memories of numerous visits to our good friends Joy and Charles' thatched cottage in Blewbury, called Nottingham Fee. The cottage had originally belonged to Joy's cousin, Susan Beatrice Pearce, a well-known illustrator in the mid-twentieth century. 'Trissy' (as Joy called her) is especially famous for her illustrations of a series of children's books, the *Ameliaranne* series. They are charming stories about a young girl who has interesting adventures. I own a few copies of the books, and Joy gave me an original crayon drawing of Ameliaranne done by her cousin. Joy had many stories about the remarkable 'Trissy' who lived to be 102 years old!

One time we stayed at Nottingham Fee with Sharon Seider; (her husband was the assistant principal at the DODDS school in Izmir, Turkey) and their daughter Shannon, who was about 18 years old at that time. We toured all around the area and took occasional day trips into London.

On one of our other visits, Joy showed us all around the village of Blewbury, sharing story after story of the cottages and their inhabitants. Joy had a remarkable memory, and her stories were fascinating.

Blewbury was also home to another famous author for at least a short time: Kenneth Grahame, creator of *The Wind in the Willows*. Joy showed us his house, but it was privately owned and not open for tours. However, there is an epitaph to him written by his cousin that I want to share:

'*To the beautiful memory of Kenneth Grahame, husband of Elspeth and father of Alistair, who passed the river on the 6th of July, 1932, leaving childhood and literature through him the more blest for all time.*'

I also had the pleasure of visiting Jane Austen's home several times over the course of our time in England. I loved to share her house with visiting friends and family. My most memorable visit however was the first one Ed and I shared with Joy and Charles. We were looking at the tiny, round mahogany table where Jane did all her writing. It was located in front of a small window that overlooked the street. As I was standing there gazing at the scene, the caretaker of the house invited me to sit on Jane's chair by the window. And I did…for several minutes. What a thrill! The scope of Jane's imagination, considering how little she actually saw of the world, still amazes me.

Ed and I were quite blessed to have Joy and Charles as friends because they introduced us to so many interesting sites and events in England including: three of Charles Dickens' homes; Winchester Cathedral; Dorchester Cathedral; Bath; York; countless Roman ruins; Stonehenge; the ruins of Avebury; Thomas Hardy country; to name a few. Because of their generosity in sharing these experiences with us, we in turn were able to share these sights again with DODDS friends who came to visit us in England over the years.

Windsor Castle

Gene and Kathy Jenkis, who were DODDS teachers with me in England, were another couple who shared special trips with us. One that I remember fondly was in June during the summer solstice, the longest day of the year. Gene and Kathy picked us up at our home and did not tell us where we were going. Gene especially liked to surprise us.

After a drive of a little more than an hour, we found ourselves in Windsor and boarding Gene's lovely motor launch on the river Thames. We motored up the river to the outskirts of Windsor castle! Then, to top it all off, Gene prepared and served us a lovely dinner on the boat as we floated on the water in front of the castle. This was an experience I never dreamed could happen to me. The water was lovely, fifty or so swans and ducks floated around us, the sky was blue with puffy white clouds, the view of the castle was so very impressive that I thought I was in heaven for a while.

Ireland

During one of our spring breaks, Ed and I traveled to Ireland with Sharon Seider. We had originally planned to drive across England to the west coast, take a ferry over to Ireland, and have our car to drive around. However, we ended up flying to Ireland and renting a car instead. We spent only a little time in

Dublin since we were most interested in the Irish countryside.

Our main goal was to visit the Bunratty Castle and the Blarney Castle, both steeped in history. And at the Blarney Castle, Sharon and I both wanted to kiss the famous 'Blarney Stone.' That was quite an unusual experience for me. Kissing that stone involves lying down on your back, with half your body over the edge of a wall and trusting the attendant to hold your legs and feet, the lower half of your body, so you don't slip over the edge into 'never never land.' I was nervous and scared to do it, but once I was in the position, I only 'pretended' to kiss the stone because it looked so unsanitary with many, many red lipstick impressions on the stone.

I don't remember specifically the other sites we saw since Ireland is so full of many wonderful old castles and beautiful quaint villages. I do distinctly remember spending the night in a home directed by nuns from the Catholic Church. The rooms were spotlessly clean, but quite sparse and simple. The nuns were friendly and caring, but in a detached sort of way.

I wish I could have spent more time in Ireland, but a week was all we had. However, I loved every bit of it!

The Ceremony of the Garter

Another dear friend who shared with us many special experiences in England was Ros Sandorek, whom I had met during my sabbatical year in England in the late 1970s. We had stayed in touch after that and when I began working for DODDS, we were able to meet together occasionally.

One day Ros called on the phone and said, "Mary, I was given some marvelous invitations and I would like to have you join me at Windsor to see part of the ceremony of the Knights of the Garter." Ros was the headmistress of a school in Windsor and as a result received invitations to special events occasionally.

I was not exactly sure what that ceremony was, but knowing Ros I assumed it was special.

"Oh, absolutely, I'd love to go, but I have a friend visiting me here from the States."

"Well," Ros answered, "I have two tickets, one for you and Ed, in addition to mine."

"Ed will probably not want to go because of all the walking and standing," I told Ros, "could I bring my friend instead?"

"That would be fine," Ros replied, and so my friend Susan Rogers, and Ros and I traveled to Windsor Castle on a bright and sunny June morning and took our place among the few people lining the walk between Windsor Castle and St. George's Chapel. Yes, I say 'few' since there were a limited number of people invited from the Town of Windsor.

The following description of the **Ceremony of the Garter** is taken from a book I have:

"*Every June, the Knights of the Garter gather at the Windsor Castle, where new knights take an oath and are invested with the insignia. A lunch is held in "Waterloo Chamber" and the Royal family and the knights, old and new, process down the winding hill to the St George's Chapel.*"

Ros, Susan and I were standing on the side of the street on that 'winding hill to St. George's Chapel.' First, the Queen Mother, riding in a royal carriage went by. The royal family, in their beautiful blue robes, were walking behind her. First the Queen, then Prince Philip, then their son Charles, Prince of Wales and the Queen's daughter. They were followed by the newly vested knights, as well as Prime Minister Margaret Thatcher and her Parliament ministers.

I was so close to the Queen as she passed by that I could have reached out and touched her, but I would never be so rude. I was surprised to see how short she was however.

Susan Rogers and I were impressed with the whole ceremony. I will never forget it, ever, or my friend Ros and her incredible generosity for sharing it with us.

And of course every summer, we had the opportunity to return home and visit family and friends for eight weeks. We spent most of our time visiting our daughter, Susan and our son, Eric and family, and Amy. Susan was in Henniker, N.H. with her wonderful caretaker and husband, John, in their little apartment. She had steadily grown worse with Multiple Sclerosis, but seemed to be managing somehow. Eric and Kelly and their growing family of two beautiful children, Kim and Michael, were in Austin, Texas and Amy was finishing up at the University of Massachusetts, and eventually went on for her Master's Degree and Doctorate. All was seemingly quite well! Ed and I were proud of our little family. They were just marvelous! My heart broke whenever I left each of them in the summer, but then, they also knew I had to live my life as well.

One summer we visited my dear friend, Paul Gayzagian, a professor at UMass Lowell, whom I had met while studying at Lowell State Teacher's College. He and I had worked together when he needed to place music students into practice teaching positions at local schools. I worked with his students in Andover.

By the time of this visit, Paul had retired from teaching and Ed and I were visiting him and his wife Doris one afternoon. Ed and Doris had gone out to look at some flowers in the garden, and I asked Paul, "What prompted you to decide to retire?"

Paul made a few 'false starts' on answers to the question, then after a few minutes of reflection, he made a statement that I've never forgotten.

"When the time comes Mary, you will know...you will know right away and there will be no question in your mind about when to retire."

Well, I left it at that and we went on to other topics when Doris and Ed returned but...I never forgot his words.

How many goodly creatures are there here!
How beauteous mankind is!
O brave new world
That has such people in it.

The Tempest
—Shakespeare

Back to England

Ed and I went back to England after another wonderful summer of touring foreign countries at the end of school and then visiting with our family in the States.

I loved England so much I felt I must have lived there in another life. Not that I had not enjoyed all the other countries and schools where I had the opportunity to teach: Okinawa, Turkey, Italy. However, there was something pulling at my heartstrings all the time in and about England. I had hoped to be able to purchase a small dwelling in England so we could have another 'pied a terre', another home in which to hang our hats. I came close to looking into one or two while in Gerrard's Cross, but, in my heart, I knew I could never afford to buy another home. Prices were high in England as compared to here at that time and even now, I've been told. I would never be able to manage the whole thing alone on one retirement salary, or, I should say two retirement salaries, one from Massachusetts and one from the government. Ed's disability paycheck per month was not very large however. So I stopped wishing and dreaming and concentrated on other things.

We continued with our traveling; we went on short trips and long trips depending on what or which holidays were upon us. I loved all of them and all of England, but I often found myself thinking of what Paul said for some reason. Not sure why, but Paul's words popped into my mind often: "One day…you will know, Mary, you will just know when it is time to retire!"

> *As we advance in life it becomes more difficult,*
> *but in fighting the difficulties*
> *the inmost strength of the heart*
> *is developed."*

> **—Vincent Van Gogh**

I carried on in the same manner with my work, teaching TAG classes in addition to the music classes, developing holiday concerts and producing another Shakespeare play, *Midsummer Night's Dream*.

In the early spring, during rehearsals for our play, word came from the DODDS Superintendent's Office. There would be a concert for all fourth, fifth and sixth grade choruses, of all the DODDS Schools in England to be held at Lakenheath Air Base, almost two hours northeast of London. All the United States major military offices were in Lakenheath plus some airports, and many DODDS schools. All the 'important' people were in those offices and the air base was huge.

That meant I had to organize and make 'ready' the students; I never left anyone out, as I have said repeatedly; I had taught all of the children to sing, and I felt they all sang well. At this point in the year all the students were capable of singing two part and three part songs, a cappella. When I broke the news to the students they were absolutely elated. Singing at Lakenheath was something we had never done before!

It would be a long trip to Lakenheath with many students, up and back and in the same day, but they felt they could manage. "Could I manage?" I wondered.

All this was a bit much for me to put together at that time of the school year, knowing we had another play going with rehearsals and the final show, plus the trip to Stratford Upon Avon, plus the annual all school Square Dance Festival as well. Sadly, my very best helper, Carol, was no longer with me, her husband having retired the previous June. They had moved back home to the States. I was a little panicked but still knew, in my heart, I could get on with it and all would be well.

Off we went on the big day, by bus, to Lakenheath! We arrived, finally, after a few hours, and the children virtually tumbled out of the buses; we found a room in which to get ready.

After a few minutes of preparation, we made our way into the school auditorium. The students had eaten their lunches on the bus, so I was not worried about them being hungry. We loosened up our bodies a bit by having a short recess before changing into our costumes, dark pants or skirts, white shirts and red caplets on their shoulders tied in the back and white paper collars and a small red bow tie with two long streamers. They looked wonderful. We then waited as other school choruses performed.

I must admit the other school choruses performed badly; yes, they did. I said nothing to my children, however, keeping all my thoughts to myself. What made them perform in a manner of which I did not approve, one may ask? Well, first of all, they used taped recordings to accompany their singing and consequently the quality was terrible. Their choice of music was equally awful, no classical music, just current popular songs. As I listened to the other choruses I realized that there was not one school chorus that sang with the same quality or tone as ours. During intermission two of my very best and brightest girl students came to me and whispered in my ear, "Mrs. Guziejka, the other students who sang sounded awful, didn't they?"

"Shhh, don't say anything more now...we will talk about everything later..." meaning I would discuss the reasons why, and how their quality of tone was not as good as I knew ours would be.

Finally, it was our turn. We sang three 'a cappella songs,' and the students' singing tones were lovely and pure as they sang in two part harmony and then the last song of this type, was in three part harmony. I directed, of course, nodding, smiling and mouthing the words to instill confidence in the singers (I dread thinking how I must have looked while mouthing the words in an exaggerated fashion, no wonder the choruses all smiled at me and felt relaxed.) I was thrilled with their sound, their pure and lovely bell like tones. Yet, at the same time, I was a nervous wreck.

Our next song was in two-part harmony and with me accompanying on the piano. Then, the students sang two more a cappella songs. We ended out portion of the concert with the Battle Hymn of the Republic with two-part harmony and piano accompaniment. The chorus looked grand in their red capelets! They resembled, in my mind, an English School Choir! I was ecstatic, absolutely thrilled with their performance. Our boys' voices had not changed which was helpful for me at the time, since there is nothing more beautiful than a boy soprano with a well trained, singing voice. Their voices tend to be richer sounding than the girls at that age, which is not to say the girls' voices were not lovely! My boys were proud of their singing, not disgraced by it as some of the boys seemed to be in the other groups. We did not have any soloists, it was asked that we not, otherwise I would have featured some of my best singers among the students. All was most successful and I felt absolutely wonderful!

After the concert, when all the groups of singers and their teachers were assembling for their buses for the long rides home, the DODDS Superintendent came to me and complimented me privately. She told me the quality of my students' singing was exemplary. I was pleased as punch. She indicated, but did not say specifically, that she was not happy with the other groups. However, she implied that they lacked the quality that my group had.

With an arm around my shoulder and a beatific like smile on her face, she went on to say, "I am going to ask you to host next year's 'All Schools Elementary Concert' in the spring of the year. It will be a three-day workshop ending with a marvelous concert. Your children sing so beautifully, I just know you will do a great job!"

This absolutely floored me! I felt limp all over…I was shocked! Whereas I felt proud and most honored by her words of praise, I realized what a huge job she was asking me to take on. I would have to do a large amount of conducting, and the choosing of songs; and some of the teaching to the large groups! Also, I would have the job of finding homes for the students from all over and also find three or four professional musicians to come in and conduct some of the classes. As well, there would most likely be mountains of paper work that would go back and forth throughout the year. I could not face all that…and that was that! I was totally overwhelmed with her accolades but, at the same time, upset about the thoughts of next year's work!

As the lovely lady stood there my mind sifted through those episodes so rapidly that I felt limp all over…thinking, "I can't do it…I cannot handle it anymore, what will I do, what will I do?"

"Thank you so very much…from the bottom of my heart…for your compliments…I feel most honored!"…I found myself saying as we…grasped, each other's hands.

I had never met the lady before, but she left me feeling quite happy on the one hand, and, on the other hand, devastated! The pictures flooding through my mind at a rapid pace were quite overwhelming! The thoughts of having to arrange another one of these for everyone, meaning all the DODDS schools in U.K., was overwhelming. To have them all come to my little school would require much assistance, many homes to take children in for three overnights and on and on…the responsibilities grew in my mind. Also, where would we perform? I would need to find money and a hall in which to work.

On the way home in the bus I was exhausted, just worn out…and I kept hearing Paul's voice running around in my head: "Mary, when the time is right, you will know…you will know right away."

The DODDS Superintendent's statement to me, while it was most complimentary, made me think how much work would be involved in this undertaking and suddenly, I realized, I could not do this anymore. The sad part was… I loved it and I loved all I taught the children and how they performed; their voices were like angels singing; I loved my school children with all my heart. (I miss them terribly now…)

I still had a lot to do at my West Ruislip school before ending the present school year, let alone worry about the next year. All I could think of was my home in Dracut and my family in New England and Texas. My lovely, first born child, Susan…her M.S. had crippled her virtually all over her body, was terribly ill, and I felt I should be with her or at least nearby in our Dracut home to see her often.

I also knew it was time to see our son and his wife, Eric and Kelly, and their two lovely children, Kim and Mike, more often. I wanted them to know us! And Amy…yes, she was graduating from college with her Masters' Degree and going on for her doctoral degree! I needed to be with her also! Strangely, as well, our home was going to be empty of tenants as of June. Also, I dislike having to mention it, but I would be 70 years old in May.

I think it was April 1, 2000, or close to the first of April, when I went into the principal's office and told her that I needed to retire at the end of this school year. Paul was most correct when he said, "You will know, Mary, you will know."

I heard his voice clearly in my mind. Suddenly, I did know. I gave my resignation paper to the principal, and finished the remainder of the school year with a simultaneously happy but very sad heart, still singing and still dancing and enjoying everything until the very last moment!

Now, today, ten years later, my problem is, I miss all my teaching and all my school children terribly but know, full well…ten years later…I could never have gone back.

It Is Not Always May
—Henry Longfellow

The sun is bright, the air is clear
The darting swallows soar and sing,
And from the stately elms I hear
The bluebird prophesying Spring.

So blue yon winding river flows
It seems an outlet from the sky
Where, waiting till the west wind blows,
The frightened clouds at anchor lie

All things are new; the buds, the leaves,
That gild the elm tree's nodding crest
And even the nest beneath the eaves;
There are no birds in last year's nest

All things rejoice in youth and love
The fullness of their first delight!
And learn from the soft heavens above
The melting tenderness of night.

Maiden, that read'st this simple rhyme
Enjoy the youth, it will not stay:
Enjoy the fragrance of thy prime
For oh, it is not always May.

Enjoy the Spring of love and youth,
To some good angel leave the rest:
For time will teach thee soon the truth,
There are no birds in last year's nest.

EPILOGUE

On October 14, 2005, I received the following e-mail from Maria McFarlane, the mother of one of my former students in West Ruislip, England. I remember the student well because he was not an easy student to manage, always 'acting out.' The letter would warm the heart of any teacher and I'd like to share it here:

Hi Mary,

I am sure you are surprised to hear from me. The other night I was talking to Diane and asked her for your e-mail. Hopefully everything is going well for you.

The reason I am writing to you is I want to let you know that Jimmy is going to Berklee College of Music in Boston. He has never put down that guitar since grade school. I just wanted to let you know that we still talk about how you are the reason he started playing the guitar in the first place.

I will never forget the day you came up to the office and told me to get an inexpensive guitar from the J.C. Penny catalogue and start him with lessons. You said you thought he had some talent and it would be beneficial for him. It was the best advice you could have ever given for Jimmy. He enjoyed high school with all the passion in the world, cared about his classes and his school work and was involved in many activities. He always made the honor roll and just thoroughly enjoyed himself. He has always had private guitar lessons since we lived in England and is continuing with private lessons in Berklee.

Thank you for caring so much about your students. There is nothing in the world like a TEACHER!!! You are the Best.

Cheers,

Maria McFarlane

In November 2011, I was invited to attend the 'Harvest Festival' at Sanborn School in Andover, an event which I had initiated in 1979 following my sabbatical year in England.

The presentation was simpler than what I had done in the beginning, but it was good to see the tradition continued. I was happy about that. After the program I decided to leave and not go into the luncheon that is traditionally offered to the teachers and the audience. As I was walking down the hallway to the front door, I heard some noise, as in...someone calling. I could not distinguish the sounds at that point, therefore I kept on walking, assuming a teacher was calling an errant child. Again though I heard the same noises, but they were sounding somewhat louder..I still did not turn to look, knowing it was not my place to step in. Finally, the words became distinguishable and I heard my name being called, "Mrs. Guziejka, Mrs. Guziejka!" I turned quickly and saw a man calling to me and rushing, almost running, down the long corridor. Finally I could hear him saying...

"It's me, it's me, David, David Birnbach," the man said. I looked at him in amazement and the next thing I knew we were in each others arms hugging. Tears welled up in my eyes as I remembered the young boy who performed on stage so many years ago...he was an exceptional student and a brilliant actor. I had not seen him since he was twelve years old.

Once we stopped hugging each other, David looked at me and said, "No one does shows the way you used to do with us." We pulled apart, looked each other over and then talked for an hour or more in the hallway of the Sanborn School. He is now 51 years old and a successful businessman in Andover. His own son attends the Sanborn School. It was recess time for his son, and he took me out to the playground to meet him. "Mrs. Guziejka, my Dad talks about you all the time," the boy blurted out, and then ran back to play with his friends. I could not believe what was happening.

I am so very grateful for all that has happened to/through me and pleased that memories of my work are still being shared with generations to come.

Appendix

Pentatonic Play

1/
Play opens with a bed and a child......

Child: (sitting in bed, puzzled expression, can't sleep,but
   sleepy and cranky)

   Mrs Guziejka keeps saying,"Pentatonic, pentatonic and I don't
know what she means. She thinks I do but I know that I don't. I try
so hard to understand but I can't seem to figure out exactly what
it means. I love to sing but I keep forgetting what the word penta
means and then I cannot do the scale, so how can I sing the song?
(A noise, or confusion is heard and the child is puzzled)
What do I hear? I think I hear music.....I wonder who it is at this
time of night?!?

(In a whirl or frenzy of confusion, five people garbed as five tones
--Penta-tonic-- arrive and start to sing the scale. All notes are
sung in $\frac{2}{4}$ and as half notes)

$\frac{2}{4}$ Do, re, mi, so, la, do....do, la, so, mi, re, do.
then into a song.

Pentatonic Play continued

27

(once through, then as a round)

Child:(utter amazement) WHO ARE YOU!!?!
DO: I am "do" of the five tone scale and here are my friends.
     (all that line is sung on one tone)
DO:(spoken) I couldn't live without them . I would be a monotone,
and how monotonous! (said as in a pun)
RE: I am"re" and I sing like this.
     (sung on the tone of re)
RE:(spoken) I am a step higher.
MI: I am "MI"(sung on mi)
MI: (spoken) It's nice to be me(then sing on so,)Here is "so".
SO: I am "so" and close to "la".
LA: I am "la" and on to DO.
DO: High Do and I sing like this(all these words sung on high Do.)
(Then all the five tones sing up the scale holding the notes for two
beats. When high Do sings, he sings it twice and then says:
Do: I like it so well, I sing it twice.

REPEAT SONG BUT WITH THE FOLLOWING WORDS.
  Do mi so do la do so
We are penta tones all five
When we sing we come alive
Do la so mi re so do.

Pentatonic scale it's true
let us show what we can do
Do mi so do la do so
Do la so mi re so do.
(Re steps out and sings on his note:)
Re:You only gave me one turn, I want to sing more.
(Do and Mi pull him back in line)
Do: Wait

Pentatonic Play continued

3/
Mi: Your
Do: Turn!

la   do   so,   la   la   do   la   so
la   la   do   la   so   mi   re   do   re   so   so
Now we've done a bit for you
You can come and sing it too!

(Invite child to join the line)
High Do: Re will come and get you.(sung on Do, do la la do do)
Child: No, I can't. I don't know how.
Re: It's easy. You've seen what I can do.(all sung on re)
Child: But, what note would I be once I have learned how? Would I
      only sing one note?
La: You're ridiculous child. It would be foolish of you to go
      around singing like this all the time.(all sung on "la")
      You need to know more than one note.
Re-So Do: Even a recitative in an opera sings on more than one note.
Child:(exasperated) Then show me what to do.
Do(speaks) Touch each of us in any order; up, down or all around.
      Once you know all five of us you will be able to sing almost anything
      in the whole world.
(Child hesitatingly walks forward and gingerly presses *Center*
                                                        of note.

LA....so...mi...re...mi...
LA....so...la...so...la...so...mi...
re...re...re...re...mi.
(Then sung in a round)

So: We have sung our tones to you...
Child:(interrupts) But something STILL seems to be missing.
Re: The words, the words....once you know the notes you need the words
to tell a story in song.
Child:(nodding his head) No wonder it didn't make any sense.
(Thinks for a second...then continues) What words can you put to
the last pretty melody that I played when I touched you?
Do: This last melody speaks of nature, life and man's search for
eternal peace.(serious speech, with an emphasis on the three items
and a pause between each.)

Pentatonic Play continued

4/

Child: (Excitedly) Let's do it all over again and this time do it
with the words.
(Notes that sing, step forward out of line andsing)

Accompaniment... first and end with accompaniment.
LA.....SO.....MI....RE

Child: (wonder and excitement repeats words of song)
      Clouds are high above
      I am down on earth below
      Looking for a dove.

Child: Ican do it, I can do it....I can sing and I know the penta
      tonic scale!

La: Enough of this simple explanation(emphasis on word"simple")
    We are going to take you on a trip. You will be able to sleep
and then waken and find yourself in the middle of JAPAN. There
will be an Oriental *implosion*.
Child: what is an Implosion? *art*
Child: I would love to go, but why Japan? *within Japan*
Re: Oriental music is built on the five tone scale . It helps to
eliminate discord and dissonance found in western music. It is unusual,
has its own flavor and comes from the East. Come with us on our
journey to Japan . We will travel slowly as did the sixteen year
old Emperor as he left Kyoto,   on his travel to Edo,which is now
called Tokyo, a long time ago. *Cymbals clash.*

Bar music Starts slowly here ! - trickle on xylophones

(The following sung in a chordal arrangement, if possible)
Close your eyes, sleep
Sleep and dream
sleep and dream,
sleep.

met.

Clocks .

Pentatonic Play continued

4 3/4 (bottom of p.4)

Scene: (Enclosed cart pulled by ox)

    (As child is about to go back to sleep, sung to sleep by the
    pentatonic scale, the mime children appear before the screens
    and with masks ● they chant.....

"A long time ago, a long time ago,
Edo was Tokyo, a long time ago
A young child from Kyoto, chose to go to Edo
A long time ago.
The young child was Lord,
The Lord of Edo, the Lord of Edo
A long time ago.
He made a slow journey, a journey to Edo
Which now is Tokyo, a long time ago.
The child began to reign, the child began to reign
Then began Tokyo, a long time ago.
The time was....a long time ago.
It was a slow journey, many, many miles,
A long time ago.
At last we had unity,
unity and peace,
peace through a child,
A child from Kyoto, journeying to Tokyo,
A long time ago."

    (All the above done by different voices, some in chorus,
    some in solo...chanting, and accompanied by different drum
    patterns and hand cymbals...ending with a tremolo on the hand
    cymbal.)

Tympani

bell

Child:(In utter amazement) Hurry and take me there...I can't wait to see
    more.How do I get there, quick, tell me, how do I get there?
    (Pentatonic chord sings CLOSE YOUR EYES, SLEEP)

Bed and child are removed from front center

Pentatonic Play continued

5/
SLIDE_TAPE PRESENTATION WHICH APPEARS ON SCREEN AFTER CHILD
IS TAKEN AWAY BY THE PENTATONIC SCALE)

Accompaniment: flutes, recorders...drum... first beat each measure...
flutes play unison, then round, music to CLOUDS

<u>Chorus speaking and/or solo:</u>
Issa spoke of nature, love, age, death and peace. I speak of the
vastness of the sky, the smallness of me on earth, striving
constantly for inner peace, happiness and contentment. I find it in
music. I find it in Art. I find it in poetry. I find it in dance.
I am a child and I am love. I express myself in all that is around
me. I am a child and I am love. I want to please and be pleased.
I want to love and be loved....I want to understand, to learn and to
be understaod. I am a child and I am love.

*****
Original haiku to be chosen and read during the flashing of slides
with xylophone etc. accomp. in background....to be read with
different voices, not all one child.

Pentatonic Play continued

6/

Kashiko: I am Kashiko. Welcome to Japan. By the aid of a vivid
imagination, a beautiful spirit and a strong determination
you will be^{at liberty} to witness many of the Festivals that occur
█████████ somewhere, on anyday, in any place in Japan, the
whole year long. Give me your hand, do not be afraid and we *will*
hear, see andtouch upon many wonders of this old world.

(Kashiko and child leave front center and find a place to
watch the proceedings)
Television Studio WJAPAN

Speaker: This is Television Japan being brought to you today and you are
about to be taken to this, the year of Festivals in Japan.
You are about to witness a brilliant array of color, poetry,
mime, dance and song.
Slide Tape - P, S - here -

Speaker: While we are waiting for our artists to be ready I think it
would be interesting for our audience to know some of the
facts about Japan as we know them today.

Speaker: Right----- For example, it is incredible for me to conceive of
four major islands being only the size of California with one
hundred and eleven million people crowded into only fifteen
percent of the country.

Speaker: It has to be that way, David, since most of the country is
mountains, hills and forests.

Speaker: Did you know that Tokyo, Japan's capital and second largest
city in the world has less space per personthan any other city
in the world? The Ginza, Tokyo's main shopping center, is as
crowded on a Monday morning as Times Square is in New York
on New Year's Eve.

Speaker: That is unbelievable. In fact, that is awesome!

Speaker: Japan is also a land of contrasts where the old world mixes with
the new world very easily. It is a blend of old and new and
East and West.

Speaker: For example, visitors have noticed that the Japanese will race
home after work, through traffic or on the Bullet train at 120
miles an hour and then, when home, change from western suits into
traditional kimonos and spend one whole hour preparing and having the
ceremonial tea!

Pentatonic Play continued

7/

Speaker: I see something very interesting about to appear on our
screen. I see some bamboo trees with some white paper
tied to the limbs and boughs. Yes, I can see now, it is
the Festival of Tanabata, the Festival of the stars.

Speaker: The old chinese legend says that on the seventh day of the
seventh moon the boy's star lying on the side of the milky
way and the girl's star on the other side meet at the milky
way. (excitedly) If you squint your eyes and peer through
your eyelashes, all the trees, strung with the paper appear
to look like the milky way. (Secretively) It is said that
the children take the first dew of the morning off a lotus
leaf to dilute the ink for writing their poems. The messages
found on the paper tell of love, kindness, nature, beauty
and simplicity. The haiku speaks of love.

TANABATA SCENE NOW UNFOLDS WITH SEVERAL BOUGHS TRIMMED WITH ORIGINAL
HAIKU. WHILE THE SONG AND ACCOMP. GOES ON THE TREE BEARERS ARE STILL
AS IF FROZEN. WHEN ALL THE SCENE HAS FINISHED, SONG, DANCE, MIME, ETC.
THEN THE TREE BEARERS WILL DISTRIBUTE POEMS OF LOVE THROUGHOUT THE AUDIENCE

Speaker: That was simply beautiful, but look, quickly to the rear, what
have we here?

Speaker: We have the dance called Tanko Bushi. It is an old dance and as
familiar to children in Japan as the Virginia Reel is in America.
Notice the delicacy and the precision of each of the movements
Each movement tells the story of the Tanko Bushi or translated
for our American audience, the Coal Miner's Dance.

(Dancers have left the aisles)

Speaker: Japan is a land of Shinto shrines and Buddhists temples. All
shrines are marked by red Torii gates. These are shaped like a
rooster's perch.

Speaker: I never knew why they had that unusual shape.

Speaker: Well, let me tell you of the old legend. It is believed that
when time began, a rooster crowed. He woke the sun goddess and
she brought light to the world. There is a children's shrine

Pentatonic Play continued

8/

visiting day all over Japan. On that day, children, dressed in their very best are taken to the shrines by their parents. They then thank t their gods for health and pray for blessings.

~~Speaker: Here is the roster and the summary intmusit istmx and x smexxx~~

SCENE: THE ROOSTER CROWED......

SCENE: LIFT THE BLINDS, LET FRIENDSHIP IN, LONG SHADOWS WILL BE CAST AGAINST THE WALL.

*Possibility of a Boon Ra Ku Puppet....

TWO JAPANESE TALES

NUMBER TWO:

NUMBER THREE:

Speaker: The humor of the Japanese about themselves is delightful. But on to the next scene. I believe we have a rice planting ceremony.

Speaker: Yes, there are many rice paddies and small farms in Japan. It is important for everyone's well being to have good crops.

There is one story that tells of the year 1603 in Akita. The young men called for the help of their gods for a good harvest by dancing all night. They danced with bamboo frames on their heads. On the frames they had paper lanterns. This was not just one hanging of lantenrs but many layers upwards intot he air. They balance all these on their heads and shoulders and on and on throughout the whole night.

Speaker: There is another Festival we are now going to see called the Day of the Rice God .

CHANTING BEGINS.....DRUM BEAT....GOD SMILES ON HIS FESTIVAL DAY
GOD SMILES ON HIS FESTIVAL DAY
SANBAI_SAMA TO YOUR DUTY
CHIYODA CALLS YOU
SANBAI SAMA TO YOUR DUTY
CHIYODA CALLS YOU.

Speaker: Thus begins the Mibu Ohana Taue....a rice transplanting ritual preserved by the Japanese Government as a national "folk culture asset"

585

Pentatonic Play continued

9/

a day of old beliefs and old ways of working the earth.
a prayer in dance and song begging the boon of another year's
fruitful crop. Flower hat dancers dip and swirl in procession.

Speaker: The flower- hat dance was once performed later in the season to
drive away the worms from the rice field. Costumes recall a
local ruse staged in 1578, when a local warlord dressed his men
as flower hat dancers and led them into the enemy's castle..
Samurai steel flashed from silk kimonos and the dancing warriors
won the victory.

SCENE   FLOWER HAT DANCER WALKS TO THE BEAT OTHROUGH THE AUDIENCE

CAST...LEADER, CHORUS, ORCHESTRA.....

Speaker: We no sooner leave one Festival that we find ourselves into another.
That is what is so exciting about Japan. The child in each of us,
children and adults alike love a parade, a festival, a remembering,
and what an excellent way to learn about one's country!

Speaker: We have ahead of us the Cormorant Fishing, an almost ageless
tradition. There is of course, much commercial fishing around Japan
since Japan is four major islands and all surrounded by the sea, but
there is another that many of us would not know about and it takes
place at Gifu.

Speaker: There is a boat, of course, and a wire basket with fire. The fire
then skims low over the water, at night, and the bright light
of the fire attracts the fish and causes them to come near to the
surface of the water. It is when they are near to the surface that
the trained cormorqat bird swoops down and catches his fish.

Speaker: But then, does he not swallow it?

Speaker: No, absolutely not, because inxthairxxxisdamyxthayxiaarnadxtaxputxa
through experience and wisdom, the Japanese fisher men learned to
put a ring around the bird's neck to prevent it from swallowing the
fish.After the bird brings the fish to land or onto the boat, then
it regurgitates the fish and the fisherman has his supper for the
next day. Of course, it could be for breakfast since the Japanese
eat mush raw fish and at any meal.

Pentatonic Play continued

10/

Speaker: How many years has this type of fishing gone on in Japan?
Speaker: For over a thousand years and people from all over the world, to this
day go to the Nagara River at Gifu, at night to watch the fishermen
and birds at work.

Scene: NIGHT TIME FISHING A YOI, YOI

Speaker: What is that coming onto the scene now? It seems to be some
small girls in traditional costume with some dolls.
Speaker: Yes, I believe we are about to witness the Hina-Matsuri which is
the doll Festival. This is a very special day for all girls in
Japan.It is on March 3rd when the girls display their collection of
ceremonial dolls which have been passed down to them for many generations. These decorative dolls are arranged in a special order
with the Emperor and Empress on the highest shelf. Here they come.

SCENE:DOLLS DISPLAYED ON ROLLING STEPS....RED CLOTH AND MUSIC IN THE
BACKGROUND...CHILDREN ACCOMPANY DOLL DISPLAY IN TRADITIONAL KIMONO AND
FREEZE IN A POSITION FOR FIVE SECONDS THEN LEAVE....

SCENE: Rain Song...sung by chorus with girls in traditional costume walking
through with umbrellas.

Sung by chorus and accompaniment....

SPEAKER: THAT was absoluely delightful. Did you know that the first umbrellas
were brought over to Japan from China. ▬▬▬▬▬▬ Also, they
are not made just for sunshade but for rain also. They are lacquered so
that the rain does not penetrate. I always thought that they were only
for the sun.
Speaker: Another dance group....what are they performing this time. Let's see
if we can figure out the title of the dance by the movements of the
bodies,....watch the arms and hands very closely.

SCENE: DANCERS PERFORMING TREES.
SPeaker: They seem to be beautiful trees swaying in the gentle breeze.
Speaker: You are exactly right. That is exactly what the program says.

Pentatonic Play continued

Speaker: We must remember here in America as well as in Japan that the past
is not forgotten. And as is true in Japan it is equally true in America. We must have a deep, profound respect for our gift of land, sun
water and ~~one another~~ *each other* in order to preserve the future of United
States, Japan and the world.

Pentatonic Play continued

11/

Speaker: Mt. Fuji has just been flashed upon our screen. What do we hear
about this enormous, sacred mountain?

Speaker: We know that it is not far from Tokyo, and that it has a perfect
cone at that top and has been extinct for over 250 years.

Speaker: Is this sacred mountain difficult to climb?

Speaker: Not at all. There are six trails and ten stations along the way where
you can rest and eat.

Speaker: What is the main purpose of the climb? I realize that we climb mount-
ins for physical fitness, and for the beauty at the top but what other
reason is there for the Japanese and others who visit there
to climb Mt. Fuji?

Speaker: The main purpose for the climb is to see the sunrise. Japan is also
called Nippon which means the land of the rising sun, and when one
reaches the height of the top of Mt. Fuji one does see a most gloriou
sight at sunrise. It is truly then the land of the rising sun.

SCENE: SONG...PANTOMIME...MT. FUJI'''...ACCOMP.

Speaker: We have yet many more Festivals to go and so little time left on
our television station. The next we are about to see is the
Bean Throwing Festival which signifies the end of Winter and the
Beans are intended to drive away the evil spirits and let the good
weather come and then the good crops.

SCENE: BEAN THROWING FESTIVAL

Optional......Festival to remember the Dead...lanterns...out on water...
end of three day festival....skit without any formal song could
be arranged. O BON FESTIVAL

End of program with carps on poles and Dragon......

Song of the Pentatonic

Cormorant Fishing

Cormorant Fishing continued

Cormorant Fishing continued

Cormorant Fishing Cont. - <u>Chant</u>   M.M.Quziejka

Fire, Fire wire basket, fire
Cormorant bird, Cormorant bird
Swim little fish 3,   (gong on rest)
swim little fish 3'
Baby need food 3
Mama need food 3
Papa need food 3
Send your fire lower over water
lower over water
Skim the surface
Skim the surface
look, bird —
Search — bird —
Search and look bird

tympani   Ah — — — — — — — — — — swoop — — —
roll   Swoop — — — — — — — — Ah — — —

Home to rest, Cormorant .
Home to rest, Cormorant .

Chorus repeats song — instruments
fade out after in reverse order.

Clouds are High Above

Lift the Blinds

Lift the Blinds continued

Lift the Blinds continued

The Rooster Crowed

The Rooster Crowed continued

The Rooster Crowed   M.M. Guziejka

The rooster crowed —— and woke the sun goddess, Japanese world be gan - - - - - .

optional: tympani mallet handles against gong

optional — sopranino Recorder introduces entire arrangement by playing the melody of the song — as in a bird singing alone to greet the dawn.

Japanese Spring Song

Japanese Spring Song continued

Japanese Spring Song continued

Little Girls' Festival

Little Girls' Festival continued

Mount Fuji

Mount Fuji continued

Tanabata

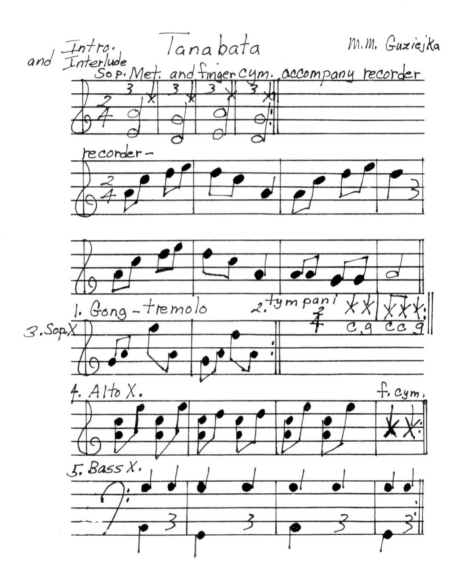

Tanabata continued

Tanabata continued

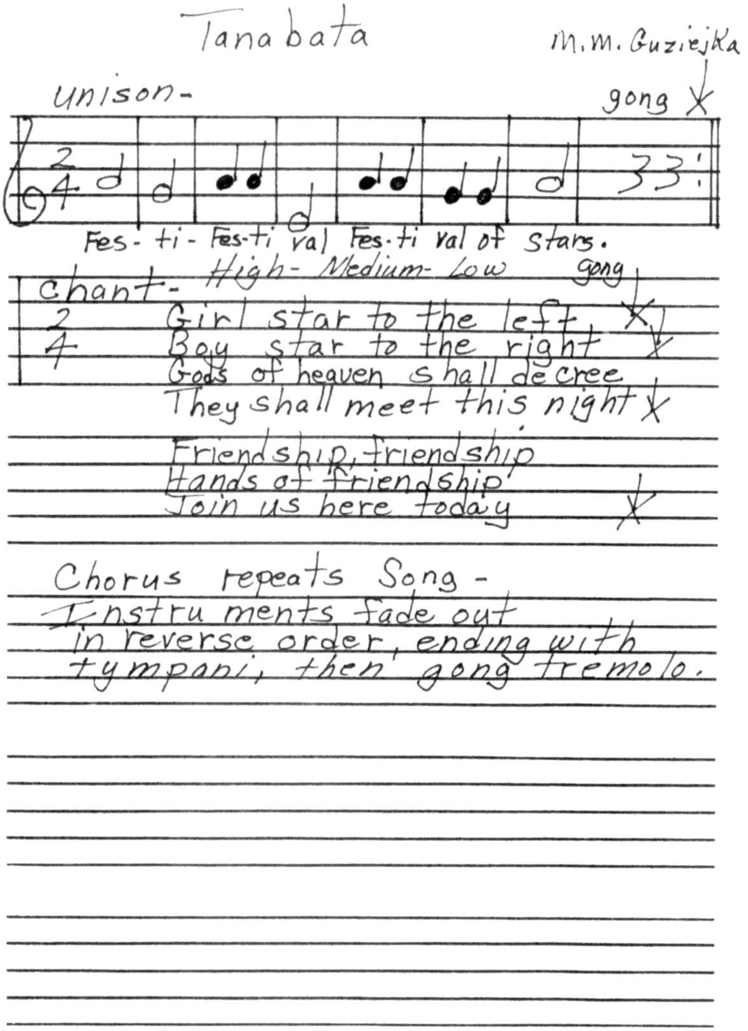

Soft, the Winds Blow

Soft, the Winds Blow continued

Rice Planting Ceremony

Rice Planting Ceremony continued

An Anthem of Peace

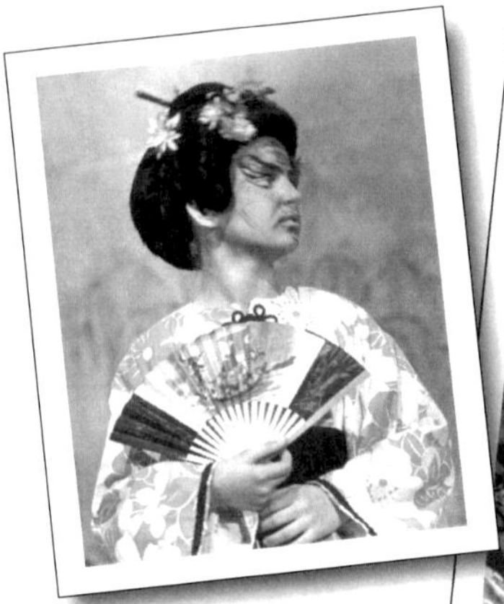

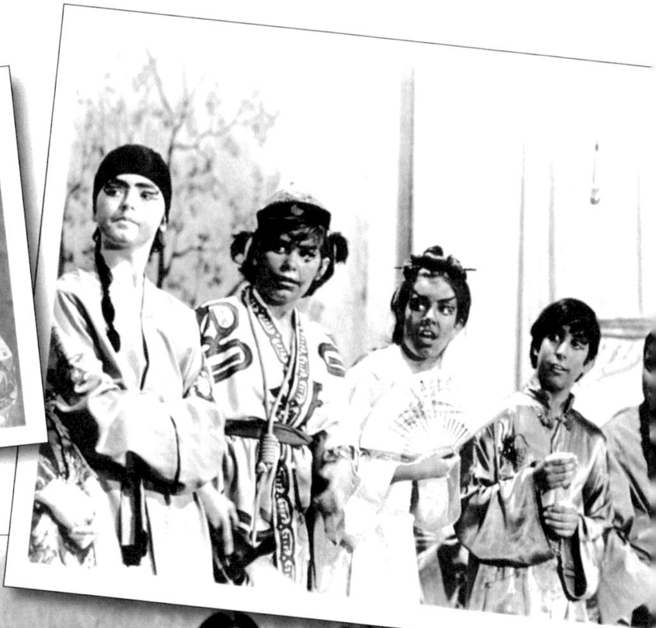

— fold-out page —

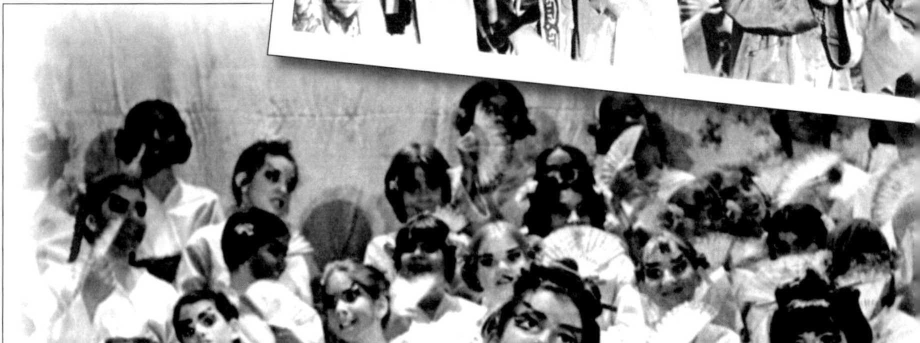

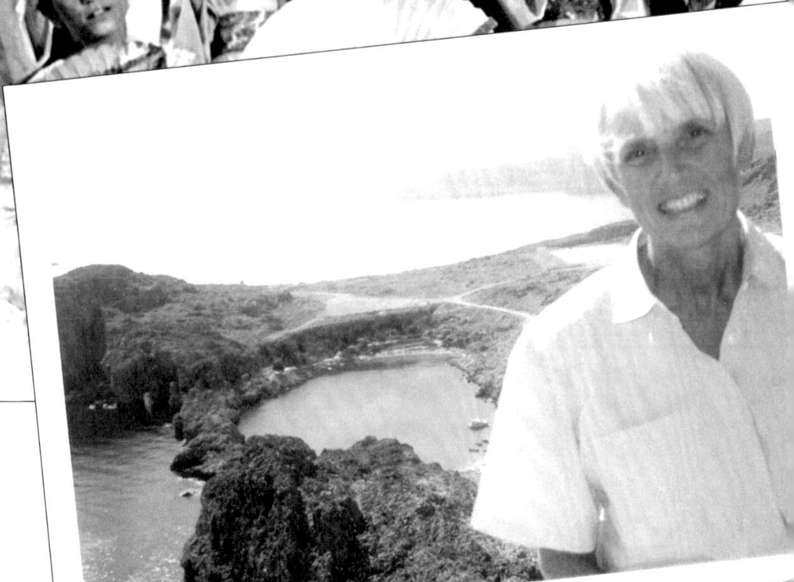